VYACHESLAV NIKONOV

THE CODE OF CIVILIZATION

ИНСТИТУТ ПЕРЕВОДА

AD VERBUM

Published with the support
of the Institute for Literary Translation, Russia

THE CODE OF CIVILIZATION

by Vyacheslav Nikonov

Translated from the Russian by Huw Davies

Publishers Maxim Hodak & Max Mendor

Book cover and interior design by Max Mendor

**Published with the support
of the Institute for Literary Translation, Russia**

© 2020, Vyacheslav Nikonov

© 2020, Glagoslav Publications

www.glagoslav.com

ISBN: 978-1-912894-81-9

First published in English by Glagoslav Publications in December 2020

A catalogue record for this book is available from the British Library.

This book is in copyright. No part of this publication may be reproduced, stored in a retrieval system or transmitted in any form or by any means without the prior permission in writing of the publisher, nor be otherwise circulated in any form of binding or cover other than that in which it is published without a similar condition, including this condition, being imposed on the subsequent purchaser.

VYACHESLAV NIKONOV

THE CODE OF CIVILIZATION

Translated from the Russian by Huw Davies

GLAGOSLAV PUBLICATIONS

CONTENTS

PROLOGUE 7

    CHAPTER 1
    PEOPLE AND CIVILIZATIONS 14

    CHAPTER 2
    UNITED STATES OF EUROPE 44

    CHAPTER 3
    EUROPEAN (DIS)UNION 82

    CHAPTER 4
    THE AMERICAN MAGNITUDE 131

    CHAPTER 5
    THE RUSSIAN MATRIX 246

    CHAPTER 6
    THE RETURN OF ASIA 352

    CHAPTER 7
    THE CHINESE PARTY 383

    CHAPTER 8
    THE COLLECTIVE OF THE RISING SUN 424

    CHAPTER 9
    THE INDIAN WAY 454

    CHAPTER 10
    THE ISLAMIC FACTOR 497

    CHAPTER 11
    LATIN-AMERICAN CHARISMA 539

    CHAPTER 12
    THE AFROCENTRISM OF HOPE 586

EPILOGUE 636

ABOUT THE AUTHOR 640

PROLOGUE

Has it ever occurred to you, dear reader, that when we describe the North Pole as being in the north, this is merely a matter of perspective? It would serve its purpose just as well if it were beneath us. And if we were to turn the globe upside down, as people living in the southern hemisphere often do, the resulting image of the world would look very different. The Antarctic and Australia would appear to be the biggest continents, while Russia and North America would look as significant as the Antarctic looks on the globe we are used to seeing.

It so happens that I have had occasion to visit around a hundred countries in my lifetime. I have done so as an academic and a delegate at conferences. I have done so as an Americanist by training, someone who has taken courses and taught classes in the USA; as a parliamentarian and a member of a large number of inter-parliamentary organizations; as the executive director, and later the chairman of the board of governors, of the "Russkiy Mir" (Russian World) foundation, which promotes the Russian culture and language all over the planet; as the chairman of the Russian national committee for researching issues related to BRICS – the association of the five largest emerging economies: Brazil, Russia, India, China and South Africa; and as the leader of the Russian delegation at the CSCAP, the Council for Security Cooperation in the Asia-Pacific, an organization with 27 member states from the Asia-Pacific Region. And as the co-host of *The Great Game* TV show, which focuses on world politics.

In each of these one hundred countries, I have had plenty of conversations with people – from a plethora of heads of state and ministers, to taxi drivers and waiters. I have read the local papers (if they were in a language I could understand) and have read books that were published there. I had a look at the museums and cultural monuments. I tried to get inside each country's mindset, its worldview, to make sense of the history of these states and of the civilizations of which they are a part. The conclusion I reached is as follows.

Even here in Russia (to say nothing of people in the West), we have grown used to looking at the world from a single point of view: from the West and North. The education that we received was, and remains, one that is north- and west-centric. After the history of the ancient world, where the East and West were given a more or less equal share of attention, our school history books then proved to be predominantly oriented towards Russia and Europe. We should be glad that the situation was not even worse than this, of course: in many countries, the history of foreign countries is not taught at all. In our lessons on Russian history, Europe played a dominant role: one minute we were defending ourselves from it, the next we were carving out a window onto it; one minute we were triumphing over it, then being integrated into it, then seeing that integration reversed. The philosophy we were taught was either Western or Marxist (the latter being of the West, too). Political science and management studies proved, all too often, to be mere transliterations of American and British textbooks (for beginners). The real authorities on all subjects, it seemed, lived in the West.

The eternal question of the Russian intelligentsia has been: what will Europe say? The main ideological dividing line boils down to this: are we the West or not, are we part of it or not? I spent a great deal of time in all of these countries in Europe and North America before I began taking a strong interest in other parts of the world.

Irrespective of one's opinion of the West, there is no doubt that it is very important. It is the only civilization that has made a mark – mainly through conquest, but not only in that way – on the whole world. But there is also the majority of mankind, about whose existence we do not often think. The mass media – the key sources of knowledge in the modern world – rarely give us any information about the events, countries and continents that are not a firm part of the system of national stereotypes. Do you stop to recall man, agriculture, civilization, statehood, cities, literacy, the world's religions, the foundations of science? All of this was born not in the West, but in the East. And, if we exclude the last two centuries, the main centers of global development and economics are also located somewhere other than in the West. Do we ever ponder the processes taking place in countries where there are far more people living today than in Russia; for instance, in Indonesia, Nigeria, Pakistan or Bangladesh? Do you ever hear anything about the wars in Africa, which are taking the lives of thousands of people every day? Even the knowledge Russians have about their own country is incredibly limited.

The modern world has been around for quite some time. Human civilization goes back several millennia. A plethora of great empires and states have passed into oblivion. A handful have kept going into modernity. The most ancient of the countries existing today – China – can point to 5,000 years of ongoing history. All of these civilizations and states, however – those that disappeared and those that live on – have made their contribution, whether large or small, self-evident or barely noticeable, to the creation of the world in which we live.

The supremacy of Western civilization began a couple of centuries ago – a moment ago in historical terms – and, it would appear, reached its apogee towards the end of the 20th century, when there were widespread celebrations of a "victory" in the "Cold War" and "the end of history", in connection with the triumph of Western values.

This triumphalism is clearly ebbing away. The world is demonstrating a multiplicity of models for development, increasingly taking into account the national, regional, historical, religious and other particularities of each country. The center of gravity for global development is increasingly shifting from the West to the East, from the north to the south, from the area of developed economies to the sphere of developing ones. Whereas 30 years ago the countries in the West accounted for 80% of the world economy, they now account for significantly less than half of it.

In 2014, for the first time since 1872, the United States ceased to be the biggest economy (in terms of purchasing power parity), after being displaced by China. In the same year, the GDP of the Western G7 states – the USA, Japan, Germany, the UK, France, Italy and Canada – proved to be less than that of the seven largest developing countries – China, India, Russia, Brazil, Mexico, Indonesia and Turkey.

The United States found itself in a debt trap, which was not something to be feared, while there was still faith in the dollar and the financial instruments created by the American government. The disappearance of a consensus on key socio-economic and moral and ethical questions is paralyzing the political mechanism, the party-political system is polarized, something which was not seen before the Civil War of 1861-1865, and is hindering the political decision-making process. Trust in the American government, and in President Donald Trump, who is unacceptable in the eyes of the vast majority of the establishment, is at a very low level. Racial conflicts, which ebbed away largely thanks to the election of the first African-American president Barack Obama, flared up again after his departure.

The USA, ever convinced of its uniqueness amongst the world's nations, will, as before, bank on global hegemony, despite having increasingly fewer resources and capabilities with which to make that happen. The key method by which they would do this will, as before, be their efforts to prevent the emergence of alternative centers of power, capable of laying down a challenge to American domination. The USA is thoroughly purging such alternatives or stirring up chaos within them: Iraq, Libya and Syria, with constant pressure on Iran. The key restraining factors for the USA in the foreseeable future will be Russia, as the main challenge in the military and strategic sphere, and China, as an economic and geopolitical challenge, and perhaps even a challenge in terms of civilization. The "dual constraint" of Russia and China may prove to be a decisive test of the USA's capabilities in the modern world.

When the USA effects regime change in various countries, this often has results which go against the interests of Washington itself, not to mention the interests of those countries themselves. This policy is likely to be continued, incidentally, given the stereotypical nature of American approaches, even though Trump can see how unproductive it is. At the same time, one gets the feeling that the overwhelming majority of humankind have grown tired of the unilateral domination that hides behind the banner of a liberal world order. The relentless aggressiveness of the United States is bad news for non-proliferation of WMD. The USA and its allies have not yet attacked countries with nuclear weapons, and this makes nuclear weapons a valuable asset in the eyes of those who do not want to fall victim to the latest "humanitarian" or other intervention.

The European Union is still recovering from the economic crisis of 2007 to 2009, and still has the slowest rate of growth on the planet. The possibilities for keeping the European social model going in the foreseeable future are melting away before our eyes. Europe will have to do a balancing act along a narrow tightrope, with the pro-Europeans and Euro-bureaucrats, on one side, striving to create a federative state, and on the other, the equally powerful desire of the Euroskeptics and nationalists of individual countries to preserve their national sovereignty, already expressed at its most obvious in Brexit. By casting Christian values aside, and backing multiculturalism and an "anything goes" morality, the leaders of the EU continue to risk losing popularity in the future, prompting a surge in nationalist and left-wing forces.

"The countries that built the liberal international order are weaker today than they have been for three generations. They no longer serve as an example to others of the strength of liberal systems of economic and political governance," writes the director of the Chatham House think-tank, Robin Niblett.[1]

---

[1] Robin Niblett, "Liberalism in Retreat: The Demise of a Dream", *Foreign Affairs*, Vol. 96, Issue 1,

The world's largest territory with the biggest reserves of natural resources, a highly educated population, a powerful defence potential, an elite with the capacity to think in global categories, and a resurgent sense of national self-esteem – all these factors make Russia a powerful geopolitical player. The country remains an independent center of power, increasingly relying on its own capabilities and partnership with the non-Western world, since it has found itself – not for the first time, of course – isolated by the West. Strategic depth will be created via the expanding Eurasian Economic Union, the Shanghai Cooperation Organization, BRICS, and regional and bilateral alliances. Russia's weaknesses are mostly of an economic and demographical nature.

Asia, which is already home to most of humanity, will become a global leader over the next decade in all key socio-economic and, possibly, technological parameters. There will be nothing new in this, incidentally: throughout the last two millennia, Asian countries, first and foremost China and India, have consistently – with the exception of two centuries – been the biggest economies in the world. Recently, Asian countries have felt the wind in their sails, and this has led to a widespread increase in national dignity, and confidence in the strength of their traditions and in their ability to change their countries and the entire world for the better.

China is going to continue to break away from all other countries in terms of its economic growth, even if not so rapidly as before. The combination of the power and good organization of the state, founded on the legacy of Empire and Communism, on the culture of Confucianism and strategic thinking, with the vast market of the world's most populous country, gives China a huge reserve of solidity and vital energy. It is China that is stepping forth into the role of the second global center of power, and the efforts of the other centers, in terms of limiting its influence, will prove to be the main constraining factor for Chinese growth. It will also serve as a stimulus for growth and the search for partners all over the world.

India is going to continue to rise up the global table of ranks, mostly by using the advantages of its demographic dividend to bring tens of millions of people out of poverty. A weak state, which has always been inherent to this "functioning anarchy", will be the main weakness of the "biggest democracy in the world". India's role in the world will increase tangibly, reflecting both its economic surge and the desire of all the main centers of power to have Delhi as a strategic partner.

....
January/February 2017. P. 24.

A burdensome historical legacy, the policy of Western countries, the American interventions in Afghanistan, Iraq, Libya and Syria, the revolutions of the "Arab Spring" supported from without, have destabilized the Islamic world in a lasting way, transforming many countries into a source of permanent conflicts and fueling the fire of Islamist extremism, far beyond its borders. The conflict between the Sunni and the Shiite Muslims backed by the rivals Saudi Arabia and Iran respectively will intensify. At the same time, the resurgence of Islam, strengthened by the oil resources in the Persian Gulf, will prompt growth both in this vast region and throughout the whole of the Muslim community.

Latin America may not yet be a civilization in its own right, but it is certainly on the way to becoming one. It will continue to be divided into states that have close relations with the USA and states that are more distant: into right-wing and left-wing governments. The recent right-wing swing is obvious. That swing could, though, be replaced by a new left-wing renaissance. Latin America is capable of showing solidarity, of becoming emancipated from the unconditional influence of the USA, of influencing global policy more actively and increasing its weight in global governance.

Africa could become the fastest-growing continent, both from a demographic point of view and an economic one. The rivalry amongst global centers of power for the hearts of the African countries, which make up the biggest voting share in the UN, and for the continent's resources, is becoming more intense. Within the continent, competition is developing between two main contenders for leadership: South Africa and Nigeria. At the same time, Africa is set to remain the poorest continent for a long time, where the majority of the population will continue to live in poverty, with the lowest levels of access to health care and the lowest life expectancy.

The era of unipolarity has proved to be fairly short-lived. History has been restarted, and the world is striving for greater diversity. The creation of strong states, as it has transpired, does not strongly go against the interests of democratic development. Rather, fewer and fewer people consider what exists in the USA to be democracy, or an example to be copied.

On a daily basis, throughout the world, we are seeing a renewed interest in cultural roots, in faith, in nature. Traditionalism, pride in the legacy of one's ancestors, national culture and moral principles, are cropping up in all quarters, taking the form of movements and/or "indigenous" revivals in Latin America, "Ubuntu" in South Africa, Confucian regeneration in China and other East Asian countries, the rise in Hindu tendencies and political forces in India. With the exception of Europe and maybe the US, where churches are becoming more and more empty, a growing number of people in the world are displaying religious feelings. This can be seen from the rapid increase in the congregations at Orthodox churches in post-Soviet Russia, the crowds in the Buddhist pagodas in China or Japan, and the re-Islamization of the Muslim world.

The contours of the new world order, as I see it, can already be made out. First and foremost, in an organization such as BRICS, which started out as a virtual reality, as a list of rapidly growing economies that were not related to one another, but quickly acquired the flesh and blood of political reality. The gradual rise of BRICS is not associated with violence or hegemonic tendencies. Each of the five countries and civilizations has its own unique place on the globe, its cultural matrices, views on development and security. Yet this diversity itself is considered to be an undoubted benefit. Brazil, Russia, India, China and South Africa, which house 44% of the planet's population, are not inclined to meddle in one another's internal affairs, and accept their partners in the way that each has been shaped over the centuries. They cooperate over and above the old dividing lines of East and West or North and South. These five states are far closer to demonstrating a model of a "concert of civilizations" than the clash of civilizations predicted by Samuel Huntington.

In tomorrow's world, leadership will be in the hands of those who have not only overwhelming economic and military strength (those two factors may coincide with one another, but not necessarily), but who have a quality of leadership, morals, motivation of the populace, state strategies, political will, and the ability to offer a new dream to mankind – these factors will decide who holds the balance of power. And, most important of all: the ones in front will be those who have truth and justice on their side.

CHAPTER 1
PEOPLE AND CIVILIZATIONS

Civilizations are capable not only of doing battle with one another, but also of cooperating with one another. For there is enough room on Earth for the whole of humanity, in all its diversity.

Mankind's Past is Full of Mystery

According to the latest scientific knowledge, everything that exists came into being some 13.7 billion years ago, at the time of the Big Bang, when, for a reason not yet known to modern science, nothing was transformed into something.[1] The part of the Universe which can be observed by astronomers is known as the Metagalaxy, and contains several hundred billion galaxies. The planet on which we have the good fortune to live is the third planet from the sun in our Solar System, which came into being 4.7 billion years ago and was cast adrift (or, to look at it another way, was not cast adrift) in its further reaches, 10,000 parsecs from the center of our galaxy, which is known as the Milky Way and contains, in addition to the Sun, another 10^{11} stars (more than the number of people living on our planet).

The majority of the earth's surface – 70.8% of it – is covered by the world's oceans, and the rest – all 149.1 million square kilometers of it – is taken up by land which forms 6 continents and a multitude of islands. Not all of the land is hospitable: 20% of it consists of deserts, 10% of glaciers, 30% of it is covered with forests, 20% with savannah and sparse woodland, and another 10% is used for farming.

Between 3 and 3.8 billion years ago, life came into being, and the biosphere began to take shape. At least 3 million years ago – probably in Africa – mankind,

---

[1] For more on this see: Robert Hazen, *The Story of Earth: The First 4.5 Billion Years, from Stardust to Living Planet*. Penguin Books, 2013.

the species that would go on to become the master of the planet, appeared. Man would prove to be far from the most assiduous of masters, and certainly a very brutal one.[2] It transpired that man was the only species that destroyed those like him and had a strong impact on his environment, and not for the better.

As Yuval Noah Harari rightfully observed in his sensational book *Sapiens*, colonization of the planet by Homo sapiens has become "one of the biggest and swiftest ecological disasters to befall the animal kingdom. Hardest hit were the large furry creatures. […] Homo sapiens drove to extinction about half of the planet's big beasts long before humans invented the wheel, writing, or iron tools. […] Long before the Industrial Revolution, Homo sapiens held the record among all organisms for driving the most plant and animal species to their extinction. We have the dubious distinction of being the deadliest species in the annals of biology."[3]

The migration of Homo sapiens to various regions of the inhabited world, pushing out pre-homo sapiens hominids who lived there, and, possibly, interbreeding with them, resulted in the emergence of multiple racial types. Mankind was divided into four major racial branches: Europeoids, Mongoloids, Negroids and Australoids. As a result, around 40,000 years ago, intelligent man became the only representative of the hominid family and became established throughout virtually the entire planet. Back then, there were probably fewer than half a million people in the world. For hunter-gatherers – each of them would have needed a territory of 10-25 square kilometers – there was no more room left. In the late Neolithic era – 10,000 years ago – the population of earth stood at around 6 million people, average life expectancy was 30, and man subsisted on a diet that would have cost 2 dollars a day in today's terms.

A particularly significant moment was the Neolithic revolution: the transition from an appropriating economy to a production economy: to agriculture and cattle rearing; metallurgy, trades, and the forerunners of the exchange of goods appeared. The central role as the protector of the home and hearth – a role played by women – began to be pushed aside by the leading role of man as a tiller of the land and a warrior. The emergence of surplus food, along with the tools of labor and other belongings, which were not distributed among the whole community but remained within the family, led to the rise of private property and inequality. A clannish elite

---

[2] See: Yuval Noah Harari, *Sapiens: A Brief History of Humankind*. Random House, 2014.
[3] Yuval Hoah Harari, *Sapiens: A Brief History of Humankind*. Random House, 2014.

formed, deciding matters at a tribal council, and military leaders and priests gained special prominence.

By the time of Plato and Aristotle (in the 4th century BC), the population of the planet was approaching 200 million, and it then stayed at that level for a long time: mankind had entered the era of intense self-destruction, exacerbated by large-scale epidemics (the most devastating of which was the plague pandemic that killed off 45% of Europe's population in the middle of the 14th century).[4] In the year 1000 CE, there were roughly 275 million people living on the planet. By about 1800, the human population had reached the billion mark. And then the demographic boom began.

In the 20th century, the planet's population doubled in size, almost twice over. In 1900, it stood at 1.6 billion people, in 1927 2 billion, and in 1950 3 billion. On 12th October 1999, the 6 billionth person was born, in Sarajevo: Adnan Nevich. Twelve years later, the 7 billionth human arrived, in the early hours of 31st October 2011, in Kaliningrad: Pyotr Nikolayev. Today, approximately 230,000 people are born every day on Earth, and in the year 2019, around 80 million babies were born. Average life expectancy is 67 years, and the average level of income is 25 dollars a day. Yet some 2.5 billion people live on less than 2 dollars a day.

The figures for the growth in population, in the billions, are amazing: it is hard to imagine so many people. Let us try to do just that, though. Imagine if all the people on the planet gathered together in one place, on an island for example, and stood shoulder to shoulder. How big would that island need to be? As big as the United Kingdom, or Japan, or Greenland? Far from it. The entire population of Earth in 1950 could have fitted onto the Isle of Wight, off the southern coast of England, which measures 381 square kilometers. For today's population, Zanzibar would suffice, measuring as it does 1,554 square kilometers, which is a little more than the area of Moscow, prior to its expansion beyond the borders of the belt-way.[5]

The peak of population growth arrived in the 1960s, when it stood at 2% a year. Today, the figure is half that. We shall not reach the next milestone – 8 billion – for another 14 years, as opposed to 12, and the next billion after that might take 18 years. The main reason for the explosive population growth in the 20th century was a string of successes in healthcare, first and foremost in the invention of antibiotics and the implementation of rules on hygiene.

....

[4] George Minois, "Too Much Life on Earth", *The New York Times*, July 13, 2011 <https://www.nytimes.com/2011/07/14/opinion/14iht-edminois14.html>.

[5] "A Tale of Three Islands", *The Economist*, October 22, 2011. P. 29.

The key distinctive characteristic of the 21st century will be a fall in the birth rate. A key factor is considered to be the development of urban communities, and of an urban culture. As demographers like to joke, "urbanization is the best form of contraceptive". Moreover, increases in the educational and professional level of women have also played a role, along with the trend for getting married at a later age and for more frequent divorces, and the absence in the cities of the economic need to have a large family, and the widespread use of abortion and contraception.

Today, experts have calmed down somewhat about the issue of over-population and the Malthusian Trap. According to the weighted-average forecast by the UN, the earth's population will reach 9.7 billion (enough to fill every inch of an island the size of Tenerife) in 2050 and 11.2 billion in 2100, before stabilizing. Eighty-three countries, which together are home to 46% of humanity, have a birth rate lower than the level of reproduction. These include, first and foremost, all the countries of Europe, and also Canada, Australia, New Zealand, Russia, China, and other states in East Asia. The second group of countries, which are home to another 46% – countries with better prospects on the demographic front – has an average level of reproduction of between 2.1 and 3: the majority of countries in South and South-east Asia, the Islamic world, and also the American continent, including the United States. This list includes India as well – the global champion in terms of population growth, where the birth rate will fall to the level of simple reproduction in 2025-2030 (when India will move into first place in the world in terms of population numbers, overtaking the current leader, China). Only 9% of the planet's inhabitants are to be found in the countries where the fertility rate is over 3, almost all of them being in sub-Saharan Africa. In a decade, say experts, there will be just three countries left in the world with a fertility rate higher than five children per one woman – Mali, Niger and Somalia.[6] Moreover, marriages are increasingly taking place at an ever later age, and growing numbers of children, particularly in developed countries, are being born outside wedlock (40% of children are born out of wedlock in the countries of the OECD).[7]

In 2100, two out of every five inhabitants of Earth will be living on the African continent – 4.4 billion people; meanwhile there will be just 646 mil-

....

[6] Robin Harding, "The End of the Malthusian Nightmare", *Financial Times*, August 11, 2015 <https://www.ft.com/content/0d7d245a-400c-11e5-b98b-87c7270955cf>.
[7] "Marriage. A More Perfect Union", *The Economist*, November 25, 2017. P. 16.

lion people in Europe.[8] Unless, of course, everyone in Africa has migrated to Europe by then.

The planet, by all accounts, will be able to sustain and keep its population fed in the 21st century and, therefore, in the 22nd century as well. Even today, the yield of most agricultural crops has risen 10-fold by comparison with the 19th century.[9] While today there are people going hungry, and 2 billion are living in poverty, this is explained not by a shortfall in resources, but by the poor distribution of these resources, i.e., first and foremost, by the poor quality of state governance.[10] And the situation varies greatly in particular parts of the world.

However, both the speed of change, and the number of changes that are unfavorable for the human race, are growing. The Holocene, which began just 16,000 years ago, turns out to be the shortest geological period in Earth's history; all the others lasted tens of millions of years. At an international congress of geological sciences held in South Africa in 2016, it was proposed that a new era – the Anthropocene – should be considered to have begun, starting in 1950. It is characterized by the increased influence of human activity on the climate, the rapid disappearance of forests, a reduction in levels of fish in the ocean, the loss of a growing number of living species, and the emission of greenhouse gases.[11]

Ethnicities, Nations, States

Each of us is part of a multitude of communities: whether territorial, ethnic, linguistic, faith-based or political, and it is not easy to count how many of them there are.

Ethnicity is about being part of a community that is held together less by shared "blood" than by the nature of the cultural stereotypes which lie at the heart of its sense of self, in the way it distinguishes between "our kind" and "others". Here, language plays an important, and often the most

---

[8] Ross Douthat, "Africa's Scramble for Europe", *The New York Times,* August 8, 2015 <https://www.nytimes.com/2015/08/09/opinion/sunday/ross-douthat-africas-scramble-for-europe.html>.

[9] Jess Lowenberg-DeBoer, "The Precision Agriculture Revolution. Making the Modern Farmer", *Foreign Affairs,* May/June 2015. P. 105.

[10] George Minois, "Too Much Life on Earth", *The New York Times,* July 13, 2011 <https://www.nytimes.com/2011/07/14/opinion/14iht-edminois14.html>.

[11] "The Anthropocene Should Bring Awe – and Act as a Warning", *Time,* September 12-17, 2016. P. 8.

important, role (although there are people who speak the same language but think of themselves as different ethnicities, such as the Serbs, the Bosnians and the Croats). According to current estimates, there are currently between 5,000 and 6,000 languages spoken on Earth. At the same time, 80% of the planet's population speaks just 80 languages between them, while the other 3,500 languages are spoken by just 0.2% of the Earth's population.

The most widely spoken languages (in millions of people) are: Chinese – 1,213; English – 514; Spanish – 425; Russian – 275; Hindi – 258; Arabic – 256; Bengali – 215; Portuguese – 194; Indonesian (Malay) – 176. Japanese and German have slipped out of the top ten in the last few years. If we look at the number of people that speak a particular language as their native tongue, however (something that has a lot to do with the numbers of each ethnicity), we see a different picture: Chinese – 1,213; Spanish – 329; English – 328; Arabic – 221 (it is the official language of 57 countries); Hindi – 182; Bengali – 181 (the official language of Bangladesh); Portuguese – 178; Russian – 144; Japanese – 125; German – 110.[12] We get another picture again if we consider the language of Internet sites. Here, English is streets ahead of all the other languages at 56.1%, with Russian unexpectedly in second place at 6%, followed by German with 5.9%, Spanish with 4.9%, Chinese with 4.5%, French with 3.9%, Japanese with 3.2%, and Portuguese with 2.2%.[13]

According to some studies, a language dies out every two weeks. In other words, 24 languages die out every year, and this trend is going to continue. In the 21st century, up to 70% of existing languages will disappear. In a couple of centuries' time, only 500-600 languages will survive. It should be said, though, that many highly-regarded academics consider such forecasts to be unfounded.

Even though the number of languages and ethnicities is falling, the number of nations is rising. The understanding of a nation as an ethnic community was reinforced in Russia with the help of those diligent students of the Austrian Marxists of the 19th century Vladimir Lenin and Josef Stalin. Such an interpretation bears no relation to modern theories of national policy or to the modern world. The universally accepted concept of a political nation is a community of citizens belonging to a particular state.

....

[12] Vladimir Yemelyanenko, "The New Russian Paradox", Russky mir.ru, January 2013. PP. 11, 13.

[13] Ksenia Kolesnikova, "Za slovom v karman" ("Never Stuck for Words"), *Kul'tura i iskusstvo* (*Culture and Art*), January 20, 2015 <http://www.cult-and-art.net/society/114310-za_slovom_v_karman>.

The formation of a nation is not a universal stage of development for all the peoples of the world. Almost all minority ethnic groups have ended up as part of larger nations. Multi-ethnicity is the norm for contemporary nation states. Many countries leave far behind even Russia, with its 180 ethnic groups. According to UN data, the number of ethnic groups in the following countries looks like this: China – 205, Cameroon – 279, India – 407, Nigeria – 470, Indonesia – 712, Papua New Guinea – 817.[14] They are all unquestionably nation states.

How many nations are there on Earth? If we define them as political nations, the number roughly corresponds to the number of states. Max Weber defined a state as a community that has a monopoly on the lawful use of force inside a particular territory. States have been formed on the basis of tribal proto-states (chiefdoms) in urban cultures, developing in the valleys of great rivers, and the first of them were the states of Sumer in the land between the Tigris and the Euphrates, where, it seems, royal rule first emerged (including hereditary rule), along with bureaucracy and literacy. Egypt in the valley of the Nile is another early state. They were followed by states along the river Indus in India and the Huang He in China. In Europe, statehood came into being with the emergence of the first Greek tribes in the Balkans in the 20th to 17th centuries BC, when Mycenae, Tiryns and Pylos appeared.

We can begin counting the number of states in the modern sense (or, at least, the modern concept of the state) from the mid-17th century. After the Protestant Reformation and the bloody Thirty Years' War, the leading European states attempted, in Westphalia, to draw up new rules for interaction and for their own legitimacy. The result was a model that had at its foundation the principle of sovereignty: the state is the source of the highest political power, exercised to the full extent within the limits of its own territory. It conducts foreign policy independently, and it respects the right of other states to act in the same way.

For the most part, the 19th century brought the creation, by the leading European states, of empires (a concept which had existed before then in many parts of the world). Contemporary authors usually interpret "empire" as "a relationship, formal or informal, in which one state controls the effective political sovereignty of another political society"; "not merely a large

---

[14] *Vidimyye ruki: Otvetstvennost' za sotsial'noye razvitiye.* Doklad issledovatel'skogo instituta po problemam sotsial'nogo razvitiya pri OON (*Visible Hands. Responsibility for Social Development.* Report by the Institute for Research into Problems of Social Development at the UN). Moscow, 2001. PP. 78-82.

polity, but a compound polity that has incorporated lesser ones"; "a composite state, in which the metropolis reigns supreme over the peripheries, against the interests of the latter."[15]

The start of the collapse of empires after the First and Second World Wars – particularly the Second, and the rise of national self-consciousness, prompted a growing trend towards the multiplication of independent states. When the UN was created in 1945, there were 51 states represented within it. Today, there are 193. A significant contribution to the process of multiplication was made by the collapse of the USSR, which resulted in 14 new countries becoming members of the UN at the same time. However, the number of so-called unrecognized states in the world is also growing. These are those which do in fact have some sovereignty, but this sovereignty is not recognized by any other state (such as the Transdniester and the Donetsk and Luhansk People's Republics), or is recognized by only a small number of countries (Abkhazia, South Ossetia) or even by a large number of countries but not enough for it to acquire the status of a member of the United Nations (such as Kosovo and Palestine). If we take the countries that are not officially recognized into account, the total number of states on the planet is over 250.

After the First World War and until the 1980s, there was a strengthening of national states. The functioning of a single global community was not possible due to the breaking up of the world into opposing blocs. The end of the Cold War and the collapse of the Socialist bloc and the Soviet Union created the prerequisite conditions for globalization. The main driving force behind it was in the West, which saw an opportunity to expand its influence in developing countries by means of economic and informational infiltration.

The State and Globalization

Globalization is generally understood to mean the dramatic acceleration of the process whereby money, goods, services, information and people cross national borders. In the 1990s, it was concepts associated with globalization that proved the inevitable weakening and gradual dying away of the state, and began to lay the Westphalian system to rest.

---

[15] Michael Doyle, *Empires*. Ithaca, 1986. P. 45; John Alexander Armstrong, *Nations Before Nationalism*. Chapel Hill, 2011. P. 131; R. G. Suni, "Empire as it Really is: the Imperial Period in Russia's History: 'National' Identity and Theories of Empire" in *Natsionalizm v mirovoi istorii* (*Nationalism in World History*), ed. by V. A. Tishkov and V. A. Shnirelman. Moscow, 2007. P. 38.

According to supporters of the concept of globalization, states started to lose their monopoly on the implementation of the functions of power. While remaining the leading actors, they were forced to share the arena of global politics with international governments and non-governmental organizations, transnational corporations, pressure groups, supra-national and sub-national institutes, and information networks.

The daily turnover of money crossing national borders greatly exceeds the annual size of the GDP of the overwhelming majority of countries in the world. The economic might of transnational corporations exceeds the capabilities of governments even in countries with middling amounts of development. The economic policy of individual states has ceased to be sovereign, and is becoming ever more influenced by the global market.

Foreign Ministries have gradually lost their customary role as the only representative of the country in the international arena. The significance of "low diplomacy" (trade, technologies, currency etc.), as opposed to "high diplomacy" (national security, military crises, summits), has grown.

Globalization has been accompanied by mass migration. In 2015, there were around 250 million international migrants, and approximately 65 million people were forced to become refugees or move elsewhere. Seventy-six million immigrants moved to Europe.[16] One of the consequences of migration was a rise in anti-immigrant feeling, which undermined one of the tenets of globalization.

Globalization has had a contradictory influence on the development of democratic institutions. On the one hand, the increasing complexity of community ties, the de-centralization of economic activity, and the ease of access to information, are leading to a situation whereby it is impossible for them to be regulated by a single center. This implies less hierarchical governance, and it is engendering a trend towards the realignment of society as a network, rather than as a hierarchy of institutions. At the same time, it is becoming clear that democracy and market liberalism, taken on their own, are not creating dependable states able to meet the challenges of globalization. The Western democracies have demonstrated worse economic growth in the last decades than the utterly undemocratic China. Democracy, the former British Prime Minister Tony Blair believes, is facing an "'efficacy' challenge": "democracy seems slow, bureaucratic and weak. In this sense it

---

[16] Fareed Zakaria, "Populism on the March. Why the West is in Trouble", *Foreign Affairs*, November/December 2016. P. 14.

is failing its citizens."[17] Lately, people in Western countries themselves have been seen as the main threat to democracy, since they are increasingly responsive to ideas characterized in Western political discourse as "populism". Brexit, and Trump's victory in the presidential elections in 2016, are seen as the symbols of its triumph.[18]

Whereas in the 1990s, democracy was seen as the main and only prerequisite for successful development, we can now add to this the notion of ensuring governability by the state and society.

Information is being accumulated about citizens and their behavior. Electronic databases are gathered about citizens' telemetric parameters, DNA structure, fingerprints, and so on. The American National Security Agency, as Edward Snowden revealed, has been eavesdropping on the whole world. Russia stands accused of meddling, via the Internet, in elections all over the world. Algorithms are compiled of our cultural and consumer preferences, based on what are known as "breadcrumbs" – the traces of information that we leave behind us in the digital world. Thus, the opportunities for interfering in peoples' private lives, and for global monitoring of their behavior, are growing dramatically. This runs counter to a host of founding democratic principles, and may require additional measures in order to protect privacy.

A serious challenge to states and democracy is posed by our modern information technologies. In 2018 there were around 8 billion mobile phones in the world, used by over 5.5 billion people, while more than 4 billion people use the Internet. Cross-border virtual communities are being created, capable of exerting an influence on governments, one that can go as far as toppling them. The number of people who have become *de facto* amateur journalists, chroniclers and bloggers, is growing exponentially. We are seeing the phenomena of flash-mobs, the "Twitter revolutions", attacks on the servers of state structures, the publication of secret materials, and the documentation of corruption. And all these people have powerful computer software at their disposal: in terms of its capabilities, even the iPhone 6 was more powerful than the fastest supercomputer on the planet in the 1990s.[19]

....

[17] Tony Blair, "Is Democracy Dead?", *The New York Times*, December 4, 2014 <https://www.nytimes.com/2014/12/04/opinion/tony-blair-is-democracy-dead.html>.

[18] Jeff D. Colgan and Robert O. Keohane, "The Liberal Order is Rigged. Fix It Now or Watch It Wither", *Foreign Affairs*, May/June 2017. P. 36.

[19] Dave Baiocchi and William Welser IV, "The Democratization of Space. New Actors Need New Rules", *Foreign Affairs*, May/June 2015. P. 99.

How best to solve the problems of social and state security while adhering to democratic principles of openness and freedom – this is by no means a trivial task.

Power: Soft, Smart and Hard

Globalization has increased the role of "soft power", associated with economics, finance and the environment. "Conventional wisdom has always held that the state with the largest military prevails, but in an information age it may be the state (or nonstates) with the best story that wins," observes Joseph Nye, one of the creators of the concepts of "soft power" and "smart power". He himself understands "soft power" as "the ability to get what you want through attraction rather than coercion or payments. It arises from the attractiveness of a country's culture, political ideas, and policies." "Smart power" means "the combination of the hard power of coercion and payment with the soft power of persuasion and attraction."[20]

Yet the factor of military force cannot be disregarded. Wars are still won and lost. Nuclear deterrence works, for it prevents major wars from happening. No-one is eager to abandon nuclear weapons; on the contrary, arsenals are being constantly upgraded. Military force was decisive in terms of defining the fate of Syria. while North Korea's growing nuclear and missile potential has stimulated the dialogue between Donald Trump and Kim Jong Un.

The accelerating cross-border flow of "know-how", and the growing chaos in international relations, are clearly increasing the danger that weapons of mass destruction will proliferate, along with missile technologies. While slowing down in Europe, arms races are intensifying in Asia. The global arms market has reached its highest volume since the days of the Cold War. According to SIPRI, three quarters of it was accounted for by the five biggest suppliers: the USA (one third of the market), Russia (23%), China (6.2%), France (6%) and Germany (5.6%). The leader in terms of imports is India, followed by Saudi Arabia (8.2%), the UAE (4.6%), China (4.5%) and Algeria (3.7%).[21]

Globalization has exacerbated a host of traditional security challenges: the proliferation of weapons of mass destruction, separatism, religious ex-

---

[20] Joseph S. Nye, Jr. *Soft Power. The Means to Success in World Politics.* N.Y., 2004. P. x; Joseph S. Nye, Jr., *The Future of Power*. PublicAffairs, 2011. P. xiii.

[21] Anton Bayev, "Mir vooruzhayetsya" ("The World is Acquiring Arms"), *RBK*, February 20, 2017 <https://www.rbc.ru/newspaper/2017/02/21/58aad8b59a794756977f5617>.

tremism, drug trafficking, cross-border organized crime, sea piracy. There has been a rise in the frequency of conflicts related to the use of forests and water resources, fishing, and the borders of economic zones. Even in armed conflicts involving states, an increasing role is being played by non-governmental organizations. Suffice it to recall private military companies, and military outsourcing, involving tens of thousands of subcontractors.

At the same time, in the last 50 years, the number of wars and armed conflicts between states has fallen steadily (though this may seem hard to believe). In the first decade of the 21st century, only 3 out of 30 major armed conflicts were between states – between India and Pakistan, Ethiopia and Eritrea, and the US's intervention in Iraq. The presence of nuclear weapons has for many decades acted as a deterrent against a major war between the great powers. The number of civil wars increased during the Cold War and in its immediate aftermath, but then it too began to decline. This can be attributed to the effective cessation of post-colonial wars and confrontations along the dividing lines between the two sides in a bipolar confrontation, and the growing role of international peace-keeping. Fifteen years after the end of the Cold War, there were more wars finished than in the 50 years preceding it. Of the 150 major civil wars that have taken place on Earth since 1945, no more than ten are still ongoing, and only in seven of these, in recent times, have more than 1,000 people died in a year. The biggest losses have been seen in Libya, Syria, Afghanistan, Ukraine and Iraq.

Wars involving the leading states are becoming increasingly technological, with ever more weapons being used that require minimal human involvement, such as unmanned drones, self-guided missiles, robotic weapons. In July 2015, a group of famous names in the world of advanced technology – Stephen Hawking, Steve Wozniak, Elon Musk – wrote an open letter calling for a ban on the use of "autonomous" weapons systems, so that we do not find ourselves facing a situation like the one depicted in the film *Terminator* (in which, should you need reminding, robot-warriors broke free from human control and set about destroying mankind). Articles were promptly written in defence of "autonomous" military technologies, which enable us to avoid mistakes typically made by human beings, and mass killings, and to save soldiers' lives and bring military action to an end instantaneously.[22] It is clear that the people and corporations working in this field are not going to stop what they are doing.

....

[22] Jerry Kaplan, "Robot Weapons: What's the Harm", *The New York Times*, August 17, 2015 <https://www.nytimes.com/2015/08/17/opinion/robot-weapons-whats-the-harm.html>.

If anything, the risk of a conflict between the great powers is increasing, as confrontation in cyber space grows.

Hundreds of books have already been written about cyber-wars and cyber-crime. State concepts on cyber-security, and cybernetic chains of command in the armed forces and intelligence services of the leading countries, have also appeared. It is now obvious that this will "blur the distinction between war and peace, because any networks or connected devices, from military systems to civilian infrastructure such as energy sources, electricity grids, health or traffic controls, or water supplies, can be hacked and attacked."[23] According to estimates, business losses alone from cyber attacks run to half a billion dollars annually. In 2015, the world spent 76.9 billion dollars on cyber security and in 2020 this amount will increase to 170 billion.[24]

The very definition of the term "war" is becoming increasingly vague. Reference is often made to the concept of "hybrid warfare", which the authors of the authoritative annual publication *Military Balance* defined as "the use of military and non-military tools in an integrated campaign, aimed at achieving the element of surprise, seizing the initiative, and acquiring psychological and physical advantages, with the use of diplomatic opportunities, rapid disinformation operations, and also electronic and cybernetic operations, military and reconnaissance actions, undercover or sometimes without cover, and economic pressure." The country most often accused of introducing "hybrid warfare" of this nature is Russia – in connection with the events in Ukraine. One cannot help observing, however, that state operations of this kind – albeit without electronic and cybernetic resources – have been used for centuries. The USA and their allies, according to Western experts' own calculations, are carrying out activities aimed at undermining the status quo in 120 states.[25]

Many conflicts in the modern world arise from state border disputes and certain ethnic groups' demands for sovereignty. The International Court of Justice is swamped with territorial dispute cases, and more and more claims on maritime boundaries delimitation are being registered within the United Nations Convention on the Law of the Sea.

---

[23] Klaus Schwab, *The Fourth Industrial Revolution*. Crown, 2017. P. 84.

[24] Ibid. P. 59.

[25] Vladimir Kotlyar, "K voprosu o 'gibridnoy voyne' i o tom, kto zhe yeye vedet na Ukraine" ("Thoughts on 'Hybrid War' and Who is Waging it in Ukraine"), *Mezhdunarodnaya zhizn'* (*International Life*), August 2015. PP. 58-60.

The reduction in the number of conflicts involving states has been accompanied by an increase in non-state conflicts. There is an increasing number of conflicts between a state and a non-state player, acting from the territory of another state. Two examples are the conflict between the Lebanese group Hezbollah and Israel, and the clash between "global Jihad" and many leading countries in the world.

The terrorist attacks on the World Trade Center and the Pentagon on 11th September 2001 shed light on the globalization of the terrorism problem. Though terrorists do not have powerful armed forces or weapons of mass destruction, they are nevertheless capable of causing damage, even to great powers, comparable in scope to the actions of army divisions. For the first time, mankind faces the threat of bio-terrorism, and the danger of nuclear, chemical, radiation and cyber terrorism is great. For the first time, terrorists are preaching their objectives through global information channels.

Since the start of the 21st century, the number of terror attacks around the world has risen 4- or 5-fold. This flaring up of terrorist activity came at the height of the War on Terror led by the USA, and most of the terrorist attacks occurred in the three countries – Iraq, Afghanistan and Pakistan – that are at the epicenter of this war.[26] The authoritative American RAND center, in a report on the state of the terrorist threat in the world, recorded 28 Islamic extremist groups in 2007 similar to Al-Qaida, which carried out around 100 attacks, and in 2013 – 49 groups and almost 1,000 attacks.[27] The terrorist group ISIL established control over a considerable swathe of the territory of Syria and Iraq for two years. Terror came to Europe.

The Fourth (De)Industrial Revolution and the Global Economy

Globalization is regarded as a process in which national economies are transformed into a unified global economy. Until recently, the United States were the main beneficiary of the globalization process, because they happened to possess the mechanism of control over investment flows, capital flows and world trade, especially since no-one tried to challenge the domination of the dollar as an international settlements and reserves currency. Therefore,

....

[26] *Rossiya v politsentrichnom mire* (*Russia in a Polycentric World*), ed. by A. A. Dynkin and N. I. Ivanova. Moscow, 2011. P. 143.

[27] Yevgeniy Antonov, "Khalify revolyutsii" ("The Caliphs of the Revolution"), *Intelros*, Issue 8, August 2014. PP. 73-74.

together with globalization, "financialization" was under way, implying a process of transforming commodities and product markets into financial markets. All things of dollar value were being turned into financial instruments traded at global financial hubs on commodity, raw materials and futures exchange markets mainly in the UK and the USA. At the same time, these markets turned into pricing centers for resources and raw materials.

"A post-industrial economy based on money, services and intellectual property rights turned information, along with money, into one of the most important productive resources: the role of digital technologies increased dramatically along with employment in knowledge-based industries."[28]

The Executive Chairman of the Davos Economic Forum, Klaus Schwab, put forward the concept of the fourth industrial revolution, and has not met with any serious objections from the expert community. The first revolution was associated with the construction of railways and the use of the steam engine; the second concerned mass production based on the use of electricity and conveyor systems; the third had to do with the introduction of computers in the 1960s. The fourth revolution began at the turn of the third millennium. Its core manifestations are the ubiquitous mobile Internet, miniature production devices, and artificial intelligence and machines that are capable of learning. Artificial intelligence is already found everywhere: from translation software and Siri to driverless cars and unmanned drones. Whereas today the impact of artificial intelligence depends on who is controlling it, in tomorrow's world it will depend on whether it will even be possible to control it.

Breakthroughs are being made in new fields of knowledge and in new technologies: the decoding of the human genome, nanotechnologies, renewable sources of energy, quantum computing. Digital technologies are already capable of cooperating very actively with both the physical world and the biological world. Schwab identified as mega-trends the creation of unmanned vehicles, 3D-printing, robot technology, and the creation of new materials with pre-programmed properties – metals with a "memory" enabling them to return to their original form, and ceramics and crystals that can transform pressure into energy. Blockchain technology will make it possible to create an extremely diverse range of applications, the most famous of which is Bitcoin.

---

[28] Alexander Losev, "Dorogoy tsarya Midasa. Kak material'nyy mir prevrashchayetsya v finansovyy" ("Following the Way of King Midas. How the Material World is Turning into the Financial"), *Kommersant. Den'gi* (*Kommersant. Money*), Issue 2, February 14, 2019. P. 17.

The industrial revolution is unfolding not like a straight line on a graph, but at an exponential rate. It took 120 years for the spindle, the symbol of the first industrial revolution, to spread throughout the planet; the Internet has done so in less than ten years. The task of decoding the human genome took 10 years and 2.7 billion dollars; today, your genome can be decoded in a matter of hours, and for the average citizen of earth, it is an affordable service. 3D production could be combined with genetic information in order to manufacture skin, bone, heart and muscle tissue.

Big companies are rising to the top ever faster and using smaller and smaller amounts of start-up capital. The average age of the companies in the S&P 500 index has fallen from 60 to 18. The greatest economic efficacy has been demonstrated by digital platforms: networks that bring together the sellers and buyers of goods and services and maximize profits using the scale effect. It took Facebook just 6 years to achieve a turnover of a billion dollars, and Google only five. The largest taxi company, Uber, does not own a single car; Facebook does not create content; the giant trade company Alibaba does not produce goods; and the biggest player in the hotel sector, Airbnb, owns no real estate.

"Information products" are provided with practically zero expenditure on storage, transportation and rollout. Instagram and WhatsApp needed virtually no financing to get started, yet tens of billions of messages are now sent using these platforms every day.

A significant part of commercial value is created with the help of exponentially expanding knowledge and information; this accumulates into enormous datasets, and that in turn spurs the development of data collecting, storage and processing technologies. Digital products – software, databases, intellectual services, games, music, video – are replicated, copied and shared on physical and virtualized data storage media. Giant datasets acquired with the help of Big Data technologies make it possible to create new services, to configure marketing, to adjust activities, to affect consumer tastes, to hold electoral and political campaigns which take into consideration the individual preferences of voters. More and more often we hear that "information has become the new oil". The monetization of digital technologies and the financialization of commodity markets and financial operations bring capital owners more profit than manufacturing.

It is no wonder that the fourth industrial revolution is creating fewer and fewer jobs. Many traditional professions face the threat of being pushed aside by digital technologies sooner than we think – not just accountants and librarians, but also insurance salesmen, financial analysts, and even drivers and journalists. In addition, material inequality in the modern world is only growing: the latest technologies bring in profits, first and foremost, to a small circle of highly-educated people. Half of all the assets in the world are controlled by 1% of humanity, and the bottom half of the world's population in terms of income possess less than 1% of the world's wealth.[29]

In the 1990s, the process of globalization was characterized, first and foremost, by companies from the USA, Western Europe and Japan actively moving into new markets – Eastern Europe, China, India, South-East Asia, Latin America – which had opened their doors to foreign investment. Since the start of the 21st century, however, the process has started moving in the other direction. More and more companies from developing countries have entered developed markets, often through mergers and acquisitions. As for the developed countries, they have started to put up impediments to prevent the "new pretenders" from advancing. Whereas in the past, issues of the development of the global economy were resolved within the framework of the G7, today these issues have become the prerogative of the G20, which includes all the major developing economies.

Dynamism has been shown by the BRICS countries, which are playing a growing role in the global economy and in politics. "The aggregate GDP of the BRIC countries has close to quadrupled since 2001, from around $3 trillion to between $11 and $12 trillion. The world economy has doubled in size since 2001, and a third of that growth has come from the BRICs. Their combined GDP increase was more than twice that of the United States and it was equivalent to the creation of another new Japan plus one Germany, or five United Kingdoms, in the space of a single decade," observed the man behind the BRICS concept, Jim O'Neil of Goldman Sachs.[30] The growth rates of Russia, Brazil and South Africa then fell, but those of India and China did not. Hot on the heels of the five BRICS countries are other developing economies, which Goldman Sachs has described as the "next eleven": Bangladesh, Egypt, Indonesia, Iran, Mexico, Nigeria, Pakistan, the Philippines, South Korea, Turkey and Vietnam.

Globalization has enabled hundreds of millions of people to break out of the poverty trap. The biggest winners from globalization, incidentally, have

---

[29] Klaus Schwab, *The Fourth Industrial Revolution*. Crown, 2017. P. 92.

[30] Jim O'Neill, *The Growth Map: Economic Opportunity in the BRICs and Beyond*. Penguin, 2011. PP. 4-5.

been the super-rich around the world, and a large proportion of the middle classes, first and foremost in China.[31]

A serious watershed in economic globalization was the global crisis in 2007-2009. Since then, growth rates in the global economy have amounted to 2.5% a year on average, whereas in the period between the Second World War and the start of the 21st century, the figure had been around 4%. In 2007, the economies of more than 65 countries grew by more than 7% a year, including such major countries as Argentina, Vietnam, India, China, Nigeria and Russia. In 2017, there were just six such countries, and they were small, such as Ivory Coast or Laos. Ruchir Sharma – a global strategist at Morgan Stanley – associates this with three main factors: a fall in the growth rate of the working-age population (from 2% a year in 1980 to 1% now), an increase in the debt burden in all countries (from 100% of GDP in the late 1980s to 300% in 2018), and deglobalization. Cross-border financial flows (mainly bank loans) fell from 16% of global GDP to 2%, a figure on a par with the early 1980s. The world fell into the grip of "debt fear". From 2008 onwards, the major countries have set up approximately 6,000 barriers of various kinds, to protect themselves from foreign competition. As a result, international trade has fallen to 55% of global GDP (30% in 1914 and 1980, 60% in 2008).[32] *The Financial Times* confirms that the amount of money crossing state borders from 2007 to 2016 fell 3-fold, with most of the funds taking the form of direct investment. The main reason was the sharp fall in the banks' international lending activity, above all that of the European banks.[33]

Not only are many voters becoming enemies of globalization, but so too are several Western governments. "Neglected by the mainstream left and right, many have opted instead to vote for populist and nativist politicians typically opposed to globalization. Isolationism is, once again, becoming a credible political alternative. Without it, there would have been no Brexit and no Trump."[34] Donald Trump won the election largely thanks to slogans advocating protectionism and protecting the country from an influx of

---

[31] "Global Inequality. Shooting an Elephant", *The Economist*, September 17, 2016. PP. 66-67.

[32] Ruchir Sharma, "The Boom Was a Blip. Getting Used to Slow Growth", *Foreign Affairs*, May/June 2017. PP. 104-108.

[33] Shawn Donnan, "Deglobalization. Ebbs and Capital Flows", *Financial Times*, August 22, 2017. P. 9; Shawn Donnan, "Globalisation in Retreat: Capital Flows Decline since Crisis", *Financial Times*, August 21, 2017 <https://www.ft.com/content/ade8ada8-83f6-11e7-94e2-c5b903247afd>.

[34] Stephen D. King, *Grave New World: The End of Globalization, the Return of History*. New Haven, 2017. P. 6.

foreign workers, and then took the United States out of negotiations on a Trans-Atlantic trade and investment partnership and the Trans-Pacific trade partnership, and initiated programs designed to support exports. Following the G20 summit in Hamburg in July 2017, Fyodor Lukyanov wrote: "For the first time, a leader has emerged who openly states that protectionism isn't a problem, but a solution."[35]

Incidentally, as the famous banker Satyajit Das rightly observed, "Support for freer trade and greater openness had in fact begun to falter well before economic nationalists like Trump and Farage took centre stage."[36] In the period 2009-2015, the number of measures taken to restrict trade was three times the number of measures designed to liberalize it. The USA, the UK, Brazil, Canada and a host of countries in the EU have chosen to back domestic producers. "Buy domestic" campaigns have taken place in the USA, England and Australia. Financial authorities have cut interest rates to a minimum level and introduced quantitative easing, to guarantee a favorable exchange rate for international competition.[37]

As a result of measures taken by the central banks to solve their own governments' debt problems, and "quantitative easing", 15 trillion dollars' worth of state obligations have come to be in the hands of just six central banks (and the equivalents thereof) – the USA's Federal Reserve System (FRS), the European Central Bank (ECB), and the Central Banks of Japan, England, Switzerland and Sweden. This is one fifth of the debt obligations of these countries, four times higher than pre-crisis levels.[38]

Ever more books and articles are being written about the end of globalization.[39] Danny Roderick, of Harvard's Kennedy School of Government, maintains that the world went too far with economic globalization, in the direction of an impractical version of "hyperglobalization", in which the destruction of barriers to trade and financial cross-flows became the goal

....

[35] Fyodor Luk'yanov, "Master po prodazham" ("The Master of Sales"), *Rossiyskaya Gazeta*, July 9, 2017 <https://rg.ru/2017/07/09/fedor-lukianov-donald-tramp-vystupil-v-kachestve-agenta-po-prodazham.html>.

[36] Satyajit Das, "The Age of Protectionism Precedes Trump", *Gulf News*, September 20, 2016 <https://gulfnews.com/business/analysis/the-age-of-protectionism-precedes-trump-1.1899069>.

[37] Ibid.

[38] Kate Allen and Keith Fray, "Decade of QE Leaves Big Central Banks Owing Fifth of Public Debt", *The Irish Times*, August 16, 2017 <https://www.irishtimes.com/business/economy/decade-of-qe-leaves-big-central-banks-owning-fifth-of-public-debt-1.3188340>.

[39] See, for instance: Stephen D. King, *Grave New World: The End of Globalization, the Return of History*. New Haven, 2017.

in and of itself, instead of being a tool with which to achieve fundamental economic and social objectives.[40]

In the fields of information technology and scientific and educational cooperation, however, globalization is successfully continuing. The quality of education varies to a decisive degree from one state to the next, and this is becoming a crucial factor in terms of competitiveness. One increasingly hears people talking about "countries with an intellectual deficit", rather than about "poor countries". The weakest states are finding it harder and harder to fend off competition in this sphere, and on top of that they are coming up against the problem of "brain drains", leading to growing economic and social inequality.

Only societies that are poorly developed can allow themselves (so to speak) to have a weak state. A host of countries in sub-Saharan Africa have extremely weak institutions of power, but this is a guarantee not of democracy and increasing wealth, but of anarchy and poverty. The taxes may be very low there, but this inevitably means that there is no adequate social policy, infrastructure or law enforcement body, and education and healthcare are poor.[41]

Globalization and the emergence of a multipolar world do not, in and of themselves, regulate the system of relations between states. Awareness of this fact is prompting the discussion of issues related to the creation of a trans-state world order.

At present, a process of integration at a regional level has become the priority. It is easier to set common rules based on similar cultural traditions and economic development at a regional, rather than a global, level. The European Union is the most advanced integration project. In Asia and in Africa, integrational processes are slower, not least because many nation states are still in their infancy. A drive towards integration can be seen with the establishment by CIS nations of the Eurasian Economic Union.

States are intensifying efforts aimed at setting up systems of global governance. The OECD, WTO, IMF, World bank, and G20 now address matters which used to be the exclusive responsibility of individual nation states. These include financial markets, corruption, specific economic policies,

---

[40] Dani Rodrik, "Put Globalization to Work for Democracies", *The New York Times*, September 17, 2016 <https://www.nytimes.com/2016/09/18/opinion/sunday/put-globalization-to-work-for-democracies.html>.

[41] Niall Ferguson, *The Ascent of Money: A Financial History of the World*. Penguin, 2008. PP. 275-277.

ecological standards, trade tariffs. But for all the widespread discontent with the weakness, fragmentation and inefficiency of the system of global governance, to date there is no common understanding of how it ought to be constructed.

As Parag Khanna rightly observes, "What we have right now, though, is global policy gridlock: the West demands interventions and human rights while the East prefers sovereignty and noninterference; the North is scared of terrorism and proliferation while the South needs food security and fair trade. Stock prices are crucial for the capital rich; commodities prices for the resource rich. Americans are suspicious of Chinese state-owned companies, while the Chinese are suspicious of American regulators. We seem as far away as ever from a new consensus. [...] But just as there is no one nation that can rule the world, there is no one institution that can run it, either."[42]

For a long time to come, the great powers will continue to have a decisive influence on the course of global affairs: such centers of power as the world's sole superpower, the USA; the European Union; China and India. Russia is a center of power as well. The global system is going to waver between attempts to build a unilateral world and the multilateral world that actually exists.

However, it is important to underline that all the great powers, along with other members of the G20, are pivotal; they are leaders of the world's civilizations.

Civilizations

In the late 20th century, it was thought, for some reason (I am exaggerating, of course), that people of various nationalities and faiths would start to merge together within the framework of some sort of cross-border community of shared humanity, founded on the principles of Western civilization. The concept of a plurality of cultures was rejected as an anti-Western idea. Huntington maintained that multiculturalism "'[is opposed to] narrow Eurocentric concepts of American democratic principles, culture, and identity'. It is basically an anti-Western ideology."[43] Francis Fukuyama talked of the

---

[42] Parag Khanna, *How to Run the World: Charting a Course to the Next Renaissance*. Random House, 2011. PP. 6, 7.

[43] Samuel P. Huntington, *Who Are We? The Challenges to America's National Identity*. N. Y.: Simon & Schuster, 2004. P. 171.

concept of the end of history as a decisive and irrevocable victory for the Western model of development on a global scale.[44]

This merging of cultures did not take place, and the world proved to be more complicated than that. People – and this is a phenomenon that can be widely observed – are in no hurry to reject not only state sovereignty, but also their own sense of self, their national and religious identity. Pankaj Mishra notes the rise in "static identities based on race, ethnicity, nationhood, and religion."[45]

Multiculturalism is now looked upon as the official basis of state policy in many countries, such as Canada and Australia. But people are increasingly seeking, and finding, sources of strength in the roots of their own civilizations, and national self-esteem is on the rise. A growing number of thinkers are appealing to an analysis of cultural and civilizational factors to explain modernization, political democratization, the behavior of ethnic groups, military strategies, and the nature of relations between various states. And this has proved to be a very productive approach. Culture does indeed matter.

There is a tendency to believe that civilization emerged in the same places as states, and that its forefathers were that same foursome – Sumer, Egypt, India, China. The latest discoveries made by scientists do not give us good grounds for considering this to have been proven. It appears that agriculture was invented on the island of New Guinea (which is now shared by Indonesia and Papua New Guinea), and in Peru, before it emerged in Sumer. It seems that writing emerged in South-West Europe and China before it developed in Sumer, too. And some incredibly old monumental edifices have been discovered in Malta.

It is difficult to pin down the exact meaning of "civilization". In Latin, the word "civilis", from which "civilization" is derived, meant "civil, of the state, political, worthy of a citizen". It was a concept that incorporated all of the civil qualities taken together, including upbringing and level of education. An equivalent concept can be found in the ancient Chinese language, which sounded like "van" and meant the most important qualities inherent to the Confucian "noble man", or the "complete man". It was in this sense that the term civilization was used by the Enlightenment thinkers of the 18th century, who spoke in favor of the development of civil society, in which freedom

---

[44] Francis Fukuyama, *The End of History and the Last Man*. Penguin, 2012.

[45] Pankaj Mishra, "The Globalization of Rage. Why Today's Extremism Looks Familiar", *Foreign Affairs*, November/December 2016. P. 51.

and law reign supreme. It was first used in print, it would seem, by the British philosopher David Hartley in his book *Observation on Man*, published in 1749, in which he contrasted "barbarity and rudeness" with "knowledge and civilization". The concept of the "barbarian" was widely used in Western Europe in the Middle Ages and the early New Age to denote the uneducated and those seen as inferior, including the Slavs, Madyars, Vikings, Saracens, Arabs, Tatars and Turks.[46] In France, the first person to write about civilization, in his work *The Friend of Man, or Treatise on Population* (1756), was the marquis Victor de Mirabeau, the father of a famous figure from the French Revolution, Honoré Mirabeau. The term initially described some sort of advanced state of cultural and intellectual development. The word was defined in a similar vein – as a stage in human progress, which came after wildness and barbarity – by Louis Morgan, Karl Marx and Max Weber.

People began talking of civilizations in the plural – as a socio-cultural phenomenon – in the first half of the 19th century, when Henry Bocle's *A History of Civilization in England*, Francois Giseau's *A History of Civilization in France*, and Raphael Altamira Y Crevea's *A History of Spain and Spanish Civilization* appeared. In these books, civilization was essentially portrayed as an equivalent concept to that of a nation, with its specific culture, mentality, history, and language. Giseau also published *A History of Civilization in Europe*.

In the 18th and 19th centuries, concepts of civilization were of a purely Europe-centric nature. "Eighteenth-century gentlemanly culture seemed a welcome revival of the spirit of Athens and Rome and, while the optimism of the French Enlightenment wilted beneath the blade of the guillotine and the carnage of the Napoleonic wars, it blossomed again the gentlemen's clubs of nineteenth-century Britain," joked the well-known English historian Roger Osborne. "[T]he wonders of Ancient Greece and Rome, of Venice and Florence, were of a piece with each other and with the marvels of industrial Britain. [...] Those who lay outside this sacred line were discounted as barbarians – and those within as civilized. The civilized world of Buckle's time was not only self-defining, it had a mission 'to suppress, to convert and to civilise' the rest of humanity, justifying the European colonization of the world as a beneficial mixture of evangelism and moral superiority."[47]

---

[46] David Cannadine, *The Undivided Past. Humanity Beyond Our Differences*. N.Y.: Knopf, 2013. PP. 219, 221.

[47] Roger Osborne, *Civilization: A New History of the Western World*. Random House, 2011. PP. 4-5.

One of the first to put forward the theory of civilizations outside the European framework was the Russian ideologue of pan-Slavism, Nikolay Danilevsky. In his book *Russia and Europe*, published in 1869, he identified nine historical types that had developed in independent civilizations, three of which belonged to "the tribes of the Semite race" – Chaldean, Hebrew and Arabic; two to indigenous tribes – Hamite (Egyptian) and Chinese, while the rest were Aryan – Indian, Persian, Greek, Roman, German. The eleventh type to emerge in the arena of world history, was, he thought, the Slavs. Danilevsky considered language and race to be defining characteristics in terms of the classification of civilizations.

In the early 20th century, the civilization-based approach – the notion of history as the totality and series of socio-cultural systems – became fairly popular. It was developed by Pitirim Sorokin, who put forward, in my view, the most exhaustive list of criteria that differentiate one civilization from another. Each of these includes an ideological collection of values, inherent systems of language, science, religion, philosophy, law, ethics, literature, art, sculpture, architecture, music, and economic, political and social theories, as well as actions, ceremonies and rituals.

The theory of civilizations was given a major boost by Oswald Spengler, whose book *The Fall of the West* had the effect of a bomb going off in Europe's intellectual world. Outlining the seven biggest civilizations in history – Egyptian, Chinese, Arabic, Greco-Roman, Mexican, Semite and Western, he measured the average life cycle of a civilization, which he found to be around 1,000 years, and astonished the public by predicting the inevitable death of Western European civilization in the same way that its great predecessors had died.

A classic author in this genre is Arnold Toynbee, who was not as pessimistic as Spengler about the West, seeing a way out in spiritual renewal. In his twelve-volume *A Study of History*, Toynbee proposed that religion and territory should be seen as the key defining traits of a civilization. Looking at civilizations as macro-cultures, Toynbee noticed in each a specific spiritual and social structure, together with institutions and elites, and stages of development including the emergence and creation of a universal state and a universal church and onwards to death and ruin. In the many volumes of his epic work, Toynbee identified between 21 and 26 civilizations in the history of mankind, and between eight and ten that were alive on earth at the time of writing. These were the 10 living civilizations, according to Toynbee: Western civilization, the Orthodox Christian Middle East, the Orthodox Christian civilization in Russia, the Islamic civilization, the Hindu civilization, the Far

Eastern civilization centered around China, the Far Eastern civilization in Japan, the Polynesian civilization, the Eskimos, and the nomadic civilization. According to Toynbee's not overly optimistic assertion, "the Polynesian and Nomad societies are now in their last agonies and that seven out of the eight others are all, in different degrees, under threat of either annihilation or assimilation by the eighth, namely, our own civilization of the West." Even Western civilization, he added, "may also have passed its zenith for all that we as yet know".[48]

In France, where the "Annales" school long dominated historical studies, Fernand Braudel was a leading figure in the study of civilizations. He saw them as a complex and well-ordered system of prohibitions, instructions and principles determining mentality and the structure of feelings and actions.

The civilization-based approach was significantly discredited during the Second World War, which saw a huge split within Western civilization (the founder of the "Annales" school, Marc Bloc, was even shot by the Gestapo), and during the Cold War, whose ideological fronts extended throughout all countries and continents and even inside individual states (for example, Germany, Korea, and Vietnam). It was rejected on both sides of the Iron Curtain. In the West, it was replaced by a concentrated view of the world as a battlefield between the forces of democracy and totalitarianism. In the Soviet Union, the preferred view of history was as the arena for class struggle.

An explosive level of interest in the theory of civilizations returned in the 1990s, following the publication of Samuel Huntington's articles and book, *A Clash of Civilizations*, in which he wrote, "In the emerging global politics, the core states of the major civilizations are supplanting the two Cold War superpowers as the principal poles of attraction and repulsion for other countries."[49] In total, Huntington identified nine major global civilizations: Western, Latin American, African, Islamic, Chinese, Hindu, Orthodox, Buddhist, and Japanese.

Huntington asserted that the future would be defined by a conflict between civilizations. "Civilizations are the ultimate human tribes, and the clash of civilizations is tribal conflict on a global scale." "It is human to hate.

---

[48] Arnold Toynbee, *A Study of History: Abridgement of Vols I-VI*. Oxford University Press, 1987. PP. 244, 276.

[49] Samuel P. Huntington, *The Clash of Civilizations and the Remaking of World Order*. N.Y. et al., 1996. P. 155.

For self-definition and motivation, people need enemies: competitors in business, rivals in achievement, opponents in politics. They naturally distrust and see as threats those who are different and have the capability to harm them. […] In the contemporary world the 'them' is more and more likely to be people from a different civilization."[50] However, Huntington left some hope for the West and the rest of humanity: "Avoidance of a global war of civilizations depends on world leaders accepting and cooperating to maintain the multicivilizational character of global politics."[51]

Contemporary authors display a certain civilizational minimalism. Adda Bozeman identified five in the pre-modern world: Western, Indian, Chinese, Byzantine and Islamic. Matthew Melko found twelve throughout the whole history of mankind, seven of which no longer exist (Mesopotamian, Egyptian, Cretan, Classical, Byzantine, Central American, Andean), with five continuing their history – Chinese, Japanese, Indian, Islamic and Western. Shmuel Eisenstadt added another to this list – Jewish.[52]

In modern Western thought, Russia is rarely identified as a representative of an independent civilization. Russia is more often associated with either Byzantine civilization – in relation to the Middle Ages – or to Western civilization. Niall Ferguson, the most oft-quoted English historian in the world, who works at Harvard, sees good reason to assert that "the Soviet Union was as much a product of Western civilization as the United States." He also argued that "in fact, it [the USSR] was the last European empire to rule over large tracts of Asia."[53]

And now let us proceed with my own perception of the landscape of modern civilizations.

What I understand by civilization is a socio-cultural community of nations and states, lasting a long time in historical terms, which incorporates a host of shared or similar parameters and characteristics.

1. A geographical region, since the environment is a basic condition for the formation of civilizations, particularly ancient ones. In this regard I share the view of Fernandez-Armesto, who defined civilizations as "a relationship

----

[50] Ibid., PP. 207, 130.

[51] Ibid., P. 21.

[52] Adda B. Bozeman, *Politics and Culture in International History: From the Ancient Near East to the Opening of the Modern Age*. N. Y., 1994; Matthew Melko, *The Nature of Civilizations*. Boston, 1969; Shmuel Eisenstadt, *Comparative Civilizations and Multiple Modernities*. Leiden, 2003.

[53] Niall Ferguson, *The Great Degeneration: How Institutions Decay and Economies Die*. Penguin, 2012. P. 23.

between one species and the rest of nature, an environment refashioned to suit human uses".[54]

Robert Kaplan, in *The Revenge of Geography*, states that the intelligentsia of both the Neo-Conservative right and the liberal left continue to proclaim that the ideas and the actions of individuals shape history – and they are certainly right. Nevertheless, it is also true that "human beings operate under constraints imposed by geography and the vast and varied phenomena that emanate from it: everything from persistent, albeit changeable, national characteristics to the location of trade routes to the life-or-death requirement for natural resources – oil, water, strategic metals and minerals."[55]

Overly favorable climatic conditions do not stimulate the development of civilization. Civilization appears in those places where, on the one hand, there are challenges to survival (for Russia, for instance, this is the challenge of the cold climate), and, on the other hand, a reasonable surplus of products can be created (by contrast with regions in the Far North, where only a nomadic culture is possible).

2. Religion. Max Weber identified five "global religions": Christianity, Islam, Hinduism, Confucianism and Buddhism. It is worth noting that all five were born in Asia. And they all, to a greater or lesser extent, form the foundations of key civilizations. Today, it is more customary to consider only three religions to be global: Buddhism, Christianity and Islam. Four fifths of humanity are religious (though not all of these necessarily believe in God, since this is not a requirement of some religions). 56% of all believers profess one of the Aramaic religions which have a single god – Christianity, Islam and Judaism. There are 2.18 billion Christians (17% of all believers on Earth are Catholics, 7.5% are Protestants and 4% are Orthodox).

More than a quarter of all those who profess a faith are Muslims (1.4 billion). Judaism is around 0.2% – 13.5 million people. The Russian Empire was home to the largest number of Jews in the early 20th century, whereas now 81% of them live in Israel and the USA, and only 205,000 live in Russia.[56] Hinduism is around 14% (870 million) of the world's population, and Buddhism (which has split into two branches – Mahayana, widespread in

---

[54] Felipe Fernández-Armesto, *Civilizations: Culture, Ambition, and the Transformation of Nature*. Simon and Schuster, 2001. P. 4.

[55] Robert D. Kaplan, *The Revenge of Geography: What the Map Tells Us About Coming Conflicts and the Battle Against Fate*. N. Y., 2013. P. 347.

[56] "Alive and Well: Special Report", *The Economist*, July 28, 2012. PP. 2-3.

China, Korea, Vietnam and Japan, and Theravada, with its more ancient roots, prevailing in Sri Lanka, South-East Asia, Tibet and Mongolia) 7.1%.

One of the obvious trends in contemporary global development is the growth in religiosity, which is also known as "God's revenge". Churches are emptying in Western Europe, but even there, mosques are overcrowded.

3. Linguistic affinity. There are a number of global languages which are common to one (or more) civilizations. This has already been covered.

4. Particularities of culture, and a system of values. Lawrence Harrison regards culture as the totality of "the values, attitudes, beliefs, orientations, and underlying assumptions prevalent among people in a society", which is "acquired-transmitted from generation to generation through the family, the church, the school, and other socializing instruments."[57]

5. Enduring characteristics in socio-political organization, and interrelations between the state and society, which are often described in terms of political culture.

6. The psychological feeling of belonging to a community, of self-identity.

7. In the modern world (and at other times), all of this is supplemented by a geopolitical vision of the elites, and a striving for regional integration.

All of the characteristics listed, of course, are different in nature, and we would not be able to find a single civilization for which they would all be fully suitable. Not all the features are equally important for the identification of a particular civilization or for self-identification by its representatives.

For instance, geography is exceptionally important in terms of defining African, Latin American and Indian civilizations, but less important for Western civilization, which is now spread far and wide across various continents (though it played a massive role for its European forefathers).

Religion is important in terms of identifying the specifics of Islamic, Western and Latin American civilizations, but could not be more important for the African civilization or that of East Asia, both of which are syncretic, i.e. based on a combination of several religions or teachings. The ancient Jewish religion, one that is found all over the world, can scarcely be defined as the basis of any modern civilization, while the state of Israel should be seen in practical terms as a part of Western civilization more than anything else.

---

[57] Lawrence E. Harrison and Samuel P. Huntington, *Culture Matters: How Values Shape Human Progress*, 2001. P. xv; Lawrence E. Harrison and Jerome Kagan, *Developing Cultures: Essays on Cultural Change*. Routledge, 2006. P. xii.

Linguistic affinity brings together the Latin American civilization (which speaks the Latin group of languages) and the Chinese civilization, but is not a determining feature for the African or Indian ones.

Civilizational self-identity is difficult to measure, since people identify themselves more in terms of their country, ethnicity, or even their continent, and only then (if at all) with a civilization.

It is my belief that there are currently nine civilizations in the world today, some of which can be broken down into sub-civilizations. Each of them has a kernel, in which its civilizational particularities are manifested at their most distinct, and a periphery, where they are vague. Each civilization and/or sub-civilization has distinctive leader-states, or one distinct leader-state, which are the sites of the crystallization of civilizational particularities and centers of attraction for the countries and peoples that are part of the civilizational community. Incidentally, if there are several leader-states inside a civilization, relations between them are not necessarily harmonious.

1. Western civilization, with various sub-civilizations: the European sub-civilization, coinciding in the main with the borders of the European Union. The central states are Germany, France, the UK, Italy and Spain; the North American sub-civilization, which, in addition to its leader, the USA, includes Canada; the Australian sub-civilization, in which Australia is the leader in relation to New Zealand and a number of adjacent island states.

2. Eastern European (Eastern Christian, Eurasian) civilization, which I am inclined to qualify as such, following Toynbee and Huntington. The central state is Russia, and the countries commonly known as the kernel of the Commonwealth of Independent States are drawn to Russia.

3. Islamic civilization: the Arabic sub-civilization, incorporating 23 countries, with Egypt and Saudi Arabia as its leaders; the Turkish sub-civilization, with Turkey as its leader; the Indo-Persian sub-civilization, including Iran and Pakistan as its leading states.

4. Indian civilization, in which, in addition to the undisputed leader, India, there are also Nepal, Bhutan and Sri Lanka.

5. Chinese civilization, for which a single country is quite sufficient: China. All the more so given that it has given a massive boost to the development of my sixth and seventh civilizations. Probably for this same reason, I would also categorize Korea as a sub-civilization.

6. Japanese civilization.

7. The civilization of South-East Asia, mainly coinciding with the ASEAN countries. This civilization is synthetic, still coming into being, far from fully-formed, polycentric, multi-ethnic and multi-religious. The country

with the greatest potential to be a leader is Indonesia, which is the biggest country, but it is also a peripheral one in the Islamic civilization.

8. African civilization, incorporating the continent to the south of the Sahara. The leader – not the most typical country in terms of the continent and its civilizational characteristics – is South Africa.

9. Latin American civilization, where the leader is Brazil, with Mexico and Argentina also playing very significant roles.

Unlike Huntington, I would suggest that it is an inherent trait of people not only to feel hatred, but also, as a bare minimum, to pursue their own interests. And this interest is evidenced less in conflict than in cooperation. I would therefore suggest that what awaits us – in the best-case scenario – could be more of a dialogue than a clash of civilizations.

What will it look like, though, and who will the participants be, given that civilizations, as a rule, do not have subjects as such? An answer comes in the fact that we can point to civilizational leaders. It is these leader-states that are, as a rule, the great powers of the modern world. I would point out that almost all the leader-states of the civilizations and sub-civilizations (except for Iran) are in the G20. This book will primarily be about them.

CHAPTER 2
UNITED STATES OF EUROPE

Western European civilization is unique in that it is the only civilization to have had a fundamental impact on the whole of the rest of the world – through conquest, resettlement, economic expansion, and ideas.

The West Has Long Been in Fashion

One view is that the West is all-powerful and that this is a big advantage, because it promotes the ideals of progress and democracy. With the collapse of the USSR, its only serious rival disappeared, the fate of the world is decided by the G7 and NATO, and they alone possess global capabilities, including military ones.

All the major non-Western economies lag far behind the West in terms of GDP per capita. Average income per capita in developed countries is $47,400, while the average in the world as a whole is $16,500.[1] The same can be said about the quality of GDP, its structure. The gross product of Western countries is created in large part in the services sector (around 80%), including science, education, healthcare, telecommunications and high-tech manufacturing. The Western countries control the international banking system and almost all the currency reserves. They are leaders in the fields of research and development, telecommunications, and the aviation industry. Western countries are the biggest consumers in the world. McDonald's and KFC, Google and Facebook have set the pace in a liberalized global market.

The leading ideologies of the last few centuries – liberalism, conservatism, Christian democracy, anarchism, Marxism, Communism, socialism, social democracy, conservatism, nationalism, chauvinism, racism, corpo-

---

[1] *The Economist. Pocket World in Figures.* 2018 Edition. L., 2017. P. 25.

ratism, fascism – these were all engendered by Western civilization. Values and doctrines that come from the West are shared by substantial segments of the elite, and sometimes by people on other continents.

Huntington called this a universal civilization, or the "Davos Culture". "Each year about a thousand businessmen, bankers, government officials, intellectuals, and journalists from scores of countries meet in the World Economic Forum in Davos, Switzerland. […] Davos people control virtually all international institutions, many of the world's governments, and the bulk of the world's economic and military capabilities."[2]

There is an alternative view, however. Western civilization is on the wane, its global political, economic and military might, by comparison with the other centers of power, is steadily falling. The indicators of the West's economic superiority are significantly lower than at any time in the last three centuries, and that downward trend will continue. The center of global dynamics is clearly switching from Europe and North America to Asia and Latin America, and the recession of 2007-2009 only served to accelerate this long-term trend.

In 2011, for the first time, the GDP of developing countries surpassed that of developed ones. The USA ceased to be the largest economy in the world, after being displaced by China. The parameters of the state debt that has been accumulating in the West stand at over 100% of GDP. Today, in terms of economic growth, Western countries, particularly in Europe, are lagging behind developing countries.

Change is occurring in geopolitics as well. The territories and populations of countries under direct Western control have dramatically shrunk in the last century. Ideas of the natural supremacy of the West are becoming less popular even in Western countries themselves.

"Doesn't the whole world crave to be western? We can no longer have any confidence in that. It was remarkably arrogant to believe the rest of the world would passively adopt our script. We must cast a sceptical eye on what we have learnt never to question," wrote Edward Luce of *The Financial Times* in 2017.[3]

Which of these two views is correct? As I see it, they both have validity. The West's domination in many spheres is undeniable today. Yet irreversible

---

[2] Samuel P. Huntington, *The Clash of Civilizations and the Remaking of World Order*. N.Y. et al., 1996. P. 57.

[3] Edward Luce, "The Siege of Western Liberalism", *The Financial Times*, May 4, 2017 <https://www.ft.com/content/c7444248-3000-11e7-9555-23ef563ecf9a>.

and fundamental shifts are taking place, leading to a reduction in the might of the West in comparison with other centers of power, above all, in Asia.

What are the distinctive characteristics of Western society? Which components of its experience can be considered definitive? The answers to these questions, which have been asked by generations of researchers, are hidden in details, but what they share is that they define the key institutes, customs, events and ideas that can be considered as pivotal for Western civilization.

At the core of the Western – originally, European – civilization lie some very diverse components: the classical legacy of the cultures of ancient Greece and Rome, the Roman Catholic Church, the culture of the Germanic tribes, the division between spiritual and secular power, political and societal pluralism, the doctrine of the rule of law, the free city, the legacy of the Renaissance, the Reformation and Protestantism, individualism, rationalism, the presence of representative bodies, liberalism and democracy, market capitalism, colonialism, militarism and nationalism.[4]

When considered separately, almost none of these characteristics were unique to the West. But their unique combination defined its particular characteristics, as did its geography.

William McNeill, in his classic work on the origins of the West, commented on such characteristics of European geography as extensive and fertile plains and an uneven coastline, providing a large number of natural curves. He noted the number of rivers suitable for transport by ship, flowing from South to North, which provided a line of communication from the Mediterranean region. He also mentioned the abundance of forests and metals. The fairly harsh, cold and damp climate made life very difficult, and this stimulated civilization, but at the same time there were comfortable conditions for travelling and trade.[5]

The authors of *Contemporary World Policy* from the Moscow State Institute of International Relations (MGIMO) make an important point that "In Europe, the limited nature of the natural resources ready for immediate use meant that a fundamentally different kind of behavior was required – not a contemplative one, but an active one, predetermining the formation of an aggressive type of society, constantly aware of the 'man versus nature' antagonism, forced to put up opposition to the outside environment and construct its

---

[4] See further: Vyacheslav Nikonov, *Sovremennyy mir i yego istoki* (*The Modern World and Its Origins*). Moscow, 2015.

[5] William H. McNeill, *The Rise of the West: A History of the Human Community*. Chicago, 1963.

way of life in accordance with this… Renewing and maintaining life demanded a constant, never-ending battle with the outside world, which became an extremely important source of philosophical thought and state institutions."[6]

Classical Debut

European civilization emerged in Greece. A leading role in Greek societies was played by the Achaean tribes, which became famous thanks to the Troy campaign, sung by Homer in *The Iliad* and *The Odyssey*. In historical times, the territory occupied by the Hellenic peoples was broken down into two thousand small, independent city states, which alternated between enmity and alliances with one another. The social systems in the various parts of Greece differed but developed along the same lines. "There was a very general development, first from monarchy to aristocracy, then to an alternation of tyranny and democracy," observed the British thinker Bertrand Russell. "The kings were not absolute, like those of Egypt and Babylonia; they were advised by the Council of Elders, and could not transgress custom with impunity. 'Tyranny' did not mean necessarily bad government, but only the rule of a man whose claim to power was not hereditary. 'Democracy' meant government by all the citizens, among whom slaves and women were not included."[7]

Socrates, Plato and Aristotle – the thinkers from antiquity who had the greatest influence on Western thought – lived in Athens in the 5th and 4th centuries BC, in other words at the time of the flourishing of democracy. All of them criticized democracy. "If the poor, for example, because they are more in number, divide among themselves the property of the rich – is not this unjust?" asked Aristotle.[8] Socrates even got into conflict with Athens' democracy, and was executed for "corrupting the youth" and "refusing to recognize the gods recognized by the state, and of introducing other new divinities".[9]

More important than that, however, was the notion maintained by the Athenians themselves, that they were a unique race. This gave them an undoubted feeling of superiority in relation to other peoples, whom they

....

[6] *Sovremennaya mirovaya politika* (*Contemporary World Politics*), ed. by A. D. Bogaturov. Moscow, 2010. PP. 336-337.
[7] Bertrand Russell, *History of Western Philosophy*. Psychology Press, 2004. P. 20.
[8] *Complete Works of Aristotle*. Volume 2. Princeton University Press, 1984. P. 2033.
[9] Cit. from: R. E. Allen, *Socrates and Legal Obligation*. Univerity of Minnesota Press, 1981. P. 3.

considered barbarians. Greece was less a country than a cultural and linguistic concept, since its component city states, as in a kaleidoscope, formed patterns of ever-changing alliances and constant wars. It was only an outside threat, primarily the incursion by the Persians at the start of the 5th century BC, that was able, for the first time and for a long time, to unite them. Only under the reign of the Philip of Macedonia, who established his hegemony over Greece after the battle of Chaeronea in 338 BC, did the city states acknowledge that they were all part of a common political whole. The age of city-states had come to an end, to be replaced by the epoch of monarchies – kingdoms and empires. The result of the conquests of Philip's son, Alexander the Great, was the supplanting of the Persian Achaemenid Empire, which had been dominant for two centuries, stretching from the Atlantic to the Bay of Bengal. Alexander's conquests led to the creation of a Hellenistic world that stretched from Spain to northern India. The Hellenistic world became a model for many future cultural and national entities, particularly in Europe.

Greek civilization was ultimately overtaken by Roman civilization. Rome first meddled in Greek matters when it started a war with Pyrrhus, the king of Epirus, who won a "Pyrrhic victory" at a great cost at the Battle of Asculum (279 BC). Last to fall at the feet of the Romans was Egypt, where the Empress Cleopatra – in spite of her tempestuous love affairs with Julius Caesar and Mark Antony – was forced to commit suicide in 30 BC. This marked the formal conclusion of the Hellenistic epoch.

The Greeks made a decisive contribution to the Western concept of the state.[10] There were other components of the ancient Greek legacy that proved to be important to Western society: ideas about democracy; a conviction about their own superiority, including from the point of view of the structure of the state and racial characteristics; the experience of creating a colossal empire; respect for art and knowledge; and critical reasoning, which strove to question everything.

Hellenistic culture did not disappear when the Romans arrived. On the contrary, the Roman Empire became the continuation of what were now Greco-Roman traditions, spreading them across Europe. When the Romans first made contact with the Greeks, they realized that by comparison with the Greeks, they were fairly coarse and unrefined. The instinctive attitude of the Greeks towards the Romans was one of scorn, which was replaced by fear: the Greeks felt themselves to be more cultured, but weaker. The Greeks

---

[10] François Chamoux, *Tsivilizatsiya drevney Gretsii* (*The Civilization of Ancient Greece*). Yekaterinburg-Moscow, 2009. P. 226.

were significantly more advanced than the Romans in trade, agriculture, art, literature, and philosophy. The Romans did not have any new literary or artistic forms to offer, nor any philosophical systems or scientific discoveries. They were clearly superior to the Greeks in the art of war, however, as well as social cohesion, including the compiling and systematization of laws, engineering, construction and the building of roads. In all other matters, the Romans recognized the achievements of the Greeks and strove to copy them.

There was no democracy in Rome. For the first two and a half centuries after the foundation of Rome by the brothers Romulus and Remus (approximately 754-753 BC) there was a monarchy. After the last king, Lucius Tarquinius Superbus (510-509 BC) was exiled, a republic was established, in which "citizen warriors" played an important role. The highest governing body was the Senate, which was dominated by representatives of the nobility and, later, the wealthiest families. By the middle of the 3rd century BC, Rome had conquered the entire Italian peninsula and entered into a successful battle for dominance in the Mediterranean. Rome officially became an empire in 27 BC, when Octavian had the title Augustus bestowed upon him by the Senate. To this day, in the Western world and elsewhere, Roman political terms and concepts continue to live on, including republic, senate, constitution, consul, prefect and the rule of law.

Starting in the 4th century BC, Rome began to pay its soldiers, who fought battles ever further away from their home. Thus, the foundations were laid for one of the most powerful professional organizations in the history of mankind – the military machine of Rome. In its nine centuries of existence, millions of people from every corner of Europe, North Africa and the Middle East passed through it. All democracies that existed in the ancient world passed into oblivion under the imperial might of Rome, and democracy would have to wait two thousand years for its next incarnation.

The Romans were constantly fighting battles on the edges of their empire, but within it there was continuous peace, which not only enabled them to spread their culture, but also helped to familiarize people with the idea of a single civilization, living under a common jurisdiction, a single government. Of course, there were great civilizations that flourished in Eurasia beyond the borders of the Roman Empire as well, such as India and China. But the Romans had the notion that they owned the whole world, beyond the borders of which there were only barbarians, whose land could also be conquered should the need arise. For most Romans, the empire expressed a shared sense of humanity; it was seen as a force for good. This prompted the 18th century British historian Edward Gibbon to remark sarcastically that: "By defending themselves, the Romans conquered the whole world."

Rome waged wars not only "for the sake of its merchants", the assertion made by the most eloquent of all Romans, Cicero, who was ultimately executed for his big mouth. The Romans were inspired to fight by their sense of honor and the glory of their motherland. They had an unwavering belief that through their victories, they would bring benefit to all mankind. The notion of a single universal culture and a single global state, governed from a single center, with a single religion, has stood behind the idea of a European elite since the days of the Roman Empire. I suggest that this is a source of the West's messianism.

The Roman era saw the addition of another key component of Western civilization – Christianity. It came from the East, with its centuries-old tradition of anxiety and desperation, which used faith in a world beyond the grave, in life after death, as a spiritual antidote. After the crucifixion of Christ, a community began to form around the Apostle Peter, spreading from Palestine to other eastern provinces of the Roman Empire: Egypt, Asia Minor, the Jewish Diaspora and the capital of the empire itself. The builder of the Christian church, the Apostle Paul (who was once a persecutor of Christians before converting and preaching Christianity in the eastern Mediterranean and in Rome), opened the community to everyone, regardless of nationality, status, or gender. His letter to the Galatians contains the line: "There is neither Jew nor Gentile, neither slave nor free, nor is there male and female, for you are all one in Christ Jesus" (Gal. 3: 28). It was thanks to Paul's efforts that it became possible for non-Jews to be welcomed into the church, something that had been resisted by a large number of early Christians. Subsequently, a single community was created with universal teachings. Paul, an educated Jew and resident of the Greco-Roman world, invested Christianity with a unique combination of Old Testament moral zeal and cerebral Greek universalism.

Huge numbers of Christian saints and martyrs were victims of the large-scale Roman purges. There were mass executions of Christians, accused by the Emperor Nero of setting fire to Rome in the year 64 CE (the year in which the Apostles Peter and Paul were martyred). Thereafter, Christianity was officially declared by Rome to be illegal for 250 years. The Christians followed Christ's teachings: "But when they persecute you in this city, flee you into another" (Matthew 10:23). The public executions served only to cement the faith within the community, and aroused interest and admiration on the part of the Gentiles. Then a miracle occurred. The Emperor Constantine became a Christian, probably in the hope that this would help him govern such a gigantic, heterogeneous empire, particularly at a time when most of his soldiers, it seems, had already become Christians. In 313 CE, the edict of Milan was adopted, which asserted that Christianity was on an equal footing with the other legal faiths within the Empire, and effectively transformed Christianity into an official ideology. The Roman Empire became a Christian empire. The Pope was proclaimed head of the Church.

It was during the Roman epoch that Germanic tribes first arrived in the historical arena; they were not literate but had in many ways found their *raison d'être* and contentment in warfare, and they began their incursions into the weakening Empire around the year 400 CE. In order to fight off one group of tribes, the Romans brought in soldiers from another group. Before long, the Emperor had more Gothic soldiers in his service than Romans, and these were now the soldiers who could put Roman leaders on the throne. In the year 476 CE, the commander of the Germanic mercenaries, Odoacer, who was in control of the largest military force in Italy, simply overthrew the Emperor Romulus Augustulus. Given that Odoacer then proclaimed himself King, rather than Emperor, the Western Roman Empire officially came to an end. After this, the Empire slowly broke apart into its component entities. The Middle Ages had begun. The Eastern Roman Empire (which had broken away from the Western half in 395) continued to exist for another millennium as the Byzantine Empire, until the Ottoman conquest of Constantinople in 1453. It played a role in the creation of the Eastern Christian civilization, of which Russia is a branch.

Through the Dark Ages

There were two main institutions that served as bridges between antiquity and Western civilization: the plethora of small kingdoms – collapsing and then re-emerging – under the control of various German tribes, and the Christian Church.

Among the German tribes who were to dominate the Western world in later centuries were the Angles, the Saxons, the Franks, the Frisians and the Alemanni, whose languages were the forebears of English, German and Dutch. The Germans in the northern group were the forefathers of today's Scandinavian peoples. The tribes that played the most important role in the fate of the Western Roman Empire were the East Germanic tribes that brought it to an end: the Ostrogoths, Visigoths, Vandals and Burgundians – who then dispersed across Europe and did not leave any linguistic legacy. Their rulers did not have any understanding of what it meant to rule a state with fixed borders, to create government structures, or collect taxes. The remnants of the Roman administration disappeared amid the chaos, while trade and cities went into a downturn. The population of Rome, which amounted to one million people at the peak of its power, fell to just 20,000 by the 7th century. Economic, political and spiritual life was rapidly moving away from the cities and into the countryside. The West underwent a transition, mainly towards a land economy of small, self-sufficient rural communities. The monasteries that sprang up (the first was created in 415 near Marseilles) became centers of rural, rather than urban, life. The kings and the aristocracy resided, in the main, in castles surrounded by hunting lands, and in country estates.

Of the German tribes that became the "heirs" to the Roman Empire, only one succeeded in building a sustainable state that can be directly traced to one that exists today in Western Europe – the Franks. It was the Franks that played a decisive role in shaping Western civilization. The Carolingian kingdom, centered around Aachen, attained its greatest majesty during the reign of Charlemagne (768-814), who dedicated his life to conquering the neighboring countries and converting them to Christianity. At its peak, the Frankish kingdom occupied the territory of modern day France (whose name derives from it) and regions in Germany, Spain and Italy – from the Pyrenees to the Oder and from the North Sea to Rome. It was the largest Western European state in history, if one discounts the short-lived empires of Napoleon and Hitler.

After the fall of Rome, the rulers of Byzantium were crowned as emperors. Taking advantage of the fact that a woman (Empress Irene) was on the throne in Constantinople, Charlemagne claimed that this broke Roman tradition and managed to secure the title of Emperor of Rome. At Christmas in the year 800, Pope Leo III, after Christmas Mass, crowned Charlemagne and proclaimed him Caesar. This was not so much an anointing of the bowed head of a king as a desperate attempt by the Pope to secure the patronage of the most powerful man in Europe and obtain influence over the destiny of the Christian world.

Following Charlemagne's death, his successors broke the empire apart. Under the Treaty of Verdun in 843, it was divided into three parts by his grandsons. Charles the Bald received the Western, Roman part, which would later become France. Ludwig of Germany acquired most of the eastern lands, which would later become Germany. Luther I was granted the title of emperor along with Austrasia, eastern Burgundy, Provence and Italy, which became known as the Middle Kingdom, a future bone of contention between France and Germany. Subsequent infighting and invasions by the Vikings broke up the Empire still further. Counts and dukes were transformed into local rulers, who depended little on the kings. "Not everything in the kingdom belongs to the king" – this was the core principle which lay at the heart of the concepts of political rights and freedom of economy, which in many ways defined the specific features of the West and its successes.

For three centuries (932-1250), Frankish knights, dressed in armor that their poorer adversaries could never have afforded, almost never tasted defeat. With control over France and western Germany, they spread throughout Europe, fending off Vikings, Arabs, Hungarian and Slavic tribes, and defeating or conquering England, parts of Wales and Ireland (the Norman conquest of 1066, which the British endow with a special historical significance, was only a small part of a broader Norman – Frankish expansion), southern Italy, Sicily, Greece, Bohemia, Moravia, Estonia, Finland, Austria, Hungary, Silesia, Castalia, and Aragon. "They brought the cult of the warrior to every corner of Europe," observed Osborne. "Brutal but honourable, greedy but loyal to one's family; avaricious but Christian – these were the characteristics of the new masters of Europe, together with a cultural addiction to the idea of war and a social structure that reflected the needs of a military society."[11] Through the capturing of land, strategic marriages, and conquest, the Frankish nobility attained material and political supremacy in almost every European kingdom. Their descendants, from wives taken from among the local elite, became national aristocracy. Along with Catholicism, Franks also brought the well-developed system of feudalism, which had developed organically in France, but was forcibly imposed on the local population in all the territories that were subjugated, thanks to agreements between kings and conquering knights, concluded even before the start of military campaigns. The eastern borders in the West were therefore defined by the 10th and 11th centuries.

The Roman Catholic Church outlived the Western Roman Empire, but its future was in other people's hands: the Popes were now isolated in Rome, which had lost its status as the capital, and they were forced to bow down either to the local – initially pagan – Gothic kings, or to Byzantium. For Western Europe, there remained as much classical culture as the Catholic Church was able to imbue it with. The prestige of the Roman Empire was

---

[11] Roger Osborne, *Civilization: A New History of the Western World*. Random House, 2011. P. 157.

the main reason why the Germans who defeated it adopted Christianity. The subsequent transformation of Christianity into the universal religion of Europe in the Middle Ages was facilitated by its openness to saints or sinners, kings or tradesmen. Everyone could be (and was required to be) a Christian.

The conquests of Charlemagne, which were accomplished with Rome's blessing and, in many ways, with the aim of spreading Christianity, changed the nature of the Church's activity. Missionary activity to convert new peoples to Christianity was supplemented with the power of the sword; emissaries from the Vatican were required to teach the populace to change their ways, to ensure that they were unscrupulously loyal to the teachings of the Church. The Pope's web tied the Western Christian world into a natural unity.

The rise of Western Europe and the papacy could not but provoke a conflict with Constantinople, which also saw itself, not without justification, as the capital of the Christian world, all the more so since Byzantium was far more advanced than the Frankish kingdoms. In 1054, a council was held in Constantinople, after which the Pope was no longer commemorated in Eastern churches. A decisive division between the churches had taken effect.[12] This event, which reinforced the split in Europe between Orthodoxy and Catholicism, between East and West, played a massive role in the destinies of the old world, and of Russia in particular. An intense rivalry began between the two churches for the soul of Europe. In the 11th to 13th centuries, Hungary, Poland, Scandinavia and the Baltic coast were converted to Western Christianity, and the eastern border of Western civilization was established in places where it was to remain largely unchanged for a long time. Kyivan Rus, Bulgaria, Romania and Moravia remained within the Byzantine commonwealth of Orthodox nations.

The ecclesiastical jurisdiction of the Pope spread throughout Europe, from Spain and Great Britain to Scandinavia and Poland. The "Dictatus papae" of Pope Gregory VII in the late 11th century proclaimed the supremacy of the Church in both religious and secular matters. One of the main reasons why monarchs in the Western Christian world consented to the supremacy of the Pope was that the Pope was at that time beyond any suspicion of having ambitions to secure secular power. Indeed, the popes had never tried to become emperors, nor did the emperors try to become popes. They were in no doubt about the need for each other's existence, and the battle between

---

[12] Yevgraf Smirnov, *Istoriya khristianskoy tserkvi* (*A History of the Christian Church*). Moscow, 2007. PP. 412-421.

them was all about the balance of power. This is an important feature of Western Europe, which differentiates it from Byzantium, for instance, where the Emperor was seen as a ruler presiding over both secular and spiritual matters, and the Patriarch was appointed with his consent.

One of the key characteristics of Western civilization was the markedly higher level of political and social pluralism and competition, both between states and within them. "Europe was also a profoundly divided continent," observes Brendan Simms. "It had been engaged in internecine conflicts throughout the Middle Ages: between emperor and pope, between the principal monarchs, between city states and territorial princes, between various barons, between rival cities, and between peasant and lord. Catholic unity had come under attack from Lollards in England, Hussites in Bohemia, Albigensians in the south of France and various other sects [...]."[13]

The sources of this pluralism are to be found in the "Dark Ages", which were characterized by the disappearance of Roman power in the absence of any other power. As Norman Davies has stressed, it was this "disorder [that] begat feudalism [...] The key elements were heavy cavalry, vassalage, enfeoffment, immunity, private castles, and chivalry."[14] The need to ensure the presence of a large class of highly qualified cavaliers – Chevaliers, Caballeros, knights, the gentry – was the very thing that tied the land to service. The king rewarded his closest associates with land. In return for this, the new elite were required to provide soldiers to the king should the need arise. The land that was given to them became known as a feud, the word from which the name of this socio-economic system is derived.

The king continued to own the land in theory, but in practice it became the inherited property of the feudal lord, who was bound only by an oath. Royal power was thus founded on the unspoken contractual nature of the relations between the ruler and his subject, and this idea has never died out in Western Europe. This predetermined the weakness of the feudal monarchs and monarchies. The central administrative figure of Frankish Europe was the count (the local landowner by birth or appointment), who collected taxes on behalf of the sovereign and himself, presided in court, and was in charge of local military mobilization. The merger of military and civil functions was a fundamental principle of the European feudal society.

Western European society proved to be hierarchical. The treaty of Verdun in 843 was based on the principle that "every man must have a master". Only

---

[13] Brendan Simms, *Europe: The Struggle for Supremacy, 1453 to the Present*. L., 2013. PP. 2-3.
[14] Norman Davies, *Europe: A History*. Pimlico, 1997. P. 311.

the Emperor and the Pope were theoretically free, although even they were considered to be servants of God. This gave each person a set of coordinates, a clearly defined cell within society, created a certain amount of protection, but also created a harsh system of subordination. Pluralism carved out a path for itself, however, in the form of the burgeoning particularism, the development of the system of immunities, the expansion of the system of contractual relations between monarchs and their vassals. The complex system of benefits, agreements, alms, charters and contracts created an interdependency between the peasant and his master. The monarchs would ultimately make everyone subordinate to them, but during the confrontation, the nobility managed to secure a large set of rights, first and foremost rights to property, which were considered inviolable.

There was a relatively independent aristocracy, a large peasantry, and a small but significant trading class. There was no democracy in the Middle Ages, of course, but the European elites, in the long run, were free, and demands for political rights were widespread among affluent sections of the population.[15]

No other civilization can boast a history of representative bodies that goes back for a millennium. Iceland's Althing, probably the oldest parliament and judicial assembly on the planet (and now probably the smallest in terms of the size of the building that houses it), was founded in 930. The purpose of having representation of the people was so that complaints could be discussed and the people could provide a votum on the budget allocations decreed by the central powers. With its help, the aristocracy, the senior priests, and in many cases the cities too, entered into a "safety contract" with the king, to whom they promised to provide military aid and support in exchange for protection from enemies and a guarantee of their land rights.

In the Middle Ages, the parliaments were not constant bodies of power and did not pass laws. In some cases, in the era of absolutism, these bodies were banned, or saw their powers significantly restricted. Yet these class-based representative institutions were the very thing that secured the forms of representation which started to evolve into the institutions of modern democracy in the New Age.

It should be stressed that a certain amount of pluralism was still present even when the monarchs, having fought against the feudal lords and the parliaments, gradually started to take the upper hand and the monarchies became absolute. Why? Because the law and representative bodies existed,

---

[15] Ibid. PP. 311–314.

and these also imposed a limit on supreme power. The concept of the rule of law had been inherited from the Romans. Or, to be more precise, from the Byzantines, since the codifying of Roman law, starting from the time of Adrian, had been initiated by the Byzantine emperor Justinian in the 6th century. At the end of the 11th century, his *Corpus Juris Civilis* was rediscovered in Italy and put at the heart of canonical law, along with the secular studies of jurisprudence in Bologna, which laid the foundations for the first real university, and for Western jurisprudence, which spread throughout the world from there.[16] Legislation in the West is so steeped in its Roman legacy that lawyers were required to understand Latin right up until the 20th century. Most of the contract law that is in place today, and the laws on property, inheritance, debt obligations, and defamation, and the rules on court procedures and witness testimony, are all variations on themes from Roman law. It is considered that the rule of law, reflected in the Magna Carta, and in the Magdeburg law, came into being six or seven centuries before the emergence of elections.

Incidentally, even the Magna Carta itself (its 800th anniversary was celebrated in 2015), often cited as the starting point of Western democracy, is a big historical myth. "By limiting the power of the king, the Magna Carta set a precedent for what would later be known as 'no taxation without representation,'" Edward Luce wrote. "This short medieval document was lost to the mists for several hundred years – Shakespeare did not even mention it in his play *King John*. Yet since the seventeenth century, when the Magna Carta was dusted off by opponents of Stuart tyranny in England, then made its way to America's thirteen colonies, it has morphed into the founding myth of Western liberalism. As Dan Jones, a historian of the Magna Carta, describes it, the year 1215 is today seen as 'year zero' of Western liberalism [...]. When the Universal Declaration of Human Rights was issued after the Second World War, Eleanor Roosevelt said that it 'may well become the international Magna Carta for all men everywhere.'"[17] In actual fact, the Magna Carta, which John was forced into signing at a time when he was in a tricky situation, stayed in force for just a couple of months and was then forgotten about for several centuries.

Among the key outposts of Western civilization were the cities, which had begun to grow once again. In the 11th century, the era of great Roman-

---

[16] Edward Luttwak, *The Grand Strategy of the Byzantine Empire*. Harvard University Press, 2009. P. 84.

[17] Edward Luce, *The Retreat of Western Liberalism*. Hachette, 2017. PP. 9-10.

esque (Roman, i.e. Byzantine) and Gothic cathedrals began. Recognition of the special status and role of cities came when Royal charters started being awarded to them. Max Weber has emphasized that "[i]n the central and northern European cities appeared the well-known principle that Stadtluft macht frei"[18](City air makes one free). Cities were governed by elected councils comprised of the most affluent and influential people, who in turn elected, from among their number, a mayor.

Western European cities were small in terms of their size and population. Professor Ian Morris of Stanford has calculated that the European city which came second to Rome with its one million population at the beginning of our era was London in the 19th century. Following the fall of Rome, the biggest city on the planet was Constantinople – 450,000 inhabitants in the year 500 AD, but thereafter its population began to fall steadily, and stood at 125,000 by the year 700. It was soon overtaken by Baghdad, Cairo and then the Spanish city of Cordoba, which, in the period 900-1000, under the control of the Arabs, was the most populated city on the European continent. From roughly the late 6th century AD until the end of the 17th century, however, the biggest cities on earth were all Chinese: Xianyang, Kaifeng, Guangzhou, Nanking and Peking. Only then did London and Istanbul enjoy a short-lived period of revenge, before once again giving way to non-European cities in the 20th century.[19] Today, the biggest city on the planet is Tokyo, while the largest Western city – New York – is only tenth in terms of population size.

The Renaissance and the Reformation

In 1500 there were more than 500 states, city-states, principalities and duchies in Europe. The autonomy of the cities grew particularly quickly in those regions where, as a consequence of the struggle between the emperors and popes, there was no centralized power – on the territory of modern day Germany and Italy. It was here that the phenomena that were to be key for the future European civilization came into being: universities, the Renaissance, the Reformation and then the Enlightenment.

At that time the Europeans realized, however, that… they did not know all that much after all. How did they come to this realization? Through

....

[18] Max Weber, *Economy and Society: An Outline of Interpretive Sociology*, Vol. 3. Bedminster Press, 1968. P. 1239.

[19] Ian Morris, *The Measures of Civilization. How Social Development Decides the Fate of Nations.* Princeton University Press, 2013. PP. 144-165.

the Crusades, and their interactions with the Arabs in southern Italy and Spain, which enabled Europe to discover the world of Byzantine and Islamic learning. At the turn of the second millennium, the countries of Islam were at a higher level of development than Europe. When European aristocrats arrived in the Holy Land during the Crusades, eminent Arabs were struck by how uncouth and poorly educated they were. After the conquest of the Middle East by Arab soldiers, classical Greek texts, having been preserved and translated into Aramaic and Persian, took on a new life in the minds and creative works of Islamic academics. The works of Plato and Aristotle became part of the Canon of the Arab world, as did the legacy of Byzantium. For a century and a half, Western Europe – in the Spanish city of Toledo, in Greece, in the Kingdom of the two Sicilies – actively set about translating into Latin previously unknown works written in Greek, Arabic and Aramaic. The West not only became acquainted once again – after 1,500 years – with the major works of Aristotle, Plato, the Neoplatonites, and Proclus, it also discovered the works of Al-Farabi, Avicenna, Averroes and many other outstanding Islamic scientists and thinkers. The enormous task of translating this literature was completed by about 1270, after which it proved possible to achieve the systematization of science and the classification of human knowledge (though not all of it, for Chinese and Indian learning, which was even more advanced, would only become known to Europe later). A special contribution in this regard was made by Thomas Aquinas.[20] It was in this period that ancient Greece and Rome were incorporated into the cultural family of Western civilization, while the Europeans themselves first became familiar with Arabic numbers (which were in fact invented in India), algebra and chemistry.

Europe could now get to grips with science, chiefly through the newly discovered works of Aristotle on logic, medicine, astronomy and mathematics, and their authority was irreproachable. Moreover, university courses included classes on the Bible, the works of Augustin, and Justinian's *Corpus Juris Civilis*, which constituted the basis for theology and law studies.

The era of the Renaissance began at the turn of the 13th and 14th centuries in Italy, and its historical significance lies in the commencement of the secularization of European society and its departure from Catholic dogma. The language and literature of ancient Rome became fashionable, and classical manuscripts were sought out and discovered. Brunelleschi and Donatello

---

[20] Maurice de Wulf, *Philosophy and Civilization in the Middle Ages*. Courier Corporation, 2012. P. 81.

spent years working on digs at Roman ruins, which had not elicited any interest earlier. In architecture, sculpture, painting and literature, the Italian Renaissance began to give gifts of creation comparable to the achievements of ancient Greece. The doctrine of rejecting worldly goods and focusing on prayer gave way to social activity and the desire to achieve success. "[Its significance] lies also in the whole vision of a world in motion, a world not rendered insignificant but made more beautiful by its transience, its erotic energy, and its ceaseless change."[21] Merchants in the era of the Renaissance spent money on works of art and wanted to feel just as charitable as their forefathers, who had donated money to churches and monasteries. The concept of civil humanism came into being, whereby the function of a moral compass began to be performed not by the church, but by a special layer of thought and feeling, encouraged by a noble tradition of republicanism, personal self-awareness, and the desire to perfect oneself.

New forms of administrative and political relations came into being in Italy. Lombardy and Tuscany served as laboratories for the Western world, where a successful experiment was conducted to create a new international commercial and industrial society – or capitalism. By the end of the 15th century, the Italians felt so superior to other Europeans that they came up with the notion of "barbarians" for all the peoples living on the other side of the Alps. The rest of Europe could sense, and recognized, this superiority. Remember that more than three quarters of William Shakespeare's plays are based on Italian plots. England became the most attentive student, showing greater mastery than all other Europeans of the economic and political lessons of the Italian Renaissance after the movement had died out in Italy itself. It was in England that this tradition developed into the concepts of the responsibility of executive power before Parliament, and industrialism, i.e. – industrial manufacturing based on the market economy.

The Renaissance was the first challenge to the world of the Middle Ages. The second was the Reformation in the 16th century. This was not only an attack on the Catholic Church, but also a revolt by the northern nations against the intellectual leadership of Italy and the reign of the Vatican at a time when, around it and inside it, events were taking place that were a long way from notions of Christian piety. To the God-fearing Germans and English, who had paid considerable amounts of money into the Pope's coffers, it became obvious that the authority of the papacy was not compatible with the recklessness and dissipation of the Borgias and the Medicis. On the

---

[21] Stephen Greenblatt, *The Swerve: How the Renaissance Began*. Random House, 2011. P. 10.

basis of Paul's letter to the Romans, which stated that man was saved by faith in Christ, Martin Luther came to the conclusion that nothing special had to be done in order to obtain salvation, least of all an appeal for help from the priests. The Reformation set itself the aim of reforming the church in line with the spirit and word of the Bible and on the basis of principles and norms from early Christian communities – meetings in modest settings, not in luxurious churches. The emergence of the Church of England, incidentally, was dictated by somewhat different circumstances: through Henry VIII Tudor's desire to wed Anne Boleyn, a move that the Vatican had sought to prevent, determined as it was not to allow him to divorce Catherine of Aragon. Protestants rejected the notion of the church as a middleman conveying the Bible's truth, affirming that each person could interpret the scriptures in his or her own way. Over the course of four decades from 1520 to 1560, a new form of preaching began to take root in northern Europe, in many German principalities, Swiss cantons, in the Netherlands, England, Scotland, Scandinavia and in parts of France. After a century and a half of bloody wars, Protestantism was established as the faith of half the people of Western Europe. Protestantism was by no means a byword for all-permissiveness. On the contrary, it required strict adherence to the Gospels. In Geneva, under the leadership of Calvin, people were put in prison for adultery, gluttony and magic, and criticism of the doctrines of Calvinism could result in the death penalty. Black magic, alchemy and wizardry, to which Catholicism had turned a blind eye, were now strictly forbidden. Witch-hunts and the burning of witches at the stake were a predominantly Protestant activity.

The Reformation and the counter-reformation that followed it – the Vatican's struggle against the freethinking reformers – brought an end to the epoch of the Renaissance as well. The very elderly Michelangelo lived to see the day when he was forbidden to depict nude bodies.

However, the Renaissance and the Reformation had already changed drastically the European worldview. There now emerged subjectivism and individualism, which were also a manifestation of greater intellectual freedom, and the growing social isolation of the individual. The pushing aside of the church as a middleman between believers and God altered the believers' perception of their relations with secular power as well. And it is no accident that Dutch and North American Calvinism proved to be closely bound to ideas of political self-determination. The notion of the right to individual choice was already playing a role in the West by the 17th century.

In the 16th century, the scientific revolution was characterised by a cry of "The ancient Greeks may have been wrong!" European scientists began to outdo them. In 1543, Nicholas Copernicus stopped thinking of the Earth as the center of the solar system. Galileo Galilei asserted – not without unpleasant consequences – that the Earth revolved on its axis. Kepler and Rene Descartes were the first scientists to pose questions about the laws of nature, in the modern sense. Isaac Newton's three laws of motion and law of gravity are still used today to calculate the orbit of the Earth and the planets, the flight parameters of rockets, and the construction of cars and buildings. At the same time, Galileo, Kepler, Descartes and Newton all based their arguments on the idea that the laws of nature were created by God.[22] In the 1600s, the merchant and scientist Antonie van Leeuwenhoek, with the help of a microscope he had made himself, became the first person to see bacteria – this was the discovery of the micro-cosmos, hitherto unknown to the world. Ideas about the world changed in an even greater way in the light of all the geographical discoveries that were being made. For the first time, the practical significance of science was recognized in connection with its usefulness in military matters. Galileo Galilei and Leonardo da Vinci were given positions in government service thanks to their modernization projects relating to artillery and fortifications. The main driver and instrument of science was the printing of books. This dramatically increased the level of interest in humanitarian knowledge. In Western Europe, in the 16th century – for the first time since classical times – political philosophy emerged. The works of Niccolo Machiavelli became widely known, as did the ideas of the Spanish Catholic philosopher Francisco Suarez on the right of kings to issue orders and the right of peoples to overthrow tyrants, and Thomas More's communist *Utopia* was published.

The Beginnings of Capitalism and Modern Democracy

As we know, new forms of administrative and political relations took shape in Lombardy and Tuscany during the Renaissance, which was marked by a previously unseen concentration of wealth in the hands of the ruling aristocracy. Initially the source of this wealth was farming, crafts and trade. Capitalism began with the start of banking operations, with a particularly important part played by the Medicis. The Medicis achieved fame as "bankers"; they sat on benches (hence the word *banchieri*) behind tables that were put out on the street.[23] However, their role was not limited to banking. Two

---

[22] Leonard Mlodinow and Stephen Hawking, *The Grand Design*. Random House, 2010. P. 29.
[23] Niall Ferguson, *The Ascent of Money: A Financial History of the World*. Penguin, 2008. P. 42.

Medicis – Leo the Tenth and Clement the Seventh – assumed the papacy; two women from the same family – Catherine and Marie – became Queens of France, and a further three were dukes – of Florence, Nemur and Tuscany.

The Italian banking model inspired those northern European nations which achieved the highest level of economic development in later centuries – the Dutch, the British, and the Swedes. Amsterdam, London and Stockholm were the first cities in which prototypes of today's central banks emerged. If the rise of banks was the first great revolution of capitalism, the second was the creation, in Florence, of securities – a promise by the government, written down on paper, to pay a particular percentage to the bearer. Securities were originally needed by the Florentines – constantly doing battle against their enemies – so that they would be able to pay their mercenary army.

In the 17th century, Amsterdam became recognized as the capital of financial innovations. Here, the Amsterdam exchange bank came into being, and with its help the Dutch managed to transform the monetary system. For instance, they solved the problem of money being spoilt by the introduction of "bank money" – the giving of credit equivalent to a coin's mint value, even when the coin had been damaged by being in circulation. The key Dutch invention, though, was the joint stock company. Dutch merchants, in their efforts to bring an end to the monopoly of the Spanish and Portuguese in trade in spices from the East, created the East India Company, by decree of His Royal Dutch Majesty, in 1602. Anyone could sign up for shares, and in the blink of an eye the Dutch East India Company became the biggest company on the planet. The company was divided up into small shares (actien).[24] A secondary market for the buying and selling of shares emerged almost immediately. For the purposes of share trading, it was decided, in 1608, that an indoor stock exchange (Beurs) should be erected on Rokin Street, not far from the Town Hall. At roughly the same time – in 1609 – the Amsterdam exchange bank was established, which supported the stock market: shares could now be acquired on credit. The joint-stock company, the stock exchange, the bank – these were the three cornerstones of the new – capitalist – economy.

The Republic of the Netherlands later moved aside to give way to a new, successful rival – England, which also became the founder of parliamentarianism and modern democracy. Fukuyama rightly observed that "contemporary liberal democracies did not emerge out of the shad-

---

[24] Ibid. PP. 126-138.

owy mists of tradition. Like communist societies, they were deliberately created by human beings at a definite point in time, on the basis of a certain theoretical understanding of man and of the appropriate political institutions [...]."[25] The principles of liberalism were formulated by John Locke in his work *Two Treatises of Government*, published in 1690. Citing the Roman idea of natural law and the opinion of the majority in the English parliament, he asserted that every person was endowed from birth with the right to life, freedom and property. Locke portrayed the state as a result of a social contract, whereby people would provide a share of their freedoms to the government in exchange for protection of their rights.

Under the Stuarts, Parliament aspired to become equal with the Crown and attempted to force Charles I to resign himself to the notion of the monarch acting as a servant of the state. The aristocrats and landed gentry of which Parliament was composed were attempting to preserve their ancient rights and privileges, for which they suggested a host of measures to restrict the powers of the king: the regular convening of Parliament, the imposing of taxes only with their consent, the independence of the courts. In so doing, they unwittingly laid the foundations for the liberal state, in which they sought a place for the rational man, imbued with a sense of his own dignity. In order for this goal to be achieved, the execution of a king and two revolutions were needed, though they were admittedly brought about with less bloodshed than those that occurred later in other states.

A massive role in the success of the West was played by another of its inventions: mass industrial production. In 1771, two English entrepreneurs – Richard Arkwright and Jedediah Strutt – constructed the first weaving factory, powered by water, in the town of Cromford, in Derbyshire, thereby initiating the factory system. Before long, Britain was the world's leading economy and the "workshop of the world", the first state to go into the industrial phase of development. Alongside this, the country secured its domestic market by means of protectionist measures, and controlled trade in the world's oceans by possessing the most powerful naval fleet on the planet. Adam Smith would formulate the principles of the free market, and they were brought to life with the help of brutal state regulation. Britain's true apogee arrived in the period between 1845 and 1870, when it produced more than 30% of the world's

---

[25] Francis Fukuyama, *The End of History and the Last Man*. Simon and Schuster, 2006. P. 153.

gross product, with one fifth of global trade turnover under its control and two fifths of the world's industrial production, despite having only 2% of the total population of Earth.[26]

Britain was the first global economic empire and the most successful state at exporting its culture. The English lifestyle was actively copied all over the world. Pushkin's Eugene Onegin is described as having "dressed like a London dandy". Almost all sports disciplines originated in England.

In fact, the 18th century saw the start of the era of Anglomania, as the French called it. Thereafter, in the other countries of Europe, there was a need to pay ever greater attention to the demands of the educated nobility, who were well read on matters of law, rights and duties, freedom and conflicts of interest. Other affluent sections of society followed them, creating a mass of pragmatic and independent individuals, aware of their responsibility for their own fate. This group would later become known as the middle class. Political ideas, spreading ever further afield as a result of the increase in literacy, became an exceptionally influential medium for social changes. Political philosophy flourished at the time of the Enlightenment, which preceded the great French Revolution towards the end of the 18th century. The key idea was declared to be the transformation of all public institutions, from politics to morals and faith – on the basis of the principles of reason. One of the most notable representatives of the Enlightenment, Denis Diderot, asserted: "Men will never be free until the last king is strangled with the entrails of the last priest." This new thinking not only threw off the yoke of the King and the Church, which had become hateful during the era of rationalism, but also resulted in great bloodshed and a dictatorship.

Incidentally, after the Great French Revolution and the coming to power and defeat of Napoleon, a fresh round of "monarchization of Europe" took place, as a result of which, in 1815, Switzerland was left as the only European country without a monarchy. The European states, meanwhile, contributed enormously to the elimination of monarchies in the rest of the world, where the creation of empires was accompanied by the destruction of the local ruling dynasties or their subordination to the colonial powers. This process was largely complete by the start of the First World War: the Sultan of Morocco was the last monarch to find himself under a colonial administration, although he retained

---

[26] Fareed Zakaria, *The Post-American World. W. W. Norton & Company,* 2008. P. 174.

his title. By the end of the 19th century, constitutional monarchies were already fairly widespread in Europe, but in most of them, like Germany or Austria-Hungary, the head of the executive was not appointed by legislators and was not answerable to them. A system whereby the executive was answerable to parliament existed in the monarchies of Britain and the Netherlands, and also in France in the time of the Third Republic.[27] "Whereas monarchy, as real concentration of power or mere ornament, was a ubiquitous feature of the nineteenth century, we have to look a little harder for the traces of democracy. It is not even altogether certain that more of the world's population than a century before had a direct influence on its political destiny. This was doubtless the case in Western Europe and America, but it has to be set against the unquantifiable barriers to participation associated with colonialism," writes the German historian Jurgen Osterhammel.[28]

The concept of the rule of law emerged in Britain and included the ideas of professional judges, the ability to contest government decisions in court, recognition by the legislative and the judiciary of individuals' rights, and freedom of speech. In the 19th century, the central idea in this concept was the protection of property. The concept did not extend, of course, to the non-white citizens of the Empire, who had no chance whatsoever of being given a fair trial – nor, incidentally, did the poorest citizens of the British Isles themselves.

The "constitutionalization" of the West began in the USA (in 1787), France (1791) and Spain (1812), and was largely brought to an end by the adoption of the imperial constitution in Germany in 1871. "The key point is that on the eve of the First World War, after a full century of constitutionalization, only a few European countries had achieved a constitutional democracy with general elections and a system of majority government answerable to a parliament: Switzerland, France, Norway, Sweden, and Britain (as late as 1911, when the power of the unelected House of Lords were curtailed)."[29]

The emergence of a relatively mass-scale electorate – in France in 1848, in Germany from 1871 onwards, and in the United Kingdom from 1884 onwards – made it necessary to form parties, which were mainly either

---

[27] Jurgen Osterhammel, *The Transformation of the World: A Global History of the Nineteenth Century.* Princeton-Oxford: Princeton University Press, 2014. PP. 577-584.

[28] Ibid. P. 593.

[29] Ibid. PP. 598-599.

conservative or liberal. When the franchise was given to those outside the privileged classes, there was also scope for creating socialist parties, inspired by the ideas of utopian communists – Tommaso Campanella, Robert Owens, Charles Fourier – as well as anarchists, and Karl Marx. And although not a single socialist party came to power in Europe before the First World War, they did a considerable amount for the democratization of the European political system.[30]

As far as electoral democracy is concerned, it developed gradually. In Great Britain, prior to the reform of 1832, only 1.8% of citizens had the right to vote; this percentage had increased to 6.4% by 1867 and 12.1% by 1884. Half a century after the USA acquired independence, only 5% of the country's adult population voted in the presidential elections.

Women were granted the right to vote for the first time in Wyoming in 1869; the first country to try out the idea was New Zealand in 1893, while in Europe, Finland was the trailblazer in 1906, when it was still part of the Russian Empire. At the end of the 19th century, there was not a single country in Europe in which women could vote, and there were only a handful of countries in which more than 45% of men could do so.

In the USA, women first began voting in 1920; restrictions on voting for African-Americans in the Southern states were abolished in the 1960s.[31] Which country was the first in the world to introduce universal suffrage and direct voting rights? It was Russia – after February 1917!

The Imperial Spirit

By the middle of the second millennium, expanding trade and technological achievements had laid the foundations for the era of global politics. Sporadic contact between civilizations gave way to an uninterrupted, all-encompassing influence on the part of the West over all other places. The conclusion of the re-conquest of the Iberian Peninsula – the last Moors were ejected from Spain in 1492 – coincided with the date on which Columbus set sail, under the patronage of the Spanish monarchs, on the voyage aimed at finding a Western route to India: all the overland routes were at that time firmly under the control of the Muslims. Instead of India, Columbus discovered America, though he never believed it. That is why the continent was named after

....

[30] Ibid. PP. 594-604.
[31] Fareed Zakaria, *The Future of Freedom: Illiberal Democracy at Home and Abroad*. W. W. Norton & Company, 2007. P. 51.

Amerigo Vespucci, who did believe. Active penetration into both Americas began on the part of the Spanish, while the Portuguese moved into Asia. They were soon followed by England, France and Holland.

Why was it specifically the Europeans, rather than anyone else, that were able to create empires and a system of global dominion?

Philipp Hoffman shows that the reason for this was Europe's politically fragmented and warlike nature, accompanied by a number of wars that is without precedent on the rest of the planet. The waging of these wars demanded the perpetual refining of arms and military machines, something that also created incentives for improving the government, legal and financial mechanisms necessary for the objectives of military mobilization. Europe in the Middle Ages began to outdo the rest of the world in terms of spending on military innovations. Although it was the Chinese that invented gunpowder, it was the Europeans that managed to create firearms – from muskets to the artillery with which ships were fitted – and organized armies. It was specifically their superiority in the use of firearms that enabled a relatively small number of Europeans to keep a vast proportion of humanity under control.[32] Military force was the key factor behind the successes of colonial politics.[33]

In Asia, where the Europeans encountered enlightened societies with well-developed economies, they initially established no more than reinforced settlements, which became centers of trade for the acquisition of spices, coffee, tea and fabrics. The inhabitants of the Western hemisphere were much less fortunate.

In the early 16th century, the population of Mesoamerica, according to some estimates, stood at around 25 million people. The local people initially welcomed the Europeans. Yet the Europeans' military culture, according to which it was considered glorious to subject oneself to danger and to attack with the intention of killing, was beyond the understanding of the aborigines. The visitors were better armed (they had firearms and horses), better organized, and more disciplined. They also took with them from Europe to the New World new, previously unknown diseases. As a result of this, the population fell to 9 million within 50 years of their arrival. The magnificent civilizations of the Aztecs and Incas were completely destroyed. The native population of North America prior to the Europeans' arrival was around 6 to

---

[32] Philip T. Hoffman, *Why Did Europe Conquer the World?*. Princeton University Press, 2017. P. 101.

[33] Ibid. P. 43.

12 million people; after their arrival, it again fell significantly. The Europeans saw the native population either as incorrigible primitive wild men, or as "proud savages", deserving only death.

On the American continent, the primary source of income was precious metals, while in the countries of the Caribbean basin, it was the sugar and tobacco plantations. The commencement of the production of sugar cane in the West Indies was the event that led to the emergence of the African slave trade; this became a large-scale and profitable business. The status of whites as free men and of blacks as slaves was enshrined in legislation by the British, and soon became the norm for the rest of America. The flourishing of Virginia and North and South Carolina in the 18th century and the construction of luxury houses and estates in the cities was financed by the profits made from tobacco, coffee and rice, which were grown by the slaves. By the time slavery was abolished, the USA was producing three quarters of the world's cotton. In the British Empire, slavery was abolished in 1833, but persisted for another generation in the United States, until 1863. Lord Macaulay once said that "there is nothing so ridiculous as the British public in a periodic fit of morality."[34]

In the 19th century, the continent of Africa was partitioned among the European powers.

For five centuries, imperialist ideas penetrated the entire life, politics and psychology of the peoples of the metropolises – from the aristocrats to the man in the street. The very word "imperialist" was spoken with respect, and was imbued with romanticism. Cecil Rhodes, in the late 19th century, was the idol of a large proportion of English society, as the man who had turned Britain into an empire on which the sun never set. "[W]e are the finest race in the world and [...] the more of the world we inhabit the better it is for the human race" – pretty much every Englishman would have signed up to these words.[35]

Huntington summed up the effect of colonial policy: "Europeans or former European colonies (in the Americas) controlled 35 percent of the earth's land surface in 1800, 67 percent in 1878, and 84 percent by 1914. By 1920 the percentage was still higher as the Ottoman Empire was divided

---

[34] Cit. from: John Bew, "Pax Anglo-Saxonica", *The American Interest*, Vol. 10, Issue 5, May/June 2015. P. 42.

[35] Cit. from: Jeremy Paxman, *Empire: What Ruling the World Did to the British*. Penguin, 2012. P. 156.

up among Britain, France, and Italy. [...] Only Russian, Japanese and Ethiopian civilizations [...] were able to resist the onslaught of the West and maintain meaningful independent existence."[36]

Pankaj Mishra rightly observes: "In post-Cold War commentary and discourse in the West, the centuries of violence and suffering induced by colonialism, slavery, civil wars, and institutionalized racism and anti-Semitism were often reduced to the story of the two world wars – which in turn were interpreted primarily as necessary if terrible stages in liberal democracy's eventual triumph over its antimodern ideological rivals. [...] [W]estern intellectuals forgot (or unlearned) that totalitarian politics had in fact emerged from turn-of-the-century ideas – eugenics, racial unity, jingoistic nationalism, imperialism, social engineering – that had appeared first in liberal states and that were immensely popular in such bastions of liberalism as France, the United Kingdom, and the United States."[37] As for whether these states were genuinely liberal, or whether their elites merely paid lip-service to the idea of being liberal – that is another matter.

The Westphalian World

The emergence of an international system dominated by the West was an extremely important event in world history after 1500. While bringing about expansion from the inside, however, Western states cooperated with one another striving to develop shared rules of the game. In the mid-17th century the first attempt – and one that is still of significance today – was made to bring order to the European system. The Emperors of the Holy Roman Empire of the German Nation were less and less inclined to see themselves subordinated to the Vatican, particularly at a time when the Protestant Reformation was sweeping the continent, representing a real threat to their power. The results of this was the devastating Thirty Years' War, which caught Germany in its grip and which sucked in Denmark, Sweden and, finally, France. The rebellious states of Europe realized that they were in need of some different legitimizing principle, other than the benediction or the will of the Holy See (particularly given that some of them stopped being Catholic).

---

[36] Samuel P. Huntington, *The Clash of Civilizations and the Remaking of World Order*. N.Y. et al., 1996. P. 51.

[37] Pankaj Mishra, "The Globalization of Rage. Why Today's Extremism Looks Familiar", *Foreign Affairs*, November/December 2016. P. 52.

Such a principle was suggested by one of the most influential politicians of that time, Cardinal Richelieu – the supreme state interest (*raison d'état*), understood in terms of the modern concept of national security, which justified the use of any methods in order to preserve the state. This was the principal that lay at the heart of the Westphalian model, which came into being during the four-year negotiations between the Holy Roman Empire of the German Nation and France in Münster, and between the Empire, on the one hand, and Sweden, together with the other German states, on the other hand, in Osnabrück. The two peace treaties signed in 1648, which brought an end to the Thirty Years' War, became known as the Westphalian peace, given that both Münster and Osnabrück were located in Westphalia. The Holy Roman Empire lost its power over Europe, which was effectively turned into a conglomerate of more than 300 independent states, with the German rulers acquiring the status of kings. France and Sweden, which were put forward as European leaders, and their allies, by contrast, procured sizeable territories and rights to intervene in the Empire's affairs. The Lutherans and Calvinists had their rights and freedoms acknowledged. Domination by one center gave way to a balance of powers on the principle of sovereignty.

Russia has been part of this community, and one of the most influential states on the continent, certainly from the start of the 18th century – from the time of the Battle of Poltava, in which Peter the Great crushed the most powerful army in Europe at the time, namely the Swedish army of Carl the Twelfth. The German philosopher Leibnitz wrote, on that day: "The Tsar henceforth will attract the consideration of Europe and will pay a big part in general affairs… You can imagine how the great revolution in the North has astounded many people. It is commonly being said that the Tsar will be formidable to the whole of Europe, that he will be as though a Turk of the North."[38] To the west of Russia's borders, people have never appeared to think of Russia as a European country. The same applies to the Ottoman Empire, which controlled as much as a quarter of what was generally referred to as Europe.

The balance of power was radically destroyed by the wars conducted by Napoleon, who tried to bring about one of the most ambitious projects in the history of Europe aimed at creating a universal state. And he did not do so through the power of arms alone. "It is not simply that the language was

---

[38] Cit. from: Andrew Rothstein, *Peter the Great and Marlborough: Politics and Diplomacy in Converging Wars*. Macmillan, 1986. P. 124.

French which makes the Napoleonic programme for European unity seem so contemporary," joked Margaret Thatcher. "For example, among Bonaparte's aims was, he said, to create 'a monetary identity throughout Europe'. He later claimed that his common legal code, and university and monetary systems, 'would have achieved a single family in Europe. No one would ever have left home while travelling.' The president of today's European Central Bank could hardly have put it better."[39]

After the fall of Napoleon, Europe set about creating a common European system of security, which found its embodiment in the European concert of powers. This was born, as Henry Kissinger wrote, out of the transformation of the idealistic suggestions of the Russian Tsar Alexander I about rejecting the use of force and resolving conflicts through arbitration between the great powers, into a more practical concept, based on the principles of the balance of power.[40] At the Vienna Congress of 1815, a kind of diplomatic oligarchy emerged, which undertook to maintain international stability and the status quo through joint efforts. At first, these were the four great powers which had made the greatest contribution to the triumph over Bonaparte – Russia, Great Britain, Austria and Prussia. After the swift return to the international arena of France (against which the Concert had initially been created, in many ways), the quartet was transformed into a "pentarchy", and, when the kingdom of Italy joined it, into a hexarchy; a kind of G6, if you will. The French historian Antonin Debidour, in the late 19th century, described the European system that he knew as follows: "The states listed did not always live in complete harmony. At times, ferocious conflicts broke out between several of them. Some of these states were stronger and acquired greater influence than in the past, while others saw something of a decline and lost their former authority. None of them, though, suffered such a loss of strength, that the others were able to destroy it or exclude it from their association. All of them continue to exist, at times guaranteeing one another in equal measure through their rivalry, and through their agreement."[41] In many ways, thanks to the existence of the concert, the 19th century proved to be the most peaceful in history. Only the major Crimean War and Fran-

---

[39] Margaret Thatcher, *Statecraft: Strategies for a Changing World*. HarperCollins, 2002. PP. 326-327.

[40] Henry Kissinger, *Diplomacy*. Simon & Schuster, 1994. PP. 75-76.

[41] Antonin Debidour, *Diplomaticheskaya istoriya Yevropy ot Venskogo do Berlinskogo kongressa (1814-1878)* [*Diplomatic History of Europe: from the Vienna Congress to the Berlin Congress (1814-1878)*], Vol. 1. Moscow, 1947. P. 25.

co-Prussian war proved unavoidable; other major conflicts took place on the European and colonial periphery, while the USA endured the Civil War.

By 1914, the world was demonstrating greater political and economic unity than at any other time in the history of mankind. The scale of international trade and foreign investment in gross worldwide product was greater than at any other time before then, and would not reach that level again until the period from the 1970s to the 1990s. The term "civilization" was applied almost exclusively in relation to the West. International law was Western. The political system was the Western Westphalian system of sovereign national states and the colonial territories under their control.

During the First World War, however, vast areas of Europe were subjected to horrifying and unprecedented destruction. The First World War put a stop to the European nations' belief in their assumed superiority and "natural progress"; according to Osborne, the war, and the tense juxtaposition of the capitalist and communist systems, showed how wrong the Europeans were to assume a moral right to dominate others.[42] For the first time, Europeans began to ponder a crisis in their civilization. In 1919, the French poet and philosopher Paul Valery wrote: "We modern civilizations, we too now know that we are mortal like the others."[43]

The decline predicted by Spengler was indeed the start of the weakening of the European component of Western civilization, but not of Western supremacy. The United States of America was breaking into the global arena at a frenzied pace; as early as 1872 it had become the world's largest economy. Having entered the First World War in April 1917 and contributed to bringing it to an end, the USA, through the efforts of President Woodrow Wilson, exerted a strong influence over the conditions of peace. The Treaty of Versailles pushed Germany out of the European system; it was said of Germany that it was: "Too big to remain at peace, and too small to achieve hegemony." There were some in Germany who did not agree with the theory about hegemony. Also excluded from the European system was Soviet Russia, which had emerged from the ruins of the Russian Empire. The Versailles system, writes Brendan Simms, "was designed to guard against a revival of German expansionism while maintaining the *Reich* as a bulwark against the spread of Bolshevism."[44] The scene for a new confrontation was set.

....

[42] Roger Osborne, *Civilization: A New History of the Western World*. Random House, 2011.

[43] Cit. from: Mary Louise Roberts, *Civilization without Sexes: Reconstructing Gender in Postwar France, 1917-1927*. University of Chicago Press, 2009. P. 3.

[44] Brendan Simms, *Europe: The Struggle for Supremacy, 1453 to the Present*. Penguin, 2014.

On top of the conflicts between nation states, there was also a clash of ideologies. Karl Marx was a Western thinker who formulated his ideas on the basis of the experience of revolutionary France and capitalist England, and wrote his works in London – long before they were put into practice in Soviet Russia. Marxism was a product of Europe, but it did not have much success there. In the 1920s, fascism reared its head in the market of ideologies; it was born in Italy, and an even more dangerous variety of it arose in Germany – National Socialism (Nazism). Although both fascism and the Communist ideology had their roots in ideas and moods from the previous century, "these were not two sides of the same coin. The nationalism, xenophobia and assumptions of white supremacy that infected late nineteenth-century Europe formed the principles of fascism, but were directly challenged by communism, which promoted internationalism and equality."[45]

As Ian Kershaw observed, "During almost the whole of the first half of the twentieth century Europe's intellectuals – its leading thinkers and writers in a variety of disciplines – were preoccupied with a society in crisis. [...] The immense disillusionment with bourgeois society and loss of faith in the political system that represented it polarized intellectual reaction. Most common was a move to the Left, towards some variant of Marxism. A minority, however, looked to the fascist Right. Common to both types of reaction, though in very different ways, was the feeling that the old must be swept away and replaced by a new society based on utopian ideas of social renewal."[46]

Nazism as a European Value

The inter-war period was marked by a narrowing of the sphere in which liberalism was able to spread in Europe.

Hannah Arendt wrote: "The constitutions of experts under which Europe came to live after the First World War were all based, to a large extent, upon the model of the American Constitution, and taken by themselves they should have worked well enough. [...] [F]ifteen years after the downfall of monarchial government on the European continent more than half of Europe lived under some sort of dictatorship [...]."[47]

....

P. 320.

[45] Roger Osborne, *Civilization: A New History of the Western World*. Random House, 2011. P. 429.

[46] Ian Kershaw, *To Hell and Back: Europe 1914-1949*. London: Allen Lane, 2015. P. 448.

[47] Hannah Arendt, *On Revolution*. Penguin, 2006. PP. 145-146.

Whereas in 1920, constitutional and elected representative bodies existed right across the continent to the west of Soviet Russia, by the start of the Second World War they had been disbanded or deprived of real powers in 17 of the 27 European states, and in a further five they ceased to exist when the war broke out. Only Britain and Finland, along with Ireland, Sweden and Switzerland, which maintained their neutrality, kept the activity of their democratic institutions going right up until 1945.[48]

A crushing blow to liberal democracy, which was already on the back foot due to the rise of communism and fascism, was dealt by the great depression of 1929 to 1933. This robbed people of their savings, and discredited the arguments put forward in favor of a free, capitalist market. Germany was hit hardest by the crisis; it was still – along with the USSR – an outcast from the European system. Its army had been forced by politicians to capitulate in 1918, and the country considered itself to have been betrayed. The crisis was an extremely important factor in enabling the Nazis to come to power in Germany in 1933; they began to form their European and world order.

In the autumn of 1933, Germany left the League of Nations. On 30th January 1935, Hitler, clearly not expecting resistance from the Western democracies, held a plebiscite in the Saars region, which was under the rule of the League of Nations, following which he restored full German control over this coal basin. On 30th March, the Führer declared Germany to be free from the obligation not to have an air force, and three days later, he signed a law on the introduction of conscription and the restoration of the Wehrmacht, which was a blatant violation of the Treaty of Versailles and a challenge to the League of Nations.

Germany was rapidly restoring and increasing its economic potential, and was helped considerably in this by the Western states. "In spite of the German machinations with the repayment of debts under the Dawes and Young plans, neither the USA nor Britain applied sanctions, fearing the collapse of the Nazi regime and the Bolshevization of Germany," wrote the historian Mikhail Meltyukov. "Having become the biggest market for the sale of raw materials and military materials in the 1930s, Germany secured for itself a relatively favorable position in its trade with Britain and the USA, which were concerned that sanctions might lead to an increase in German exports, and strengthen competition. All the more so given that by 1935,

....

[48] Roger Osborne, *Civilization: A New History of the Western World*. Random House, 2011. P. 438.

Germany had become the biggest importer of raw material and military materials from the USA and Britain."[49]

In 1934, the Polish leader Pilsudski signed a non-aggression treaty with Germany, altering the country's traditional pro-French orientation. On 24th October 1936, Hitler and Mussolini proclaimed the creation of the Berlin-Rome axis, and on 5th November, the German interior Minister, Neirat, and his Japanese counterpart, Mushakoji, entered into the Anti-Comintern Pact in Berlin. Hitler openly stated that he would now be able to defeat not only socialism, but the whole of Europe. On 30th January 1937, he uttered the famous phrase in the Reichstag: "Germany is removing its signature from the Treaty of Versailles." Meanwhile the Spanish Civil War had broken out, in which the Soviet Union provided military assistance to the legitimate Republican government and helped with the formation of international brigades to battle with the pro-fascist rebels of General Franco, while the Western democracies essentially refused to become involved.

The British Prime Minister Neville Chamberlain said, "For us, of course, the best outcome of all would be for these mad dogs – Hitler and Stalin – to do battle with one another and tear each other apart."[50] Italy, with the Western capitals looking on in almost complete silence, seized Ethiopia, and then Albania. Germany – with the USSR objecting, and the West staying silent – carried out the "Anschluss" of Austria. In September 1938, in Munich, Hitler, Mussolini, Chamberlain and Deladieu signed a death sentence for Czechoslovakia, by prohibiting it from putting up resistance or asking for Soviet aid. In Moscow, the Munich policy was interpreted unambiguously as the appeasement of an aggressive Hitler, with the aim of directing him towards the USSR. Poland, meanwhile, took part in the dividing up of Czechoslovakia and received assurances from Goering, that in the event of convocations with Russia, Poland could count on the most effective assistance on the part of Germany.

Hitler decided to take a different path, however. His strategy, devised by the start of 1939, consisted in crushing all of his adversaries one by one, so as to avoid waging war on two fronts. Of the two biggest antagonists on the

---

[49] Mikhail Meltyukhov, *Upushchennyy shans Stalina: Sovetskiy Soyuz i bor'ba za Yevropu 1939-1941 gg.* (*Stalin's Missed Chance. The Soviet Union and the Fight for Europe 1939-1941*). Moscow: Veche, 2008. P. 21.

[50] Cit. from: Valeriy N. Gorokhov, *Istoriya mezhdunarodnykh otnosheniy 1918-1939* (*A History of International Relations 1918-1939*). Moscow, 2004. P. 188.

continent, the USSR and France, the latter was considered the weaker, and therefore ought to be dealt with first. The plan was to finish off Czechoslovakia in March, then Poland before autumn came, then in 1940 to crush France and, if possible, Britain, and then by 1941 to carry out the "main objective" – to destroy the USSR. In the middle of March 1939, Germany liquidated Czechoslovakia as an independent state. On 3rd April, a directive was issued on the preparedness of the German troops to attack Poland by 1st September 1939, and on 11th April, Hitler signed the corresponding plan, the "Weiss" plan.

In the days when Germany was preparing to invade Poland, the USSR was already waging a fully-fledged war against the Japanese. The USSR, naturally, was interested in keeping Poland as a buffer state, separating it from Germany. For this to happen, though, Poland would have to allow itself to be helped, by accepting guarantees of its security from the Soviet side, and it ultimately refused to do so. Poland could have been helped by France and Great Britain, if those two countries had made it abundantly clear to Berlin that they were genuinely prepared to go to war with Germany were it to attack Poland. On the contrary, Hitler received reassuring signals from the West, that they would declare war but would not start fighting. The USSR was still not considered in Paris and London as a state with which "reputable" countries could become allies.

On the night of 23rd August, a non-aggression pact was signed between the Soviets and the Germans, along with an addendum thereto. On 1st September 1939, the bloodiest war in the history of mankind began, with Germany's invasion of Poland.

In his book, *The World of Yesterday: Memoirs of a European*, Stephan Zweig described the 20th century as he had known it: "I have been a defenceless, helpless witness of the unimaginable relapse of mankind into what was believed to be long-forgotten barbarity, with its deliberate programme of inhuman dogma. It was for our generation, after hundreds of years, to see again wars without actual declarations of war, concentration camps, torture, mass theft and the bombing of defenceless cities, bestiality unknown for the last fifty generations, and it is to be hoped that future generations will not see them again."[51]

The historian Andrew Roberts has calculated that the Second World War lasted 2174 days, cost some $1.5 trillion and took the lives of more than 50

---

[51] Stefan Zweig, *The World of Yesterday: Memoirs of a European*. London: Pushkin Press, 2009. P. 20.

million people. That means that over the course of six years, 23,000 people were killed every day, or six people every minute.[52] More than half of that number were citizens of the Soviet Union. Admittedly, Roberts clearly underestimated the losses suffered by China.

The Western Pole

"The conclusion of the Second World War marked the end of Europe's worldwide hegemony. It was a momentous transition. The antagonism between the United States and the Soviet Union that was to define global politics for close to half a century came into existence," writes Anthony Giddens, who for many years was the director of the London School of Economics.[53] The start of decolonization reduced Europe's influence still further. From a phase of one-sided influence on the part of one civilization over all the others, mankind was now shifting to a stage of intensive and multifaceted mutual relations between all civilizations. As historians put it, the "expansion of the West" had ended, and the "revolt against the West" had begun.

Europe had grown weaker, but the United States had not. In the 1940s, the American phase of Western domination began, along with the period of the most close-knit unity in Western civilization. A crucial factor in the unifying of the Western world was the Soviet threat, which was interpreted as an existential one. The USSR had ambitions not only to expand its sphere of influence (this had been standard behavior for great powers since the dawn of time), but also to bring to life its alternative project of social organization. The word "West" began to be understood as one of the sides in a bipolar construction of the world, while the word "East" referred to the Soviet Union and its partners in the socialist camp. The other states found themselves lumped together in a broad category of "Third World" countries.

A symbol of the military and political unity of the West and of the growing, long-term engagement of the USA in European affairs was the formation in 1949 of the North Atlantic Treaty Organization (NATO). "NATO was a new departure in the establishment of European security," Kissinger remarked. "The international order no longer was characterized by the traditional European balance of power, distilled from shifting coalitions of multiple states.

---

[52] Andrew Roberts, *The Storm of War: A New History of the Second World War*. Allen Lane, 2009. P. 579.

[53] Anthony Giddens, *Turbulent and Mighty Continent: What Future for Europe?*. Polity Press, 2014. P. 186.

Rather, whatever equilibrium prevailed had been reduced to that existing between the two nuclear superpowers. If either disappeared or failed to engage, the equilibrium would be lost, and its opponent would become dominant. [...] The nations joining the North Atlantic Treaty Organization provided some military forces but more in the nature of an admission ticket for a shelter under America's nuclear umbrella than as an instrument of local defense."[54]

Atlantic solidarity and the USA's military presence in the countries of the Old World became crucially important tenets of Western civilization. The unofficial formula of the alliance would become: "America in, Germany down, Russia out." Sure enough, this defined the character of relations between Russia and the Western system. An arms race began that was to cost mankind 45 years and 18.45 trillion dollars (based on the value of the dollar in 2014).[55]

Transatlantic solidarity was put to the test several times during the Cold War. The USA did not support the Anglo-French intervention in the region of the Suez Canal in the mid-1950s, seeing it as a display of neo-colonialism. Serious cracks appeared during the years of the American incursion into Indo-China in the 1960s and 1970s, when the USA was not able to count on the support of many allies, and the French president Charles de Gaulle even went so far as to take his country out of the military organization of NATO. The mass anti-war protests which broke out after the USA was defeated, "Vietnamese syndrome", economic difficulties triggered by the decision of the OPEC countries in 1974 to reduce oil extraction, leading to a surge in energy prices – all of this once again prompted a wave of discussions about the crisis of the West.

In the 1980s, however, attitudes shifted. A new, conservative, consensus emerged, embodied by the US President Ronald Reagan and the British Prime Minister Margaret Thatcher. They dispelled the recent pessimism, restoring ideas of superpower status, military might, Messianism, and faith in Western values. People started to feel proud to be part of Western civilization. Ideas about a free market laid the foundations for the supply-side economy, monetarism and the "Washington consensus". Great advances in military construction were proclaimed, with the aim of achieving a decisive advantage over the USSR. It was as a triumph of precisely this policy that the collapse of the socialist camp and the Soviet Union, in the late 1980s and the 1990s, was

---

[54] Henry Kissinger, *World Order: Reflections on the Character of Nations and the Course of History*. Penguin, 2014. PP. 282-283.

[55] Samuel Charap and Jeremy Shapiro, "Consequences of a New Cold War", *Survival*, Volume 57, Issue 2, 2015. P. 41.

interpreted. Many experts suggest that the peak of Western influence took place precisely at that moment, in the 1990s, when the USA became the only global superpower.

At the same time, the question of the West's borders took on a new, practical significance: there was a need to define how far eastwards the Europeans and Euro-Atlantic institutions – the EU and NATO – should be expanded. In my view, Huntington provided a good explanation of the logic behind the search for a solution in civilization-based terms. He suggested that the idea of the West boundary gives us "the historical line that has existed for centuries separating Western Christian peoples from Muslim and Orthodox peoples. This line dates back to the division of the Roman Empire in the fourth century and to the creation of the Holy Roman Empire in the tenth century. It has been in roughly its current place for at least five hundred years. Beginning in the north, it runs along what are now the borders between Finland and Russia and the Baltic states (Estonia, Latvia, Lithuania), through Western Belarus, through Ukraine separating the Uniate west from the Orthodox East, through Romania between Transylvania with its Catholic Hungarian population and the rest of the country, and through the former Yugoslavia along the border separating Slovenia and Croatia from the other republics. In the Balkans, of course, this line coincides with the historical division between the Austro-Hungarian and Ottoman empires. It is the cultural border of Europe, and in the post-Cold War world it is also the political and economic border of Europe and the West. [...] Europe ends where Western Christianity ends and Islam and Orthodoxy begin."[56] It is not difficult to see that it was almost exactly along these same lines that the eastern boundary of NATO and the European Union was established, and that the divisions in Ukraine are now taking place.

One of the paradoxical results of the West's triumph in the Cold War and the expansion of its integration institutions was a marked weakening of its internal unity. Even during the height of Gorbachev's "Perestroika", one of its ideologues, a member of the Politburo named Alexander Yakovlev, said that the Soviet Union was going to do the most fearful thing of all for the West – it would disappear as a threat. The disappearance of the USSR deprived the Western countries of a plethora of internal supports that held it together. Moïsi is entirely justified in asserting that to characterize this shift in brief, one could say that the disregard that America felt towards Europe grew, at a

....

[56] Samuel P. Huntington, *The Clash of Civilizations and the Remaking of World Order*. N.Y. et al., 1996. P. 158.

time when the Europeans sensed that their need for America was weakening.[57] The European Union tried to rely heavily on "soft power", the "pool of sovereignties" and the blurring of state borders and sovereignties. The USA relied far more on "hard power" – its willingness to apply military force, including preventive force – and the inviolability of its own sovereignty. The American neo-conservative Robert Kagan believed that the Americans were from Mars and that their ideal was might, while the Europeans were from Venus and strove to achieve heaven on Earth.[58]

At present the word "West" mostly means what was called Western Christianity in the past. This is the only part of humanity which defines itself in reference to a corner of the earth rather than a people, religion or area name.

Can Russia be conceived of as being part of the West? We have had a fair few people in this country who have advocated such an idea. There have been some in the West too, but only a handful. I would suggest that the events pertaining to Ukraine, which led to a full-on collision between the interests of Russia and the West, have reduced their numbers even more.

The period of triumphalism in the West after the end of the Cold War proved short-lived, however. The West is losing its dynamism and its absolute domination. As Stephen D. King notes: "Economic power is shifting eastwards and, as it does so, new alliances are being created, typically between countries that are not natural cheerleaders for Western political and economic values. There are signs that the pre-Columbus versions of globalization – in which power was centered on Eurasia, not the West – are making a tentative reappearance."[59]

He continues, "[W]e are all, in some sense, slaves to our own versions of history. For those of us living in the West, we have found it all too easy to claim that our own good fortune will continue and that, in time, it will inevitably spread far and wide. It's time to wake up to reality."[60]

---

[57] Dominique Moïsi, *The Geopolitics of Emotion: How Cultures of Fear, Humiliation and Hope are Reshaping the World*. Random House, 2009.

[58] Robert Kagan, *Paradise and Power: America and Europe in the New World Order*. London: Atlantic Books, 2004. P. 3.

[59] Stephen D. King, *Grave New World: The End of Globalization, the Return of History*. New Haven, 2017. P. 5.

[60] Ibid. P. 7.

CHAPTER 3
EUROPEAN (DIS)UNION

Can you name the biggest city in Europe? The correct answer is Moscow (Istanbul is bigger, but a substantial portion of it is located on the Asian side of the Bosporus). Once we have established this, it is not difficult to answer the question "Which is the biggest country in Europe – both in terms of territory, and in terms of population?" Yet those in Brussels, London or Berlin, when they utter the word Europe, do not have Russia in mind. The geographical Europe and the political Europe are two different entities.

European Integration: From Success to Success

Europe is understood to mean, first and foremost, 28 countries – the members of the European Union (one of which, the United Kingdom, is on its way out). In addition to them, though, there are also several developed countries in Western Europe that decided not to join the EU: Norway, Switzerland, Iceland, and the smallest countries in Western Europe: Andorra, Liechtenstein, and others. One can then identify a group of countries that aspire to membership of the EU, but are not part of it, in the Balkans: Albania, Bosnia and Herzegovina, Macedonia, Serbia, Montenegro and also Kosovo, which has not yet officially been recognized. Those with ambitions to join include Iceland and, to an increasingly lesser extent, Turkey. The next circle of countries includes the post-Soviet states – Belarus, Moldova, Ukraine, Armenia, Georgia, Azerbaijan, and Russia, which are not among the official candidates to join the EU, though Ukraine and Moldova have declared on more than one occasion the desire to become members and have signed associate partnership agreements.

The European Union is 4,000,000 km² of densely populated territory with a population of 507 million people. This is the most integrated expanse in the world. Things were not always like this on the continent – one that has given the world the largest number of wars, including both world wars. Moreover, the idea of a common European system has been expressed in one form or another many times. None other than Vladimir Lenin, in 1915, wrote an article entitled "On the slogan 'The United States of Europe.'"

European integration has inextricably been linked to the movement for a united Europe, which emerged after the end of the Second World War, with the main aim of avoiding a new military conflict.

Key tensions on the continent remained those between France and Germany. When Germany was divided into West Germany and East Germany, the well-known French writer François Mauriac commented: "My love for Germany is so great that it gladdens me to see that there are now two of them." The United States helped Europe to deal with the strategic choice that it faced. Only political and military unification of Europe could stop the USSR and take the burden of protecting the Old World away – one that Washington had been carrying practically on its own. Central to this approach was the restoration of German power and its re-militarization. State Secretary Dean Achison argued: "You cannot have any sort of security in western Europe without using German power."[1]

London and Paris were not at all happy with the idea of rearming Germany. The USA made a proposal: if (but only if) Britain and France were to agree to the creation of substantial German Armed Forces within the framework of NATO, the USA would increase its military presence in Europe. At the same time, it was felt in Washington that the project of a unified Europe was essential in order to restrain resurgent German might. Thus, the unifying of Europe was seen as an instrument of dual restraint – on Germany and the Soviet Union.

The United States provided not only diplomatic assistance, but also financial aid and information support to the European project. The Central Intelligence Agency (CIA) and the Information Research Department (IRD) – the fastest growing subdivision of the British Foreign Office – demonstrated a high degree of inventiveness. Their operations included the creation of anti-Communist and anti-Soviet labor unions, liberal and left-wing organizations. "The centerpiece of this covert campaign was the Congress for Cultural Freedom, run by CIA agent Michael Josselson […]. At its peak, the Congress for Cultural Freedom had offices in thirty-five countries, employed dozens of personnel, published over twenty prestige

---

[1] Christopher Gehrz, "Dean Acheson, the JCS and the 'Single Package': American Policy on German Rearmament, 1950", *Diplomacy and Statecraft*, Vol. 12, Issue 1, 2001. P. 141.

magazines, held art exhibitions, owned a news and features service, organized high-profile international conferences, and rewarded musicians and artists with prizes and public performances. Its mission was to nudge the intelligentsia of western Europe away from its lingering fasciation with Marxism and Communism towards a view more accommodating of 'the American way'. [...] Whether they liked it or not, whether they knew it or not, there were few writers, poets, artists, historians scientists or critics in post-war Europe whose names were not in some way linked to this covert enterprise. Unchallenged, undetected for over twenty years, America's spying establishment operated a sophisticated, substantially endowed cultural front in the West, for the West, in the name of freedom of expression," writes the scrupulous British historian Frances Stonor Saunders.[2]

In Munich, the radio station "Free Europe" was created, and classic anti-Soviet works were prepared. The IRD financed the writing and publication of George Orwell's *Animal Farm*. In order to maintain the moral spirit during the Cold War, the European Convention on Human Rights was drawn up in 1950, setting out a new selection of ideas that became known as the "European values", which had supposedly been an inherent part of the Old World – democracy, freedom of expression and human rights.[3]

Western Europe also thought of an integration project of its own. The Western European countries, most of which had been on the losing side in the Second World War, found it hard to cope with the downgrading of their status on the world stage, the loss of their colonies, the growing influence of the USA and USSR, and therefore they strove to move towards one another, hoping to acquire strength in unity. The practical path towards European integration was opened by a declaration by French Foreign Minister Schumann on 9th May 1950, in which it was proposed that a new chapter be opened in the relations between countries, by handing over all of the coal and steel smelting industries in France and West Germany to a supranational body. Western Europe did not start to redraw the borders, as it had done after the First World War, but it did change the very nature of the borders, encouraging the free flow of capital, goods and people. "Political maps fell

---

[2] Frances Stonor Saunders, *The Cultural Cold War: The CIA and the World of Arts and Letters*. The New Press, 2013. PP. 1-2.

[3] Scott Lukas, *Freedom's War: The US Crusade Against the Soviet Union, 1945-56*. Manchester: Manchester University Press, 1999. P. 81; Volker R. Berghahn, *America and the Intellectual Cold Wars in Europe: Shepard Stone Between Philanthropy, Academy, and Diplomacy*. Princeton-Oxford: Princeton University Press, 2001. PP. 108-151; Samuel Moyn, *The Last Utopia: Human Rights in History*. Cambridge-London, 2010. PP. 78-79.

out of fashion; economic graphs took their place. Diplomats in Brussels came to see economic interdependence, international legal institutions, and mutual interference in one another's domestic politics as their primary source of security."[4]

In drawing up the concept of the European construction, a sizeable role was played by another prominent French "Europeanist" – Jean Monnet, who maintained: "Europe has never existed. It is not the addition of national sovereignties in a conclave which creates an entity. One must genuinely create Europe."[5] Instead of a Europe beset by nationalism, Monnet and Schumann's concept involved forming a unified, peaceful Europe on principles of democracy, economic prosperity, social consensus, peace and mutual cooperation. There were plenty of West European states that did not at first adopt the Monnet – Schumann concept – chief among them was Great Britain, which, in 1960, created the European Free Trade Association, together with Austria, Denmark, Norway, Portugal, Switzerland and Sweden.

Although the European integration plan was presented as a purely economic one, there were strategic ideas at its heart: putting Germany's Armed Forces under international control, given that the Americans were so insistent on their re-emergence. "In effect," writes Brendan Simms, "Paris wanted to Europeanize Germany, before it Germanized Europe."[6] Britain, as one would expect, was extremely skeptical, fearing a loss of sovereignty. Konrad Adenauer supported Schumann's plan, counting on bringing Germany to the table of great powers with genuine faith in a shared European destiny.

The agreement on the establishment of the European Coal and Steel Community was drawn up pursuant to decisions taken at an international conference in Paris in June 1950, attended by France, Germany, Belgium, the Netherlands, Luxembourg, and Italy, and was signed on 18th April 1951 for a term of 50 years. Through the efforts of the "Euro-enthusiasts", European integration moved forwards – from a customs union to a single market with free movement of goods, services, workforce and capital, and thereafter to an economic and currency union, which in turn evolved into a political union.

The movement towards a unified Europe was accompanied by the formation of a shared set of rules (*acquis communautaire*) and a system of in-

---

[4] Ivan Krastev and Mark Leonard, "Europe's Shattered Dream of Order", *Foreign Affairs*, Vol. 94, Issue 3, May/June, 2015. P. 49.

[5] Cit. from: Anne-Wil Harzing and Joris Van Ruysseveldt, *International Human Resource Management*. SAGE, 2004. P. 168.

[6] Brendan Simms, *Europe: The Struggle for Supremacy, 1453 to the Present*. L., 2014.

stitutions, to which the greater part of the sovereign rights of member states were delegated, something that differentiates the EU from other integration associations.

On 25th March 1957, the same six original founding states signed agreements in Rome, which established the European Economic Community (EEC) and the European Atomic Energy Community (EURATOM). At the same time, the Parliamentary Assembly and Supreme Court of the EEC were created. Most significant of all was the establishment of the EEC, which immediately strove to achieve tighter integration. There were to be four stages of integration.

The first, a free-trade zone, i.e. the abolition of customs tariffs, quotas and other restrictions on trade between member states. The second, a customs union involving a common external customs tariff and transition towards a single trade policy in relation to third-party countries. The third, a single internal, common market, which would have, in addition to the customs union, free movement of services, capital and manpower. The fourth: economic and currency union – the single market, with the addition of a harmonized and coordinated economic policy among member states, the replacement of national currencies with a single currency, and a common monetary policy.

On 8th April 1965, an agreement was signed in Brussels which established the Council and the Commission of the European Communities. The act, usually referred to as the Merger Treaty, united the institutions of three communities into the unified structure of the Communities. These three were: the Council and Commission, the European Parliament, and the Supreme Court. In June 1969, yet another round of negotiations – successful ones, this time – began on the accession to the European Community of the United Kingdom, Denmark and Ireland. On 1st January 1973, "the six" became "the nine".

The development of integration led to a new institution being created in 1974 – the European Council, at the level of heads of state and heads of government. The Community brought in a policy of providing financial and technical aid to individual regions. In 1978-79, the European currency system was introduced, whose primary mechanisms were supporting stable exchange rates for national currencies and a common monetary unit for the EEC: the ECU. In 1979, the first direct elections to the European Parliament took place. In 1984, a common agricultural policy was commenced, and the First Framework Program for Scientific and Technical Development was adopted.

It was Europe that was the birthplace of détente, and where increasingly noisy criticism of the USA's aggressive policy in Vietnam was voiced, and where people spoke out in favor of a normalization of relations between all states on the continent. Back in the 1960s, the French President Charles de Gaulle put forward the idea of creating a shared security zone stretching "from the Atlantic to the Urals". France and West Germany seized the initiative from Washington in the shaping of the West's policy in relation to the socialist countries. The German chancellor Willy Brandt proposed the notion that a unified Germany could be achieved by drawing closer to the USSR and the countries in Eastern Europe. On 12th August, 1970, Brandt signed the Moscow Agreement, which recognized Poland's Western borders along the Oder and Neisse Rivers, as well as the borders between the two German states.

The Helsinki Final Act of 1975, largely inspired by de Gaulle's ideas, though it was not a legally binding document, played a significant role in strengthening security in a bilateral world, and created a European-wide structure, for the first time – the Conference for Security and Cooperation in Europe (later renamed the Organization for Security and Cooperation in Europe, OSCE), which included all of the Old World countries on both sides of the Iron Curtain.

The European idea was spoken of with renewed vigor in 1985, when Jacques Delors took over as chairman of the European Commission, and Mikhail Gorbachev became the leader of the USSR. The possibility of overcoming the continental divide, and of bringing an end to the Cold War, roused minds.

There were active discussions taking place about the idea of a unified Europe that might also include the USSR and its allies. Thatcher was the first to express a formula for a Euro-Atlantic security zone "from Vancouver to Vladivostok". Gorbachev talked of a "common European home", which might include the Soviet Union. Thereafter, however, these formulae, which contained a strong dose of idealism, were not persisted with.

The European Union's new strategy for development after the end of the Cold War was devised in way that took two key circumstances into account. Firstly, after the successful creation of the common market, the prospects for further integration seemed limitless. Secondly, the end of the Cold War and the transformations in the countries of Central and Eastern Europe (CEE) opened up opportunities for a dramatic expansion of the EU. Hence the strategy of simultaneous deepening and expansion. The pro-Europeans were for a long time victorious over the Euroskeptics.

Meanwhile, European construction continued not only without Russia, but in many ways against her.

The objectives and the manifesto for the development of "in-depth" integration were defined in the Treaty on European Union, signed in Maastricht on 7th February, 1992, and supplemented by decisions of the European Council in Amsterdam in 1997 and in Nice in 2000. The aims of the Maastricht Treaty were to create an economic and currency union, and also to transition towards a common foreign and defence policy and cooperation in the fields of home affairs policy and law and order. The treaty introduced citizenship of the Union.

"By the late 1990 the debate about Europe's architecture appeared to be settled in favour of the view that European integration had transformed a network of sovereign national states into a system of multilevel governance," notes the Danish political scholar Rebecca Adler-Nissen.[7] After the Maastricht Treaty, the notion of the three "pillars" was brought in, to delineate the areas of activity of the EU: the customs union, a single internal market, economic and currency union; a single foreign policy and security policy; and cooperation in the field of home affairs policy and justice.

The first pillar soon acquired a real embodiment: in 2001, a shared currency came into being – the Euro. This was a mostly political construction. Chancellor Helmut Kohl "saw himself as the last 'good German' – that is, the last German chancellor with personal memories of World War II. He told his partners that Europe had to hurry to complete the process of post Cold War integration and the creation of the euro because after him it would be too late […]."[8]

The other motive for bringing in the Euro, according to the economic correspondent at Reuters, Alan Whitely, was a desire to "increase European standing in the world and diminish the exorbitant privilege of the United States that had rankled, especially with the French, over the years. […] Protected by its single currency, Europe would be less exposed to the volatility of the dollar and no longer vulnerable to the US exchange-rate weapon."[9]

---

[7] Rebecca Adler-Nissen, *Opting Out of the European Union: Diplomacy, Sovereignty and European Integration*. Cambridge, 2014. P. 179.

[8] Dominique Moïsi, *The Geopolitics of Emotion: How Cultures of Fear, Humiliation and Hope are Reshaping the World*. Random House, 2009.

[9] Alan Wheatley, "The Pretenders to the Dollar's Crown" in *The Power of Currencies and*

Things were more complex when it came to the pillar of security. The fall of the Berlin Wall, and the collapse of socialism and the USSR, did not bring lasting peace to Europe. On the contrary, war broke out on the continent, for the first time since 1945, in the Balkans. In order to re-establish peace, intervention by the United States and NATO, in the shape of the bombing of Serbia, was required. Against this backdrop, many suggested that a solution to the problems of stability in Europe was to create European structures for ensuring security and for the future expansion of the European Union – a gentlemen's club with values of peace, vibrancy, and ethnic acceptance. In order to avoid the Balkanization of the whole of Europe, Central and Eastern Europe needed to be Europeanized.

At a meeting of the EU Council in Cologne in June 1999, the goal of implementing a European Security and Defence Policy (ESDP) was set, to which end the Committee on Political Security, the European Military Committee and the European Union Military Staff were created, and Javier Solana was appointed High Representative of the Union for Foreign Affairs and Security Policy. In December 1999, in Nice, the decision was taken to open accession negotiations with a big group of countries all at the same time.[10]

Whereas in the past, the EU had expanded in small doses (in the 1980s, it welcomed Greece, Spain and Portugal, which were now rid of dictatorships, and in the 1990s Austria, Sweden and Finland), there was then an explosion in growth, which reflected the desire to bring the countries of Central and Eastern Europe firmly within the West's orbit. The largest wave of expansion of the EU took place in 2004: Hungary, Cyprus, Latvia, Lithuania, Malta, Poland, Slovakia, Slovenia, the Czech Republic and Estonia all joined. In 2007, it was the turn of Bulgaria and Romania. In 2013, the seventh wave of expansion occurred: Croatia joined the EU. These successes in expansion were accompanied by sizeable problems, however. As Moïsi has underlined, "[M]ost Western Europeans have been unenthusiastic about expansion, seeing it more as a moral and historic duty, and a political and economic risk, rather than as an occasion for optimism and celebration."[11]

Over time, there was not much more enthusiasm about Europe in the countries of Eastern Europe. The popularity of the idea of national sovereignty, wrote Schroeder, "is growing among the Eastern European countries

---

Currencies of Power, ed. by Alan Wheatley, Routledge, 2013. P. 46.

[10] Brendan Simms, *Europe: The Struggle for Supremacy, 1453 to the Present*. L., 2013.

[11] Dominique Moïsi, *The Geopolitics of Emotion: How Cultures of Fear, Humiliation and Hope are Reshaping the World*. Random House, 2009.

which are members of the EU, too: after the collapse of the Warsaw Pact, they acquired sovereignty and were reluctant to give away their sovereign state rights at the European level."[12] The mega-expansion of the EU resulted in unprecedented diversity and heterogeneity.

The EU in the 21st Century: From Bad to Worse

Mega-expansion ought to have been followed by mega-deepening – the adoption of a common Constitution. Major problems emerged here, too. In 2005, the French and the Dutch said "no" to a European Constitution, and in 2008 the Irish rejected the idea as well.

Having come crashing up against a wave of referenda, the project for European integration required a rethink before the threat of the retrograde movement. From the texts of the EU's founding documents, all references to the flag, anthem and logo of the European Union were removed. The words "constitution", "European law" and "family of peoples", disappeared. What remained was the assertion of "the creation of a closer union among the peoples of Europe" based on shared values: dignity, freedom, democracy, equality, the rule of law and human rights. The result of these revisions was the Lisbon Treaty, which came into force on 1st December 2009, and which gave the project of European integration a breather. The vision of a single Europe in the form of a federation, which was shared by the Euro-enthusiasts, remained unrealized.

The chances of implementing it, it seemed, only began to melt away under the impact of the blows dealt by the economic crisis of 2007-2009 and the lengthy depression that followed it. At the same time, however, in the search for ways out of the economic problems, a plethora of initiatives emerged, aimed at lending a fresh impetus to integration. Before addressing them, however, let us answer the question: how integrated is Europe today? How much national sovereignty is currently in Brussels, and how much is in the national capitals?

The functioning and development of the EU is ensured by a branched and at times muddled system of institutions, norms, methods and procedures, created and rolled out over decades: the European Council, the European Parliament, the European Commission, the European Court of Human Rights, the Court of Auditors, the Council of the European Union, the Eu-

---

[12] Gerhard Schroeder, *Resheniya. Moya zhizn' v politike* (*Decisions. My Life in Politics*). Moscow, 2007. PP. 314-315.

ropean Central Bank, the European Economic and Social Council. And that is not an exhaustive list – far from it.

The EU has made rapid advances in the matter of unifying the legislation of the member states. More than half of all new laws are drawn up in Brussels and then incorporated into the national legislation. The member states are continuing to maintain their prerogatives on a wide range of issues, however.

The Director of the Institute of European Studies in Brussels, Paul Magnette, has stressed that of the four key functions of the modern state – protecting the borders, a source of national identity, the defining of the political structure of society, and market regulation – only the latter is subject to supra-national regulation.[13] The common EU budget amounts to just over 1% of the union's GDP. Brussels does not have the right to collect taxes independently. The member states hold their coffers far away from Brussels. Niall Ferguson said that the EU "resemble[s] not so much the Rome of the Emperors as the Rome of the Pope – of whom Stalin famously asked: 'How many divisions has he?'"[14]

At the same time, a growing number of critics of the EU are pointing to its democratic deficit, given that more and more powers are being put into the hands of the Brussels bureaucracy. The European Parliament remains the only body that is directly elected, but, though it does have wide-ranging powers, the parliament does not determine the community's policy, and it is no coincidence that interest in its formation and activity is waning. In 1979, 65% of the electorate took part in the elections for the European Parliament, but in 2009 only 42.5% voted. Far more real is the power that is concentrated in the corridors of the European Commission, in whose formation voters are not involved; all the fateful decisions stem from the political leaders of the biggest countries.

There is a growing mountain of publications about the Brussels bureaucracy – the fastest-growing, most highly-paid and probably the most wasteful bureaucracy on the planet. A quarter of the 35,000 EU civil servants receive a salary that is higher than that of a federal minister in Germany. Merely to keep the building of the European Parliament in Strasbourg in good working condition, 212 million Euros are spent each year. There, 46 days a year, the 754 Members of the European Parliament convene (on a salary of 8,000 Euros a month, plus daily allowances, travel

---

[13] Timofey Bordachev, "Sovereignty and Integration", *Rossiya v global'noy politike* (*Russia in Global Affairs*), Vol. 5, Issue 1, January/February 2007. PP. 66-67.

[14] Niall Ferguson, *Empire: How Britain Made the Modern World*. London: Penguin, 2003. P. 367.

costs, taxi expenses, a bonus payment if they live a long way away, and 20,000 for their aides).[15]

The European Union usurped the right to speak in the name of all Europe and to articulate European values. It is hardly surprising that millions of people consider Europe and the EU to be the same thing, and that they have been putting the blame for their accumulating problems at Brussels' door. When the then UK Prime Minister David Cameron announced that a referendum was to be held on the issue of Brexit, Herman Van Rompuy, the head of the Council of the EU at the time, called it "the worst policy decision in decades". The Nobel laureate Joseph Stiglitz said on this issue: "In so saying, he revealed a deep antipathy towards democratic accountability. Understandably so: as we have noted, in most of the cases in which voters have been directly turned to, they have rejected the euro, the European Union, and the European constitution."[16]

Leadership has been an extremely challenging problem in the EU. It has transpired that in order to lead the European Union, one must either have lost elections in Luxembourg, like Jean-Claude Juncker, or represent a minority Polish party, like Donald Tusk. "Its institutional leaders are too weak to battle its crises; its heads of government see little advantage in defending its achievements and are plagued by disagreements."[17]

As far as the truly all-European institution OSCE is concerned, it initially included three baskets: security, the economy and humanitarian problems. Security, to a considerable degree, went to NATO; the economy to the EU; and the humanitarian agenda almost disappeared (cultural problems, minorities, languages), and what was left was overseeing elections further east than the EU and NATO. In the mid-1990s, Russia proposed that the OSCE should become the European Security System. The proposal was rejected at the time as a Russian plot aimed at undermining NATO, and the OSCE has increasingly turned into a virtual organization. The OSCE, though, which now has 55 member states – including non-European ones – is not a hopeless

---

[15] "The Dragon in the Room. The European Union's Inexplicable Fear of Exposing Corruption", *The Economist*, April 26, 2014. P. 28; Aleksey Slavin, "Yevrotranzhiry zhiveye vsekh zhivykh" ("Eurospenders are More Alive Than Anyone Else"), *Ekho Planety* (*Echo of the Planet*), Issue 47, 2013. PP. 26-27.

[16] Cit. from: Joseph E. Stiglitz, *The Euro: And its Threat to the Future of Europe*. Penguin, 2016. PP. 327-328.

[17] "State of Disunion. Cheerleading for Europe has Become an Almost Impossible Job", *The Economist*, September 15, 2016 <https://www.economist.com/europe/2016/09/15/state-of-disunion>.

case, if an attempt can be made to revive it as it was initially supposed to be, and to fill all three baskets with actual content. In Ukraine, since 2014, the OSCE has tried to play the role of a middleman and observer but has not yet done so with any great success.

The Debt Economy

European identity manifests itself in what is known as the European economic and social model. It has a variety of forms in different countries, but it differs markedly from the American model, for instance. Its characteristic features are: a higher level of state expenditure, a higher overall level of taxation, higher social welfare payments, and strong state regulation, particularly in labor markets. Furthermore, within the framework of the EU alone, there is a monetary and credit union, and most of the member states are in the Eurozone. Today, however, more and more analysts are debating the limits and efficiency of this model, due to the serious economic difficulties that Europe has gone through.

In 2011, the former prime minister of the UK, Gordon Brown, wrote: "Once Europe represented half the output of the world. By 1980 this had fallen to one quarter. Now it is less than one fifth – just 19 percent. Soon it will be little more than a tenth – 11 percent by 2030 – and then it will fall to 7 percent. By 2050 – less than four decades from now – the European economy could be smaller than that of Latin America. If European growth continues to run so far behind its competitors, then by midcentury it may be as small as Africa."[18]

What happened? Sergey Karaganov provided a succinct answer: "The Europe of the EU will be forced to pay for the triumphalism and mistakes of the past. For the overly rapid expansion of the Union and the Eurozone, almost without conditions. For the rejection by most of the countries (except for Germany and a number of northern European states) of structural reforms on the wave of euphoria prompted by the extensive expansion of markets following the fall of the iron curtain and the economic opening of China."[19] Over the course of the two decades preceding the crisis in 2007-

---

[18] Gordon Brown, "Europe's Real Problems", *The New York Times,* July 2011 <https://www.nytimes.com/2011/07/12/opinion/12iht-edbrown12.html>.

[19] Sergey Karaganov, "Yevropa: khoroshiye novosti" ("Europe: Good News"), *Rossiya v global'noy politike (Russia in Global Affairs),* July 13, 2012 <https://globalaffairs.ru/pubcol/Evropa-khoroshie-novosti-15613>.

2009, average rates of growth in GDP in the EU countries amounted to 1.9%. In this same period the EU's share of world exports has gradually fallen. GDP could only grow at the expense of domestic demand, essentially consumer demand, which was increasing faster than GDP itself. The digital revolution helped with successes in trade: computers, music players, mobile phones and other kinds of technology that are frequently updated, Internet traffic. Increased sales were achieved through a long-term reduction in inflation and interest rates. Commercial banks lent more and more money, paying no heed to whether or not borrowers were actually capable of paying them back.

The crisis of 2007-2009 came to Europe from the USA, but the EU countries were among those that suffered the most: in 2009, their aggregate GDP fell by an average of 4.1%, against an average worldwide fall of around 3%. In terms of the nature of the anti-crisis measures that were taken, the Old World was divided into two groups. States where expenditure had previously been increased continued to do this at the expense of internal and external loans, not stopping when faced with a sharp increase in the budget deficit. Almost all the EU countries went far above the 3% threshold for the budget deficit. The states with the highest deficits rushed to seek assistance from their more thrifty partners, but the latter saw no reason to encourage someone else's wastefulness.

The American journalist Michael Lewis has shown, with great clarity, how, for example, the Greek government was able to engage in almost unrestricted borrowing in the economy, when their country became a member of the Eurozone and was given the highest credit rating. "In the last 12 years alone, the salary fund of the state sector of the Greek economy doubled in real terms – without taking into account bribes paid to civil servants," Lewis wrote in his book *Boomerang: Travels to the New Third World*. The average salary in the state sector was almost three times higher than the average salary in the private sector. Annual income from the state railways amounts to 100 million Euros, and 400 million is spent on salaries, not to mention other spending amounting to 300 million. It would be cheaper to provide all the passengers on the Greek railway network with taxi rides. The Greek system of state schools was utterly devoid of efficiency: though one of the worst in Europe, it nevertheless employs four times more teachers per pupil than the Finish system, one of Europe's best education systems.

When Greece's new finance minister, Giorgos Papakonstantinou, who had worked at the OECD for ten years, took office in October 2009, the government was sure that the Greek budget deficit stood at 3.7%. It did not take him long to establish, after just two weeks, that the deficit was in fact 14% of GDP.[20] Europe was shocked.

A second group of states, by contrast, resorted to tax rises and tough cuts in state spending, but here again, the results were far from reassuring. The most decisive moves were made by the Baltic states. In 2009, Lithuania cut the spending side of its budget by 30%, public sector salaries by 20-30%, and pensions by 11%; all excise duties were increased, on everything from medicines to alcohol. As a result, Vilnius managed to keep the deficit at the level of 9% of GDP, but the consequences were 14% unemployment, a 15% fall in production, a mass outflow of manpower and a doubling of the number of suicides. Germany and a number of countries in northern Europe went down the same route, but they too were unable to escape the crisis. It transpired that German banks were the main creditors to Greece and the biggest investors in the American, Irish and Icelandic mortgage and finance bubbles.

In 2010, economic growth was restored. However, the maximum level – no more than 3% of GDP for the deficit – was exceeded by 22 states (12 of which were members of the Eurozone), and the average budget deficit across the EU was over 6%.

The disastrous financial situation in Greece, and shortly afterwards in Ireland and Portugal, put the Euro under threat, along with economic and currency union as a whole. Faced with a choice between two evils – excluding them from the Eurozone, with the threat of a chain reaction, or giving them colossal amounts of aid – the EU leaders chose the lesser one – coming to their aid. The European Financial Stability Facility was set up in the summer of 2010, and was able to provide loans amounting to 440 billion Euros and guarantees worth 780 billion Euros. Another instrument was the European financial stabilization mechanism, with the help of which the European Commission was able to use resources in the financial markets (up to 60 billion Euros), starting in 2013.

The second aspect of the anti-crisis strategy was the announcement of financial stabilization, and the instrument used for this was the series of national stabilization programs (for the countries in the Eurozone) or convergence (for the other members of the EU) for 2011-2014. Common to all these countries was the transition to a restrictive budget policy, underpinned by structural reforms, leading to increased income for the state.

---

[20]   Gordon Brown, "Europe's Real Problems", *The New York Times,* July 12, 2011 <https://www.nytimes.com/2011/07/12/opinion/12iht-edbrown12.html>.

Many experts began warning, not without justification, that self-restriction of the budget could result in a more drawn-out depression, high unemployment and social protest. The Eurozone countries did indeed fall into the trap. The debt of the problem countries proved to be so high that financiers were fearful of lending money not only to the countries of the "European financial periphery" – Greece, Ireland and Portugal, but also to such large economies as Spain and Italy. When debts are high, one can of course lower the budget deficit, i.e. reduce spending and try to increase revenues. In addition to this, since they did not have their own currencies, the problem countries could not resort to such anti-crisis mechanisms as devaluations or emissions.

In 2012, a recession began once again, and the sovereign credit ratings not only of the main debtor states, but also of the Eurozone as a whole, collapsed. Forecasts regarding the end of the era of the Euro were no longer looked upon as extravagant.

At the summit of the European Council in June 2012, a Pact for Growth and Employment was adopted, with a budget of 120 billion Euros. The key outcome of the summit, though, was the decision to create a common banking regulator. In the first stage, this task was seen as a restructuring of the banking sector (around 8,500 banks) and stabilization of the lending market. The European stabilization mechanism was given the right to conduct a recapitalization of problem banks directly, rather than, as previously, through governments.[21]

In the autumn of 2012, the Project for a "deeper and fairer Economic and Monetary Union" was presented; it was an ambitious plan for a five-year period to create a full economic, banking and budgetary (fiscal) union.

As the European economy restored its slow growth, the incentives for further transformations disappeared. The ECB, as a stimulating measure and a way of overcoming deflation, resorted to the policy of quantitative easing. "The euro-zone crisis has cooled, easing the pressure for reform," observed *The Economist* in March 2014. "Euroscepticism is on the march […]."[22]

Euro-skepticism was given a huge stimulus by the Greek crisis. The danger of a default by Greece or of its departure from the Eurozone ("Grexit")

---

[21] "Inching Towards Integration", *The Economist*, July 7, 2012. PP.15-16; Yekaterina Kravchenko, "Poradovali soglasiyem" ("Delighted with the Agreement"), *Vedomosti*, July 2, 2012 <https://www.vedomosti.ru/newspaper/articles/2012/07/02/poradovali_soglasiem>.

[22] "Wooing Mrs. Merkel", *The Economist*, March 1, 2014. P. 32.

intensified after the coming to power of the radical left-wing party Syriza in January 2015. The Prime Minister Alexis Tsipras made it abundantly clear that the regime of austere savings and docility was a thing of the past, and that Greece would not put the country's future at threat for the sake of repayment of its foreign debt as a *sine qua non*. In the referendum, the terms for the provision of aid were rejected.

Jochen Bittner of *Die Zeit* described an opinion that was popular on the continent at the time: "When the Greeks held a referendum, demanding to end this madness, Germany responded by blackmailing them: Accept an even tougher austerity program or leave the euro. The same Germany that had its debt written off after World War II is willing to smother Europe's south unless it bends to Berlin's will. The European Union as an economic Fourth Reich? Europeans, resist!"[23]

Under these conditions, Tsipras "was forced to make a great U-turn, which, however, brought him into conflict with members of his own party, resulting in the loss of his coalition's parliamentary majority."[24] It is all the more surprising that policy in relation to Greece was not subject to any serious public discussion in the EU. The terms of the deal were dictated by Germany.

Mark Mazower claimed that the Greek crisis had "revealed the shallowness of any sense of political solidarity across the continent and the limited legitimacy of the EU's political institutions. The Greeks complain about German meanness, the Germans about Greek profligacy; the French and Italians are driven by the worry that if Greece goes they may be next; while across Eastern Europe people are asking why their money should go to prop up a standard of living in Athens that remains several notches higher than their own."[25]

Tusk asserted that it was precisely the issue of solving Greek debt that had made anti-EU and anti-German sentiment "part of mainstream political discourse."[26] The steps taken by the EU's leaders themselves did not bring any tangible results. There was an enormous "Greek bail-out", but it was

....

[23]   Jochen Bittner, "Europe's Civil War of Words", *The New York Times*, August 18, 2015 <https://www.nytimes.com/2015/08/19/opinion/jochen-bittner-europes-civil-war-of-words.html>.

[24]   Nikos Konstandaras, "Gambling for Stability", *Kathimerini*, August 20, 2015 <http://www.ekathimerini.com/200768/opinion/ekathimerini/comment/gambling-for-stability>.

[25]   Mark Mazower, "Why the Eurozone Crisis is Just Part of Our Long Struggle for Peace", *The Guardian Weekly*, July 17, 2015. P. 18.

[26]   Peter Spiegel, "Greece: Donald Tusk Warns of Extremist Political Contagion", *The Financial Times*, July 16, 2015 <https://www.ft.com/content/f6872342-2bd2-11e5-acfb-cbd2e1c81cca>.

actually a bail-out of German and French banks. "Most of the money went to Greece and then right away went back to Germany and France," claimed Stiglitz.[27] And what happened?

In August 2018, the program of "aid" to Greece – credits worth 320 billion Euros – from the European Union ended. The results were shocking. In eight years, GDP fell by a quarter, investment by two thirds. The number of people living in poverty has doubled to one third of the country's 10 million population. One in five people is out of work and cannot afford to pay for housing, electricity and interest on loans. In a third of families, at least one of its adult members is jobless. Salaries were the lowest in the EU. Household income fell by more than 30%. A lot of people just left the country. The national debt is 180% of GDP.[28]

By 2017, compared with the figures from a decade ago, "the German economy has grown by almost 7%, whereas the economies of Belgium, France, and the Netherlands have remained stagnant, and those of Finland, Greece, Ireland, Italy, and Portugal have all contracted more than they did during the Great Depression. Inequality has also increased within countries – to a stunning degree in the worst-performing ones, such as Greece, but even in Germany, too," wrote Andrew Moravcsik of Princeton.[29]

Growth in 2017 surpassed all expectations, rising above the 2% mark for the first time in a decade. Unemployment also fell to its lowest level, but on the periphery of the Eurozone it rose to 10%, and one in every five young Europeans is unemployed. Inflation did not come close to the figure of 2% targeted by the European Central Bank. The main factors in terms of restoring growth were cheap money and the policy of quantitative easing. Growth was most noticeable in the countries of Eastern Europe. Industry still stayed at pre-crisis level.[30] But by 2018 growth slowed again

---

[27] Peter S. Goodman, "How a Currency Meant to Unite Europe Wound Up Dividing It", *The New York Times*, July 27, 2016 <https://www.nytimes.com/2016/07/28/business/international/how-a-currency-intended-to-unite-europe-wound-up-dividing-it.html>.

[28] "Greece Has Many Rivers to Cross", *Kathimerini*, August 20, 2018; "The Greece-y Pole", *The Economist*, August 4, 2018. P. 8; Liz Alderman, "Greece's Bailout is Ending. The Pain is Far From Over", *The New York Times*, August 19, 2018 <https://www.nytimes.com/2018/08/19/business/greece-bailout-financial-crisis.html>.

[29] Andrew Moravcsik, "Europe's Ugly Future. Muddling Through Austerity", *Foreign Affairs*, November/December 2016. P. 139.

[30] "The Eurozone Revival Heralds Spring Cheer", *The Financial Times*, May 3, 2017 <https://www.ft.com/content/8565a966-2ff6-11e7-9555-23ef563ecf9a>; James Shotter, "Central Europe Records Strong Growth", *The Financial Times*, August 17, 2017. P. 4; Tim Wallace, "Eurozone Industrial Output Slumps", *The Daily Telegraph*, August 15, 2017. P. 31; Jana Randow, Samuel

to 0.3-0.4% in the first half of the year, and "the index for expectations entered negative territory for the first time since 2012".[31] And this slowdown continued into 2019.

Europeans are increasingly laying the blame for low growth on Germany, the main engine of Euro-integration. "Germany cannot be blamed for wanting a strong currency and a balanced budget," writes the famous financier George Soros. "But it can be blamed for imposing its predilection on other countries that have different needs and preferences – like Procrustes in Greek mythology, who forced other people to lie in his bed and stretched them or cut off their legs to make them fit. The Procrustes bed in which the eurozone has to lie is called austerity and, ultimately, deflation."[32] Lord Giddens has noted the rise in anti-German sentiment: Germany is "leading but is not loved". In spite of all the political correctness, in the newspapers – particularly those in southern European countries – headlines are appearing which feature the phrase "the fourth Reich". Demonstrators in Italy, Spain, Greece and Cyprus are carrying pictures of Merkel with a moustache and a swastika drawn onto them.[33]

Discussions about the future of the Euro and the Eurozone have intensified. Michael Mandelbaum believes that "the euro, may be said to be Providence's way of reminding the world of the pervasive presence in human affairs of unintended consequences. The euro has produced, on a great and damaging scale, the opposite of what its architects and champions sought to accomplish."[34]

Joseph Stiglitz believes: "The euro was supposed to 'serve' the European people; now they are asked to accept lower wages, higher taxes, and lower social benefits, in order to save the euro." "A common currency is threatening the future of Europe. Muddling through will not work. And the European

---

Potter, Cormac Mullen, and Blaise Robinson, "Emerging From a Lost Decade", *Bloomberg Businessweek*, November 20, 2017. PP. 36-37; Nicholas Megaw, "Jobs Growth and Orders at 17-year Highs as Eurozone Enjoys 'Boom'", *The Financial Times: Europe*, November 24, 2017. P. 1.

[31] Claire Jones and Adam Samson, "Eurozone Business Confidence Hit by Trade Fears", *The Financial Times*, August 2, 2018 <https://www.ft.com/content/0160ae04-9648-11e8-b67b-b8205561c3fe>.

[32] George Soros and Gregor Schmitz, *The Tragedy of the European Union: Disintegration or Revival?* PublicAffairs, 2014. P. 25.

[33] Anthony Giddens, *Turbulent and Mighty Continent: What Future for Europe?* Polity Press, 2013. PP. 213-214.

[34] Michael Mandelbaum, "Euromess", *The American Interest*, Vol. 11, Issue 1, August 2015 <https://www.the-american-interest.com/2015/08/01/euromess/>.

project is too important to be sacrificed on the cross of the euro. Europe – the world – deserves better."[35]

However, Eurozone collapse prophecies turned out to be wrong. Leaving the Eurozone is something that comes at an extremely high price. Therefore, in all surveys, most people in the Eurozone believe that the introduction of a common currency has caused harm to their countries, but the majority are not in favor of leaving the Euro.

The EU remains a powerful economic player. Its share of the world's population is one fourteenth, but the EU accounts for one fifth of global GDP, and from one third to two fifths of international exchange of goods and services.[36] Finland, the Netherlands, Germany, the UK and Sweden are among the top ten most competitive economies in the world.[37]

Is It Easy to Be a European?

Western Europe is rightly proud of its successes in creating a model for a social state, which has transformed it into one of the most affluent regions in the world. The level of social stratification is relatively low. A high level of security is being provided (there are four times fewer murders in the EU than in the United States).

In recent years, however, social tension on the continent has been growing, and one of the main reasons for this is the inability of the EU countries to maintain their former standards of social welfare in the new circumstances. Angela Merkel has expressed concern about the fact that the EU has 7% of the world's population and accounts for half of all social spending.[38]

Here are just a few citations from Philippe Legrand's book *The European Spring*: in Greece, "Children scavenge through rubbish bins for scraps for food, while hospitals run short of medicine"; in Spain, "suicide is now the top cause of death after natural causes"; and across Europe, "fifteen million

---

[35] Joseph E. Stiglitz, *The Euro: And its Threat to the Future of Europe*. Penguin, 2016. PP. 306, 326.

[36] Igor Gladkov, "Yevropeyskiy Soyuz v sisteme sovremennoy mezhdunarodnoy torgovli" ("The European Union in the System of Modern International Trade", *Sovremennaya Yevropa (Modern Europe)*, Issue 1, 2016. PP. 85-86.

[37] Mark Leonard and Hans Kundnani, "Think Again: European Decline", *Foreign Policy*, May/June 2013. P. 47.

[38] "The Next Supermodel", *The Economist*, February 2, 2013. P. 9.

people below the age of thirty are neither in employment nor education."[39] In Germany, a country where the level of inequality exceeds that of the other states in the Eurozone, the poorest 40% of citizens do not even have any savings in their bank accounts.[40]

Europe is getting older. The sizeable generation born during the "baby-boom" years is reaching pension age. Since 2014, the active population has begun to decline.[41] In 1970, there were four to five people of working age for each pensioner. By 2030, the ratio of workers to pensioners, for example in Germany, will be 2:1. If one considers that no more than 65% of Europe's working population are in employment anyway (the biggest groups among the not employed are students and housewives), there will be three people in work for every two pensioners. Current systems of social welfare were not designed for this kind of ratio.

At the turn of the millennium, the main source of growth for the EU's population was immigration. In recent years, the population has been swelled by 3-4 million new arrivals each year. The nature of immigration has changed, meanwhile: the backbone of it is formed by people from poor countries in Asia and Africa, mainly Muslim countries. The tumultuous events in the Middle East and North Africa are only adding to their numbers.

The new immigrants have brought with them a mentality, a way of life and a system of values that do not fit in well with the customs of the indigenous population of the Old World. They increasingly see themselves as a separate ethno-cultural community, defending their right to "otherness" using political and legal instruments. The most popular name for boys born in the European Union is Mohammed. Among the latest wave of immigrants, there has been a considerable proportion that have no education or professional skills, so that they are permanently on benefits paid by the taxpayer. No wonder that a widespread antipathy is growing among the native population towards these foreigners, an antipathy which sometimes grows into intolerance, xenophobia and anti-immigrant sentiment.

....

[39] Cit. from: Philippe Legrain, *European Spring: Why Our Economies and Politics are in a Mess – and How to Put Them Right*. CB Books, 2014. PP. xiv-xv.

[40] Stefan Wagstyl, "Germany: the Hidden Divide in Europe's Richest Country", *The Financial Times*, August 17, 2017 <https://www.ft.com/content/db8e0b28-7ec3-11e7-9108-edda0bcbc928>.

[41] *Demography Report 2010: Older, More Numerous and Diverse Europeans. Commission staff working document* by Directorate-General for Employment, Social Affairs and Inclusion (European Commission), Eurostat (European Commission). Luxembourg: Publications Office of the European Union, 2011. P. 2.

The problem became particularly acute after Germany took the decision to let a record number of refugees from the Middle East enter the country in 2015. Under the Dublin Regulation, refugees were required to ask for asylum in the EU country in which they arrived. In September 2015, the European Commission decided, without holding discussions, to redistribute 160,000 refugees from the main countries in which they had arrived – Greece, Hungary and Italy – to all the others. This prompted a highly sensitive reaction in many countries, and in Eastern European ones in particular.[42]

For many years, the official policy of member states and the EU as a whole was oriented towards not allowing a rise in nationalist trends. Two or three decades ago, the word "Motherland" and its equivalents disappeared from the European lexicon altogether. However, the atmosphere of total political correctness and tolerance that was thereby created led to a situation in which acute ethnic and religious problems found themselves outside the framework of public discussion. Great hopes were placed on the introduction into the public consciousness of the values of multiculturalism, which were intended to replace the traditional approach whereby minorities were assimilated. In 2011, however, the leaders of several European countries – Angela Merkel, Nicolas Sarkozy, and David Cameron – expressed the view that multiculturalism was dead.

Shockwaves were sent through the extremely politically correct Germany by a book written by a former member of the government in Berlin, Thilo Sarrazin, *Germany Abolishes Itself*, in which he expressed concern about the fact that people were not even allowed to hint at the consequences of the falling birth rate and uncontrolled immigration. "Germany will not die suddenly and quickly. It will quietly be extinguished together with the Germans and the demographically conditioned exhaustion of their intellectual potential."[43]

On 22nd July, 2011, Anders Breivik blew up a bomb in the government district of Oslo, and then sailed to an island housing a youth camp of the Workers' Party. He shot dead more than 70 of the participants. By doing so, the 32-year-old Norwegian intended to rouse Europe from its slumbers, which were not allowing it to see the threat posed by the influx of Muslims and the left-wingers and liberals who pandered to them.

---

[42] "Leading From the Front. Through Yet Another Crisis, the EU is Groping Towards the Expansion of Its Powers", *The Economist*, September 12, 2015. P. 28.

[43] Thilo Sarrazin, *Germaniya. Samolikvidatsiya* (*Germany Abolishes Itself*). Moscow, 2013. PP. 14-15, 343.

A growing problem is that of migrants not only from outside the continent, but also from within Europe itself. In 2011, Polish became the second most widely spoken language in England, overtaking the languages of the former colonies.[44] The ubiquitous "Polish plumber" became not only a figure of speech, but also an argument in the political struggle. There is no less sympathy in Western Europe for immigrants from Romania, Bulgaria or Ukraine.

Against this backdrop, there is a growing number of protests by nationalist parties, combining anti-immigrant slogans with criticism of the EU and the Euro. The British National Party, France's Front National, the Dutch and Austrian Freedom Parties, the "True Finns", Alternative for Germany and other influential right-wing European radicals are actively converting more and more supporters to the cause of the Euro skeptics.[45] The traditional right-of-center parties – the Conservatives, the Christian Democrats – have also armed themselves with anti-Brussels slogans, the most striking example of which was the UK Conservative Party's rash support for the idea of holding a referendum on leaving the EU.

At the same time, ultra-left-wing parties gained influence, and the party systems have become polarized. In the first round of the presidential elections in France, in April 2012 the far-left and the far-right combined received 29% of the vote, more than Nicolas Sarkozy or Francois Hollande. The Front National came first in the elections for the European Parliament. Its leader, Marine Le Pen, made use of allusions to Joan of Arc, declaring: "France does not control anything, not its budget, not its currency, not its frontiers. It is time to say 'stop' to the EU."[46]

In the UK, to the horror of the establishment, the Labour Party elected Jeremy Corbyn as its leader in September 2015, a man who was accused of being an admirer of Hugo Chavez, Putin, Greece's SYRIZA party, Lebanon's Hamas and China's economic policy, and who was said to be against interference by NATO in the politics of Ukraine.[47] In the elections to the European Parliament in 2014, the right-wing UK Independence Party led

---

[44] Robert Booth, "Polish Becomes England's Second Language", *The Guardian*, January 30, 2013 <https://www.theguardian.com/uk/2013/jan/30/polish-becomes-englands-second-language>.

[45] See: Igor Uznarodov, "Yevroskeptitsizm posle krizisa" ("Euroskepticism After the Crisis"), *Sovremennaya Yevropa (Modern Europe)*, Issue 1, 2015. PP. 26-36.

[46] Hugh Carnegy, "Le Pen Kicks Off Campaign with Call for 'Patriots' to Reject Brussels", *The Financial Times*, May 2, 2014. P. 8.

[47] "Backward, Comrades! Jeremy Corbyn is Leading Britain's Left into a Political Timewarp", *The Economist*, September 19, 2015. P. 9.

the field – the first time since 1906 that any party had beaten both Labour and the Conservatives.

In March 2016, Alternative for Germany won 25% of the vote in Saxony, and in May, Norbert Hofer, representing the right-wing Freedom Party, very nearly won the presidential elections in Austria. In June, the British voted for Brexit. In December, Italy's Matteo Renzi lost to the left- and right-wing opposition in a referendum on the issue of reforms to the system of local government.

"Where next? After the one-two punch of Brexit and Trump, Europeans are watching every coming election, from Austria to the Netherlands to France, for fear it could become the next staging post in the long march to illiberalism. Europe's centrists have begun to see themselves as modern-day defenders of the Alamo, desperately standing their ground as marauding populists advance on all sides" – that was how *The Economist* conveyed the mood among liberal internationalists at the end of 2016.[48]

In autumn 2017, Alternative for Germany was elected to the Bundestag for the first time. By 2018, its popularity had reached 16%, and it actually caught up with the Social Democrats. In March 2018, the Euroskeptic Five Star Movement won 32% of the vote in the Italian elections, and the center-right coalition, which included the League of the North, "Forward Italy!" of Silvio Berlusconi, and the movement "Italian Brothers", won 36.9%. In June, a coalition of these parties took power, and the League's leader Matteo Salvini headed the Ministry of the Interior. The coalition raised questions about a rejection of the Euro, a ban on immigration to the country, and the lifting of sanctions against Russia, thereby immediately provoking fears among the liberal community and investors of the collapse of the Eurozone and a deepening of the EU crisis. The anti-immigrant group Swedish Democrats, headed by Jimmy Okesson, took third place in the September elections with a record result of 17.6%. The long-term leader of the right movement in the Netherlands – the Freedom party of Geert Wilders – found himself with an even more right-wing rival – the Forum for Democracy, which already in 2018 was supported by 8% of citizens. The Greek far-right Golden Dawn party had a 2018 rating of 9%.[49]

---

[48] "Running Scared. Even Without Winning Elections, Populists Are Setting Europe's Pace", *The Economist*, November 26, 2016. P. 24.

[49] Nataliya Portyakova and Yekaterina Postnikova, "Smyagchit' po-ital'yanski" ("To Soften in the Italian Style"), *Izvestiya*, May 23, 2018 <https://www.pressreader.com/russia/izvestia/20180523/281479277076718>; Mikhail Overchenko and Alexey Nevelsky, "Italiya pugayet rynki" ("Italy Scares the Markets"), *Vedomosti*, May 30, 2018 <https://vedomosti.

Euroskepticism spread far and wide throughout Eastern Europe. Professor Jean-Werner Muller, of Princeton, came to this conclusion: "Democracy is struggling: nearly all the countries that joined the EU during the last decade are experiencing profound political crises. [...] Yet it has become clear that at least some of this success story was a fairy tale that many in the EU chose to believe despite a lot of worrisome evidence of its falsity. [...] But for eastern Europe, the great investment boom ended around 2007. The public's faith in democracy plummeted along with the economy [...]."[50] The governments of Poland, Hungary, the Czech Republic and Slovakia have spoken out against the dictates of the European Commission on numerous occasions. Brands of goods which hark back to the Socialist era have become popular in Eastern European countries, and the press has commented on the "communist nostalgia".[51]

The Hungarian leader, Viktor Orban, has compared the EU to a colonial power, and declared a "war for independence" from Brussels: "I believe that Brexit is a colossal opportunity, an opportunity for a cultural counter-revolution. We need to talk about the importance of national and religious values, we need to preserve them and enshrine them in European documents. The British have said that they want to be British."[52] Orban is now seen as a dangerous populist, although he was comfortably re-elected in April 2018.

The ruling party in Poland, Jarosław Kaczyński's Law and Justice Party, provoked Brussels' wrath by restricting the powers of the Constitutional Court, and putting its people in senior managerial positions in the biggest media organizations. The clamp-down on the press is particularly troubling for the Germans, who own dozens of regional Polish publications. Warsaw has been accused of human rights violations and infringing the principle of the distribution of powers. Brussels does not like the fact that there are many believers among Poles (88% of the population describe themselves

---

profkiosk.ru/article.aspx?aid=648162>; "Hot Under the Collar", *The Economist*, July 28, 2018. P. 21; Yekaterina Mareyeva and Anna Chistyakova, "Shvetsii pridetsya smeshchat'sya vpravo" ("Sweden will Have to Move to the Right"), *Kommersant*, September 11, 2018 <https://www.kommersant.ru/doc/3737981>.

[50] Jan-Werner Mueller, "Eastern Europe Goes South. Disappearing Democracy in the EU's Newest Members", *Foreign Affairs*, Vol. 93, Issue 2, March/April 2014. P. 14, 15, 16.

[51] "Post-Communist Chic. You Must Remember This", *The Economist*, September 17, 2016. P. 25.

[52] Ariadna Rokossovskaya, "Varshava zanyalas' 'konekradstvom'" ("Warsaw has Engaged in 'Horse-Theft'"), *Rossiyskaya Gazeta*, September 13, 2016 <https://rg.profkiosk.ru/article.aspx?aid=497036>.

as Catholics, and 48% attend church on Sundays), the fact that a ban on abortions has been in effect since 1993, and the country's negative attitude towards same-sex marriages. In November 2017, in connection with suspicions that the country had been violating European values, the European Parliament asked for a mechanism to be brought in that would take away its right to a vote in the EU Council. Poland disapproves of the fact that half of the subsidies from Brussels go back to German firms or to the EU's budget, only three out of fifteen of the biggest retailers have Polish owners, and that (as they see it) the EU talks down to the country. People have stopped being shy of the Polish flag. Whereas recently Poland had only one enemy, in the form of Russia, now the EU and (in particular) Germany have been added.[53] On 27th July 2017, Kaczyński announced that preparations were being made to bring a lawsuit against Germany for reparations. Poland, which lost one fifth of its population during the Second World War, intends to demand compensation to the tune of 6 trillion Euros. The idea is backed by two thirds of the population.[54]

The key word in Warsaw is "repolonization", which refers to the return to Polish hands of enterprises which in the 1990s moved to foreign investors. In 2018, for the first time since 1999, more than half of bank capital was in Polish ownership, while nationalization of the shipbuilding and pharmaceutical industries and the media is under way. As the Prime Minister Mateusz Morawiecki said, Poland is bringing home the "family silver".[55]

In the Czech Republic, fewer than a third of citizens consider membership of the EU to be a "good thing" and only a quarter support the transition to the Euro. The elections in October 2017 were won by the billionaire Andrej Babis, who accused the traditional parties of corruption and incompetency, and advocated closing the borders to immigrants with the help of NATO, and distancing the country from Brussels, which he compared to the Soviet Union.[56]

In 2016, 13.7% of the seats in the parliaments of the European Union were held by right-wing populists, to use Fareed Zakaria's terminology, and 11.5%

---

[53] Ariadna Rokossovskaya, "Pol'sha: trudnosti perevoda" ("Poland: Lost in Translation"), *Rossiyskaya Gazeta* (*Russian Newspaper*), February 25, 2016 <https://rg.ru/2016/02/25/sobkor-rg-rasskazala-o-peremenah-proishodiashchih-v-polshe.html>.

[54] "Reparations for Poland. Upping the Ante", *The Economist*, August 19, 2017. P. 18.; Kamil Zwolski, "Poland's Foreign Policy Turn", *Survival*, Vol. 59, Issue 4, April/September 2017. P. 167.

[55] "Poland. Buying Back the Family Silver", *The Economist*, August 11, 2018. P. 23.

[56] Ladka Bauerova and David Rocks, "Gaining From the EU But Hating It Anyway", *Bloomberg Businessweek*, September 11, 2017. PP. 38-39.

by left-wing populists.⁵⁷ By 2017, parties that were called "populist" had secured more than 10% of the vote in elections in 16 European countries. On average, 16.5% of the electorate voted for them – from 65% in Hungary to 1% in Luxembourg. "Populists" hold the largest share of seats in the parliaments of Greece, Hungary, Italy, Poland, Slovakia and Switzerland. In Hungary, Italy and Slovakia, they secured more than half of all votes. In Hungary, the right-wing Fidesz and the left-wing Jobbik are both referred to as populist. In three countries – Finland, Lithuania and Norway – populists have become part of the ruling coalition.⁵⁸

Against the backdrop of economic problems, the issue of separatism has intensified. Flanders is growing ever more determined in its wish to break away from the less affluent Wallonia (for the time being, the break-up of Belgium is being held back, mainly, by the two parties' inability to share Brussels). In a consultative referendum in Veneto and Lombardy in October 2017, an overwhelming majority voted for independence from Italy. In Catalonia, the elections held in November 2012 were won by parties which are in favor of seceding from the rest – the less affluent part – of Spain. In November 2014, the referendum in Catalonia returned a "yes" vote for independence, but the vote was not recognized by Spain's constitutional court.

A new referendum was set for 1ˢᵗ October, 2017, and Catalan authorities headed by Carles Puigdemont were taking success for granted. The government of Mariano Rajoy was determined not to allow the referendum to take place. A strong police presence was deployed to disrupt it, with polling stations closed down, leading to violent clashes. Ninety percent of those who voted in the referendum, which was declared illegal, voted for independence.

Rajoy announced a decision to revoke Catalonia's autonomy, remove Catalonia's government from office, and hold fresh elections there. This provoked the parliament in Catalonia to go ahead and proclaim independence, whereupon the president and parliament of Spain removed the province's autonomy, the Constitutional Court abolished the declaration of independence, and the courts accused the deposed autonomous government of causing riots. Puigdemont and several ministers fled to Brussels, and others were arrested.⁵⁹

....

[57] Fareed Zakaria, "Populism on the March. Why the West Is in Trouble", *Foreign Affairs*, November/December 2016. P. 10.

[58] Cas Mudde, "Europe's Populist Surge: A Long Time in the Making", *Foreign Affairs*, November/December 2016. P. 26.

[59] Alyona Akimova, "Zakonno izgnannoye pravitel'stvo" ("A Legitimately Dismissed Government"),

On 1st June 2018, Prime Minister Mariano Rajoy was impeached as a result of a corruption scandal (although the Catalan crisis also played an important role in the fall of the Cabinet). He was replaced by Pedro Sánchez, who led a minority government – in Congress the Socialists held 87 seats out of 350. Sánchez was ready to sit down with the Catalans at the negotiating table. Among the compromise options, he named the transformation of Spain into a federation, with the provision of additional rights to Catalonia.

In Catalonia, the regional elections of 2017 brought victory to the separatist parties, and the Cabinet was headed by the head of the coalition "Together for Catalonia" Kim Torra. Torra is a supporter of independence, and on 8th December 2018 he suggested that the region follow the "Slovenian scenario" (in June 1991, Slovenia announced its unilateral withdrawal from Yugoslavia).[60]

A referendum was held in Scotland on 18th September 2014, in which almost half the population voted for independence from the UK. The results of the referendum on Brexit only exacerbated the problem: in Scotland, 62% of the electorate voted to remain in the EU. Of the 59 Scottish MPs in the British parliament, only two represent the Labour Party or the Conservatives; the rest are members of national parties. Scotland's government is in favor of holding a fresh referendum on leaving the United Kingdom, and polls indicate that this idea is backed by a majority of Scottish voters, who feel that it is the only way to stay in the European Union.[61] There is growing separatist sentiment in Wales. No-one can say with any certainty how long Bosnia-Herzegovina is going to remain united.

"The biggest problem for the modern Eurozone is the loss of the European idea and the vagueness of European identity," stresses the MGIMO professor Olga Butorina.[62] Its leaders have not been able to provide a convincing answer to the question of what it means to be European today. The European values listed in the Lisbon Treaty – freedom, democracy, human rights, the rule of law – are universal for the whole of the civilized world,

---

Kommersant, November 1, 2017 <https://www.kommersant.ru/doc/3455514>.

[60] "The Catalan Question. In Two Minds", *The Economist's Special Report on Spain*, July 28, 2018. PP. 6-7; Yekaterina Mareyeva, "Kataloniyu sderzhivayut polumerami" ("Catalonia is Restrained with Half Measures"), *Kommersant*, December 13, 2018 <https://www.kommersant.ru/doc/3828309>.

[61] "Britain is Sliding towards Scoxit", *The Economist*, February 18, 2017. PP. 8-9.

[62] Olga Butorina, "Yevropa bez Yevrosoyuza" ("Europe Without the EU"), *Rossiya v global'noy politike* (*Russia in Global Affairs*), November/December 2011 <https://globalaffairs.ru/number/Evropa-bez-Evrosoyuza-15407>.

without having any traits of "Europeanness". The EU is reluctant to talk to its citizens about the issues you read about above: Europe's Christian roots, the legacy of the Crusades, the conflicts between the popes and the kings, the Renaissance, the Reformation and the religious wars, colonialism or the Enlightenment. The period of socialism, in the history of the countries of Central Europe, is subject to an unspoken ban. The Old World has less and less of a sense of the root of its own civilization, but many people are nostalgic for them.

The terror attacks against the Paris-based satirical journal *Charlie Hebdo* were seen as a serious wake-up call for millions of Europeans, who took to the streets of cities in January 2015 to say "no" to extremism and "yes" to their national roots and traditions.

According to Hubert Vedrine, a former foreign minister of France, only 15-20% of Europeans are Europhiles, while roughly the same percentage reject the EU outright, and the remaining 60% are suffering from a "Euro-allergy". Agreeing with this assessment, the former head of Spain's Foreign Affairs Ministry, Ana Palacio, explains the reason: "Put simply, for much of the public, EU institutions lack legitimacy. The reasons are well known: poor communication, a democratic deficit, finger pointing between member states and the Commission, a flawed institutional architecture."[63]

On the Waves of Brexit

The most serious blow to unity in the EU was dealt by the departure from it of the United Kingdom, which had always been the most Euroskeptic country in the EU, and had demanded special terms for itself and refrained from joining the single currency. Supporters of Brexit described the EU "as interfering, borderline corrupt, and practically incompetent, incapable of coping with stresses in the eurozone and the influx of refugees." They warned that the EU is being transformed into a super-state, taking away from Britain the responsibility for ensuring its security and weakening its defence capabilities and connections to the United States. The referendum in June 2016 brought success to those advocating a departure from the EU, after which the desire in Brussels to punish Britain was strong.

Theresa May called a general election in the hope of strengthening her party's position – the polls were giving the Conservatives a 20-point lead

---

[63] Ana Palacio, "The End of the European Supernation?", *Gulf Times*, September 21, 2016 <https://gulfnews.com/opinion/op-eds/the-end-of-the-european-supernation-1.1901348>.

over their rivals – and uniting the nation on the eve of the negotiations with the EU over Brexit. The outcome, however, was the direct opposite. Only 42% of the electorate voted for the Tories, with 40% voting for Labour, and no party won a majority, resulting in a "hung parliament". May clung on as PM, and the country was governed by a minority government propped up by the Democratic Unionist Party – the only party with whom the Tories were able to form an alliance.[64]

Brexit negotiations between London and Brussels (who were determined to punish London as harshly as possible in order to demotivate other members from leaving the EU) hit problems from the very start. London's European partners were actively transferring their assets to Paris, Frankfurt am Main and Dublin, and its position as the world's leading financial center was challenged by Singapore, New York and Dubai. In 2017, European money pulled from London totalled 350 billion Euros.[65] Around forty conservative MPs supported a motion of no confidence in their party leader. Debates intensified on whether the UK should give up the Brexit idea altogether, or pursue a no-deal scenario.[66]

In July 2018 foreign secretary Boris Johnson resigned from the cabinet, protesting against May's Chequers plan of a "soft Brexit", which left the tools to control the EU-British economic ties in the hands of Brussels. Polls found that voters preferred no deal to Chequers by two to one.[67]

At the Tories' annual conference, Boris Johnson excoriated May's road map to exiting the EU as a sad, weak and dangerous mistake, and called her approach not only "politically humiliating" but "a cheat" against everyone who had voted for Brexit. Britain's foreign secretary, Jeremy Hunt, compared the EU to the Soviet Union: "The EU was set up to protect freedom. It was the Soviet Union that stopped people leaving. If you turn the EU club into a prison, the desire to get out won't diminish, it will grow, and we won't be the only prisoner that will want to escape."[68]

---

[64] Oleg Okhoshin, "Dosrochnyye vybory v Britanii: vzglyad iz kel'tskikh regionov" ("Early Elections in Britain: A View from the Celtic Regions"), *Mezhdunarodnaya zhizn'* (*International Life*), July 2017. PP. 101-102.

[65] Kristina Akopova, "Pobeg s Al'biona" ("Running Away from Albion"), *Rossiyskaya Gazeta* (*Russian Newspaper*), September 18, 2018 <https://rg.profkiosk.ru/673317>.

[66] Ian Bremmer, "Theresa May's Britain Is Headed for a Brexit Train Wreck", *Time*, November 27 – December 4, 2017. P. 10; "Brexit. Decisions, Decisions", *The Economist*, November 16, 2017. PP. 30-31.

[67] "Brexit with no Deal. Ready or Not", *The Economist*, August 4, 2018. P. 25.

[68] William Booth, "Boris Johnson Trashes Theresa May's Brexit Plan as a Sad, 'Politically

In November 2018 the EU and May reached an agreed deal on Brexit. However, opposition to the deal in the British Parliament and in the Conservative party proved to be insurmountable. On 15th January 2019, May suffered the biggest defeat of her political career: Parliament rejected the Brexit plan agreed with the EU by 432 votes to 202 – the biggest parliamentary defeat suffered by any UK government in a hundred years. Corbyn immediately raised the issue of a vote of no confidence in the government, but the vote (325:306) went in favor of May. Parliament made her drain the cup of Brexit – with all its bickering and costs – to the dregs. In July 2019 May resigned, and Johnson took over as prime minister, with a no-deal Brexit clearly in his mind.

According to Fyodor Lukyanov, "Joining the EEC was a reaction to the dismantling of the Empire, an attempt to overcome the syndrome of 'little Britain', which swept the UK in the 1960s... The UK's exit from the EU does not turn it into a global player; on the contrary, the question arises of what noticeable role, if any, the UK can play in the world. Not to mention the fact that leaving the EU creates serious risks to the integrity of the UK." [69]

"Today Britain is a shadow of its former self: inward-looking and anxiety-ridden, stagnant and expensive, split down the middle and fearful of the future," admits *The Economist*.[70]

Against the backdrop of Brexit and Donald Trump's victory in the US, the elections in France in 2017 were looked upon as a decisive clash between the forces of good and evil on a global scale. A unique fact testified to the extent of the dissatisfaction with the French establishment: none of the traditional parties managed to get their candidates through to the second round of the elections. Meanwhile, the leader of the En Marche! party, created just a year earlier, Emmanuel Macron, did make it through to the second round, as did the leader of the Front National, Marine Le Pen, with her appeal to the "forgotten French".

....

Humiliating' Cheat at Party Confab", *The Washington Post*, October 2, 2018 <https://www.washingtonpost.com/world/europe/boris-johnson-trashes-theresa-mays-brexit-plan-as-a-sad-politically-humiliating-cheat-at-party-confab/2018/10/02/c63f2964-c643-11e8-b1ed-1d2d65b86d0c_story.html?utm_term=.8ad5c0620f3e>.

[69] Fyodor Luk'yanov, "Rastvoreniye utopii" ("The Dissolution of Utopia"), *Rossiyskaya Gazeta*, January 17, 2019 <https://rg.profkiosk.ru/article.aspx?aid=700597>.

[70] "Bagehot: Britain has Fretted about Decline Before, but Never like This", *The Economist*, July 28, 2018 <https://www.economist.com/britain/2018/07/28/britain-has-fretted-about-decline-before-but-never-like-this>.

Macron won. "Fortunately, reason and hope prevailed over anger and fear," wrote Dominique Moisi. "But he got where he is because the Socialist Party of Francois Mitterrand is dead, and the conservative Les Republicains are in a shambles."[71] After the presidential elections, Macron opted for "creating a brand-new party from scratch out of a list of candidates it must pull from established parties and from outside politics."[72]

Macron's party won a landslide victory in the parliamentary elections, securing 308 of the 577 seats in the Assemblée Nationale, mainly with candidates who were completely new to politics. But then the ruling party started having problems. Defence spending cuts resulted in the resignation of the popular Chief of the Defence Staff General Pierre de Villiers. Serious damage was inflicted by budget cuts – especially housing allowances for the poor – against the backdrop of the tax cuts for the rich. Many deputies from the ruling party showed their amateurism and incompetence. Relations with trade unions were spoiled by changes in labor legislation in favor of entrepreneurs and in the status of the personnel of the national railway company SNCF.

By August 2017, Macron's rating had fallen to 36% – the most rapid decline in the history of the Fifth Republic. In 2018, 71% of French people considered Macron's domestic policy unfair, and 65% ineffective. His prestige was further undermined by the case of Alexander Benalla, the head of the presidential security service, who was convicted of the brutal beating of demonstrators.[73] Marine Le Pen complained that literally every day her party is "persecuted" by the authorities. "Every day – searches, every day – a criminal case." Such, she asserted, is the fate of dissidents, against which the entire arsenal of the means of suppression is used.[74]

---

[71] Dominique Moisi, "Resisting the temptations of Bonapartism", *Gulf News,* May 6, 2017 <https://gulfnews.com/opinion/op-eds/resisting-the-temptations-of-bonapartism-1.2022717>.

[72] Josh Lowe, "Can France's New President Emmanuel Macron Really Create a Brand-New Party?", *Newsweek,* May 10, 2017 <https://www.newsweek.com/2017/05/26/france-french-elections-emmanuel-macron-parliamentary-elections-manuel-valls-606721.html>.

[73] Lyubov' Glazunova, "Makron Bonapart. Chego dobilsya prezident Frantsii za pervyye sto dney pravleniya?" ("Macron Bonaparte. What has the President of France Achieved During His First Hundred Days in Office?"), *Moskovskiy komsomolets,* Issue 18, August/September 2017. P. 10; "France's Ambitious President Macron Stumbles", *The Economist,* August 26, 2017. PP. 21-22; Yekaterina Zabrodina, "Nemedovyy mesyats" ("Not a Honeymoon"), *Rossiyskaya gazeta* (*Russian Newspaper*), Issue 159, July 2014 <https://rg.profkiosk.ru/article.aspx?aid=661684>; Jonathan Fenby, "The Benalla Affair Has Brought Macron to Earth", *The Financial Times,* Weekend, August 3, 2018 <https://www.ft.com/content/db23ec12-964f-11e8-95f8-8640db9060a7>.

[74] Vyacheslav Prokof'yev, "Pressing po-frantsuzski" ("Pressure, French Style"), *Rossiyskaya Gazeta* (*Russian Newspaper*), October 3, 2018 <https://rg.profkiosk.ru/article.aspx?aid=677489>.

"Macron's vision of France has at its heart a deeply integrated Europe, with France as the continent's leader alongside Germany. Macron wants the European Union to become an economic powerhouse that will play a crucial role in a multipolar world order."[75] Speaking to both houses of Parliament in Versailles in July 2018, the President said: "I want France to become a power of the 21st century."[76]

Macron actively took up the strengthening of the European Union, proposing that the Eurozone move towards a closer financial union with a common budget and regulatory authorities, and defending tougher anti-dumping procedures and measures to control the flow of foreign capital. However, his first major initiative – that workers from Eastern Europe should not receive inferior wages and social benefits in Western countries to those of indigenous citizens caused acute conflict and an exchange of accusations with the leadership of Poland.[77]

In November 2018, Macron, along with world leaders, stood at the Arc de Triomphe in Paris, marking the 100th anniversary of the end of World War I. Shortly afterwards, the Arc was damaged by participants in the "Yellow Vests" protests.

Such mass actions had not been seen in France for half a century. The immediate cause of the protests was the rise in gasoline prices, and more widely – the perception of Macron as the President of the rich, after he launched multi-billion programs in support of business. Initially, the Yellow Vests required an increase in the minimum wage, the return of the luxury tax, and a reduction in the retirement age. But then they started to call for the resignation of Macron, exit from the European Union and NATO, and a halt to immigration. The protest movement could not be

....

[75] Ronald Tiersky, "Macron's World", *Foreign Affairs*, January/February 2018. P. 88.

[76] Gregory Viscusi and William Horobin, "Macron Defends Record, Saying He Hasn't Forgotten France's Poor", *Bloomberg*, July 9, 2018 <https://www.bloomberg.com/news/articles/2018-07-09/macron-defends-record-pledging-to-continue-to-transform-france>.

[77] Martin Sandbu, "Emmanuel Macron's Risky Vision of a Euro Bargain", *The Financial Times*, August 21, 2017 <https://www.ft.com/content/de225ddc-865f-11e7-bf50-e1c239b45787>; Anne-Sylvaine Chassany, "Macron Gears Up for Contentious French Labour Reform", *The Financial Times*, August 24, 2017 <https://www.ft.com/content/62f80b24-88ae-11e7-8bb1-5ba57d47eff7>; Henry Samuel and Justin Huggler, "Macron Hosts EU Power Summit as Clouds Gather Over Presidency", *The Sunday Telegraph*, August 27, 2017; Vyacheslav Prokof'yev, "Makron grezit o velichii" ("Macron's Dreams of Greatness"), *Rossiyskaya gazeta (Russian Newspaper)*, Issue 148, July 11, 2018 <https://rg.profkiosk.ru/article.aspx?aid=658212>.

brought under control because it did not have leadership and did not involve trade unions and/or opposition parties.

Macron immediately called the protesters "a movement of demagogues and a disgrace to France." His response was one of harsh suppression, with an unprecedented number of detainees arrested, which only weakened his own position. Seventy-four percent of the populace shared the mood of the Yellow Vests. And in December 2018, only 23% rated the work of Macron positively – a rating equal to the lowest achieved by the most unpopular president in the history of the country – Francois Hollande. Only 11% believed that Macron understood the aspirations of ordinary French people.

The general election in Germany in 2017 took place in a somewhat calmer setting than in France, and became known as the "sleepy campaign". Merkel and the leader of the socialists, Martin Schulz, went to great lengths to avoid attacking one another, so as not to provoke a counter-attack from the other side. They carefully side-stepped pressing issues, above all those associated with migration and crime among immigrants.[78]

Schultz began his campaign in January with a 17-point lead, but his party started to dramatically lose support, above all, among the working class in depressed industrial regions, who moved over to Alternative for Germany *en masse*. Workers make up only 17% of the SPD electorate, but represent 34% of the Alternative for Germany voters.[79] This was a reflection of the general trend in Europe, where social democrats everywhere are ceasing to be seen as the party that protects social rights. The socialists have lost all the most recent elections. Schultz went on a mild offensive at the end of his campaign, trying to portray Merkel as Trump's supporter who would plunge Germany into a new arms race at Trump's prompting, and was failing to take a tough line with the American president.[80]

One of Merkel's political consultants, Thomas Strerath, summed up her campaign in two words: "Angst and Gemütlichkeit, or, in rough translation, 'anxiety' and 'coziness.'"[81] The German chancellor rejected the role offered to

---

[78] Stefan Wagstyl, "Main German Parties' Silence on Refugees Risks Boosting Far Right", *The Financial Times*, August 21, 2017. P.2.

[79] Guy Chazan, "Germany's working class turns away from SPD", *The Financial Times*, August 21, 2017 <https://www.ft.com/content/ac8f5060-7da7-11e7-9108-edda0bcbc928>.

[80] Guy Chazan, "Flagging Schulz goes on the offensive against Merkel", *The Financial Times*, August 22, 2017 <https://www.ft.com/content/ed476412-8711-11e7-bf50-e1c239b45787>.

[81] Cit. from: Simon Shuster, "The Two Words That Explain Merkel's Shrewd Campaign", *Time Magazine*, September 25, 2017 <https://www.magzter.com/articles/11134/243151/59bfbc90348a3>.

her after Trump's election, that of "the leader of the free world" and opted instead – for the first time ever – to roll out her campaign in the colors of Germany's national flag.[82]

The party Alternative for Germany won seats in the Bundestag for the first time, under the leadership of Alexander Gauland; the party was already represented in 13 out of 16 land governments.[83] Alternative for Germany attracted a considerable number of voters who would normally vote for the main parties, and finished third with 12% of the vote. Merkel called the election results a catastrophe. The negotiations which followed, on the creation of a government coalition consisting of the CDU/CSU, the FDP and the Green Party (known as the "Jamaica coalition" as the parties' colors are those of the Jamaican flag), came to nothing due to disagreements: above all on the issue of the status of migrants. This brought about the first genuine crisis of government in Germany's post-war history, and created something akin to panic with regard to the future of the EU. *The New York Times* wrote of a "profound crisis of leadership for Europe and a protracted period of uncertainty, at a time when it can least afford it. […] Ms. Merkel has been the indispensable leader in Europe. Any weakening of her political position at home, or domestic preoccupation, is a serious blow to a bloc still struggling to salvage its future. […] Mr. Macron has audacity, but he is too new and viewed too skeptically by other leaders, including those from Central Europe, to actually 'lead Europe', if Europe can in fact be led."[84] A rush by Brussels and Washington to Merkel's rescue resulted in talks on the resurrection of a big coalition with the SPD, although at first Schulz strongly opposed the idea of re-joining the alliance on the grounds that membership of the alliance had caused the popularity of his party to fall to an all-time low – receiving, as it did, just 20.5% of the vote.

For more than six months, Germany lived without a government: Angela Merkel and her ministers performed only their official duties. The outcome of the negotiations on the creation of yet another coalition was decided by a vote of ordinary members of the SPD, who supported, in the end, the

---

[82] Simon Shuster, "The Two Words That Explain Merkel's Shrewd Campaign", *Time Magazine*, September 25, 2017. PP. 10-11.

[83] "Alternative for Germany. Fifty Shades of Blue", *The Economist*, August 26, 2017. P. 22.

[84] Steven Erlanger, "Merkel's Troubles May Spell Trouble for All of Europe", *The New York Times*, November 21, 2017 <https://www.nytimes.com/2017/11/21/world/europe/merkel-germany-european-union.html?auth=login-email&login=email>.

formation of a coalition government led by Merkel. However, this did not calm the country much. In Eastern Germany, clashes between right-wing radicals and immigrants have become more frequent, taking the most acute forms in Saxony. And the popularity of Alternative for Germany surpassed that of the SDP in the Eastern lands.

The ruling "big coalition" still has the majority of votes in only one age group – voters over 65 years old. In all other age groups, the vibrant Greens (who are not afraid to act against the shift to the right) and Alternative for Germany, which is leading the right-wing movement, are making a strong showing.[85]

After extremely unsatisfactory elections for the CSU in one of its strongholds – in the land of Hessen, where support for the party fell from 38% to 27% – at the end of October 2018, Merkel announced her resignation from the post of party leader and her unwillingness to run for Chancellor in 2021.

The frontrunner in the struggle for the post of leader of the CDU was the longstanding leader of Saar, Annegret Kramp-Karrenbauer, also known as AKK and (since she was considered as an alter ego of Frau Chancellor) the "Mini-Merkel". But AKK – a Catholic and mother of three children – has her own agenda: she is against same-sex marriage and takes a tougher stance than Merkel on migration.[86] The future of the governing coalition remains uncertain.

No wonder that the crisis in the European Union is one of the central subjects in Western discourse. "The EU's architects created a head without a body: they built a unified political and administrative bureaucracy but not a united European nation. The EU aspired to transcend nation-states, but its fatal flaw has been its consistent failure to recognize the persistence of national differences and the importance of addressing threats on its frontiers," writes Jakub Grygiel of the Center for European Policy Analysis.[87]

Jean-Claude Juncker agreed: "I think the European Union gave the impression that we are in command of everything. We were trying to have

---

[85] Fyodor Luk'yanov, "Obshchestva v zhiletakh" ("Societies in Vests"), *Rossiyskaya Gazeta (Russian Newspaper)*, December 4, 2018 <https://rg.ru/2018/12/04/lukianov-fenomen-zheltyh-zhiletov-privodit-v-zameshatelstvo-vlasti.html>.

[86] Timofey Borisov, "Ostalis' lish' dvoye" ("Only Two Remained"), *Rossiyskaya Gazeta (Russian Newspaper)*, Issue 276, December 6, 2018 <https://rg.ru/2018/12/06/germaniia-uznaet-imia-svoego-vozmozhnogo-budushchego-kanclera.html>; Mary Kaye Schilling, "Annegret Kramp-Karrenbauer?", *Newsweek*, December 2018. P. 17.

[87] Jakub Grygiel, "The Return of Europe's Nation-States. The Upside to the EU's Crisis", *Foreign Affairs*, September/October 2016. P. 97.

influence in so many things that are better in the hands of national, local and regional authorities."[88]

Yet on 13th November 2017, in Brussels, 23 EU member states took a step towards military integration by signing the Permanent Structured Cooperation (PESCO), with the USA and the UK objecting, as they have traditionally done, due to concerns that it would result in a weakening of NATO.

In June 2018, during German-French inter-governmental consultations, the idea of creating an EU Security Council was voiced. In October, Merkel repeated it, focusing on the principle of rotation: Germany and France were to be present in the Council permanently, while other countries would rotate. This has the look of a move to abandon unanimity in decision-making in the EU.[89]

A new round of discussions about the future of the European Union has begun, and the talks promise to be far from straightforward. The director of Chatham House, Robin Niblett, writes: "Other countries will probably not follow the United Kingdom out of the EU. But few European leaders appear willing to continue relinquishing their countries' sovereignty."[90]

European Pole

Through centuries, global history was made in Europe, and control over the Old World effectively became a synonym for global supremacy. This period has come to an end.

In the days when Henry Kissinger was the USA's Secretary of State, in the 1970s, when the idea of a common European foreign policy was first mooted, Kissinger asked for a phone number to call in order to find out all the essential parts of such a policy. At present, such number is still nowhere to be found. From the US's perspective, the modern European approach to foreign and defence policy, to quote Charles Kupchan, appears "schizophrenic": "On the one hand, the Lisbon Treaty provides Europe with institutions meant to enhance its ability to take on a new level of international leadership and responsibility. […] On the other hand, the renationalization of Europe is

---

[88] Charlotte McDonald-Gibson, "The EU's Chief Executive on Trump, Populism and Russia", *Time*, February 16, 2017 <https://time.com/4673011/the-e-u-s-chief-executive-on-trump-populism-and-russia/>.

[89] Ariadna Rokossovskaya, "Sovet ot kantslera" ("Advice from the Chancellor"), *Rossiyskaya Gazeta (Russian Newspaper)*, October 3, 2018 <https://rg.profkiosk.ru/677488>.

[90] Robin Niblett, "Liberalism in Retreat: The Demise of a Dream", *Foreign Affairs*, January/February 2017. P. 20.

undercutting the EU's aspirations to fashion a more collective and robust foreign policy."[91]

At the same time, Western Europe remains a serious player in foreign and military-political affairs. It accounts for 20% of global defence spending, compared with 8% for China, 4% for Russia and 3% for India.[92] There are tens of thousands of European soldiers based in Sierra Leone, the Democratic Republic of Congo, the Ivory Coast, Chad, Lebanon and Mali. The EU has 17% of global trade (as compared with the USA's 12%) and half of all foreign aid programs (the USA provides 20% of these).[93]

The USA and the countries of Western Europe see each other as key partners and allies in the modern world. The elites of the European countries were educated in the USA in big numbers or recruited with the involvement of American governmental and non-governmental structures, and are part of the general "Davos culture".

At the same time, the European Union's role in the American leadership's strategic calculations has waned in recent decades. Richard Haas stresses that "the critical elements of Europe's transformation over the past 70 years – the democratization of Germany, Franco-German reconciliation, economic integration – are so robust that they can reasonably be taken for granted. Europe's parochialism and military weakness may make the region a poor partner for the United States in global affairs, but the continent itself is no longer a security problem, which is a huge advance on the past."[94] Moreover, the United States is satisfied with the system that has taken shape for organizing security in Europe, which has NATO at its apex.

The US itself, meanwhile, which is experiencing debt problems of its own, and is increasingly concerned by matters of security in other regions of the planet, has reduced its military presence in the Old World for now. At the same time, the deployment of a modified ABM system, with an enhanced naval component, has begun, in spite of strong objections from Russia. Since March 2011, Europe's seas have been patrolled by American ships equipped with the Aegis Combat System.

---

[91] Charles A. Kupchan, *No One's World. The West, the Rising Rest, and the Coming Global Truth.* Oxford, 2012. P. 176.

[92] Mark Leonard and Hans Kundnani, "Think Again: European Decline", *Foreign Policy*, May/June 2013. P. 48; Bastian Giegerich and Christoph Schwegmann, "Sustaining Europe's Security", *Survival*, August/September 2014. P. 43.

[93] Joseph S. Nye, *The Future of Power*. PublicAffairs, 2011. P. 162.

[94] Richard N. Haas, "The Unraveling", *Foreign Affairs*, November/December 2014. P. 72.

NATO remains at the kernel of Euro-Atlantic integration. In theory, with the disappearance of the USSR, there were no more dangers left in the Euro-Atlantic zone that called for the preservation of the largest military-political bloc on the planet. How, though, could one disband an alliance that had "defeated" the West's main enemy so triumphantly, without a single shot being fired?

The need to have a fully-fledged and unifying mission, alongside a desire to strengthen the geopolitical changes in favor of the West which took place in Europe after the collapse of the Soviet Union, were the reasons behind a large-scale expansion of NATO. In the period 1999-2004, ten new members joined NATO, and in 2009, Albania and Croatia acceded to the alliance, while Montenegro did so in 2017, and Macedonia is on its way as well. At present, the only member states of the EU that are not in NATO are Austria, Finland, Sweden, Ireland, Cyprus, and Malta. Expansion through the acquisition of a large number of weak member states has not strengthened unity and military firepower. The European veterans of the alliance were annoyed by the fact that its tone was now set by states which had only recently joined. The newcomers, in turn, placed more faith in guarantees of security from the USA than in the "lily-livered" Western European grandees.

The war in Yugoslavia in 1999 was NATO's first military campaign in history. Europe neutralized this "hotspot" at its borders, and the USA tested the bloc's fitness-for-purpose as a military instrument – and were clearly disappointed by the fighting capabilities of their allies. After the terror attacks of 11th September 2001, in response to the proposal made by Europeans to apply a clause on collective defence, the USA opted instead to act outside the framework of the bloc in the first instance, relying on a "coalition of the willing".

Germany and France were against the invasion of Iraq in 2003. The German government did not support the bombing of Libya, and considerable differences existed within the Alliance in relation to the use of force against Syria. There is less and less enthusiasm about the ability to promote democracy in various corners of the planet, particularly through military force.

Washington is increasingly irritated by the insufficient defence efforts of the EU countries. Today, 75% of NATO's costs are paid for by the USA, in comparison with 63% in 2001.[95] Robert Gates maintained, when he headed

---

[95] Steven Erlanger, "Shrinking Europe Military Spending Stirs Concern", *The New York Times*, April 23, 2013 <https://www.nytimes.com/2013/04/23/world/europe/europes-shrinking-military-spending-under-scrutiny.html>.

the US's Defence Ministry, that the Europeans "'the military capabilities simply aren't there' for European states to conduct a serious campaign".[96]

By all accounts, this phase of hasty expansion has come to an end. As soon as a measure of resistance to further expansion was encountered, as was the case with Ukraine and Georgia, it transpired that nobody within NATO was prepared to take any risks, and much less suffer any casualties.

The crisis in Ukraine did, however, give NATO new life. NATO's Foreign Ministers agreed that "Russia's illegal military intervention in Ukraine and Russia's violation of Ukraine's sovereignty and territorial integrity" provided grounds to cease "all practical civil and military cooperation between NATO and Russia".[97] Rasmussen declared that Russia's aggression in Ukraine puts freedom and peace in Europe in jeopardy and "[t]oday we will show our firm commitment with the joint defense – and defense starts with restraint."[98] Resources were increased for an aerial mission patrolling the Baltic states.

As part of the Baltic Air Policing program, which began in March 2014 in Latvia, Lithuania and Estonia, the activity of 15 member states of NATO increased by a factor of 1240 in terms of airplane-days.[99]

Additional forces were engaged for reconnaissance flights over Poland and Romania, and large-scale military exercises held. At a summit in Wales in September 2014, the Alliance re-engaged functions that it had performed in the days of the Cold War. It was decided that the shrinking of military budgets had to end. A Readiness Action Plan (RAP) was adopted, in which Russia was identified as a "threat to Euro-Atlantic security". In essence, the Alliance, after a long search for a new mission, has gone back to its old one: deterring Russia. Expansion is taking place – in violation of the Founding Act between Russia and NATO – of the military presence in Latvia, Lithuania, Estonia, Romania and Poland, where NATO Force Integration Units are located. Rapid-response forces are being created, based at the German-Dutch corps, headquartered in Munster. There have been reports that 150 tanks were supplied from the USA, with the proposed deployment of most of them in Poland, Romania or the Baltic states. American para-

---

[96] Cit. from: Øystein Tunsjø, "Europe's Favorable Isolation", *Survival*, Vol. 55, Issue 6, 2013. P. 96.

[97] "Statement by NATO Foreign Ministers", NATO, April 1, 2014 <https://www.nato.int/cps/en/natolive/news_108501.htm>.

[98] "NATO Secretary General calls Russia for dialogue", Bulgarian National Radio, April 1, 2014 <https://bnr.bg/en/post/100381966/nato-secretary-general-calls-russia-for-dialogue>.

[99] Lyudmila Glazkova, "NATO idet na Vostok" ("NATO is Moving to the East"), *RF Today*, Issue 17, 2015. PP. 14-17.

troopers have officially appeared in Ukraine.[100] Some have said that "NATO no longer has the luxury of reducing reliance on nuclear weapons for its own sake [...]."[101] In the immediate vicinity of Russia's borders, there are more than 150 US military bases and satellites thereof, and this number is growing. And this is despite the fact that Russia does not have a single base in the Western hemisphere.

"With the decisions taken at the Warsaw Summit in July 2016, NATO crossed a new symbolic threshold," writes the former head of political planning at the office of the secretary general of NATO, Fabrice Pothier. "For the first time since the end of the Cold War, NATO will deploy, on a quasi-permanent basis, troops on the eastern flank of the Alliance. This move, touted by the Alliance as historic, is meant to reassure nervous allies and to deter Russia from crossing the sacred border of NATO territory."[102] Particular attention is being paid to the strategy for overcoming the system for protecting Russian territory from the penetration of military might on its territory (anti-access/area denial – A2/AD).

Trump, who described NATO during his election campaign as an outdated organization that had lost its reason to exist, changed his mind 80 days after taking office and told the Secretary General of the Alliance: "It's no longer obsolete."[103] Nevertheless, at the NATO summit in May 2017, the president put forward two central ideas. Firstly, an increase in Europe's contribution to collective defence and the fulfilment of the obligations undertaken in Wales on increasing military spending to at least 2% of GDP by 2024, with 20% of that amount going to the primary forms of armaments

---

[100] Yelena Chernenko, "NATO navodyat na staruyu tsel'" ("NATO is Aiming at an Old Target"), *Kommersant*, Issue 49, March 25, 2014 <https://www.kommersant.ru/doc/2437286>; Statement of NATO Foreign Ministers, April 1, 2014 <https://www.nato.int/cps/en/natolive/news_108501.htm>; "NATO perekhodit k sderzhivaniyu" ("NATO is Shifting Towards Restraint"), *Kommersant*, Issue 55, April 2, 2014 <https://www.kommersant.ru/doc/2443469>; Yelena Chernenko, "NATO rasshiryayetsya nazad. Severoatlanticheskiy al'yans vozvrashchayetsya k strategii sderzhivaniya Rossii" ("NATO is Expanding Backwards. The North Atlantic Alliance Returns to Its Strategy of Restraining Russia"), *Kommersant*, Issue 158, September 4, 2014 <https://www.kommersant.ru/doc/2559207>; Yevgeniy Grigor'yev, "NATO razmeshchayet shtaby na Vostoke" ("NATO is Locating its Headquarters in the East)", *Nezavisimaya Gazeta* (*Independent Newspaper*), February 3, 2015 <http://nvo.ng.ru/world/2015-02-03/2_nato.html>.

[101] Matthew Kroenig, "Facing Reality: Getting NATO Ready for a New Cold War", *Survival*, Vol. 57, Issue 1, 2015. P. 64.

[102] Fabrice Pothier, "An Area-Access Strategy for NATO", *Survival*, Vol. 59, Issue 3, 2017. P. 73.

[103] Peter Baker, "Trump's Previous View of NATO Is Now Obsolete", *The New York Times*, April 13, 2017 <https://www.nytimes.com/2017/04/13/world/europe/nato-trump.html>.

(the "2/20" formula). Secondly, the declaration that NATO's key priority was the global war on terror.[104]

At the NATO summit in July 2018, a joint initiative was approved to increase the mobility of the Alliance's armed forces, called "four by thirty": by 2020, to have 30 mechanized battalions, 30 air squadrons and 30 warships ready for use within 30 days to counter the "Russian threat". Already, eight NATO members were ready to spend 2% of GDP on defence: the USA, Great Britain, Greece, Poland, Latvia, Estonia, Romania and Lithuania.[105]

Since 2012, negotiations have been ongoing on the subjects of creating a free-trade zone between the EU and the USA and a Trans-Atlantic trade and investment partnership (TTIP). This powerhouse economic pact was supposed to "consolidate the economic and technological power of the West and the US for at least another generation, if not longer."[106] Its adversaries didn't stay idle, and Donald Trump was among them. Trump, on coming to power, simply buried the TTIP with one of his first executive orders among a number of protectionist measures.

The election of Trump prompted an extremely negative reaction in Europe. In France, for example, 75% of voters had a negative opinion of him. "Trump's style is also anathema to the French. The view from Paris is that Trump is a vulgar plutocrat who came to office by pandering to the unsophisticated masses and who might leave office early in scandal."[107]

David Goodhart of Policy Exchange identified three different camps when it comes to European attitudes to Trump. "The first and largest sees him as a living fossil, the sort of 'ugly American' common enough in earlier eras, focused less on responsible global leadership than on nativism, mercantilism, and gunboat diplomacy. […]. A second, smaller camp is more pragmatic. Its members point out that the Trump administration's actions have been more conventional than its rhetoric and that the president's tweets have not represented U.S. policy. The third, smallest camp includes Trump's European supporters, populists and nationalists across the continent who are delighted by such an emphatic vindication of their worldview from such an

---

[104] Dmitri Danilov, "NATO: neformal'nyy sammit ili novyy format?" ("NATO: an Informal Summit or a New Format?"), *International Affairs*, August 2017. PP. 50-53.

[105] Maxim Makarychev, "Tramp protiv vsekh" ("Trump Against All"), *Rossiyskaya Gazeta*, Issue 148, July 11, 2018 <https://rg.profkiosk.ru/article.aspx?aid=658211>.

[106] Ashley J. Tellis, "The Geopolitics of the TTIP and the TPP", in *Power Shifts and New Blocks in the Global Trading System*, ed. by Sanjaya Baru and Suvi Dogra. London, 2015. P. 110.

[107] Natalie Nougayrede, "France's Gamble. As America Retreats, Macron Steps Up", *Foreign Affairs*, September/October 2017. P. 3.

unexpected source. Germany is the epicenter of the continent's anti-Trump feelings [...]."[108] Which is hardly surprising.

"For the first time since the middle of the last century, Europe is confronted with an American administration, for which Germany, for instance, is first and foremost not a strategic partner, but a competitor in the markets."[109] Trump wrote about Germany: "We have a MASSIVE trade deficit with Germany, plus they pay FAR LESS than they should on NATO & military. Very bad for U.S. This will change."[110]

At the July 2018 NATO summit, Trump said that the purchase of gas from Gazprom made Germany "hostage to Russia", and again attacked the surplus in Berlin's trade with the United States and Germany's unwillingness to sharply increase military spending. "Germany has emerged as Mr Trump's favorite whipping boy, the epitome of all the dislikes about NATO, globalized trade and immigration. And his punchbag of choice is Angela Merkel," wrote *The Financial Times*.[111]

For Merkel, a staunch supporter of transatlantic solidarity and a fan of the United States, the new reality is very painful. "What we've taken for granted for decades, the idea that the US is the global superpower, in good and bad times, is no longer so certain in the future We can't simply rely on the US to uphold the global order," Merkel said in July 2018.[112]

Europe was outraged by the US withdrawal from the Paris climate agreement and the Iranian nuclear deal, and the introduction of tariffs on European steel and aluminum.

In March 2018, Washington introduced import duties for all metal suppliers in the US, granting the EU, however, a delay until 1st May (extended to 1st June). Brussels has threatened tariffs on American products. "Looking at the latest decisions of Donald Trump, someone could even think: with friends like that who needs enemies," said Donald Tusk. "But frankly, EU should be grateful. Thanks to him we got rid of all illusions."[113]

....

[108] David Goodhart, "The United Kingdom's Trump Trap: How Special a Relationship?", *Foreign Affairs*, September/October 2017. P. 17.

[109] Fyodor Luk'yanov, "Vremya protektsii" ("The Time of Protection"), *Rossiyskaya Gazeta* (*Russian Newspaper*), July 5, 2017 <https://globalaffairs.ru/redcol/Vremya-protektcii-18825>.

[110] Cit. from: Stefan Theil, "Berlin's Balancing Act: Merkel Needs Trump – but Also Needs to Keep Her Distance", *Foreign Affairs*, September/October 2017. P. 9.

[111] Guy Chazan, "How Germany Became Donald Trump's European Punchbag", *The Financial Times*, August 2, 2018 <https://www.ft.com/content/8f87c03c-93dc-11e8-b67b-b8205561c3fe>.

[112] Ibid.

[113] Alex Barker and Jim Brunsden, "Europe's Leaders Patch Differences to Tackle Trump on

In late July, Trump and Jean-Claude Juncker agreed to suspend the trade war. It was decided to abandon the introduction of new duties, start negotiations on the abolition of trade barriers, and agree on the size of duties on steel and aluminum. An intention to move to zero duties on industrial products not related to the automotive industry, to increase trade in services was announced. The EU promised to increase purchases of liquefied gas and soybeans. There were threats of joint efforts to put China in its place. However, even after these agreements, protectionist American duties on European metals remained in force, and European business complained of extreme uncertainty and instability in world trade.[114]

One more serious trouble spot emerged after the USA quit the nuclear deal with Iran. In Europe, work began on a mechanism to protect business transactions between EU countries and Iran from US sanctions. The so-called blocking law was passed, which prohibits European companies from carrying out the restrictive measures imposed by the US against Iran, and allows them not to recognize extraterritorial court decisions on this issue. However, the EU's determination to confront the United States over Iran should not be exaggerated, nor should the determination of European business, which has no guarantee of immunity from the American courts or of escaping the effects of US sanctions.

A lot of noise was generated by the initiative of Steve Bannon, chief strategist of Trump's election campaign but later dismissed from the White House, to engage in the promotion and consolidation of right-wing parties in Europe. He created a foundation called the Movement, which was intended to be an alternative to George Soros's "Open Society". Bannon's goal was to create a right-wing "supergroup" during the European Parliament elections of May 2019, turning them into a referendum on migration and the dominance of Islam in the Old World. Bannon looked to Viktor Orban to be a leader of the movement. However, the creation of an alliance of

....
Trade", *The Financial Times*, May 16, 2018 <https://www.ft.com/content/bb39b6fc-5914-11e8-bdb7-f6677d2e1ce8>.

[114] Natal'ya Il'ina, "Dotorgovalis' do mira" ("A Bargain for Peace"), *Vedomosti*, Issue 137, July 27, 2018 <https://vedomosti.profkiosk.ru/article.aspx?aid=662373>; Yevgeniy Shestakov, "Yunker sbit" ("Juncker Brought Down"), *Rossiyskaya Gazeta* (*Russian Newspaper*), Issue 163, July 27, 2018 <https://rg.ru/2018/07/26/iunker-i-tramp-dogovorilis-druzhit-protiv-kitaia.html>; Jack Ewing, "Europe Feels the Squeeze of the Trump Trade Tariffs", *The New York Times*, August 2, 2018 <https://www.nytimes.com/2018/08/02/business/economy/europe-trade-trump-tariffs.html>.

right-wing European parties was seen by experts as a difficult goal, given the serious differences between them.[115]

Trump's lukewarm attitude to the EU and NATO is, in turn, strengthening the trend towards consolidation in Europe, including in the military sphere, on the basis of Franco-German cooperation. At the same time, it is helping to support those forces in the United Kingdom that are in favor of Brexit.

If the USA and the Trans-Atlantic partnership remain the key political vector in the EU's foreign policy, the EU's main economic partner in recent years has started to be the Asian countries, first and foremost China. In 1996, under an initiative led by France and Singapore, the Asia-Europe forum (ASEM) was launched, and it is held once every two years, attended by dignitaries of the highest rank.

The way the EU looks on China is markedly different from America's approach, which is based on a demand that China unambiguously accepts Western rules, with any other kind of behavior seen as "revisionism".

"Unlike the USA, Brussels didn't alienate China, and despite long-time human rights issues in China and the Dalai Lama's visits to Europe, there are no ideological debates in its relations with Beijing. Their economies are highly developed and quite compatible, thus ensuring a balance of interests; and geographical remoteness excludes the possibility of any strategic military differences."[116] The theme of the "Chinese threat" – one of the central ideas in American literature – is expressed far more mildly in the European Union.[117]

Strategic dialogue between the EU and China began in 1994. Since 1998, annual bilateral summits have been held. For the EU, the main problem is the colossal deficit in trade with China. Trade turnover was in excess of $667 billion in 2017, and Chinese exports to EU countries are three times higher than European exports to China. Brussels considers that the cause of this is the low exchange rate for the yuan, which helps Chinese exporters. Since 2009 the EU has been building tariff walls as a barrier to cheap Chinese

....

[115] Maxim Makarychev, "Revolyutsiya dlya Yevropy" ("Revolution for Europe"), *Rossiyskaya Gazeta* (*Russian Newspaper*), Issue 159, July 24, 2018 <https://rg.profkiosk.ru/article.aspx?aid=661681>; Ivan Krastev, "Steve Bannon's New Best Friend", *The New York Times*, August 20, 2018. P. A21(L).

[116] Mikhail Nosov, "YeS i Kitay: torgovlya ili strategiya" ("EU and China: Trade or Strategy"), *Sovremennaya Evropa* (*Modern Europe*), Issue 6, 2018. P. 15.

[117] Sebastian Hellmann and Dirk H. Schmidt, *China's Foreign Political and Economic Relations: An Unconventional Global Power*. Lanham (MD), 2014.

goods in order to save its own manufacturers. When the volume of Chinese investment in EU countries reached 35 billion Euros in 2016 – an increase of two thirds in just a year – those in Brussels became keen to adopt measures against Chinese acquisitions and takeovers, particularly in the sectors of infrastructure and energy.[118]

As a result, in 2017, the amount of Chinese investment fell to 6 billion Euros. In the first half of 2018, the figure began to grow again, and amounted to $12 billion, while investments from China to the United States decreased by 92% to $2 billion. In July 2018, a very remarkable EU-China summit was held. Mutual understanding was reached on the issues of WTO reform and safeguarding it from what were seen as threats posed by Donald Trump, and negotiations on the further opening up of markets for investments were unblocked. In addition, the European Union has reached a mutual understanding with China on climate change. At the same time, Beijing has been building a separate nexus of relations with the countries of Central and Eastern Europe, according to the formula 16+1 (11 of the 16 partnership countries are in the EU), which is considered by Brussels to be China's attempt to split the European Union.[119]

A Clash of Values?

Anti-Russian sentiment in the countries of the EU is unprecedentedly strong. But in relations between Russia and the European Union there are a number of constants that define the framework conditions of interaction and are not subject to dramatic changes. The actions and words of the leaders of the EU and the member states often testify to the fact that they have not rid themselves of their sense of being the victor in the Cold War, of the tendency to view Russia as the rump of the losing side in that war, the Soviet Union. Hence a reluctance to acknowledge the fact that Russia has its own national interests, the expansion of Western military structures in the post-Soviet space, the efforts to minimize Russia's influence in its neighboring states, and aspirations to the right to influence her domestic political development.

---

[118] Jim Brunsden, "Brussels seeks tighter vetting of foreign takeovers", *The Financial Times*, August 13, 2017 <https://www.ft.com/content/04fa752c-7dda-11e7-ab01-a13271d1ee9c>.

[119] "Relations with the European Union. The Youth and the Rich Old Man", *The Economist*, July 21, 2018. PP. 43-44; Ian Bremmer, "The E.U. Looks East to Shield Itself from the Fallout of Trump's Trade War", *Time*, July 30, 2018. P. 19.

Russian proposals for the development of cooperation (whether it be a common economic space, or a pact on European security), have been utterly ignored. In exchange, nothing whatsoever has been put forward, and this demonstrates the absence of an inclusive strategy with regard to Russia. At the same time, the post-Soviet states are increasingly being drawn into various forms of cooperation which exclude Russia.

A serious source of disagreement has been the "Eastern Partnership" program, which was proposed to countries further east than the EU and NATO – Azerbaijan, Armenia, Belarus, Georgia, Moldova and Ukraine – in accordance with a traditional EU model of development assistance conditional upon democratic reforms. Russia declined to take part in the program, seeing it, not unjustifiably, as a mechanism by which new, independent states could break away from the CIS.

The Russian Federation is a key trade partner for the EU, although the imposition of sanctions has caused the volume of trade to fall significantly. Three countries stand out: the Netherlands, Germany and Italy are behind only China in terms of foreign trade relations with Russia. Poland, the UK, France and Finland are much further behind.

European countries have also been the main foreign investors in Russia. It should be remembered, though, that foreign investment registered in Luxembourg or Cyprus will often represent Russia's own assets, taken out of the country either legally or illegally. Estimates suggest that up to one third of "European" investment in Russia is in fact investment of Russian capital.

A change towards a tougher stance in dealings with Russia was noted in the EU – particularly in its engine, Germany – even before the Ukrainian crisis, from the moment Putin returned to the Kremlin in 2012. A campaign took place in the German media to discredit the "apologists" for Russia in the political class and the expert community. Berlin went from being a supporter of closer ties with Russia to being openly against Moscow in all areas. Ukraine took this cooling of relations to its logical conclusion.

The agenda for relations with Russia, as *The Economist* put it, did not look very promising. Firstly, in response to the "Russian threat", the EU states demonstrated their readiness to increase their military spending. Secondly, they persisted with policies aimed at lessening their energy dependence and any other dependence on Russia. Thirdly, the sanctions against Russia are going to be maintained, and possibly stepped up, although they are damaging not only Russia, but also the unstable Western

European economy.¹²⁰ Indeed, according to UN experts in the autumn of 2017, after the introduction of sanctions, the EU's economy lost more than 100 billion dollars, and Russia lost approximately 55 billion.¹²¹

The demonization of Putin and Russia has reached anecdotal dimensions. Russia has increasingly been accused of meddling in European countries' domestic affairs. In France, Germany and Italy, there have been many claims at the highest level about Russian interference in elections. Norway accused Russian hackers of carrying out attacks on its ministries and parties. The UK's Defence Minister accused Moscow of "weaponizing disinformation". The Dutch asserted that two groups of hackers who stole secrets from the National Committee of the Democratic Party, in the USA, did the same thing in the Netherlands.¹²²

The issues are not confined to Ukraine and the elusive Russian hackers. The cultural and civilizational gulf is deepening, too. "A conflict is taking place on the battlefield of liberal values, and if one looks closely, the split is occurring because of different worldviews," says a thoughtful German expert, Alexander Rahr. "The West has for a long time been living in a post-Christian world, while Russia is trying to develop in a spirit of neo-Christianity, after the Communist persecution of religion throughout almost the whole of the 20th century.

No-one will say this openly in the West, but Western intellectuals consider 'Putin's authoritarian regime' to be illegitimate. They are hoping that a more 'enlightened' generation will come to power in Russia, and then cooperation will be renewed in accordance with a Western scenario. In response to the Russian elite's criticism that the West is undermining the principles of state sovereignty, and thereby violating international law, the answer comes back: the global order has changed, and when human rights are being violated somewhere, the liberal West has the moral right to intervene in the domestic affairs of other states, protecting the weak from the tyranny of dictators."¹²³

---

[120] "The World in 2015", *The Economist*, 2015. P. 37.

[121] Anastasiya Bashkatova, "YeS stradayet iz-za antirossiyskikh sanktsiy bol'she, chem RF" ("EU is Suffering from Anti-Russian Sanctions More than Russia"), *Nezavisimaya Gazeta* (*Independent Newspaper*), September 14, 2017 <http://www.ng.ru/economics/2017-09-14/1_7073_eu.html>.

[122] Andrew Higgins, "Fake News, Fake Ukrainians: How a Group of Russians Tilted a Dutch Vote", *The New York Times*, February 16, 2017 <https://www.nytimes.com/2017/02/16/world/europe/russia-ukraine-fake-news-dutch-vote.html>.

[123] Alexander Rahr, "Yevropa – Rossiya: na chem stavim krest" ("Europe – Russia: What We're Saying Goodbye to"), *Rossiyskaya Gazeta*, September 11, 2012 <https://rg.ru/2012/09/11/rossia.html>.

Incidentally, the internal European unity that was seen in the early stages of the Ukrainian crisis, founded on a common anti-Russian stance, is starting to weaken. There is a group of states that is clearly not prepared to extend the sanctions indefinitely: Greece, Cyprus, Hungary, the Czech Republic, Slovakia, Austria, and Italy. European business overwhelmingly supports the lifting of sanctions. Despite strong opposition from Washington, Warsaw and Kyiv, construction of the Nord Stream 2 gas pipeline from Russia to Germany has continued.

Dialogue with Moscow is being renewed in many areas, and Berlin and Paris have taken serious steps towards a peaceful resolution in eastern Ukraine, as part of the Minsk-2 process. The euphoria in European capitals caused by the results of the Ukrainian revolution has passed, and Kyiv is being deprived of the indulgence seen in the past for the committing of military crimes.

Lukyanov draws attention to the complexities for Moscow of relations with the EU: "The political weight 20 years ago of individual countries in the Old World – France, Germany, the UK, Italy – was greater than that of united Europe today. One cannot therefore rely on it as a strong player. But it is impossible to reach pragmatic agreements, since the EU's assessment of its own worth is extremely high. It sees itself as the pinnacle of peace-making, and bases its approach on the presumption of its own moral rectitude, so that everyone else must act on the basis of the rules it sets. Yet Europe is not capable of achieving internal unity, turning its relations with external partners into a tortuous farce."[124]

Modern Europe feels that it is going through a crisis, not just economically, but also psychologically. Dominique Moïsi described these feelings as being in the categories of fear. "It is the fear that Europe is condemned to become a sort of museum, a bigger version of Venice, an oasis of sophisticated 'good life' and culture that people from more dynamic continents enjoy visiting or retiring to, but no longer a centre of creativity […]."[125]

Robert Kaplan has called the EU an "empire". "The EU has been such an ambitious enterprise mainly because it has sought a union over the former Carolingian, Prussian, Hapsburg, Byzantine and Ottoman domains, all with starkly different histories and development patterns. To accomplish that,

---

[124] Fyodor Luk'yanov, "Gasnushchiy mayak" ("The Fading Beacon"), *Rossiyskaya Gazeta*, Issue 118, May 28, 2014 <https://rg.ru/2014/05/28/europa.html>.

[125] Dominique Moïsi, *The Geopolitics of Emotion: How Cultures of Fear, Humiliation and Hope are Reshaping the World*. Random House, 2009.

the EU has had, in effect, to replace the functionality of those former empires. Even inside the open borders of the Schengen Area, within which EU citizens are guaranteed free movement, the union represents a sprawling territory, governed by a remote and only partly democratic bureaucracy, with many of its people demanding more direct representation."[126]

At the same time, serious analysts agree that Europe is going through a period of remarkable uncertainty. Simms wonders: "Will Europeans persist in regarding the EU as a modern-day Holy Roman Empire, which enables them to coexist more easily than ever before but is incapable of effective collective actions, or will they conclude that all these problems can only be mastered by establishing a new constitutional settlement on the lines pioneered by the Anglo-Americans in the eighteenth century: a mighty union based on a common debt, strong central institutions responsible to a directly elected parliament and a common defence against common enemies?"[127] Only time will tell.

---

[126] Robert D. Kaplan, "The Necessary Empire", The New York Times, May 5, 2017 <https://www.nytimes.com/2017/05/05/opinion/robert-kaplan-european-union-balkans.html>.

[127] Brendan Simms, *Europe: The Struggle for Supremacy, 1453 to the Present*. Penguin, 2014. P. 532.

CHAPTER 4
THE AMERICAN MAGNITUDE

The USA is an indispensable state in the sense that not a single serious global problem is resolved without it, yet it produces a substantial share of these problems itself. This is because the USA is now the only superpower, with global interests, and the capacity to apply force in all corners of the planet.

Colonial Duality

Optimism, idealism, individualism, the cult of superiority, a conviction about its own uniqueness – these have been the key components to the success of the country which saw itself more as a construction site for the new world than the embodiment of a European tradition which had to be preserved or overcome. America (how much more poetic this sounded than the United States!) was to become a new country, turning its back on Europe both metaphorically and culturally. "Unlike Europeans, the Americans are not preoccupied by the ghost of their past," suggests Moïsi.[1] While the first generation of European immigrants still had their roots in the homelands, the children did not have the same attachment to their country of origin. Incidentally, the campaign to have statues taken down in 2017 seemingly confirms that the ghost of the past has arrived in the USA, too – along with its history.

The American branch of Western civilization began to grow from Spain. Until the late 16th century, both the Americas belonged to Spain. The only European settlements in North America by 1600 were the Spanish fortresses of San Juan on the territory of what is now New Mexico state, and San Augustin in Florida. In the 17th century, the weakened Spain jealously protected

---

[1] Dominique Moïsi, *The Geopolitics of Emotion: How Cultures of Fear, Humiliation and Hope are Reshaping the World*. Random House, 2009.

its position in South and Central America, but not in the thinly populated northern part of the continent, to where the British, French and Dutch went hurrying. Before long, England had an invincible ace up its sleeve: as a result of revolution and religious persecution in England, a far greater number of people moved to the New World than from France. As a result, by 1750, thirteen British colonies "had 1.5 million people compared to a mere 60,000 in French Canada and 10,000 in Louisiana. Still fewer Spaniards lived in Arizona, Florida, Texas, and new Mexico."[2]

Right back in the pre-revolutionary era, the special DNA of the American culture, which determined its many essential features, was formed. From the very beginning, it was dualistic, reflecting historical consciousness and historical experience.

Anglo-American civilization, as Alexis de Tocqueville asserted, "is the result [...] of two quite distinct elements, which elsewhere have often been at war but in America have somehow been incorporated into one another and marvelously combined. I allude to the *spirit of religion* and the *spirit of liberty*.

The founders of New England were at once ardent sectarians and impassioned innovators."[3]

The religious zealotry of the first settlers became the foundation of the messianic-idealistic tradition, which had its roots in 17th century Britain, when philosophers and public figures expressed the idea that the Anglo-Saxons were preordained to colonize the New World and other parts of the planet, and thereby bring civilization and a true puritan faith to them. Initially, it was suggested that America's destiny was to become a moral example to the rest of humanity. This was particularly true of the pilgrims of Massachusetts Bay, who, according to the historian Daniel McInerney, were the first Americans to become aware of their special mission and to position themselves as part of the savior nation, which was called upon to become an example for the rest of the world. Such a model did not allow a different way of thinking. The Puritans did not reject the idea of religious freedom, but only acknowledged it for themselves – so as to live and act in accordance with their own God.[4] It is hardly surprising that it was in Massachusetts that the notorious "witch-hunts" began, the highlight of which was the Salem

---

[2] Alan Taylor, *American Revolutions. A Continental History, 1750-1804.* N.Y.C.: W.W.Norton & Company, 2016. P. 20.

[3] Alexis de Tocqueville, *Democracy in America.* Library of America, 2004. P. 48.

[4] Daniel J. McInerney, *A Traveller's History of the USA.* Interlink Books, 2001.

trial, when around a hundred people – mostly elderly women – were brought before a court of law, and 20 of them were sentenced to death.

In the Puritanical vision of the colony's Governor, John Winthrop, of the "City upon a hill", to which all other nations would turn their gaze, and of America as the Lord's country, America was to have the role not of a humble petitioner for God's charity towards mankind, but as the supreme arbiter of other nations, endowed with a special capacity for penetrating divine providence. Of course, in the 17th and 18th centuries, ideas about America's global mission did not correspond at all to its capabilities or to its weight in the global system. At this stage, they were used to justify the colonization of the continent.

Given the extreme weakness of colonial administration, principles for organizing governance, law and education had to be devised by the settlers themselves, and they drew heavily on European experience of self-governance. Each American colony came into being as a settlement that was governed by people elected by the whole community. The town councils reported back to their electorate at open assembly meetings, where decisions of town-wide importance were taken. In rural areas, individual farm holdings dominated, and villages in the European style did not emerge; accordingly, there were no peasant communes. Isolated farmstead settlements became the main model for most of the country.

The Seven Years' War, fought in North America as well as in Europe (where Russian forces of the Empress Elizabeth entered Berlin after victory over Frederick the Great), proved to be the catalyst for the American Revolution. Maintaining a military presence in the American colonies was too expensive, however. Britain decided to reorganize the administration and tax the North American colonies, since the people living there had the formal status of subjects of the British Crown. They were special subjects, though: by this time, each colony had its own assembly composed of representatives of the towns.

The British prohibition on settling further west than the Appalachians, and the introduction, through The Stamp Act, of a commodity duty, provoked a boycott of English goods, and to the meting out of rough justice to British customs officials at the ports: they were smeared with tar and had feathers stuck to their bodies. In October 1765, nine colonies sent delegates to the first general forum – the Stamp Act Congress, the slogan for which was "no taxation without representation". The Stamp Act was abolished, but under an initiative by the Chancellor of the British Treasury, Charles Townshend, taxes were introduced on glass, paper, paint and tea, so that the colonial judges and governors could be paid. In 1770, as a result of protests by the settlers, the British Parliament abolished taxes on all these items except for tea. On 16th December 1773, a group of colonists, disguised as Native Americans, boarded three boats that were moored in Boston Harbor, and threw 342 chests of tea into the sea. This was the famous "Boston Tea Party". The British king, George III, ordered that the port be closed until compensation for the damage had been paid in full, banned the town councils, and appointed a British general as governor of Massachusetts.

In September 1774, delegates from all 13 colonies gathered together in Philadelphia for the first Continental Congress, which declared itself to be in favor of a boycott of British goods, and of joint action in the event of an attack against them, and demanded representation in the British Parliament. On 19th April 1775, the British general Gage went on a march from Boston to Concord, in order to seize the rebels' underground arms cache. The armed American rebels organized resistance in Lexington and Concord, forcing Gage to retreat, with some 250 men killed or wounded. The War of Independence had begun.

In 1776, fresh impetus was given to the battle by a pamphlet called *Common Sense*, written by Thomas Paine, who had recently arrived from England. Half a million copies were distributed across colonies that now had a total population of 2.5 million people. Paine asserted that Americans, like most Europeans, lived under the yoke of tyranny and that they faced a choice: either to resign themselves to being ruled by an unelected monarch, or to fight for their freedom. The founding fathers studied all the philosophical tomes about republicanism and democracy on which they could lay their hands. In June 1776, the Continental Congress in Philadelphia set up a committee of five men – John Adams, Benjamin Franklin, Thomas Jefferson, Robert Livingston, and Roger Sherman – to draw up a draft document on independence. On 4th July 1776, the Congress adopted the Declaration of Independence, written by Jefferson, with a number of amendments by Franklin, which spoke of the right of each person to "life, liberty and the pursuit of happiness", and which proclaimed the country's independence from Britain. "The Constitution of the United States was not the first written constitution in the history of the world. The world's first written, popularly ratified constitutions were drafted by the American states, beginning in 1776. Having dismantled their own governments, they took seriously – literally – the idea that they needed to create them anew, as if they had been returned to a state of nature."[5]

---

[5] Jill Lepore, *These Truths. A History of the United States*. N.Y.C. W.W.Norton & Company,

Thirteen united states of America established an independent nation state, which now faced the small matter of defeating the forces of the "mother country". Congress appointed a plantation owner from Virginia, George Washington, as commander-in-chief; he proved to be an indifferent field-marshal but a talented leader and inspiring figure, just the kind that was needed by the army of volunteers going into battle against a trained army. After winning the first few battles, Washington began to suffer heavy defeats, until, in October 1777, he forced 6,000 British soldiers to surrender at Saratoga. This proved to be enough to convince the French, who were being courted by the USA's ambassador in Paris, Franklin, to join the war. In October 1781, the English general Cornwallis was surrounded and forced to capitulate in Yorktown, after which the outcome of the war was a foregone conclusion. A formal peace agreement was signed in February 1783.

In May 1787, 55 delegates from the 13 states gathered in Philadelphia to adopt a Constitution. Fernand Braudel has observed: "It has long been said: the founding fathers created a constitution 'based on the philosophy of Hobbes and the religion of Calvin'. But they also supposed that 'man is a wolf to man', that his 'bodily spirit' is contrary to the spirit of God… But the main idea that preoccupied and conditioned the actions of these property owners, these businessmen, these lawmakers, these plantation owners, speculators and financiers, these 'aristocrats', was the idea that it was essential to protect property, wealth, and social privileges."[6]

The main discussion was centered around two key issues: the prerogatives of the federal government and the states, and the elections to Congress. Some delegates preferred the idea that the legislature be elected by the state assemblies. The idea that prevailed, though, was for direct elections to Congress, and for the president to be elected by an electoral college. Only men were given the vote (women, Native Americans, and slaves had no political rights), and only those men who had full ownership of property subject to tax of 40 shillings or more. The delegates asserted that only property owners had a conscious interest in the prosperity of the country, and that people had fought not for democracy but for constitutional rule. The Constitution defined the relations between the legislature, the executive and the judiciary, and also the full range of powers of the federal government. All other mat-

---

2018. P. 111.

[6] Fernand Braudel, *Grammatika tsivilizatsiy* (*Grammar of Civilizations*). Moscow, 2008. P. 449.

ters were to be dealt with by the states themselves. After 17 weeks of secret discussions, the document was adopted.

When the Constitution was sent for ratification, legislative assemblies in various states, led by Massachusetts, expressed the wish that additional guarantees of citizens' rights should be added to it. James Madison drew up amendments to the Constitution, ten of which were accepted and became known as the Bill of Rights, stipulating the right to freedom of speech and peaceful assembly, the right to bear arms, the right to refuse to testify against oneself (the oft-used fifth Amendment), and the right to trial by jury. Naturally, the rights and freedoms that were declared did not apply to slaves or the indigenous population of Native Americans, whose numbers were over 6 million, compared to the 2.5 million whites. If one considers that there were roughly 1 million white men, and that during the first 50 years of American democracy, 5% of them made use of their right to vote, it can be said that this was a democracy for around 50,000 people out of a population of 9 million. Nonetheless, the USA, from the moment it came into being, had far broader electoral rights than any European country.[7]

At the same time, America proved to be an overtly racist country. The text of the Constitution as it was approved legalized slavery. The very first naturalization law, passed in 1790, decreed that only white immigrants could become citizens. It was not until the 1960s that African Americans were given the right to vote throughout the whole country. "In fact, liberal democracy – with full adult suffrage and broad protection of civil and political liberties – is a relatively recent development in the United States," wrote a group of authoritative researchers into problems faced by democracy. "By contemporary standards, the country became fully democratic only in the 1970s."[8]

Yet the USA emerged as a unique template, for that time, of an egalitarian society, with a weak aristocracy and formal equality among citizens. The political system created by the Constitution enabled the United States to remain a stable entity for over two centuries, in the course of which time it changed beyond recognition, and was transformed into the most powerful country in the world.

---

[7] Francis Fukuyama, *Political Order and Political Decay. From the Industrial Revolution to the Globalization of Democracy*. L., 2014. P. 140.

[8] Robert Mickey, Steven Levitsky, and Lucan Ahmad Way, "Is America Still Safe for Democracy? Why the United States Is in Danger of Backsliding", *Foreign Affairs*, May/June 2017. PP. 22-23.

Two-Party Foundations

The first American President, George Washington, was not a party candidate. In his farewell address to the nation, he warned in the grandest possible way against the party spirit, which was the worst enemy of a democratic government.[9] It was specifically during Washington's presidency, however, that the parties came into being.

The initial duality of the American tradition, manifested in the colonial era, was continued in practical politics and in the ideologies of the independent United States of America.

In the domestic political sphere, the dichotomy was manifested above all in the answer to the question of the role of the government and its regulating powers. It is commonly thought that the USA is a country of classic private entrepreneurship, and that this was the fundamental reason for its phenomenal successes. This is not quite the case.

George Washington himself was inclined towards strong central power, as was the Treasury Secretary Alexander Hamilton, who was accused of having monarchist inclinations and the snobbery of an aristocrat. "For the Hamiltonians, the national government was the grand instrument by which to transform a pastoral economy into a booming industrial nation."[10] Casting aside "Adam Smith's fantasies", and describing the idea of a self-regulating economy as a "wild speculative paradox", Hamilton wrote, in his seventh article in *The Federalist*, that the spirit of entrepreneurship, if not restricted by anything, "would naturally lead to outrages, and these to reprisals and wars".[11] His ideas became the foundation of economic realism, acknowledging the government's role in economic regulation, and of the Federalist Party's ideology.

Meanwhile, the opposition had gained strength; its leaders were James Madison, and also Thomas Jefferson, who saw the America of the future as a paradise of small farmsteads, a rural Arcadia, where every free landowner would feel safe beside his vineyard and fig tree. Jefferson never acknowledged the need for banks or a stock exchange, and this

---

[9] Yekaterina Glagoleva, *Washington*. Moscow, 2013. P. 434.

[10] Arthur M. Schlesinger Jr., *The Cycles of American History*. Houghton Mifflin Company, 1986. P. 220.

[11] Alexander Hamilton, James Madison, and John Jay, *The Federalist, on the New Constitution*. R. Wilson Desilver, 1847. P. 22.

was the cause of endless criticism from the supporters of Hamilton.[12] Jefferson, who considered Adam Smith's *The Wealth of Nations* to be "the best book of our times" on political economy, maintained: "Were we directed from Washington when to sow and when to reap, we should soon want bread."

These ideas lay at the heart of the ideology of the party of Jefferson's Republicans – a broad and paradoxical coalition come together under the aegis of a small number of plantation owners and staking a claim for the title of protector of the interests of ordinary people from the encroachments of the privileged few. The common ideological traits of this coalition, notes the prominent Americanist Vladimir Pechatnov, were "the famous ideals of 'Jeffersonian democracy' – a democratic republic of freeholders, founded on principles of individual freedom and equal rights (for the white male population, at least), minimum interference by the state, local autonomy and the inalienable rights of the states."[13]

The two-party system became the distinctive feature of the United States. Why? The well-known historian Clinton Rossiter identified a number of reasons which can be broken down into three broad categories. *Psychology.* The two-party system corresponds to the natural order of things, since duality, for and against, always exists in life. *Sociology.* Alternative, third forces have never been strong: "The bounty of the American economy, the fluidity of American society, the remarkable unity of principle of the American people, and, most important, the success of the American experiment have all militated against the emergence of large dissenting groups that would seek satisfaction of their special needs through the formation of political parties."[14] *The constitutional structure.* The polarizing effect of single mandate electoral districts and the system for electing the president (the winner takes all, and the person who comes third will not have any chance of being elected to any position), the distribution of power between the Federation and the states (each party is a conglomerate of 50 parties, one in each state, so creating a national organization from scratch is simply unrealistic). The entire electoral system – the election legislation, the practice of hoarding campaigns – all of this works against

---

[12] Arthur M. Schlesinger Jr., *The Cycles of American History.* Houghton Mifflin Company, 1986. PP. 221-223.

[13] Vladimir Pechatnov, *Ot Dzheffersona do Klintona. Demokraticheskaya partiya SShA* (*From Jefferson to Clinton. The US Democrats in the battle for the Electorate*). Moscow, 2008. P. 15.

[14] Clinton Rossiter, *Parties and Politics in America.* Cornell University Press, 2018. P. 8.

third parties. Over time, the two-party system became part of the American political tradition.[15]

Wider political engagement became possible after the Jacksonian Revolution of the 1830s. "The propertied classes, until then mostly large landowners, no longer made up the totality of politically responsible citizens, as America abandoned the old idea, taken over from European republicanism, that only property ownership guaranteed independence and qualified people for rational political judgment. Now the autonomy of citizens rested upon ownership of their own person; property qualifications largely ceased to apply. Unusually high rates of electoral participation (often over 80 percent) were signs of the energy now invested in politics."[16]

Right up until the Civil War of 1861 to 1865, the essentially Federalist policy of industrialization prevailed. In the 1840s, the North American continent, which had seemed so impossible to encompass to the first settlers, began to be criss-crossed with railroads, stretching across it like threads, and canals. Their construction would have been unthinkable without government finance. In little more than a century, the United States managed to transform itself from relatively small coastal economies into an economic and cultural giant.

The sources of foreign policy traditions are also to be found in the 18th and 19th centuries. Henry Kissinger described the dichotomy of foreign policy thinking as follows: "The singularities that America has ascribed to itself throughout its history have produced two contradictory attitudes towards foreign policy. The first is that America serves its values best by perfecting democracy at home, thereby acting as a beacon for the rest of mankind; the second, that America's values impose on it an obligation to crusade for them around the world."[17] The first can be seen in the ideas of those usually described as belonging to the school of Realpolitik, and the second in the views of those who preach the active mission of America to change the world – from liberal internationalists to neo-conservatives. It should be stressed, meanwhile, that there has never been an impenetrable barrier between the various schools; they have been seen, at times, in a diverse range of combinations and mixtures.

---

[15] Ibid. P. 10.

[16] Jurgen Osterhammel, *The Transformation of the World: A Global History of the Nineteenth Century*. Princeton-Oxford: Princeton University Press, 2014. PP. 601-602.

[17] Henry Kissinger, *Diplomacy*. Simon and Schuster, 1994. P. 18.

Alexander Hamilton, defending the creation of a strong, centralized government, saw it as needed in order to "concur in erecting one great American system, superior to the control of all transatlantic forces or influence, and able to dictate the terms of the connection between the old and the new world."[18] This position was not universally understood, and there were concerns that it would require a huge army, and that it was freighted with overtones of tyranny. Initially, Congress did not want to give its consent to the creation of a permanent army. Hamilton was forced to provide a warning from the pages of *The Federalist*: "[T]he United States would then exhibit the most extraordinary spectacle, which the world has yet seen – that of a nation incapacitated by its Constitution to prepare for defence, before it was actually invaded."[19]

In his farewell address in 1796, George Washington said the future was in favor of the American dream, and the rest of the world, sooner or later, would have to adjust itself to its ideals. For the time being, he, like the other Federalists, felt that maintaining the balance of powers in Europe was the approach that best suited the USA's national interests.

The political course adopted by George Washington and, John Adams, and Thomas Jefferson was to refuse to be drawn into European wars. By contrast, President Madison declared war on Britain in an attempt to crush the Anglophile Federalists and in response to pressure from members of Congress from the new states and settlers, who could not wait to set about the annexation of Canada.[20] The result of this was the capture of Washington and the burning down of the White House by British troops in 1814. The USA achieved a decisive victory at New Orleans in January 1815, when the war was already officially over. The war strengthened the conviction of the American elite that until their country had adequate military power, engaging in clashes with the leading European powers was premature to say the least. America did not become entangled in a single European conflict for a century. "During the nineteenth century, American goals abroad were defined first as splendid isolation (non-entanglement) and then as a mission to expand, occasionally reinforced

---

[18] Alexander Hamilton, James Madison, and John Jay, *The Federalist, on the New Constitution*. R. Wilson Desilver, 1847. P. 42.

[19] Ibid. P. 96.

[20] M. O. Troyanovskaya, "Anglo-amerikanskiy konflikt 1812 g. i nachalo vtoroy voyny za nezavisimost' SShA" ("The Anglo-American Conflict of 1812 and the Beginning of the Second US War of Independence"), *SShA. Kanada. Ekonomika — politika — kul'tura* (*USA. Canada. Economy – Politics – Culture*), Issue 3, 2013. PP. 85-86.

by strong doses of jingoism," observed Zbigniew Brzezinski.[21] The new country turned its back on the Atlantic and began to expand its borders in the West and South.

For a long time, the quintessence of American foreign policy was the Monroe Doctrine. On 2nd December 1823, President James Monroe, in an address to Congress, announced that in the light of the superiority of American political institutions over those of Europe, and the USA's direct vested interest in cherishing "sentiments the most friendly in favour of the liberty and happiness of their fellowmen on that side of the Atlantic", the United States would consider any attempt by European countries that were members of the holy alliance to "extend their political system to any portion of either continent without endangering our peace and happiness."[22] This became a tool for justifying "exclusive rights" to creating the USA's own sphere of influence.

Ideas about the "destiny" of the USA to expand across the whole American continent permeated the rhetoric and activity of Andrew Jackson. He believed that Providence had chosen the American people as "the guardians of freedom, to preserve it for the benefit of the human race".[23] It was he who coined the phrase "the extending the area of freedom". This was understood to mean the conquest of vast territories in the Wild West, primarily by taking land belonging to the Native Americans.

Ideas about an "American mission" were voiced in the press, particularly in the Democratic Review, edited by G. O'Sullivan. He was the first writer to talk of "Manifest Destiny". Initially, the doctrine was based on the need to annex Texas and territory in Oregon, "by the right of our manifest destiny to overspread and to possess the whole of the continent which Providence has given us for the development of the great experiment of Liberty and federated self-government entrusted to us."[24]

Under this banner, the USA annexed Texas and, after the war with Mexico in 1848, added a vast territory stretching from what is now Arizona to the Pacific Ocean. By an irony of fate, "the expansion of the zone of freedom",

....

[21] Zbigniew Brzezinski, *The Choice. Global Domination or Global Leadership.* Basic Books, 2004. P. 196.

[22] *A Compilation of the Messages and Papers of the Presidents.* Forgotten Books, 2018. Vol. II. PP. 267, 268.

[23] *Memoirs of General Andrew Jackson.* J. C. Derby, 1845. P. 240.

[24] "Exceptionalism – Manifest Destiny", *Encyclopedia of American Foreign Policy.* Vol. II. P. 526 <https://www.americanforeignrelations.com/E-N/Exceptionalism-Manifest-destiny.html>.

which moved in a south-westerly direction, in fact resulted in an expansion of the zone of slavery.

A Peculiar Institution

In 1820, Thomas Jefferson wrote of the slave trade: "I considered it at once as the knell of the Union." In the mid-19th century there were around 380,000 slave-owners; but the system that was known as a "peculiar institution" lay at the heart of the whole of Southern society; owning slaves had become a natural part of life for the white population. Ordinary citizens held slaves as servants or cooks, as builders or manual laborers. America was made a great power at first by tobacco, then by the cotton grown and picked by the slaves. The industrial revolution in England created what appeared to be an unlimited demand for American cotton: manufacturing of cotton doubled every ten years from 1820 onwards, and in 1860 cotton accounted for three fifths of all American exports and three quarters of its worldwide supplies.[25] Demand for cotton led to a surge in the number of slaves – from 800,000 in 1776 to 1.5 million in 1820 and 4 million in 1860. In addition to the profits they made from cotton, sugar cane and tobacco, southerners made good money from the slave trade itself. At a time when slavery was disappearing throughout the rest of the world, the American South increasingly saw itself as a special region on the planet with a culture that was different from the northern states, and resisted all interference in its internal affairs, invoking the Jeffersonian doctrine of the rights of states.

The Northerners (the Yankees) were not supporters of slavery, but were not willing to give their lives for its abolition: factories in the north-east made quite a lot of money by manufacturing clothes and shoes using raw materials received from the South, which was also a good market for the sale of the finished goods. Attitudes were changed by immigration. On the very same ships which took them to America, immigrants to the North, who had been victims of persecution in their own homelands, could see black slaves in chains and shackles. The confrontation between southern tradition, of which owning slaves was an integral part, and northern tradition, which saw America as a free country, only increased. The trade and financial hub of the north-east became extremely uneasy as the slave trade expanded.

....

[25] James McPherson, *Battle Cry Freedom. The Civil War 1961-1865*. Oxford University Press, 2003. P. 39.

The emergence of the Republican Party in 1854 was the logical outcome of the growing movement towards restricting – not abolishing – the expansion of slavery. Abraham Lincoln accepted the challenge: "'A house divided against itself cannot stand.' I believe this government cannot endure, permanently half *slave* and half *free*. I do not expect the Union to be *dissolved* – I do not expect the House to *fall* – but I *do* expect it will cease to be divided. It will become *all* one thing or *all* the other."[26] The victory of Lincoln in the election of 1860 provoked a conflict. Those advocating a breakaway departed from the "narrow" interpretation of the American Constitution and the doctrine of the states' rights. "The union was formed as a voluntary association of states, bearing on their shoulders all the burdens of the War of Independence, which entailed the right, at their own discretion and at any time, to break the ties that bound them."[27] The southern states proclaimed a secession and the formation of an independent Confederacy, with Richmond, Virginia, as its capital. This news was met with astonishment in the North, while reports from the South about people poking fun at the stars and stripes caused outrage. Union, by that time, was already a symbol of American life, for which people were taught to show piety in history lessons, at church, and through the celebrating of Independence Day.

Lincoln declared the war to be a battle that would decide the question of whether "We shall nobly save or meanly lose the last, best hope of Earth" in the shape of a unified United States.[28]

To achieve victory, late in 1862 Lincoln declared that slavery was illegal, and that slaves were free men. Slaves were now running away from the plantations, some of them intending to fight in the Northerners' army. By the end of the war, there were up to 200,000 black soldiers fighting. The South, which had no military industry of its own, was doomed.

The Civil War did not, however, resolve the race issue. At that time, "the majority of white Americans were 100% convinced of the supremacy of their own race." Under such circumstances, attempts to ensure equality for blacks or Native Americans were doomed to fail. The Southerners' response was to create a militant organization by the name of the Ku Klux Klan in 1866.

....

[26] Eric Toner, *The Fiery Trial. Abraham Lincoln and American Slavery*. N.Y., W.W.Norton & Company, 2010. PP. 99-100.

[27] Alexander Kormilets and Sergey Porshakov, *Krizis dvukhpartiynoy sistemy SShA* (*The Crisis in the USA's Two-Party System on the Eve of the Civil War*). Moscow, 1987. P. 72.

[28] Reinhold Niebuhr and Alan Heimert, *A Nation So Conceived: Reflections on the History of America from Its Early Visions to Its Present Power*. N. Y., 1963. P. 126.

During the Reconstruction which followed the Civil War, a system of racial segregation began to take shape. As the prominent activist in the negritude movement, William Du Bois, would later put it: "The slave went free; stood a brief moment in the sun; then moved back again toward slavery."[29] "Reconstructions demise," Eric Foner believes, "and the emergence of blacks as a disenfranchised class of dependent laborers greatly facilitated racism's further spread, until by the early twentieth century it had become more deeply embedded in the nations culture and politics than at any time since the beginning of the antislavery crusade and perhaps in out entire history."[30]

In 1883, the Supreme Court ruled that the federal administration was not entitled to impose a ban on segregation on the part of private individuals; in 1896 it affirmed the right of states to segregation in public areas; and in 1899 it allowed the states to open new whites-only schools. The Supreme Court's logic may be illustrated by its decision in the case of Plessy v. Ferguson, in which it declared that the political rights of all people are identical, but this does not cancel out the inherent inferiority of black people, which defines their social status accordingly. After this, most of the southern states introduced segregation at public institutions, on trains, in schools and on public transport, and brought in laws prohibiting contact between whites and blacks and effectively depriving Afro-Americans of the right to vote. The creation of a racist mass culture began. "In the first half of the twentieth century, white and black southerners were born in separate hospitals, educated in separate schools, married in separate churches and buried in separate cemeteries; and every bus, school, diner, boarding house, waiting room, hospital, drinking fountain and prison was either for whites or for blacks, but never for both," writes Osborne.[31]

The fate of the indigenous inhabitants of the New World, towards whom the British colonists were initially well disposed, proved to be even more tragic. The first major problem for the Native Americans was the array of new diseases that they faced – influenza, German measles, and the plague – which took away hundreds of thousands of lives. There was then a need to acquire

---

[29] W. E. B. Du Bois, *Black Reconstruction in America: Toward a History of the Part which Black Folk Played in the Attempt to Reconstruct Democracy in America, 1860-1880*. Transaction Publishers, 2013. P. 26.

[30] Eric Foner, *Reconstruction. America's Unfinished Revolution. 1863-1877*. N. Y., 1988. P. 604.

[31] Roger Osborne, *Civilization: A New History of the Western World*. Random House, 2011. P. 383.

land. The settling of whites on American land had turned into a fairly easy activity, given the white man's military superiority. The true destroyers of the traditions of America proved to be farmers. The mass genocide of Native Americans began after the Civil War. In 1865, the army was ordered to purge the Great Plains of Native American tribes. The authorities set about killing herds of bison, thus destroying the basis of the Native American economy (in 1870, there were around 15 million bison grazing on the plains of the American West; a decade later, a few hundred were left). The battle of Wounded Knee in the late 1880s was the symbolic finale of the destruction of the Native Americans' way of life. "For all the wars and crises that were to come, never again would the authority of western civilization to rule America be challenged."[32]

The Triumph of Will and Capital

The Civil War resulted in a huge increase in government orders and the growth of a capital market which enabled the accumulation of major private fortunes in areas other than plantation slavery, the basis of which had been undermined. The upwardly mobile capitalist class dictated the direction of economic policy: protectionism and the rejection of state regulation inside the country. "So far as there can be said to be any theory on the subject in a land which gets on without theories, laissez alter has been the orthodox and accepted doctrine in the sphere of both Federal and of State legislation," wrote Lord Bryce in 1888. American society was built on the conviction that the "right to the employment of what he has earned, and to the free expression of his opinions, are primordial and sacred," "the less of government the better," and "[t]he functions of government must be kept at their minimum."[33]

In the fifty years after 1865, mass immigration, the conquest of the West and the growth of the cities created the continental state we know today. Americans stopped talking about the United States in the plural, switching instead to the singular ("is" rather than "are"). In the space of just two generations, a country with a predominantly rural economy developed into an urbanized industrial society. In the 1870s and 1880s, four major railroads from the East to the West were built. All the trans-

---

[32] Ibid. P. 386.

[33] James Bryce, *The American Commonwealth*. Vol. 4: Illustrations and Reflections & Social Institutions. Jazzybee Verlag, 2017. PP. 96, 94.

continental railroads – except for the great Northern Railroad – were provided with state-owned land free of charge. The problem of how to take cattle from America's remote pastures to the capital markets was now solved: the cattle could be herded to the nearest terminus of the railroad line somewhere in Wyoming and taken from there to the cattle yards of Chicago. The figure of the cowboy came into being, in Westerns, with their sharpshooting gunslingers and ubiquitous saloons. In fact, these men were reclusive loners, who spent their lives in the saddle, a long way from populated areas, and the era of the cowboys lasted only from the end of the Civil War until the 1890s, when the railroad network connected the whole country and herds began to be put in enclosures. Steamships replaced sailing boats on the main routes across the ocean; the journey time was halved and the crossings became far safer. In 1914, the construction of the Panama Canal, linking the Atlantic with the Pacific, was completed.

During the Civil War, the government brought in import duties with the aim of covering the cost of war. After the war, these customs duties were transformed into a mechanism for protectionism, which remained in place until American industry was in a dominant position in the world. There was not yet any anti-trust legislation that might have helped to maintain competition. The courts almost automatically delivered their verdicts in favor of entrepreneurs and against labor unions, in favor of creditors over debtors, and railroad companies over farmers whose land had been taken away from them. The American version of laissez-faire economics permitted the provision of government aid to business, but precluded interference by the government in business activity.

The government, seeking to grow the network of railroads, allocated money and land to the railroad companies, and these companies, making tidy profits from government contracts, sold off the plots at an enormous profit and bought off politicians. According to the famous historian Richard Hofstadter, "Before business learned to buy statesmen at wholesale, it had to buy privileges at retail. Fabulous sums were spent."[34] Andrew Carnegie bought up most of America's sources of coal and iron ore, supplying it solely to his own companies, which produced 70% of America's steel, effectively closing off the sector to everyone else. In 1901, he sold his

---

[34] Richard Hofstadter, *The American Political Tradition, and the Men Who Made It*. N. Y., 1974. P. 219.

business to JP Morgan. Another example of a monopoly was Standard Oil, which belonged to the Rockefeller family.

This was the period of the "robber-barons", who dominated the business world. The biggest cities were centers of crime, corruption and poverty (very much as they were depicted in the film *Gangs of New York*), but none of this discouraged the millions of immigrants who travelled to the country which they saw as the land of opportunity. Whereas in 1882, 90% of immigrants still came from the North and West of Europe, in the early 20th century, 80% were from the South and East of the Old World. The immigrants strove to stay close to one another, creating a kaleidoscope of ethnic communities in different districts within the USA's biggest cities – Italian, Irish, Polish, Jewish or Russian communities.

The existence of a national press and spread of mass culture played a large part in welding together the new American nation. In Europe, newspapers were read by the educated nobility and reflected the views of the ruling elites. The American press traditionally had an independent and critical attitude towards the authorities, going right back to the time of Benjamin Franklin and his *Philadelphia Gazette*. The press bound together a multi-ethnic country through a single language and culture, having developed a distinctive American style – skeptical, optimistic, romantic, patriotic, pathetic – and dryly mocking any excessive pathos.

Fukuyama has identified the adoption of the Pendleton law in 1883 as the beginning of the formation of a fully-fledged bureaucracy that spread its jurisdiction throughout the country; he has also written that the creation of a modern European-style state in America did not take place until the end of the Second World War. The three main characteristics of the USA's political system compared with other democracies, according to Fukuyama, are: the considerably greater role of the legislative and the authority of the courts at the expense of the executive; the powerful influence of interest groups and lobbyists; and "vetocracy" – the possibility that the decisions of one branch of power can be cancelled out by other branches.[35] As we shall see, these characteristics would later prove to be among America's weaknesses.

The late 19th century became a golden era for political parties. Their organizational structures and internal discipline were better than at any other time in American history, as was the turnout at elections, which was as high as 82%. The heroic legacy of the Civil War, dependable financial support

---

[35] Francis Fukuyama, "The Decay of American Political Institutions", *The American Interest*, Winter (January/February), 2014. PP. 7, 8, 10, 12.

from the world of business, and the Protestant church, enabled the Republicans, during the second half of the 19th and early 20th centuries, to remain the party of the majority. By the end of the 19th century, the Republican Party, breaking away from the initial American tradition of isolationism, became the key carrier of ideas of expansion. In the last quarter of the 19th century, the big industrial companies turned their gaze ever more insistently on external sales markets and new sources of raw materials.

A belief in the idea that every person was capable of achieving great pinnacles of success in their lives was nourished by almost constant economic growth. On the eve of the Civil War, the total value of the goods produced in the United States amounted to $1.6 billion, and in 1899 – $13 billion, making the country the biggest economy in the world.

It was easy enough to make Americans believe that "the fittest" – in Charles Darwin's term – lived in the USA. "Although Darwinism was not the primary source of the belligerent ideology and dogmatic racism of the late nineteenth century," wrote Richard Hofstadter, "it did become a new instrument in the hands of the theorists of race and struggle."[36] A plethora of philosophers, historians and theologians argued in favor of combining social Darwinism with ideas about "American exceptionalism".

In the late 1890s, the concept of "the White man's burden" – "the civilizing mission" of the USA and humanitarian aid to less developed nations – became widely popular; it was the notion defended by a host of popular publicists and writers, including the talented English poet and prose writer Rudyard Kipling.

By 1898, when the USA became engaged in a war against the Spanish over their territories, the idea that Anglo-Saxons had a special mission to civilize and govern in the world had already firmly taken root in the American consciousness.[37] The groundwork for achieving broad popular consent to the establishment of US rule in the Philippines, Guam and Puerto Rico, and of the protectorate in Cuba, had already been done. When the matter of annexing Hawaii arose, President William McKinley (1897 to 1901) did not spend long seeking justification for his decision: "We need Hawaii just as much and a good deal more than we did California. It is Manifest Destiny."[38]

---

[36] Richard Hofstadter, *Social Darwinism in American Thought*. Boston, 1955. P. 172.

[37] P. Boller, *American Thought in Transition: The Impact of Evolutionary Naturalism, 1865-1900*. Chicago, 1971. P. 215.

[38] E. Tompkins, *Anti-Imperialism in the United States: The Great Debate, 1890-1920*. Philadelphia, 1972. P. 102.

In the early 20th century, the emphasis switched from territorial expansionism to economic and ideological: "[W]e intend to do all we can to help all the nations of mankind... to rise... toward an orderly and self-respecting and law-abiding civilization [...]," declared President Theodore Roosevelt.[39] His name is also associated with a new interpretation of the "Monroe Doctrine", which was now used to justify USA's right to start using a "big stick" in Latin America.

Roosevelt – the heir to the Hamilton tradition – maintained that the might of corporations represented a threat to democracy, arguing that control over this irresponsible and antisocial force could be exercised in the interests of the whole nation in only one way – through the provision of the proper powers to the sole institution capable of using them – the federal government. Teddy Roosevelt was the first president to put in place anti-crisis measures. During the banking panic of 1907, the administration lowered interest rates and increased emission, to help the banking system. Antitrust legislation came into being as well.

Before the First World War, a concept of state interference in the economy already existed. The war served to strengthen such understanding: it did not occur to anyone to seek answers to the challenges facing America in the doctrine of unregulated markets. Now, the Democratic administration of Woodrow Wilson (1913 to 1921) expanded military production, brought in control over production and the allocation of foodstuffs, regulated private investment, and even nationalized the railroads, the telegraph system and telephone network. Federal expenditure during the five years of the war rose from $726 million to $18.5 billion (the equivalent of $17.2 billion to $253 billion in 2015), and in 1921 Congress asked the President to bring in a draft budget for the first time in history.[40]

Washington dealt very decisively with the leftist threat that had flared up in Russia and was in the process of doing so in Europe. Using as a pretext the fact that, in June 1919, a number of senior officials received parcels containing explosive matter in the post – they were sent by anarchists, as it transpired – the prosecutor general Mitchell Palmer ordered his assistant Edgar Hoover to create a special body for countering radical movements. Their agents quickly compiled dossiers on 150,000 people, after which the Palmer raids began – mass raids involving searches and arrests in the labor unions, and communist and socialist organizations. More than 10,000

---

[39] *The Writings of Theodore Roosevelt*, ed. by W. Harbauch. Indianapolis; N. Y., 1967. P. 77.
[40] "Fun on the Budget", *The Economist*, February 7, 2015. P. 40.

people were arrested, and around 600 foreigners were expelled from the country as a result of this "red scare". Laws were passed in 30 states on the countering of the left-wing danger, and all socialist deputies were driven out of legislative bodies at all levels. By the time the Palmer raids came to an end, the membership of socialist and communist organizations had fallen by 80%. The leader of the Socialists, Eugene Debs, was put in prison for two and a half years for protesting against the USA's participation in the war.[41]

Hollywood upon the Hill

During World War I the USA was gripped by a surge in foreign policy activism. Woodrow Wilson's name is associated with the ideology of liberal internationalism. As professor of political science at Princeton and as governor of New Jersey, he often talked about America as "the City on the hill". "In that part of the world, upon that new-found half of the globe, mankind, late in its history, was thus afforded an opportunity to set up a new civilization; here it was strangely privileged to make a new human experiment," wrote Wilson in his book *The New Freedom*.[42] When the war broke out in 1914, the president successfully made use of slogans about the special mission of the USA in terms of bringing in universal peace, in order to prepare public opinion for the overcoming of isolationist feelings and an entry into military action (the first time in American history) in the Old World. The USA entered the war at a decisive moment – in April 1917 – when both of the warring sides were exhausted, and this allowed the USA to take up a position as global arbiter without suffering heavy losses. At Versailles, Wilson made a bid for a special role in determining mankind's destiny. "At last, the world knows America as the savior of the world," he declared upon his return from the peace conference.[43] Wilson regarded the League of Nations as the leading instrument in the USA's battle for global leadership. The Senate, however, refused to ratify the Treaty of Versailles and to sanction the US's accession to the League of Nations.

This defeat for Wilson's "internationalism", along with the success in the presidential elections of 1920 of the Republican candidate Warren

---

[41] Viktor Sogrin, *Istoricheskiy opyt SShA* (*The Historical Experience of the USA*). Moscow, 2010. PP. 325-326.

[42] Woodrow Wilson, *The New Freedom: A Call For the Emancipation of the Generous Energies of a People*. N. Y., 1961. P. 161.

[43] S. Freud and W. Bullitt, *Thomas Woodrow Wilson*. Boston, 1967. P. 287.

Harding, amounted to a changing of the guard: right up until the country joined the Second World War, the decisive role was played by the concept of isolationism. Yet the idea of the United States fully departing from world affairs was by now out of the question. The key principle of isolationism was to have a "free hand" to strengthen the USA's economic and political position, which was in many ways made easier by the fact that half of the world was now in America's debt.

It was during the terms in office of the Republican administrations of Harding, Calvin Coolidge and Herbert Hoover, that the period of so-called "prosperity" occurred. These men are seen by posterity as the proponents of individualistic principles. "What's good for General Motors is good for America!" became the slogan of the era. Government interference was limited to helping with "the self-regulation of business".

America was no longer merely the biggest economy; it had started to set the standard in various aspects of life. More and more affordable for ordinary consumers, a personal car became the symbol of the era and the driving force for all branches of industry. Photography, the telephone, cinematography and the radio were invented in Europe, but it was in the US that they were applied on a grand scale, becoming a distinctive characteristic of the country. Movie theaters began to be constructed, and by 1926 there were already 20,000 of them; more than a hundred million people attended them every week – almost half the country's population. The film industry was created, primarily, by Jews, many of whom were immigrants from Russia. Initially, the sector was based in New York, but the climate there was too capricious for film shoots. From 1907 onwards, films were produced in the vicinity of Los Angeles, where, in 1911, a company known as Nestor built the first permanent studio to the North-West of the city. Within ten years, there were 760 studios in the Hollywood district, producing no less than 80% of all the movies on the planet.

Another powerful cultural instrument was the recording of sound. In Europe, recordings usually featured popular operatic arias and classical music. America chose a path of its own, not least because of segregation. African Americans were not permitted to become involved in painting, architecture, literature or cinematography, but they did have musical instruments, with which they created inspired performances of songs in a strange style known as the blues. The endless variations that they created around a basic theme became the distinctive features of Western music in the 20th century. New Orleans was the birthplace of jazz, and black musicians such as Willie Smith and Louis Armstrong became the first true jazz stars. Through the efforts of white composers like Irving Berlin and George Gershwin, on the basis of blues, jazz and ragtime, a new type of popular music and song was created. In Texas and in the rest of the South, white musicians started to refashion the compositions of their black colleagues, and thus country music was born – a white version of the blues, permeated with melodies from folk dances. The sentimental love song – whether of the Broadway, cowboy or swing variety – spread from America and began conquering the world.

Faith in the all-powerful nature of American values and of an unregulated market became one of the key reasons for the stock exchange crash on Wall Street 1929, which was followed by the biggest depression in the history of the capitalist world, the Great Depression. Between 1929 and 1933, 20% of all American banks – 15,000 in total – went bust. The monetization of the economy was reduced, prices fell by one third, real interest rates exceeded 10%, destroying the credit institutions and households that were in debt.[44]

"The depression dealt a mean blow to America's confidence in the uniqueness of its civilization," emphasized the authoritative historian William Leuchtenburg. "It was hard to draw a contrast between America's good fortune and the misery of Europe when the United States had so many of the social ills it had long believed were endemic in the Old World."[45] The pages of newspapers and speeches by public figures were filled with gloomy predictions of "a fall in American greatness", and with doubts about whether the USA's social system was adequate. Even when the level of unemployment in the USA reached 25%, however, in 1931, Herbert Hoover refused to try to support employment, arguing that the only function of government is the creation of conditions which might favor private entrepreneurship.[46]

The presidency of Franklin Roosevelt (1933 to 1945), who was elected four times, marked the start of a new era in domestic policy, the primary features of which were strengthening the role of government and long-term domination by the Democratic Party.

---

[44] Niall Ferguson, *Civilization: The West and the Rest*. Penguin, 2011. PP. 230-231.

[45] William Leuchtenburg, "The Great Depression", *The Comparative Approach to American History*, 1968. P. 297.

[46] Herbert Hoover, *State Papers and Other Public Writings*, ed. by W. S. Myers. N. Y., 1934. Vol. 2. PP. 8-9.

His New Deal laid the basis for a new liberal policy, the political and economic foundation of which was Keynesianism, involving government regulation of demand in accordance with the dynamics of the market. It was under Roosevelt that the doctrine of social responsibility of the government began to acquire practical embodiment; a system of Social security emerged in America. In Roosevelt's "Economic Bill of Rights", it was declared that the goals of state policy were guarantees of rights in the workplace, a decent wage, and the right to housing, medical services, education, and social welfare in the event of illness, unemployment and in old age.

Foreign policy was dominated by isolationism and a policy of "non-interference", which helped the Axis powers' aggression in Europe and in the Far East: It is here at home that we must rescue democracy. Conservative politicians and businessmen expressed the concern that the powers of the federal government, which had already grown sharply during the years of FDR's New Deal, might grow even more as a result of new military adventures, and might jeopardize the basis of "true Americanism" – the system of free entrepreneurship.[47]

Even after Germany's invasion of Poland, which marked the start of the Second World War, isolationist feelings continued to prevail in the USA. It was only the attack by the Japanese air force at Pearl Harbor on 7th December 1941 that decided the dispute between the isolationists and the "internationalists". Roosevelt took America into the Second World War, and this marked the threshold after which the United States was transformed into a superpower, not just in economic terms, but also in military terms (particularly after it acquired a nuclear monopoly in 1945), and in political terms.

In a book published in 1941 called *The American Century*, the newspaper magnate Henry Luce foresaw the USA's mission as it was to be interpreted in the years of the Cold War. He reflected that the 20th century would be "America's first century as a dominant power in the world."[48] During the Second World War, the groundwork was laid for the creation of a foreign policy founded on the conviction that America was to play a decisive role in the system of international relations.

The greatest source of discontent for the West after the war was the policy of the USSR in Eastern Europe, which the West fairly quickly began to refashion in accordance with its own vision of geopolitics (in the same way

---

[47] Charles Alexander, *Nationalism in American Thought, 1930-1945*. Chicago, 1971. PP. 164-172.

[48] Henry Luce, *The American Century*, Life, February 17, 1941. PP. 61-65.

that the Western allies behaved in Western Europe, incidentally). Roosevelt understood the inevitability of new spheres of influence for the great powers, yet at the same time hoped to keep the Soviet sphere of influence open for American capital, goods and propaganda. The Cold War became unavoidable, Richard Sakwa believes, "as it became clear that Soviet power had come to stay in the eastern European countries liberated from fascism by the Red Army, but now to be subordinated to the great Soviet communist experiment."[49]

The Superpower

If we wish to uncover the origins of the Cold War, it is useful to take a look at Washington in the mid-1940s.

After the war, the USA took a dominant position in the global arena, against the backdrop of the devastation wrought on Europe and the Soviet Union. The USA accounted for 60% of the world's GDP, and had four fifths of the gold reserves and two thirds of all trade on the planet. Its armed forces consisted of more than 12.5 million people, its naval fleet was bigger than those of all the other countries in the world put together, and so were its capabilities in terms of strategic aviation. Military expenditure, which accounted for only 1% of the budget in the early 20th century and 3% in the 1930s, rose to as much as 40% during the war and stayed at this level. Boeing and General Motors held on to their defence divisions.[50] This unprecedented potential for projecting power was safeguarded by the United States nuclear monopoly. "It was thereby able to define leadership," wrote Henry Kissinger, "as essentially practical progress along lines modeled on the American domestic experience; alliances as Wilsonian concept of collective security; and governance as programs of economic recovery and democratic reform."[51]

On the other hand, the experience of the two world wars, and the shock of Pearl Harbor, engendered a vulnerability complex in the USA, and concerns for the safety of its own territory. Decisions were taken to keep US military industrial potential and battle-readiness at a level sufficient to defeat any potential adversary, to deliver preemptive strikes against such an adver-

---

[49] Richard Sakwa, *Communism in Russia*. Red Globe Press, 2010. P. 76.
[50] William J. Lynn III, "The End of the Military-Industrial Complex", *Foreign Affairs*, November/December 2014. PP. 105-106.
[51] Henry Kissinger, *World Order: Reflections on the Character of Nations and the Course of History*. Penguin, 2014. P. 278.

sary, and to keep military action as far away as possible from American soil. The idea of defence at "long-distance" led to a transition from the pre-war concept of continental defence – defence of the Western hemisphere – to the concept of a permanent military presence in key regions of the world and maintaining the potential for a global projection of power. Such a role met the criteria for what had become "the traditional American concern with preventing the domination of either Europe or Asia by any single power," as Samuel Huntington has noted.[52]

Meanwhile, under a school of geopolitical thought that has become popular (Mackinder, Spykman), the main source of strategic threat was considered to be the vast territory of Eurasia, control over which by states hostile to the USA was considered to represent a threat to American vital interests. Of particular interest were the so-called rim lands of Eurasia; from there, power could be projected into the heart of Eurasia. The USA's plan of post-war force deployment, prepared in 1943, stipulated that strategic perimeter defence should be provided far beyond the bounds of the Western hemisphere, requiring dominance in both the Atlantic and Pacific oceans. By the fall of 1945, the Chiefs of Staff presented the new deployment plan, in which was proposed the positioning of key military bases around the entire perimeter of the Pacific Ocean (from New Zealand via the Philippines to Alaska and the Aleutian Islands), in the Arctic (Newfoundland and Iceland), in the East Atlantic (the Azores), the Caribbean basin, and around the Panama Canal. Safe transit would have to be ensured on the following route: Manila – Bangkok – Rangoon – Calcutta – Delhi – Karachi – Darkhan – Cairo – Tripoli – Casablanca.

Pechatnov has observed: "The messianism that had become traditional for the Republic across the ocean, with its belief in the universality of American principles and the benevolence of American might, was now backed up, for the first time, by the world's most powerful military and economic potential."[53] However, in order for such a global strategy to retain full support from both government and society, there was one thing missing: an enemy.

By the spring and summer of 1945, the role of "enemy" began to be attributed, in private assessments, to the Soviet Union, if for no other reason than because it alone had the set of characteristics that one could ascribe

[52] Samuel P. Huntington, *The Clash of Civilizations and the Remaking of World Order*. N.Y. et al., 1996. P. 232.

[53] Vladimir Pechatnov and Alexander Manykin, *Istoriya vneshney politiki SShA* (*The History of the USA's Foreign Policy*). Moscow, 2012. P. 369.

to a global rival: a position at the center of Eurasia, military might, and an ideology and social order that were unacceptable to the USA.

There was also a host of important factors that forced the USA to seek out a serious enemy and to find it specifically in the Soviet Union. Pechatnov has rightly pointed to the "major concerns among those at the top of the Pentagon in relation to the potential dramatic demobilization and disassembly of the entire military industrial scientific complex of the USA, created during the war and now finding itself obsolete in the eyes of a large portion of American society."[54]

Ideas about American exceptionalism took on a decidedly anti-Soviet hue. "Confident that Providence had appointed us its chosen instrument to frustrate Communism wherever it threatened peace, stability and morality, we took our stance at Armageddon and battled for the Lord," wrote Henry Commager. "Those who were not with us were against us, we said, and we used our prodigious resources of money and influence and, eventually, of military power to strike down the wicked and to inspire and arm the righteous, thus dividing the world into two hostile camps on the basis of morality."[55]

In the fall of 1945, the Joint Chiefs of Staff (JCS) drew up a new Strategic Concept and Plan for use of the armed forces of the USA, which asserted that the only major power with whom America could enter into a conflict (incapable of resolution within the framework of the UN) was the USSR. The Strategic Concept of the Defeat of Russia was quickly fleshed out with specific military plans. The first of these was devised in October 1945; it stipulated nuclear bombing raids against 20 major cities in the Soviet Union. By the start of 1946, the main goals of Soviet policy were interpreted at the Pentagon as being indistinguishable from fascist ones, which meant that the principles applied during the war against the Axis states would be needed again: no appeasement, negotiations would be futile; the USA must prepare for the destruction by force of the aggressor.

Stalin responded with a speech on 9th February 1946, in which he resurrected the notion that capitalism was a source of war and called upon the Soviet people to make a fresh leap forward, so as to be ready "for any surprises". In the West, the speech was interpreted as a refusal by the USSR to cooperate. The State Department asked for the opinion of its embassy in

---

[54] Ibid. P. 302.

[55] Henry Commager, *The Defeat of America: Presidential Power and the National Character*. N.Y., 1974. P. 10.

Moscow on this score, and received a "long telegram" on the causes of Soviet behavior. George Cannon created the demonic image of the Soviet Union that proved to be so necessary in the US administration: a force that was inherently hostile to the West, propelled by ideas of expansion and requiring external enemies in order to rescue its totalitarian system. The leadership of the USSR understood only the logic of force, and for that reason must be restrained by the overwhelming force of the West. The strategy had become clear: resisting "Soviet expansion" throughout the whole world, rejecting any compromise with the USSR, and forceful pressure – containment.

On 5th March, Winston Churchill gave his famous Fulton speech, approved by Truman and read out in his presence. Churchill talked about the totalitarian regime that had come to the fore, and spoke of an "iron curtain", declaring that it was necessary to renew Anglo-American military and strategic cooperation so as to destroy this curtain.

The toughening of the West's stance was not limited to rhetoric. It took the form of the creation of a unified military command, the "re-mobilization" of industry, the expansion of nuclear potential, the enlargement of the network of military bases, the creation of "auxiliary forces" from former German and Japanese prisoners of war, and the drafting of joint plans for war against the USSR. The "Pincher", drawn up by the summer of 1946, stipulated the dropping of atomic bombs on the USSR from British bases located in the British Isles themselves and in Egypt. Agreements on military bases were signed with Portugal (the Azores), and Iceland, and it was decided that bases should be set up in Okinawa, on the Caroline, Marshall and Mariana Islands, and in the Philippines.

On 18th March 1947, the Truman doctrine was announced, whereby financial and military aid was allocated to Greece and Turkey, over whom the Soviet military threat was supposedly dangling. In June 1947, US Secretary of State George Marshall, addressing a graduation ceremony at Harvard, proposed lending money to Europe. This would solve a number of problems simultaneously: it would prevent an economic collapse there, create a market for American goods, and weaken the influence of Communist parties, which were actively making their presence felt, particularly in France and Italy.

The Cold War quickly spread to the Far East as well. The Chinese revolution, with Soviet help, achieved victory in 1949, leading to the formation of the People's Republic of China and the emigration of the Kuomintang, led by Chiang Kai-shek, to Taiwan. The "two Chinas" had come into being.

Then came the Korean War, in which the USSR backed North Korea. Soldiers moving from the North into the South of the peninsula were halted when American troops engaged those wearing light blue UN helmets, and were then pushed back north of the 38th parallel. The North Korean forces would have inevitably suffered complete defeat thereafter, but were saved from this by Chinese intervention. The Korean War demonstrated that the forces of the two superpowers – the USSR and the USA – were roughly equal, and served as the prologue to their global confrontation in all parts of the world. Within the USA, meanwhile, it engendered a new "red scare", and McCarthyism.

In 1950, a previously unknown Republican Senator from Wisconsin, Joe McCarthy, explained why the Soviets had acquired the bomb so quickly, and how the communists had seized power in China. It was not because the enemy (the USSR) had sent soldiers to conquer their shores, but because of "the traitorous actions of those [...] who have had all the ben efits that the wealthiest nation on earth has had to offer – the finest homes, the finest college educations, and the finest jobs in Government we can give."[56] The enemy was in the government!

On 24th July 1950, J. Edgar Hoover secured Truman's approval for the expansion of the powers of the FBI in investigating "espionage, sabotage, subversive activities and related matters", affecting the national security of the USA. Left-wing views, and also homosexuality (which was seen as an abnormality that the enemy could take advantage of for recruitment), became grounds for immediate dismissal from state service and the removal of any prospects in other forms of activity. As part of Hoover's secret "Responsibilities Program", universities, colleges and schools were purged of hundreds of teachers suspected of having left-wing views.[57]

The FBI, the CIA, and the National Security Agency monitored White House staff, journalists, political opponents, and activists. Between 1956 and 1971, the FBI alone launched more than 2000 operations to discredit and disrupt black protest organizations, anti-war groups, and other perceived threats.[58]

The expansion of the USA's sphere of strategic interests found its embodiment in the creation, under its aegis, of a system of military-political blocs

---

[56] David M. Oshinsky, *A Conspiracy So Immense: The World of Joe McCarthy*. N. Y., 2005. PP. 108-109.

[57] Tim Weiner, *Enemies: A History of the FBI*. Penguin, 2013. PP. 171, 176.

[58] Robert Mickey, Steven Levitsky, and Lucan Ahmad Way, "Is America Still Safe for Democracy? Why the United States Is in Danger of Backsliding", *Foreign Affairs*, May/June 2017. PP. 23-24.

and alliances. The symbol of the military-political unity of the West and of the growing, long-term influence of the USA in European affairs was the formation of NATO. Military blocs, oriented, one way or another, against the USSR, were created in other regions of the world too: the Rio de Janeiro Pact, ANZUS, CENTO, SEATO. Networks of bilateral military agreements between the USA and various countries were expanded, as was the financial-economic system (the IMF, the World Bank, GATT, OECD), in which the US also dominated.

It is often said in the USA that the USA successfully introduced democratization in Germany and Japan, and ensured the flourishing of these countries. "This was true, but the examples were rather misleading," writes Fukuyama. "Germany and Japan *were* transformed into model democracies after 1945, but they started out as highly developed countries with strong states whose cores for the most survived the war intact."[59] At the same time, the United States controlled the Philippines for almost 50 years, and yet its successes in terms of democracy and the economy there were dubious. The USA has invaded Cuba, Nicaragua, the Dominican Republic, Haiti, Afghanistan, and Iraq, without succeeding in creating sustainable democratic and market institutions in any of these countries.

The most significant of all the documents from the early years of the Cold War was NSC68, a report drafted by the National Security Council in 1950, which set out the core philosophy, an algorithm for the actions of government bodies, the nature of military planning, and the content of propaganda for the entire period up to the start of the 1990s. It is notable that the task of containing the Soviet "slave state" came second in the list of priorities, with first place going to the objective which has remained unchanged to this day in the USA's national security strategy: creating a stable international system that safeguards the USA pre-eminence and its global domination. Military force was seen not only as a resource to be deployed (different "thresholds of sensitivity" for the use of force had existed at different times), but also as a tool for achieving political and economic objectives.

The presidential election of 1952 was won by a Republican, Dwight Eisenhower. His domestic policy stuck to the course of "enlightened conservatism" or "New Republicanism". The economic crisis that began in the summer of 1953 forced him to take action. The government cannot stand aloof from the private economy; it must show willingness to take energetic steps in support

---

[59] Francis Fukuyama, *America at the Crossroads: Democracy, Power, and the Neoconservative Legacy*. Yale University Press, 2006. P. 132.

of stable prosperity, explained the chairman of the Council of Economic Advisors, Arthur Burns.[60] The Republican administration mobilized financial levers of state to stimulate growth: taxes on corporations and private income were cut, and access to bank loans was eased. Growth in state expenditure and the budget deficit in the 1950s were now part of the arsenal not just of the Democrats, but also of the Republicans. Major construction projects to build expressways and housing took place, and the route along the St Lawrence River was renovated. State expenditure rose from $42.5 billion in 1950 to $92.2 billion in 1960.

Ideas about internationalism in the spirit of the American mission were espoused by Eisenhower and his Secretary of State, John Foster Dulles. In its election platform in 1952, the "Grand Old Party" had promised to put an end to the "negative, futile and immoral policy of containment, which abandons countless human beings to despotism and godless terrorism", and to encourage liberating trends in socialist countries.[61]

"McCarthyism" reached its climax in this period. A total of ten million people underwent investigation under various "loyalty" programs, and by the middle of 1954, around 7000 civil servants had been fired. The Communist Party of the USA was declared by law to be "an agent of a foreign, hostile state" and was stripped of its political rights. The strategy of containing communism was now replaced by a doctrine of "liberation", reinforced by the expansion of the American military presence, and mass economic and cultural pressure.

A dedication to the ideas of the USA's global responsibility was reflected in the theory of the "power vacuum": in those parts of the world from whence the "old" colonial empires had been banished as a result of a national liberation struggle, empty spaces came into being, which it was the USA's duty to fill. This theory lay at the heart of the "Eisenhower doctrine".

In 1950, popular uprisings were suppressed in the Philippines, and the CIA put Ramon Magsaysay in power in the country. In 1952, King Farouk of Egypt was overthrown with the help of US intelligence, and the man who came to power was the former Abwehr agent and future hero of the Soviet Union, Gamal Abdel Nasser. One year later, a CIA expert on the Middle East and the son of the late President, Kermit Roosevelt, planned and executed an operation to depose the elected leader of Iran, Moham-

---

[60] *US News and World Report*. October 29, 1954. P. 46.

[61] Cit. from: James M. Scott, "Reagan's Doctrine? The Formulation of an American Foreign Policy Strategy", *Presidential Studies Quarterly*, Vol. 26, Issue 4, 1996. P. 1059.

mad Mossadegh, and restore Shah Mohammad Reza Pahlavi to the throne. In 1954, the president of Guatemala, Jacobo Árbenz, was overthrown as a result of a CIA operation.

The USA's belief in the superiority of its nuclear weapons and air delivery systems lay at the heart of the doctrine of "Massive Retaliation", which was first postulated by Dulles on 12th January 1954. If the country were to attempt to fight back against "aggression", guided, as the Truman administration had been, by a "willingness to fight anywhere"… then that could not go on for long without leading to serious budgetary, economic and social consequences. Hence the following conclusion: Rely "primarily upon a great capacity to retaliate, instantly, by means and at places of our choosing."[62]

By the end of the 1950s, as a result of "Dulles's pactomania", the USA was at the head of four military-political blocs which incorporated, in addition to themselves, a further 39 countries around the world, to say nothing of a multitude of bilateral military agreements. The system of military bases was expanded, and the USA did not make a big secret out of their intended purpose: The European and Asian bases were particularly important in the 1950s, since they amounted to outposts from which American strategic bombers could strike at the heart of the communist monolith.[63]

The document NSC-5412, adopted in December 1954, set out the powers of the CIA when conducting "espionage and counter espionage operations abroad": creating and using in its interests problems that are difficult to solve for international communism, discrediting the ideology and prestige of international communism and reducing the strength of its parties and other elements, reducing international communism's control over all areas of the world, creating underground resistance and assisting with secret and partisan operations, and supporting the activities of these forces in the event of war. It was recommended that all "covert operations" should be conducted in such a way that "US government's responsibility for them is not evident… and if uncovered the United States government can plausibly disclaim any responsibility for them." NSC-5412 proposed, as potential methods for such operations: propaganda; political action; economic war; preventative direct action, including sabotage and counter-sabotage; measures aimed at destruction and at

....

[62] John Foster Dulles, "The Nation: The New Focus", *Time*, March 29, 1954 <http://content.time.com/time/magazine/article/0,9171,819642,00.html>.

[63] Ch. Kegley and E. Wittkopf, *American Foreign Policy. Pattern and Process*. N. Y., 1982. P. 101.

encouraging emigration; activity aimed at undermining hostile states or groups, including aiding the underground resistance, guerrilla and emigrant groups; supporting nationalist and anti-communist elements; planning and implementing slander operations.[64]

At the same time, a number of positive breakthroughs emerged in relations between the USSR and the West. Just two weeks after the death of Stalin – on 19th March 1953 – the government of the USSR approved a policy of ending the war on the Korean peninsula. For its part, the commander-in-chief of the American forces in Korea, general Ridgeway, asserted that an attack on the North, on the borders of Manchuria, would cost the USA 350,000 to 400,000 men, killed or wounded. In July 1953, an armistice was signed. Signs of a shift in the trend towards confrontation were seen at a summit in Berlin of the foreign ministers of the USSR, the UK, the USA and France in January – February 1954, and also at the great powers' summit in Genève in July 1955.

The launch of the first Soviet *sputnik* in 1957 had the effect of a bomb going off in the USA. For the first time, the Soviet Union had shown that it possessed the most effective method of delivering a nuclear weapon – inter-continental ballistic missiles (ICBMs). The USA's invulnerability had become a thing of the past. "This Soviet achievement was impressive," said Eisenhower, recalling the effect made by the launch of the Soviet satellite. "The size of the thrust required to propel a satellite of this weight came as a distinct surprise to us."[65] This new state of affairs rendered the threat of "mass retaliation" unrealistic.

October 1959 saw the first visit in history by a Soviet leader – Nikita Khrushchev – to the USA. Prior to Eisenhower's return visit to Moscow, the decision was taken to convene a summit of the four major powers in Paris. On 1st May 1960, however, a U2 plane, flying from Pakistan and tasked with crossing the USSR from South to North for reconnaissance purposes, was shot down over Sverdlovsk. The top-level meeting in Paris was cut short: Khrushchev caused a ferocious row, slamming the door shut as he left. The US President's visit to the USSR was no longer possible. Moscow, meanwhile, had taken advantage of the coming to power of Fidel Castro in 1959 to create a foothold in Latin America.

....

[64] Blanche Wiesen Cook, *The Declassified Eisenhower: A Divided Legacy*. Doubleday, 1981. PP. 182-183.

[65] Dwight Eisenhower, *The White House Years. Waging Peace. 1956-1961*. Garden City, 1965. P. 205.

At the end of the 1950s, the time came for the Eisenhower administration to face up to the storm of criticism for its "indifference" to the assertion of the ideals of "Pax Americana". The man who emerged as one of the most dogged critics of Republican policy was Senator John Kennedy, a Democrat, who called to "put an end this depression of our national spirit" and come to "rendezvous with destiny".[66] Ideas of global leadership could be heard in the inaugural address by the new master of the White House: "Let every nation know, whether it wishes us well or ill, that we shall pay any price, bear any burden, meet any hardship, support any friend, oppose any foe, in order to assure the survival and success of liberty."[67]

A Flexible Response

Rapid advances were made in military build-up, enabling the USA to maintain its nuclear superiority until the end of the 1960s. "Massive Retaliation" was replaced by the doctrine of "Flexible Response", which placed the emphasis on expanding the range of wars for which the USA ought to make ready. Kennedy's activism had not only a military side, but also a reformist aspect, designed to demonstrate that the United States cared about developing countries.

Kennedy did not wish to have a constant thorn in his side in the shape of pro-Soviet Cuba, and in the spring of 1961 he ordered an invasion at the Bay of Pigs, which ended in failure. In the summer of 1962, in response to the positioning of American missiles in Turkey, medium-range Soviet rockets were sent to Cuba. When news of this reached Washington, Kennedy announced a naval blockade around the island. The USA began to build up its forces in the Caribbean Sea and made battle-ready its troops stationed in Europe, the 6th and 7th fleets, the airborne forces, the infantry and armored tank divisions, and the air force. The USSR responded in kind. The world was a hair's breadth from catastrophe. A compromise was found at the very last moment. Moscow withdrew the missiles. Washington promised to leave Cuba in peace.

After the Cuban missile crisis – the most dangerous crisis in the whole Cold War – both states opted for a policy whereby they did not allow relations to reach such a dangerous threshold. In August 1963, representatives

---

[66] Cit. from: Edmund Ions, *The Politics of John F. Kennedy*. Routledge, 2013. PP. 30, 31.
[67] Cit. from: Richard Dean Burns and Joseph M. Siracusa, *Historical Dictionary of the Kennedy-Johnson Era*. Rowman & Littlefield, 7 May 2015. P. 4.

of the USSR, the USA and the UK met in Moscow to sign the "Treaty Banning Nuclear Weapons Tests in the Atmosphere, in Outer Space and Under Water".

During the presidency of Lyndon Johnson, who took up the post after the assassination of Kennedy in Dallas, the reformist element of foreign policy began to take a back seat, while the role of military force increased. US aggression in Indochina was explained not only by the USA's interests in South-East Asia, but also by the belief in their exceptional right "to extend its hegemony over the world community and to stop every form of revolutionary movement which refuses to accept the predominant role of the United States."[68] After the Gulf of Tonkin incident, inspired by Washington in February 1965, the USA began intensive bombing campaigns against North Vietnam (the DRV); a month later, American troops arrived in South Vietnam to engage in military action against the National Front for the Liberation of South Vietnam. By December 1965, there were 400,000 US soldiers in the country. The USSR and China responded by supplying arms to North Vietnam.

In May 1965, a group of Soviet military advisers travelled to the DRV, and in August, anti-aircraft forces shot down their first American planes with the help of "surface-to-air" missile systems supplied from the USSR.

By the end of the 1960s, the Soviet Union had achieved military and strategic parity with the USA. The Third world had inflicted tangible blows on America's international status and prestige, specifically through increases in oil prices imposed by members of OPEC in 1973. Countless anti-war protest movements began taking place within the country. Prominent experts sought to show that the US had become an "ordinary" state. Daniel Bell wrote: "[B]elief in American exceptionalism has vanished with the end of empire, the weakening of power, the loss of faith in the nation's future. There are clear signs that America is being displaced as the paramount country [...]."[69]

The theme of the decline of American power was fairly widespread, and had some justification. Military spending from 1968 through to 1975 fell by 40%, and the nation's armed forces fell in size from three and a half million to two million. Henry Kissinger bemoaned the fact that "never has America been weaker". Nixon felt that comparisons with ancient Greece and Rome

---

[68] Gabriel Kolko, *The Roots of American Foreign Policy: An Analysis of Power and Purpose*. Beacon Press, 1969. P. 132.

[69] Daniel Bell, "The End of American Exceptionalism", *The Public Interest*, Fall, 1975. P. 197.

were appropriate, of which nothing but columns remained. Donald Rumsfeld – Defence Secretary under the Ford administration – wrote in 1976: "The Soviets have a strong momentum, while we have a strong downward momentum." The Iranian Shah assured those around him that the USA could be turned into a "fifth- or even tenth-rate power". The subject of the protection of rights was somewhere in the background. Kissinger did not believe that the USSR could be destroyed by increasing "circulation of newspapers and so on."[70] Instead of "superiority", Nixon began talking about "sufficiency": "The United States and the Soviet Union have now reached a point where the small numerical advantages in strategic forces have little military relevance."[71]

The primary political document that defined the contours of the Republican administration's new military and political strategy was the Nixon Doctrine, or the Guam Doctrine (announced in July 1969 on the island of Guam). Explaining its essence to Congress, Nixon said: "Its central thesis is that the United States will participate in the defense and development of allies and friends, but that America cannot – and will not – conceive all the plans, design all the programs, execute all the decisions and undertake all the defense of the free nations of the world. We will help where it makes a real difference and is considered in our interest."[72]

In the context of this doctrine, a new military strategy was proposed – that of "Realistic Deterrence". Under this strategy, Nixon's government demanded that its allies support not only the USA, but also their own military forces. This concerned not only the US's partners in Asia, where, under the "Vietnamization" and "Koreanization" schemes, American armed forces had begun to be replaced by local militaries, but also the US's allies in NATO. Nixon announced that in military construction, the guiding policy would be to ensure that the USA was capable of waging not two-and-a-half wars, as before (major wars in Europe and Asia and a small war in any part of the globe), but one-and-a-half. No secret was made of the fact that the United States was ruling out the idea of waging a "major Asian war", i.e. a war against China.

....

[70] Cit. from: Hal Brands, *Making the Unipolar Moment: US Foreign Policy and the Rise of the Post-Cold War Order*. Cornell University Press, 2016. PP. 27, 17, 44-45, 29.

[71] *United States Foreign Policy for the 1970's: Building for Peace. A Report to Congress by Richard Nixon*. Harper & Row, 1971. P. 139.

[72] "Report by President Nixon to the Congress" in *Foreign Relations of the United States, 1969-1976*, Vol. I, Foundations of Foreign Policy, 1969-1972. March 2, 1970 <https://history.state.gov/historicaldocuments/frus1969-76v01/d60>.

Closer relations with China became one of the fundamental aspects of Nixon's foreign policy, and he was the first American president to visit Beijing. "Should the Soviet Union succeed in reducing China to impotence, the impact on the world balance of power would be scarcely less catastrophic than a Soviet conquest of Europe" – that was how Henry Kissinger explained the administration's thinking.[73] He also observed that the USA's policy of having closer ties with both the USSR and China was also seen as a way of preventing these two countries from moving closer to one another.

None of this prevented the drawing up of dozens of treaties and agreements with Moscow. At the same time, détente did not signify the end of the Cold War. Kissinger described the limits of détente in October 1973: "This administration has never had any illusions about the Soviet system. We have always insisted that progress in technical fields, such as trade, had to follow – and reflect – progress toward more stable international relations. We have maintained a strong military balance and a flexible defense posture as a buttress of stability."[74]

The early 1970s saw the launch of new programs to develop strategic armaments; these programs were to bear fruit in the decades to come. "After the signature of SALT I, our defense budget increased," Kissinger noted, "and the Nixon and Ford administrations put through the strategic weapons (MX missile, B-1 bomber, cruise missiles, Trident submarines, and more advanced warheads) that even a decade later are the backbone of our defense programs and that had been stymied in the Congress *prior* to the easing of our relations with Moscow."[75]

During Nixon's second visit to Moscow, from 27th June – 3rd July 1974, the Treaty on the Limitation of Underground Nuclear Weapons Tests, and the protocol to the Anti-Ballistic Missile Treaty (ABMT), drawn up in 1972, were signed. After this summit, however, which took place just a month after Nixon was forced to resign amidst the Watergate scandal, difficult times arrived for the détente.

Gerald Ford, who became president after Nixon's departure, strove to preserve the structure of the negotiations on arms control. His meeting with Brezhnev in Vladivostok in November 1974 confirmed the parties' intention to draw up a new Strategic Arms Limitation Treaty (SALT-2). In 1975, the

---

[73] Henry Kissinger, *Years of Upheaval: The Second Volume of His Classic Memoirs*. Boston, 1982. PP. 53, 54.
[74] Ibid. P. 239.
[75] Ibid. P. 237.

Biological and Chemical Weapons Convention (which included the destruction of existing stocks), came into force. Evidence that it was possible for the two countries to cooperate was seen in the joint space flight and the space link between the Soyuz and Apollo spaceships in July 1975.

The negative trends in Soviet-American relations were clear for all to see, however. Representatives of the US Administration, including Kissinger, began talking about "disillusionment with détente", accusing the USSR of violating its "rules" and moving into a stage of "global imperialist expansion". In 1974, Congress, at the initiative of Henry Jackson, adopted an amendment which linked the most favored nation regime in trade with a change in Soviet emigration policy.

America was losing the war in Indochina, and, not without due cause, it laid the blame at the USSR's door. In April 1974, the pro-American regime in Cambodia capitulated; Saigon fell, and the Temporary Revolutionary Government of South Vietnam took power. In December 1975, a People's Democratic Republic was proclaimed in Laos, and in September, the SEATO council decided to disband the bloc. There was then a dramatic exchange of accusations in connection with events in Angola, where the USA was assisting anti-government factions. Support from the Soviet Union for national liberation movements was seen as "a violation of the code of détente".

In March 1976, Ford refused to use the term "détente", stating that from now on, the USA was going to implement a policy of peace, backed up by force.

At the start of the presidency of Jimmy Carter, there was a short-lived thaw in Soviet-American relations. A new round of bitter disagreements arrived, concerning conflict in the Horn of Africa, successful revolutions in Afghanistan and in South Yemen, and outbreaks of civil war in Zaire, and, lastly, the toppling of the pro-American Shahdom in Iran. The President's national security adviser, Zbigniew Brzezinski, spoke of the problem of an "arc of instability" covering South-West Asia and the Middle East, areas which had been destabilized by the Soviet Union. The whole region was declared to be critical to the vital interests of the USA.

Reaching an agreement on arms control was becoming more and more difficult. Carter had to endure a fair amount of criticism over pacifying the aggressor. The SALT-2 Agreement, signed in the summer of 1979, established an equal number of strategic defensive weapons for both parties. Later, however, at a NATO meeting in Brussels, it was decided that medium-range Pershing-2 ballistic missiles and Tomahawk cruise missiles were to be deployed in five Western European countries. The USSR's response was to put on alert a Pioneer (SS-20 in the Western classification) mobile ICBM complex in 1981.

The ratification of SALT-2 dragged on, and the final blow to it was the dispatching of Soviet troops into Afghanistan in 1979. The USA played a significant role in enticing the USSR there. Brzezinski subsequently acknowledged in an interview that Washington's interference in Afghanistan had begun even before the USSR sent troops into the country. Later, in order to hamper the Soviets, it was deemed necessary to provide "more money as well as arms shipments to the rebels" in "concert with Islamic countries in a covert action campaign," supported by the UK, France and Pakistan.[76]

The coming to power of Ronald Reagan signalled a revival of messianism. "We will again be the exemplar of freedom and a beacon of hope for those who do not now have freedom," Reagan said in his inauguration speech.[77] He repeated several times a phrase that had supposedly been said at the end of the Second World War by Pope Pius XII: "[I]nto the hands of America, God has placed the destinies of an afflicted humanity."[78] He regarded the revival of Americans' belief in their moral superiority and self-efficacy as his main goal – evidenced, for instance, in a reduction of government regulation.

Reagan described détente as a "one-way street that the Soviet Union has used to pursue its aims." His famous and oft-quoted line about the USSR being an evil empire was to follow just over a year later.

The Reagan administration strove to create the kind of weapons systems which the Soviets will find it hard to neutralize, which will provoke disproportionate expenditure on their side, open new areas of military rivalry, and render all previous Soviet spending worthless.[79] The president's plan for devising an anti-missile defence system with space components ("Star Wars") as a means of destroying any threat from strategic nuclear weapons had a large backing.

Fukuyama reasonably wrote that "The United States and the international community together have developed an impressive range of political

---

[76] Cit. from: Bruce Riedel, *Kings and Presidents: Saudi Arabia and the United States since FDR*. Brookings Institution Press, 2019. P. 75.

[77] *Public Papers of the Presidents. Ronald Reagan. 1981*. Washington, 1982. P. 3.

[78] *Public Papers of the Presidents of the United States: Ronald Reagan, 1986*. Best Books, 1988. P. 807.

[79] *Eagle Defiant: United States Foreign Policy in the 1980s*, ed. by K. Oye et al., 1983.

tools for supporting democratic regime change since the early 1980s."[80] Under the pretext of protecting democracy, interference took place in the affairs of Afro-Asian and Latin American countries. There was also active support for "Solidarity", which dealt a blow to the Polish regime. The Reagan administration also decided to toughen up the restrictions imposed on trade with the USSR, in the hope of weakening it economically.

The meeting between Gorbachev and Reagan in November 1985 in Geneva was the starting point for bilateral dialogue between Moscow and Washington. On 11th and 12th October 1986, in Reykjavik, Gorbachev put forward proposals, aimed at a reduction in, and, further down the line, the complete destruction of, strategic weapons, and the destruction of medium range missiles in Europe, in exchange for a moratorium on "star wars". As Kissinger noted, Gorbachev "simply overplayed his hand."[81] During a visit to Washington, however, from 7th to 10th December 1987, Gorbachev managed to reach an agreement on the Intermediate Range Nuclear Forces Treaty. This was the first instance of nuclear missile disarmament. Gorbachev was delighted with this "new thinking", but Reagan pressed ahead with the same old geopolitics.

In January 1988, Reagan had all the grounds to say: "[W]e have left behind us the days of retreat. America is again a vigorous leader of the free world, a nation that acts decisively and firmly in the furtherance of her principles and vital interests. No legacy would make me more proud than leaving in place a bipartisan consensus for the cause of world freedom, a consensus that prevents a paralysis of American power from ever occurring again."[82]

Reagan's general agenda was furthered by George Bush Senior. At the Republican National Convention in 1988, he stressed: "This has been called the American century, because in it we were the dominant force for good in the world. [...] Now we are on the verge of a new century, and what country's name will it bear? I say it will be another American century."[83]

The bipolar world was coming to an end. A few days after Bush entered the White House, Soviet troops were pulled out of Afghani-

....

[80] Francis Fukuyama, *America at the Crossroads: Democracy, Power, and the Neoconservative Legacy*. Yale University Press, 2006. P. 131.

[81] Henry Kissinger, *Diplomacy*. Simon and Schuster, 1994. P. 783.

[82] *Public Papers of the Presidents of the United States: Ronald Reagan, 1988-1989*. Best Books, 1990. P. 90.

[83] Douglas B. Harris and Lonce H. Bailey, *The Republican Party: Documents Decoded*. ABC-CLIO, 2014. P. 162.

stan. Did it even occur to Bush himself, however, that the USSR and the socialist system would soon collapse? At the same time, the Bush administration, before resuming the dialogue with Gorbachev, openly supported the protest movements in Eastern Europe. "Democracy-support organizations like the NED and NGOs like the American Center for Labor Solidarity (affiliated with AFL-CIO) were critical in providing support to the Solidarity labor union in Poland [...] Broadcasting, through agencies like Radio Free Europe/Radio Liberty and the Voice of America, was an important means of providing people in the communist world with alternative sources of information about their own countries and the outside world."[84] In the summer of 1989, the Polish "Solidarity" movement secured the introduction of the first free elections in the socialist realm, and in September, formed the first non-Communist government in the Soviet bloc. On 9th November 1989, the Berlin Wall came down.

The USA displayed far greater caution in its attitude towards China, though, where the protest on Tiananmen Square was put down by tanks on 4th June 1989. Bush did not want to jeopardize his strategic partnership with Beijing, although the sympathies of ordinary Americans and of Congress lay with the Chinese protesters. He opted for a relatively mild condemnation, after which his National Security Advisor Brent Scowcroft was sent on a secret mission to Beijing, to provide assurances that the American response would be formal in nature, and that the Polish model was not applicable to China.

The crisis in the Soviet system meant that the United States was able to do as it pleased in Central America, where a purge of anti-American governments began. After US soldiers were parachuted into Panama in December 1989, President Noriega ended up in handcuffs in an American jail. In 1990, the rebel movement organized by leftists in Salvador and the civil conflict in Nicaragua were put down, and the cessation of Soviet economic aid to Cuba led to a crisis for Castro's regime.

After Iraq invaded Kuwait in August 1990, Bush created an anti-Iraq coalition. In mid-January 1991, the United States began operation "Desert Storm", which led to the defeat of Saddam Hussein's army and the liberation of Kuwait. This success was to have far-reaching consequences. As Richard Betts has observed, "[T]he U.S. military's stunningly quick, cheap, and sweeping victory in the 1991 Gulf War raised policymakers'

---

[84] Francis Fukuyama, *After the Neocons: America at the Crossroads*. Profile Books, 2006. P. 136.

expectations about what force could accomplish at low cost [...]."[85] Interventionism acquired a large number of supporters in both parties.

The meeting between Bush and Gorbachev in December 1989, held on two military ships near Malta, was to be an historic one. Gorbachev and Bush officially declared that the Cold War was over. The Soviets agreed to give their official recognition to the coups in Eastern Europe, and a consultation process began which was to lead, within the year, to the reunification of Germany, practically on the West's terms. "Bush's performance deserve the highest praise," writes Brzezinski. "He cajoled, reassured, flattered, and subtly threatened his Soviet counterpart. He had to seduce Gorbachev with visions of a global partnership while encouraging his acquiescence to the collapse of the Soviet empire in Europe."[86]

At a meeting at the White House on 31st May 1990, Gorbachev gave his full consent to the reunification of Germany (which duly took place in October), receiving in exchange a promise of financial support and cooperation. The circumstances of the deal are the subject of dispute to this day, but, by all appearances, Gorbachev agreed to a reunified Germany acceding to NATO in exchange for a promise from US Secretary of State James Baker that the alliance would not expand further eastwards.[87]

In August 1991, Bush visited Moscow, and then, during a speech in Kyiv, he said that he would not help those who "promote a suicidal nationalism based upon ethnic hatred", acknowledged the merits of "greater autonomy" (but not independence) and declared that America's "businessmen look forward to doing business in the Soviet Union, including the Ukraine".[88] This speech was interpreted as an attempt to preserve the Soviet Union. William Safire, writing for the *New York Times*, called it a "Chicken Kiev".[89] To this day, historians of the period are convinced that Bush Sr. "did almost everything diplomatically possible to keep the Soviet

---

[85] Richard K. Betts, "Pick Your Battles: Ending America's Era of Permanent War", *Foreign Affairs*, Issue 6, November/December 2014 <https://www.foreignaffairs.com/articles/united-states/2014-10-20/pick-your-battles>.

[86] Zbigniew Brzezinski, *Second Chance: Three Presidents and the Crisis of American Superpower*. Hachette UK, 2008.

[87] George Bush and Brent Scowcroft, *A World Transformed*. N.Y., 1998. P. 239; James M. Goldgeier, *Not Whether, But When: The US Decision to Enlarge NATO*. Brookings Institution Press, 2010. P. 15.

[88] President George H.W. Bush's speech to a session of the Supreme Soviet of Ukraine, 1 August 1991 <https://en.wikisource.org/wiki/Chicken_Kiev_speech>.

[89] William Safire, *Safir's Political Dictionary*. Oxford University Press, 2008. P. 608.

Union alive."⁹⁰ Yet in fact the president applied maximum effort to make it collapse.

The period of "Gorbo-mania" proved to be short-lived. A time came when it was decided, in Washington, that Gorbachev should be dropped as a partner, like used goods. "CIA was another cheerleader for Yeltsin", and supported him not so much in words, but by means of a series of assessments which emphasized his popularity both in Russia and elsewhere and his initiatives in the field of reforms, said the USA's then Defence Secretary, Robert Gates.⁹¹ All that remained for Gorbachev to do was to rue the ungrateful, conservative portion of the American leadership: "It appears to have believed that a weakened Russia under Yeltsin was more in line with the USA's interests than the prospect of a renewal of the Union, for which Gorbachev was fighting."⁹² I would suggest that it was less the prospect of Gorbachev that was not to the USA's liking, than the prospect of the USSR.

Unipolarity and the Great Recession

The main objective of national security policy after the Cold War, whose end was interpreted unambiguously as a victory for the USA and a triumph for the policy of containment, was stated, in new doctrinal documents, to "preclude the emergence of a hostile power that could present a global security threat comparable to the one posed by the Soviet Union". The emphasis was placed on strengthening democratic institutions in Russia, so as to prevent the rise of a "hostile non-democratic powers from dominating regions critical to our interests".⁹³

NATO was still referred to as the key link in the chain of European security, and the preconditions for its expansion were laid down: "The most promising avenues for anchoring the East-Central Europeans into the West and for stabilizing their democratic institutions are their participation in Western political and economic organizations. East-Central European membership in the (European Community) at the earliest opportunity, and ex-

....

⁹⁰   Cit. from: Serhii Plokhy, *The Last Empire: The Final Days of the Soviet Union*. Basic Books, 2014. P. 206.

⁹¹   Robert M. Gates, *From the Shadow: The Ultimate Insider's Story of Five Presidents and How They Won the Cold War*. Simon and Schuster, 2007. PP. 503-504.

⁹²   Mikhail Gorbachev, *Alone with Myself*. Moscow, 2012. P. 595.

⁹³   Cit. from: Patricia L. Dunmire, *Projecting the Future Through Political Discourse: The Case of the Bush Doctrine*. John Benjamins Publishing, 2011. P. 156.

panded NATO liaison. [...] Should there be a re-emergence of a threat from the Soviet Union's successor state, we should plan to defend against such a threat in Eastern Europe, should there be an alliance decision to do so."[94]

The Pentagon's budget stood at around half of the total global military expenditure. Practically all developed countries were allies of the USA. America dominated in the leading international financial and economic institutions, which defined the rules of the game in the global economy. All of this gave the USA grounds to claim the role of the sole superpower in the system of international relations.

Thanks to his youth, intelligence and eloquence, Bill Clinton, who took up residence at the White House in 1993, became a symbol of benevolent, all-powerful America. In his inaugural address, he declared that "there is no longer a clear division between what is foreign and what is domestic. The world economy, the world environment, the world AIDs crisis, the world arms race – they affects us all. [...] America must continue to lead the world we did so much to make."[95]

Clinton's eight years as president was a successful period for the American economy, and in terms of its rate of growth, the USA outpaced other developed countries for the first time in decades: 4.1% in the second half of the 1990s, with unemployment falling from 6% to 4%. This was brought about by a very responsible macro-economic policy: in 1998, there was a surplus in the federal budget, and federal debt fell from 64.4% of GDP to 57.9%. The faith that was put in human capital paid dividends – faith in a knowledge economy, in industrial policy, and in the accelerated development of information technologies and the transformation of the "electronics economy" into an engine of growth.[96] A role was also played by the expanding opportunity to enjoy the benefits of globalization on a global scale, actively moving into markets in the Eastern European and post-Soviet states.

Meanwhile, there was a steady deterioration in relations with Russia. Many problems arose from American assessments of the causes and effects of the end of the Cold War and the declaration that NATO was to be expanded in 1994. Dimitri Simes wrote: "Underlying the United States'

---

[94] Cit. from: "Excerpts from Pentagon's Plan: 'Prevent the Re-Emergence of a New Rival'", *The New York Times*, March 8, 1992 <https://www.nytimes.com/1992/03/08/world/excerpts-from-pentagon-s-plan-prevent-the-re-emergence-of-a-new-rival.html>.

[95] Bill Clinton, *My Life*. Random House, 2010. P. 477.

[96] Viktor Sogrin, *Istoricheskiy opyt SShA* (*The Historical Experience of the USA*). Moscow, 2010. PP. 424-428.

mishandling of Russia is the conventional wisdom in Washington, which holds that the Reagan administration won the Cold War largely on its own. [...] Washington's self-congratulatory historical narrative lies at the core of its subsequent failures in dealing with Moscow in the post-Cold War era. [...] They seemed to forget that Russia had not been occupied by U.S. soldiers or devastated by atomic bombs. Russia was transformed, not defeated. This profoundly shaped its responses to the United States."[97]

In March 1999, bombing raids against Yugoslavia began, as well as the forcing out of the Serbs from Kosovo. This was followed by a regime change operation in Belgrade, using the "colored revolution" method; the United States did not make too much effort to hide its role in this. "With colleague Joschka Fischer and others, I urged Serb opposition leaders to build a real political organization and focus on pushing Milošević out," former secretary of state Madeleine Albright recalled. "[...] I met with prodemocracy mayors and found ways they could secure aid for their people without it being siphoned off by the federal government. [...] As anti-Milošević demonstrators swarmed into Belgrade, many coming from the democratic municipalities we had helped, I worked nonstop to intensify diplomatic pressure."[98]

The administrations of Clinton and George Bush Junior developed the technologies of "color revolutions" to the fullest extent. "By the early twenty-first century, a vast international infrastructure had emerged to help societies make the initial transition from authoritarian government to democracy, and to help consolidate democratic institutions once the initial transition was completed," writes Fukuyama. "The impact of these international soft-power instruments was clearly evident in the three major democratic transitions that took place in Europe in the new millennium – the fall of Slobodan Milošević in Serbia in 2000, The Rose Revolution in Georgia in 2003, and the Orange Revolution in Ukraine in 2004-5. [...] External support was critical in each of these cases."[99]

After winning the election in 2000, George Bush Jr. declared himself the heir of Reagan, combining ideas of rolling out the initiative of a free

---

[97] Dimitri K. Simes, "Losing Russia: The Costs of Renewed Confrontation", *Foreign Affairs*, Vol. 86, Issue 6, November/December 2007 <https://www.foreignaffairs.com/articles/russia-fsu/2007-11-01/losing-russia>.

[98] Madeleine Albright, *Madam Secretary. A Memoir*. Harper Perennial, 2013. PP. 502-503.

[99] Francis Fukuyama, *America at the Crossroads: Democracy, Power, and the Neoconservative*. Yale University Press, 2007. P. 136.

market with the concept of American global dominance underpinned by means of foreign policy activism and military might.

The domination of the Neo-Conservative agenda was a consequence of the tragedy of 11th September 2001, when the USA – for the first time since the Anglo-American War of 1812-1814 – found itself under attack on its own territory. American society came together around the President, and Bush was given carte-blanche to adopt whatever policy he saw fit. A new body was created – the Department of Homeland Security. Congress passed the Patriot Act, which gave the forces of law and order within the country greater powers in its actions against suspected terrorists, prompting protests from those committed to protecting civil liberties. A consensus emerged that it was necessary – and that America had the right – to destroy the Taliban regime in Afghanistan, where Osama bin Laden was hiding, and then to remove Saddam Hussein in Iraq, allegedly in order to destroy weapons of mass destruction. In 2006, the retired former director of the CIA's European division, Tyler Drumheller, wrote a book called *On the Brink: An Insider's Account of How the White House Compromised American Intelligence*, in which he revealed what he had told his superiors about the mental instability of the source that had confirmed the presence of WMDs in Iraq. Yet it was to no avail. "The policy was set. The war in Iraq was coming, and they were looking for intelligence to fit into the policy [...]."[100]

On the strategic front, the "war on terror" in fact reflected a desire to maintain control over the resources in the Persian Gulf, and a desire to strengthen Israel's security by removing the threat posed by Iraq.

Speeches made at West Point and the American Enterprise Institute in June 2002 and February 2003, and the "National Security Strategy", published in September 2002, were collectively given the informal name of "the Bush doctrine", which resounded in unison with the ideas of neo-conservatism. The President himself formulated it as follows: "First, make no distinction between the terrorists and the nations that harbor them — and hold both to account. Second, take the fight to the enemy overseas before they can attacks us again here at home. Third, confront threats before they fully materialize. And fourth, advance liberty and hope as an alternative to the enemy's ideology of repression and fear."[101] Henceforth, Fukuyama

---

[100] Sam Roberts, "Tyler Drumheller, Ex-C.I.A. Official Who Disputed Bush, Dies at 63", *The New York Times*, August 10, 2015 <https://www.nytimes.com/2015/08/10/us/tyler-drumheller-ex-cia-official-who-disputed-bush-dies-at-63.html>.

[101] George W. Bush, *Decision Points*. Random House, 2010. PP. 396-397.

asserted, the administration was inextricably bound to such concepts as "regime change, benevolent hegemony, unipolarity, preemption, and American exceptionalism that were came to be hallmarks of the Bush administration's foreign policy."[102]

The President had clearly not foreseen the serious negative reaction in the world to his interventionist policy, or the consequences of the Iraq campaign. Although US troops reached Baghdad fairly quickly in 2003, they were not able to establish control over the country. Moral and material expenses rose. Over the next few years, the enduring nature of the Iraq problem in the highest echelons of power overshadowed all of the other foreign policy issues that America faced. Brzezinski suggested that the war in Iraq "discredited America's global leadership. America was able neither to rally the world to its cause nor to decisively prevail by the use of arms. Its actions have divided its allies, united its enemies, and created opportunities for its rivals and ill wishers."[103]

The Foreign Affairs editor Gideon Rose believes: "By the end of George W. Bush's first term, his eponymous doctrine was a dead letter, with each of its three pillars – 'preemption', regime change, and a Manichaean division between friends and enemies – discredited and discarded. [...] It was a classic cautionary tale of unchecked power goaded into hubris, followed by folly, followed by nemesis. And as a result, Bush bequeathed to his successor a divided country, an economic catastrophe, and two ongoing wars, one of them heading in the wrong direction."[104] I wonder which one he felt was going in the right direction.

Relations with Russia became far from straightforward. Although during the first meeting between the leaders of the two countries in Ljubljana in 2001, Bush said that he gazed into Putin's soul and found it to be entirely satisfactory.

Russia actively supported the war on terror, but as early as 2002, the USA left the ABM Treaty, which limited the creation of an anti-ballistic missile system. Moscow – along with Germany and France – openly spoke out against the war in Iraq, where no weapons of mass destruction were found.

---

[102] Francis Fukuyama, *America at the Crossroads: Democracy, Power, and the Neoconservative.* Yale University Press, 2007. P. 3.

[103] Zbigniew Brzezinski, *Second Chance: Three Presidents and the Crisis of American Superpower.* Hachette UK, 2008.

[104] Gideon Rose, "What Obama Gets Right. Keep Calm and Carry the Liberal Order On", *Foreign Affairs*, September/October 2015. P. 6.

In 2004, another seven countries joined NATO, and at a NATO summit in Bucharest in 2008, Bush insisted, decisively, that Ukraine and Georgia should immediately be invited into the Alliance, and only the skepticism of Merkel and Sarkozy prevented him from going ahead with this plan.[105] The war in South Ossetia in August 2008 took Russo-American relations almost to freezing point.

The Secretary of State in the administration of George Bush Jr., Condoleezza Rice, saw the main problem in relations with Russia as Russia's inability to reconcile itself to the order that was established after the Cold War.[106] Bush himself complained, in his memoirs: "Over the course of eight years, Russia's newfound wealth affected Putin. He became aggressive abroad and more defensive about the record at home."[107]

The operations in Afghanistan and Iraq required major expenditure. For the first time in American history, however, a war was being waged not only without an increase in taxes, but against the backdrop of a tax cut. The Bush administration brought in the biggest cuts in income tax in US history in 2001 and 2003, wishing to stimulate business, and this led to a fall of roughly a quarter in the federal government's income. At the same time, state spending not only did not fall, but rose substantially. Military spending on Iraq and Afghanistan (over 1 trillion dollars) became an additional reason for rapid growth in the budget deficit. As a result, the budget surplus that had existed under Clinton quickly turned into a deficit. Economic growth and private consumption were financed to a significant extent by means of foreign investment in US Treasury bonds.

It was not just the government that saw an increase in its debts: the banks did too, and so did the people. The debts of the five biggest investment banks – Lehman Brothers, Bear Stearns, Merrill Lynch, Goldman Sachs and Morgan Stanley – reached 4.1 trillion dollars in the period 2004-2007. Only the latter two managed to survive the financial crisis. The deregulation of the financial markets, implemented in a neo-liberal vein, led to the onset of a wave of speculation, primarily in the market for tertiary financial instruments (derivatives), tied to mortgages, as a result of which a colossal gap emerged between the cost of certain types of securities and their actual value. Leading banks and investment companies found themselves embroiled in this game of speculation.

---

[105] George W. Bush, *Decision Points*. Random House, 2010. PP. 430-431.
[106] Condoleezza Rice, *No Higher Honor. My Years in Washington*. N. Y., 2011. P. 693.
[107] George W. Bush, *Decision Points*. Random House, 2010. P. 432.

Nouriel Roubini emphasizes: "Politicians and policy-makers, far from standing in the way of these get-rich-quick schemes, encouraged them. [...] Financial innovations and experimentation were hailed for their tremendous contributions to economic growth, and new kinds of financial firms emerged to market little-understood securities to inexperienced investors and to make extensive lines of credit available to millions of borrowers."[108]

This was precisely the policy that ultimately led to the economic crisis of 2007-2009, whose consequences were felt the world over. At any rate, among the world's experts and politicians, it is generally accepted that "responsibility" for the crisis which became known as the "Great Recession" lies with the USA, its financial system and its regulatory bodies.

The Republican administration decisively rejected its party's traditional ideas about non-intervention by the government. The leaders of the financial bloc – the Secretary of Treasury, Henry Paulson, and of the FRS, Ben Bernanke – managed to persuade Bush that without far more decisive additional steps, the country would face the collapse of markets, and a crisis on the scale of the Great Depression, with 25% unemployment. It was proposed that 700 billion dollars of additional liquidity should be put into the market, by increasing the state deficit. "Within days, political officials in Washington had assumed responsibility for decisions normally made by the markets in New York, a momentous shift in economic and financial power from America's capital of finance to its capital of politics," noted Ian Bremmer.[109]

The financial and economic crisis lasted 18 months (until June 2009), and proved to be the longest crisis since the Great Depression of 1929-1933. The crisis resulted in the USA's banking system being written off, and the loss of a gigantic amount in assets – more than a trillion dollars (or more than 8% of all assets, as against 3.6% in Europe). The destruction of the credit system led to an avalanche-like fall in sales of automobiles, homes and other goods with long-term demand, and this was reflected in the manufacturing sector all over the world.

The Great Recession led to a crisis of confidence in the political course steered by Bush, in state and economic institutions, and to American society losing its characteristic optimism and belief in the future. America was now ready for change of the most dramatic kind.

---

[108] Nouriel Roubini and Stephen Mihm, *Crisis Economics: A Crash Course in the Future of Finance*. Allen Lane, 2010. P. 13.

[109] Ian Bremmer, *The End of the Free Market. Who Wins the War Between States and Corporations?* L., 2010. PP. 1-2.

Obamamania

The political pendulum swung sharply towards the side of the Democrats, leading not only to Barack Obama's victory over John McCain in the presidential elections in 2008, but also to the Democrats establishing control over both houses of Congress. The election of the nation's first black president reflected the serious socio-cultural advances in American society – an unprecedented activation, against the backdrop of the crisis, of groups within the electorate who had long been waiting for change – young people, black people and ethnic minorities, and women. Obama won 43% of the vote among white Americans, 95% among Afro-Americans, 66% among Hispanics, and 64% among Asians.

At the center of his economic policy were three main tasks: stimulating growth, increasing employment, and overcoming the huge budget deficit. The steps towards implementing this often contradicted one another, and growth was stimulated at the expense of an increase in the deficit. In spite of all stimulatory measures, growth remained scarcely higher than 2%. The problem was not the lack of access to credit, but insufficient demand from investors and consumers: the corporations showed caution, in no rush to expand production and increase the number of people employed, although record profits were being recorded, first and foremost through cost-reductions achieved via the firing of staff during the crisis.[110] From 2011 onwards, the focus was on creating jobs in education and in advanced technology sectors, incentivizing investment in new equipment, and large-scale expenditure on top-priority projects: education, innovation and R&D, and the development of infrastructure.

In August 2011, after an extremely intense battle between the parties and at a time when there was a very real threat of default by the US Treasury, debt having reached the maximum level permitted by law (14.3 trillion dollars), the Budget Control Act was signed into law. The official upper limit for the USA's state debt was raised by 2.1 trillion dollars. At the same time, the law provided for a tough plan to reduce state spending. For the first time since the 1990s, military spending was to be cut – by 350 billion dollars over 10 years. Salaries for federal civil servants were frozen for two years, and funding was reduced or stopped altogether for more than 200 federal programs.

---

[110] "February Federal Budget Deficit Sets Record", Associated Press, *The Daily Herald*, Thursday, March 10, 2011 <https://www.dailyherald.com/article/20110310/news/110319927/>.

Through this one-of-a-kind, risky monetary saturation of the global market, conducted so as to save the position of the dollar and keep inflation at a minimum, the collapse of the global financial system was avoided, and the global status of America's currency was, if anything, strengthened.

In 2012, Obama's economic policy began to bear fruit: there were renewed signs of life in the housing market and in the automobile industry.

The government and the FRS decisively increased the scope of the use of financial and administrative instruments. The FRS, acting at the limit of what was permitted by law, spent 16 trillion dollars in the two years after the crisis on supporting the biggest American and overseas financial institutions. By the end of 2012, during "Operation Twist" (the replacement of short-term securities by long-term instruments), around 85 billion dollars were being poured into the economy every month. A mechanism was launched in January 2013 for the automatic reduction of the federal budget by a total of 2.4 trillion dollars. At the same time, the expiry of certain tax breaks, adopted in the early 2000s and extended by president Obama for two years in 2010, offered a growth in tax revenues. The combination of a brutal reduction in budget spending – by law, in 2013 alone, the reduction was to amount to 240 billion dollars, or almost a quarter of all discretionary expenses – with an increase in taxes led to a situation that became known as a "fiscal cliff".

The president called on Congress to extend the existing tax breaks for the middle class, but to cancel them for the richest 2% of Americans, i.e. for families with an income of over 250,000 dollars a year. Moreover, he insisted on a strengthening of the progressive system of taxation. Republicans spoke out against the cancellation of the tax breaks and the more progressive taxation system, and were in favor of cuts to various social programs, but not cuts in spending on the military.[111]

The dramatic finale to all this came on New Year's Eve, when the country managed to avoid the "fiscal cliff". None of the sides ended up getting what they wanted, and the fundamental problems within the American economy remained unresolved.

---

[111] *Rossiya i mir: 2013. Ekonomika i vneshnyaya politika. Yezhegodnyy prognoz* (*Russia and the World: 2013. Economic and Foreign Policy. Annual Forecast*), ed. by A. A. Dynkin, V. G. Baranovsky. Moscow, 2012. PP. 63-67.

Resource-Constrained Environment Strategy

Within the first two years of Barack Obama's presidency, extensive work was conducted in order to redefine the conceptual framework of political and military strategy. During 2010 and 2011 a sizeable set of doctrinal documents concerning national security and defence was published.[112]

The authors assumed that the USA and the rest of the world had entered the third post-1945 "strategic era", the first being cold war, with its bipolar confrontation, and the second, a short-lived period between the collapse of the USSR and the beginning of the global war against terrorism, marked by American total dominance. Previous strategic guidelines concerning long-term American dominance turned out to be incompatible with America's entanglement in local conflicts in Iraq and Afghanistan, and with the rapid rise of large emerging economies, and economic depression.

Gideon Rose described Obama as "an ideological liberal with a conservative temperament – somebody who felt that after a period of reckless overexpansion and belligerent unilateralism, the country's long-term foreign policy goals could best be furthered by short-term retrenchment."[113]

A policy of the unilateral use of force was at least theoretically replaced by a new strategy based on "smart power". The author of this concept Joseph Nye described it as "providing things that people and governments in all quarters of the world want but cannot attain in the absence of American leadership".[114] Hillary Clinton translated it into political language: "For me, smart power meant choosing the right combination of tools – diplomatic, economic, military, political, legal, and cultural – for each situation. The goal of smart power and our expanded focus on technology, public-private partnerships, energy, economics, and other areas beyond the Sate Department's standard portfolio was to complement more traditional diplomatic tools and priorities, not replace them."[115]

---

[112] Quadrennial Defense Review, February 2010; Ballistic Missile Defense Review Report, February 2010; Nuclear Posture Review, April 2010; National Security Strategy, May 2010; National Space Policy, June 2010; National Security Space Strategy, January 2011; National Military Strategy, February 2011.

[113] Gideon Rose, "What Obama Gets Right. Keep Calm and Carry the Liberal Order On", *Foreign Affairs*, September/October 2015. P. 2.

[114] *CSIS Commission on Smart Power*. Cochairs: Richard L. Armitage, Joseph S. Nye, Jr. Center for Strategic and International Studies, 2007. P. 5.

[115] Hillary Rodham Clinton, *Hard Choices*. Simon and Schuster, 2014. P. 31.

The "leadership from behind" concept was one more strategic innovation which became particularly apparent in the West's operations in Libya and Syria; these were undoubtedly orchestrated by a Washington which preferred to avoid direct involvement.

The Pentagon remained the largest employer in the USA and the largest owner of real estate, with more than 800 military facilities all over the world at its disposal. From the end of the cold war until 2015, the USA spent about $12 trillion in order to sustain their global military dominance.[116] At the same time, American military planning was more and more shaped by financial constraints; in many documents can be found recognition of the necessity to act in the present "resource-constrained environment" – and of the fact that the experience in Iraq and Afghanistan had been a bad one.

A new strategy, which its author Leon Panetta described as a "defense strategy for the 21st century", included five main innovations: the reduction of the army to 490,000 soldiers over the coming decade, with greater emphasis on the National Guard and reservists; a shift in the center of gravity of the US military presence towards Asia, using the "rotational model" of military presence; no deployment of large forces of occupation in the foreseeable future; the "two wars" concept, in which the military would fitted with the capability to fight (and win) a full-scale war (in Europe or in the Asia-Pacific), and at the same time at least damage the military aspirations of another adversary in a second region; and an increase in the capabilities of special operations, cyber and space-based forces.[117]

Furthermore, a key joint air-sea concept involving the integration of air and ground forces across a whole operational theatre was developed.

Principles governing the use of nuclear weapons outlined in the Nuclear Posture Review led to the conclusion that the role of nuclear weapons in the USA's military strategy had declined in importance to some extent. Commitment to the "global zero" principle voiced by Obama was reaffirmed, although the President's critics in the military establishment considered it to be naïve.

At the same time, emphasis was placed on deployment of the ABM system. Prominent experts had no doubt that the American strategic ABM system targeted not only the "rogue states" but China and Russia as well,

---

[116] David A. Shlapak, "Towards a More Modest American Strategy", *Survival*, Vol. 57, April/May 2015. PP. 61-62.

[117] Leon Panetta and Jim Newton, *Worthy Fights. A Memoir of Leadership in War and Peace.* Penguin, 2014. PP. 382-384.

and this was confirmed by the choice of location of four interrelated components – the USA, Europe, the Middle East, and North-West Asia.

Special attention was given to the deployment of Prompt Global Strike – a new class of a non-nuclear missile system located on USA territory and capable of delivering a precision-guided conventional weapons strike anywhere in the world within one hour.

However, what is sometimes said to have been the most important change of the last decade concerned American special operations. During the war on terrorism, the lines between the special forces and the military operations became blurred. "Since its creation in 1947, the CIA has steadily evolved from an agency devoted to its mission of spying on foreign governments to one whose current priority is tracking and killing individual militants in an increasing number of countries. It has been well documented that the agency's growing scope and depth of influence in the counterterrorism fight reflects its growing skill at hunting America's enemies from Pakistan to Yemen."[118]

Pulitzer Prize-winning *The New York Times* reporter Mark Mazetti, in his book *The Way of the Knife*, writes: "No longer a traditional espionage service devoted to stealing the secrets of foreign governments, the Central Intelligence Agency has become a killing machine, an organization consumed with man hunting."[119] In Pakistan alone, more than 5,000 people have been killed by the CIA.

Within U.S. Strategic Command, Obama established the special Cyber Command (USCYBERCOM) in 2010. This body plans, coordinates, integrates, synchronizes, and in general directs the operations of Department of Defence information networks, and conducts military cyberspace operations designed to provide support to military missions, to ensure US/Allied freedom of action in cyberspace, and to disable enemy cyber weapons.[120]

Obama regarded Europe as a key partner. In 2010 he wrote, "With no other region does the United States have such a close alignment of values, interests, capabilities and goals."[121]

---

[118] Yochi Dreazen and Sean D. Naylor, "Mission Unstoppable", *Foreign Policy*, May/June 2015. P. 38.

[119] Mark Mazzetti, *The Way of the Knife: The CIA, a Secret Army, and a War at the Ends of the Earth*. Penguin, 2013. P. 4.

[120] U.S. Cyber Command Fact Sheet 2010. US Department of Defense, May 25, 2010 <https://nsarchive2.gwu.edu/NSAEBB/NSAEBB424/docs/Cyber-038.pdf>.

[121] Barack Obama, "Europe and America, Aligned for the Future", *The International Herald Tribune*, November 19, 2010. Also available at <https://www.nytimes.com/2010/11/19/opinion/19iht-edobama.html>.

Obama set up a group to analyze relations with NATO. The group's main conclusions boiled down to this: NATO, as the party that won the Cold War, should continue to play a key role in reinforcing Euro-Atlantic unity and ensuring security; an approved, shared approach for the entire bloc must be drawn up, for relations with key countries that are not in the alliance: in Europe – Russia, Serbia, and the "neutrals"; in the Middle East – the Arab countries; in South Asia – India, Iran and Afghanistan. The USA's desire to use the Ukrainian crisis to increase European countries' military spending became clear. It was the USA that was forcing through tougher sanctions against Russia in Europe. Vice-President Joseph Biden wrote that "the combination of our $3.4 billion European Reassurance Initiative and NATO's new forward deployments in Poland and the Baltics will strengthen our European allies and provide a bulwark against further Russian aggression."[122]

The United States under Obama was engaged in creating two new trade blocks simultaneously: a transatlantic partnership with EU countries (the TTIP, described earlier), and a corresponding transpacific partnership (the TPP). Taking part in the TPP negotiations were the USA, Canada, Mexico, Chile, Peru, Australia, New Zealand, Vietnam, Singapore, Malaysia, and Brunei. A geopolitical explanation of the perceived need for the TPP was suggested in 2012 by Edward Luttwack – that it would be a key element of joint efforts made by countries concerned about the rise of China and keen to "contain" it using geo-economic methods.[123] Or, as the former head of the White House staff, William Daley, put it, "If we don't set the rules for commerce in the Asia-Pacific region, China will."[124] Beijing understood this and took steps to counter the American plans.

America's trading relationships with East Asian countries have for a long time been closer than those with Europe, but Obama's positioning of himself as the first Pacific President of the United States and the "pivot to Asia", as the President and Hillary Clinton jointly described it, were nevertheless highly symbolic. "The president shared my determination to make Asia a focal point of the administration's foreign policy," Clinton recalled. "Born

---

[122] Joseph R. Biden, Jr., "Building on Success. Opportunities for the Next Administration", *Foreign Affairs*, September/October 2016. P. 51.

[123] Edward Luttwack, *The Rise of China vs. the Logic of Strategy*. Cambridge (Mass.), 2012. PP. 38, 42.

[124] William M. Daley, "Free Trade Is Not the Enemy", *The New York Times*, May 19, 2015 <https://www.nytimes.com/2015/05/19/opinion/free-trade-is-not-the-enemy.html>.

in Hawaii, and having spent formative years in Indonesia, he felt a strong personal connection to the region and understood its significance. [...] Over the next four years we practiced what I called 'forward-deployed diplomacy' in Asia, borrowing a term from our military colleagues."[125]

The numbers behind this shift in American policy were given by US Defence Minister Leon Panetta in June 2012 at the Shangri-La conference in Singapore: by 2020, 60% of the USA's military ships, including six aircraft carrier groups, were to be based in the Asia-Pacific.[126] Robert Kaplan drew attention to the fact that by locating American marines in Australia and a fleet in Singapore, the United States coordinated their military and naval presence in two oceans – the Indian and the Pacific. Henceforth, wrote Kaplan, "the maritime security systems of the Greater Middle East and East Asia would begin to merge into one grand geography uniting the southern Eurasian rimland."[127]

The first question on the agenda had become the strengthening of China, the USA's key strategic rival in the 21st century. The crisis of 2007-2009 had a considerable impact on the development of bilateral relations, revealing the high degree of interdependency between the world's biggest consumer economy and its biggest manufacturing economy.

China was the major lender to the United States and the engine of the global recovery from the recession. In his 2009 book, Zachary Karabell coined a term which went into common parlance: Chimerica, meaning a symbiosis of the two economies.[128] There was also talk – thanks to Brzezinski – of a G2, an informal alliance of the USA and China, capable of deciding the world's destiny. Obama's team also set out a new approach to American-Chinese relations – "strategic assurance", stipulating a tolerant position on the part of the USA in relation to China's increased geopolitical might and influence in the world, in exchange for cooperation with the USA on key security issues.[129]

....

[125] Hillary Rodham Clinton, *Hard Choices*. Simon and Schuster, 2014. PP. 42-43.

[126] Leon Panetta with Jim Newton, *Worthy Fights. A Memoir of Leadership in War and Peace*. N. Y., 2014. P. 384.

[127] Robert D. Kaplan, *Asia's Cauldron. The South China Sea and the End of a Stable Pacific*. Random House, 2015. P. 181.

[128] Zahary Karabell, *Superfusion: How China and America Became One Economy and Why the World's Prosperity Depends on It*. Simon and Schuster, 2009. PP. 11-13.

[129] Yang Peng, "'Strategic Reassurance' and the Future of China-U. S. Relations", *CIR*, September/October 2010. PP. 17-19; James Steinberg and Michael O'Hanlon, *Strategic Reassurance and Resolve: U. S.-China Relations in the Twenty-First Century*. Princeton (N. J.), 2014.

China found itself at the center of the United States' military planning. Beijing was perfectly well aware of the anti-Chinese orientation of the concept of the Air-Sea Battle plan, and expressed concern on this score several times.[130] In the United States, discussions about various scenarios for military action (including action in cyberspace) against China have become commonplace, though rivalry with China in cyberspace was seen as something which could only bring a "hot war" closer.[131]

In April 2014, Obama went on a voyage to East Asia, during which he signed a new military agreement with the Philippines. America's military cooperation with Japan, Korea, Australia and Singapore intensified. Statements were made about the desire to secure the capability for a "temporary military presence" of the USA in Vietnam, Indonesia and Malaysia. The Pentagon began actively reviving American and Japanese aerodromes from the time of the Second World War in the Pacific.[132]

Washington was carefully monitoring the rise of India, which since the 2000s was regarded as a potential strategic partner, a counterweight to the Chinese and, perhaps, to Russian and Iranian influence, and an ally in the fight against radical Islam. Seeing India as a potential exporter of security "to the Indian Ocean and beyond", the United States was nonetheless not prepared to give it decisive strategic backing in the region, confirming instead its dedication to long-term strategic partnership with Pakistan, built on the foundation of mutual interests and joint efforts.

The Middle East continued to be regarded as a source of key threat to US national security. In the first few months of his presidency, Obama tried to show reverence towards the Arab-Islam world, a symbol of which was a speech he gave at Cairo University, which genuinely resonated in a positive way among Muslims. The consequence of this, however, was that Obama's popularity rating fell to 5% in Israel, and this was a threat to the electoral coalition of the Democratic Party, in which Jews play a significant role. The result was a clear departure from the orientation initially declared, and a return to more traditional approaches.

---

[130] Zhao Jinjun, "Objectively Viewing 'Air-Sea Battle'", *Beijing Zhanyou Bao*, June 30, 2012. P. 3; "Not to Be Misunderstood – Air-Sea Battle is Officially Directed at China", *Global Times*, January 12, 2012.

[131] David C. Gompert and Martin Libicki, "Cyber Warfare and Sino-American Crisis Instability", *Survival*, August/September 2014. PP. 7-22.

[132] Geoff Dyer, "US Eyes Pacific Islands as Part of Military Strategy: Pivot to Asia", *The Financial Times*, April 29, 2014. P. 6.

The Obama administration focused a great deal on Afghanistan, where whole groups of the population which had formerly remained neutral were now increasingly supporting the Taliban. At the same time, some Afghans managed to establish mutually beneficial relations with the occupying forces, primarily through the drugs business, in which the local power brokers and American drugs cartels were involved. In 2010, the Obama administration dramatically increased the number of American troops in Afghanistan, in a bid to secure a decisive military victory. No particular successes were achieved, however, and the USA began the withdrawal of troops.

The stabilization of the situation in a problematic region or country (examples might be Germany and Japan after World War II) is by no means always the objective of USA policy; often its interests appear to include long-term destabilization, and not allowing an adversary who is down to get back on to its feet. To all appearances, this is the USA's approach in Afghanistan.

It was believed in the USA that the Iraqi security forces would be able to maintain order. After the American troops left, however, the country once again teetered towards civil war. At the start of Obama's presidency, there were 180,000 American troops in Afghanistan and Iraq, and in early 2015 fewer than 15,000.[133] The USA spent between 4 and 6 trillion dollars on the wars in these two countries, and its losses amounted to 6,700 killed and 51,000 wounded.[134] The United States has never kept count of the other side's losses, but in Iraq alone, the number of people killed, according to data from local sources, is over a million.

The USA's reckless policy in Syria, where Obama supported groups close to Al-Qaida in an attempt to overthrow the regime of Bashar Assad, ultimately turned into a huge headache for everybody. The Islamic State of Iraq and the Levant (ISIL) seized a considerable portion of the territory of Syria and Iraq, and this required a fresh military intervention on the part of the USA. "[…] President Obama boasted of putting together a coalition of Sunni powers such as Turkey, Saudi Arabia, Qatar, Jordan, United Arab Emirates and Bahrain to oppose Isis, but these all have different agendas to the US in which destroying IS is not the first priority," noted the British expert on

---

[133] *National Security Strategy*. The White House, February 2015. Washington, 2015. P. 7. <https://obamawhitehouse.archives.gov/sites/default/files/docs/2015_national_security_strategy_2.pdf>.

[134] David A. Shlapak, "Towards a More Modest American Strategy", *Survival*, April/May, 2015. P. 61.

the matter Patrick Cockburn. "[T]hey like the fact that ISIS creates more problems for the Shia."¹³⁵

Iran's role as a regional power had grown considerably as a result of the weakening of its age-old rival, Iraq, its ability to influence the policy of its Shiite leaders, and scientific breakthroughs and advances in its nuclear program. At the same time, the USA created the impression that it was capable of successfully conducting a regime change operation in Tehran. After President Ahmadinejad left the political scene, the White House renewed its dialogue with Rouhani's government. This decision, however, and the deal that was eventually reached (Iran's rejection of its nuclear program in exchange for the removal of sanctions), caused serious annoyance for the pro-Israeli lobby in Washington and in the Sunni countries that are USA's partners in the Middle East.

The revolutionary events in Tunisia, Egypt and Libya, and the turmoil in Algeria, Yemen, Syria and Bahrain, have put some basic assumptions underlying the USA's regional strategy in doubt. "The support for the Arab Spring, desperate in terms of its lack of sense, and dictated by an utterly transparent hope that the position of Western democracy would be strengthened in the world, resulted in the weakening, primarily, of pro-American regimes. The Middle East has become significantly less stable."¹³⁶

The results of American policy in the region were far from expected. "As the former administration official Philip Gordon has noted, 'In Iraq, the U.S. intervened and occupied, and the result was a costly disaster. In Libya, the U.S. intervened and did not occupy, and the result was a costly disaster. In Syria, the U.S. neither intervened nor occupied, and the result is a costly disaster.' And in Yemen, one might add, the United States relied on drone strikes and active diplomacy, and the result is a costly disaster."¹³⁷

Latin America warmed to the USA for the first time in decades, when Obama restored diplomatic relations with Cuba. By 2013, the number of Latin Americans with a favorable opinion of the United States had

---

¹³⁵ Patrick Cockburn, "War against Isis: US Air Strategy in Tatters as Militants March on", *The Independent*, October 12, 2014 <https://www.independent.co.uk/voices/comment/war-against-isis-us-strategy-in-tatters-as-militants-march-on-9789230.html>.

¹³⁶ Sergey Karaganov, "Rossiya – SShA: dolgoye protivostoyaniye?" ("Russia – USA: a Long Confrontation?"), *Rossiya v global'noy politike* (*Russia in Global Affairs*), Issue 4, July/August 2014. P. 78.

¹³⁷ Gideon Rose, "What Obama Gets Right. Keep Calm and Carry the Liberal Order On", *Foreign Affairs*, September/October 2015. P. 9.

reached 58%.[138] "Obama's policy towards Africa has been something of a disappointment," wrote Nicolas van de Walle of Cornell University, who has conducted research into it. Rather limited assistance, as it turned out, was provided to corrupt regimes, mostly in the form of military supplies.[139]

In his memoirs, published in 2014, Robert Gates gave a fairly critical assessment of the USA's policy towards Russia, stressing that "[f]rom 1993 onward, the West, and particularly the United States, had badly underestimated the magnitude of Russian humiliation in losing the Cold War and then in the dissolution of the Soviet Union, which amounted to the end of the centuries-old Russian Empire. The arrogance, after the collapse, of American government officials, academicians, businessmen, and politicians in telling the Russians how to conduct their domestic and international affairs (not to mention the internal psychological impact of their precipitous fall from superpower status) had led to deep and long-term resentment and bitterness. […] [M]oving so quickly after the collapse of the Soviet Union to incorporate so many of its formerly subjugated states into NATO was a mistake. […] When Russia was weak in the 1990s and beyond, we did not take Russian interests seriously. We did a poor job of seeing the world from their point of view, and of managing the relationship for the long term."[140]

Russia proved to be relatively high up in the foreign policy priorities of the Obama administration. The White House called a halt to the plans to bring Ukraine and Georgia into NATO, while maintaining military cooperation at a level necessary for effective preparation for membership. Meanwhile, as the President of the USA and Canada Institute, Sergey Rogov, rightly warned, "The strategic partnership between Russia and the USA lacks domestic political basics."[141]

The war in South Ossetia in 2008 was taken as evidence of the rebirth of the authoritarian and aggressive Russia. Planning of conventional military actions against Russia in case of "aggression" against the Baltic states, and a program of air and sea exercises in the immediate vicinity of Russian borders in the spring and autumn of 2010 was pointedly resumed.

---

[138] Michael Reid, "Obama and Latin America", *Foreign Affairs*, September/October 2015. P. 52.

[139] Nicolas van de Walle, "Obama and Africa. Lots of Hope, Not Much Change", *Foreign Affairs*, September/October 2015. PP. 54-55.

[140] Robert M. Gates, *Duty. Memoirs of a Secretary at War*. Random House, 2015. PP. 157, 158.

[141] Sergey Rogov, "Politika SShA i rossiysko-amerikanskiye otnosheniya v nachale XXI veka" ("US Politics and Russo-American Relations in the Early 21st Century"), *Rossiya v global'nom mire, 2000-2011* (*Russia's Foreign Policy: 2000-2011*). Vol. 3. Moscow, 2012. PP. 12-31.

At the same time, a "reset" has proved possible. At its heart, believed Andrew Kuchins, lay three main reasons: "(1) the growing urgency of resolving the Iranian nuclear issue; (2) the need for additional transport routes into Afghanistan, to support the growing military presence and (3) a return to a more multilateral approach so as to ensure nuclear security and strengthen the non-proliferation regime."[142]

The renewed deterioration in relations was connected with the election cycle in 2011-2012 in Russia and the return of Putin to the presidency, a wave of accusations against Moscow of dictatorial trends and human rights violations, and, finally, with Russia's intervention in Syria. There was talk in the USA about the start of a new Cold War, with plenty of epithets deployed against Russia.

During the presidential campaign in 2012, the Republican candidate, Mitt Romney, called Russia "geopolitical enemy number one". The Edward Snowden affair, which the USA saw as a slap in the face, also contributed to troubled relations.

The attack on Russian interests continued in the form of Washington's participation in regime change in Kyiv. As Assistant Secretary of State Victoria Newland admitted, the USA alone spent $5 billion on "supporting democracy" in Ukraine. For Russia, this was not a geopolitical threat – it was an existential threat, and Moscow behaved accordingly. The referendum on the reunification of Crimea and Russia, and Moscow's support for local forces in Donbass who took up arms to protect their land from a punitive operation organized by Kyiv, proved a serious challenge for the US leadership.

The question "What should be done about Putin's Russia?" became one of the central issues, if not the central one, in American foreign policy, and a whole range of potential answers was put forward.

As in many other cases, Obama's policy in relation to Russia was a combination of the recipes of Neo-Conservative and liberal interventionists. "Through its provocative – from the American point of view – non-systemic actions in the Crimea, Moscow has effectively put a question mark over Washington's ability, as a world leader, to achieve the goals that it sets, and to maintain the norms and principles of the world order that took shape after 1991... Therefore, the 'wilfulness of a revisionist state' must be curtailed decisively. The turn towards a policy of containing Russia, within the con-

---

[142] *Russia after the Global Economic Crisis*, ed. by Andes Aslund, Sergey Guriev, and Andrew C. Kuchins. Washington, 2010. P. 244.

text of such an interpretation of the situation, was inevitable."[143] Sanctions were brought in against many representatives of the Russian elite, in Russia's oil and gas, defence, and banking sectors. Starting in the autumn of 2014, Barack Obama began to describe Russia, in all his speeches, as one of the three main threats to the security of mankind, alongside Islamic State and the Ebola virus.

In the second year of the conflict, discussions on policy towards Russia became slightly more balanced, although it remained anti-Russian. More and more experts asserted, however, that the moment was long overdue to enter into a political dialogue with Moscow on the principles of security in Europe, since "[g]ratuitously seeking confrontation with Russia could lead to Armageddon."[144] One of the politicians who felt that way was Donald Trump.

Who Won in 2016?

The 2016 election campaign was expected to be a rather ordinary one. Among Democrats Hillary Clinton had the best chance of nomination. The Republicans were giving the palm to former Florida Governor Jeb Bush. A new Clinton versus Bush competition was foreseen. That is not what happened. America witnessed the most surprising campaign in history: in both parties, candidates who had no connections with the party leadership or the establishment took the lead.

In March 2015, Trump's prospects of becoming president were discussed only on TV comedy shows. His popularity rating back then among Republican voters was no higher than 1-2%. The bookmakers were offering odds of 150-1 on Trump winning the nomination, whereas Jeb Bush's odds were 4-1. In June, Trump announced his candidacy, immediately levelling accusations at everyone – from "Mexican rapists" to good for nothing American politicians. He certainly did not have any voter recognition problems to worry about. "He'd been in the spotlight nearly all of his adult life. He was still in his thirties when he became a single-name celebrity, like Madonna or Beyoncé, like a rock star or a president, his name, in ALL CAPS, gold plated, on buildings and airplanes and shirts and wine bottles (even though he says

....

[143] Eduard Solov'yev, "'Smena rezhima' v Ukraine i problemy evolyutsii rossiysko-amerikanskikh otnosheniy" ("Regime Change in Ukraine and the Problem of the Evolution of Russo-American Relations"), *Mezhdunarodnaya zhizn'* (*International Life*), Issue 10, October 2014. P. 82.

[144] Samuel Charap and Jeremy Shapiro, "Consequences of a New Cold War", *Survival*, Vol. 57, Issue 2, 2015. P. 37.

he's never had a drink in his life). He was the rare billionaire who shunned privacy [...]. He was, almost from the start, his own brand. [...] He knew how to be famous, he knew how to win numbers, get ratings, make people take notice. More than three decades before he decided he wanted to be president, he showed up on Gallup's list of the ten men Americans most admired, running behind only the pope and some presidents. [...] He was a proud, boastful winner who had also failed at more businesses than many moguls start in a lifetime."[145] He didn't have a computer on his office table, he had no time to read long reports, he has always preferred short oral messages.

His very first campaign speech sent his popularity rating up to 11%. After the first Republican Party debates in August 2015, Trump was supported by 24% of voters, 10% more than Bush. In second place was Ben Carson, the favorite of the Tea Party movement, a black surgeon who had never been involved in politics before.[146]

Red baseball caps bearing the white slogan: "Make America great again" became the symbol of what was a nightmare for some and a new hope for others. Trump told stories, portraying himself as a man of the people, who found taxi drivers and metal-workers more interesting than rich and powerful elites. In violation of all the rules, Trump ignored the leadership of his own party, did not conduct public opinion polls, spent hardly any money on advertising, and did no preparation for debates. He said he did not need consultants because he already knew what was going on in the economy, and as far as military issues were concerned, he felt that it was quite enough to watch TV with its talking heads. What was the reason for Trump's success? One of his aides offered two reasons: "One is the total revulsion of American voters with politicians and the entire political system. And secondarily, just the belief that he can't be bought."[147]

However Trump's chances were regarded as minimal. It was believed that "the Trump balloon will burst" before the caucuses in Iowa.[148] The entire Republican establishment rose up to fight against him, asserting that he was unpredictable, that he would break the party apart. They were a long way off

---

[145] Michael Kranish and Marc Fisher, *Trump Revealed. An American Journey of Ambition, Ego, Money and Power*. Simon and Schuster, 2017. P. 3.

[146] Demetri Sevastopulo, "Trump Reveals Staying Power as He Consolidate Lead in Republican Race", *The Financial Times*, August 20, 2015. P. 4.

[147] Michael Scherer, "The Donald Has Landed", *Time*, August 31, 2015. PP. 20-25.

[148] Albert R. Hunt, "Republicans Battle for the Right in Iowa", *The New York Times*, August 10, 2015 <https://www.nytimes.com/2015/08/10/us/republicans-battle-for-the-right-in-iowa.html>.

the mark. Fareed Zakaria wrote: "Trump's political genius was to realize that many Republican voters were unmoved by the standard party gospel of free trade, low taxes, deregulation, and entitlement reform but would respond well to a different appeal based on cultural fears and nationalist sentiment."[149] Trump proposed cutting taxes, abolishing Obamacare, supporting US producers, protecting the country from migrants, building a wall along the border with Mexico, looking after America rather than the rest of the world, putting pressure on China and Iran, pulling out of Afghanistan, making a deal with Russia, making America's allies pay for their own defence, and withdrawing from planned trade alliances. He retained pole position in the race to be the Republican candidate.

In the Democratic Party, it seemed as though nothing could threaten Hillary Clinton: her level of support across the country before the campaign began was as high as 63%. The Democrats unequivocally backed her, without lining up an alternative option, although she had always been a fairly divisive figure. And after she announced that she and Bill had been completely bankrupt when they left the White House in 2001, her level of support dropped as low as 53%. In March 2015 *The New York Times* discovered that Clinton had used an unprotected communications system while she was Secretary of State. She strongly denied the fact, but the scandal was very damaging. Two months later a book called *The Clintons' Cash* was published, which disclosed how she had used her official position to top up the Clinton Fund.

"Taken together, these three should have set off warning sirens within the Democratic Party that the frontrunner was damaged goods – a tone-deaf spokesperson with serious ethical and moral issues that might blow up in her and her party's faces," John Podhoretz wrote.[150] However, these warnings were rejected as Republican propaganda.

A serious alternative within the Democratic Party arose in the shape of the 73-year-old senator from Vermont, Bernie Sanders. He vowed to break up the banks, bring down the billionaire class and smash the political establishment. A Senator from the tiny state of Vermont, Sanders joined the Democratic Party only in April 2015. In September of that year, Sam Frizell of *Time* magazine wrote: "Without a single TV ad – or a single congressional

---

[149] Fareed Zakaria, "Populism on the March. Why the West Is in Trouble", *Foreign Affairs*, November/December 2016. P. 14.

[150] John Podhoretz, "The Liberal Establishment's Clinton Obsession is Blowing up in its Face", *The New York Post*, September 17, 2016 <https://nypost.com/2016/09/17/the-liberal-establishments-clinton-obsession-is-blowing-up-in-its-face/>.

endorsement – Sanders has exposed the weakness of the party's Clintonian establishment while at the same time spotlighting its hunger for an ideological savior."[151]

Both Trump and Clinton won their nominations via extremely hard-fought and uncompromising contests within their own parties, during which masses of compromising stories were slung at them. The campaign was unprecedented in its brutality.

A summarised list of objections to Trump can derived from a biography of him written by David K. Johnson. According to Johnson, Trump is obsessed solely by money, the cobbling together of wealth at any price. The things he has said about women are politically incorrect in the extreme, and he rejects all social norms and niceties, thereby making himself a hero to some and a pariah to others. He has a huge number of acquaintances in the criminal world among gangsters, bandits and drug-dealers. He is intolerant of a free press, constantly attacks journalists and does not accept criticism. He is a world-class narcissist. He has deep and often dubious financial operations across the world, including in Canada, Europe, Russia and the Middle East, and contractual relations with foreign governments; he is friends with kings, sheikhs and dictators in many countries. He has ties to the Russian mafia, and he had said the kind things about the "murderous autocrat" Vladimir Putin.[152]

Foreign policy matters did not play a major role in the election campaign, apart from the problems of trade and migration. And, of course, the Russian factor. As the program director of the Valdai Discussion Club, Dmitriy Suslov, said at the time: "The entire American elite unambiguously sees Russia as its enemy. They see any politician who sees this differently as a system error which needs to be corrected, as was the case with Trump."[153] In the summer of 2016, in connection with the Internet publication of correspondence between the Democratic National Committee on the subject of the discrediting of Sanders, "America's intelligence agencies have assessed with 'high confidence' that Russia's government was behind the hack, and private security companies have identified two Russian teams of hackers

---

[151] Sam Frizell, "The Gospel of Bernie", *Time*, September, 2015. P. 34.

[152] David Cay Johnson, *The Making of Donald Trump*. Brooklyn-L., 2017. PP. 208-212.

[153] Nina Il'ina, "Donal'da Trampa prodolzhayut obvinyat' v porochashchikh svyazyakh s Rossiyey" ("Donald Trump Still Accused of Sordid Ties with Russia"), *Vedomosti*, August 15, 2016 <https://www.vedomosti.ru/politics/articles/2016/08/16/653142-donalda-trampa-prodolzhayut-obvinyat-porochaschih-svyazyah-rossiei>.

that were inside D.N.C. computers."[154] One team is called Cozy Bear and is linked to the FSB, the successor to the KGB, and another is called Fancy Bear is linked to the GRU, or Russian military intelligence.[155] Trump joked on that point, suggesting that Russian intelligence services should double their efforts.

His opponents were not amused at all. *The New York Times* indignantly wrote: "On Wednesday, Mr. Trump crossed a new line by practically inviting Russia, an increasingly aggressive American adversary, to interfere in the presidential election by cyberspying on Hillary Clinton's email correspondence when she was secretary of state. [...] He was, in effect, urging Russia to commit a crime that would damage national security."[156]

The mud-slinging campaign against Trump in the liberal press reached new heights. Trump responded with promises to put Clinton in jail for having misappropriated the State Department's secrets, and warned of a sweeping conspiracy against him, which included groups "of faceless global elites, named media organizations, bankers, elements of the federal government and even his own party's leadership." He encouraged supporters to "watch" the polls in predominantly minority neighborhoods. "This is a conspiracy against you, the American people."[157]

The main group of voters to which Trump owed his victory were the white workers of the "Rust belt", who were former members of labor unions and former Democrat supporters. Almost a quarter of the white working class people who had voted for Obama in 2008 voted for Trump in 2016, and this was the decisive factor in Trump's success.[158] The best predictor of how people would vote was the extent to which they were concerned by the issue of race.[159]

As noted by the well-known conservative Newt Gingrich, Trump united traditional Republican voters who believe in free markets, a "small" govern-

---

[154] Nicholas Kristof, "Did Putin Try to Steal an American Election?", *The New York Times*, July 28, 2016 <https://www.nytimes.com/2016/07/28/opinion/did-putin-try-to-steal-an-american-election.html>.

[155] Ibid.

[156] "What Was Mr. Trump Thinking", *The New York Times*, July 28, 2016 <https://www.nytimes.com/2016/07/28/opinion/what-was-mr-trump-thinking.html>.

[157] Zeke J. Miller, "How Trump Plans to Win-Even If He Loses the Election", *Time*, October 31, 2016 <https://time.com/4540117/how-trump-plans-win-election/>.

[158] Edward Luce, "When West Isn't Best", *The Financial Times*, May 6, 2017. P. 1.

[159] Nate Cohn, "The Obama-Trump Voters Are Real. Here's What They Think.", *The New York Times*, August 15, 2017 <https://www.nytimes.com/2017/08/15/upshot/the-obama-trump-voters-are-real-heres-what-they-think.html>.

ment, and traditional morality, with a recently activated group of "blue-collar" Democrats, as well as disgruntled rural voters fed up with the elites of both parties.[160]

Drain the Washington Swamp

Trump became President by promising to give back power to the people, by draining the "Washington swamp", but the establishment, in turn, was utterly determined to sink Trump. He proved to be ideologically alien to all the traditional groupings. Indeed, Trump has never shown any interest in the principles of libertarianism, traditionalism, neo-conservatism or the party's other ideological tenets. Trump himself described his ideology as "'common sense' conservatism" and said he wished to model himself as President on Andrew Jackson.[161] Newt Gingrich, speaking about the principles of Trump, suggested that one imagine a rectangular table, one side of which is "extremely anti-left", the other – "anti-stupid", the third – "anti-politically correct" and, the fourth – "pro-American".[162]

Trump actively set about implementing his agenda. In the first week of his presidency, he signed executive orders on the abolition of Obamacare, on leaving the Trans-Pacific Partnership, on the start of the construction of a wall on the border with Mexico, on the prohibition of foreign organizations promoting abortions, and on restricting migration from seven Muslim countries.

The sabotaging of the Administration's activity began right away. Enraged by what he supposed to be the scheming of internal wreckers, the President and his surrogates have responded by claiming to be victims of the "deep state", a powerful, unelected bureaucracy secretly promoting an agenda of their own.[163] However, Jon D. Michaels of the University of California, Los Angeles suggested that "bureaucratic problems come not from an insidious, undemocratic 'deep state' but simply from the state –

---

[160] Newt Gingrich, *Understanding Trump*. Hachette UK, 2017.

[161] Charles R. Kesler, "Donald Trump Is a Real Republican, and that's a Good Thing", *The New York Times*, April 26, 2017 <https://www.nytimes.com/2017/04/26/opinion/donald-trump-is-a-real-republican-and-thats-a-good-thing.html>.

[162] Newt Gingrich, *Understanding Trump*. Hachette UK, 2017.

[163] Jon D. Michaels, "Trump and the 'Deep State'. The Government Strikes Back", *Foreign Affairs*, September/October 2017. P. 52.

the large, complex hive of people and procedures that constitute the U.S. federal government."[164]

Judges from four federal district courts froze the implementation of the executive order banning immigrants on entering the USA. Protest demonstrations took place throughout the country against the President. The Democrats in Congress have become a fierce opposition. Indeed, many Republicans have begun to actively distance themselves from their President.

Jeff Bergner of the University of Virginia wrote: "The country's current political divisions compound the normal complexities of executive-legislative relations. [...] Congressional committees frequently investigate presidents: Ronald Reagan over Iran-contra, Clinton over Monica Lewinsky, Obama over Benghazi. But it is unusual for a president to be under investigation by four separate committees, led by members of his own party, in the first year of his term."[165] John McCain complained about the chaos in the White House: "Who's in charge? Who's making policy? Who's making decisions?"[166] It was indeed difficult to answer these questions.

The forming of the administration took place extremely slowly, and was accompanied by countless scandals. National Security Adviser Michael Flynn was the first to lose his post – he fell victim to deliberate leaks from the intelligence services about his close and potentially criminal ties to the Russians. Flynn was fired 24 days into his job. And thus "Kremlingate" began.[167]

After Trump fired James Comey, the director of the FBI, who had been investigating the Trump circle's ties to Russia, there was a storm of protest. 46% of Americans were convinced that Comey had been fired due to his investigation into the "Russia probe".[168] Robert Mueller was appointed as special prosecutor to investigate Trump's dealings with Moscow.

....

[164] Ibid. PP. 52-53.

[165] Jeff Bergner, "The Congressional Apprentice. How Trump is Approaching Capitol Hill", *Foreign Affairs*, September/October 2017. PP. 100, 105 <https://www.foreignaffairs.com/articles/2017-07-31/congressional-apprentice>.

[166] Cit. from: Philip Elliott, "Inside Donald Trump's White House Chaos", *Time*, February 16, 2017 <https://time.com/magazine/south-pacific/4673149/february-27th-2017-vol-189-no-7-8-asia-europe-middle-east-and-africa-south-pacific/>.

[167] Max Boot, "The Drip Drip Drip of Kremlingate", *USA Today*, February 20, 2017 <https://eu.usatoday.com/story/opinion/2017/02/20/flynn-trump-russa-leaks-kremlin-max-boot-column/98131530/>.

[168] Emily Cadei, "Cirque Du Comey", *Newsweek*, May 26, 2017 <https://www.magzter.com/article/Business/Newsweek/Cirque-DU-Comey>.

Turnover in the Trump administration was at a record high. In the first 16 months of the presidency, two national security advisers, the White House Chief of Staff and his deputy, the Secretary of State, advisers on strategy, internal security, and economic policy, three communications directors and many lower-ranking officials were all replaced. The percentage of staff turnover was 34% in the first year of the presidency (Reagan – 19%, Bush, sr. – 7%, Clinton – 11%, Bush, Jr. – 6%, Obama – 9%).

Acute disagreements over internal politics made it extremely difficult for the administration to implement its legislative agenda, because its prospects mostly depended on Congress, which was as polarized as society itself. Right-wing Democrats and left-wing Republicans who share more or less common views and thus make up a two-party political center were becoming endangered species. In the 1960s, nearly one third of members of Congress of both parties were centrist; this figures stands at present in the region of one fifth. Readiness to offer a helping hand to the rival party tends to be regarded as betrayal. Even Republicans themselves, who retained a majority in Congress, were no less divided than the Democrats, and more deeply than they themselves had ever been before.

The central issue on Trump's legislative agenda was tax reform. The proposals concerned a massive cut in taxes, designed to stimulate growth and provide additional profits of $7 trillion in a decade. Critics hastened to claim that the plan would lead to "a multitrillion-dollar shift from federal coffers to America's richest families and their heirs, setting up a politically fraught battle over how best to use the government's already strained resources".[169]

The Tax Cuts and Jobs Act was approved by Congress and signed by Trump on 22nd December 2017. It retained the current seven-bracket structure, but lowered most individual income tax rates. The marginal corporate tax rate was reduced from 35% to 21%, thus being at its lowest since 1939. It would seem that business benefitted from the Act more than ordinary citizens.[170]

---

[169] Alan Rappeport, "Trump's Tax Plan Is a Reckoning for Republican Deficit Hawks", *The New York Times*, April 26, 2017 <https://www.nytimes.com/2017/04/26/us/politics/trump-tax-plan-budget-deficit.html>; Julie Hirschfeld Davis and Patricia Cohen, "Trump Tax Plan Would Shift Trillions from U.S. Coffers to the Richest", *The New York Times*, April 27, 2017 <https://www.nytimes.com/2017/04/27/us/politics/individual-business-tax-wealth.html>.

[170] Viktor Supyan, "SShA: globaliziruyushchayasya ekonomika v globaliziruyushchemsya mire" ("USA: Globalizing Economy in the Globalizing World"), *Mezhdunarodnaya zhizn'* (*International Life*), April 2018. PP. 97-98.

The Republicans had a few other legislative victories, when they acted together. Through the infrequently applied 1996 Congressional Review Act, they were able to reverse a number of regulatory measures in the oil, gas, coal and telecommunications industries adopted in the final months of Obama's presidency.

Internal party unity was manifested on the issue of forming the judiciary. With the appointment of Neil Gorsuch to the Supreme Court, the President set about changing the make-up of the federal courts to bring in "his" judges and shift the balance back to the conservatives.[171] However during the first year of Trump's presidency The Senate confirmed only 12 new federal judges, leaving vacant nearly 150 positions. Besides, Trump's administration still had to fill two thirds of key jobs which required congressional approval.

In the area of social legislation, the most acute struggle predictably unfolded around health insurance. The idea to cancel Obamacare, as Trump had promised during the election campaign, failed. In October 2017, seeing the impasse in the Senate, Trump unilaterally decided to stop subsidies to the insurers who insured people on low incomes.

However, there were initiatives that enjoyed bipartisan support. Even in such a contentious area as the adoption of the budget and the raising of public debt, it is obvious that Trump did not adhere to the traditional Republican ideas about the need to reduce budget spending. "Republicans who entered politics to cut the state and say 'freedom' a lot are marooned by the rise of Trump."[172]

Many analysts were skeptical about the results of the interaction between Trump and lawmakers. "Undisciplined and unpopular, Trump has been largely unable to advance his agenda on Capitol Hill despite Republican control of both houses of Congress," wrote Sarah Binder from the George Washington University, on the results of the first year of Trump's presidency.[173] It is not, however, that simple.

Trump has clearly strengthened his position in Congress and in the party. "Congressional Republicans know that Mr Trump's voters like him more than the party; they are right to worry that this gives him room to ma-

---

[171] "Here Come the Trump Judges", *The Wall Street Journal*, May 9, 2017 <https://www.wsj.com/articles/here-come-the-trump-judges-1494286213>.

[172] Janan Ganesh, "After Trump, the GOP Must Accept a New Kind of Republicanism", *The Irish Times*, August 2, 2018 <https://www.irishtimes.com/news/world/uk/after-trump-the-gop-must-accept-a-new-kind-of-republicanism-1.3583595>.

[173] Sarah Binder, "How to Waste a Congressional Majority. Trump and the Republican Congress", *Foreign Affairs*, January/February 2018. P. 78.

noeuvre."¹⁷⁴ Talk of impeaching the President with the help of votes from Republican lawmakers has fallen silent on the understanding that a Trump impeachment would most likely split the Republican party as it is today, which would be the party's undoing.

In the draft budget for the fiscal year 2018, Trump proposed to abolish more than 60 government programs. In fact, only a small number were eliminated. Fiscal hawks in the Republican Party – Bob Corker, Rand Paul, John McCain – sounded the alarm about the sharp increase in the budget deficit.

When the draft budget for 2019 was submitted in February 2018, Mick Mulvaney, head of the Office of Management and Budget, gave assurances that over the next ten years the US intended to reduce the budget deficit by $3 trillion. At the same time, the cost of fighting drugs, social assistance to the military, defence, and protection of the border with Mexico all increased significantly. $200 billion was allocated to infrastructure investment. Reductions were envisaged for the programs of the State Department and environmental protection.

The USA entered the 11th year of continuous economic growth. It is the longest expansion period in American history. High growth rates, record-breaking corporate profits, and the large-scale redemption of bonds by the issuing companies have become inter-related factors in unprecedented stock-market growth.¹⁷⁵ On 2nd August 2018, Apple became the world's first trillion-dollar public company. Economic growth gave a boost to consumer spending. Americans started to buy more cars, clothing and footwear, and to pay more for utility and medical services.

However, criticism of Trump's economic policy and skepticism concerning growth sustainability and long-term perspectives of the American economy run deep as well. Investors were concerned about plans to raise the Federal Reserve rate. In late February 2018, Trump spoke of a trade war for the first time. Tariff wars have pushed up the prices of steel and aluminum and have raised costs for companies that produce cars, tractors, washing machines and dishwashers, and packaging. Naturally, companies hurried to pass these costs on to the customers, at the same time blaming Trump

---

[174] "Trump and Congress: Just One of Those Things", *The Economist*, September 16, 2017. P. 37.

[175] Robin Wigglesworth and Nicole Bullock, "US Bull Market Continues to Ride out Trump Risks", *The Financial Times*, August 10, 2008 <https://www.ft.com/content/9c42685a-9c19-11e8-9702-5946bae86e6d>.

and his policy for the increase in prices.[176] Direct foreign investment in the American economy dropped by two thirds in the first quarter of 2018 in comparison to early 2016.

Foreign investors and central banks became reluctant to buy US Treasury securities. In autumn 2016, a decline in foreign demand sparked a sell-off. As a result, yields on 10-year bonds jumped as high as 3.23% in October, and stocks fell. Mostly, investors were concerned with the USA budget deficit. According to Moody's Investors Service, by the year 2028 the budget deficit was expected to rise to 8% of GDP from today's 4%.[177]

Stock markets faced serious problems. In November 2018, the S&P and Dow Jones indexes were well down. Apple's stock alone fell by 24% from its October high, and lost 250 billion dollars in market capitalization. The possibility of a world-wide recession in the midst of a trade wars between USA and China, sanctions against Iran, and Trump's plans to tighten restrictions on technology exports turned out to be bad news for investors.[178]

The year of 2018 was dominated by the mid-term elections, perhaps the most turbulent in American history. The stakes were extremely high. The Democrats' victory made the prospect of Trump's impeachment conceivable.

In 2018, Trump's support from Republican voters was unprecedentedly high compared to any other President from his party – 90%. The unprecedented aggression of the media and the mainstream towards the President, and a willingness to inflate any action of his into a scandal has had the opposite effect to that intended – the Republican core is consolidated in opposition to the attack.[179] Republicans have focused on the main achievement of the Trump administration – the economy. The problem was Trump's approval rating, which fell to 39% – the lowest for any president since Eisenhower (Obama's rating in 2010 was 46%, although unemployment reached 10%).[180]

---

[176] Peter Eavis, "Customers Pay for Trump's Trade War", *The New York Times*, July 30, 2018 <https://www.nytimes.com/2018/07/30/business/dealbook/trade-war-customers-pay.html>.

[177] Daniel Kruger and Ira Iosebashvili, "Foreign Buying of U.S. Treasurys Softens, Unsettling Financial Markets", *The Wall Street Journal*, October 23, 2018 <https://www.wsj.com/articles/foreign-buying-of-u-s-treasurys-softens-unsettling-financial-markets-1540303515>.

[178] Tat'yana Gladysheva and Irina Tsyruleva, "Birzha idet ko dnu: rynki perezhili 'chernyy' den'" ("The Stock Market Goes Down"), *Izvestiya*, November 22, 2018 <https://iz.ru/814982/tatiana-gladysheva-irina-tcyruleva/birzha-idet-ko-dnu-rynki-perezhili-chernyi-den>.

[179] Nate Cohn and Alicia Parlapiano, "How Broad, and How Happy, Is the Trump Coalition?", *The New York Times*, August 9, 2018 <https://www.nytimes.com/interactive/2018/08/09/upshot/trump-voters-how-theyve-changed.html>.

[180] Marc A. Thiessen, "What Trump Needs to Do to Avoid Being a One-Term President", *The Washington Post*, November 20, 2018 <https://www.washingtonpost.com/opinions/what-

The administration was jarred by scandals. On 6th September 2018, an unprecedented, unsigned article appeared in *The New York Times* on behalf of a senior member of the administration or perhaps even Trump's own staff. "The dilemma – which he does not fully grasp – is that many of the senior officials in his own administration are working diligently from within to frustrate parts of his agenda and his worst inclinations. I would know. I am one of them."[181] Trump responded with a one-worded tweet: "Treason".

The Democrats' negativity against Trump was rife. However, they had an important problem to solve: how to restore the trust of ordinary Americans in more rural areas, where it was perceived as a party of the political establishment and disliked even more than the big business. There was also a lack of positive ideas. The leader of the House congressional minority, Nancy Pelosi, turned out to be unacceptable to almost all socialist Democrats in many parts of the country, and this fact demonstrated that the problems of anti-Washington sentiments and the deep division within the Democratic Party still loom large. As a result, the party preferred not to wage a centralized campaign, and ran many independent campaigns in states and congressional districts.[182] The former leaders of the party – Barack Obama and Hillary Clinton – took an active part in the mid-term election campaign, which is not typical for the United States.

Both parties did not so much discuss the country's problems as blame each other. Trump focused on immigration, without response from the leaders of the Democrats; Democrats devoted much of their effort to the positive promotion of health issues that were of no concern to Republicans.

However, there were some circumstances that did not work in Trump's favour. Prominent Democrats and Trump opponents began to receive improvised explosive devices in the mail. The whole country was horrified by the threat of terrorist attacks. The perpetrator of the failed attacks, César Sayok, was arrested in Florida. His van at the time of detention was pasted over with posters with images of Trump and Pence and filled with Republi-

---

trump-needs-to-do-to-avoid-being-a-one-term-president/2018/11/20/c26bf67c-ecdc-11e8-96d4-0d23f2aaad09_story.html>.

[181] "I Am Part of the Resistance inside the Trump Administration", *The New York Times*, September 5, 2018 <https://www.nytimes.com/2018/09/05/opinion/trump-white-house-anonymous-resistance.html>.

[182] Sheril Stalberg and Nicholas Fandos, "Democrats Discard Washington Platform in Bid for House Control", *The New York Times*, August 15, 2018 <https://www.nytimes.com/2018/08/15/us/politics/democrats-house-midterm-campaign.html>.

can Party propaganda. A day later, 46-year-old Robert Bowers entered the synagogue Tree of Life in Pittsburgh and killed eleven people and wounded five, including three police officers.

Democrats used these events against Trump. Their leaders in both Houses issued a joint statement accusing Trump of cultivating an atmosphere of violence and hatred.

Trump responded with demands to strengthen security in connection with the approach to the US's southern border of a caravan of 7,000 migrants from Guatemala, Honduras and El Salvador, which the president called the invasion of the United States and a threat to national security.

Disaster for Trump was averted. The Republicans held the Senate, the Democrats won a majority in the House of Representatives. "The combination of a Senate map that heavily favored Republicans, and Trump's success in turning out his 2016 base, produced a red wall that held up pretty well against the blue wave," Mark Thyssen wrote in *The Washington Post*.[183]

"The Democrats got an effective tool to attack the Republican President, but not enough to bring him down..." wrote Fyodor Lukyanov.[184]

And that is exactly how things turned out.

Trump's decision at the end of 2018 to withdraw American troops from Syria and the Secretary of Defence's resignation caused another political scandal, turning the whole establishment against Trump. The administration made it clear, though, that it relied first and foremost on voters. Mulvaney admitted: "We recognize the fact that this is unpopular within the Beltway. We recognize the fact that it's unpopular within the Defense Department. It's very popular with ordinary American people."[185]

Democrats in the House of Representatives decided to multiply their investigations of Trump's activities.

....

[183] Marc A. Thiessen, "What Trump Needs to Do to Avoid Being a One-Term President", *The Washington Post*, November 20, 2018 <https://www.washingtonpost.com/opinions/what-trump-needs-to-do-to-avoid-being-a-one-term-president/2018/11/20/c26bf67c-ecdc-11e8-96d4-0d23f2aaad09_story.html>.

[184] Fyodor Luk'yanov, "Nevnyatnyy referendum" ("Unclear Referendum"), *Rossiyskaya Gazeta (Russian Newspaper)*, November 8, 2018 <https://globalaffairs.ru/redcol/Nevnyatnyi-referendum-19818>.

[185] Cit. from: Quint Forgey, "Mulvaney Goes to Bat for Trump over Syria Withdrawal", *Politico*, December 23, 2018 <https://www.politico.com/story/2018/12/23/mulvaney-trump-syria-withdrawal-1074505>.

The Trump Doctrine

In Trump's foreign policy, there are obvious elements of continuity. The course towards American dominance has been affirmed. Resistance to rising, alternative, uncontrolled centers of power are still at the center of policy. Again, there is a focus on the demonstration of force, and a jump in defence spending. The military budget in 2018 returned to the 600 billion dollar mark, and the proposed 2020 budget amounted to 750 billion dollars. A program of total modernization of the country's nuclear capability continues, with $1 trillion to be spent on it in the next 30 years. New nuclear capabilities and delivery systems are planned: 100 new strategic B-21 Raider bombers, 1,000-1,100 cruise missiles, 12 new Columbia-class nuclear submarines, 400 new intercontinental ballistic missiles, and seven new types of nuclear warhead.[186]

The USA spends about two thirds of its defence budget on technology and research and on weapons and military equipment (European countries spend 20% and BRICS 25%). According to SIPRI, of the 100 largest arms manufacturers, 45 are American companies; they account for 65% weapons sales worldwide, with the main customer being the Pentagon.

What is extremely pertinent though, is that Trump declared that he did not wish to be president of the whole world. Newt Gingrich stressed: "Trump candidly expressed to the American people something politicians have willfully ignored for decades: most of our policy decisions – both in trade and defense – are based on a world that no longer exists. The era of the post-World War II, ultrarich America that faced little economic competition on the world stage is over."[187]

That makes many in America unhappy. Stewart M. Patrick, of the Council on Foreign Relations, argued: "Since the administration of Franklin Roosevelt, 13 successive U.S. presidents have agreed that the United States must assume the mantle of global leadership… That is about to change."[188] Walter Russell Mead wrote: "For the first time in 70 years, the American people have elected a president who disparages the policies, ideas, and institutions at the heart of postwar U.S. foreign policy."[189]

---

[186] James E. Doyle, *Renewing America's Nuclear Arsenal: Options for the 21st Century*. L., 2017.
[187] Newt Gingrich, *Understanding Trump*. Center Street, 2017. P. 119.
[188] Stewart M. Patrick, "Trump and World Order", *Foreign Affairs*, March/April 2017. P. 52.
[189] Walter Russell Mead, "The Jacksonian Revolt. American Populism and the Liberal Order", *Foreign Affairs*, March/April 2017. PP. 2-3.

G. John Ikenberry of Princeton was horrified by the fact that "the world's most powerful state has begun to sabotage the order it created. A hostile revisionist power has indeed arrived on the scene, but it sits in the Oval Office, the beating heart of the free world. [...] U.S. President Donald Trump's every instinct runs counter to the ideas that have underpinned the postwar international system. Trade, alliances, international law, multilateralism, environmental protection, torture, and human rights – on all these core issues, Trump has made pronouncements that, if acted on, would bring to an end the United States' role as a guarantor of the liberal world order."[190]

Trump's personal diplomatic style affects policy as well. "Mr Trump is transactional, not institutional. He views foreign policy like a dealmaker and does not care whether the outcomes fit America's traditional practice of building systems that advance its interests and values," noted Robert Zoellick. "He is the first president in my experience who does not believe the office is larger than himself."[191]

The economic focus in US foreign policy has grown stronger under Trump. As Zoellick observed, "He proudly embraced protectionism in his inaugural address, the first president since Herbert Hoover to make such a public stand."[192] During his first foreign visit – to Saudi Arabia – Trump signed an arms deal worth several billion dollars. The USA began actively promoting its energy resources in the global market, including in Europe, calculating that it would be able to push Russian suppliers out of the European market. A package of sanctions which could be imposed on European companies participating in the "Nord Stream 2" project can be used as an example of how far the administration is willing to go in pursuit of American commercial interests.

There has been less emphasis on human rights, with Trump declaring that America itself is not so innocent; his stance has caused causing much consternation. "All U.S. presidents have, to varying degrees, downplayed and even overlooked concerns about human rights in order to get things done with unsavory foreign partners. But none has seemed so eager as

---

[190] G. John Ikenberry, "The Plot against American Foreign Policy. Can the Liberal Order Survive?", *Foreign Affairs*, May/June 2017. PP. 2-3.

[191] Robert Zoellick, "The Conflict at the Heart of Trump's Foreign Policy", *The Financial Times*, August 23, 2017 <https://www.ft.com/content/896ff946-868e-11e7-8bb1-5ba57d47eff7>.

[192] Ibid.

Trump to align with autocrats as a matter of course," wrote Sarah Margon, Washington Director of Human Rights Watch.[193]

Trump regards America as a model state, but not as a regime-changing corporation. The connection with the domestic political agenda is also clear: Trump's objective is a party realignment in the USA, and as far as his own target group – the white working class – is concerned, matters such as protecting American manufacturing, immigration and the building of a wall on the border with Mexico really are important. Hence the President's much-publicized isolationism and protectionism.

This is a very serious distinction between Trump and the "Davos culture". Richard Haas wrote: "The Davos crowd sees globalization as a good thing, in no small part because it has been very good to them. With few exceptions, these are highly educated, wealthy, successful and mobile. [...] [T]he 45th President, apostle of 'America first', sees globalization as bad for domestic prosperity and security and a direct threat to Washington's sovereignty. He genuinely believes that the costs of U.S. leadership far outweigh the benefits."[194]

The Trump administration has a clear reluctance to tie its hands with bilateral and multilateral obligations. Trump called NAFTA "the worst trade deal of all time", and reviewed the agreement. This same tendency was shown in the way the negotiations on the creation of the TTP and TTIP were curtailed at a moment's notice, and in the obvious unwillingness to make any agreements whatsoever on arms control.[195]

Trump is paying attention to the civilizational particularities of the modern world, and existing value orientations. It was no mere coincidence that for his first foreign policy tour, he chose the centers of three world religions – Saudi Arabia, Israel and Rome.[196]

Important changes have taken place in US doctrinal documents. Especially symptomatic was the National Security Strategy, the first to be released.

---

[193] Sarah Margon, "Giving up the High Ground: America's Retreat on Human Rights", *Foreign Affairs*, March/April 2018. P. 39.

[194] Richard Haass, "What the Global Elite Can Learn from the Donald", *Time*, February 5, 2018. P. 27.

[195] Shaun Polczer, "Nafta 2.0: Dealing with the Devil", *The Petroleum Economist*, October 12, 2017 <https://www.petroleum-economist.com/articles/politics-economics/north-america/2017/nafta-20-dealing-with-the-devil>.

[196] Mark Landler and Peter Baker, "Saudi Arabia and Israel Will Be on Itinerary of Trump's First Foreign Trip", *The New York Times*, May 4, 2017 <https://www.nytimes.com/2017/05/04/us/politics/trump-to-visit-saudi-arabia-and-israel-in-first-foreign-trip.html>.

For the Obama administration, the world was heading in the right direction – towards freedom, democracy and open global markets – and it needed only assistance under American leadership. Regimes that had not yet understood the benefits of the game played by American rules were to be educated and engaged, and the erring – isolated. Trump's Strategy, on the contrary, comes from the fact that the world is not going the American way. The interests of the US and the rest of the world are not identical. The world is dangerous. Global competitors, especially China and Russia, are deliberately hatching long-term plans "to erode American security and prosperity." Therefore, the conflict with Beijing and Moscow is "existential".[197] It is rooted in a clash of social models – a free-world and a neo-authoritarian world, so the return to rivalry is inevitable.

The National Security Strategy of 2010 constantly appealed to the "international system" as a global reality and the main instrument of American policy. In Trump's 2017 National Security Strategy (2017 NSS), the actors are separate, competing sovereign nations. The emphasis – unusual for America – is on the concept of sovereignty, which in the interpretation of Trump, means self-sufficiency, remoteness, and independence from the global system.

The principles of the division into "us" and "them" also changed. For Obama, a key principle was commitment to "common values, democracy and progress", whereas Trump's strategy sees "common interests" in terms of the willingness to support the interests of America. The most common word in Obama's Strategy was "engagement", in Trump's – "competition".

For Obama, US power was primarily in the allies and American-led alliances, and secondarily in military potential and competitiveness. For Trump, military power and competitiveness are the only factors. In the 2017 NSS, "soft power" is not even mentioned. At the same time, the concept of "principle-based realism" has been introduced as a guide to decision-making. In the list of foreign policy tools America plans to use in support of peace, the maintenance of diplomacy is in last place, and allies are given no more than a passing mention.[198]

---

[197] *National Security Strategy of the United States of America.* The White House, December 2017. PP. 2, 25 <https://www.whitehouse.gov/wp-content/uploads/2017/12/NSS-Final-12-18-2017-0905.pdf>.

[198] Andrey Bezrukov, "Razvod s mirom i yego posledstviya" ("Divorce from the World and Its Consequences"), *Rossiya v global'noy politike* (*Russia in Global Affairs*), Issue 1, January 18, 2018. PP. 131-135.

The Defence Strategy and Nuclear Posture published later fully confirmed the line set out in the initial document. The Defence Strategy also put China and Russia above Islamist extremism in the list of threats to America.[199]

Trump sees the Western countries not only as allies, but also as competitors. Unlike Obama, who campaigned against Brexit, Trump welcomed it. He has no wish to spend money on defending allies, and is trying to compel them to increase their defence contributions.

Trump's debut at his first NATO summit was seen by many as a failure. "The allies had hoped to hear a robust endorsement of the NATO Treaty's Article 5, which commits them to a 'one-for-all, all-for-one' principle that has been the foundation of the alliance since it was established. What they got instead was a vague promise to 'never forsake the friends who stood by our side'," complained *The New York Times*.[200]

Attitudes towards Trump in EU countries remain negative. In 2017, only 22% of Germans felt that the United States was a reliable ally, whereas 59% had thought so one year earlier.[201]

In reality, Washington is not taking any steps to make concessions requested by the EU, whether in the security sector (the Iran deal, the exit from the INF Treaty), the economy (trade wars and pressure on partners); nor is he even prepared to make general soothing declarations of political unity. In October 2018, Deputy Secretary of State Wes Mitchell said at the Atlantic Council: "The West must reclaim the tradition of supporting the nation state as its own and work harder to ensure that international institutions reflect the democratic will of nations, or expect institutions to lose influence and relevance."[202] "If Washington puts it that way, then in fact, the basic principles of contemporary Europe are called into question."[203]

---

[199] "The Next War: The Growing Danger of Great-Power Conflict", *The Economist*, January 27, 2018. P. 9.

[200] "President Trump Fails NATO", *The New York Times*, May 26, 2017 <https://www.nytimes.com/2017/05/26/opinion/donald-trump-nato-russia.html>.

[201] Jeff D. Colgan and Robert O. Keohane, "The Liberal Order is Rigged. Fix It Now or Watch It Wither", *Foreign Affairs*, May/June 2017. PP. 37-38.

[202] "Winning the Competition for Influence in Central and Eastern Europe: US Assistant Secretary of State A. Wess Mitchell", *Atlantic Council*, October 19, 2018 <https://www.atlanticcouncil.org/commentary/transcript/winning-the-competition-for-influence-in-central-and-eastern-europe-us-assistant-secretary-of-state-a-wess-mitchell/>.

[203] Fyodor Luk'yanov, "Smena formy pered smenoy soderzhaniya" ("Changing the Form before Changing the Content"), *Rossiyskaya Gazeta* (*Russian Newspaper*), October 31, 2018 <https://globalaffairs.ru/redcol/Smena-formy-pered-smenoi-soderzhaniya-19811>.

During the election of 2016, Trump spared no epithets in relation to China. "China is bilking us for hundreds of billions of dollars by manipulating and devaluing its currency. Despite all the happy talk in Washington, the Chinese leaders are not our friends. [...] And yet, with China beating us like a punching bag daily [...]."[204]

Predictions of a rise in American-Chinese confrontation are heard ever more frequently; the well-known expert Graham Allison of Harvard has dedicated recent writings to this subject. "[T]ensions between American and Chinese values, traditions and philosophies will aggravate the fundamental structural stresses that occur whenever a rising power, such as China, threatens to displace the established power, such as the United States." Allison called this "Thucydides' Trap"; Thucydides once wrote that the rise of Athens and the fear that it caused in Sparta had made war inevitable. "In the case of the United States and China, Thucydidean risks are compounded by civilizational incompatibility between the two countries, which exacerbates their competition and makes it more difficult to achieve rapprochement. This mismatch is most easily observed in the profound differences between the American and Chinese conceptions of the state, economics, the role of individuals, relations among nations, and the nature of time."[205]

Aaron L. Friedberg from Princeton argues, "It is impossible to make sense of the ambitions, fears, strategy and tactics of China's present régime without reference to its authoritarian, illiberal character and distinctive, Leninist roots. [...] The two powers are separated not only by divergent interests, some of which could conceivably be reconciled, but by incompatible visions for the future of Asia and the world."[206]

Henry Kissinger's words about China having its own well-established national interests and its roots being a few millennia older than Lenin are not of use in current American liberal thought.

The formal doctrines of the Trump administration have adopted an unprecedentedly tough stance against China. The National Security Strategy characterized China as a "revisionist power [...] that seeks to displace the United States in the Indo-Pacific region [...]."[207] For the first time during

---

[204] Donald Trump, *Time to Get Tough: Make America Great Again!* Simon and Schuster, 2011. PP. 2, 3.

[205] Graham Allison, "China vs. America. Managing the Next Clash of Civilizations", *Foreign Affairs*, September/October 2017. PP. 80-81.

[206] Aaron L. Friedberg, "Competing with China", *Survival*, Issue 3, June/July 2018, PP. 8, 9.

[207] *National Security Strategy of the United States of America*. The White House, December 2017.

the 40 years since the re-establishment of diplomatic ties, economic relations were described as antagonistic, not complimentary. In the National Defence Strategy of 2018, China is viewed as "a strategic competitor" that is using "predatory economics" and growing military capabilities "to intimidate its neighbors". America should rid itself of illusions and prepare itself for a "long-term strategic competition" with Beijing. That will require "the seamless integration of multiple elements of national power", which includes diplomacy, information, economics and military potential.[208]

According to Vasiliy Kashin from the Institute of Far Eastern Studies in Moscow, "Thus far the United States have no illusions that the 'China problem' will work itself out. The USA is seeking to crush China and make it abandon its attempts to change its position in the international system of labor division. If the USA fails in this aim, it will have to switch to a hard-line containment strategy, driving Chinese companies from the market, blocking their access to technologies, and restricting investment opportunities altogether with an increase in military and political pressure."[209]

The US trade war with China has undoubtedly become the most important world event in 2018-2020. In initiating it, Trump surely took into consideration the relevant statistics. In 2017, China exported $505 billion worth of goods to the US and imported $130 billion from America. However, China-US economic interactions go far beyond import and export. China hosts many American multinational businesses, while similar global Chinese companies – national champions – are already blossoming in China. Of great importance is technological competition in the most promising areas – from quantum technology to 5G and artificial intelligence. The trade war with China also had an obvious domestic political dimension: tough criticism of China resonates well with public sentiment in the United States and is a proven election tactic.[210]

....
P. 25 <https://www.whitehouse.gov/wp-content/uploads/2017/12/NSS-Final-12-18-2017-0905.pdf>.

[208] *Summary of the 2018 National Defense Strategy of the United States of America*. US Department of Defense, 2018. PP. 1, 4 <https://www.hsdl.org/?abstract&did=807329>.

[209] Vasiliy Kashin, "Torgovaya voyna s bol'shimi posledstviyami" ("A Trade War with Great Consequences"), *Izvestiya*, July 10, 2018 <https://iz.ru/764532/vasilii-kashin/torgovaia-voina-s-bolshimi-posledstviiami>.

[210] Ibid.; Demetri Sevastopulo and Shawn Donnan, "Yrump Zeroes in on China after Trade Truce with Europe", *The Financial Times*, August 2, 2018 <https://www.ft.com/content/425448b8-9674-11e8-b747-fb1e803ee64e>.

In 2018, Washington began with an increase in the tariff for Chinese steel. China, in response on 2nd April, increased trade duties on 128 goods imported from the United States. The choice of goods for the initial US duties was such so that the average consumer in the US did not feel the rise in prices. China imposed tariffs mostly on goods from the 5 states which voted for Trump – soybeans, cars from the Midwest, and oil products from the two Dakotas and Texas. In early July 2018, the countries introduced import duties on each other's goods worth $34 billion each. At the same time, Beijing reduced import charges on cars from other countries from 25% to 15%. When one door is closing another opens up, as Xi Jinping put it.[211] On his part, Trump threatened to impose tariffs on all the Chinese imports.

A full-fledged war broke out in the electronic equipment market. A conflict between the U.S. and the Chinese ZTE company lasted from March until July 2018. As a result, ZTE had to pay a 1.2 billion dollar fine for supplying American equipment to Iran, North Korea and Syria, and to allow American inspectors into its management. In August, Trump banned all US government organizations working with personal data to use Huawei and ZTE products. A similar ban was also introduced by Australia, New Zealand and Japan.[212] In September, the US Treasury imposed sanctions against the office for the development of military equipment of the Central Military Council of China's army and its chief, Lee Shanfu. For the first time ever, the USA implemented sanctions against a Chinese official institution and against a country buying Russian weapons in accordance with CAATSA act.[213]

And then a trade war broke out on a scale unprecedented since 1930s. On 24th September, Trump introduced new duties of 10% on Chinese imports worth $200 billion, to be increased to 25% from the beginning of 2019 if Beijing did not make concessions on trade and intellectual property protection issues. The President also promised the introduction of additional duties on imports valued at 267 billion. China's Ministry of Commerce said that "to protect its legitimate rights and interests and order in international free

---

[211] Mikhail Overchenko, "Voyna protiv torgovli" ("A War Against Trade"), *Vedomosti*. July 9, 2018 <https://vedomosti.profkiosk.ru/657592>.

[212] Mikhail Korostikov, "Oborudovaniye povyshennoy neblagonadezhnosti" ("Highly Untrustworthy Equipment"), *Kommersant* (*The Businessman*), December 11, 2018 <https://www.kommersant.ru/doc/3826868>.

[213] Aleksey Nikol'skiy, "Kitay nakazan za Rossiyu" ("China Punished for Russia"), *Vedomosti*, September 24, 2018 <https://vedomosti.profkiosk.ru/674537>; Vasiliy Kashin, "Sanktsii postfaktum" ("Sanctions Post Factum"), *Izvestiya*, September 24, 2018 <https://iz.ru/792298/vasilii-kashin/sanktcii-postfaktum>.

trade, China is left with no choice but to retaliate simultaneously".²¹⁴ Another statement followed that "China would not negotiate 'with a gun pointed to its head'" and tariffs ranging from 5% to 10% on $60 billion worth of U.S. goods were raised, including a 10% charge on American LNG. China also pledged to increase tariffs once more in January if America did not change its mind.²¹⁵

More than half of US corporations operating in China reported in September that they had begun to experience non-tariff restrictions, such as delays in customs clearance and an increase in the number of inspections. Farmers and other business organizations in the United States have created a coalition preparing lawsuits in court to block the actions of the Trump administration.²¹⁶

Vice-president Michael Pence, at the Hudson Institute, unveiled a new doctrine of relations with China. "First, it called out the Chinese government for perpetrating a multi-faceted, well-resourced and shady campaign of foreign influence operations on U.S. soil. Second, it placed that campaign in the context of a global competition between the United States and China that is being waged on every continent and in every realm."²¹⁷ The experienced Walter Russell Mead, who is difficult to surprise, immediately said that this was the beginning of Cold War II and the most fundamental turn in US-China relations since Henry Kissinger's visit to Beijing in 1971.²¹⁸

The APEC summit in November, held in Papua New Guinea, for the first time in the history of the organization ended without the adoption of a final Declaration, because of the contradictions between the US and China. The star of the summit was again Michael Pence, who said that Beijing was drag-

---

[214] "China Says it will Retaliate after Trump Imposes Fresh Tariffs", *The Economic Times*, September 2018 <https://economictimes.indiatimes.com/news/international/business/china-says-it-will-retaliate-after-trump-imposes-fresh-tariffs/articleshow/65854648.cms?from=mdr>.

[215] "China Won't Just Play Defence in Trade War, Global Times Says", *Reuters*, September 17, 2018 <https://www.reuters.com/article/usa-trade-china-idUSL3N1W31A1>.

[216] Yelizaveta Bazanova and Mikhail Overchenko, "SShA obyavlyayut voynu" ("US Declares War"), *Vedomosti*, Issue 175, September 19, 2018 <https://vedomosti.profkiosk.ru/article.aspx?aid=673525>.

[217] Josh Rogin, "The Trump Administration Just 'Reset' the U.S.-China Relationship", *The Washington Post*, October 4, 2018 <https://www.washingtonpost.com/opinions/global-opinions/the-trump-administration-just-reset-the-us-china-relationship/2018/10/04/c727266e-c810-11e8-b2b5-79270f9cce17_story.html>.

[218] Walter Russell Mead, "Mike Pence Announces Cold War II", *The Wall Street Journal*, October 8, 2018 <https://www.wsj.com/articles/mike-pence-announces-cold-war-ii-1539039480>.

ging the participants in its Belt and Road program into the trap of foreign debt. Pence called the Chinese initiative "a constricting belt and a one-way road" whereas "the inspiring American model of globalization contributes to the development of national finance markets and implies lending from private banks to private companies but not state loans".[219]

The meeting between Trump and Xi at the G20 summit in Argentina was supposed to ease tensions. It lasted for two hours and a half instead of the scheduled one hour, and resulted in a trade war truce between the USA and China. The White House announced that within the next three months the two countries would tackle their differences over such issues as China's economic policy, forced technology transfers, intellectual property protection, non-tariff barriers, cyberespionage, the service sector, and agriculture. Chinese officials mentioned only that negotiations on mutual removal of trade restrictions were on the agenda".[220]

However, the summit was hardly over when a new round of the trade war started. In Canada, at the request of the New York district court, the Huawei CFO and a representative of the powerful financial clan Meng Wanzhou were detained, accused of promoting the export of American technology to Iran.

Negotiations dragged on, and markets on both sides of the Pacific were shaken by the trade war.

At the start of Trump's presidency, the crisis concerning North Korea had reached maximum intensity, with the North Korean leadership carrying out tests of nuclear missiles in response to Trump's bellicose rhetoric and the joint American and South Korean military exercises on its borders. The President announced that an aircraft carrier was to be sent to the Korean peninsula, which, admittedly, then returned home. Trump's promises to use "fire and fury" against North Korea caused great alarm, especially in Seoul and Tokyo. Privately, representatives of the administration let it be understood that they were willing to engage in dialogue with Pyongyang, and Trump did not rule out talks with Kim Jong Un.[221] On 1st April and 9th

....

[219] Dmitriy Butrin, "Pust' rassudyat papuasy" ("Let the Papuans Judge"), *Kommersant. Den'gi (The Businessman. Money)*, Issue 52, November 28, 2018. PP. 10-11.

[220] Mikhail Overchenko, "Novyy god ne nachnetsya s torgovoy voyny" ("New Year Won't Start with a Trade War"), *Vedomosti*, December 3, 2018 <https://vedomosti.profkiosk.ru/690869>.

[221] Brian Harris, "What's at Stake in the South Korea Election?", *The Financial Times*, May 6, 2017 <https://www.ft.com/content/871c2f32-3145-11e7-9555-23ef563ecf9a>; Mark Landler, "Following 'Fire and Fury,' Trump Looks to Ease Tensions in Asia", *The New York Times*, August 14, 2017 <https://www.nytimes.com/2017/08/14/us/politics/trump-north-korea-china-trade.>

May 2018, CIA Director Pompeo visited North Korea to discuss the possibility of the first US-North Korean summit. On 12th June 2018, in Singapore, there was a meeting between Trump and Kim Jong Un, which initiated the unfreezing of relations. However, neither in Singapore nor during the new summit in Hanoi in February 2019, was any significant progress was made with regard to the denuclearization of the Korean Peninsula.

Trump was a supporter of rapprochement with India, feeling personal sympathy for Narendra Modi and striving to create a counterweight to China. New Delhi made it clear that its crises and conflicts with Washington were in the past. India needs US investment for Modi's "Make in India program". In October 2017, Rex Tillerson held talks in Delhi, which many viewed as a turning point of US policy in South Asia. The place of a key ally of Washington, formerly owned by Pakistan, passed to India.

In September 2018, the first ever meeting of the heads of defence and diplomatic ministries of the United States and India, in the format of "two plus two", was held. At its conclusion, there was a signed Communications Compatibility and Security Agreement (COMCASA), which allowed New Delhi access to high-tech equipment for highly secure communication systems. It is one of four agreements constituting the legal base of the countries' bilateral relations in the security sphere. Pompeo, during the visit, said that the provisions of the CAATSA sanctions law would apply where it "would make sense". Indians were confident that Trump would not impose sanctions.

On 21st August 2017, Trump – after 16 years of the lengthiest war in American history – put forward his policy on Afghanistan and Southern Asia. He came to the conclusion that simply leaving would create a vacuum for terrorists, including ISIL and Al-Qaida. It was proposed that approximately 4,000 military personnel would be added to the 8,400 who were already there (at the height of the campaign, in 2010, there was a contingent of 100,000 servicemen and women in Afghanistan). Trump narrowed the strategic goals of the USA's policy in Afghanistan: "We are not nation-building again; we are killing terrorists."[222] A new factor was stepping up the pressure on Pakistan, with the aim of forcing it to refrain from supporting "its" terrorists in Afghanistan – under the threat of a reduction in military aid, sanctions

---

html>; Bill Powell, "Trump's Korean Cold War", *Newsweek*, September 22, 2017. P. 11.

[222] "Remarks by President Trump on the Strategy in Afghanistan and South Asia". The White House, August 21, 2017 <https://www.whitehouse.gov/briefings-statements/remarks-president-trump-strategy-afghanistan-south-asia/>.

for Pakistani officials, and possible US air strikes on Pakistani territory. A symptomatic note was struck, against this background, by the invitation that was extended to India to take a more active role in Afghanistan's post-war recovery, and to the NATO partners – to step up their military efforts.[223]

Tensions between the USA and Turkey escalated considerably. Erdogan's political reforms were seen as stifling democratic freedoms and asserting authoritarianism, and a tough campaign in the Western media began against him. In addition, the Turkish leadership greatly angered the US by deciding to buy an S-400 anti-missile system from Russia, and by the arrest of Protestant pastor Andrew Brunson for participating in the Gülen conspiracy. Turkey, for its part, criticized the United States for supporting the Kurds, to whom, according to Ankara, in recent years American weapons have been supplied on 5,000 trucks and 2,000 aircraft.

The US raised tariffs on Turkish steel and aluminum, and sanctions under the law of Magnitsky were introduced against Turkey's Ministers of Justice and Interior. Congress voted to withhold the delivery of a consignment of F-35 jet fighters, and urged to international financial institutions to freeze lending to Turkey. Ankara responded with mirror counter-sanctions. The pro-government Turkish media have called for the closure of an American military base in Incirlik.[224] Erdogan openly warned: "Unless the United States starts respecting Turkey's sovereignty and proves that it understands

---

[223] Julie H. Davis and Mark Lander, "Trump Outlines New Afghanistan War Strategy With Few Details", *The New York Times*, August 21, 2017 <https://www.nytimes.com/2017/08/21/world/asia/afghanistan-troops-trump.html>; Michael R. Gordon, "Trump's Strategy May Help in Afghanistan, but Few Expect 'Outright Victory'", *The New York Times*, August 21, 2017 <https://www.nytimes.com/2017/08/21/world/asia/trump-strategy-afghanistan.html>; Zalmay Khalilzad, "Why Trump Is Right to Get Tough With Pakistan", *The New York Times*, August 23, 2017 <https://www.nytimes.com/2017/08/23/opinion/trump-afghanistan-pakistan-strategy.html>; Roger Cohen, "Trump's Afghan Illusions", *The New York Times*, August 23, 2017 <https://www.nytimes.com/2017/08/23/opinion/trump-afghanistan-strategy.html>; Ben Farmer, Henry Samuel, and Justin Huggler, "Nato Allies Shy away from Trump's Demand for More Afghanistan Troops", *The Daily Telegraph*, August 22, 2017 <https://www.telegraph.co.uk/news/2017/08/22/nato-allies-shy-away-trumps-demand-afghanistan-troops/>; Mazzetti and Salman Masood, "Trump Tilts the Political Balance in South Asia", *The New York Times*, International Edition, August 24, 2017. P. 1.

[224] Amberin Zaman, "Understanding the Failed Deal With Turkey That Sparked Trump's Fury", *The New York Times*, August 7, 2018 <https://www.nytimes.com/2018/08/07/opinion/turkey-andrew-brunson-prison.html>; "Turkey's Downward Spiral", *The New York Times*, August 10, 2018 <https://www.nytimes.com/2018/08/10/opinion/turkey-united-states-trump-erdogan.html>; Ruchir Sharma, "Worried About Turkey's Economic Problems? China's Could Be Worse", *The New York Times*, August 15, 2018 <https://www.nytimes.com/2018/08/15/opinion/turkey-economy-lira-china-currency-erdogan.html>.

the dangers that our nation faces, our partnership could be in jeopardy. […] Failure to reverse this trend of unilateralism and disrespect will require us to start looking for new friends and allies."[225] This is perhaps the most serious conflict within NATO since France's withdrawal from the military organization in the 1960s.

Trump's decision to move the American Embassy to Jerusalem, recognizing it officially as the capital of Israel, was rejected by the rest of the world community and sharply aggravated the situation in the Middle East. The third intifada began, and the Organization of Islamic States officially recognized East Jerusalem as the capital of Palestine on 13th December 2017.

Trump threatened to suspend aid to the Palestinians if they did not establish peace with Israel. But Palestinian President Mahmoud Abbas said that the United States had "taken itself 'off the table'" as a possible mediator.[226] The Palestinians' attempt to reverse the American decision in the UN Security Council came up against a veto by Washington. Edward Luce rightly observed that by removing the final status of the Holy City from the table, Mr. Trump almost guaranteed that the Palestinians would not come to the table. He had also complicated the lives of his Arab friends.[227]

One can scarcely describe the policy in Syria as a success, where the USA was not so much fighting ISIL as helping the internal opposition in their attempts to overthrow Assad. The US air force and American advisers helped in the liberation of Raqqa, but most of the country found itself under the control of government forces, backed by Russia. "By now, hopes of getting rid of Assad or securing a reformed government are far-fetched fantasies, and so support for anti-government factions should be off the table. […] There is, however, one way in which the United States can still do good: easing the suffering of the millions of Syrian refugees outside the country," the former US ambassador to Syria, Robert Ford, reported in late 2017.[228]

---

[225] Recep Tayyip Erdogan, "Erdogan: How Turkey Sees the Crisis with the U.S.", *The New York Times*, August 10, 2018 <https://www.nytimes.com/2018/08/10/opinion/turkey-erdogan-trump-crisis-sanctions.html>.

[226] "Abbas Committed to Serious Negotiations", *Gulf Times*, February 3, 2018 <https://www.gulf-times.com/story/580347/Abbas-committed-to-serious-negotiations>.

[227] Edward Luce, "Donald Trump is Playing with Matches in the Middle East", *The Financial Times*, May 16, 2018 <https://www.ft.com/content/ff2cbeba-5863-11e8-b8b2-d6ceb45fa9d0>.

[228] Robert S. Ford, "Keeping Out of Syria. The Least Bad Option", *Foreign Affairs*, November/December 2017. P. 16.

Trump's unexpected decision in December 2018 to withdraw troops from Syria, which led to resignation of Defence Secretary Jim Mattis, also created serious problems for the main US partner in Syria – the Kurdish-Arab Alliance "Syrian Democratic Forces". To avoid immediate military aggression by Turkey, the SDF was forced to urgently switch to cooperating with the Assad government.[229] John Bolton went to Turkey and Israel to reassure partners: Washington will maintain its presence in the region. One of the main goals was to continue work on the creation of an anti-Iranian coalition, which would include the Gulf countries as well as Israel. Saudi Arabia and Israel share the anti-Iranian phobia. Other regional players would prefer the resumption of normal dialogue between Washington and Tehran, as well as Washington and Damascus.[230]

Trump, who branded Tehran as the main problem of the Middle East and the whole world, once again exacerbated the tensions between Iran and the United States. Iran's support of the Assad regime and several political factions which are regarded as terrorist organizations in the USA (like Hezbollah in Lebanon, the Shia militia in Iraq, Lebanon and Syria, and the Houthi in Yemen), its missile program, and its good relationship with Moscow are a significant source of irritation to Washington. Besides, the American establishment, as well as Israel and the Arab monarchies of Persian Gulf, still strongly believe that Iran is continuing with its nuclear program.

Trump's announcement in October 2017 that the USA might unilaterally quit the Joint Comprehensive Plan of Action (JCPOA) agreement was supported by Israel, Saudi Arabia, Bahrain and the Emirates, but caused consternation in other states, including the USA's European allies, who were concerned that a new crisis could occur in the Middle East and that obstacles might arise that prevented Western business from penetrating the Iranian market.[231] Brussels considered JCPOA to be "the EU's signature foreign-policy achievement", and argued for its preservation.[232] Russia and

---

[229] Varvara Podrugina, "Siriya gotovitsya k peredelu" ("Syria is Preparing for Repartition"), *Vedomosti*, Issue 243, December 25, 2018 <https://vedomosti.profkiosk.ru/article.aspx?aid=696714>.

[230] Marianna Belen'kaya, "SShA uspokaivayut soyuznikov" ("The US Calms its Allies"), *Kommersant (The Businessman)*, Issue 1, January 9, 2019 <https://www.kommersant.ru/doc/3849667>.

[231] Sergey Strokan', "Iranskaya strategiya SShA perekraivayet al'yansy" ("The USA's Iranian Strategy is Remaking the Alliances"), *Kommersant (The Businessman)*, Issue 192, October 16, 2017 <https://www.kommersant.ru/doc/3440332>.

[232] "Splits over the Iran Nuclear Deal are Testing the Transatlantic Bond", *The Economist*,

China opposed the breaking of the deal. Nevertheless, in early May 2018, Trump announced his withdrawal from the JCPOA and offered to start discussing a new deal. The United States put forward 12 conditions for Iran to conclude a new agreement, which was no longer limited to Tehran's refusal to create nuclear weapons, but demanded a revision of their entire foreign policy: an end to their ballistic missile program, the withdrawal of forces from Syria, a cessation of Iranian support for Hezbollah and Hamas. Otherwise, "unprecedented financial pressure" was promised.

Tehran responded with a clear refusal, not seeing the slightest reason for the revoking of the JCPOA. IAEA Director General Yukiya Amano confirmed that Iran was fully complying with its obligations under the nuclear deal.

After the exit from the deal in May 2018, employees of the US State Department and the Treasury visited two dozen countries with unambiguous messages: it is dangerous to do business with Tehran. Over the summer, Brian Hook, who carried an Iranian brief within the State Department, paid a visit to several Asian and European countries, after which a statement was made that more than 50 international corporations intended to curtail their activities in Iran. The French company Total was hardest hit by this, having as it did a large presence in Iranian energy projects.

Europeans tried to show independence. The German foreign Minister Haiko Maas initiated the creation of an independent monetary fund and a system of interbank payments with Iran, which was supported by the EU. On 7th July in Vienna, Iran, Russia, China, Germany, France and the United Kingdom confirmed their readiness to comply with the agreements reached in 2015.[233]

On 6th August, Trump announced a resumption of sanctions against the Iranian car industry, gold trade, and the transfer of dollar assets. The EU recommended to European corporations that they ignore the sanctions and bring claims for damages against the USA. However, Trump's threat to sanction anyone doing business with Iran from doing business with America was taken seriously by European companies.[234]

....
January 27, 2018. P. 25.

[233] Pavel Tarasenko and Yelena Chernenko, "Partneram Irana dali 180 dney na razmyshleniye" ("Iran's Partners Given 180 Days to Think"), *Kommersant* (*The Businessman*), Issue 78, May 10, 2018 <https://www.kommersant.ru/doc/3623837>; Igor' Dunayevskiy, "Sanktsii vmesto strategii" ("Sanctions Instead of Strategy"), *Rossiyskaya Gazeta* (*Russian Newspaper*), Issue 109, May 23, 2018 <https://rg.profkiosk.ru/article.aspx?aid=646853>.

[234] "America and Iran: The Pain of No Deal", *The Economist*, August 11, 2018. P. 29.

On 5th November 2018, sanctions against Iran's energy sector and secondary sanctions against third party companies who continued to cooperate with Tehran were re-imposed. China continued to buy Iranian oil. India, Turkey and Iraq still had hopes of persuading the USA to grant them exemption from the sanctions regime. However, by the end of November, France and Germany took the bold step of creating a payments channel known as a Special Purpose Vehicle, or SPV, and using "a system of credits to facilitate compensation for goods traded between Iran and Europe – allowing some trade to proceed without the need for European commercial banks to make or receive payments to Iran".[235]

The murder and dismemberment in the Saudi Consulate in Istanbul of leading political analyst and columnist for *The Washington Post*, Jamal Khashoggi, has put the West, who were only recently worried about the health of Mr. Skripal, in a rather ticklish position. Although the involvement of the Saudi intelligence agencies in this crime was established beyond doubt, and there is a very high probability that the Crown Prince Mohammed bin Salman was involved, strategic considerations in this case clearly took precedence over morals and ethics. United States opposition insisted on firm action being taken against Riyadh, including sanctions within the global Magnitsky Act.

Trump reminded them that the victim was not a US citizen, and that the incident took place in Turkey. He also frankly declared himself unhappy with the fact that the USA might lose a $110 billion investment from Saudi Arabia to Russia, China or somewhere else.[236] European capitals were quick to let the scandal drop as well. Germany was the only country which responded by halting arms sales to Riyadh.[237] The Saudis will very likely make up the German shortfall from the USA. Middle East experts said the goal for Mr. Trump and the Saudis was clear: get the Saudi role in Mr. Khashoggi's to disappear from the headlines and renew focus on the Iranians.[238]

....

[235] Laurence Norman, "France and Germany Step In to Circumvent Iran Sanctions", *The Wall Street Journal*, November 26, 2018 <https://www.wsj.com/articles/france-and-germany-step-in-to-circumvent-iran-sanctions-1543251650>.

[236] Yevgeniy Shestakov, "Trampa vzyali v 'zalozhniki'" ("Trump Taken Hostage"), *Rossiyskaya Gazeta (Russian Newspaper)*, Issue 231, October 16, 2018 <https://rg.profkiosk.ru/article.aspx?aid=679930>.

[237] Bojan Pancevski and Laurence Norman, "Germany to Halt Arms Sales to Saudi Arabia Over Khashoggi Killing", *The Wall Street Journal*, November 19, 2018 <https://www.wsj.com/articles/germany-to-halt-arms-sales-to-saudi-arabia-over-khashoggi-killing-1542640934>.

[238] David E. Sanger, "Khashoggi Disappearance May Disrupt Trump Administration's Plans to

The rapprochement between the USA and Latin America ended with Trump. At the end of September 2017, his administration decided to call home 60% of its diplomatic staff in Havana due to concerns over their health, in connection with some mysterious "acoustic attacks", and also to stop issuing entry visas to the USA to Cuban citizens. The State Department called on Americans to refrain from travelling to Cuba, an idea that was not supported, incidentally, by the USA's tour operators and airlines companies, who offer increasingly popular tours to the island.[239]

Trump has done significant damage to relations with Mexico. "The Mexicans think we are domineering and imperialist, and we think they are corrupt," an American expert put it, explaining the essence of the dispute.[240] Trump declared NAFTA to be "the worst trade deal in history", and announced that "Mexico is killing us economically". He called Mexican immigrants "criminals" and "rapists", who steal jobs from Americans and pose a threat to their lives. He has spoken in favor of the mass deportation of "criminal aliens" and demanded that the Mexican government pay for the construction of a wall along the USA's southern border.[241]

Hopes that the USA would continue to draw closer to the continent's countries emerged during the crisis in Venezuela, when mass protests against president Maduro started and the opposition won a majority in parliament. After the presidential election organized by Maduro on 30th July 2018, sanctions were introduced against the constitutional judges who recognized them, and against Maduro personally.[242] However, Trump's statement in August about the possibility of using military force against Venezuela alienated the majority of countries of the continent once again. Vice-president Pence was forced to reassure Latin American leaders during his tour of Chile, Panama and Argentina. In 2019 the USA

Squeeze Iran", *The New York Times*, October 16, 2018 <https://www.nytimes.com/2018/10/16/us/politics/khashoggi-trump-iran-sanctions.html>.

[239] Yevgeniy Bay, "Amerika razorvala otnosheniya s kubintsami" ("America has Torn up Its Relations with the Cubans"), *Kommersant (The Businessman)*, October 2, 2017 <https://www.kommersant.ru/doc/3427451>.

[240] Azam Ahmed and Damien Cave, "'El Chapo' Guzmán's Escape in Mexico Adds to Strains with U.S.", *The New York Times*, July 14, 2015 <https://www.nytimes.com/2015/07/15/world/americas/mexico-hunts-joaquin-chapo-guzman-united-states-offer-help.html>.

[241] Shannon O'Neil, "The Mexican Standoff. Trump and the Art of the Workaround", *Foreign Affairs*, September/October 2017. PP. 43-44.

[242] Nicholas Casey, "Trump's Threat against Maduro Unites Latin America, Against U.S.", *The New York Times*, August 16, 2017 <https://www.nytimes.com/2017/08/14/world/americas/trump-venezuela-maduro-latin-america.html>.

continued their efforts to overthrow Maduro, and unprecedently recognized National Assembly interim speaker Juan Guaido as Venezuelan president while at the same time imposing a harsh economic blockade on Venezuela. This ended in political stalemate and brought suffering to the people of Venezuela.

In the first two years of his presidency, Trump has not come up with any major initiatives in relation to Africa. The first visit to Africa was made only in October 2018, and then not by the President himself but by the First lady, Melania Trump, who embarked on a goodwill tour. The proportion of the federal budget directed towards non-military internal aid to Africa has been cut, overall, from 5% in the 1960s to 1%. Grants aimed at supporting development and the fight against AIDS in Africa were the major victims of these cuts. It is obvious that the USA's interest in the developing world and aid programs is decreasing.

The Trump-Russia Affair

In January 2017, during his election campaign, Trump tweeted: "Having a good relationship with Russia is a good thing, not a bad thing. Only 'stupid' people, or fools, would think that it is bad!" He ridiculed the American intelligence agencies over their stories about Russian cyber-attacks, and several times spoke favorably of Putin. In Trump's eyes, unlike many members of his team, Russia was not enemy No. 1.

In America's foreign policy and, unusually, domestic policy, Russia has moved into first position. The Russian theme has become the core of the political battle, and a possible way of commencing an impeachment procedure. "President Trump certainly seems to have a strange case of Russophilia. He has surrounded himself with aides who have Russian ties. Those aides were talking to Russian agents during the campaign, and some are now pushing a dubious peace deal in Ukraine. Trump recently went so far as to equate the United States and Vladimir Putin's murderous regime. [...] [I]t would indeed be a worse scandal than Watergate," famous journalist David Leonhardt wrote.[243] "The Russification of America under Trump has proceeded apace. Vladimir Putin's macho authoritarianism, disdain for the press, and mockery of the truth has installed itself on the Potomac," wrote the equally

---

[243] David Leonhardt, "Trump's Russia Motives", *The New York Times*, February 21, 2017 <https://www.nytimes.com/2017/02/21/opinion/trumps-russia-motives.html>.

well-known Roger Cohen.[244] The rise in Russia's authority – whether with a plus or minus sign – is clear to see.

Moscow, if you listen to what American journalists and politicians are saying, changes American presidents. With a single telephone call from the embassy, it can have anyone of the President's aides fired. It is already clear how you can get rid of any civil servant in the USA: all you need is a call from the embassy or simply from Moscow and the words "sorry, wrong number". All Russians are under suspicion. Perhaps we have not moved so very far from the days of McCarthyism…?

Russia is accused of all the deadly sins and of being to blame for all of America's woes – from interfering in the election and launching an assault on American democracy, to provoking racial unrest in the USA and having aggressive intentions in relation to its Baltic neighbors. According to the former US ambassador to NATO, Ivo H. Daalder, Moscow has turned into "a systematic challenge to the West. The goal is to weaken the bonds between Europe and the United States and among EU members, undermine NATO's solidarity, and strengthen Russia's strategic position in its immediate neighborhood and beyond. Putin wants nothing less than to return Russia to the center of global politics by challenging the primacy that the United States has enjoyed since the end of the Cold War."[245] Pressure is being put on Moscow from every direction. The unprecedented seizure of Russian ambassadorial property prompted retaliatory steps aimed at taking away some of the USA's property in Moscow, and the expulsion of diplomats has proceeded on a scale not seen even during the Cold War.

Although Ukraine is not a central element of Trump's politics and is in many ways a game started by the Obama administration, military aid to that country is increasing. Russian journalists from *RT* and *Sputnik* have been forced to register as foreign agents, and were denied entry to Congress. Measures mirroring these were then taken in Moscow against *Voice of America* and *Radio Freedom*.

The agenda is the narrowest one there has ever been. Rex Tillerson, in his first speech as Secretary of State, said: "Today, there is almost no trust be-

---

[244] Roger Cohen, "The Russification of America", *The New York Times*, February 21, 2017 <https://www.nytimes.com/2017/02/21/opinion/the-russification-of-america.html?searchResultPosition=6>.

[245] Ivo H. Daalder, "Responding to Russia's Resurgence. Not Quiet on the Eastern Front", *Foreign Affairs*, November/December 2017. P. 30.

tween us."²⁴⁶ The meeting between Putin and Trump during the G20 summit in Hamburg in July 2017 did not greatly broaden this agenda, which was kept to the barest agreement on military operations in Syria, contact concerning Ukraine, and an exchange of views on the North Korean problem.

Russian Deputy Foreign Minister Sergey Ryabkov observed: "In an unprecedented manner, using Russia as the bogeyman, using relations with Russia as a tool, as a sledge-hammer with which to smash Trump's presidency to bits, the Democrats have undermined for many years to come the possibility of building rational relations with them. It is regrettable that this is the case. And whoever the President of the USA might be, whoever wins the next election, he or she will be in a situation whereby the law passed by both chambers of Congress will have been brought in, and will feel extremely constrained from the point of view of bringing in a more reasonable policy in relation to Russia."²⁴⁷

Sure enough, the summer package of sanctions in 2017 was notable for its diversity and scale, reflecting a reluctance to cooperate with Russia on any matters whatsoever. Russia is being turned into a "radioactive country", with which it is dangerous to do business without inciting America's wrath. The sanctions include a restriction on the supply of goods, services and technologies for new projects in the extraction of Arctic, deep-water and shale oil; the possibility of bringing in restrictions on investment in the construction of export pipelines with Russian involvement; a reduction of the periods for which loans can be provided to Russian banks; sanctions against individuals who undermine the USA's cyber-security; investigation of the assets and income of Russian politicians, oligarchs and their relatives; and the possibility of personal commercial and financial sanctions against Russian politicians and businessmen.²⁴⁸ These sanctions were extraterritorial in nature – the restrictions applied to companies and citizens of any state.

At the end of October 2017, the special prosecutor Robert Mueller, investigating Russian interference in American domestic policy, made his first accusations – against the former head of Trump's election campaign

---

²⁴⁶ Gardiner Harris, "Tillerson: It's Time to Restore 'Balance' With Other Countries", *The New York Times*, May 4, 2017 <https://www.nytimes.com/2017/05/03/us/rex-tillerson-state-department.html>.

²⁴⁷ Sergey Ryabkov, "SShA s godami vse men'she i men'she sklonny iskat' kompromissy" ("As the years go by, the US is less and less inclined to seek compromises"), *Mezhdunarodnaya zhizn'* (*International Life*), August 31, 2017. P. 8.

²⁴⁸ Alexander Barinov and Arkady Kuznetsov, "Revizory iz Kapitoliya" ("The Auditors from the Capitol"), *Profile*, Issue 29-30, July 30, 2017. PP. 9-10.

team, Paul Manafort, and his business partner Rick Gates – of conspiring against the USA, money-laundering, and tax evasion.[249] Admittedly, it is not clear what this has to do with Russia. The only connection is that Manafort worked for Yanukovych, who was the "pro-Russian" president of Ukraine. The extent of Mr. Yanukovych's pro-Russia orientation has been significantly exaggerated. I would never call him a pro-Russian politician: his political consultants were Americans led by Manafort who, in every possible way, pushed Yanukovych away from Russia. And if this whole story clarified anything, it was the direct and visible intervention of the United States in the internal affairs of Ukraine and the greed of American political consultants.

Russia, which has repeatedly denied any interference in the US election, has no idea how to respond to such accusations. Moreover, Moscow has not received any official documents, requests or evidence from overseas. The tangle – hackers, fake news, Internet trolls, collusion of Trump and the Kremlin, ambassadors-spies – is unlikely to be unraveled in the foreseeable future. In Russia, all of this is perceived as, to put it mildly, complete inadequacy.

Russian assessments of the ongoing deterioration of relations are unambiguous. Here is a fairly typical opinion of Sergey Karaganov: "The losing political elites of the United States and Europe especially hate Trump as a symbol of their defeat. The chances that Trump will be able to overcome this current Russophobia are almost zero. The American and some of the Western elite unilaterally unleashed a 'cold war' against Russia and China… These elites have offset themselves solidly against what is happening in the world – the decline of the power of the United States and its immediate environment. So we're seeing an evil defensive reaction."[250]

In a message to the Federal Assembly on 1st March 2018, Putin spoke about new types of Russian strategic weapons capable of overcoming any conceivable missile defence system. And he addressed Washington: "To those who over the past 15 years have been trying to inflate the arms race, trying to obtain unilateral advantages against Russia, imposing internationally illegal restrictions and sanctions… in order to restrain the

---

[249] Sergey Strokan and Yelena Fedotova, "Donal'du Trampu predyavili obvinyayemykh" ("Donald Trump was Presented with the Accused"), *Kommersant* (*The Businessman*), October 31, 2017 <https://www.kommersant.ru/doc/3454613>.

[250] Sergey Karaganov, "Vidimo, Putin i Tramp o chem-to dogovorilis" ("Apparently, Putin and Trump Have Agreed on Something"), *Rossiyskaya Gazeta* (*Russian Newspaper*), Issue 154, July 17, 2018 <https://rg.ru/2018/07/17/karaganov-pochti-net-shansov-chto-tramp-preodoleet-rusofobiiu-zapadnyh-elit.html>.

development of our country, including in the military field, I will say: 'Everything you have tried to prevent, happened. Containment of Russia failed!'"[251]

Russia has sharply reduced its investment in US public debt, which, in 2013, exceeded $150 billion.[252] Selling American government bonds worth $80 billion in April and May 2018 alone, Russia reduced her portfolio to a mere $14.9 billion.[253]

The first Russian-American summit of the Trump era took place on 16th July 2018, in Helsinki, in the Presidential Palace, which was once the Palace of the Russian Emperor. In September 1990, Gorbachev and Bush Sr. met there. At the press conference, the leaders, in their statements, sounded optimistic. Putin called the talks the first step in "clearing the rubble" in relations between Russia and the United States. Trump asserted that although relations between the countries had never been worse, after the summit the situation had changed. The Russian President voiced proposals for a dialogue on strategic stability, the fight against terrorism, cyber security and the creation of high-level groups for dialogue on economic issues and bilateral relations.

However the American establishment and journalists were not impressed. They were hoping for revelations concerning a criminal association between Russia and Trump's election campaign. Putin dismissed all speculation about Russian intervention, although he did not hide the fact that during the election he was personally sympathetic to Trump. And here, Trump replied that he had no reason not to believe Putin. This ran against many reports of American intelligence about such interference.[254]

In the traditional diplomatic system of coordinates, the results of the summit could be assessed as moderately successful: the prolonged pause in formal contact between the leaders of the two countries was interrupted. The reaction of all world capitals – except Ottawa – was moderately positive. However, in the US the reaction turned out to be disastrous for Trump. The head of the American state, together with a foreign leader who is accused

---

[251] *Poslaniye Prezidenta Rossiyskoy Federatsii Federal'nomu Sobraniyu* (*Message from the President of the Russian Federation to the Federal Assembly*). Moscow, 2018. P. 66.

[252] Tat'yana Lomskaya, "Rossiya otdayet dolg SShA" ("Russia Pays off the US Debt"), *Vedomosti*, Issue 131, July 19, 2018 <https://vedomosti.profkiosk.ru/article.aspx?aid=660515>.

[253] Ibid.

[254] Kira Latukhina, "Myach v igre" ("The Ball is in Play"), *Rossiyskaya Gazeta* (*Russian Newspaper*), July 16, 2018 <https://rg.ru/2018/07/16/kak-proshla-vstrecha-vladimira-putina-i-donalda-trampa-v-helsinki.html>.

of plotting against America, had confronted his own intelligence services. Trump was met with a real tsunami of accusations, including weakness and incompetence – the most innocent, and more often – treason.[255]

This was followed by a statement by Washington on its withdrawal from the INF Treaty. Since at least 2011, Russia and the United States had exchanged accusations of violation at different levels. The claims of Washington concerned the development of a new cruise missile, the 9M729. Moscow claimed that the missile had never been tested for a range prohibited by the Treaty. Counter-claims made by Russia concerned the Mk41 units in Poland and Romania, which are capable of launching not only anti-missiles, but also offensive cruise missiles; the use – as targets to test missile defences – of systems that fall under the definition of medium-range ballistic missiles; and the use of the long-range attack drones Predator and Raptor. On 21st October 2018, Trump announced that the USA had quit INF Treaty.

The first reaction on this issue seemed to leave the United States in diplomatic isolation. The EU called for the preservation of the Treaty. Subsequently, though, the US's European allies, within the framework of Euro-Atlantic solidarity, sharply changed their positions, allowing themselves to be persuaded that the culprit of the destruction of the Treaty was Russia.

How did Moscow retaliate? Putin replied: "Simple: we will do the same. Let me remind you that this year, before the US Congress announced the US withdrawal from this Treaty, it allocated money for R&D to create these missiles. That is, the decision was made long ago, but was kept quiet. […] Russia is not the one to blame. We are against the destruction of this Treaty. But if this happens, we will respond accordingly."[256]

More and more often we hear a talk about a new cold war, about the destruction of what is left of arms control. Yes, the cold war was resumed – by the West, and, in my opinion, in more dangerous and irreversible forms than in the past. According to Aleksey Pushkov, "The Western alliance is waging this war against Russia. They can't stop the restoration of Russia's position as a great power by political means, so they try to do it by means of economic war. The Western alliance is more and more resorting to military pressure as well. The presence of American and NATO armed forces in the Baltic republics, in the Baltic sea, the deployment of military bases and

---

[255] Brian Bennett, "A Crisis of His Own Making", *Time*, July 30, 2018. PP. 24-27.

[256] "Otvety na voprosy zhurnalistov 5 dekabrya 2018 goda" (Answers to journalists' questions on December 5, 2018), Prezidentskaya biblioteka (Presidential Library) <https://www.prlib.ru/item/1181226>.

ABM bases in Eastern Europe, can be regarded as instruments of military pressure on Russia. For the foreseeable future, there is no reason to believe that the US and NATO will abandon this policy; on the contrary, it may well be further strengthened."[257]

At present, rapprochement between Moscow and Washington is hardly to be expected. In the foreseeable future, even the most favorable deal between the US and Russia is impossible, because it will be perceived by the American establishment and the public opinion as a surrender to "Putin's authoritarian regime". Washington is not ready for any arrangement with the Russian side, other than the unconditional surrender of Moscow.[258] But surrender is definitely not on the Russian agenda.

It is now evident that Russia is of increased significance in US politics. A liberal journalist, Maxim Trudolyubov of *Vedomosti*, rightly noticed that in the past, for the majority of Americans, "Russia did not exist as a political issue; and if she was mentioned during election campaigns, then it was in negative sense… A simple political logic dictated: either bad or nothing about Russia. Today Russia, or more precisely a certain image of Russia, has found itself at the center of political discussion. Now it's either bad or good about Russia. The Russian theme is one out of two or three issues which determine one's place in today's political confrontations."[259]

The Dollar Economy

The USA is an economic super-power, even if we assume that China has already overtaken the US in GDP. The American economic model is characterized by a relatively low degree of involvement, by the government, in the economy. The level of taxation and government revenues in the USA is lower than in Europe, and stands at roughly 30% of GDP, whereas in many European states it is 45-50%. This is one of the reasons for the high level of private consumption in the USA.

The level of government spending in the USA is also fairly low – roughly 35% of GDP (admittedly, it rose to 43% of GDP during the recession). In

---

[257] Aleksey Pushkov, "The Global'nyye Shahmaty. Russkaya partiya"("The Global Chess Game. Russian Perspective"). Moscow, 2018. P. 339.

[258] Strategy. Issue 4, 2018. P. 21.

[259] Maxim Trudolyubov, "Novyy konservatizm" ("New Conservatism"), *Vedomosti*, Issue 137, July 27, 2018 <https://vedomosti.profkiosk.ru/article.aspx?aid=662364>.

the structure of expenditures, defence costs are traditionally high, up to 6% of GDP, which is three times higher than in the EU. Spending on social welfare, healthcare and education, by contrast, is lower – 15% in the USA and 30% in the EU countries. The largest ring-fenced components in the budget are the four key programs: Social Security, pensions and benefits to widows, orphans and the disabled; Medicaid, which provides medical services to the needy; Medicare, which finances healthcare services for pensioners and the disabled; and Welfare. In total, 56% of federal spending went to these ring-fenced components, only 38% to others, while 6% went on interest payments.

From 1948 through to 2000, America's GDP per head rose by 2.3% a year, on average. In this century, the rate of growth has fallen to 1%. From 1985 through to 2000, the total number of paid hours of work in the USA rose by 35%, and over the following 15 years to 2015 by just 4%. Geographical mobility has fallen considerably: the number of Americans who cross the borders of their state has halved by comparison with 1960. Entrepreneurial activity is slowing down: the proportion of Americans aged 30 and under who have their own business has fallen by 65% since the 1980s. In 1983, 69% of 17-year-olds had a driver's license, whereas now only half of Americans obtain a license by the age of 18.[260]

America, once the land of unlimited opportunity, has now seen a significant fall in social mobility across all statistical indicators. "A child born in the bottom quintile of incomes in the United States has only a 4 percent chance of rising to the top quintile, according to a Pew study. A separate study found that in Britain, such a boy has about a 12 percent chance. [...] [S]ocial mobility is twice as great for Canada as for the United States."[261]

Since 1979, the income of the richest 1% of Americans has risen by 138%, while that of the remaining 90% by only 15%. From 2002 through to 2013, only two categories of households – the families of college graduates and young people under 30 – have not faced a fall in their real-terms salary. Meanwhile, for more than a quarter of a century, growth in the cost of housing, education and healthcare has outstripped inflation.[262] Average income

....

[260] David Brooks, "This Century Is Broken", *The New York Times*, February 21, 2017 <https://www.nytimes.com/2017/02/21/opinion/this-century-is-broken.html>.

[261] Nicholas Kristof, "U.S.A., Land of Limitations?", *The New York Times*, August 8, 2015 <https://www.nytimes.com/2015/08/09/opinion/sunday/nicholas-kristof-usa-land-of-limitations.html>.

[262] Michael Scherer, "Up With People", *Time*, July 20, 2015. P. 30.

only reached pre-recession levels at the end of 2015, and it is still lower than at the start of the century. Almost half of Americans describe themselves as "lower class", whereas in the early 2000s only a third did so.[263] In 2016, *The Atlantic* conducted a survey of Americans, asking them how they would cover an unforeseen expense of 400 dollars. 47% of the respondents said that they would need to take out a loan or sell something in order to do so.[264]

In 1970, a third of those in employment worked in an industry concentrated mainly in the Midwest; by 2010, only one in ten people were doing so.[265] Due to the movement of industrial enterprises to other countries, the USA lost 5.6 million jobs in 10 years, and its share of global industrial production fell from 27% to 19%, whereas China's rose from 7% to 19.7%. Hi-tech manufacturing is concentrated inside the country – for the aerospace, medical, military, telecommunications, computing and pharmaceuticals sectors.

In recent years, however, America's growth has been secured to a considerable extent by three factors. First: America has been on an "oil needle", something that we in Russia have been trying to avoid for many years. The highest growth has been seen in traditional sectors of the economy and in states which produce oil and gas. American analysts have noted that "the big winners in the current economy are the 'Material Boys' – the people who grow grain, drill for fuel and lay pipeline."[266]

One cannot but mention the shale revolution. The development of shale technologies enabled the USA to become the biggest gas-producing country in the world as early as 2013, and in the first half of 2014 to become the world's leading extractor of oil. Falling oil prices had a dual effect on the American economy. On the one hand, cheaper fuel revived entrepreneurial and consumer activities. On the other, the drilling of new shale gas boreholes went into decline, because shale gas production was becoming un-

---

[263] Edward Luce, "Electorates' Sharp Right Turn is Symptomatic: When West Isn't Best", *The Financial Times*, May 12, 2017 <https://www.ft.com/content/995426de-340e-11e7-99bd-13beb0903fa3>.

[264] Andrey Shitov, "Pochemu Tramp 'na kone'?" ("Why is Trump 'Sitting Pretty'?"), *Rossiyskaya Gazeta (Russian Newspaper)*, April 27, 2016 <https://rg.ru/2016/04/25/pochti-polovine-amerikancev-nechego-otkladyvat-na-chernyj-den.html>.

[265] "America's Industrial Heartland. Reinvention of the Rust Belt", *The Economist*, July 11, 2015. P. 35.

[266] David Brooks, "Revolution of the Axis of Ennui", *The International Herald Tribune*, March 13, 2013. P. 6.

profitable.²⁶⁷ Ten years ago the USA imported nearly two thirds of oil they consumed; nowadays that figure is only one fifth. The country has become the biggest exporter of ready fuel; it began exporting oil and gas in 2016, and became a net exporter of energy in 2019.²⁶⁸

The USA is the second-largest exporter in the world (behind China). Energy supplies lead the way when it comes to the growth rates of American exports – petrol, kerosene, diesel fuel and coal have a growth rate of 114% in 2013-2014, followed by oil and gas show a growth rate of 68.3%. On average, commodities export increased by 32.7%. By contrast, America's share in the global export of manufactured goods fell from 19% to 11% (while the European Union's share decreased from 22% to 20% and at the same time China's share increased from 7% to 21%).

The second growth factor is information technologies, which has enabled American IT companies to rise to the top by reference to market capitalization. One of the USA's competitive advantages is its leadership in science and technology. The USA accounted for one third of global spending on scientific research.

The third factor in America's economic growth was "quantitative easing". The USA has increased the amount of money in circulation: the Federal Reserve System actively bought up the government's debt securities and held the interest rate at the lowest possible level.

The most powerful tool in the US economy is the dollar, which for almost 90 years has been the primary, and for 70 years the near-monopolistic means of payment, and instrument for saving and lending. The exchange rate for the dollar does not cause the FRS much concern when it conducts monetary policy. The dollar can be used as payment in all corners of the world. It is used to pay for goods exported from the US. A good American product, which produces nigh on the largest pure profit, is paper dollars (they cost the Treasury no more than the price of the paper and the printing), 60% of which are in circulation outside the United States. There would be even more of them, if it were not for the 500 Euro note, which is more popular among drug dealers, smugglers and other international criminals.²⁶⁹ In 2010, the dollar's share in international transactions stood at 86%; in international

---

[267] "The New Oil Order", *The Wall Street Journal*, December 1, 2014. P. 12.

[268] Meghan L. O'Sullivan, "Harness the Energy Boom", *The New York Times*, September 15, 2017 <https://www.nytimes.com/20 How Trump Can Harness the U.S. Energy Boom17/09/15/opinion/trump-energy-boom.html>.

[269] *The Power of Currencies and Currencies of Power*, ed. by Alan Wheatley. L., 2013. P. 30.

reserves – 64%; in foreign banknotes in circulation abroad – 65%; in preserved debt liabilities – 46%.²⁷⁰ At the same time, the appearance of the Euro meant that the dollar's relative position declined, and growing interest in the Yuan is also contributing to this process.

From the 1980s onwards, the USA has been consuming more than it produces, thereby running up increasing debt. US state debt is enormous. Over the last 20 years, it has increased from $5.1 trillion to $22.5 trillion. In 2017, the cost of servicing interest on public debt amounted to $263 billion, – 6.6% of all government spending and 1.4% of GDP. In 2018 the national debt grew, along with interest rates and inflation, and the cost of servicing it increased by 20%. According to the forecast of the Budget Office of the Congress, by 2028 interest payments will increase to 915 billion dollars, which will be 13% of all expenses and 3.1% of GDP. In 2020, the national debt will grow from the current 78% of GDP to 96.2%.²⁷¹

However, the benefits of the global role of the dollar helped to cover the shortfall of the budget, through the issue of Treasury bonds, without risk to the stability of the U.S. financial system. Moreover, in terms of monetary assets, the stock market is much larger that the banking sector. Ordinary citizens, American financial institutions, foreign central banks, and companies constantly consume U.S. Treasury bonds, which are regarded as low-risk assets necessary for any investment portfolio. Remarkably, the day never comes when these debts have to be paid off. With the lack of other attractive investment instruments, demand for Treasury bonds stays high, and it is permitted to exchange matured bonds for new ones.

The USA are still ahead of other countries in terms of market capitalization. They account for more than 40% of the global financial market. 10% of all stock market assets are concentrated in the hands of 5 companies – Apple, Google, Microsoft, Amazon and Facebook. The American economy is still weakly globalized – the export of goods and services accounts for 14% of GDP, whereas in the EU it accounts for 26%.²⁷²

The USA is experiencing intensive processes of capital and property concentration. Mergers and acquisitions have doubled since the 1990s.

....

[270] *Reserve Accumulation and International Monetary Stability*. International Monetary Fund, April 13, 2010. P. 8 <https://www.imf.org/external/np/pp/eng/2010/041310.pdf>.

[271] Kate Davidson and Daniel Kruger, "U.S. on a Course to Spend More on Debt than Defense", *The Wall Street Journal*, November 11, 2018 <https://www.wsj.com/articles/u-s-on-a-course-to-spend-more-on-debt-than-defense-1541937600>.

[272] "Growth in America. Careful Now", *The Economist*, April 11, 2015. PP. 65-66.

The share of GDP generated by the 100 largest companies has increased from 33% in 1994 to nearly 50%. The five biggest banks own 45% of bank assets, while in 2000 their share was only 25%. The number of start-ups has dropped to its lowest since the 1970s; every day more companies cease to exist than those being newly established. Heads of small companies dream of selling their businesses to giant corporations, but not of growing into a giant themselves.

About 30% of foreign investments come from "offshores" locations. Large companies widely use "transfer pricing" in order to disguise the geography of profits. Giant corporations hire armies of lobbyists using the same technologies which they perfected in Washington in Brussels, where 30,000 lobbyists swarm the corridors.[273] The high profits of large corporations do not mean that they create many jobs. The IT companies have rather few employees.

A serious source of concern for the American elite is the degradation of infrastructure. "While China is building new airports and highways, and Europe, Japan, and now China possess advanced high-speed rails, America's equivalents are sliding back into the twentieth century," noted Zbigniew Brzezinski. "China alone has bullet trains on almost 5,000 kilometers of rails, while the United States has none. Beijing and Shanghai airports are decades ahead in efficiency as well as elegance of their equivalents in Washington and in New York, both of which increasingly smack embarrassingly of the third world."[274]

The American Society of Civil Engineers estimates that a quarter of all the bridges in the USA are not used or are out of service. A report from the American Road & Transportation Builders Association in January 2018 reckoned that 54,259 of the country's 612,677 bridges were "structurally deficient". These problem bridges had an average age of 67 years and were crossed by 174 million vehicles every day.[275] The federal excise duty on petrol, 18.4 cents per gallon, which is the main source of funds for the development of infrastructure, has not increased since 1993, and in real terms has fallen by 40%. The USA spends 2% of its GDP on infrastructure, whereas the EU countries

---

[273] Ian Traynor, "30,000 Lobbyists and Counting: is Brussels under Corporate Sway?", *The Guardian*, May 8, 2014 <https://www.theguardian.com/world/2014/may/08/lobbyists-european-parliament-brussels-corporate#:~:text=According%20to%20Corporate%20Europe%20Observatory,those%20seeking%20to%20affect%20legislation>.

[274] Zbigniew Brzezinski, *Strategic Vision: America and the Crisis of Global Power*. Basic Books, 2013. P. 51.

[275] "Construction Technology. A Bridge Too Far", *The Economist*, August 18, 2018. P. 63.

spend 5%.²⁷⁶ The United States, which once had the best infrastructure in the world, is now 16th in the World Economic Forum's infrastructure ratings.²⁷⁷

The United States has a significant demographic dividend, thanks largely to its immigrants. Though, in recent years, the rate of population growth has fallen due to unemployment in colored families, and to young people deciding to postpone getting married or having a child. Today, the fertility rate in the USA stands at 1.9, which is less than in France or the UK.²⁷⁸ The family institution is going through serious changes. 46% of children under the age of 18 live at home with heterosexual parents in a first marriage. In 1960, this figure stood at 73%.²⁷⁹

In the education system, some things are far from perfect. In terms of the level of secondary education, the United States is not even in the top twenty most successful countries, and is behind Poland and Estonia. In the PISA rankings for mathematical ability among 15 year-olds, the United States came only 36th out of 69 nations.²⁸⁰ When it comes to higher education, however, America is still the outright leader. Fareed Zakaria writes that higher education is "America's best industry. […] In no other field is the America's advantage so overwhelming".²⁸¹ In fact, American universities dominate the top positions of all the world ratings. However, we also have to take into consideration the fact that either the rating systems themselves or the assessment criteria are worked out in the USA. 7% of GDP is spent on education, and the proportion of people with a degree among the workforce is 30%, while the average number of years that an American spends in education is around 13.²⁸²

The USA is the absolute leader in terms of aggregate spending on healthcare (around 18% of GDP, as compared with 11% on average among the OECD countries). Only 29% of Americans, however, are covered by com-

....

²⁷⁶ For details see: Henry Petroski, *The Road Taken: The History and Future of American Infrastructure*. N.Y., 2016.

²⁷⁷ Francis Fukuyama, "Too Much Law and Too Little Infrastructure", *American Interest*, January/February 2017. P. 31.

²⁷⁸ "Virility Symbols", *The Economist*, August 11, 2012. P. 34.

²⁷⁹ Kareem Abdul-Jabbar, "Politically Incorrect? Or Master Strategists? Try Both", *Time*, September 12-19, 2016. P. 22.

²⁸⁰ "Education. Can't Be Asked", *The Economist*, August 19, 2017. P. 29.

²⁸¹ Fareed Zakaria, *The Post-American World*. W. W. Norton & Company, 2008. P. 190.

²⁸² Viktor Supyan, "SShA v mirovoy tabeli o rangakh: ekonomicheskiye pokazateli" ("The USA in the Global Table of Ranks: Economic Indicators"), *Mezhdunarodnaya zhizn'* (*International Life*), Issue 8, August 2013. P. 142.

pulsory medical insurance, and this is the lowest figure among all the OECD countries, while 16.7% of the US population do not have any medical insurance (the figure is 46% among those who do not have citizenship).

While acknowledging the socio-economic problems in the US, one should also underline that the US economy still accounts for roughly one-fifth of global GDP, and that consumption by American citizens alone accounts for 15% of the planet's GDP. The real (applied) scientific and technical progress in the world is in many ways focused in the United States.

The Empire of Lawyers and Lobbyists

The theme of the paralysis of the American political system has become something that crops up again and again in the works of analysts. Niall Ferguson maintains: "Americans could once boast proudly that their system set the benchmark for the world; the United States *was* the rule of law. But now what we see is the rule of *lawyers*, which is something different." The USA, in his opinion, is behind the rest of the world in such aspects as the efficiency of the political system, the clarity of laws, the sufficiency of regulation, the effectiveness of the legal system, and flexibility in the firing and hiring of personnel.[283]

The legislative and the judiciary branches still have the most important part to play, to the detriment of the executive, and this renders the decision-making process on any serious issue a long-drawn-out battle that has a paralyzing effect on those in power, according to Fukuyama. "conflicts that in Sweden or Japan would be solved through quiet consultations between interested parties in the bureaucracy are fought out through formal litigation in the U.S. court system. […] In the United States, by contrast, policy is made piecemeal in a highly specialized and therefore non-transparent process by judges who are unelected and usually serve with lifetime tenure."[284]

As Fukuyama puts it, the role of interest groups and lobbyists remains high and is still growing, and this "has distorted democratic processes and eroded the ability of the government to operate effectively". Hardly any corporation pays taxes at established rates, because almost all the major

---

[283] Niall Ferguson, *The Great Degeneration. How Institutions Decay and Economies Die*. L., 2012. PP. 108-100.

[284] Francis Fukuyama, "The Decay of American Political Institutions", *The American Interest*, January/February, Vol. 9, Issue 3, 2014 <https://www.the-american-interest.com/2013/12/08/the-decay-of-american-political-institutions/>.

firms have secured, through the lobbyists, various loopholes and exemptions. The state has become enormous, but the least efficient among all the democracies. "At a time of sharp political polarization, this decentralized system is less and less able to represent majority interests, but gives excessive representation to the views of interest groups and activist organizations that collectively do not add up to a sovereign American people."[285]

National security aside, the executive branch of federal government is fairly transparent. However, most of the government's work is outsourced to subcontractors, on whom, unlike the government, no demands for transparency are placed.[286]

Fukuyama also notes that by comparison with other parliamentary systems, the US Constitution is unique insofar as it divides and duplicates power, creating a large number of in-built "veto players". "These veto players include a separately elected President with equal democratic legitimacy to Congress; a powerful upper house of Congress whose approval is needed on virtually all legislation; an independent judiciary that can overturn legislative acts; and a complex Federal system that allocates powers to state and local governments. Most parliamentary systems have far fewer veto players, and are therefore able to pass legislation more easily. […]

The U.S. system has all but ground to a halt as a result of two phenomena occurring in the broader society. The first is the rise of polarization, both in the way that Americans live and interact, and in their representative institutions, where there is virtually no ideological overlap between Republicans and Democrats today. The second has to do with the rise of a large number of well-resourced and professionally organized interest groups, representing everything from corporations to unions to social movements to victims of individual diseases."[287]

Polarization is forcing politicians and their supporters to look on their adversaries as illegitimate, and at times even as an existential threat.[288] Over the last 20 years, the media have become increasingly polarized. "The rise

....

[285] Ibid.

[286] Francis Fukuyama, "Why Transparency Can Be a Dirty Word", *The Financial Times*, August 9, 2015 <https://www.ft.com/content/1d78c194-2c8d-11e5-acfb-cbd2e1c81cca>.

[287] Francis Fukuyama, "Too Much Law and Too Little Infrastructure", *American Interest*, January/February 2017 <https://www.the-american-interest.com/2016/11/08/too-much-law-and-too-little-infrastructure/>.

[288] Robert Mickey, Steven Levitsky, and Lucan Ahmad Way, "Is America Still Safe for Democracy? Why the United States Is in Danger of Backsliding", *Foreign Affairs*, May/June 2017. P. 24.

of Fox News kicked off the era of partisan news channels. The Internet, meanwhile, has made it easier for people to seek out news that confirms their existing beliefs and has played a role in the widespread closure of local and regional newspapers. Today, Democrats and Republicans consume news from starkly different sources [...]. As polarization increases, Congress passes fewer and fewer laws and leaves important issues unresolved. Such dysfunction has eroded public trust in political institutions, and along partisan lines."[289] Almost 60% of Americans believe that the country is suffering from an excess of political correctness, while only 18% think that there is not enough of it.

The degree of regulation of various aspects of life is off the charts, and Trump has a point fighting with that. I have never had to fill in as many forms as I did when commencing a temporary job at the California Institute of Technology, not even in the Administration of the President of the USSR. The tax code, if one includes all the regulations, contains 73,000 pages. The number of regulatory acts from federal, state and local governments is too big to count. In a study of competitiveness conducted by the World Economic Forum, the USA was in 76th place in terms of the "burden of government regulation".

One in six Americans considers military rule acceptable, whereas in 1995 only one in sixteen people felt that way. A democratic order was seen as an essential by 70% of Americans born in the 1930s, but by only 30% of those born in the 1980s.[290]

What Happened to the Melting Pot

Throughout its history, the United States has been a model of a "melting pot", to which people from various countries and cultures were able to relocate successfully, merging into a single American nation. Since the end of the 20th century, however, there has been talk of "cultural and political fragmentation", of an "erosion of national identity". According to Huntington, this has had four consequences: "[T]he popularity of the doctrines of multiculturalism and diversity among some elite elements, and special interests that elevated racial, ethnic, gender, and other subnational identities over national identity; the weakness or absence of the factors that previously promoted

....

[289] Ibid. PP. 26-27.

[290] Gideon Rachman, "The Authoritarian Wave Reaches the West", *The Financial Times*, February 20, 2017 <https://www.ft.com/content/6b57d7ae-f74a-11e6-bd4e-68d53499ed71>.

immigrant assimilation combined with the increased tendency of immigrants to maintain dual identities, loyalties, and citizenships; the dominance among immigrants of speakers, largely Mexican, of a single non-English language (a phenomenon without precedent in American history), with the resulting tendencies toward Hispanicization and the transformation of America into a bilingual, bicultural society; the denationalization of important segments of the America's elite, with a growing gap between their cosmopolitan and transnational commitments and the still highly nationalist and patriotic values of the American public."[291]

Inequality along racial lines is growing. The income of the average black family has fallen from 64% to 58% of that of the average white family since 2000 (for an Afro-American family it stands at $33,000 a year, and for a white family $55,000). In terms of accumulated wealth, Afro-American families on average owned 11 times less than white families in 2005, and in 2009, after the mortgage bubble burst, 20 times less. The alarm was sounded back in the 1960s about the fact that 25% of black children were being born outside of wedlock. Today, that figure stands at 72% (for white children it is 29%), and it is almost always a case of the mother being single. Schools for Afro-Americans are under-financed, and the average 17-year-old pupil from a black family has the same reading age and arithmetic skills as a 13-year-old white pupil. 45% of whites aged 18 to 24 go to college, compared with 36% of blacks. Unemployment among Afro-Americans stands at 15%, significantly higher than among whites.

The law enforcement system discriminates against black people. By the age of 30-34, one in ten Afro-Americans has been behind bars (37% of the entire prison population), and among whites, the figure is one in 61.[292] "America has changed significantly since the Civil Rights Act," asserts John Skrentny, a sociologist from the University of California. "But we are still a long way from the day when race no longer plays a role in society."[293]

There are now more than 50 million Spanish-speaking people in the USA, more than the population of Spain itself. The TV network Univision, which broadcasts content in Spanish, is competing with the major American TV companies. Meanwhile, the English language has been protected with the status of the official language in 20 states, and Trump's idea of

....

[291] Samuel Huntington, *Who Are We? The Challenges to American National Identity*. Simon and Schuster, 2004. P. 138.
[292] "Chasing the Dream", *The Economist*, August 24, 2013. P. 10.
[293] John D. Skrentny, "Only Minorities Need Apply", *The New York Times*, May 7, 2014. P. 25.

building a wall on the border with Mexico has serious support in some parts of society.²⁹⁴

America's indigenous people are rarely mentioned. Today, there are around 6 million Native Americans, fewer than there were at the time the USA was founded. This is 1.6% of the population. They are confronted with the whole spectrum of discrimination – from pennilessness and rape, to the disappearance of their languages and traditions. One in four Native Americans is living in poverty. Only 36% of men have a permanent job. Native American women are raped 3.5 times more often than other American women. One in ten Native Americans over the age of 12 are victims of violence every year. They are killed by the police twice as often, and their chances of ending up in prison are three times higher. The suicide rate among Native Americans is 2.5 times higher than the average for America, and Native Americans are six times more likely to contract tuberculosis. The government refuses to grant the status of indigenous people to many tribes. According to UNESCO, 130 languages spoken by Native Americans are under threat of disappearing, with the threat deemed to be critical in 74 cases.

In comparison with the 1980s, the number of immigrants from Africa has increased 10-fold, and accounts for 14% of the total number of immigrants. Interestingly, among African immigrants – mostly Ethiopians and Eritreans – 35% have a bachelor's degree, whereas in the United States this rate is 30%, and among the blacks born in America 19%.²⁹⁵

The number of Americans born overseas has risen from 5% in 1970 to 14%. The problem of illegal immigration is a pressing one. 65% of white Americans said that they would support a party that would engage with "stopping mass immigration, providing American jobs to American workers, preserving America's Christian heritage and stopping the threat of Islam" (phrases modelled on the manifesto of the British National Party).²⁹⁶ The problems of white America have also come to the fore.

"A stunning U-turn in the fortunes of poor and working-class whites began in the 1970s, as deindustrialization, automation, globalization, and the growth of the high-technology and service sectors transformed the U.S. economy. In the decades since, many blue-collar jobs have vanished, wages

---

²⁹⁴ Simon Romero, "Spanish Finds Fertile Soil in the U.S.", *The New York Times*, International Edition, August 18, 2017. P. 1.

²⁹⁵ "Building Afromerica", *The Economist*, July 11, 2015. P. 37.

²⁹⁶ Fareed Zakaria, "Populism on the March. Why the West Is in Trouble", *Foreign Affairs*, November/December 2016. PP. 15, 10.

have stagnated for less educated Americans, wealth has accumulated at the top of the economic food chain, and social mobility has become vastly harder to achieve." The winners from these changes have been the big urban centers on the coast, while the once industrial South and Midwest proved to be the losers. Ultimately, three times more Hispanic people than whites in America believe in a better future. Poor African Americans are three times more optimistic in their outlook than poor white people.[297]

America has ceased to be a land of white Christians: the proportion of them in the population has fallen from 54% in 2008 to 43% in 2017. White Evangelists who believe in the teachings of the Bible make up one fifth of the American population, mainly in the South. They genuinely saw Bill and Hillary Clinton as "the Antichrist", and viewed the Supreme Court's decision to legalize same-sex marriages as the embodiment of sin.[298] Many white Southerners believe that black people, immigrants, women's rights activists and gays are taking the American dream away from them. They are aware of the scornful attitude that those in the north have of them. They see themselves as the main victims of the fall in wages and the stagnation in industry. They think of themselves as proud people in a world where the traditional sources of their pride – faith, independence and loyalty – are ceasing to be valued. Trump offered them some meaning in life.[299]

Ethnic and cultural polarization is unprecedented. "The current term of art among black intellectuals is *white privilege* and the current concern is police brutality. Among Latinos, the concern is bigotry and violence inflicted by gringo yahoos. Meanwhile, working-class whites are convinced that immigrants are taking their jobs and that blacks have long been coddled by public assistance."[300]

Robert Jones, of the Public Religion Research Institute, writes: "The recent survey data provides troubling evidence that a shared sense of national identity is unraveling, with two mutually exclusive narratives emerging along party lines. At the heart of this divide are opposing reactions to changing demographics and culture. The shock waves from these

---

[297] Jefferson Cowie, "The Great White Nope. Poor, Working Class, and Left Behind in America", *Foreign Affairs*, November/December 2016. P. 147.

[298] For details see: Frances FitzGerald, *The Evangelicals: The Struggle to Shape America*. Simon & Schuster, 2017. P. 435.

[299] Arlie Russell Hochschild, *Strangers in Their Own Land: Anger and Mourning on the American Right*. N.Y., 2016. PP. 221-230.

[300] Joe Klein, "Don't Believe the New Myths About America's White Working Class", *Time*, September 12-19, 2016. P. 24.

transformations – harnessed effectively by Donald Trump's campaign – are reorienting the political parties from the more familiar liberal-versus-conservative alignment to new poles of cultural pluralism and monism."[301]

66% of Democrats believe that the mingling of various cultures and values is very important for American identity, while among Republicans, the figure is only 35%. 64% of Republicans consider the Christian religion important for their identity, while only 32% of Democrats share the same view. The vast majority of Democrats believe that minorities – Afro-Americans, immigrants, Muslims and homosexuals – face discrimination in the USA, whereas only 27% of Republicans have the same view. 48% of Republicans and 20% of Democrats believe that whites and Christians are discriminated against. In the Democratic Party's electorate, only 29% are white Christians, while three quarters of the Republican Party's electorate are white Christians. There is one thing that the two parties agree on: roughly 70% of both Democrats and Republicans believe that America is losing its identity.[302]

In the 1950s, 72% of Americans did not care whether their daughter married a Republican or a Democrat, while in 2016 this figure fell to 45%.[303] Economic status is by no means as sure a way of explaining electoral behavior as are voters' views on such moral and ethical issues as abortions or same-sex marriages.[304]

In August 2017, in Charlottesville, Virginia, a protest march was held by southerners who were fans of the Confederacy against the removal of a statue of one of their cult heroes – the southern general Robert Lee. The march, during which racist and Nazi slogans were heard, was universally condemned. Trump, however, in his first statement, called for restraint, condemning both those who were taking down statues, and those who were sowing hatred and racism. According to one of the polls conducted, 68% of Republicans shared the view that both sides were to blame for the disorder. For the liberals and democrats, however, the fact that the President adopted such a position was a clear manifestation of racism.[305] A couple of days later

---

[301] Robert P. Jones, "The Collapse of American Identity", *The New York Times*, May 2, 2017 <https://www.nytimes.com/2017/05/02/opinion/the-collapse-of-american-identity.html>.

[302] Ibid.

[303] Suzanne Mettler, "Democracy on the Brink. Protecting the Republic in Trump's America", *Foreign Affairs*, May/June 2017. P. 122.

[304] Fareed Zakaria, "Populism on the March. Why the West Is in Trouble", *Foreign Affairs*, November/December 2016. PP. 15, 10.

[305] Gideon Rachman, "Steve Bannon's Ideas will Survive and Thrive in the White House", *The Financial Times*, August 21, 2017 <https://www.ft.com/content/f6cf2e64-864b-11e7-bf50-

he tried to back-track, describing racism as an "evil", and strongly condemning "the KKK, neo-Nazis, white supremacists and other hate groups that are repugnant to everything we hold dear as Americans."[306] But it was too late. The liberal media went on the attack against Trump the racist. The President, in turn, poured vitriol on the "fake news", accusing it of provoking internal divisions.[307]

The liberal media were flooded by publications stressing the need to remove the 1500 statues of Confederate figures who were white supremacists. Journalists argued that the monuments were constructed in 1890s when the history of the Civil War was rewritten and racist practices were restored and Jim Crow laws were being adopted, and in the 1950s during a period of mass Southern resistance to the civil rights movement. Trump assumed that Washington and Jefferson monuments might be next to be dismantled. Why not? They were prominent slave-owners after all.[308]

Those who advocated preserving the statues and tombs claimed that the South had fought the war in order to preserve a "legacy", not slavery; but the memorials to the confederates have already begun to be taken down throughout the country. People then began taking the heads of statues of Columbus, who is accused of having had a racist approach to indigenous Americans. Next came the turn of the national symbols. In September 2017, in Cleveland, eight black players demonstratively "took a knee" before an NFL match, refusing to remain standing while the national anthem was played. A considerable number of popular athletes followed suit in the sporting world, causing a huge row and strong condemnation from Trump. He questioned their patriotism and called them "privileged millionaires", who had no respect for their country and were ungrateful to it.[309]

....

e1c239b45787>.

[306] Cit. from: Ayesha Rascoe, "A Year after Charlottesville, Not Much Has Changed For Trump", *NPR*, August 11, 2018 <https://www.npr.org/2018/08/11/637665414/a-year-after-charlottesville-not-much-has-changed-for-trump>.

[307] Glenn Thrush, "New Outcry as Trump Rebukes Charlottesville Racists 2 Days Later", *The New York Times*, August 14, 2017 <https://www.nytimes.com/2017/08/14/us/politics/trump-charlottesville-protest.html>.

[308] Jennifer Schuessler, "Historians Question Trump's Comments on Confederate Monuments", *The New York Times*, August 15, 2017 <https://www.nytimes.com/2017/08/15/arts/design/trump-robert-e-lee-george-washington-thomas-jefferson.html>; Jon Meacham, "Why Lee Should Go, and Washington Should Stay", *The New York Times*, August 21, 2017 <https://www.nytimes.com/2017/08/21/opinion/why-lee-should-go-and-washington-should-stay.html>.

[309] Yevgeniy Shestakov, "Flag – sleduyushchiy?" ("Is the Flag Next?"), *Rossiyskaya Gazeta*

The mass media was filled with reports of disorder on university campuses, when crowds of students disrupted the lessons of professors whose views seemed conservative, and of the extremely lenient response to the protestors on the part of the boards of academic institutions.[310]

Internet providers started shutting down large numbers of sites that they deemed not to be politically correct – either racist or nationalist. This, in turn, caused outrage, as a misuse by organizations in the information business of the right of censorship and an attack on freedom of speech and freedom of discussion.[311]

Paul Krugman wrote that Trump was far more loathsome than Caligula, since the bloodthirsty Roman emperor had at least refrained from approving of violence on ethnic grounds inside the empire.[312]

It would appear that the ghosts of the Civil War, race riots and civil clashes are returning to haunt the USA. America's history is coming home to roost.

The United States, David Brooks underlines, has always been united by a shared national history: the country as the City on the Hill, as last best hope of humankind. "It was an explicitly Judeo-Christian story, built on a certain view of God's providential plan. But that civic mythology no longer unifies. American confidence is in tatters and we live in a secular culture. As a result, we're suffering through a national identity crisis. Different groups see themselves living out different national stories and often feel they are living in different nations."[313]

Above all, a dividing line has emerged between the parties and the electorates on matters of faith and morality, on which, out of principle, there can be no compromise. Faith and morality are uncompromising, and this was the precursor to even greater and more lasting political polarization in America.

(*Russian Newspaper*), September 5, 2017 <https://rg.profkiosk.ru/586546>; Alex Altman and Sean Gregory, "Trump's Offensive Playbook", *Time*, October 9, 2017. PP. 34-39.

[310] Arthur C. Brooks, "Don't Shun Conservative Professors", *The New York Times*, September 15, 2017 <https://www.nytimes.com/2017/09/15/opinion/conservative-professors.html>.

[311] "Don't Kick Neo-Nazis Off the Internet", *Bloomberg Businessweek*, September 11, 2017. P. 14.

[312] Paul Krugman, "Trump Makes Caligula Look Pretty Good", *The New York Times*, August 18, 2017 <https://www.nytimes.com/2017/08/18/opinion/trump-caligula-republican-congress.html>.

[313] David Brooks, "The Four American Narratives", *The New York Times*, May 26, 2017 <https://www.nytimes.com/2017/05/26/opinion/the-four-american-narratives.html>.

The Sources of American Behaviour

What are the "sources of American behaviour"? The dean of the political science department at MGIMO, Aleksey Bogaturov, has identified a number of universal components to the USA's foreign policy mindset: "Belief in their superiority is the first and, perhaps, the key characteristic of the American worldview... The machine of American patriotism hangs on the idea of their supremacy: there is a great deal that needs to be changed in America, but it is the best country in the world. The idea of superiority is just as integral a part of the American consciousness as the sense of vulnerability (taking offence at itself) is part of the modern Russian consciousness. In this sense, Americans are the opposite of Russians. The flip side of American patriotism is a genuine, at times blind and frightening conviction that the predetermined destiny of the United States is not only to "serve as an example to the whole world, but also actually to 'help' the world come into line with American ideas about good and evil."[314]

The idea of "freedom-democracy" (liberty) is easily transformed into the idea of "the freedom for America", which implies not only the USA's right to be free, but also its right to act freely. The notion of America's just superiority gives it the ability to throw off all doubt as to the appropriateness of expansive interpretations of the USA's rights and global responsibility. Americans find it hard to understand why other countries do not want to copy their practices and institutions. The desire to "turn nations to democracy" against their will (in Iraq or Afghanistan) is a painful feature of the American worldview. Jokes on this subject provoke puzzlement or cold detachment in America.

Washington considers the entire world to be the sphere of America's exclusive interests. Moreover, no other country is to have military-political interests in the Western hemisphere, North America, in the Middle East. Americans are not ready to admit that Russia and China have strategic interests of their own even in the vicinity of their borders.

International life is the last thing that interests Americans: they are swallowed up by their own domestic affairs, unless the issue in question is a major war. Even a war like the one in Iraq, though, is a domestic matter as far as Americans are concerned. What matters in the news reports from flashpoints is not the suffering of Iraqis, Afghans, Libyans or Syrians, but

---

[314] *Sovremennaya mirovaya politika* (*Contemporary World Politics*), ed. by A. D. Bogaturov. Moscow, 2010.

how many more American soldiers might die, and is the price of fuel going to rise? "Ideas about the geography, history, and cultural particularities of the outside world do not interest Americans very much. Anything that is not American is significant only insofar as it is capable of competing with America."[315] It is genuinely thought there that if there is something of value in the world, then the USA will buy it.

Because of isolation, Americans have a poor understanding of the world outside their own country, as Fareed Zakaria maintains. Americans hardly speak any foreign languages, know almost nothing about foreign cultures, and it still has not even occurred to them that this situation ought to be changed. Americans rarely compare anything with global standards, because they are certain that the path they have taken, specifically, is the best and most progressive one. American politicians are constantly and without any selectivity making demands, slandering, imposing sanctions and damning entire countries for their mistakes and failings. In the last years alone, the US has imposed sanctions on half the population of the planet. It is the only country that publishes an annual report on the behavior of all the other countries. Washington D.C. is like a bubble, inflated with self-satisfaction, and there is little understanding there whatsoever of what is going on in the outside world.[316]

In 2014 only one in six Americans could point out Ukraine on a map, while the average distance by which those surveyed fell wide of the mark was 1800 miles. Support for the idea of American military interference there is mainly expressed by the same Americans who thought Ukraine was in Latin America or in Australia. When asked whether or not America should bomb Agrabah (the country that was home to Disney's Aladdin), a third of Republicans replied in the affirmative, 13% were against, and among the Democrats surveyed, 36% were against and 19% were in favor. These people had no idea that Agrabah did not even exist. As Tom Nichols of the US Naval War College observed, in his comments on these findings, "Americans have reached a point where ignorance, at least regarding what is generally considered established knowledge in public policy – is seen as an actual virtue. To reject the advice of experts is to assert autonomy, a way for Americans to demonstrate their independence from nefarious elites [...]. I fear we are moving beyond a natural skepticism regarding expert claims to the death of the ideal of expertise itself: a Google-fueled, Wikipedia-based, blog-sodden

---

[315] Ibid. PP. 356-362.

[316] Fareed Zakaria, *The Post-American World*. W. W. Norton & Company, 2008. P. 47.

collapse of any division between professionals and laypeople, teachers and students, knowers and wonderers – in other words, between those with achievement in an area and those with none."[317]

The concept of "American exceptionalism" is not only alive and well but is becoming increasingly popular. Fastidious analysts have calculated that this term appeared in national publications 457 times in the period 1980-2000, 2,558 times in 2000-2010, and 4,172 times in 2010-2012, becoming almost the central question in the electoral debates between Romney and Obama. "Exceptionalism is not merely a rhetorical device," writes the president of MapStory Foundation, Robert Tomes. "It is not just one concept or argument, but an interwoven bundle of ideas that together represent an American creed or ideology. American exceptionalism implies a belief that the United States is unique among nations – and, for some, even superior to others."[318]

It makes no sense to condemn America, let alone to try to change it. It is what it is, and it is not likely to change in the foreseeable future. One must simply understand it, and one's own policy must be constructed in a way that takes this understanding into account.

---

[317] Tom Nichols, "How America Lost Faith in Expertise. And Why That's a Giant Problem", *Foreign Affairs*, March/April 2017. PP. 60-61.

[318] Robert R. Tomes, "American Exceptionalism in the Twenty-First Century", *Survival*, February/March, 2014. PP. 27-28.

CHAPTER 5
THE RUSSIAN MATRIX

Russia is one of only a handful of states on the planet (there are only two or three) that can boast of having enjoyed five centuries of continuous sovereign existence, without any conquest from outside and without finding itself under anyone else's control.

The Geography of the Russian Fate

The key factor that has determined Russia's fate is that it is the most northerly and the coldest country in the world. Two thirds of its territory is covered with snow for two thirds of the year. "The offshoot of the Orthodox Christian civilization in Russia was exposed to a challenge from forests and rains and frosts still more severe than that with which our Western civilization had to contend," stressed Toynbee.[1] The average temperature in the USSR is -2°C (in China it is +25, in Germany +15). In the Russian Federation, deprived of a host of warm regions, the average temperature falls to -5.5°. Moscow – a relatively warm place by Russian standards – is the coldest capital in the world (ahead of Ottawa and Ulaanbaatar). The sharp continental climate means that it is destined to have a vast range in temperatures. While along the Earth's equator there is practically no difference between the average temperature in winter and in summer, and while in Great Britain, France or Spain there is a difference of 10° to 15°, in the Moscow area it is more than 30°, and between Yenisey and the Stanovoi Ridge in Siberia it reaches 65°. The coldest place on the globe is also located here – in the Verkhoyansk region.

---

[1] Arnold Toynbee, *A Study of History: Abridgement of Vols I-VI*. Oxford University Press, 1987. P. 79.

Such a position had its positive sides. The harsh winter protected Russia from tropical diseases which ravaged other parts of the earth. The forests in the North were rich with wildlife, and there has always been high demand for furs around the world; the forests provided wood, of which almost all Russian real estate has been built for centuries, and from which the fleet was created. The forests provided a small degree of protection from nomads. Yet the country's dimensions and climate took their own additional tax from any activity. The woods and marshlands created a plethora of unforeseen dangers at every step. This taught people to pay close attention to nature, encouraging caution and resourcefulness in difficult circumstances, and the habit of patiently overcoming setbacks and privations. "There is no other people in Europe that is less spoilt and pretentious, that is accustomed to expect less from nature and from fate, or that is more durable," noted the famous historian Vasily Klyuchevsky.[2]

The East European plain is a fairly inhospitable area for agriculture, the primary activity of its population. Whereas in Western Europe, agricultural work is possible 300 days of the year, from February through November (with a two-month barren season), in Russia there are only 130 days in the year that are suitable for such activity, of which 30 days are for haymaking and 100 for arable farming. The land that was tilled had low levels of fertility, and for centuries on each landlords' arable land where a seed was sown, two to three would grow, while on peasant lands the rate was even lower. In England, where snow is quite a rarity, the harvest might see 10 times as many seeds growing as were sown. The short period of time in which the fields could be tilled left no room for innovation and experimentation: one false step, and the loss of several days – and the threat of famine would loom large.[3]

The farming activity of the Russian peasants, who accounted for more than 85% of the population even at the start of the 20th century, was based on a compressed cycle of fieldwork and required a capacity for heavy and heroic labor during the brief agricultural season. For six or seven months a year, however, farming was impossible due to the weather conditions. The peasants manufactured furniture and domestic utensils, spun yarn, wove

---

[2] Vasiliy Klyuchevskiy, *Kurs russkoy istorii* (*The Course of Russian History*). Vol. 1. Moscow, 1987. P. 312.

[3] For details see: Leonid Milov, *Velikorusskiy pakhar' i osobennosti rossiyskogo istoricheskogo protsessa* (*The Great Russian Ploughman and the Peculiarities of the Russian Historical Process*). Moscow, 1998.

clothes, prepared firewood and reared cattle, and all of this created a certain type of person, developed in the multifaceted way, patient, energetic, but not necessarily prepared for systematic work. It is as a result of this, I would suggest, that somewhat unrestrained forms of relaxation were often seen – in moments of leisure and during the long winter months.

The larger part of Russian territory is located in an area of high risk for agriculture, where harvests are by no means guaranteed. The lack of a harvest often resulted in terrible famines, when people died in the thousands and hundreds of thousands. There was also a special form of technology-related catastrophe: wooden Russia (in most of the regions of the East European plain there is no stone suitable for construction) would from time to time go up in flames. Hence the people's exceptional endurance in the face of the blows dealt by fate: for centuries, people were equally ready to expect gifts and disasters from nature.

The extreme weakness of individual farming was compensated for by the huge role played by the peasant community. All difficulties – disease, death of cattle, fire, plagues of insects, droughts, plunging temperatures – could create a threat to existence. The peasants needed a community because of the need for mutual aid: in restoring the house that had burnt down, or in collecting the harvest for a neighbor who had fallen ill. There was a great deal of land in the country, but, as the rector of Moscow University during the pre-revolutionary years, Matvey Lybavsky has rightly observed, "There was relatively little granary land". The impact of the land shortage was to some extent lessened by the low density of the population; during the early Middle Ages it was roughly three to six times lower in Russia than in the West.[4] The consequence of this was extensive production and the need for the plowing of more and more new plots of land. Hence the algorithm for Russian development that Klyuchevsky observed: "The history of Russia is the history of a country colonizing itself."[5]

This colonization, which was by no means merely a process of searching for new fertile land, predetermined the dimensions of Russia, which ended up covering 11 time zones (although today, for convenience, there are officially only nine), and this too became an extremely important component of the Russian matrix, leaving its mark on all aspects of the country's exis-

---

[4] Matvey Lyubavskiy, *Obrazovaniye osnovnoy gosudarstvennoy territorii velikorusskoy narodnosti* (*Formation of the Main State Territory of the Great Russian People*). Leningrad, 1929. P. 38.

[5] Vasiliy Klyuchevskiy, *Izbrannyye trudy* (*Selected Works*). Moscow, 2010. P. 57.

tence. "The landscape of the Russian soul corresponds to the landscape of the Russian land: that same limitless nurse, shapeless mass, striving towards endlessness, that breadth," as the Russian philosopher Nikolay Berdyayev maintained.[6]

Russian civilization was a river-based civilization. The rivers were both the main source of communication and crucial lines of protection, creating natural barriers. In the winter, though, they froze over. And they also showed the way to invading forces, indicating where they should look for Russian towns, which were located on the banks of the rivers.

The Russian territory has always been particularly vulnerable to invaders. And Russia's geopolitical environment has never been characterized by tranquility and peacefulness. No other state in the world can be compared with it in terms of the number of neighboring people it has, not all of which are known for being peace-loving. Rus was located at the point where Europe and Asia met – in this "thoroughfare" for humanity. The borders were unstable and vulnerable, and were reinforced along practically the entire perimeter, at all the points where a real or potential enemy could operate, and this meant: in the South, in the West, and in the East.

The masterful military strategist Carl von Clausewitz, who served in the Russian army in 1812, observed that from a strategic point of view Russia was undefendable. Clausewitz believed that Russia's saving grace was the circumstance of the freezing temperatures, because there were few people who wished to linger there, let alone live there. And also its vast expanse. "The Russian state is so large, that one is able to play a game of cat and mouse with an enemy army; it is on this that the idea of defending it against the superior forces of the enemy should mainly be based. Retreat into the depths of the country entices the enemy army to move in the same direction, leaving vast areas in its rear, which they are not capable of occupying."[7] Peter the Great would act in this way in his war against the Swedes, as would Alexander I and Stalin, when resisting the armed forces of the majority of the continental European states brought over by Napoleon and Hitler.

Things were somewhat more complicated as regards the southern borders, where, on the plains stretching from Mongolia to the Carpathians, from the 7th century BC until the 18th century AD, warlike nomadic tribes enjoyed an undisputed rule. For a long time, the Great Steppes were the

....

[6] Nikolay Berdyayev, *Istoki i smysl russkogo kommunizma* (*The Origins and Meaning of Russian Communism*). Moscow, 1990. P. 8.
[7] Carl von Clausewitz, *1812*. Moscow, 1937. PP. 93-94, 92.

determining factor in Russian history. In the history of Rus in the Middle Ages, though, one can only point to a period of just over two decades in the 11th century – the reign of Yaroslav the Wise and the start of his sons' reign – when it did not experience a direct threat from the South. And those were the years of the true bloom of Kyivan Rus.

The country could be subjected at any moment to a devastating invasion – not only for the purpose of plundering, but with the aim of wiping out the population or forcing it into slavery. This dictated the need, above all, to be able to mobilize as many soldiers as possible in the shortest possible time. Western European kings could live in palaces outside the city, and the dukes could live in castles in the countryside, providing the urban population with a degree of self-rule, because the most dangerous enemies for them could only be a neighboring king or duke, and the biggest threat – the payment of taxes to him. Russian "kings and dukes" were forced to live in fortified towns, whose entire population was required not only to engage in trade and crafts, but also to be prepared to take to the fortress walls, so as to protect the lives of themselves and their families, with a weapon in their hands. The alternative to this was either death or slavery. The citizens were duly organized not into guilds, as in Western Europe, but as in war – into "hundreds" and "thousands". And there was no reason to surrender.

The need to safeguard the survival and battle-readiness of a large territory, located in a complex geopolitical environment, meant that there was a requirement for mobilization and the re-distribution of resources from the extremely poor and relatively small population. This led, above all, to a high degree of centralization of power. Thus, the type of statehood that dominated large parts of Russian history was dictated by the search for the optimum method of organizing administration and survival in extremely difficult climatic and geographical conditions, a dangerous geopolitical environment (given the extremely weak material bases of society), and the poverty of the populace.

Initial Rus

Stories about the first Eastern Slavic state are of a semi-mythical character and are connected with the annalistic evidence about the decision of several tribes, mired in infighting, to invite three brothers to rule them; one of the brothers – Rurik – began running Novgorod in 862. To this day, this is considered the start of Russian statehood, and of the Rurik dynasty.

A short time later, Oleg, the Regent ruling on behalf of Igor, Rurik's young son, seized power in Kyiv too, prompting the formation of a single ancient Russian state – Kyivan Rus. The Prince was the leader of a professional army, and, by all accounts, was also the supreme priest. Efforts were then made to create a centralized state, as a result of which Igor was killed while attempting to collect taxes from Drevlyane tribe. His widow Olga not only reaped brutal revenge, but was also the first to establish by law the time and place of tax collections.

The origins of the name Rus and the role played in its creation by German and Scandinavian tribes is the subject of much debate, founded on the vagueness and contradictory nature of accounts in the manuscripts, foreign sources and data from archaeologists, which are open to interpretation. Nestor the Chronicler, who posed the question in the 11th century "From whence did the Russian land come?" is often referred to as the founder of the Norman theory, whereby Rus takes its name from a Varangian from Scandinavia, who created the first state. In the mild form, the Varangians were indeed Scandinavians, but they do not play a very big role in the creation of the Russian state – the Norman theory of the origin of the Russian state almost prevails. Among those who adhere to it, the word Rus is usually said to have been derived from the Finnish word "ruotsi" – meaning "oarsmen". The anti-Normanists, while acknowledging very strong contact with the Scandinavians, usually consider the Varangians to be Vends, i.e. Baltic Slavs. They claim that the name Rus is derived from the multiple rivers with similar names – Ros, Rus, Rosa, Rusa, Rusna, Roska, Porusie, etc. – throughout Eastern Europe, which reflected the cult of water among the people living beside the river channels ("ruslo" in Russian), with their mermaids ("rusalka" in Russian). Contemporary archaeologists have not been able to confirm any kind of significant Scandinavian presence in the 9th to the early 10th centuries; they have established an almost ubiquitous Baltic-Slavic presence, and Scandinavian people were among the Prince's men-at-arms in northern Rus.[8]

There are no strong grounds for claiming that statehood was brought from without; the Scandinavian states came into being later – in the late 10th and early 11th centuries. At the same time, a considerable influence on

....

[8] Nikolay Makarov, "Istoricheskiye svidetel'stva i arkheologicheskiye realii: v poiskakh sootvetstviya" ("Historical Evidence and Archeological Realities: In Search of Matching"), in *Rus' v IX–X vekakh: arkheologicheskaya panorama* (*Russia in IX–X Centuries: Archaeological Panorama*). Moscow-Vologda, 2012. P. 456

the process of state formation was exerted by the fact that the first Russian princes had a strong political kernel at their disposal – the *druzhina* (or "retinue"), which had a Norman component. The Princes and the *druzhina* constituted the Russian nobility, which ruled initially through tax collection, and from the 10th century onwards began to become major landowners.[9]

The specifics of statehood were determined in many ways by the system of succession adopted in Kyivan Rus. Starting during the reign of the son of Igor and Olga, Svyatoslav, it became a political tradition for the sons of the Great Prince to be appointed leaders of separate principalities – in order of seniority in accordance with the significance of each region – with the right to collect taxes independently, some of which would be sent to the capital. This type of rule was reinforced by Svyatoslav's son, Vladimir (980-1015), who ruled over Kyiv himself, but allowed his sons to have power in the regions. If the eldest of the brothers died, his principality would be passed on to the next eldest, and all the other brothers would move up one step in the hierarchy, receiving a more prestigious principality. This system made it possible to preserve state unity, but was a cause of serious enmity, particularly at the time when the Great Prince of Kyiv died; a power struggle broke out between his brothers and sons over the throne.

Yaroslav the Wise (1019-1054), whose name is associated with the first document of written law – *Russkaya Pravda* – managed to remove his brothers from power, replacing them with his own sons. After Yaroslav's death, an important role in the process of succession began to be played by the Kyiv town council – the Veche, which appointed or overthrew princes numerous times. The power struggle between Yaroslav's sons and grandsons, in which Cuman troops took part, ended in 1097 with the Council of Liubech (the Congress of Rus Princes), where the principle "Unto each his fiefdom" reigned supreme. This meant that the land owned by the father would be passed on to the son. This provided the impetus for the breaking up of a unified country into 12 self-regulated principalities with their own dynasties, each of which became more vulnerable to outside invaders.

Olga was the first ruler to adopt Christianity. During her reign, as Sergey Karpov of the Russian Academy of Sciences, a leading specialist on Byzantium, underlines, "Byzantium, without question, surpassed any country in Western Europe at the time in a cultural, economic and political regard. Constantinople was acknowledged as the 'master of the world', the most

---

[9] Anton Gorskiy, *Russkoye Srednevekov'ye* (*The Russian Middle Ages*). Moscow, 2010. PP. 34-35, 42, 68.

highly-populated, wealthy, and attractive city in Europe... Imperial power, power over the entire habitable globe, knew no rivals before Charlemagne, and even after him, the power of the emperor of the West remained, in the eyes of the Byzantines and the peoples that surrounded them, the power of a mighty state, yes, but merely the 'basileus of the Franks', by contrast with the 'basileus of the Romans', i.e. of the entire oecumene." Byzantium was attractive as the keeper of the traditions of the Roman Empire, too, and of the true synodic Apostolic Church.[10]

Christianity came to be the main factor in Byzantium's influence. Typical of this is the official history of the adoption of Christianity by Rus; the initiator of the adoption was Prince Vladimir (the official date of the Baptism of Rus was 988). It was selected, not least on account of the persuasive argument of the might of the Byzantine Empire, after the religions of neighboring nations – Judaism and Islam – had been considered. Rus received from Byzantium the tenets of the doctrine, Scripture and lore, the liturgical practices, and then the chronicles and the theological and philosophical treatises. Knowledge for the building of towns, architecture, mosaics, frescos, icons, and decorative and applied art were all brought to Rus from Byzantium. As a result of the liturgical and literary activity of the Greeks Cyril and Methodius and their followers in Kyivan Rus in the 10th and early 11th centuries, the Slavic language became – alongside Latin and Greek – one of the three written and liturgical languages of Christianity in the Middle Ages. The Old Church Slavonic language, despite all the changes that it underwent, remained the main literary language of Russia until the end of the 17th century.

After the adoption of Christianity, Kyivan Rus became part of a kind of "Byzantine Commonwealth of nations". It was one of the last states to have adopted Byzantine Christianity, but also the biggest. Constantinople had no tradition of exerting political control over Rus, nor did it have the ability to do so, and Kyiv was not politically subordinate to Constantinople. What is more, Rus provided military resources and material assistance to Byzantium when it was afflicted by invasions or natural disasters.

Rus – unlike a host of other nations – was able to absorb Christianity in its mother tongue. A veritable turning point as far as translations and

---

[10] Sergey Karpov, "Rol' vizantiyskogo naslediya na Rusi v formirovanii rossiyskoy gosudarstvennosti i russkoy kul'tury" ("The Role of the Byzantine Legacy in Rus in the Shaping of Russian Statehood and Russian Culture"), in *Rossiyskaya gosudarstvennost': istoricheskiye traditsii i vyzovy XXI veka* (*Russian Statehood: Historical Traditions and Challenges of the 21st Century*). Moscow, 2013. PP. 59-60.

the Christian enlightenment were concerned took place under Yaroslav the Wise. It was thanks to him that the first library in Rus came into being, located at Saint Sophia's Cathedral in Kyiv.[11] Sadly, less than 1% of all the manuscripts that existed in Kyivan Rus have survived to the present day: the climate had a devastating effect on parchment, and fires, civil strife, wars and natural disasters also played a role.

One of the books from this library was preserved in the French city of Reims. This was the Gospel in Glagolitic script that was taken there by Yaroslav's daughter Anna, and on which generations of French kings took the oath ascending the throne. Needless to say, Anna was far better educated than her spouse, King Henry I: unlike the king and his entourage, she could read and write in Latin, among other languages.

The cities of Kyivan Rus had a high degree of literacy. Monasteries played an enormous role in spiritual life, as they became key centers for the writing of chronicles and translations, and the spread of literacy. In the medieval Russian education system, however, key elements of the Western system – Aristotle, Augustin of Hippo, Roman law – were either left out altogether, or included only to a minimal extent.

The Western Ulus

In 1237 the Russian principalities fell victim to an invasion led by the grandson of Genghis Khan, Batu. Dozens of flourishing towns were reduced to ashes, and their inhabitants were killed to a man and woman – "from the old man to the suckling baby!" – as one of the chroniclers mournfully exclaimed. Many traditional trades and crafts vanished for one and a half to two centuries, if not forever: cloisonné enamel, niello, granulation and the polychrome glazing technique in construction. The use of stone in construction work almost came to an end.[12] The main collections of books perished in the fires, and many centers of manuscript writing, icon painting, and artistic trades died out. The manuscripts that survived paint a horrifying picture of the moral degradation of Russian society. It was at this time that the Russians became part of the international slave trade; the word "slave" began to be associated with the word "Slavic".

---

[11] Aleksey Karpov, *Yaroslav Mudryy* (*Yaroslav the Wise*). Moscow, 2010. PP. 313-315.

[12] Vadim Kargalov, *Mongolo-tatarskoye nashestviye na Rus'. XIII vek* (*The Mongol-Tatar Invasion of Rus. 13th Century*). Moscow, 2012. PP. 112-113.

The Mongols' plans, incidentally, did not include the complete elimination of the population in order to seize the land, because the forests were not suitable for nomads. The Russians were to be used chiefly as a source of constant enrichment and the addition of a workforce and military force. In 1243, the Prince of Vladimir, Yaroslav Vsevolodovich, set off to pay his respects to Batu, and the latter, in complete harmony with the Mongol tradition whereby the leading position in the hierarchy of the leaders of subjugated tribes was given to the one who was first to display his loyalty, appointed him the "senior figure" ahead of the other Russian princes. Initially, supreme power was in the hands of the great Mongol Khans, located in the capital of the Mongol Empire – Karakorum, to where Alexander Nevsky, Yaroslav's son, was also required to travel six times in order to pay his respects.

In the 1260s, the Western Ulus of the Mongol Empire (which the Mongols called Ulus Juchi, naming it after Batu's father, while the Russians called it the Horde) became an independent state with a wandering capital, which existed at the same time as the permanent one – the city of Sarai on the Lower Volga. By contrast with China or Iran, for example, where Genghis Khan's descendants replaced local rulers, Rus remained under the control of its own Princes, not becoming directly part of the Horde, but recognizing the Horde's Khan as a legitimate sovereign – a Tsar. This dependency was expressed first and foremost by the Khans helping to reinforce the princes' reigns by issuing them with the appropriate titles. As a rule, the Khan did not violate the existing traditions in the laws of succession, but had the decisive word in conflicts within the Rurik dynasty. The princes were required to provide military assistance to the Mongols. Starting in 1250s, a tax was imposed – the *vykhod* – along with other levies.[13] In 1257, a census began in which everything was counted: people, homes, pastures, cattle, crops. The Horde exempted only priests and monks from the census, so as not to provoke the wrath of the religious.[14]

During the difficult years of the Mongol yoke, an event occurred that did not prompt great interest among contemporaries but which was to have an exceptionally strong influence on the future course of Russian history. Pursuant to a decree by Alexander Nevsky, in the 1260s to 1270s, a new principality was separated from the Vladimir princedom – the final one in Russian

---

[13] Anton Gorskiy, *Russkoye Srednevekov'ye* (*The Russian Middle Ages*). Moscow, 2010. PP. 135-136, 143, 146, 192-193.

[14] Alexander Degtyaryov, *Izbrannyye trudy po russkoy istorii* (*Selected Works on Russian History*). Vol. 2. Moscow, 2006. P. 238.

history – with its center in the small town of Moscow. The descendants of Alexander Nevsky's youngest son, Daniil, who ruled it, proved to be adept diplomats and politicians, who enjoyed greater success than others in "the collection of lands" – through the annexation of unclaimed principalities, the making of alliances, purchases, the receipt of titles, and by conquering territories. They were given much assistance in seizing power over Rus by the Mongol troops that were invited to the country. Moscow's princes became the political leaders of the newly emergent Rus.

A significant influence on the Muscovite state was exerted by the experience of government organization under Genghis Khan's Empire. "The Horde's rulers brought in a fairly sensible policy, making use of the services of Chinese, Uighur and Khoresmian civil servants, who had accumulated a wealth of experience in managing vast territories. The postal and courier service, ensuring security on the roads, the collection and registration of taxes and the census of the population, the issuing of coins and paper currency, the distribution of titles and the personal dependency on the Khan of the rulers who received them, reporting by civil servants to the central authorities, well-organized armed forces, special services for collecting and storing foodstuffs and foraged goods, the erection of bridges and laying of roads – all of this was delivered in China in ancient times and the Middle Ages, and then in the Mongol state, to a level that was unknown in Europe," asserts the historian Aleksey Karpov.[15] With its borrowed practices, Russia would never attain the Chinese level of organization, but some of the contours of Muscovite statehood would retain Mongol traits.

During the period of the Mongol reign, the country participated in 300 wars and battles – against the Horde itself, the Lithuanians, the Livonian Order, and Sweden. This served as an incentive for rapid growth in the military arts. All the new methods of waging war were studied, both Western and Eastern; skills related to the use of siege equipment emerged, and military armor was perfected. From the Mongols came the centralized army on the principle of military conscription, and intelligence, and the death penalty (something that did not exist in Kyivan Rus) and torture, along with the word *palach* ("executioner"). When the Horde began to fall apart, many Tatars fled to Rus, to serve the Great Prince. Veteran Tatars would go on to form the backbone of the Muscovite cavalry. According to accounts written by Europeans who visited the Muscovite state in the 15th and 16th centuries, it was hard to distinguish a Russian cavalryman from

---

[15] Aleksey Karpov, *Batyy (Batu Khan)*. Moscow, 2011. P. 161.

a nomadic one, both in terms of outward appearance, and in terms of the tactics used in battle.

Once the Moscow principality had grown stronger, it proved capable of successfully resisting the Mongols. In 1380, Dmitry Donskoy delivered a crushing blow to the "usurper" (not descended from the Genghis race) Mamai, at the Battle of Kulikovo Field. During the reigns of Vasily II and Ivan III, when the Horde clearly grew weaker, the idea that came to dominate was that of a transition of royal glory from the Byzantine Empire to the Great Princes of Moscow, a notion that was not compatible with recognizing any dependency on the Khan.

The fact that Rus had been part of the Genghis Empire – the largest empire in history, which bound the people and history of East Asia and Europe – made it a participant in global politics. And in later times, Russia's revenge would make it the inheritor of the northern part of the Mongol Empire.

The Moscow Tsardom

Independence from the Horde was secured once and for all in 1490 under Ivan III. In the mid-15th century, the territory of the Moscow principality was 430,000 km^2, in which there were around 3 million people living. In less than a couple of centuries, this young state was destined to become the largest country in the world in terms of territory. In the 16th to 19th centuries, not only did the ancient lands of Rus become part of the state, but so did the Tatar Khanates of the Volga Region, Siberia, the Far East, Alaska, the Urals, North Caucasus, Ukraine, the Baltic area, the Black Sea region, Poland, Finland, Bessarabia, the Caucasus and Central Asia. At the height of its period of expansion, Russia was almost 50 times bigger than its initial size.

Why and how did that happen? Ivan III was not only a Great Muscovite Prince, but also the first "Tsar and Grand Prince of All Russia", who was himself described as a Tsar and autocrat (back then, this meant that he ruled the state on his own – independently from the Mongols). The centralized Russian state became a sovereign center of power, ruled by an all-powerful sovereign, under whom there was a permanent advisory body in the form of the aristocratic Boyar Assembly. Ivan the third's second wife was the niece of the last Byzantine emperor, Princess Sophia Palaeologus, after which Rus began to see itself as the direct heir to Byzantium, which had fallen to the Ottomans in 1453, and whose coat of arms – the two-headed eagle – became the national emblem of Russia. It was at this time that a widespread belief took root about Russia's special mission as a state chosen by God, as the "Third Rome" (the second being Constantinople), with a calling to become the most pious and powerful Christian state of all.

Russia also experienced the influence of the Italian Renaissance at its height, obvious evidence of which is provided by the Kremlin in Moscow, whose walls and towers were built by Italian masters. Russians also have Renaissance Italy to thank for the arrival of several rationalist heresies, vodka and venereal diseases.

Why was it that Russia was to be the builder of an empire, though, rather than, for instance, Lithuania or Poland, which at that time were larger, stronger, and had bigger populations, better armaments and were actively striving to expand their borders ("from the sea to the sea")? First of all, the degree of militarization of the Russian state, which still was forced to maintain an active defence in all three directions, was significantly higher than that of its nearest neighbors to the West. The political structure that had taken shape in Rus by the mid-15th century made it possible to implement far harsher mobilization measures, so as to concentrate the nation's forces and resources into a single "fist", so to speak.[16] Secondly, in the East – the primary direction of Russia's expansion in the 16th to 17th centuries – their serious rivals were the remnants of the weakened Horde. Russia was given a unique opportunity to fill the geopolitical vacuum that formed in Eurasia after the fall of the Genghis Empire.

The expansion of the state of Muscovy began in the West, however. Ivan III, who saw himself as the heir to the princes of Kyivan Rus, set the goal of unifying all the lands that had once been part of the ancient Russian state and had then found themselves part of the Grand Duchy of Lithuania or in Poland. In 1492, Ivan invaded Lithuania, which was ultimately forced to recognize Russia's territorial acquisitions. His son, Vasily III, had a free hand in relation to the last independent Russian principalities. In 1510, the city-republic of Pskov was brought under his rule, and in 1521, so too was the Great Ryazan principality, which had now broken free from Lithuanian rule. During the reigns of Ivan III and Vasily III, Moscow unified practically all the Russian lands, and the dimensions

---

[16] Nikolay Nikitin, "Rasshireniye territorii kak geopoliticheskiy faktor rossiyskoy gosudarstvennosti: kontseptual'nyye voprosy" ("The Expansion of Territory as a Geopolitical Factor of Russian Statehood: Conceptual Questions"), in *Rossiyskaya Imperiya ot istokov do nachala XIX veka. Ocherki sotsial'no-politicheskoy i ekonomicheskoy istorii* (*Russian Empire from its Origins to the Beginning of the 19th Century: Essays on Socio-Political and Economic History*). Moscow, 2011. P. 32.

of the state amounted to 2.8 million square kilometers, with a population of 4.5 to 6 million.[17]

After its liberation from the Horde, attempts were made to bring Russia into the Western system, as a vassal. Several offers were made to Ivan III and his son, at the initiative of the Pope and the German Nation's Holy Roman Emperor, of a coronation in Rome with adoption of Catholicism alongside. The offers were rejected. It was from this moment – the early 16th century – that in the West, and first and foremost in Poland, which was then doing battle with Moscow, the image of Russia as a barbarian, wild, godless, backward and hostile state began to take shape – and it is an image that has remained unchanged to this day. Even more significantly, this perception of Russia became part of the Western matrix; the country performed the role of a polar opposite, with the West extolling its own system of values as it turned its gaze upon Russia.

For the West, to lose such a perception would have amounted to losing part of its own identity. In Russia, in turn, a complex of self-isolation emerged, as a response to the constant threats from without and as a legacy of its belief in its own spiritual superiority. Its self-isolation, even in the 16th to 17th centuries, was not absolute, but the contact that was made with the West did not reflect an acknowledgement of Western supremacy or a desire to merge with the West, but, on the contrary, strengthened ideas about Russia's sovereignty.

The grandson of Ivan III, Ivan IV, better known as Ivan the Terrible (he ruled from 1533 to 1584, and the exact translation of his nickname should be "the Stern" rather than "the Terrible") was officially crowned as Tsar and as God's anointed sovereign. Under his reign, the strong supreme power of the autocrat was maintained, along with elements of a monarchy with class (estate) representation. A standard state bureaucracy was created, along with a professional army of *streltsy*, and boyars who showed signs of disobedience and separatist tendencies suffered brutal persecution. At the same time, the Tsar ruled the country with the help of a Boyar Duma, which differed little from its counterparts in Western Europe. The *Zemsky Sobors* (Land Assemblies) played a hugely important role. Questions of war and peace were decided depending on the opinions it expressed. "And although the Assembly was not granted the right to elect the ministers, it nonetheless had a far more important right: the right to elect the Tsar. In that regard, it

....

[17] Ibid. P. 28.

could have no reason to envy either the British Parliament, or the French États Généraux," famous lawyer Maxim Kovalevskiy asserted.[18]

Under Ivan IV, the system of landowner property, with serfdom for half of the peasant population, took shape. As was the case in the early feudalism of Western Europe, this made sense for military reasons. In order to counter new enemies – Lithuania, Poland, Sweden – a well-armed and well-trained elite cavalry was required. Until the end of the 15th century, ancestral domains had dominated, and the traditional ancestral rights imposed no restrictions on the nobleman's rights to dispose of his land, nor did they entail any duty to do military service. After the expropriation of the boyars' land under Ivan III, a colossal fund of state-owned lands took shape, which were passed on by the exchequer to the nobility in Moscow and to the children of boyars, on condition that they performed mandatory military or civil service. The Code of Laws for 1550 established that the children of boyars, by dint of their office and by birth, could no longer have their own personal freedom. Men liable to government service were required to start serving at the age of 15 and to remain in office until they died or until they were unfit for office on account of old age or severe injury.[19] Noblemen were required, when first called up, to join the cavalry, infantry or artillery corps. They could only live off the income from their estate, but their peasants often simply ran away. In order to maintain a battle-ready army, the government began to bind the peasants to the land, starting in 1497 with the Code of Laws, by means of decrees on entailed interests and statutes of limitations; serfdom was definitively introduced in the Council Code of 1648.

The making of Russia as an empire also begins, many historians agree, under the rule of Ivan the Terrible, with the conquest of the Khanates of Kazan and Astrakhan. The bolstering of the Ottoman Empire, which, after taking Constantinople, moved into the Balkans and the areas north of the Black Sea, prompted the activation of the Crimean Khanate, an Ottoman vassal which was openly hostile to Russia and coordinated its efforts with those of Kazan and Astrakhan. Incursions from the south were once again a curse for Russia. Kazan was taken in 1556, and it was in honor of this victory that the Church of Vasily the Blessed (better known as Saint Ba-

---

[18] Maxim Kovalevskiy, *Ocherki po istorii politicheskikh uchrezhdeniy Rossii* (*Sketches on the History of Russia's Political Establishments*). Moscow, 2007. PP. 71-72.

[19] Matvey Lyubavskiy, *Russkaya istoriya ot Skifii do Moskovii* (*Russian History from the Scythians to Muscovy*). Moscow, 2012. PP. 322-323.

sil's Cathedral) was erected on Moscow's Red Square. When they invaded Astrakhan, Russian forces moved into the North Caucasus, getting as far as Terek and the Caspian Sea.

Then came the turn of Siberia. The initial impulse for expansion eastwards arose in the 16th century through trade, and colonization by traders, led by the Stroganovs, merchants who supplied the equipment for the first expedition of Ermak. After this, the authorities took on the task. The conquest of Siberia proceeded along the rivers and "was like a military occupation in nature, and was expressed in the construction of Russian cities, towns and palisades on the local people's lands."[20]

Ivan the Terrible's son, Fyodor, was the last Tsar in the Rurik dynasty. He became known for establishing an independent Patriarchate in Russia, which also made it possible to create his own church metropolises. The death of Fyodor in 1598, who had no heir, and the election of Boris Godunov by the *Zemsky Sobor*, marked the start of the Time of Troubles (*Smuta*), when the country was caught in the grip of a bloody civil war, in which Poland and Sweden actively intervened. Those nations were still stronger than Russia and were competing with it for the title of Eastern Europe's superpower. During the Time of Troubles, the plan to bring Russia into the European system very nearly came to fruition, through subordination to Poland and union with it. Russia was on the verge of defeat but was saved by a mass mobilization of the people led by Prince Pozharsky and the elder from Nizhny Novgorod, Minin, who liberated Moscow's Kremlin from the Poles in 1612.

The man elected Tsar was the founder of a new dynasty – Mikhail Romanov (1613-1645). He governed the country with the help of the *Zemsky Sobor*, which met on a regular basis, and a system of decrees. Territorial expansion continued. Seafarers and explorers discovered and conquered land along the coast of the Arctic Ocean – right up to Chukotka. As the walrus tusks and sable fur reserves hunted for in the northern latitudes became depleted, however, the trailblazers moved further south. In 1643, the brigade led by Kurbat Ivanov, a Cossack explorer from Yakutsk, reached Baikal. At the same time, another brigade of experienced servicemen from Yakutsk, led by Vasiliy Poyarkov, discovered fertile land along the River Amur. Thereafter, it was the turn of the coastland, which was attractive by

---

[20] Matvey Lyubavskiy, *Obzor istorii russkoy kolonizatsii s drevneyshikh vremen i do XX veka* (*An Overview of the History of Russian Colonization from Ancient Times until the 20th Century*). Moscow, 1996. PP. 448, 455, 562.

dint of its favorable maritime climate: the Amur region proved to have the largest contingent of Russians in the Transbaikal.[21]

Russia's territorial expansion had reached the geographical boundaries beyond which it could no longer take the form of the filling of a geopolitical vacuum. In the East, its borders were strictly limited by the interests of China, in the South by those of the Ottoman empire, and in the West by those of Poland, Sweden and the Germanic states. Thereafter, almost all the territorial acquisitions that Russia made were accompanied by wars and/or were the results of wars. Even in those cases when a voluntary annexation occurred, the land in question was already dependent on someone else in some shape or form.

At the time of the formation of the Westphalian system, its participants did not recognize Russia as a partner, thinking of it as one of the barbarian states that they ought to conquer, like the American or African continents. Alexei Mikhailovich, "who had succeeded in the same decade as Louis XIV," observed Davis, "was an obscure Muscovite prince of whom, at Versailles, little was even known."[22] I suspect that this fact did not trouble Alexei Mikhailovich in the slightest, incidentally. In Russia, the first political experience of the new age – the English revolution and parliamentarianism – clearly did not go down well. When Charles I was beheaded by decision of Parliament in 1649, the Tsar was so offended that he banished all British merchants from Russia (something that played into the hands of the German and Dutch tradesmen). And while Charles II was in exile, Alexei sent him money and conveyed his most tender regards to "the disconsolate widow of that glorious martyr, King Charles I."[23]

In Russia, irritation at Western arrogance began to be combined with an appreciation of the need to learn from Western ways of doing things. In the second half of the 17th century, the secularization of culture started to take place, a genre of secular literature and poetry emerged, and secular painting came into being. In 1649, the Council Code was prepared, which was declared to be the highest law, and the principle of equality before the law was proclaimed; an objective was set whereby "the courts and justice

---

[21] N. I. Nikitin, "Prisoyedineniye Sibiri" ("The Annexation of Siberia"), in *Rossiyskaya Imperiya ot istokov do nachala XIX veka. Ocherki sotsial'no-politicheskoy i ekonomicheskoy istorii* (*Russian Empire from its Origins to the Beginning of the 19th Century: Essays on Socio-Political and Economic History*). Moscow, 2011.

[22] Norman Davies, *Europe: A History*. Pimlico, 1997. P. 649.

[23] Robert Massie, *Peter the Great*. Head of Zeus, 2016. P. 13.

should be equal for all in all matters".[24] A reform brought in by Alexei and the Patriarch Nikon, which stipulated a change to the church rituals and books in line with the rules of the Greek church, was to have serious consequences: it led to a split, whereby the "Old Believers", who refused to recognize the new developments, broke away from the official church.

More active expansion into the South began, first as a defence mechanism against incursions by Crimeans. The southern Russian cities were initially exclusively fortresses, protected by the cavalry of the nobility and by servicemen. In the South, the *Zasechnaya cherta* was created, which historian Vyacheslav Kozlyakov has described as a kind of Great Wall of China in the Russian style: "Only it was made not to last for centuries, out of stone, but out of the nearest resources to hand – the forests and the land, through the construction of piles of rubble and blocks, protected by specially recruited guards, and also by the local population." The second defensive line – the Belgorod line – was finally completed in the reign of Alexei Mikhailovich.[25] Peaceful colonization by peasants of the southern steppes, which were to be transformed, over time, into the main agricultural areas of Russia, only began in the 18th century.

Reunification with Ukraine, which had been ruled by the Poles, began after the *Pereyaslavl Rada*, which decided, in 1653, to move the "Left-Bank" of Ukraine under the protection of Russia. The *Zemsky Sobor* gave Alexei Mikhailovich its consent "for the Hetman Bogdan Khmelnitsky and all the troops of Zaporozhe, with the cities and the territories, to be taken under their sovereign wing for the Orthodox Christian faith and the saints of the Divine Churches."[26] This automatically prompted a war with Poland, after which Russia, under the Andrusovsky Treaty of 1667, obtained Kyiv and the Right-Bank of the Dnieper, Chernigov, and also Smolensk. At first, Ukraine enjoyed a large amount of autonomy. Its leader was the Hetman, elected at the Cossack Council and approved by Moscow; he was responsible for supreme governance and for justice, with support from the Council of Elders.

Kamchatka was first investigated in the winter of 1696 by an expedition from Chukotka led by the explorer Vladimir Atlasov, "in order to seek out new people, not subject to the *yasak* tax". Thereafter, in addition to Kamchatka, the Kuril Islands and Sakhalin were annexed, and Russian settlements

---

[24] Alexander Bokhanov, *Tsar Alexei Mikhailovich*. Moscow, 2012. PP. 178-198.

[25] Vyacheslav Kozlyakov, *Mikhail Fyodorovich*. Moscow, 2010. PP. 178-198.

[26] Ivan Belyayev, *Zemskiye sobory na Rusi: ot Ivana Groznogo do Yekateriny Velikoy* (*Land Assemblies in Rus: From Ivan the Terrible to Catherine the Great*). Moscow, 2013. PP. 60-61.

appeared in North America – in Alaska and on the West Coast – all the way up to Fort Ross, in the territory of what is now San Francisco. The areas where indigenous peoples dwelled were declared the property of the Tsar, and the main duty of the military commanders and servicemen sent there was to obtain, without inciting conflict, a *yasak*, a tribute paid in furs and collected regularly from the administrative districts, which were severally categorized as *volosts*, *ulus* or *yurts*.

The Great Power

Peter I became head of state in 1696 and ruled until 1725. Influenced by the exigencies of waging a large-scale war with Sweden and by his familiarization with the experiences of a host of Western countries – The Netherlands and England first and foremost – he decisively adopted a path of Westernization, which was implemented by means of brutal measures. Westernization manifested itself in all areas of life – from the shaving of beards and the introduction of European-style clothes to reforms in government administration, industry and the military. A new capital was built: St. Petersburg, as a symbol of a breakthrough towards Europe. The Senate was created as a replacement for the Boyar Duma, the country was divided into governorates, *prikaz* were replaced with collegiums, and the Academy of Sciences was created, along with theatres, the first newspaper, and hundreds of new plants and factories. A regular army and navy were created, and conscription was introduced, together with compulsory education for the children of the nobility in state academic institutions or abroad; compulsory life-long service in the military or in the civil service was reintroduced for the nobility.

The *Zemsky Sobors* ceased to convene, and Peter took as his model the absolutist state power that reigned supreme in most European countries in his day. At the same time, the monarchy would be constrained by the senior bureaucrats, the need to delegate powers, riots by the people and coups from within the royal court. "Paradoxically, by their insistence on the monopoly of political power Russian autocrats secured less effective authority than their constitutional counterparts in the west."[27]

Russia became a great European power after defeating Sweden at the battle of Poltava in 1709, and since then it has never lost this status, earning itself the position of a serious player in big politics in the Old World. Russia was declared an Empire by Peter the Great in 1721, after the decisive

---

[27] Richard Pipes, *Russia Under the Old Regime*. Penguin, 1995. P. 115.

victory over the Swedes in the Northern War and the attachment of land in the Eastern Baltic Region. Later, the governorates of this region – Lifland, Kurland and Estland – were unified into the Baltic General-Governorate. The basic principle of these governorates' administration was preserving the privileges of the Baltic barons, who served the throne of the Russian emperors truly and faithfully.

During the reign of Peter's daughter Elizabeth, Russia, after entering the Seven Years' War, defeated the mightiest military force in Europe – Prussia, and Russian troops entered Berlin. "It will need the whole of Europe to keep those gentlemen within bounds," said the despairing Frederick the Great.[28] He was saved by the Brandenburg miracle – the death of Elizabeth and the accession to the throne of Peter III, who considered the Prussian king a great genius, hero and mentor.

The country made its next great leap forward under Catherine the Great. Guided by the principles of free trade, the Empress granted to all classes the right to create manufacturing enterprises, and, via the Manifesto of 1775, industrial concerns. The peasants actively became involved in trade, capturing most of the market for foodstuffs, household goods and agricultural implements. The number of plants and factories increased 4-fold during Catherine II's reign. In 1768, the Manifesto was published, along with the edict signed by the Tsarina to the Senate "On the founding in St. Petersburg and Moscow of State Banks for the exchange of payment orders". The development of the seafaring trade, the establishment of foreign consulates, and the drawing up of trade conventions injected new life into foreign trade.

In terms of the number of wars, Catherine's reign is almost the record-holder in Russian history: there were three wars against Poland, two against Turkey and one each against Persia and Sweden. The prospect of a clash with France later reared its head. The art of military strategy reached new heights, thanks in no small part to such masters as Rumyantsev, Suvorov and Kutuzov. Under a treaty signed in Kuchuk-Kainarji in 1774, and the Treaty of Jassy of 1791, Turkey abandoned all claims to the Crimea, and Russia acquired Kuban and Novorossiya – from Bug to Dniester.

When the British colonies in America began their uprising in the 1770s, the British King George III asked Catherine to send an army and a fleet to quell the unrest. Potemkin allegedly said: "If England needed 20,000 soldiers, Russia could give them to her without a problem." Those 20,000 soldiers would probably have been enough to suppress the uprising and

---

[28] Cit. from: Norman Davies, *Europe: A History*. Pimlico, 1997. P. 649.

to postpone Independence Day in the USA by many decades. Catherine, however, had not forgotten George's refusal to sign a treaty of alliance, or to support her in Turkey or Poland. England was to go on harboring a grudge against Russia over this decision for a long time, though it was of course appreciated by the Americans fighting for independence.

On 13th October 1795, an agreement was signed on the third partition of Poland, between Russia, Prussia and Austria. Russia's acquisitions extended to the line that marks the Eastern border of present-day Poland. "Thus," notes Helene Carrere d'Encausse from the French Academy, "Russia restored to its borders the lands that were ruled over in the past by the ancestors of Rurik."[29] The division of Poland alone gave Russia 7.5 million new subjects (the entire population at the start of Catherine's reign was no more than 20 million). In the Ukrainian lands that were reattached, the Hetmanship was abolished, and the legal and taxation systems were aligned with those in place throughout Russia, as were the Ukrainian Cossack forces.

Russia's foreign policy exploits, seen as unqualified successes by its people, were viewed in an altogether different way by the outside world. As Henry Kissinger observed in *Diplomacy*, Russia provoked a dual attitude towards it: part hope and part fear, and this has been its lot right up until the present day.[30] The rise of Russia as a great power did not inspire any great feelings of sympathy for it in Europe.

Radical changes to the European system were brought about by the French Revolution, which blew up into a major international war. The main organizer of the three anti-French coalitions was the United Kingdom, while the backbone of the armed forces was supplied by Russia, Austria and Prussia. The Austrians fought without much success against the revolutionary soldiers in the Netherlands, and also in Northern Italy, where Bonaparte's star rose. It was in this period that Russia lost its great female ruler.

Paul I was ready, from an emotional perspective, to lead the forces fighting off revolution, which he saw as an absolute evil, as the machinations of the anti-Christ.[31] When Bonaparte seized Malta in 1798 and proclaimed the destruction of the Order of Saint John of Jerusalem, which was based there, Paul agreed to assume the title of Grand Master. When the French took Rome, they overthrew, robbed and carried back to France the Pope, Pius

---

[29] Helene Carrere d'Encausse, *Yekaterina II. Zolotoy vek v istorii Rossii* (*Catherine II. A Golden Age in Russian History*). Moscow, 2006. P. 342.
[30] Henry Kissinger, *Diplomacy*. Simon and Schuster, 1994. P. 74.
[31] Alexander Bokhanov, *Paul I*. Moscow, 1997. P. 62.

VI; Paul led his troops to Italy to liberate Rome, seeing it as his mission to be "the restorer of thrones and of defaced altars". Victories over the French in Northern Italy followed, along with a successful expedition by admiral Ushakov, who sailed to Naples and liberated Rome. Pius VII would later call Paul "a friend of humanity and a selfless protector and benefactor to the oppressed and downtrodden".[32]

Before long, however, after growing disillusioned with his unreliable allies, who treated even the Russian soldiers that had fought for them as second-class people, Paul effected a dramatic change of policy, and began smoothing over relations with France, where Bonaparte had restored order after the revolution, become the sole ruler, and brought an end to the persecution of the church. For his part, Napoleon saw the prospect of a powerful coalition, capable of destroying the global might of the British, and proposed, as the object of their first joint strike, "the pearl of the British Empire" – India. Paul responded by sending a corps of Cossacks to India.

Paul was against "privileges through birthright", and demanded that all the nobles serve the country irreproachably and unconditionally, and even permitted the use of corporal punishment against them. Paul's policy, which was brought in brutally and unceremoniously, made enemies of the influential Catherine-era elite. London spared no expense in its plans for a regime change operation in Russia, something that had been done in many other countries, and found some reliable partners in the royal court.

The grandson of Catherine the Great, Alexander I, who took the throne after the plot that led to the death of the Emperor Paul I, was determined to reform Russia during the first years of his reign: he decided to bring in a constitution and abolish serfdom. His decree "On free grain farmers" of 1803 was the first step in this direction. The collegiums brought in by Peter were replaced with ministries, and the State Council was founded as a body for discussing and preparing bills. Universities were opened, and the Lycée came into being, with its first set of graduates, led by Alexander Pushkin, greatly distinguishing itself; free primary education was established. Later, however, the reforms were brought to an end. For the umpteenth time, the reasons were resistance from the aristocracy to the weakening of the prerogatives of the monarch and to the abolition of serfdom, and the fact that a number of wars were taking place simultaneously: against Sweden, Persia, Turkey and, of course, against Napoleonic France.

---

[32] Cit. from: Alexander Bokhanov, *Paul I*. Moscow, 2010. P. 273.

The annexation of Finland can be explained as an attempt to move the border with Sweden, which was trying yet again to exact revenge for Poltava, further away from St. Petersburg. The special status of the Great Principality of Finland was established; it was so special, indeed, that officials could not agree on what exactly it was – an independent state, in a close union with Russia, or an autonomous province.

The protection of the Christians in the Caucasus was considered in Russia to be a sacred duty that was not open to debate. The Tsar of the unified Kartli-Kakhetia, Irakli II, signed the Treaty of Georgievsk in 1783, whereby Russia began to rule over its protectorate. His son, Georgy XII, opened negotiations about a full accession to the Russian Empire, the result of which was the corresponding manifesto of 1801. Persia and the Ottoman Empire saw this as a direct threat to their interests, while Britain saw it as an indirect and potential one. Russian troops had to be sent into the Caucasus, and this prompted a war with Persia, and then with Turkey. Land in Eastern Armenia that was divided up between these two countries came under the control of Russia in 1805-1828, forming the Erivan Governorate. Land in Azerbaijan became the battlefields of the Russo-Persian war. Under the Treaty of Gulistan of 1813, Persia acknowledged the inclusion of Georgia and the Azerbaijani khanates in the Russian Empire. The rear and supply lines of the Russian army in the Caucasus were constantly under threat from the primeval world of Circassian and Adygean tribes in the North Caucasus, most of whom were already allied to Turkey by that time. The effort to subdue these peoples turned into the 60-year Caucasian War (it has still not completely ended even today, one might add). Russia became bogged down in the Caucasus.

An overestimation of Russia's military capabilities forced Alexander I to join the ranks of the third anti-Napoleon coalition. The Tsar was made all too aware of the hastiness of his decision in 1805 at Austerlitz, where Russian forces suffered a humiliating defeat. Serious conclusions were drawn from this debacle, resulting in the Russian army borrowing tactics of military organization from France. By 1812, the number of Russian soldiers had reached 620,000 men, of which 210,000 to 220,000 were located on the western border. They were up against the Grande Armée, which had 610,000 men. There were few outside Russia who doubted that Napoleon would achieve yet another victory.

Alexander and his War Minister, Barclay de Tolly, had other ideas, though. Thanks to an extremely effective intelligence system, they were kept well informed about Napoleon's plans and capabilities and they drew up a three-year strategic plan, involving long drawn out skirmishes in the depths of Russian territory in 1812, followed by the shifting of the war outside the border in 1813 and 1814. Napoleon, after invading Russia, gradually scattered his forces, setting up communications along the route to Moscow, while the Russian high command, avoiding a decisive battle for a long time, was able to increase its readiness significantly.

After depleting Napoleon's troops in the decisive battle at Borodino, the Russian high command decided not to defend Moscow. Napoleon was not a self-critical man, putting his later failures down to the climate.[33] While waiting for the start of peace talks in Moscow, he lost a catastrophic amount of time: his army began to fall apart and melt away, and winter was approaching. The result of the patriotic War of 1812 was the almost complete destruction of the Grande Armée. Clausewitz has calculated that of the 610,000 men, 552,000 were either killed or taken prisoner in Russia.[34] Only the sluggishness of the Russian high command at Berezino prevented the complete destruction of the French army. In December 1812, Napoleon, who had survived by some miracle, repeated several times in Warsaw: "It is only one step from the sublime to the ridiculous."

In the European Concert of Powers

The Russian forces set off to "catch the monster in its lair". Russia's position at the time was strong enough to secure the signing of the second Paris agreement in November 1815, signed after Napoleon's capitulation on behalf of a vanquished France by the Duke Armand-Emmanuel de Richelieu (better known in Russia as Emmanuil Osipovich) – a lieutenant-general in the Russian army and founder of the city of Odessa, who was at that time prime minister of France under King Louis XVIII.

Alexander I was the man who initiated the creation of the Holy Alliance, intended to preserve the new political status quo in Europe; the deed creating this alliance was written with his hand. It was an alliance of Christian states, originally Russia, Austria and Prussia, which was subject to "the divine truths taught by the eternal law of God the Savior". The Prince Regent of England, George, Prince of Wales, later joined the alliance (as the Hanover Regent), and so too did the French, Swedish and Norwegian kings, and the kings of Denmark, the Netherlands, Sardinia, the two Sicilies, Spain, Portu-

---

[33] Napoleon Bonaparte, *Put' k imperii* (*The Road to Empire*). Moscow, 2011. P. 449.
[34] Carl von Clausewitz, *1812*. Moscow, 1937. P. 229.

gal, the states and free cities of Germany, and the Swiss union. Only Turkey remained outside the framework of the common European-wide system.

This marked the start of the European concert of powers, which gave the Old World the most peaceful century in its history. What preserved the relative peace was the balance of powers, an important component of which was Russia, without whom, as people said at the time, not a single cannon was fired in Europe.

During the reign of Nicholas I (1825-1855), which began to the sound of firing by the insurgent Decembrists, as they sought to bring about either a first ever revolution, or one last court coup in the style of the previous century, talk of reform was forgotten.[35]

An attempt was made to devise a new state ideology, which took the form of a theory of "official national ethos", in which Orthodoxy, sovereign autocracy, and national ethos were declared to be the traditional pillars of Russian statehood. During Nicholas' thirty-year reign, if there was any following of the European model, then it was in the techniques of state governance. For the first time, the emphasis was placed on the apparatus of state, the backbone of which was provided by the military, who had shown their loyalty in battle. The legislation was codified, technical and military education were introduced, and the first shareholders' charter emerged. Construction began on the railways, and a state-of-the-art observatory was built at Pulkovo.

Nicholas I, who is referred to, not without some justification, as Europe's last knight, was extremely true to the monarchic principle and to his obligations as an ally to Prussia and Austria, even sending troops to crush the Hungarian uprising in 1849. Excessive activity in the Caucasus, however, and the establishment of a protectorate over the Orthodox Danube principalities and attempts to establish a protectorate over the Christian Holy sites in Palestine, which were located in territory ruled by the Ottomans, led to the unsuccessful Crimean War against a powerful anti-Russian coalition consisting of Britain, France and other states, during which the Emperor died. Cast to the side of European politics, Russia, as the Chancellor Alexander Gorchakov put it, did not take offence. It was gathering its strength.

Alexander II (1855-1881) undertook a grandiose social experiment, amounting to a revolution from the top down. The Manifesto on the abolition of serfdom in 1861 marked the start of a whole series of profound transformations. Among these was trial by jury. The elected *zemstvo* (local self-governing bodies) came into being, thanks to which doctors, agrono-

---

[35] Alexander Bokhanov, *Nikolay I*. Moscow, 2008. PP. 10, 9.

mists, veterinarians and elementary schools were introduced into the villages, along with statistical analysis. Public self-governance appeared in the cities as well, with elected assemblies, Dumas, and city councils. An expansion of freedom of expression, of education, and of academic research became the basis for the successes of Russian science, enabling an increase in the level of literacy in society and the attainment of some of the greatest heights in Russian culture: Dostoevsky, Tolstoy, Tchaikovsky.

Petersburg was firmly on the side of the North in the Civil War that was raging in the USA. The presence of the Atlantic fleet under Rear Admiral Stepan Lesovsky in the port of New York, and of the Pacific fleet of Rear Admiral Andrey Popov in San Francisco, prevented interference by the British.[36] Uncertain of his ability to maintain control over Alaska, and keen to secure closer ties with Washington, Alexander II saw fit to sell the region to America in 1867 for the sum of 7 million dollars.

The Russo-Turkish War of 1877-1878 gave independence to Montenegro, Serbia and Romania, and autonomy to Bulgaria; Russia annexed the mouth of the Danube, Batum, Kars, and Ardagan. The Russian Empire advanced into Central Asia, to where Russian troops had penetrated, chasing off the local semi-criminal brigades that were troubling the settlements and fortresses of the Caspian, the Southern Urals and Kazakhstan. Moreover, Russia was concerned by the military and political incursion into the region by Great Britain. In 1868, the Russian forces took Khiva, and in 1884 Merv. The amount of money spent by Russia on supporting its mid-Asian acquisitions was three times higher than the income it derived from them. Railways began to be laid there, along with European-style construction in the cities, and the slave trade was abolished.

On 13th March 1881, Alexander II, the "Tsar the Liberator", was blown up by a terrorist from *Narodnaya volya* ("The Will of the People"). Russia was the motherland of terror. One of the organizers of the attack was a student from Petersburg University, Alexander Ulyanov, the brother of Vladimir Lenin. On the day of his brother's execution, Lenin would declare that he was going to take a different path.

Alexander III (1881-1894) felt no piety in respect of the intelligentsia (which welcomed the assassination of the Tsar), and the intelligentsia, in turn, claimed that the Emperor lacked common sense and any understand-

---

[36] Yuriy Bulatov, "'Tam, gde podnyat russkii flag, on uzhe opuskat'sya ne dolzhen.' Kto i zachem prodal Russkuyu Ameriku?" ("Wherever the Russian Flag is Raised, It Must Not be Lowered"), *Mezhdunarodnaya zhizn'* (*International Life*), April 2015. P. 134.

ing of progress. "Emperor Alexander III believed that most Russian disasters stemmed from the inappropriate liberalism of our civil servants and from the exclusive characteristic of Russian diplomacy to give in to all manner of foreign influences," recalled the Great Prince Alexander Mikhailovich.[37]

Alexander III saw no need for radical change, the reason being that abroad, he was not only not criticized (as every single other Russian ruler had been criticized, no matter what they did), but was even held up as an example to copy. The German Chancellor, Bismarck, even spoke in favor of "the Russian path of development" as the right course for his country. The state once again began to reinforce its role in the economy; one of the measures introduced was a ban on the building and operating of railroads by private companies. A tough customs system was rolled out – the country was moving from free trade to protectionism. In the 1880s, a real industrial boom began, changing the face of the country in a serious way: it created annual growth of 5% right up until 1914.

Alexander III outlined his foreign policy credo: "I understand one policy: to extract from everything all that is necessary and of use to Russia, and to be less shy about extracting that benefit, but to act directly and decisively. Our policy will be purely Russian, national… we can have no other…"[38] As Sergey Witte would later write of Alexander III, "His gigantic frame, which appeared to be some sort of giant incapable of turning back, with its extremely benevolent physiognomy and infinitely kind eyes, instilled in Europe what seemed to be fear, on the one hand, and bewilderment on the other: what is this? Everyone was afraid lest this giant should suddenly start roaring."[39]

In the late 18th and early 19th centuries, the foundations of Russia's intellectual tradition were laid, too. The main intellectual trends and philosophy in Russia came into being as a reaction to European thought. Foreign theories were initially taken as the gospel truth and as a roadmap for action, without any need for critical or skeptical analysis. Russian thought did not create a philosophical system of its own, understood in the abstract, a purely intellectual systematization of knowledge. Philosophy was closely related to life

---

[37] "Aleksandr Mikhaylovich (vel. knyaz'). Kniga vospominaniy" ("The Great Prince Alexander Mikhailovich. Memoirs"), in *Aleksandr Tretiy. Vospominaniya. Dnevniki. Pis'ma* (*Alexander III: Memoirs. Diaries. Letters*). St. Petersburg, 2001. P. 108.

[38] Cit. from: Oleg Ayrapetov, *Istoriya vneshney politiki Rossiyskoy imperii. 1801-1914* (*The Foreign Policy of the Russian Empire. 1801-1914*). Moscow, 2006. P. 361.

[39] Sergey Witte, *Vospominaniya. Polnoye izdaniye v odnom tome* (*Memoirs. Complete Edition in One Volume*). Moscow, 2010. P. 313.

and moralizing, and therefore it was more often discovered in literature and political journalism than in academic treatises.

The spectrum of politics and ideas in Russia – the distance between the left and the right – was already, in the 19th century, a good deal broader than anywhere else, and this pluralism was to be reproduced in post-Soviet Russia. The ideological delineating lines of today can in many ways be traced back to this period.

One can consider as the founder of the conservative tradition Nikolay Karamzin, who, appalled by the brutality of the French Revolution, harbored a strong preference for Russia's organic roots. The key carriers of the conservative tradition were Slavophiles – the followers of Aleksey Khomyakov, who saw in Russia's primordial nature an advantage – the Orthodox belief, the principles of *zemstvo* and estate division, the peasant commune, the absence of a class struggle. Conservatism also continued as an intellectual trend that was not related to the Slavophile movement (Pushkin in his later period, Gogol, Tyutchev, Dostoyevsky). The conservative, protective trend was associated with the activity of the last Russian emperors, and its ideologues were Uvarov, Katkov and Pobedonostsev. Nationalism took on an extreme form in the shape of the Black Hundreds.

Liberalism, by all accounts, began with Alexander Radishchev, who was nourished by ideas from the French enlightenment and attached great emphasis to empathy and love of one's fellow men. A large number of liberals found themselves among the ranks of the Westerners (of whom I consider Pyotr Chaadayev to be the first), who objected to serfdom, autocracy, bureaucracy, the fact that the country lagged behind other states, and illiteracy, and called on the country to take England and France as examples. It was out of liberal Westernism, after it had been given a dose of Marxism, anarchy and nationalist ideas, that Russian socialism was to take root and grow; it was foretold by Vissarion Belinsky, and its main proponents, ideologues and practitioners were to be Vladimir Lenin (Ulyanov) and Josef Stalin (Dzhugashvili). During Soviet times, the Socialist idea, in its Communist form – with the addition of the dictatorship of the proletariat – was to remain the only recognized ideology, although all the other trends immediately made themselves manifest upon the first signs of a thaw.

The development of market relations, the emergence of independent centers of economic might, and the start of the construction of civil society required great polycentrism, swift decision-making, the legal mechanisms for the channeling of initiatives and protest from below, and social mobility.

Nicholas II (1894-1917) understood this, too. He began to introduce reforms with cautious steps, demonstrating the style that was soon to become his calling card, which Ivan Solonevich characterized as follows: "Slowly, as ever, and as ever with a huge amount of stubbornness – without breaking anything straight away, but gradually re-doing everything."[40] Nicholas made concessions to the demands made by students, restoring the autonomy of the universities. Laws began to be developed, making it easier for peasants to depart from communes, incentivizing the building of farmsteads, and farmsteads became private property. Nicholas considered the expansion of the rights of the *zemstvo*, which was protesting against bureaucratic supervision, to be an important factor in the modernization of the country.

The Russian liberals, who were forced to compete with the extremely radical socialist organizations for the sympathies of the people, themselves took up far more left-wing positions than similar groups in Western Europe.

Russia's failings in the war with Japan in 1904-1905 led initially to serious discontent among the intelligentsia and liberal nobility, and then to mass protests in the cities, armed clashes and peasant revolts. "[R]ussian dreams of an Asian destiny had metamorphosed into a nightmare of military defeat and revolution."[41] Against the backdrop of the nationwide strike in the autumn of 1905, the Emperor Nicholas II agreed to a serious liberalization of the political system.

Russia acquired a constitution, political freedoms, and a two-chamber parliament, and became a constitutional monarchy. The first two State Dumas, in which the liberal party of constitutional democrats (cadets) held a majority, were so dominated by the opposition that their assemblies turned into an endless demonstration against the government, and they were dissolved after just a few months' work. Only the Third Duma, elected in 1907, in which the leading party was the more moderate Octobrist party, got on with the business of lawmaking and completed its full five-year term. The uprisings in the country continued until 1907 and were suppressed through the efforts of the Prime Minister, Pyotr Stolypin, using force. Under Stolypin, Russia made a powerful surge forward on the economic front, but he was killed in Kyiv in 1911 by a socialist revolutionary.

---

[40] Ivan Solonevich, *Velikaya fal'shivka fevralya* (*The Great Falsehood of February*). Moscow, 2007. P. 21.

[41] David S. van der Oye, *Toward the Rising Sun: Russian Ideologies of Empire and the Path to War with Japan*. Nothern Illinois University Press, 2001. P. 109.

Russia found itself drawn into the First World War on account of its obligations with respect to its allies in the Entente, whose other members were Britain and France; and because of its own geopolitical interests in the Balkans and its allies in the Slavic states, which were increasingly threatened by Austria-Hungary, Germany and the Ottoman Empire.

The Collapse of Russia – 1917

There are still a large number of myths surrounding the First World War and the revolution that followed it in 1917. The view most commonly held, particularly in Soviet times, was this: a weak and poor Russia suffered defeat in the First World War, its economy collapsed, the army fell apart, the country's human resources were depleted, famine struck the country, the hopelessly incompetent and arrogant government led the country along the way of treason, and because of that the bourgeoisie overthrew it in February, before itself being overthrown in October by the proletariat and the peasantry. All this is a long way from the truth!

In the early 20th century, Russia was not a superpower, but it was one of the great powers. 22.4 million square kilometers (the area of the present-day Russian Federation is around 17 million square kilometers). The population was around 170 million people, or one in every eight people on the planet (today it is one in every 50). The Russian economic miracle was a reality. According to overall statistics on industrial development, Russia was fourth in the world, and its share of global industrial production amounted to 8.2%.[42]

Russia was no longer an absolutist monarchy, and Nicholas II was a competent ruler of the country. He demonstrated courage when he assumed command of the army in August 1915, after which its battle-readiness increased. On the domestic front, he tried to demonstrate his will, the fact that he was not subordinate to the demands of the Duma and, at the same time, to maneuver his way forward, agreeing to make concessions here and there to opposition demands, resulting in frequent changes in the cabinet, a phenomenon that was not helpful at a time of war.

At the start of the war, Russian business actively encouraged the transition to an economic focus on military matters, and played an active part in forming military and industrial committees and town and country unions (*Zemgors*), which undertook to provide multi-faceted support to the front line. These organizations, however, were to become one of the most import-

---

[42] P. Kennedy, *The Rise and Fall of the Great Powers*. N. Y., 1987. P. 202.

ant instruments for the destabilization of imperial power. In the *Zemgor* circles, lists of names for a future government were drawn up as early as in 1915, almost completely matching the composition of the first Provisional government, which came into being after the February revolution. The *Zemgor* circles also gave rise to the concept of the "bloc of black forces", which spread far and wide throughout the country: the Germanophile royalist set, which was in favor of a separate peace. It was declared that the Empress Alexandra Fyodorovna and Georgy Rasputin were its leaders, although nobody found any evidence of their treachery.

The leading social group that brought the revolution closer was the intelligentsia. During the war, defeatist, anti-government feeling among the intelligentsia proved to be fairly widespread, and many felt that patriotism was the refuge of scoundrels. It was from among the intelligentsia that all the opposition political parties were mainly formed: from the liberals to the extremist and terrorist parties, including the Bolsheviks.

As the war dragged on, the proletariat and the peasantry began to ask questions about the justness of its aims, about the correctness of government policy, and they were not always satisfied with the answers they were given.

Foreign forces played a role in the Russian revolution. Like the other countries fighting in the war, Russia was the subject of behind-the-scenes diplomacy, efforts by intelligence services to undermine it, international PR campaigns, and financial machinations. The Central powers actively tried to undermine Russia as part of an "orange peel strategy": to break Russia apart "like an orange, with no knife or wound, into its natural historical and ethnic components" – Finland, Poland, Bessarabia, the Baltic region, Ukraine, the Caucasus, and Turkestan, which were to become independent states under German control.[43] The Institute for the Study of the Social Consequences of the War in Copenhagen, a body that was financed by Germany and led by Gelfand (Parvus) sponsored not only Lenin and the Bolsheviks, but other opponents of the regime as well. A contribution to the growing revolutionary trends was also made by Russia's allies, whose policy had three layers to it, at least. At the level of the heads of state, the degree of trust was high (though this did not prevent them from betraying Nicholas II). At the second level, among the elite, people held a dim view of Russia, considering it to be a dictatorship, and believing Russians to be a semi-barbarian tribe. Hence

---

[43] Gerhard Schiesser and Jochen Trauptmann, *Russkaya ruletka. Nemetskiye den'gi dlya russkoy revolyutsii* (*Russian Roulette: German Money for the Russian Revolution*). Moscow, 2004. PP. 19-21.

the bad press that Russia and its ruler were given. At the third level, the political one, the foreign powers provided support to the opposition inside the country. When, one might well ask, has the West's policy towards Russia been any different?

By the time of the February Revolution, Russia was prepared militarily and economically for a successful continuation of its military actions. The size of the field army, which had no more than 4 million soldiers in 1915, stood at 7 million by the end of 1916. The country grew its own defence industry significantly. Difficulties with the supply of foodstuffs were smaller in scale in Russia than in the other countries fighting in the war, and were only seen in the big cities, not affecting the bulk of the population – the peasantry – at all. The total number of men killed, wounded or who died from their wounds (5.5 million) was lower than the number in Germany (6.05 million), which had fought on two fronts. As a percentage of the total number of men mobilized, it was the smallest of all the main warring countries. It was already clear that the United States was soon going to enter the war on the side of the Entente.

We can only speculate as to how long the First World War might have lasted, and how it might have ended, had the revolution not occurred – a revolution that had as a consequence a shameful defeat for Russia and the enforced and humiliating Treaty of Brest-Litovsk. What we do know, however, is how the war did in fact end: Germany surrendered in November 1918. It seems reasonable to suppose that had Russia remained among the warring countries, and had the strategic plans agreed between the allies been implemented, the war might have ended in the same way – with victory for the Entente – only a good deal earlier, and with Russia being among the winners.

The Russian empire fell victim to a number of destructive tides which came together in two points: on the streets of the capital and at the military's General Headquarters. All of these tides took the form of barely concealed plots, which were hatched in circles of the Duma, the aristocracy, the *Zemgor*, and Socialist groups, and by this time fully involved those at the top of the army. The leader of the General Headquarters of High Command, the infantry general Mikhail Alekseev, an advocate of replacing Nicholas II with his brother, Mikhail, presented the Tsar with the most persuasive argument of all in favor of abdicating: the stance adopted by the leaders of the army.

The Provisional Government was established, whose ministers were members of the *Zemgor*, the Progressive bloc in the Duma, and of Masonic lodges. At the same time, though, socialist parties formed a Soviet of worker and soldier deputies, which supervised the government, and this created a diarchy. Rule by the oligarchic and intellectual elite, which did not fully understand the nature of power or of the country, led to a situation whereby, during the course of a few days in February – March, 1917, the Russian state disappeared. "Russia in the spring of 1917 may well represent a unique instance of a government born of a revolution dissolving the machinery of administration before it had a chance to replace it with one of its own creation," Richard Pipes noted in utter astonishment.[44]

The collapse of the state was exploited by the radical left-wing party, the Bolsheviks, which had a majority in the Soviets by the fall; relying on these Soviets, Lenin declared that he had supreme power. The Bolsheviks engendered hope for obtaining both peace and land, and this gave them the ladder to clamber up to power: the army. The idea of expropriating the expropriators found a shorter path to the soul of the people than the concept of constitutionalism. Bolshevism also filled the widely felt need for order. According to Nikolay Berdyayev, "Russia faced the threat of complete anarchy, an anarchical collapse; it was established as a Communist dictatorship, which found slogans to which the people agreed to subordinate themselves."[45] In the first instance, Lenin's government had almost no-one to fight against. And, indeed, no-one was in a hurry to offer resistance, since there was a strong belief that the Bolsheviks would be "king for a day" and would only last until the Constituent Assembly, at most. They lasted 74 years.

The USSR

Bolshevism in power was an eclectic product with many composite parts, nurtured in the objective conditions of Russian daily life, in the international isolation that had emerged, and which also reflected the attempts of the zealously fanatical Bolshevik party to bring to life Russified Marxist principles using traditional Russian methods. The Soviet Union was an ideocratic state. For the first time, an ideological construction had come into being which consciously went against mankind's entire previous experience.

The ideology of Soviet Socialism in its pure form stipulated the seizure by the state of key positions in the economy and the introduction of planning in the economy. The main difference between the Soviet economic model and the pre-revolutionary one was the matter of property. In 1914, the state

---

[44] Richard Pipes, *The Russian Revolution*. FontanaPress, 1992. P. 322.

[45] Nikolay Berdyayev, *Istoki i smysl russkogo kommunizma* (*The Origins and Meaning of Russian Communism*). Moscow, 1990. P. 109.

owned 8.3% of capital and 10% of all industrial enterprises. The Soviet state gradually took possession of all of the country's enterprises and capital.

The main principle in foreign policy was proletarian internationalism: subordination of the interests of the proletarian struggle in one country to the interests of this same struggle on a worldwide scale; being ready and willing, on behalf of a nation that had achieved a victory over the bourgeoisie, to make sacrifices for the sake of toppling international capital. The Communist International was seen as a crushing force in world revolution, uniting Communist Parties created with the Bolsheviks' support all over the planet. One must not underestimate the pragmatism of the leaders of Soviet Russia, however, or their need to come to terms with reality.

After the revolution of 1917, Russia collapsed. Poland, Finland, Lithuania, Latvia and Estonia departed, and Romania took possession of Bessarabia. Early in 1918, Germany and her allies recognized Ukraine as an independent state, the front in the Caucasus collapsed, and the Georgians, Armenians and Azerbaijanis proclaimed an independent Caucasian Federation on the land that had not yet been conquered by the Turks. Separatist movements flared up in Central Asia; Siberia announced its independence and expressed the hope that it would one day be united with a de-Bolshevized Russia. By the summer of 1918, there were at least 30 governments on the territory of the former Russian Empire. A bloody Civil War began.

Attempts to bring in volunteer-militia principles in the building of the army, undertaken at the dawn of Soviet rule, soon failed, and were replaced with proper military organization, enabling the Bolshevik Red Army to achieve victory in the Civil War over the White Armies, which were supported by the Western countries. The war cost 8 million lives, set the country's economy back fifty years, and led to a maximum centralization of power and militarization in the consciousness of the Bolshevik leaders. Through steel, blood and diplomacy, the state was partially restored.

In 1920-1921, agreements were concluded with the Russian, Ukrainian and Belarusian Soviet Republics, and the Bukharan and Khoresm People's Soviet Republics and the Far Eastern Republic. The agreements ensured "independence and sovereignty", stipulating the joining of forces for the purposes of defence and construction of the economy. The biggest problems were created by Georgia, which even then was weighed down by close relations with all its neighbors. Only in March 1922 did Moscow manage to draw it into a union with Azerbaijan and Armenia, by concluding an agreement on the Caucasian Federation, which also became part of an alliance with the RSFSR. The actual unity of these formally independent countries was conditioned less by the agreements than by the fact that they were all ruled by the Bolshevik Party. In December 1922, an agreement was signed on the creation of the USSR as a state, open for the addition to it of other socialist republics.

Soviet federalism did not mean the delegating of political and economic power to the republics, but it took the interests of the separate nations into account in the process of administrative and territorial division and in its policy. The American expert on the matter, Terry Martin, suggests that such a model should be called "internationalist nationalism" or "affirmative action". The leaders of the Soviet Union created national elites in the places where there were none or where they were weak, encouraging and supporting various forms of national culture and identity wherever it was pertinent to do so, and they enabled the "territorialization" of ethnicity, creating national territories at various levels and establishing new official languages.[46]

Economic collapse in the conditions of the "military communism" of the Civil War, and mass armed riots by the peasantry forced Lenin, in 1921, to push through the adoption of the "New Economic Policy" (the NEP), which stipulated that market relations could be used as long as the state's commanding position in industry was preserved. Thanks to the NEP, the problem of famine was solved and economic growth was restored by the mid-1920s, but the Kremlin (the capital having been moved from St. Petersburg back to Moscow in 1918) was not able to accumulate substantial resources with which to create heavy industry and a defence industry. The NEP was also widely criticized within the Communist party as an anti-Marxist diversion.

After Lenin's death in 1924, an intense power struggle took place among the country's leaders, in which Stalin and his henchmen triumphed over both the extreme left-wing communists – the supporters of Trotsky, Kamenev and Zinoviev, who had insisted on an immediate push for worldwide revolution and the enforced rejection of market relations, and those further to the right – Rykov and Bukharin, who were no less ardent advocates of worldwide revolution, but were against the idea of rejecting the NEP. As for Stalin, he proposed the concept of "the triumph of socialism in one country", postponing worldwide revolution until better times.

He crushed real and imagined opposition through purges, cast the NEP aside, and introduced the forcible modernization of the country through industrialization and the creation of large collective farms in rural areas.

---

[46] Terry Martin, *The Affirmative Action Empire: Nations and Nationalism in the Soviet Union, 1923-1939*. Cornell University Press, 2001. PP. 430-431.

Industrialization, collectivization and a cultural revolution were portrayed as a single and mutually related whole, synchronized in time. Increased appropriation of grain from the countryside and foreign loans were supposed to facilitate a rapid industrial advance, making it possible, with the help of new teams of engineers and workers, and by buying up state-of-the-art equipment from the West, to create modern industrial sectors, a defence complex, and also a fleet of agricultural machinery.

The collective farms were to be saturated with machinery and workforces, so that they became more efficient than those owned by the so-called "grasping fists" (*kulaks*). In this way, peasants of average means would gradually be enticed into the collective farms. This, in turn, was supposed to provide the raw material of industry, to ensure a guaranteed supply of foodstuffs to industrial centers that were rapidly expanding into the countryside, and make it possible to increase grain exports.

The Soviet cultural revolution resulted in almost universal literacy among the population, and the creation of serious scientific and technical potential. And as a result of the first few five-year-plans, the Soviet Union did indeed create a powerful heavy industry, which enabled it to begin the mechanization of agriculture and dramatically increase its defensive might.

Industrialization and collectivization were implemented at an exceptionally high cost, accompanied by the elimination of the *kulaks*, the Gulag forced labor camps, and cleansing purges, which were explained away not least as part of an effort to prevent a "fifth column" from emerging as the prospect of war with Hitler's Germany loomed.

From the moment Hitler came to power, there was never the slightest doubt that war with Germany was inevitable: documents from the NSDAP setting out its plans referred in no uncertain terms to the capture and colonization of the Soviet Union and the extermination of the majority of its "racially sub-standard" population. From the early 1930s onwards, the USSR was in a state of intense conflict with Japan, which had invaded China. To counter the growing military threat, the USSR managed to join the League of Nations, and promoted the initiative of an Eastern Pact (the idea was rejected by Germany and Poland), and provided help to the republicans in Spain. Moscow offered the Western states, and was itself willing to provide, guarantees of security to the Eastern European countries that were under threat from Germany, but France and Britain favored a policy of trying to pacify the aggressor, the symbol of which became Munich.

The Soviet Union was arming itself at a rapid pace; it had the highest rate of growth in defence spending of all countries, barring perhaps Germany in one particular year – 1938.⁴⁷ The third five-year-plan was drawn up to take into account the Anti-Comintern Pact between Germany, Italy and Japan – and the possibility of a military coalition between all its members, which also could include Poland and Romania.

In 1939, the USSR was willing and able to help Poland, which was openly hostile at the time. In order for this to happen, it would have to accept guarantees of its security from the Soviet side. Nobody proved able to persuade Warsaw to agree to this, however. Naturally, Moscow would have preferred an alliance with the Western democracies, and it proposed this several times. Negotiations were held in Moscow in the summer of 1939, but the British and French representatives did not even have any authority to draw up any kind of agreement.

On the night of 23rd August, the Soviet-German non-aggression treaty was signed, better-known as the Molotov-Ribbentrop Pact. The Soviet leaders resorted to this because there were mere days remaining until the German invasion of Poland, and for Moscow, the issue was about where the German troops would stop. The pact, as Winston Churchill wrote, was as cynical as it was a coldly calculated political step. It gave the USSR a chance not to have to engage in war with the Germans immediately, and to grow its military capabilities – in two years, the Soviet Union's defence potential doubled. It also meant the war could be started with more strategically acceptable borders. The Soviet Union by no means became an ally of Germany, it merely stole some breathing space.

By the start of the Great Patriotic War, the USSR has become a highly industrialized country capable of surpassing almost all the European economy, which worked for Hitler's Germany, in military production. From March 1941, the economy started to function according to a wartime regime.

After the beginning of WWII, Moscow divided spheres of influence with Germany, becoming reunited with Western Ukraine, Western Belarus, Bessarabia and the Baltic states, which it had lost during the Civil War. There were many tragedies for these states and their citizens. Would things have been better for them, though, if they been occupied by the Nazis in August 1939?

The invasion of the USSR on 22nd June 1941 initially brought success to the German troops, of whom there were some 5.5 million. Marshal Georgiy Zhukov wrote about the failures of the first stage of the war: "The main

---

⁴⁷ Paul Kennedy, *The Rise and Fall of the Great Powers*. N. Y., 1987. P. 296.

reasons were that the war caught our armed forces while they were still reorganizing and re-arming themselves with better weaponry; and that our soldiers on the border had not yet been put on a war footing, had not been made fully ready for battle, and were not deployed in accordance with all the rules of operative art for maintaining an active strategic defence... The nature of the strike itself – a sudden offensive on a grand scale, and, moreover, by all the existing forces and all those deployed earlier along the most important strategic routes, had not been taken into account by us to the full extent."[48]

After wearing down the enemy with defensive battles, the Red Army went on the counter-attack outside Moscow in late 1941. And although the following year saw successes for the Nazis on the southern flank and they penetrated as far as Stalingrad, the counter strikes by Soviet forces enabled them in 1944 to liberate the territories captured by the Germans, to conduct military action in Eastern Europe, and, in early May 1945, to raise the Banner of Victory above the Reichstag.

The role played by the USSR in the war was clear for all to see: it destroyed 80% of the German divisions, losing 27 million lives in the fascists' extermination machine. It was the greatest Victory in the history of mankind, achieved over the most terrifying enemy in the history of mankind, at the greatest cost in the history of mankind. Not a single family was left untouched by the tragedy of the war. The Soviet Union won the war and considered itself entitled to play a considerable role in forming the conditions of life in the post-war world.

Moscow established an extensive sphere of control in Eastern Europe, historically within the realm of the West, and this was one of the causes of the Cold War. The other reason was the American leaders' chosen course of securing global dominance and preventing the emergence of a power capable of interfering with this ambition. The Western system was built against the USSR, specifically, as part of the strategy of "containment", or, at the very least, on the basis of an attempt to keep the Soviet Union outside its framework. The Soviet threat was seen as an existential one. The USSR was laying claim not only to an expansion of its field of influence (this had been the standard behavior of great powers since time immemorial), but also bringing to fruition an alternative project for social organization.

....

[48] Georgiy Zhukov, Memuary i Razmyshleniya (*Memoirs and Reflections*). Vol. 1. Moscow, 2013. PP. 280, 281.

The Historic Alternative

The Soviet Union became a superpower as a result of creating a global socialist system, acquiring a thermonuclear weapon, and the fact that it broke new ground in science. The USSR was a pioneer in space exploration, launching the first satellite in 1957 and sending Yuriy Gagarin into orbit in 1961, and in the creation of atomic energy. Dominic Lieven wrote of the USSR: "From 1945 to 1991 it was recognized as one of the world's two superpowers."[49] The USSR not only embodied the great socialist idea; it also led the resistance, in the 20th century, to the liberal, capitalist global order, to the values for which that world order stood, and its main bastion – the mighty Anglo-American military-political bloc. Soviet Socialism openly laid claim to the title of an utterly new civilization of universal scale, and of global proliferation. It laid claim to being the herald of the end of history. It was an empire whose influence and ambitions were genuinely grandiose.[50]

Stalin died in 1953 in mysterious circumstances, which leave us unable to rule out the possibility that he suffered a violent death at the hands of his colleagues, among whom most suspicion must fall on Beria, who was also executed that year. Power was now concentrated in the hands of Khrushchev, who became first secretary of the Central Committee, Malenkov, the Prime Minister, and Bulganin, the man who later replaced Malenkov as premier.

Khrushchev set about introducing radical reforms, starting with agriculture. It was announced that the key would be to master the virgin lands and long-fallow land in Kazakhstan, Siberia, the Urals, and other steppe areas. In the first few years, the virgin lands provided grain. Thereafter, however, the fertile layer of soil began to erode quickly, carried away by black dust-storms. It was also decided that small farm-holdings must be wiped out. "The peasants began slaughtering their cattle, and the countryside set off for meat, butter and milk to Leningrad, and to Moscow. The non-Black Earth belt began to decay. The countryside was de-peasantized," wrote Politburo member Dmitriy Shepilov.[51]

Of huge significance for the country's destiny was the 20th Party Congress, during which Khrushchev astonished those present with his report

---

[49] Dominic Lieven, *Empire: The Russian Empire and its Rivals*. Yale University Press, 2002. P. 289.
[50] Ibid. PP. 289-290.
[51] *I Shepilov, kotoryy prisoyedinilsya k nim: pravda o cheloveke, uchenom, voine, politike* (*And Shepilov, who Joined Them. The Truth about the Man, Scientist, Soldier, Politician*). Moscow, 1998.

on Stalin's crimes, hoping to strengthen his authority in the country and the party and to strike a blow to the prestige of the old guard, who were now his rivals. The resonance of the speech went beyond all expectations. "Khrushchev let a genie out of a bottle: waving at his adversaries the sword of political revelations, he destroyed, without wanting to, the ideological discipline and like-mindedness which were an integral part of the communist ideology," the historian Rudolf Pikhoya has observed.[52]

Many of the transformations that took place were presented as measures designed to democratize government: expanding the economic rights of the republics, bringing the government closer to the "regions", reducing the size of the apparatus of power. For the first time in centuries, the branch-based system of government was replaced with a territorial one. Early in 1957, the Union ministries were abolished, and the enterprises that were subordinate to them were handed over to the regional *Sovnarkhoz* (Councils of National Economy; CNE), which managed many different sectors of industry simultaneously on the territory under their control.

Tensions flared among those at the very top of the party. A struggle between Khrushchev and the majority of the Presidium, led by Molotov, Malenkov and Kaganovich, took place in the middle of 1957. Khrushchev was accused of economic mismanagement, vigilantism, of taking decisions unilaterally, of incorrect steps in the field of agriculture, and of reading out a speech that had not been approved by the Presidium at the 20th Party Congress, and he was asked to step down. At an emergency plenum convened in June 1957, however, Khrushchev, after being given the backing of the local party elite, the Central Committee apparatus, and the Ministry of Defence, won the day.

Khrushchev repayed the party apparatus, weakening the iron grip it had had until recently over discipline and ideological uniformity. Richard Sakwa has suggested that from that time, two processes began destroying the system from within: "An acquisitive mentality seized the elite, and society as a whole became more oriented to consumerism. This was a struggle that the Soviet Union could not win, since in a battle over whether capitalism or communism could deliver the goods the former won hands down. [...] The second process was connected with the first, namely the

---

[52] Rudol'f Pikhoya, "O vnutripoliticheskoy bor'be v sovetskom rukovodstve. 1945-1958" ("On the Internal Political Struggle in the Soviet Leadership. 1945-1958"), *Novaya i noveyshaya istoriya* (*New and Recent History*), Issue 6, 1995. P. 13.

ideological erosion of the system."[53] The process of the self-destruction of the Soviet system and the Soviet Union had been launched.

Until the late 1950s, Khrushchev's policy appeared to be bearing fruit: the volume of industrial production rose by one-and-a-half times. In many ways, this growth could be explained by the multiplying effect of the mass construction of housing in the cities. The fuel and energy complex began to make an increasingly large contribution to the budget. In the early 1960s, however, the growth rate of the economy slowed down. The idea of creating Councils of National Economy did not appear to have paid off. The USSR was once again importing technologies. In sectors such as electronics, in which the transfer of new technologies was restricted by the West out of military and strategic concerns, it became clear that the USSR was lagging behind. The problem with foodstuffs became far more serious. In 1963 the country started buying grain from other countries. As a result, Khrushchev found that both the party apparatus and the defence and security structures were against him.

Khrushchev was an advocate of a dramatic reduction in the size of the Soviet military machine: "If the military are not controlled, and are given the opportunity to evolve as they see fit, they will take the country's budget to its grave."[54] He felt that the USSR's capability of launching a nuclear missile strike allowed it to have far more compact armed forces, and these were cut back from just over five million to two and a half million people. Logic of this kind proved rash in the days of the aforementioned Cuban missile crisis, when the world was a hair's breadth from catastrophe. It did not take long to persuade the army and the military-industrial complex that Khrushchev ought to be removed from power.

After the October Plenum of the Central Committee in 1964, he was dismissed from office. He was initially succeeded by a triumvirate: Leonid Brezhnev, who had been elected first secretary of the Central Committee, Aleksey Kosygin, the chairman of the government, and Nikolay Podgorny – the chairman of the Presidium of the Supreme Soviet of the USSR. The CNEs were immediately abolished and sector-specific ministries were brought back. These no longer had the weight and independence they had enjoyed of old, however, since they were not able to take important decisions without the approval of the sector-specific departments of the CPSU's Central Com-

---

[53] Richard Sakwa, *Communism in Russia: An Interpretative Essay*. Palgrave Macmillan, 2010. P. 104.

[54] Nikita Khrushchev, *Vospominaniya (Recollections)*. Moscow, 1997. PP. 441, 471.

mittee (CC), which were maintained and strengthened. Clashes between the ministries and the CC were one of the key reasons for the delays in bringing in economic reforms in the 1960s, reforms which were associated with the name of Kosygin and were designed to give enterprises greater independence. Brezhnev increasingly concentrated the decision-making process in his hands, despite having neither the manners of a dictator nor the qualities of a major public politician.

Today, the era of the late USSR is looked upon as a period of stagnation, which led to the collapse of the state. Yet in that period – the 1960s and 1970s – everything looked rather different. It was during this time that the country achieved its highest share of global GDP – 12.3% (the Russian Federation accounts for just over 3% today).[55] States in the West seemed to be growing ever less governable, there was no talk of any new countries going through a transition to democracy, and socialist (or pseudo-socialist) regimes proliferated all over the place, against the backdrop of the USSR's major breakthroughs in space exploration and the victories of national liberation movements in the Third world.

The Soviet regime ensured political stability, and in order to do so, administrative measures were used: the arrest, exile (internal or overseas), and detention in prison or in psychiatric clinics of a few hundred, or at most a few thousand people. Censorship lived on in the mass media and in the field of culture. At the same time, economic growth slowed, in many ways due to an imbalance in favour of the military-industrial sector and the strengthening of the army. It was in the period under Brezhnev that the USSR achieved military and strategic parity with the USA and NATO, which (together with the "Vietnam Syndrome" in Washington) was an important reason for the start of the policy of detente and the signing of a series of Russian-American treaties on arms control. Resources were also required for the USSR's active foreign policy of supporting countries in the socialist camp and its efforts to expand its economic and political influence in the third world. By the time Brezhnev died in 1982, the rule of the collapsing General Secretary was the subject of much mockery, and the country was suffering from constant shortages of a large number of products.

The death of the next two leaders in quick succession – Yuriy Andropov and Konstantin Chernenko – led, in 1985, to a representative of the "men of the sixties" coming to power in 1985 – Mikhail Gorbachev.

....

[55] Joseph Nye, Jr., *The Future of Power*. PublicAffairs, 2011. P. 162.

He was full of good intentions: he wanted to bring an end to the Cold War unilaterally – and he did indeed end it, and he achieved the democratization of the Soviet system of governance, something that would never have occurred to his predecessors. He intended to improve the economic position by allowing some elements of a market economy, reducing the burden on the economy of the over-large military and industrial sector, and ridding the country of the old communist elite, which was preventing him from moving away from the odious extremes of the Soviet regime and adapting to the challenges of growth. Gorbachev's plans certainly did not include, however, the collapse of the "Socialist system", the removal from power of the Communist Party of the Soviet Union (and of himself along with it), nor indeed the collapse of the USSR. This was in many ways an unexpected side-effect of his activity.

Perestroika was the embodiment of a particular political philosophy: its supporters were deeply committed advocates of common humanitarian values, of socialism with a human face, and of state ownership and democracy, which were being prevented from affirming themselves by the remnants of Stalinism, the party apparatus (or the conservative portion of it, at least), and the special services. All it would take would be to let people say all the things they were thinking, and elect their bosses, and socialism would be able to be rolled out in all its Leninist glory. This set of ideas, typical of an entire generation of intellectuals holding senior posts in the party, in government bodies, and in the mass media in the 1980s, would give rise to a model of state governance that was not – and possibly never could have been – fit for purpose.

What exactly do I mean by that? There have been, and there exist today, democracies with market economies, which are fit for purpose – obvious examples can be found in the countries of the West. There are functioning authoritarian states with planned economies, a leading role among whom was played by the Soviet Union. There have been fully-functioning authoritarian states with market economies: the Russian Empire, modern-day China, or the Asian "tigers". Nowhere, though, has anyone – with the exception of the Soviet Union as it went through perestroika – ever attempted to combine democracy with a non-market, planned economy. The main problem with such a model is as follows.

When, in the conditions of a democracy, people are allowed to ask questions, the first question they ask, in the absence of a market, is: "So where's the food?" This was the question that proved to be fatal – and the last question of all – for Gorbachev.

The Soviet Union was also somehow pre-programmed for collapse by the very formula of its national, state structure. At the heart of it was the dividing up of peoples into categories with unequal status. The "first-class" categories included the sizeable ethnicities which were positioned close to the borders of the state: they were given the status of "nations" and the right to form republics within the Union. Those that were smaller in size and were not located next to the border were considered as "peoples" and were granted autonomy. Thus, the status of a nationality was strongly tied, in the minds of the masses and the elite, with the acquisition of some form of statehood. This construct was married to "the right of a nation to self-determination, right up to secession," which they did not intend to exercise. This constitutional principle was immediately invoked when the leading ties that bound together the Soviet state – the Communist party and the special services – lost the might they had once wielded.

In December 1991, the USSR ceased to exist, giving birth to 15 new independent states.

Yeltsinism

The collapse of the USSR triggered a fundamentally new stage in the country's history. The global system, founded on a bipolar confrontation, was now a thing of the past, and Russia had ceased to be one of its poles. At the same time, it had lost its status as a superpower, the status previously enjoyed by the Soviet Union. The Russian Federation, the successor to the USSR, inherited four fifths of its territory, but only around half of its population and economic potential. Now covering one eighth of the land mass of the planet, as opposed to one sixth, Russia nonetheless remained the biggest country in the world. Now an even more northerly country than the Russian Empire or the USSR, the country found itself spatially "shifted away" from Western and Central Europe, the Middle East, and Southern Asia.

Having shrunk considerably in size, Russia discovered in the West the ever-expanding European Union and NATO; in the East a rapidly-growing China; and in the South the world of Islam, which was growing increasingly radical. "For the first time since its emergence from the dark forests of Muscovy, Russia finds itself surrounded by states and political groupings that are economically, demographically, and politically more dynamic than itself," Andrew Kuchins has written.[56]

---

[56] Andrew C. Kuchins, "US-Russia Relations: Constraints of Mismatched Strategic Out-

Boris Yeltsin restored the backbone of the state mechanism that had been destroyed along with the Soviet Union, launched democratic institutes, and crushed the old party apparatus. He took control of the Congress of People's Deputies, and did not hold back from having the parliament shot at by tanks in the fall of 1993, and the destruction of one of the key attributes of the preceding era: the Soviets. After this, a new Constitution was prepared, and new legislation was brought in whereby a new two-chamber parliament was elected: the Council of the Federation and the State Duma. The Constitution, forced through via a referendum, established fundamental rights and freedoms, but endowed the President with the kind of powers that all of his counterparts would have envied. Yeltsin stoically put up with criticism, though, and did not do anything that could have given rise to suspicions of an attack on freedom of speech. Yet he spent months at a time away from his desk. The extra-institutional center that was the President's "family" sometimes played a bigger role than the institutions appointed according to the Constitution. Through its channels, big business took part in the governance of the country, the appointment of ministers, the adopting of laws, and the election of governors in its "patrimonial" territories, and enjoyed wide-ranging access to state resources, without acquiring the habit of paying taxes.

The giving of sovereignty to the regions, a policy underpinned by the President, went so far that the integrity of the country found itself under threat, and the tragedy of Chechnya became possible; the war there cost tens of thousands of lives, and terror flared up inside the country. Attempting to counter the threats to Russia's security, without much success, were the poorly-paid intelligence services, disorganized by countless reforms, and a demoralized army which had not been given new weapons.

Yeltsin rescued the economy, by launching market forces into it. Starting in 1992, prices were liberalized. The reforms of the deputy Prime Minister Yegor Gaidar were characterized by a desire to assert the market principles of the free setting of prices and the facilitation of competition, to encourage private initiative and individual responsibility, to abide by the rules of the game (even if these rules often changed) in relations with business, and to integrate the country into the global economic community. "Gaidar's 'shock therapy', as the wags would soon note, was 'all shock and no therapy'. [...] By the end, a huge superpower had been reduced to the status of an impoverished Third World country," remarked the famous American journalist

---

looks", in *Russia After the Global Economic Crisis*, ed. by Anders Aslund, Sergei Guriev, and Andrew Kuchins. Peterson Institute for International Economics, 2010. PP. 245, 246.

Paul Klebnikov, who was later killed in Moscow.[57] Yeltsin sensed that the basis of the government's support had fallen to a dangerous new low, and he opted to pass on the position of Prime Minister to an experienced economic executive and the creator of Gazprom, Viktor Chernomyrdin. A group of young reformers remained in the cabinet, however. And this group – with Anatole Chubais playing the main role – was the driving force of the policy of privatization. A vast country, in which everything – from a nuclear power station to a nail – had belonged to the state, now fell into private hands. The winners of this game were those among the survivors who managed to convince the bureaucrats to appoint them, rather than anyone else, as billionaires. They resorted to actions which are defined all over the world as "corruption"; the temptations proved too powerful to resist.

Privatization was implemented in many ways for ideological purposes, so as to break the back of the socialist economy and create a new class of major property owners. At first, small companies were handed over to collectives of workers, and from them to the directors and the *nouveau-riches* associated with them.

As for foreign policy, the Foreign Minister Andrey Kozyrev defined it as follows: "Orienting ourselves towards the highly developed democratic countries and joining their club – their club alone, and none other – as an equal partner, with dignity, with our own face. Therein lies the whole concept." The policy of the early 1990s was marked by an obvious "America-centrism". "The hegemony of the United States, that people are scaremongering about, and the talk of a single superpower – all that is just stereotypes and narrow-mindedness. There is not just one single superpower," stressed Kozyrev, while promoting the plan of a strategic alliance with the USA, which would later mutate into the idea of a strategic partnership.[58] Russia was making a bid to become a member of the Western system. The second most important task was to "create a belt of good neighbors around the perimeter of the Russian borders."[59] Finally, the importance of relations with

....

[57] Paul Klebnikov, *The Godfather of the Kremlin: Boris Berezovsky and the Looting of Russia*. New York: Harcourt, 2000. P. 80.

[58] "Interv'yu s Andreyem Kozyrevym" ("An Interview with Andrey Kozyrev"), *Moskovskiye novosti* (*Moscow News*), June 14, 1992. P. 11 <https://yeltsin.ru/uploads/upload/newspaper/1992/mn06_14_92/index.html>.

[59] Andrey Kozyrev, "Interesy Rossii i vneshnyaya politika. Andrey Kozyrev: k slovu 'patriotizm' prilagatel'nyye ne nuzhny" ("Russia's Interests and Foreign Policy. The Word 'Patriotism' Requires No Adjectives"), *Krasnaya Zvezda* (*Red Star*), Issue 270, November 26, 1992 <https://dlib.eastview.com/browse/doc/3356614>.

third-world countries, which were developing without ideological dogmas, was also stressed, and in reality, this signified Russia's departure from most of the developing states.

With the signing of large-scale agreements on arms control, from reducing conventional weapons under the CFE treaty, to destroying intermediate range missiles and cutting deterrence forces under the START-2 agreement, the key principles of strategic stability were established. Russo-American cooperation helped to transform Ukraine, Belarus and Kazakhstan into countries that were free of nuclear weapons. Soon, however, disillusionment in the "Kozyrev doctrine" emerged.

Attitudes towards Russia were in many ways defined by the view that the losing party in the Cold War had put itself at the mercy of the victors. Jack Matlock wrote: "'We won the Cold War, so we can do as we please. The Russians will just have to get used to the fact that they are no longer a Great Power, and that we have no need to pay attention to their views.' This attitude led many Russians to conclude that the 'West' would not accept Russia as a partner but only as a subservient appendage."[60] Pro-Western gestures were seen as a given, and any activity on the part of Russia, particularly in relation to the CIS, was looked on as a display of "neo-imperialism".

The issue of where the borders of the Western system lay once again came to the fore. "Some historians reckon that after the collapse of the Soviet Union in 1989, the central Europe that had been formed in the Middle Ages reappeared," writes Jacques Le Goff, the well-known French medievalist.[61] The matter immediately took on a practical aspect: how far to the east should the European and Euro-Atlantic institutes – the EU and NATO – be pushed. It is not hard to see that the Western system did indeed reproduce itself in accordance with the civilization matrix from the Middle Ages, which did not include Russia.

Kozyrev's policy suffered a serious blow when NATO began considering the prospect of expansion, despite the multiple assurances that were made by Western leaders, even to Gorbachev when he was in power, that this would never happen. Yeltsin changed the tone of Russian diplomacy. In an address to the Federal Assembly, the President declared: "In 1994, we must put an end to the sinful practice of unilateral concessions."[62] There was no longer

---

[60] Jack F. Matlock Jr., *Superpower Illusions: How Myths and False Ideologies Led America Astray – and How to Return to Reality*. Yale University Press, 2010. P. 5.

[61] Jacques Le Goff, *The Birth of Europe*. Blackwell Publishing, 2005. P. 92.

[62] "Strategicheskaya tsel' – sdelat' Rossiyu protsvetayushchey stranoy" ("The Strategic Aim

any talk of joining the "Western club". The Kremlin assiduously sought an alternative to NATO expansion, proposing "far-reaching initiatives for the formation of a new Europe". Each time, however, the words, efforts and demarche of Moscow were disproved by reality, with one "principled stance" giving way to another. On the eve of the presidential elections in 1996, Yeltsin put the Ministry of Foreign Affairs in the hands of Yevgeniy Primakov, enabling him to cover the foreign policy front in the run-up to the election.

Only through an exceptionally brutal anti-Communist campaign played outside the rules, injections of cash, the consolidation of the elite and the security structures, and some miracles in the electoral precincts enabled Yeltsin to be re-elected over the Communist Gennadiy Zuganov for a new term in July 1996. Between the two rounds of the election, Yeltsin suffered a heart attack. The campaign ended without a candidate, but the country was not aware of this.

After undergoing heart surgery, Yeltsin brought in a new round of liberal reforms. "It seemed to me that after the elections in 1996, a new era had begun. An era of construction."[63] Wide scale privatization was launched, using the scheme of "loans-for-shares", as a result of which a host of major financial structures (which had risen to prominence using money from the state budget), for $1.1 billion established control over the biggest enterprises, which became part of new private holdings – YUKOS, Norilsk Nickel, TNK etc. Firstly, though, as these assets were given to the new owners of the symbolic price, this often resulted simply in the selling on of the assets and the closing of production. Secondly, the fact that entry into the market was essentially cost-free led to a focus on immediate profit and a lack of attention to long-term goals. Thirdly, the construction of new production capacity became nonsensical, since before long their losses meant that they were unable to compete with the firms that were privatized almost for free. Fourthly, the fact that access to privatization was only provided to "cronies", meant that the flow of foreign capital into the Russian market was restricted.[64]

The "invisible hand of the market", on which such great hopes had been placed, remained exactly that – unseen. It was not able to manufacture a single ship, nuclear reactor, new plane or motorway, and it did not resolve the

....
Is to Make Russia a Prosperous Country. Boris Yeltsin's Speech at the Federal Assembly"), *Rossiyskaya Gazeta* (*Russian Newspaper*), February 25, 1994.

[63] Boris Yel'tsin, *Prezidentskiy marafon* (*The Presidential Marathon*). Moscow, 2000. P. 85.

[64] Vladislav Inozemtsev, "Slovo i delo: Privatizatsiya po-rossiyski" ("Privatization, Russian Style"), *Vedomosti*, January 24, 2011. P. 4.

problems of the degradation of education and healthcare. "In the process of a market-based and spontaneous, to a considerable extent, transformation, it was the most liquid sectors that survived, associated with exports of unprocessed raw materials and semi-finished goods. In effect, we went through a large-scale process of deindustrialization," Vladimir Putin would later write.[65] People went for months without receiving their salary or pension.

Foreign policy began to look more sensible in the second term of Yeltsin's presidency. Primakov declared: "The model of a guided country is not acceptable for Russia."[66] As a counterweight to this he effectively proclaimed a doctrine of his own: the prioritizing of Russian interests and the rejection of the role of "smaller partner" in relations with the USA and the West, while not allowing the deterioration of relations or the emergence of new lines of division; the establishment of a multipolar world, a multi-vectored approach to foreign policy and the adopting, in a host of pressing international matters, of a stance that was an alternative to that of the USA (hence the shifting of emphasis towards developing relations with the countries of Western Europe, the attempts to create a "Moscow – Beijing – Delhi axis", and the independent stance in relation to Iran, Iraq and Yugoslavia); the continued integration of Russia into a globalizing world; the integration of the CIS "at different speeds".

Russia was given a membership card to the Paris club and the London club, and acceded to APEC; an agreement on partnership and cooperation between Russia and the EU was ratified; and the NATO-Russia Founding Act was signed. In 1996, the Commonwealth of Belarus and Russia was created (it was later transformed into the Union). The "Primakov doctrine" was put to the test during the battle over the expansion of NATO in 1996 to 1997, the Iraq crisis in 1997-1998, and during the West's war against Yugoslavia in the spring of 1999. In practically every case, Russia had to step back, making do with symbolic compensatory measures.

In March 1998, the third attempt to bring in Yeltsin's liberal reforms was made, with the dismissal of Viktor Chernomyrdin's cabinet and the appointment of Sergey Kiriyenko as Prime Minister. In August, there was a default. Banks, companies and private individuals lost vast sums of money,

---

[65] Vladimir Putin, "O nashikh ekonomicheskikh zadachakh" ("On Our Economic Tasks"), *Vedomosti*, January 30, 2012 <https://www.vedomosti.ru/politics/articles/2012/01/30/o_nashih_ekonomicheskih_zadachah>.

[66] Yevgeniy Primakov, *Mir posle 11 sentyabrya* (*The World after September 11*). Moscow, 2002. PP. 184-185.

and prices shot up once again. Yeltsin, now a "lame duck", brought a team of heavyweights into the government, led by Yevgeniy Primakov. Thereafter, the main source of political intrigue was the question of who would succeed Yeltsin. The idea of Primakov in that role? "Those around the President understood that I would not agree to play in an orchestra conducted by the oligarchs," wrote Primakov.[67] For a short time, Sergey Stepashin served as Prime Minister, but his approval ratings did not satisfy the President. Yeltsin's choice instead fell on Vladimir Putin.

During Yeltsin's presidency, the economy shrank to half its initial size, and fell to 14th place in the world; GDP was reduced to $300 billion. Russia walked along the edge of a precipice in the 1990s, surviving by some miracle. In an article entitled "Russia at the Turn of the Millennium", published on 30th December 1999 – the day before Yeltsin retired – Putin observed: "Russia is going through one of the most difficult periods in its centuries-old history. For probably the first time in the last 200 to 300 years, it faces the danger of finding itself in the second, or even the third layer of states in the world."[68] On 26th March 2000, the country elected a new President.

The Country Rises from its Knees

At the heart of Putin's initial strategy was pragmatism: the need to solve the issue of the country's survival.

In the Federal Assembly, a working pro-presidential majority was secured, for the first time in the post-Soviet era. It was thanks to this that the right to own land, and a taxation system with a 13% flat-rate income tax, appeared in Russia, and normal social infrastructure began to be created.

At the heart of Putin's strategy in the field of federal relations lay the alignment of regional legislation with the federal laws and the Constitution, and this was done with the help of a powerful new institution: authorized representatives of the President in seven federal districts. Through these authorized representatives, he was also able to lock into Moscow the branches of federal executive power operating in the regions, which in the 1990s found themselves under the direct control of the governors.

---

[67] Yevgeniy Primakov, *Vstrechi na perekrostkakh* (*Meetings at the Crossroads*). Moscow, 2015. P. 525.

[68] Vladimir Putin, "Rossiya na rubezhe tysyacheletiy" ("Russia at the Turn of the Millennium"), *Nezavisimaya Gazeta* (*Independent Newspaper*), December 30, 1999 <https://www.ng.ru/politics/1999-12-30/4_millenium.html>.

To stimulate the creation of parties, the bans prohibiting representatives of executive power from being members of a party were lifted, and there was a transition to elections for the State Duma on the basis of party lists. The President saw no problem with the existence of a large, dominant party – *Yedinaya Rossiya* ("United Russia") – which enabled him to consolidate a core pro-government electorate and governmental elite, and also to bring in reforms and facilitate the continuity of policy.

Putin's economic program stipulated the doubling of GDP within ten years. What Putin's team achieved in terms of cutting taxes, bringing in private ownership of land, opening the economy up for global competition, and bringing in communal, social, pension, and other reforms, went significantly further than the ideas of reformers from the early Yeltsin days.

Some are of the view that the growth in Russia's economy and in the wealth of its citizens was secured solely through an increase in oil prices. The economic advance at the start of the 21st century in fact had nothing to do with oil at all, the price of which was as follows: 28.5 dollars a barrel in 2000, 24.4 dollars in 2001, 25 dollars in 2002, 28.8 dollars in 2003. Additional income from the exporting of hydrocarbons accounted for only around 28% of the increase in citizens' income and only 12% of the rise in GDP. The driver of the economy was the consumer sector. The Kremlin significantly increased the tax burden on exporters of energy, and by doing so was able to lighten it for sectors oriented towards internal demand – trade, construction, the services and processing sectors.[69] There were other important internal factors, too: a responsible macroeconomic policy, market price formation, private ownership of land.

At the same time, Putin's strategy, particularly during his second term as President, involved preserving or even strengthening state control over several strategic sectors, including energy. Much faith was put into creating large, state corporations and vertically integrated holdings: Rostechnology, Rosatom, the United Aircraft Corporation, the United Shipbuilding Corporation. The aim was to halt the break-up of the advanced technology sectors, preserve manufacturing potential through the centralization of management, and gradually to bring together assets which formally belonged to the state and which had often lost their connection to scientific and construction centers.

---

[69] Mikhail Losev, "Rost na kazennykh kharchakh" ("Growth on the State Foodstuffs"), *RBK*, Issue 8, August 2012. PP. 25-26.

At the same time, Putin sent several "missives" with an unambiguous message to the biggest businesses: pay your taxes and demonstrate social responsibility; federal policy is the Kremlin's concern; and none of the oligarchs would be given special treatment. The moguls Gusinsky and Berezovsky were forced to leave the country. In 2003, it was the turn of Mikhail Khodorkovsky, whose increased political activity prompted increased interest on the part of the law enforcers in the truly crude tax avoidance schemes that his company YUKOS was using.

Eight years of economic growth – the fastest growth in Europe – led to a dramatic rise in currency reserves, a budget surplus, and resources for a stabilization fund. Putin showed himself to be an advocate of budgetary conservatism, however, refusing to sanction large-scale spending programs. In 2007, Russia outstripped Italy and France in terms of the size of its GDP, calculated in terms of purchasing power parity (PPP), and was in the top seven biggest economies in the world.[70] The Strategy-2020 stipulated that Russia was to break into the top five economies. The pages of the newspapers and the reports of the investment funds were filled with colorful predictions of growth.

Aware of the relative weakening of the country's potential, Putin brought in the independent, proactive, multi-vector policy of a pragmatic "father of the nation", who was at the same time concerned with the majesty of this nation.

High on his list of priorities were the CIS countries, in relations with whom the concept of integration at different speeds remained key. In his relations with the countries of the West, Putin was willing to draw as close to them and to their organizations as the West was willing to draw closer to Russia. A boost was given to cooperation with the European Union, and this was evident in the annual Russia-EU summits. In spite of objections from many quarters, Putin opted for a thaw in relations with the North Atlantic bloc – relations which had been broken off after the bombings in Yugoslavia. By establishing a mutual understanding with parliament, the President achieved the ratification of several crucial agreements – START-2, the Nuclear Test Ban Treaty – which had been

---

[70] Vladimir Putin, "Vystupleniye na rasshirennom zasedanii Gossoveta 'O strategii razvitiya Rossii do 2020 goda'" ("Speech at the Extended Session of the State Council 'On Russia's Development Strategy Until 2020'"), The Russian President's official website, February 8, 2008 <http://www.kremlin.ru/events/president/transcripts/24825>.

lying dormant in parliament for several years under Yeltsin. The strategic partnership with China and India was given a serious boost.

A significant watershed in world politics was the terrorist attack on the World Trade Center in New York, and on the Pentagon, on 11th September 2001. Putin was the first world leader to send his condolences and to offer all possible support to the American President George W. Bush in his anti-terrorist campaign. By an irony of fate, this proved possible thanks to the presence of a "hotline" between Moscow and Washington, created during the Cold War in order to prevent possible misunderstandings in the nuclear stand-off. At a summit in Washington and in Crawford in November 2001, a long-term partnership between the two countries was declared.

After the USA quit the ABM Treaty, Putin expressed regret, but no more than that. Russia signed the Strategic Offensive Reductions Treaty (SORT). The resolution adopted at the NATO summit in Prague (in 2002) on the accession of seven countries in Central and Eastern Europe to the bloc, including the Baltic states, was described as "useless", but did not prompt any diplomatic complications. Russia supported the USA by organizing and arming the anti-Taliban Northern Alliance, providing intelligence, air corridors for military planes, and access to bases in the former Soviet republics, and supplies of humanitarian aid.

Thereafter, however, relations with the West began to grow more complicated. "A serious blow was dealt to Russo-American relations by the USA's invasion of Iraq, which was roundly condemned not only by Moscow, but also by Berlin and Paris. New tests for relations with the West arrived in 2004, when the wave of the 'Orange Revolution' broke over Ukraine, and in 2008, when, at the NATO summit in Bucharest, the alliance promised to admit Ukraine and Georgia into its ranks.

Bush's refusal to adopt Putin's proposal on cooperation in the field of anti-missile defence, which he voiced in 2007 at a summit in Kennebunkport, the curtailing of Russian and American exercises aimed at defence against ballistic missiles, the USA's effective rejection of the agreement to create joint centers for tracking launches of rockets, signed in 2000, and the decision to base missile shield facilities in Poland – all of this was interpreted by Moscow as a sign of a toughening of policy in relation to Russia. The US Senate refused to ratify the Comprehensive Test Ban Treaty, and consequently it did not come into force. The CFE was ratified by only four countries – all from the CIS, and without a single one from the West – and the moment arrived when Russia decided for itself that it would cease to be part of it.

Putin expressed his disappointment with the results of cooperation with the West at the Munich Conference on 10th February 2007, resorting to huge criticism of the practice of a unipolar world: "However this term is dressed up, it ultimately means, in practice, only one thing: that there is one center of power, one center of force, one center of decision-making. It is a world with one master, one sovereign. And ultimately it is deadly not just for all those who are inside the framework of this system, but also for that sovereign itself, because it destroys it from within."[71] This speech caused serious shock. Talk of the prospect of a new Cold War began. There were more serious tests still to come, though.

In 2008, Putin's second term came to an end. Not wanting to alter the Constitution, which stipulates that a President cannot have more than two consecutive terms of office, Putin put forward as his successor the former head of the Administration and deputy Prime Minister, Dmitriy Medvedev.

The course steered by Medvedev was indeed one that picked up where Putin had left off, but at the same time they were not twins. He put at the forefront the improvement of human capital and the creation of a civilized legal environment: the rule of law, the rooting out of corruption and the practice of iniquitous verdicts, the humanizing of law and order. Strong emphasis was placed on respect for property rights, protecting small and big business from an administrative free-for-all. Medvedev went into the elections offering a modernization program founded on the four "I's": institutions, investment, innovations and infrastructure. The dramatic events of 2008, however, forced him to make significant adjustments. The focus of his attention now had to be the crises: the economic crisis, the crisis around South Ossetia, and the crisis in relations with the West.

The global recession affected Russia primarily through a fall in demand for raw materials and energy in the countries of the European Union, and it hit Russia harder than most of the other major economies: the country suffered an 8% fall in GDP (only Japan saw a greater decline). The Russian government adopted a host of measures designed to add liquidity to the banking system. It provided assistance to those corporations and banking organizations which had taken out loans in the global market and now had to pay them back. The program of anti-crisis measures also included an

---

[71] Vladimir Putin, "Vystupleniye i diskussiya na Myunkhenskoy konferentsii po voprosam politiki bezopasnosti" ("Speech and Discussion at the Munich Conference on Matters of Security Policy"), The Russian President's official website, February 10, 2007 <http://www.kremlin.ru/events/president/transcripts/24034>.

increase in social spending, pensions, unemployment benefits, support for creating jobs, the organization of public works, help in opening one's own business, dealing with the situation in single-industry towns, the stimulating of private demand, and an increase in the size of guarantees on individual deposits.

During the Georgian aggression in South Ossetia in August 2008, when dozens of Russian peacekeepers were shot dead, force was applied in order to impose peace on Saakashvili, who had overstepped the line. By securing victory and reinforcing it with a recognition of the independence of South Ossetia and Abkhazia, Russia decisively regained its seat at the table of the great geopolitical game.

Having come up against yet more problems in its dealings with the West, Russia began to increase its strategic depth in all other areas. Steps were taken towards the establishment of a Customs Union for Russia, Belarus and Kazakhstan. Brazil, Russia, India and China decided to formalize their relations within the framework of BRIC, and this duly occurred in 2009 in Yekaterinburg.

After the "Georgian crisis", the situation in the West changed, too. In the USA, it was declared that there was a need for a "reset" in Russo-American relations. The Strategic Arms Reduction Treaty (START) III was concluded, establishing new final figures on nuclear weapons (1500 – 1675 for warheads and 500 – 1100 for delivery systems).

Putin 2.0

Politics, in the form of fierce street demonstrations, returned to Russia the moment Putin announced, in September 2011, that he intended to run for President once again. The US Vice-President, Joseph Biden, in a speech made shortly before this at Moscow State University, warned that another term in office would be "damaging" for Putin and for Russia (I would imagine that this statement became, for Putin, the final argument that convinced him to return: he could not have followed the tactless advice of the American Vice-President). A coordinated internal and external attack began on the leader of the country and on his party *Yedinaya Rossiya*.

The theme of corruption became the launch mechanism for protests during the campaign for the Duma in 2011, with the tone being set by the three main political forces – the ultra-communists, the nationalists, and the liberals. Putin proved to be a more serious fortress than his multiple domestic opponents and their foreign benefactors and sponsors had reckoned with. The protests also helped to consolidate the pro-Putin electorate, who suddenly realized that the outcome of the vote was far from being a foregone conclusion. The mass demonstrations resulted in even bigger pro-government demonstrations. In the first round of the presidential elections in March 2012, 63.6% of the vote went to Putin. By the summer of 2012, Putin had managed to wrestle back the initiative and restore stability.

The pace of reform in the political sphere accelerated, creating a more competitive environment and an opportunity for protest activity within the framework of the legitimate political process. In Russia – the only country in Europe where this happens, incidentally – direct elections of governors began to be held again. Single-mandate districts were brought back in the elections for the State Duma, along with party lists.

In the West, however, the obvious defeat of the domestic Russian opposition was interpreted as just more evidence, not to say definitive proof, of the assertion in Russia of an "authoritarian dictatorship", and a ferocious information campaign was waged against it. Cancelling the notorious Jackson-Vanik amendment, Washington replaced it with the Magnitsky Act, bringing in personal sanctions against the individuals who had allegedly poisoned the tax consultant of the known financial speculator William Browder. The response was the "Guantanamo List", when Russian sanctions were brought in against Americans guilty of mass torture. The adoption of Russian children by American families was also banned, taking into account the multiple reports of deaths among the children who had travelled over there and the failure of the American side to react to them. Against the backdrop of the USA's interference in Russia's domestic affairs and Washington's increasing belligerence in relation to Syria, in the summer of 2013 the USA topped the list of the countries which Russian citizens saw as the most hostile towards Russia.

The biggest test for relations between Russia and the West was yet to come, however: the Ukrainian crisis. Geopolitical rivalry over Kyivan Rus has been going strong for a millennium already, and many in Moscow see a continuation of it in what is taking place now in Ukraine. In the autumn of 2013, protests broke out in Kyiv, allegedly in the name of asserting European values, and they ended with the overthrow of President Viktor Yanukovich. "Regime change in Ukraine was prepared by the undermining activity that has gone on for several years," wrote the German analyst Wolfgang Bittner. "The US government and its intelligence agencies have spent more than five billion dollars on this. The Western alliance's strategy right from the start was aimed at turning Ukraine into a staging ground, one with great geopolitical significance and one that is at the same time a significant economic space and a gateway to Russia's resources."[72]

The Western leaders can call what happened in Ukraine whatever they want – even a triumph of democracy. But for the Russian authorities and a substantial portion of Ukrainians, it was an anti-constitutional, armed coup, organized mainly by the United States in order to achieve the objective of weakening Russia. Europe, in this case as so often, played the role of a support group. When President Viktor Yanukovich was overthrown and a new government was formed, international agreements from 21st February 2014 were violated (constitutional reform, early presidential elections), even though they had been signed by the foreign ministers of Germany, France and Poland, and so too were all manner of norms enshrined in the Ukrainian Constitution.

The Russians living in East and South Ukraine were right, as we can see from the tragic events of the civil war in the Donbass, to fear for their lives and their rights. Ultra-nationalist armed yobs from the Right Sector, UNA-UNSO, and execution battalions started trying to lay down the law across the country.

For Moscow, the transformation of Ukraine into an anti-Russian state and a foothold for American military and naval presence represented not just a geopolitical challenge, but an existential one, and Putin behaved accordingly. On 26th February 2014, the legitimate parliament of Crimea put forward the initiative of holding a referendum on whether or not to break away from Ukraine. On 18th March, two new federal subjects acceded to the Russian Federation: the Republic of Crimea and the city of Sebastopol. Territories which had always been with Russia spiritually and culturally, came back on the basis of the open expression of the will of the people of Crimea. The reunification was supported by 96% of the Crimeans who voted, and 92% of the Russians.

Protests broke out in the South and East of Ukraine, which had in the past been granted to Kyiv by Vladimir Lenin, statues of whom were amicably taken down throughout Ukraine. The voices of the activists protesting in the South-East were completely ignored. The Ukrainian army was sent there, along with Special Forces, hired foreign soldiers and fighters from volunteer

---

[72] Wolfgang Bittner, *SShA zavoyevyvayut Yevropu: strategiya destabilizatsii, eskalatsii i militarizatsii na primere sobytiy na Ukraine* (*The USA is Conquering Europe: A Strategy of Destabilization, Escalation and Militarization Based on the Example of the Events in Ukraine*). Moscow, 2016. P. 162.

battalions, who formed a National Guard. A bloody civil war began in the Donetsk Basin (Donbass). The conflict has resulted in many thousands being killed, and created hundreds of thousands of refugees. Russia could not simply remain on the sidelines here, either. Humanitarian convoys rescued residents of the self-proclaimed Donetsk and Lugansk People's Republics, saving them from dying of starvation. Completely cut off from Ukraine, the DPR and the LPR were in essence turned into a rubble zone by the Kyiv regime, and into a Russian humanitarian and educational zone.

It was Putin who initiated the process of national reconciliation in Ukraine, which ended in the signing of the Minsk-2 accords on 12th February 2015 within the framework of the "Normandy four" – Russia, Germany, France and Ukraine – with the involvement of representatives of the DPR and LPR. The set of measures aimed at implementing the Minsk accords involved a ceasefire, the withdrawal of heavy artillery, an amnesty on participants in the armed fighting, a prisoner exchange based on the principle of "all of ours for all of yours", the start of a dialogue on the holding of local elections in the Donbass, the complete restoration of socio-economic ties (including the payment of pensions and welfare benefits), the resumption of the banking system there, the adoption of a new Ukrainian Constitution with sweeping decentralization, the restoration of Ukrainian control of the border after the local elections.[73] None of this was implemented by Kyiv.

In the West, however, it was Russia that was accused of all the deadly sins – from direct military aggression against Ukraine to the destruction of a Malaysian Boeing.

The United States, Canada, the EU member states and Japan introduced sanctions against Russia, damaging the banking, oil, and military-industrial sectors. Access to Western technologies was shut off. Moreover, personal sanctions were imposed which was an unprecedented step: personal sanctions had never been applied before – not even at the height of the Cold War. Military pressure also started to be put on Russia, and NATO moved its military infrastructure close to Russia's borders.

Sanctions were added to other factors that were unfavorable for the Russian economy. The weak point of the Russian economy proved to be the ruble, and its exchange rate fell sharply at the end of 2014. The reasons for this lay in the fall in oil prices around the world, the deficit in

---

[73] "Kompleks mer po vypolneniyu Minskikh soglasheniy" ("A Set of Measures for the Implementation of the Minsk Protocols"), The Russian President's official website, February 12, 2015 <http://kremlin.ru/supplement/4804>.

liquidity in dollars and Euros prompted by the sanctions, capital flight from Russia, and the tardy action taken by Russia's financial authorities. The difficulties with the economy had an impact on both incomes and the quality of life.

Russia responded with counter-sanctions that were small but highly pain-inducing, banning exports of agricultural products to Russia from the same countries that had imposed sanctions against Russia.

The priorities of the anti-crisis policy were: support for exports of non-raw materials and import-substitution, support for businesses in the risk zone, optimizing budget and finance policy, improving the business environment, and supporting the needy. The Western sanctions created additional incentives for reducing dependency on imports and/or meeting demand through the country's own production. Measures designed to give financial support to businesses were also used, such as the provision of subsidies, state guarantees, the financing of research and development, and measures to stimulate demand, including state procurement.[74] Inefficient state spending was carefully reduced.

The fact that some Russian banks had been cut off from the international payments system proved to be a powerful incentive for the creation, at long last, of a national payment system, "Mir". The presidential program of advanced development areas began to take shape, while further progress was made in the creation of special economic zones, industrial and technological parks, and free ports.

Russia's economy was not torn to shreds, as Barack Obama said it was – far from it. Russia's dependency on imports was reduced significantly. The departure of Western firms from the Russian market meant that their place was taken by companies from other countries and from within Russia itself. Credit resources turned out to be less accessible in the West, but certainly not inaccessible. China became the number one supplier of external capital.[75]

Industrial production and the exchange rate of the national currency stabilized, on the whole, and there was a lowering of inflation and a significant reduction in capital flight. Non-raw materials increased their

---

[74] "Otchet o rezul'tatakh deyatel'nosti Pravitel'stva Rossiyskoy Federatsii za 2015 god" ("A Report on the Results of the Activity of the Government of the Russian Federation for 2015"). Analytical Center for the Government of the Russian Federation, 2015. PP. 23, 14-15.

[75] Anastasiya Alekseyevskikh, "Rossiya perestala kreditovat'sya na Zapade" ("Russia Stopped Borrowing in the West"), *Izvestiya*, August 19, 2014 <https://iz.ru/news/575434>.

share of exports. Sustainable growth was demonstrated by the chemicals industry, pharmaceuticals, engineering, the defence sector, residential housing construction, agriculture, the food industry, green energy, and the tourism industry. Record amounts of oil are being extracted – thanks to a reduction in costs and tax changes. The nation's port capabilities are growing. Domestic air traffic now exceeds external.

Dozens of new factories have been put into operation, manufacturing automobile engines, construction materials, machine tools, armaments, industrial robots, and unmanned drones. There has been a sharp rise in exports of rocket engines and computer components. A national technological initiative is being implemented. All the preconditions have been created for renewing growth by relying on our own resources.

The deterioration of relations with the West compelled the Kremlin to develop alliances more actively and accelerate Russia's shift of focus towards the East. Moscow's policy has noticeably been activated within BRICS and the Shanghai Cooperation Organization (SCO), particularly in 2015, the year in which Russia presided over these organizations.

At the International Economic Forum in St. Petersburg in June 2016, Vladimir Putin announced the launch of the "Bolshaya Evraziya" ("Great Eurasia") project, which is open for everyone – China and the ASEAN countries, and the EU as well. During a subsequent visit to China, talks commenced on the creation of an all-encompassing trade and economic partnership in Eurasia, based on the Eurasian Union and the Chinese "Belt & Road" project. This idea received backing from South-East Asian leaders in May 2016 at the Russia-ASEAN summit in Sochi.

The more prominent role being played by Russia in global affairs has been facilitated by its uniquely active position with regard to countering international terrorism and its policy in relation to the Middle East. Moscow has no wish to see a new "Caliphate" being created, along the lines of ISIL and international terrorism, whose next target may well be Russia. This has become one of the main reasons why the decision was taken to involve the Russian Air Force in operations against terrorists in Syria.

Whatever Putin does, though, he is scarcely likely to be able to change the minds of those who see him as a "roadblock on the path of progress", an "enemy of democracy", or something even worse. It remains the case, however, that the majority of Russian society consists of people who consider Putin to be one of the most successful and propitious leaders. And there are a multitude of grounds for believing this to be so.

The Code of Russia

The Russian Federation has several distinctive features which are rooted in its history and which define its cultural code. The matrix of centuries-old Russian statehood can be defined as an estate-based (professional and national) territorial-representative autocracy with strong self-governance and a sense of man's individual freedom.

In Russian political culture, both before and after the Bolshevik Revolution, a strongly expressed statist orientation was typical. The state is not the "night-watchman", nor is it a mechanism of governance, founded on the principle of the *contrat social*, for the implementation of which the citizens delegate part of their natural sovereignty. The state is often seen as fully synonymous with the concepts of Russia or the Motherland.

In the Russian model, as in the Western one, there were elements of social and political pluralism, but many of the Western factors and institutions were present more weakly or were not present at all. In terms of its degree of pluralism, Kyivan Rus, where the Prince, the Boyar Duma, and the *veche* were integral components of the system of governance, was at least on a par with Western Europe, if not superior to it. At the same time, in Ancient Rus and the State of Muscovy, relations between the monarch and his vassals were not enshrined in a contract, and no major efforts were made to restrict the prerogatives of supreme power by means of legislation. No aristocracy, in the Western sense, developed; it did not have economic independence, being strongly dependent on the executive.

All these traits taken together meant that there was no real division of power in Russia into the executive, the legislative and the judiciary; their functions were always interwoven. Supreme power in Russia – after the convening of *Zemsky Sobor* and the Boyar Duma came to an end – was undivided. "Order comes from the Tsar"; "only the supreme power is capable of saving and building the country", "woe to the kingdom that is ruled by many", "better a terrifying Tsar than rule by seven Boyars". Those are Russian sayings. In imperial Russia, the Emperor had full rights to state power (until the Primary Laws of 1906, which created representative bodies). In the USSR, the Soviets embodied the idea of joining the executive and legislative branches of power. In contemporary Russia, under the Constitution of 1993, the institution of very strong presidential power has existed, placed over and above a system of the separation of powers.

Among the distinctive features of the Russian system are its non-institutionalized nature and the fact that it is embodied in one man. It is less the institutions of power that are important than the people in power. In Russia, supreme rulers were forgiven everything. Except weakness. A ruler who was seen as weak could face extreme forms of protest. Typical examples of this are the fates of Nicholas II and Mikhail Gorbachev.

At the same time, the notion of the all-powerful nature of Russian government at all times should not be overemphasized. Even in the age of absolutism (the 18th – 19th centuries), the capacity of monarchs to construct the life of the country as they saw fit, and to reform it, was very limited: their prerogatives were restrained by the presence of tradition, an influential bureaucracy, the imperial family, the landed gentry, the military top brass, and the prospect of potential coups within the royal court, and popular rebellions.

The system of governance since time immemorial was never clearly delineated, and the functions of various state bodies have traditionally been interwoven and confused. The habit, which Klyuchevsky described as inherited, "for administrative side rooms, cells and annexes" was passed down in unchanged form from the home-style habits of Moscow's rulers to the present day. Power was never fully formalized, there was a discrepancy between the actual decision-making processes and those prescribed by the law. It became a Russian tradition for there to be a narrow, intra-institutional circle of people who in practice took the place of formal state institutions. This circle took the form of the Near Duma, the Elected Rada, the Secret Council, the Private Council, the narrow circle of the Politburo, the small Council of People's Commissars, Boris Yeltsin's "family", and so on.

One can consider as a kind of birthmark of Russian statehood the division of supreme power, which was concentrated in the hands of the Great Prince, the Tsar, the Emperor, the General Secretary of the CC CPSU, the President, and the supreme executive power, in the hands of the highest office: the Boyar Duma, the Senate, the State Council, the Council of Ministers, the Council of People's Commissars, the Government. Control over the army, the intelligence services and the diplomatic service, meanwhile, unfailingly remained in the hands of supreme power.

For most of its history, Russia had a system of representative bodies: the *veche*, the *Zemsky Sobor*, the State Duma, the Supreme Soviet. In the period after the sun set on the *veche*, which represented in one way or another the whole population of separate cities and the land adjoining them, representation bore a estate-based and territorial nature: individuals called upon by the supreme power represented separate social and professional groups and regions in the country. Such a form of representation was characteristic of the pre-revolutionary period, the Soviet period and the modern system of representative (and legislative) power, in which, in the opinion of both the executive and society, the bosses, the intellectuals, the workers, and peasants from all corners of the country ought to be included. The representative (or legislative) bodies in Russia have always been, with a few exceptions, less a counterweight than an extension of supreme power, a support for it, and the executive itself has set the agenda to a decisive degree.

The Russian system of law was initially – through the first legal codes of Kyivan Rus – associated with Byzantine nomocanons, including church rules, and civil legislation, and through these to the system of Roman law. For a long time, judicial functions were in the hands of executive power, but at the regional and local levels there have been elected judicial bodies since days of yore. The codification of laws remained a weak spot, with conflicts between the various legislative norms commonplace. The legal system was not universal in nature; there was a serious lack of any symmetry, which might take into account the particular features of individual regions with their specific national characteristics. The idea of law is associated less with state legislative acts and formal law, than with an understanding of justice and people's *pravda* ("truth"). The law was often contrasted with truth as the highest justice, and there was a large amount of forgiveness towards those who broke the law.

The state acts as the solitary space of power which is distributed on a hierarchical basis. The provision of the powers of a ruler goes from the highest echelons of the hierarchy to the lowest, with vertical ties considered more important than horizontal ones or networks. On the ground, the indivisibility of power is apparent, too. The pendulum has constantly wavered between a desire to solve everything from the capital with the help of the bodies of central governance, and the creation of relatively independent bodies of local government and autonomy. At the same time, the system of relations between the center and the provinces has always been marked by an increased level of centralized control, a high proportion of national wealth, concentrated in the capital, and asymmetry in the status of the various subjects, associated with their ethnic composition (non-Russian areas having more autonomy).

Self-rule in the cities and in the provinces existed for centuries. Though limited rights of elected representatives in the cities, particularly in the southern and eastern frontiers, where a large role was played by servicemen (the Streltsy, the Cossacks), meant that the cities were not able to be the flagships of capitalist relations. While experimenting with Western methods of city governance and self-governance, Russia, prior to the 1930s, did not even get close to the Western level of urbanization. Russian civilization was a rural one, and mentally it in many respects remains so, as is confirmed today by the sheer number of *dachas* (country houses) and household farming by city dwellers, not seen anywhere else in the world.

Russia's colonizing was in many respects similar to that of the West, and the Russian servicemen and resettlers were no angels. Having said that, the Russians did not destroy a single civilization, in the way the Spanish did with the Aztecs and Incas; the victims of their colonial exploits are not counted in the tens of millions, as is the case with Western colonization. The Russian colonial powers left the indigenous peoples in the areas where they usually resided, rather than chasing them into reservations or destroying them, as was the case in the United States. No new subjects were turned into slaves, and there was no slave trade on a global scale, as was the case in the European colonial powers.

Often, in the places that were colonized, a unified, syncretic culture was formed, when the Russians borrowed the cuisine, clothing or even the language and aspects of religion (shamanism, animism) of the local people. "Under Russia's reconciliatory domestic policy, the peoples that were brought into the fold occupied a harmonious place within a single state, with their physical existence, natural environment, religion, culture and authenticity preserved," emphasized the Nobel prize-winner Alexander Solzhenitsyn.[76]

Since the times of Ivan the Terrible, the government has not refined the matter of the formal status of a new territory. It was considered sufficient for one or other region to be included into one of the highest state symbols – a title of the Tsar, the imperial coat of arms, finding itself within the sphere of activity of the central institutions, being part of some kind of administrative whole – a province, a governorate, a vicegerency, or for it to follow Russia-wide legislation, and its people would pay their taxes and perform the obligations imposed on them.[77]

The system of governance of non-Russian regions was characterized by a combination of the maximum possible preservation of the local characteris-

---

[76] Alexander Solzhenitsyn, *Rossiya v obvale* (*Russia is an Avalanche*). Moscow, 1998. P. 112.

[77] V. V. Trepavlov, "Kategoriya 'rossiyskaya tsivilizatsiya' i fenomen polietnichnosti" ("The Category 'Russian Civilization' and the Phenomenon of Poly-Ethnicity"), in *Fenomen identichnosti v sovremennom gumanitarnom znanii: k 70-letiyu akademika V.A. Tishkova* (*The Phenomenon of Identity in Modern Human Knowledge: Celebrating the 70th Birthday of the Academy Member V. A. Tishkov*). Moscow, 2011. PP. 132-133.

tics and standards of living, and non-interference by civil servants in fields regulated by tradition and customs. For all people, there was a common legal environment, which, if it was in any way different for individual territories and peoples, then only in a good way (with the exception of the "pales of settlement" for Jews). There was no system of national dominance on the part of an "imperial nation", namely the Russians – against whom, on the contrary, the toughest duties and forms of discrimination were imposed, from serfdom and forced conscription to purges and the lack of ethnic statehood. The ruling class was always multi-ethnic, with Russians themselves having a disproportionately low level of representation. The outlying areas were not a source of enrichment; on the contrary, the center was the source of investment. Professor Oleg Matveychev believes: "Russia is an anti-empire, since empires suck everyone up from their colonies, whereas Russia, on the contrary, sucked up itself for the sake of developing the 'colonies.'"[78]

Behind Russification, there often lay concealed not "colonialism", but an objective need for a modern society, built into a single economic and cultural space. The Russian language spread not only as a result of being imposed artificially, but also because knowledge of the state language, which was one of the global languages, opened up broader prospects in life.

In pre-revolutionary and Soviet thought, the concept of a nation had a socio-cultural, rather than a political, interpretation, by contrast with Western Europe, where, in the new age, nation was understood to mean civil solidarity, and the people as a source of power.

For five centuries, Russia was among the top ten biggest economies in the world. The only exceptions were the Times of Troubles, the Civil War, and the 1990s, when it fell out of the top ten but remained in the top twenty. At the same time, the country has always lagged behind the leading states of its day in terms of the qualitative economic, technological, and standard of living parameters. In Russia, the institution of private property, which formed the quintessence of Western society, was not able fully to take shape. The merchant class remained very closed off and depended heavily on the mercy of the government. The low productivity of agriculture in Russia, especially given that up to half of the peasantry were under serfdom for almost four centuries, meant that agriculture was not able to give rise to capitalism, as happened in England or the USA.

The role of the state in the regulation of the economy was always big. State entrepreneurship became widespread, developing in parallel to the central-

---

[78] Oleg Matveychev, *Suverenitet dukha* (*Sovereignty of the Spirit*). Moscow, 2007. P. 197.

ization of power and to the bringing under state control of a large amount of property, in the form of land. Private wealth was seen as a consequence of government mercy and often was exactly that.

The spirit of free entrepreneurship and the practices of business lagged behind those in the West. For too long, trade gravitated towards a natural commodity exchange. Foreign capital always played a larger role inside Russia than did Russian capital overseas. The banking system remained fairly undeveloped at all times, and there was no readily accessible credit. A distinctive characteristic was the poor development of transport infrastructure.

In accordance with traditions of early Christianity, wealth was considered a sin. People did not feel an inclination to organize a private business, and were not fond of the rich and successful; the intellectual elite were scornful of trade and industry. Even in contemporary Russia, it is easy to discern a lack of respect for property, bureaucratic entrepreneurship, state service as a source of personal enrichment, a negative attitude towards business, and relatively low indicators per head of the population. Also characteristic of the Russian consciousness is its non-market orientation, its poorly developed "motivation for achievement". Russians tend to have a more patient and compassionate attitude than people in the West towards the poor and disadvantaged. People do not like routine work, even if it pays well. Russians have never lived merely for material goals; ideally, they would rather be driven by some lofty goal.

In Russia – even at the peak of demographic activity – there was always a contradiction between the relatively small size of the population and the colossal dimensions of the territory, the length of the borders, the scale of the areas that required mastering, the underdevelopment of the network of settled places. The small numbers of staff in the civil service, for such a large territory, also predetermined the weakness of the power vertical: in provincial towns and parishes, to say nothing of villages, representatives of central power might not be seen for centuries.

How, then, was the country governed? The answer lies in the fact that rural self-governance (*mir*) existed in Russia for centuries. The peasants' *mir* (which means "world", "community", "peace" in Russian) had the broadest powers and capabilities for deciding all community problems on the basis of common law. The heads of households always had the final say. A life in *mir* did not guarantee harmony – passions often boiled over in the villagers – but it did presuppose a search for consent in the name of the common good. Western consciousness looks upon competition and conflict as a defining value. For the Russian consciousness, the lack of conflict was a greater value. "Live in mir (peace) – live with *mir* (community)," as a Russian saying goes.[79]

The Russian countryside did not know the institution of private ownership of land, whether by peasants, individuals or households. The land was seen as belonging to the Lord, not to man. The peasants used their allotted land, provided by the commune, which, throughout its existence, all the way up until the formation of the collective farms in the 1930s, retained the principle of periodical redistributions, for the sake of fairness.[80]

The community-oriented worldview was not limited to rural communities; it manifested itself in the principles behind the organization of labor and in industry. The community was a collective, and the community's consciousness was a collective one. Even the Salvation was seen as a collective enterprise, not an individual one.

In Russia, however, the individual by no means melted away into society, as was the case in the Orient. The people were always drawn towards individualization, man's desire to "be of himself". Byzantine sources commented on the Slavs' love of freedom, their tendency to differ from one another in their opinions and to be mutually, passionately uncompromising (the works of Byzantine Emperor Maurice and Procopius of Scythopolis). Throughout all ages, people have cast off the beast of burden and gone off to freedom, to the steppes and forests. Hence the plethora of "free, wandering people", people with no settled abode, with no household of their own.

The Russian consciousness differs from that of the West in its interpretation of freedom and justice. In the West, freedom is the exercise of rights in combination with duties, and justice is a synonym for legality. In Russia, freedom is also volition, will, the lack of responsibility; justice is equality for all and a strong, paternal state. The idea of the natural rights of man practically did not exist in the form of something divided from the state. Whereas in the West, ideally, rights and freedoms had to be protected from the state, in the Russian tradition, rights were bestowed by state power, which was also required to protect them.

---

[79] Vladimir Dal', *Izbrannyye poslovitsy russkogo naroda* (*Selected Proverbs of the Russian People*). Moscow, 2012. P. 148.

[80] S. D. Skazkin, *Izbrannyye trudy po istorii* (*Selected Works on History*). Moscow, 1973. PP. 64-65; O. Yu. Yakhshiyan, "Krest'yanskaya obshchina i mestnoye samoupravleniye v Rossii" ("The Peasant Community and Self-Governance in Russia"), in *Rossiyskaya gosudarstvennost': istoricheskiye traditsii i vyzovy XXI veka* (*Russian Statehood: Historical Traditions and Challenges of the 21st Century*). Moscow, 2013. PP. 538-551.

Russians have a fairly well-developed national pride, but they do not have a national swagger, ambitions for messianic exceptionalism. Meanwhile, they are very critical in relation to themselves. Russians tend to have a self-deprecating detachment. Alexander Herzen called one of the properties of the Russian spirit "the ability, from time to time, to concentrate on oneself, to break away from one's past, to look at it with a deep, sincere, relentless irony, while having the courage to talk about this openly, without cynicism… and without hypocrisy, accusing oneself in order to receive justification from others."[81] At the same time, in no other country have there been such heated disputes about the past, and nowhere have the history textbooks been re-written quite so many times.

On the whole, Russia was historically a country of strong faith. Yet people, by and large, were less consciously religious than mystical, and faith was associated less with theological knowledge than with ritualism. There was a powerful anti-religious movement in the Russian elite and the intelligentsia from the 18th century, imbued with ideas of positivism and socialism. The country retained a high degree of tolerance for other faiths for centuries, and there was nothing similar to inquisition or witch-hunt. The missionary cause was far less well-developed than in the West, and there was never any question of imposing a faith through force of arms.

Oppression of other faiths, persecution of heretics and even the harassment of the Old Believers were far smaller in scale than the persecution in Western Europe. Russia never experienced religious wars. Other Christian denominations always existed and still do; and Islam, Buddhism and Judaism are officially traditional religions in Russia. If persecution of these religions did occur, it bore less a religious than a political character, and it was often smaller in scale than persecution against the Russian Orthodox Church (particularly in the Soviet era).

At a time, in the 16th century, when intellectual activity in the West broke out of the framework of classical knowledge and modern science began to be created, Russian thought for a long time continued to develop in the religious canons, rejecting Western learning. Only in relation to the era of Peter the Great can one talk about the emergence of scientific knowledge and an intellectual milieu, which developed in many ways through the efforts of the European academics invited to the country. The Russian educated class, to a significantly greater extent than in the West, was very remote from the

---

[81] Alexander Herzen, *Sobraniye sochineniy v 8 tomakh* (*Collected Works in 8 Vol.*). Vol. 8. Moscow, 1975. P. 27.

rest of the people, and even dressed and spoke differently. Moreover, there was no connection between the level of education and the level of wealth, and intellectuals at times lived in poverty and felt anti-bourgeois feelings.

A sense of alienation from power and property, the pressure of living circumstances, the censors' restrictions, the absence of a democratic tradition and the presence of a critical intellectual one all lent the intelligentsia an anti-state character and radicalism. The intelligentsia has at all times remained in opposition to power, and its opposition has always grown in circumstances of the liberalization of the regime, which was criticized over the inadequacy or insincerity of the liberalization. Whereas a Western intellectual would offer the product of his labor and try to capitalize it, trying to use the government for his own ends, a representative of Russian intelligentsia would seek justice and work towards the weakening or overthrowing of any government. At all times, the characteristics of the authors of *Vekhi* ("Milestones"), given by the Russian intelligentsia, have been just: detachment from life, beautiful indifference, conceit, refusal to accept different ways of thinking, dogmatism, heroic dichotomous thinking, historic intolerance, the lack of a sense of connection with the country's past.

Relations with the outside world have always been complicated. It was seen, above all, as a source of threats, against which a strong army could provide protection. The countries to the East and South were seen as less well developed and as a constant source of threat. The countries to the West were seen as better developed, but no less dangerous. At the same time, foreigners were feared, and people were particularly cautious with regard to religious matters. A great deal was borrowed from foreigners, but the things that were borrowed were of a specific character. Yuriy Pivovarov has noted that the nature of Russian government "presupposes" borrowing, and the borrowing, above all, of whatever does not exist in Russian life. The borrowing was functional, however, and not substantial.[82]

Russia borrowed ways of doing things, as a rule, from its strongest adversary. A great deal was borrowed from Byzantium and the Mongols. Peter I borrowed the Swedish state model, Alexander I borrowed the French military model. Soviet Russia borrowed the form of organizing economic life from its enemy in the First World War – Germany. Russia copied its liberal government and economic model from its chief adversary in

---

[82] Yuriy Pivovarov, *Politika v yeye istoricheskom i kul'turnom otnosheniyakh* (*Russian Politics in its Historical and Cultural Respects*). Moscow, 2006. PP. 116-117.

the cold war – the USA. In all cases, the systems adopted from overseas worked worse in Russia than the original versions and much more worse than Russian indigenous models.

Was Russia part of the Western political system? For most of its history, it undoubtedly was not. The borders of the West, at the turn of the 1st and 2nd millennia, were defined by the spread of Catholicism, the Latin language and Franc conquests. Yet Rus, Russia, was a strong state in Europe, played an important role in the eastern periphery of the Western world, and several times became the subject of efforts to include it in that world. From the time of the reign of Olga of Kyiv, Rus became the subject of rivalry between Byzantium and Rome, and when the preference was given to Constantinople, it was a moment of civilizational choice (the Ukrainians for some reason believe that they are making such a choice right now). After the Napoleonic Wars, Russia was one of the creators and the main bearing structure of the Vienna System and the European Concert of Powers, and the Westernization of the educated class attained its highest point. With the victory of the Bolshevik revolution, a regime came to power in a major country, for the first time, which not only openly rejected Western values, but offered a radical alternative to them, on a global scale.

Opinions vary as to the condition of statehood in today's Russia: from democracy, or undeveloped democracy, to fierce authoritarianism. But what's really is going on here?

Democracy in Russia?!

Putin and Medvedev themselves are sure that democracy exists in Russia, albeit not in the perfect form (where in the world is it perfect?). The elections reflect the structure of electoral preferences. The media was so independent that for a time, 60% of media organizations had foreign owners. Opposition supporters, while slinging mud at the "bloody, dictatorial regime" at demonstrations, in parliament or in prime-time TV shows, are safe in the knowledge that their limousines will then bring them to their *dachas*, rather than the fact that they will be packed off to Siberia. Nobody oppresses the ethnic minorities. Russia is not Saudi Arabia, it is not China and it is not even Turkey, but the Russian democratic process is developing in a complicated way.

Democratic values were in many ways discredited by the era of Yeltsinism. In 2012, Richard Pipes confirmed: "When it comes to the political system, the Russians are distrustful of democracy and equate it to chaos and the spread of crime."[83] In Russia, the level of political activity of citizens is relatively low, and the turnout at elections is not higher than the average global figures.[84] For all that, Russians do not want to go back to how things were in the past. They understand "order" to mean not a rejection of democratic principles, but political and economic stability, compliance with the law, an end to the plundering of the country, the ability of each person to exercise their rights.

In Moscow alone, there are at least 5,000 professional revolutionaries, for whom the battle to overthrow the government by violent means is their *raison d'être*, their calling and a well-paid profession. Efforts to destabilize the state are also being made from the outside. After the adoption of the law on "foreign agents", there was a sharp increase in official funding of their political activity from overseas: from 4 billion rubles up to 80 billion rubles.

From a formal perspective, Russia definitely has a democratic Constitution. Enshrined in it are the principles of the division of power, ideological and political pluralism, equality of citizens before the law, and man's rights and freedoms in accordance with the generally recognized principles and norms of international law. The executive is the Government, the legislature is the State Duma and the Council of Federations, and the judiciary is the Constitutional Court, along with the Supreme Court and the Higher Court of Arbitration (before they were merged). Where does the President fit in? The President is outside the system of the division of powers. Yet he too has executive rights, since he forms the Government and in fact defines the guidelines of its work. And legislative powers, since he issues decrees and orders. And judicial ones, since he can act as an arbiter in disputes between federal and regional governments.

Alongside the post of an almighty President, the Constitution created the position of a strong Prime Minister, something that Putin clearly showed when he held the role in 2008-2012. Yet the Government is not spoken of as the highest body of executive power, and it depends on the President far more than it depends on the parliament. The Russian courts still face the same accusations levelled at them as in the Soviet era, and the pre-Soviet era: selective justice, an accusatory bias, political influence on the judges,

---

[83] Richard Pipes, "Delo ne v tsikle, a v kul'ture" ("It's Not a Question of Cycles, but of Culture"), *Vedomosti*, December 21, 2012 <https://www.vedomosti.ru/opinion/articles/2012/12/21/delo_ne_v_ciklah_a_v_kulture>.

[84] *Ot plebistsita – k vyboram: Kak i pochemu rossiyane golosovali na vyborakh 2011-2012 gg. (From the Referendum to the Election. How and Why Russians Voted in the Elections in 2011-2012)*, ed. by Valeriy Fyodorov. Moscow, 2013. P. 410.

corruption. Many of these accusations are impossible to confirm or refute, but this is the general perception.

The political history of post-Soviet Russia is the history of the rise, fall, and rise once again of a vast number of parties. In the 1990s, there were about two hundred officially registered, nationwide public associations which had the right to take part in elections, despite the fact that there were regulations directly prohibiting the holders of leading state positions to be members of parties or involved in their activities. In 2002, a law was adopted in relation to parties, which was an attempt to make them stronger. Tougher requirements were brought in on the registration of parties, and the incentivizing of major parties through state financing led to a situation whereby small parties began to disappear. The Kremlin adroitly constructed a party of power, by combining the main elite groups from *Yedintsvo* ("Unity") and *Otechestvo – vsya Rossiya* ("Homeland – All Russia") into the ranks of *Yedinaya Rossiya* ("United Russia"). The legislation on parties and elections was changed several times, with a view to narrowing the field for political competition. All this played into the hands of the major parties, the total number of which fell to seven.

At the same time, this flare-up of protest tendencies forced the Kremlin to make changes to the laws on parties and elections. In 2012, the procedure for registering new national political parties was made far easier – instead of 50,000 members, as in the past, only 500 members were needed. In the autumn of 2012, 24 parties fought for seats in the regional parliaments, and in September 2013, 54 did so, representing the entire political spectrum. By early 2019, the Ministry of Justice had registered 63 parties which were entitled to take part in the elections.[85] Fourteen of them automatically get into the ballot at nation-wide elections since they are represented in regional legislatures.

At the same time, the authorities did not shy away from creating a storm of opposition criticism over "unpopular" measures aimed at toughening punishments for unauthorized demonstrations, bringing in a registration requirement for political NGOs receiving foreign funding, the monitoring of websites offering child pornography or narcotics or promoting suicide. It must be said though that, judging by public opinion polls, these measures are very popular, and each of them is supported by at least two thirds of the electorate. The biggest problem is still corruption, although its size is not

....

[85] Alexander Povorin, "Yest' takiye partii" ("Such Parties Exist"), *Rossiyskaya Gazeta* (*Russian Newspaper*), May 18, 2015 <https://rg.ru/2015/05/19/partii.html>.

easy to measure. Annual income and property declarations, the introduction of a ban on foreign accounts and reports on overseas property for senior officials and the members of parliament have already forced many to prefer their property and accounts abroad to civil service.

In post-Soviet Russia, the main symbol of liberalism was Boris Yeltsin, whereas now, it is a motley alliance of forces without an obvious leader, which is calling for Russia to follow the Western model. The problem facing the liberal, pro-Western part of the electorate is not that it is small – it stands at around 10% – but that it is fragmented. The liberals had a disastrous result in the elections to the State Duma in 2003, and were unable to win back seats in 2007, 2011 or 2016.

Yedinaya Rossiya did not face any serious problems in 2016, receiving 54.2% of the vote, followed by the Communist Party of the Russian Federation with 13.34%, the Liberal Democratic Party of Russia with 13.14% and *Spravedlivaya Rossiya* ("A Just Russia") with 6.22%. Grigoriy Yavlinsky's liberal *Yabloko* party came 6th with 1.99%, while Mikhail Kasyanov's PARNAS came 11th with 0.73%. Having also secured an overwhelming majority in the single-mandate districts, *Yedinaya Rossiya* acquired a comfortable constitutional majority. *Yedinaya Rossiya* is the main bearer of conservative tradition, while Gennadiy Zyuganov's Communist Party performs the same role for the communist tradition, Sergey Mironov's *Spravedlivaya Rossiya* for the social-democratic tradition, and Vladimir Zhirinovsky's Liberal Democratic Party of Russia for the nationalist. Turnout in parliamentary elections fell from 63.7% in 2007 to 48% in 2016.[86]

The traditional distribution of the electorate was confirmed in the presidential elections in March 2018. With a turnout of 67.5%, Putin had no problem getting the support of 76.7% of voters, while his closest rival – Communist candidate Pavel Grudinin – only polled 11.8%, and Zhirinovsky 5.7%. All other candidates (and in total in the ballot there were 8 surnames) gathered less than 2% of votes.

However, such a high rating of the President only lasted until the autumn of 2018, when pension reform began: a gradual increase in the retirement age for men from 60 to 65 years, and for women from 55 to 60 years. This change, which could not be avoided, was regarded by many as a kind of violation of the social contract. Both Putin and *Yedinaya Rossiya* lost the

---

[86] Nikolay Kalinin, "Odnikh prizyvov malo" ("Calls to Arms are Not Enough"), *Parlamentskaya gazeta* (*Parliamentary Newspaper*), October 11, 2016 <https://www.pnp.ru/politics/odnikh-prizyvov-malo.html>.

support of up to 20% of its supporters, and candidates of the ruling party were defeated in some regional elections, where the voters preferred the candidates from the Communist party and the LDPR. The request for social justice has generated a major shift to the left.[87]

What terms can we use to describe Putin's mindset? Unlike the liberals, he does not deny the national traditions – talking about families, about moral and religious values. He is the advocate of a strong state. At the same time, he is committed to the principles of evolutionary development, a free market, democracy, strong statehood, Russian sovereignty, and traditionalism. This combination is characteristic of conservatism. Putin has confirmed as much himself. When asked about his ideological orientation, he replied once: "I think one can definitely say that I am a pragmatist with a conservative inclination…"[88]

Growth Is Seen in Comparisons

Based on figures for 2018, the IMF evaluated Russia's GDP at 4.2 trillion dollars, in terms of PPP, and Russia turned out to be the sixth biggest economy on the planet for this indicator, after China (25.2 trillion), the USA (20.4 trillion), India (10.5 trillion), Japan (5.5 trillion), and Germany (4.3 trillion). In terms of the figures for GDP per head of the population, Russia, with 10,700 dollars based on the exchange rate and 27,900 dollars based on PPP, corresponds to the level of countries such as Greece, Hungary or Poland.[89]

There is a clear slowing down in the rate of economic growth, which began even before Western sanctions were brought in. The rise in GDP in 2012 stood at 3.4%, and in 2013 at 1.3%. In 2014, it rose by 0.6%. The factors that have slowed growth down were budget austerity, the high interest rate set by the Central Bank, the reduction in investment and the slowing down of the monetization of the economy, the fall in oil prices and, yes, the sanctions. In 2015, GDP fell by 2.8%, and in 2016 by 0.2%. However, growth has resumed since 2017 (2%), and continued in 2018 with 2.2%.

---

[87] Yelena Mukhametshina, "Otvernulis' ot Putina" ("They have Turned Their Backs on Putin"), *Vedomosti*, Issue 188, October 8, 2018 <https://vedomosti.profkiosk.ru/article.aspx?aid=678251>.

[88] "Eksklyuzivnoye interv'yu V.Putina Pervomu kanalu i agentstvu 'Assoshieyted Press'" ("An Exclusive Interview with V. Putin for Channel One and the Associated Press Agency"), Pervyy kanal (Channel One), September 4, 2013 <http://www.1tv.ru/news/social/241135>.

[89] "The World in 2018", *The Economist*, 2018. PP. 110-112.

Russia, unlike other major economies, has maintained a budget surplus for many years. Only at the end of the first third of 2015 did the budget see a deficit, of 4.4% of GDP, since when this deficit has only been reducing.[90] The budget surplus at the end of 2018 amounted to 2.1% of GDP.[91]

Foreign exchange reserves at the end of 2013 were worth 511 billion dollars, in May 2015 356 billion, and in December 2018 464 billion. In 2014, Russia began increasing the proportion of gold in its reserves, disposing of dollars at the same time.

At 13.5% of GDP, Russia's combined state debt (meaning its aggregated domestic and foreign debt) remains the lowest of all the developed countries. The main reason is its low level of foreign debt, which for many years did not exceed 10% of GDP and is now at 4%.[92] The government also launched a complex plan for reducing the debts of the regions, which includes the restructuring of loans, the simplifying of access to cheap loans from the budget, and additional federal aid.[93]

The banking system is, on the whole, in a satisfactory condition. As of the start of 2017, Russians had a total of 24.2 trillion rubles of savings in the banks, whereas in 2014 this figure stood at 17 trillion, and in 2006 at 2.7 trillion. This can be explained in large part by the rapid proliferation of bank payment cards. The consumer borrowing market has grown dramatically, with total loans taken out by individuals as of the start of 2017 exceeding 10.8 trillion rubles, or 12.5% of GDP, including mortgage loans.[94] Given that in the EU, mortgage loans amount to 51.7% of GDP, the Russian market clearly still has scope to keep growing. In the meantime, analysts are starting to sound the alarm over the increased number of "bad borrowers". There has been increased tension in the currency market: growth in the monetary mass has slowed, interest rates on loans are high, as well as the price of money on the

---

[90] Vadim Visloguzov, "Minus trillion" ("Minus a Trillion"), *Kommersant* (*The Businessman*), May 19, 2015 <https://www.kommersant.ru/doc/2729241>.

[91] Economic indicators for 2018 are are based on the press conference of Putin on December 20, 2018. The Russian President's official website, 2018 <http://www.kremlin.ru/events/president/news/59455>.

[92] Yuliya Titova, "Risk defolta Rossii snizilsya do minimuma" ("The Risk of a Russian Default is at Its Lowest Level"), *RBK*, September 4, 2017 <https://www.rbc.ru/newspaper/2017/09/05/59ad48889a79476d6f595d3d>.

[93] Alina Yevstigneyeva and Valentina Dorokhova, "Regiony gasyat dolgi" ("The Regions are Paying Off Their Debts"), *Izvestiya*, October 2, 2017 <https://iz.ru/652588/alina-evstigneeva-valentina-dorokhova/minfin-dolgov-ne-proshchaet>.

[94] *Rossiya v tsifrakh. 2017* (*Russia in Figures. 2017*). Moscow, 2017. PP. 378-379.

inter-bank market. The ready availability of short-term money goes hand in hand with an acute shortage of long-term investment resources.

A serious problem for Russia is capital outflow. In 2014, it stood at $154.1 billion, in 2015 $57.5 billion, and in 2016 $15.4 billion. The improvement in this indicator is linked to renewed interest in the Russian market among foreign investors, and the improved status of the ruble; Bloomberg stated that the Russian ruble was the best performing currency in the first three months of 2015. An amnesty on capital repatriated also had a positive effect, as did the actions of foreign states in preventing the return of funds to Russia (particularly from British and Spanish jurisdictions). Since 2017, the outflow has started to rise again, exceeding $30 billion in 2017 and $60 billion in 2018, which was associated, primarily, with the fact that the Russian banks continued to reduce foreign debt.

Russia is a major player in the investment market; this investment goes to companies in the raw materials, energy, metals and telecommunications sectors. For many years, the biggest investor in Russia's economy was… Cyprus. It was followed by investors from Switzerland, the Netherlands, Luxembourg, the Bahamas, Jersey, and the British Virgin Isles; these are off-shore tax havens, and this obviously points to the Russian origins of this investment. Today, interest in investing in the Russian market is distinctly limited in the West, though growing in the East. One cannot fail to notice the 400 billion dollar contract with China for the *Sila Sibiri* (Force of Siberia) gas pipeline, which will enable a diversification of the transportation routes for Russian gas.

In the Doing Business rating, Russia rose from 120th place in 2011 to 35th place in 2017. It was some distance behind its rivals by reference to ease of acquiring permits for construction, and foreign trade, which is not surprising, given the Western sanctions.[95]

The data on foreign trade in goods prior to 2014 showed a constant increase in volumes: from 149.9 billion dollars in 2000 to 867.6 billion in 2013.[96] Thereafter, however, under the sanctions and the Russian counter-sanctions, an obvious fall in foreign trade turnover began to be seen – to 784.5 billion dollars in 2014 and 467.8 billion in 2016. Even after this, however, the net surplus in foreign trade remained higher than 100 billion dollars. In

---

[95] Anton Feynberg, "Plyus pyat'" ("Plus Five"), *RBK*, October 31, 2017 <https://www.rbc.ru/newspaper/2017/11/01/59f735d39a79471f78aa5311>.

[96] *Rossiya v tsifrakh. 2014* (*Russia in Figures. 2014*). Moscow, 2014. P. 517.

2017 there was a 25% increase in turnover, to $591 billion.[97] The net surplus reached $190 billion in 2018. The biggest foreign trade partners are China, the Netherlands, Germany, Belarus, and Italy. The structure of exports leaves a lot to be desired, and it is not getting any better. The proportion of mineral resources (oil, oil products, gas, coal, ores) rose from 42.5% in 1995 to 71.6% in 2013, and then to 60% in 2017. The greatest growth was seen in exports of metallurgical products, products from the engineering and wood processing industries, and products from the agricultural sector – particularly to countries in the Asia-Pacific.[98]

Russia is an energy superpower. This has nothing to do with its development strategy. It is simply a fact. But it is also true that the main investments are still in oil and gas production. A dozen majors provide more than half of all capital investments made by large businesses, while all other industries feel a lack of investment.[99] However, we have to take into consideration the fact that modern production and transportation of energy is a high-tech industry.

For several years in a row, the volumes of oil extracted have been rising, and the country now accounts for more than 12% of global oil production. In 2017, 546 million tons of oil and gas condensate were extracted. As an oil exporter, Russia is second only to the Saudis. Russia is the world's second-biggest extractor of natural gas (691 billion cubic meters), trailing only the USA.[100] The biggest single gas company in the world, however, is Gazprom.

The USSR was a pioneer in nuclear energy, and today Russia is a leading figure in the market for the construction of nuclear power stations. Rosatom has more contracts for the planning and construction of nuclear power stations than all its competitors around the world put together. Rosatom's portfolio of foreign orders alone includes 36 energy facilities in China, India, Turkey, Belarus, Bangladesh, Finland, Vietnam, Armenia, Hungary, and Egypt. As *The Economist* put it, "[F]or now Russia has no serious rivals in the export of nuclear technology."[101]

---

[97] *Rossiya v tsifrakh. 2018* (*Russia in Figures. 2018*). Moscow, 2018. P. 482.

[98] *Rossiya v tsifrakh. 2017* (*Russia in Figures. 2017*). Moscow, 2017. PP. 474-475; Aleksey Tyupanov, "Sformirovan yedinyy institut podderzhki eksporta" ("The United Institute for the Support of Exports has been Formed"), *RBK*, September 5, 2017 <https://plus.rbc.ru/news/59ad84ae7a8aa91a58b19391>.

[99] Yevgeniy Ogorodnikov and Maxim Remizov, "Za krayem neftegazovogo gorizonta" ("Beyond the Oil and Gas Horizon"), *Ekspert* (*Expert*), Issue 42, October 15-20, 2018. PP. 24-28.

[100] *Rossiya v tsifrakh. 2018* (*Russia in Figures. 2018*). Moscow, 2018. P. 233.

[101] Kira Latukhina, "Atom idet na Vostok" ("Atom is Heading Eastwards"), *Rossiyskaya Gazeta*

In 2014-2018, rapid growth continued in the pharmaceutical and medical industries, in agricultural engineering, and in production in all the defence sectors: in the radio electronics industry, in aviation, in shipbuilding, and in the missile and aerospace industry.[102] Russia maintains its leadership in space the industry. Russia operates about 10% of all global orbital spacecraft. When the USA brought in its anti-Russian sanctions, it did not extend them to the aerospace sector, realizing that it was too dependent on cooperation with Moscow. American astronauts were taken to the International Space Station by the "Soyuz". It proved impossible for the US to manage without Russian rocket engines. Boeing jets are made using Russian titanium, and the software for them is built in Moscow.

The contribution of the digital economy to GDP grew by the end of 2018 to 5.1%. By then, there were already more than 90 million Internet users in Russia, or 75.4% of the adult population; among young people the figure was 99%. Two thirds of users access the network via mobile devices, the number of which per capita in Russia is much higher than in the US or Japan.[103]

While the USSR, in the final decades of its existence, was an importer of foodstuffs, Russia, in recent years, has become a major exporter, and the largest exporter of grain. In the 2016/17 season, exports of grain reached 35.1 million tons, out of a harvest of 120.7 million tons.[104] Whereas in 2013, only 24% of the agricultural machinery acquired was made in Russia, in 2017 this proportion rose to 56%.[105] In many ways, progress in the agricultural sector

....

(*Russian Newspaper*), September 2016 <https://rg.profkiosk.ru/497005>; Il'ya Dashkovskiy, "Verkhom na yadre" ("Riding the Core"), *Kommersant. Den'gi* (*The Businessman. Money*), October 17-23, 2016. PP. 23-26; "Russia and Nuclear Power. The Global Supplier", *The Economist*, August 4-10, 2018. P. 25.

[102] "Otchot pravitel'stva o rezul'tatakh raboty v 2014 godu" ("Government Report on the Results of Work in 2014"), *Parlamentskaya Gazeta* (*Parliamentary Newspaper*), April 23, 2015 <https://yandex.ru/turbo/s/pnp.ru/archive/2015/04/23/otchyot-pravitelstva-orezultatakh-raboty-v-2014-godu.html>.

[103] Dmitriy Shestoperov, "Internet-pol'zovateli vykhodyat iz-za stola" ("Internet Users Leave the Table"), *Kommersant* (*The Businessman*), Issue 6, January 16, 2019 <https://www.kommersant.ru/doc/3854727>.

[104] Yekaterina Burlakova, "Rekord poshel na eksport" ("The Record Went to Exports"), *Vedomosti*, June 2017 <https://vedomosti.profkiosk.ru/571528>.

[105] Dmitriy Goncharuk, "Otechestvennyye traktory i kombayny dostupny vypuskat' po goszakazu" ("Russian-Made Tractors and Combine Harvesters are Being Released under State Commissions"), *Parlamentskaya Gazeta* (*Parliamentary Newspaper*), October 16, 2017 <https://yandex.ru/turbo/s/pnp.ru/economics/otechestvennye-traktory-i-kombayny-stanut-vypuskat-po-goszakazu.html>.

was stimulated by Moscow's response to the sanctions, which included a ban on the supply of many types of foodstuffs from Western states.

Putin, however, is not satisfied at all with the current rates of growth; nor is the general populace, whose living standard is stagnant.

A Revival

In 1913, the Russian Empire contained roughly 9% of the world's population. In 1950, the share of Russia alone (and this was after the war) stood at around 4%, with the USSR having around 8%. Today, Russia has just 2.4% of the world's population. In 1913 the Russian Empire was behind only China and India in terms of population size. In 1950 Russia, taken within its current borders, was fourth behind China, India and the USA. Today Russia has a population of 146 million people and is only the ninth most populous country in the world: it has been overtaken by Indonesia, Brazil, Pakistan, Bangladesh and Nigeria.

No forecast is predicting that Russia's population is going to rise. Some analysts do not see any major problems in this. They point out that Canada has a relatively small population too, yet it is doing pretty well. It is hard to share such optimism. There is an obvious discrepancy between the size of the population and the dimensions of its territory, the length of its borders, the scale of the spaces which need to be mastered. It is simply going to be difficult to maintain control over the territory.

The fall in the birth rate in Russia in the 1990s had to do with the economic situation, to a considerable degree. The lowest figure – 1.215 million births – was recorded in 1999, after the default. Since then, it has risen. In 2015, 1.94 million children were born. A decrease then followed, because a relatively small cohort of those born in the 1990s reached childbearing age. In 2017 1.69 million children were born. In 1999, each woman had an average of 1.16 children; in 2011, this figure had risen to 1.58. The most common age at which women gave birth rose from 21 to 25-26.[106]

An incentivizing role has been played by child benefit, provided on the birth of a second child and any subsequent children, and by the opening of a large number of regional and federal perinatal centers. In the last 25 years, infant mortality has fallen almost 4-fold, from 22.5 to 5.6 per 1000 babies

---

[106] *Naseleniye Rossii 2010-2011: yezhegodnyy demograficheskiy doklad* (*The Population of Russia 2010-2011. Annual Demographic Report*), ed. by A. G. Vishnevskiy. Moscow, 2013. PP. 278, 294.

born alive, and the mortality rate among mothers has fallen by 71% over the last 10 years.¹⁰⁷ An important factor in increasing the birth rate is the promotion of family values and large families, and the campaign against abortion. Russia has the most liberal laws on abortions in the world. It should be noted, though, that since 1988, there has been a constant decline in the number of abortions, which had fallen 4-fold by 2011. Even allowing for this, though, the problem remains: the number of future young parents is extremely small. In the early 2020s, due to the demographic decline of the 1990s, there will be a third fewer mothers aged 20 to 35 than there were at the start of the 21st century. In 2018, child benefit was brought in for first-born children as well.

The mortality rate rose dramatically in the 1990s, particularly among men. The primary reason for this was vodka and surrogate versions of it. Moreover, a large number of people are killed on Russia's roads: 15,000 in 2016. Almost the same number commit suicide each year. In terms of suicides per head of the population, Russia was in 12th place in the world in 2013.¹⁰⁸

Since 2003, Russia has seen the longest continuous fall in the mortality rate: from 16.4 deaths per 1000 people to 12.4 in 2017. In 2000, the natural decrease in the population stood at 958,000 people; in 2012, for the first time, there was no net decrease in population size, and in 2013, a natural increase was recorded for the first time. In 2017 the decline resumed. Average life expectancy has risen from 65.3 to 73 since the start of the century, and among women it stands at 77.6 – the highest level in the country's history, while among men it is 67.5. Demographers link the rise in life expectancy, above all, to the reduction in the consumption of strong alcohol.¹⁰⁹ The cessation of the war in the North Caucasus was also a contributing factor. Let us not forget that in 2014 Crimeans added to Russia's population – more than two million people – and there has been an influx of hundreds of thousands of refugees from the Donbass.

Trying to ensure population growth by means of measures to reduce mortality and increase the birth rate is a hopeless affair. It is impossible without migrant inflow. Russia in fact has the second largest number of im-

---

¹⁰⁷ Elina Khetagurova and Yevgeniya Pertseva, "Prodolzhitel'nost' zhizni v Rossii vyrosla do 71,8 goda" ("Life Expectancy Reaches 71.8 Years Old"), *Izvestiya*, June 29, 2017 <https://iz.ru/612100/elina-khetagurova/raznitca-po-prodolzhitelnosti-zhizni-v-regionakh-16-let>; *Rossiya v tsifrakh. 2018* (*Russia in Figures. 2018*). Moscow, 2018. PP. 79-84.

¹⁰⁸ Irina Krasnopol'skaya, "Liniya smerti" ("The Death Line"), *Rossiyskaya Gazeta* (*Russian Newspaper*), 15 March 2013. P. 1.

¹⁰⁹ *Rossiya v tsifrakh. 2018* (*Russia in Figures. 2018*). Moscow, 2018. PP. 79-81.

migrants in the world (behind the USA and ahead of Germany). Estimates of the number of foreign workers in Russia vary from 8 million to 12 million. Working migrants from Ukraine and Belarus are seen by the native population as "our kind": they can speak Russian, they do not look different outwardly, and they do not form national enclaves. Objections sometimes arise against people from Central Asia, the South Caucasus and even the North Caucasus, areas which are part of the RF; Russians expects these people to adhere to commonly-accepted standards of behavior in Russia, and they do not always do so. The real problem is not how to restrict migration, though, but how to make it as legitimate and as useful as possible for the country.

When the great American ballet maestro George Balanchine was asked about his nationality, he replied: "I am a Georgian by blood, a Russian by culture, and a St. Petersburger by nationality." This speaks volumes as to Russian self-identification, in which ethnicity, culture and one's place of residence are all interwoven.

The Russian government is currently promoting the notion of "common citizenship" – the sense of a community of citizens of the Russian state – through such concepts as the "Russian nation", the "single people of Russia", the "multi-ethnic Russian nation".[110] According to various studies, between 80% and 95% of Russians identify themselves as "citizens of Russia". The most powerful consolidating factor is the state, followed by pride in one's history and culture.[111] A factor that fights against the concept of the single Russian nation is ethnic nationalism, especially Russian with its slogan "Russia is for Russians".

The collapse of the USSR led to a marked rise in religious sentiment. Whereas in Western Europe, congregations and the number of religious people are steadily falling, in Russia, they are growing. Religion is taking its revenge. All the traditional religions and a plethora of non-traditional ones are showing this trend. The profession of a faith has become a public matter, and religion is "in fashion".

Whereas in the late 1980s, two thirds of Russians considered themselves atheists, and 30% described themselves as Orthodox, the figures for 2013 were as follows: 79% said they were followers of the Orthodox faith, 4% were

---

[110] Natal'ya Gorodetskaya, "Russkiy narod probuyetsya na ob"yedinyayushchuyu rol'" ("The Russian Population is Auditioning for a Unifying Role"), *Kommersant* (*The Businessman*), October 18, 2012 <https://www.kommersant.ru/doc/2047014>.

[111] Leokadiya Drobizheva, "Rossiyskaya identichnost': faktory integratsii i problemy razvitiya" ("Russian Identity: Factors of Integration and Problems of Development"), *Sotsiologicheskaya nauka i sotsial'naya praktika* (*Sociological Science and Social Practice*), Issue 1, 2013. PP. 74-84.

followers of Islam, 9% believed in some higher power and 7% subscribed to atheist views. Since the end of the 20th century, the proportion of Russians who have never attended a church, a mosque or a synagogue has fallen from 42% to 26%. At the same time, only 4% of the population describe themselves as deeply committed to their faith, adhering to all the norms of the church.[112] In 2010, 23,494 religious entities were registered in Russia. Most part of them – 12,941 – belong to the Russian Orthodox Church of the Moscow Patriarchate; 4127 are Muslim; 291 are Jewish, 208 are Buddhist, 4438 Protestant and 1489 belong to other religious denominations.[113]

Under Patriarch Kirill, the Russian Orthodox Church (ROC) has adopted a new, energetic, one might even say aggressive strategy, actively entering socio-political life.[114] Meanwhile, the church has come under strong criticism lately from the liberal and ultra-communist opposition, which accuses the ROC of cooperating too closely with the government, and of obscurantism.

Russia is one of the world's biggest Islamic countries. In August 2003, President Putin attended a summit of the Organization of Islamic Cooperation in Kuala Lumpur, where he described Russia not only as a bastion of Orthodoxy, but also as a country in which Islam is a historic religion. After the fall of the USSR, there was essentially an Islamic rebirth in Russia. Thousands of mosques have been opened, a system of religious education is being created, and contact with overseas Muslims has been established. There are two major concentrations of Muslims in Russia. One is in the Caucasus, while the other is in the Volga region. There is no particular difference in the orientations of the two main groups of Russian Muslims. They are Sunnis, but the Tatars and Bashkirs are closer in mentality to Turkey, whereas the Muslims in the North Caucasus have more in common with the Arab countries.[115] The majority of Muslim communities in Russia are fairly moderate, modernist or traditional.

....

[112] Boris Dubin, "Otnosheniye k vere analogichno otnosheniyu k gosudarstvu – statistika" ("The Relationship to Faith is Analogous to the Relationship to the State"), *RBK*, August 2012. P. 22.

[113] Vladimir Zorin, "Gosudarstvennaya natsional'naya politika v Rossii na sovremennom etape" ("Governmental National Policy in Modern Russia"), in *Fenomen identichnosti v sovremennom gumanitarnom znanii* (*Identity Phenomemom in Modern Human Sciences*). Moscow, 2011. P. 257.

[114] Aleksey Malashenko, "Zaklyucheniye" ("Conclusion") in *Pravoslavnaya tserkov' pri novom patriarkhe* (*The Russian Orthodox Church Under the New Patriarch*), ed. by A. Malashenko and S. Filatov. Moscow, 2012. PP. 402-403.

[115] Rinat Mukhametov, "Rossiyskiye musul'mane i vneshnyaya politika" ("Russian Muslims and Foreign Policy"), *Rossiya v global'noy politike* (*Russia in Global Affairs*), May/June, 2012.

The standard of living has risen continuously in the 21st century. From 2000 through to 2018, average salaries and pensions, in current money, saw a 14-fold increase, a 4.7-fold increase in real terms. General consumer costs have risen almost 10-fold at face value. However, the consumer activity index was stagnant in the period 2014-2019. Unemployment has been at the level of 5.5% for some years now.

Russia had one of the lowest retirement ages in the world: 60 for men and 55 for women. In 2018 the Government introduced a pension reform bill which proposed a gradual increase in the retirement age for men to 65 years, and for women to 60 years. The initiative was extremely unpopular, with 90% of Russian citizens against it. However, *Yedinaya Rossiya* supported it, considering the changes inevitable from an economic perspective because now there are only two people in work for every one retiree.

By comparison with the 1990s, the number of people living in abject poverty has fallen by more than two and a half times, though around 15% of people are still below poverty level. If one goes by the standards of the World Bank, however, which defines the poorest as those living on less than two dollars a day, there are no such people at all in Russia.

At present, more than 80% of Russian families have a higher level of consumption than the average Soviet family. In 1995, people spent 49% of their income on food. In 2010 the figure was 29,8%, whereas in 2016 it was 32.4%. Expenditure on housing and utilities rose from 4.2% to 10.1% of people's income.[116]

The construction of new housing has increased in recent decades, from 41.5 million square meters in 1992 to 85.3 million in 2015 (a record in the country's history) and 79.2 million in 2017. Russians' access to housing has increased by 40%, from 16.8 to 25.2 square meters per person.[117] This puts it in 32nd place in the world by reference to this indicator, between Slovakia and Serbia (Australia tops the list with 89 square meters per person).[118]

58% of households have a car, compared with only 27% in 2000. In terms of the total number of cars Russia holds the 5th place in the world, and the 52nd with its 317 cars per 1000 persons.

P. 117.

[116] *Rossiya v tsifrakh. 2018* (*Russia in Figures. 2018*). Moscow, 2018. PP. 128-129.

[117] Ibid. PP. 285, 131.

[118] "Zhilishchno-kommunal'nyy mir" ("Housing and Communal World"), *Kommersant. Den'gi* (*The Businessman. Money*), December 1-7, 2014. PP. 64-65.

Over the last 10 years, a sizeable middle class has formed, although it is hard to establish its exact size at the moment. In 1998, it consisted of between 5% and 10% of the population – less than in the late USSR. It now includes at least 30% of the population, in terms of income level.[119] Russia is 7th on the list of countries whose citizens spend the most on travel, ahead of Japan and Italy.[120]

At the same time, there has been an increase in social inequality in Russia. The ratio between the average earnings of the richest 10% and the poorest 10% was 8:1 in 1992; it is now 16.2:1, effectively mimicking the position in the USA. During the last 20 years, the incomes of the richest 20% of Russians have doubled, while incomes of the poorest 20% have nearly halved in real terms.[121] Inequality in the standard of living between the various regions is particularly high. The most affluent region, the Tyumen oblast, is 25 times richer than the poorest, the Republic of Ingushetia, in terms of income per head of the population.

The high level of social inequality is reflected in the rankings of the top billionaires. Russia has the highest ratio of billionaires to total GDP in the world.[122]

Education and science were hit hard in the 1990s by insufficient funding, an outflow of qualified staff, a departure from Soviet standards in education, the degradation of the science-heavy sectors of industry, and the rapid realignment of education from the natural sciences towards the humanities. There was a sharp decline in the number of people employed in research and development, from 1.7 million in 1991 to 807,000 in 2006. No more than 1% of university graduates applied for jobs at research organizations.[123]

---

[119] Aleksey Shapovalov, "Sredniy klass trebuyet novoy raboty" ("The Middle Class Demands New Jobs"), *Kommersant* (*The Businessman*), March 27, 2014 <https://www.kommersant.ru/doc/2438702>.

[120] "Zarubezhnyye postupleniya" ("Foreign Incomes"), *Kompaniya* (*The Firm*), February 25, 2013. P. 12.

[121] Olga Kuvshinova, "Dve Rossii" ("Two Russias"), *Vedomosti*, April 11, 2011 <https://web.archive.org/web/20110413062833/http://www.vedomosti.ru/newspaper/article/258225/dve_rossii>.

[122] Chrystia Freeland, *Plutocrats: The Rise of the New Global Super-Rich and the Fall of Everyone Else*. N. Y., 2012. P. 149.

[123] A. V. Todosiychuk, "O disproportsiyakh v rossiyskoy sisteme podgotovki nauchnykh kadrov i putyakh ikh preodoleniya" ("On the Disproportions in the Russian System of Training Scientific Staff and the Paths for Overcoming Them"), *Naukovedcheskiye issledovaniya* (*Scientific Research*). Moscow, 2010. PP. 26-28.

Though it has suffered tangible setbacks, Russian science has managed to survive. Grant support programs have begun to be introduced for developers of state-of-the-art technologies. Development institutes have started searching for and selecting projects with potential, providing financial support to innovative firms. A center for innovative research has been created in Skolkovo. Since the turn of the century, funding for science from the federal budget has increased – from 17 billion rubles in 2000 to 439.4 billion in 2015, and from all sources taken together, from 76.7 billion to 943.8 billion.[124] In terms of share of GDP, however, this is significantly lower than in most developed countries. Since 2013, the number of people working in science has grown, thanks to both the arrival of young scholars and the return of scientists who had previously lived overseas.

From my position as Chairman of the State Duma's Committee on Education and Science, the education system in Russia looks as follows. Nursery education has become a standard part of the education system. Russia compares favourably with many other countries in this regard. The problem of providing kindergarten places for all children aged between 3 and 7 has been solved. Now the same must be done for those aged under 3. Once the kindergarten construction program has been completed, a program for the construction of new schools will be launched.

Elementary education in Russia is outstanding. In inter-country comparisons, according to the PIRLS ratings, we are on top. In 2017, Russia topped the world in this field. The same ratings, however, when applied to our secondary schools, are less positive. Russia still makes it into the top ten, however, ahead of many Western countries, but behind the "East Asian dragons". A drop in quality can be seen at high school (though Russia's bright kids still win most international competitions in maths, physics, chemistry and programming). This is largely because schoolchildren simply stop studying a whole range of subjects, in which they do not plan to take the Unified State Exam.

The education provided at bachelor level at decent Russian higher education institutions is comparable to Western standards. It remains more formalized, however, and provides less variation in the programs offered, so that there is less scope for devising customized education trajectories. In the West and in the East one would be hard-pressed to find two people who, despite having studied at the same department, took an identical set of subjects. Here in Russia, by contrast, it is hard to find people who managed to take strikingly different paths while being students in the same department.

---

[124] *Rossiya v tsifrakh. 2017* (*Russia in Figures. 2017*). Moscow, 2017. PP. 338, 343-345.

There is still a fairly inflexible system of specializations and professionalization in place at Russia's universities, although it is gradually becoming more flexible and varied.

The number of universities and students in modern Russia has risen many times over. In 1991, there were 514 universities with 2.8 million students; in the 2008/09 academic year there were 1134, with 7.5 million. All this has led to a drop in the overall quality of higher education. Regrettably, many higher education institutions, particularly private ones, merely take people's money and hand out diplomas. In 2017-2018, there were 766 institutions left in the country, and 4.2 million students.[125] Meanwhile, due to the baby boom of the 1990s, in just ten years, the number of high school leavers halved, and 57% of them are guaranteed university places funded by the government.

Among Russian nationals aged 25 to 64, 60% have completed university and college education; in this parameter, Russia has overtaken Canada (52.6%), Japan (46.6%), Israel (46.4%), and the USA (43.1%). Experts from the OECD have declared Russia to be the most educated of all the states of the G20. Higher education has gone from being a social mobility tool for the few to a norm to which the majority strive.[126]

Graduates from Russian universities successfully continue their studies and work all over the world – you will not find a single decent university in the West that does not employ Russian professors. It is in large part thanks to Russians that the famous Silicon Valley is making such giant strides. Russia has lost a whole generation of teachers and academics, who have fled to more lucrative professions than science or to places where scientists are paid well. In 2018 the level of salaries for university academics reached 200% of the regional average, in line with a proposal made by Vladimir Putin. He also named education and science among the priorities of his most recent term as President.

"Polite People"

The Eastern Slavs would have been wiped out by the tide of history, had they not possessed military organization, in which all adult men were included. The nation's extremely vulnerable geopolitical location, bordering on the

---

[125] *Rossiya v tsifrakh. 2018* (*Russia in Figures. 2018*). Moscow, 2018. P. 141.

[126] Pavel Aptekar', "Ot redaktsii: Vysokiye zaprosy" ("Editorial: High Demands"), *Vedomosti*, April 24, 2014 <https://www.vedomosti.ru/newspaper/articles/2014/04/25/vysokie-zaprosy>; "Rossiya na pervom meste po vysshemu obrazovaniyu" ("Russia in First Place for Higher Education"), *Argumenty nedeli* (*Arguments of the Week*), September 25, 2014 <https://argumenti.ru/talks/n456/367013>.

steppes, transformed the interests of defence into an absolute priority for state policy. War became the norm in the life of the country, and its militarization became the distinctive feature of the Russian matrix. The fact that Russia lagged behind its enemies, particularly those in the West, in a technological and tactical sense, was compensated for by the country's ability to mobilize large number of human resources, equipped with extraordinary levels of endurance and courage, and to concentrate disproportionately large forces and resources for the objectives of defence in a centralized manner. Whereas the principle of hiring men for military service was typical of Western Europe, for Russia, the principle of conscription was in place, namely the obligation of each man from the manorial and patrimonial lands – first and foremost the elite – to serve his country. Later, a system of universal, systematic military service was introduced, in 1874.

Since the days of Peter the Great, the Russian army has gradually been becoming one of the most powerful on the planet, capable of resisting – with some or other degree of success – any other great power or a coalition of great powers. Yet the army's independent, political role was more the exception (in the 18th century) than the rule.

After the collapse of the USSR, Russia went through an extremely radical process of demilitarization. The army was made three times smaller than before. Troops were withdrawn altogether from East Germany, Poland, Czechoslovakia, Hungary, Lithuania, Latvia, Estonia, Georgia, Azerbaijan, and Mongolia, and military bases in Cuba and Vietnam were closed. The withdrawal of troops happened so quickly that there was nowhere to accommodate the returning soldiers. The war in Chechnya had a strong impact on the morale of the army. Constant reforms to the army have been taking place, which have ended in nothing other than the reorganization of troop command.

Defence spending has been falling constantly. By 2008, production of military planes in Russia had fallen 17-fold by comparison with 1992, production of military helicopters 5-fold, missiles 23-fold, and ammunition more than 100-fold.[127] As of 2008, the length of compulsory military service was cut to one year, whereas by the time of the collapse of the USSR, it had been two years, and prior to the 1970s it was three years.

Putin wrote: "We began with the most pressing matters. We restored systems of elementary social guarantees for the military, got rid of the con-

---

[127] *Rossiya v politsentrichnom mire* (*Russia in a Polycentric World*), ed. by A. A. Dynkin and N. I. Ivanova. Moscow, 2011. P. 109.

stant delays in the payment of the monetary allowance. Year on year, we increased the amount spent on the Army and Navy; and after all, there had been times when there was not enough money for the most pressing needs. [...] In all strategic areas, divisions that were constantly battle-ready were formed, complemented by contractors."[128] The armed forces have increased their battle-readiness, as has been demonstrated already by the war with Georgia in 2008. After the war, reforms began in earnest.

The military doctrine of the Russian Federation, adopted on 5th February 2010, for the first time, did not stipulate preparations for a major war (in the 1970s and 1980s, this had meant a war against NATO or China, or both). At the same time, seven of the eleven sources of threat identified were in some way tied to the West and to NATO. The preservation and strengthening of the nuclear arsenal was characterized, in the military doctrine, as "an extremely important defensive factor".[129] The doctrine was updated in 2014. The assessment of threats had not greatly changed. The main foreign military danger was "the growing military potential of the North Atlantic Treaty Organization (NATO) and the endowing of it with global functions, and the nearing of the military infrastructure of NATO's member states to the borders of the Russian Federation."[130]

Russia is a nuclear superpower, one of only two countries capable of destroying every living thing on the planet, and in terms of the number of nuclear warheads in its possession (including tactical ones), it continues to be first in the world. This will be achieved through the rolling out of the "Topol" and "Yars" intercontinental ballistic missiles, the commissioning of "Borey" submarines with "Bulava" missiles, and the renewed production of strategic bombers. Being unable to compete with USA and NATO in terms of overall army strength and quantities of armaments, Russia has

---

[128] Vladimir Putin, "Byt' sil'nymi: garantii natsional'noy bezopasnosti dlya Rossii" ("Being Strong: Guarantees for Russia's National Security"), *Rossiyskaya Gazeta* (*Russian Newspaper*, February 20, 2012 <https://rg.ru/2012/02/20/putin-armiya.html>.

[129] Decree of the President of the Russian Federation of February 5, 2010, No. 146 "O Voyennoy doktrine Rossiyskoy Federatsii" ("On the Military Doctrine of the Russian Federation"), The Russian President's official website <http://www.kremlin.ru/acts/bank/30593>. For details on the reaction to the doctrine see: D. O. Novikova, "Rossiyskaya voyennaya doktrina v redaktsii 2010 g.: reaktsii i otsenki ofitsial'nykh i ekspertnykh krugov Zapada" ("Russian Military Doctrine, 2010 Edition: Reactions and Assessments from Political and Expert Circles in the West"), *Vestnik MGIMO-Universiteta* (*MGIMO-University Bulletin*), Issue 4, 2010. PP. 41-46.

[130] "Voyennaya doktrina Rossiyskoy Federatsii" ("The Military Doctrine of the Russian Federation"), *Rossiyskaya Gazeta* (*Russian Newspaper*), December 30, 2014 <https://rg.ru/2014/12/30/doktrina-dok.html>.

managed to obtain qualitative superiority in strategic deterrent forces, having created "Sarmat" ICBM, hypersonic weapon systems, missiles with nuclear engines and unlimited range, submarine strike systems, and laser systems.

Russia has maintained a limited military presence in Armenia, Abkhazia and South Ossetia, Transdniestria, Tajikistan, and Kyrgyzstan, and has increased its military presence in Syria. Moreover, Russia has small non-battle contingents, servicing sites in Belarus (communications centers), Azerbaijan (the radio-location station), and Kazakhstan (the space center).

In terms of the number of servicemen and women in its armed forces – 831,000 people – Russia is fifth in the world, behind China, the US, India, and North Korea. According to the IISS, Russia's military budget, calculated on the basis of the exchange rate, amounted to 45.3 billion dollars (the USA's is 643.2 billion, China's is 168 billion, Saudi Arabia is 82.9, the UK's is 56.1 billion, India's is 57.9 billion, that of France is 53.4 billion and that of Japan is 47.3 billion dollars).[131] After 2014, national defence spending rose, in their ruble expression, by almost a quarter.

Successes in military construction were clearly demonstrated by the reunification with the Crimea, where "polite people" managed to create conditions for a referendum and conduct a peaceful transition on the peninsula to Russian jurisdiction without the loss of a single life. The magazine *Survival* wrote: "Despite claims to the contrary, Russia is much closer to having the military it needs than has often been suggested. [...] It is time to abandon hyperbole about Russian military ascendance or decay."[132]

Under sanctions, problems in the defence industry have grown more acute, since imported components and materials were used in the production of a significant number of Russian military systems. Import substitution, which took two to three years, is due to be implemented for 826 types of armament and military machinery.[133]

In terms of its overall military might, Russia is currently in second place on the planet, behind only the United States. Russia is also second

---

[131] *The Military Balance. 2019. The Annual Assessment of Global Military Capabilities and Defence Economics.* London, 2019. PP. 513-518.

[132] Bettina Renz, "Russian Military Capabilities after 20 Years of Reform", *Survival*, Vol. 56, Issue 3, 2014. PP. 62, 79.

[133] Andrey Frolov, "Svoy vmesto chuzhikh" ("Our Own Rather than Someone Else's"), *Rossiya v global'noy politike* (*Russia in Global Affairs*), November/December 2016. PP. 190-191.

in the global arms market. It accounts for a quarter of global military exports. Russian machinery and weapons systems are bought by 55 states, and military and technical cooperation is taking place with more than 80 states around the world.

Early in 2012, a Cyber command of the Armed Forces was set up. The task of coordinating efforts to ensure cybersecurity was entrusted to the intelligence services – first and foremost, the FSB. On 15th January 2013, Putin signed a directive on the creation of a state system for discovery, warning, and neutralization of computer attacks on the country's information resources. The size of the problem is huge: each day, there are up to 10,000 attacks on the websites of the President, the State Duma and the Council of Federations alone.[134]

The activity of terrorist groups and cells in the North Caucasus, associated with international terrorism structures, remains a serious threat to the security of the Russian Federation.

The normalization strategy consists, on the one hand, in the unconditional destruction of the terrorist bands, the cutting off of their financing and the silencing of radical Islamic propaganda; and on the other, in the transfer of a large number of powers and responsibilities to local government bodies, a program of economic growth, and the creation of new jobs. Support for the clergy, imams, and muftis who preach traditional Islam, rejecting extremism, is seen as an important factor.

Crime rates in Russia decrease steadily, partly owing to the efforts of "polite people". In 2005, 3.55 million crimes were recorded, of which 30,800 were murders. In 2017, the corresponding figures were 2.05 million crimes and 9,700 murders. The number of convictions fell from 1.18 million in 2000 to 697,000 in 2016, with the number of people convicted for murder falling from 19,400 to 8,000. In 27.8% of cases, the punishment for those convicted was a prison sentence.[135] The crime rate in Moscow is currently lower than that of New York, London and Paris, and is at the same level as that of Berlin.[136]

---

[134] Ivan Yegorov, "FSB raskinet set'" ("The FSB will Spread out the Net"), *Rossiyskaya Gazeta (Russian Newspaper)*, February 20, 2013 <https://rg.ru/2013/02/20/patrushev.html>.

[135] *Rossiya v tsifrakh. 2017* (*Russia in Figures. 2017*). Moscow, 2017. PP. 174-177.

[136] Lyubov' Protsenko, "V Moskve vyrosla raskryvayemost' tyazhkikh i osobo tyazhkikh prestupleniy" ("Has Been an Increase in the Solving of Serious and Especially Aggravated Crimes in Moscow"), *Rossiyskaya Gazeta (Russian Newspaper)*, January 28, 2016 <https://rg.ru/2016/01/28/zasedanie-sobyanin-site.html>.

The End of History? Not Just Yet

Moscow assumes that serious transformations are taking place in the world. "There can be no doubt now that when the Cold War ended, the longest stage of global development – one that lasted 400-500 years – came to an end; during this time, European civilization played a dominant role in the world," wrote Russia's Foreign Minister, Sergey Lavrov, in 2008. "There are two fundamental approaches that can be adopted if one wishes to assess what the content of the new stage in mankind's development will be. The first is that the world, through the adoption of Western values, must gradually become a sort of Greater West. This would be an 'end of history', of sorts. The other approach – and this is the one to which we subscribe – is that competition will take on a truly global nature and a civilizational dimension. In other words, things like values and growth models will become subjects of competition."[137]

The Kremlin believes that Russia is one of a handful of countries in the world that are capable of playing, and will indeed play, their own foreign policy game; that Russia will be an independent center of power, preserving its sovereignty in domestic and international affairs. There is some potential for this: Russia is the only Euro-Pacific permanent member of the UN's Security Council, an energy, nuclear, space and resources superpower, which has made a sizeable contribution to the development of global civilization over the last millennium. Russia has retained significant internal institutional resources, based on the high professionalism of its Foreign Ministry, its foreign intelligence service, and an expert analytical community, capable of thinking in global terms.

Putin stated that Russia "has almost always enjoyed the privilege of being able to have an independent foreign policy. This will be the case in the future, too. Moreover, I am convinced that security can only be provided in the world if others work together with Russia, rather than trying to make it 'step aside', to weaken its geopolitical position, to damage its defensive capabilities."[138] Moscow acknowledges the right of every state to sovereignty, free from foreign interference, and is in favor of a strengthening of the bases of international relations.

---

[137] Sergey Lavrov, *Mezhdu proshlym i budushchim. Rossiyskaya diplomatiya v menyayushchemsya mire* (*Between the Past and the Future. Russian Diplomacy in a Changing World*). Moscow, 2011. PP. 67-68.

[138] Vladimir Putin, "Rossiya i menyayushchiysya mir" ("Russia and a Changing World"), *Moskovskiye novosti* (*Moscow News*), February 27, 2012 <https://www.mn.ru/politics/78738>.

The polycentric nature of the modern world calls for a multifaceted foreign policy – a positive agenda in relations with all the global and regional centers. The CIS countries are top regional priority.

The suddenness of the collapse of the USSR made the gathering together of its pieces an extremely complicated matter. The CIS became the arena for a clash of interests between Russia and the West, who have diametrically opposed definitions of success when it comes to the Post-Soviet states. For Russia, success means strengthening integrational ties, drawing closer to our neighbors, reinforcing our cooperation. For the West, by contrast, success means distancing the newly independent states from Russia, with the aim of preventing "the rebirth of the Russian empire".

Experts have been trying to write an obituary for the CIS throughout its entire existence. Nonetheless, as Vladimir Putin has emphasized, "The experience of the CIS is the very thing that enabled us to launch a multi-level and multi-paced integration process in the post-Soviet region, to create such necessary formats as the Union State of Russia and Belarus, the Collective Security Treaty Organization, the Eurasian Economic Community, the Customs Union and, lastly, the Common Economic Space."[139] In 2010, the Customs Union of Russia, Kazakhstan and Belarus took effect.

The three states decided to effect a shift towards a higher form of integration – the Common Economic Space, and since 2015, the Eurasian Economic Union has been in operation; in addition to these three, it also includes Armenia and Kyrgyzstan. Given the growing threat to the southern borders of the Commonwealth, the activity of the Collective Security Treaty Organization is of increasing significance.

From Russia's point of view, the West is an important and unavoidable partner. Its attitude towards Russia has changed little in the last five centuries. The West is not a uniform place, however. The EU consists of an "old Europe", more inclined towards dialogue with Russia, and a "new" one, which retains anti-Russian phobias to a greater extent. "Old Europe" can be divided into the South, which is less Russophobe, and the North.

The West filled the geopolitical vacuum that was left after the disappearance of the USSR and the Warsaw Pact, seeing Russia as a defeated state, one capable of protesting, but no more than that. The re-emergent

---

[139] Vladimir Putin, "Novyy integratsionnyy proyekt dlya Yevrazii – budushcheye, kotoroye rozhdayetsya segodnya" ("A New Integration Project for Eurasia – a Future that is Born Today"), *Izvestiya*, October 4, 2011 <http://www.izvestia.ru/news/502761>.

Russia under Putin, which is seen as an authoritarian country, and which adopts an independent stance on all matters of global policy, often not coinciding with that of the West, is regarded as representing a growing challenge.

Even those Western books in which authors have suggested the idea of admitting Russia into a common Euro-Atlantic realm imply that Russia as it is now cannot count on cooperation from the West. It has to be some other Wonderland Russia – without Vladimir Putin, completely open to foreign investment and in absolute solidarity with the West concerning key international issues.

The main drawback of a situation in which NATO has become the European security system, from the Russian perspective, is obvious: we are not part of it. In theory, sympathy for a military bloc that one is not part of is perverse. Particularly if that bloc is the most powerful in the world and is drawing closer to Russia's borders, in spite of years of desperate objections. In NATO's operative military planning, Russia has not stopped being seen as an adversary, has not been taken off the short hit-list of targets for nuclear or cyber-attacks, and is seen "as the main 'object' of nuclear deterrence".[140]

The NATO-Russia Founding Act did not change much, since its role is limited merely to non-binding consultations. The crises in Ossetia in 2008 and Ukraine in 2014 are a good illustration: during a period of crisis, a mechanism that was created to resolve crises was frozen by the Western side. Those who think Russia could become a member of NATO are living in a dreamland, and it is equally unlikely to join the EU. It is impossible to incorporate Russia into NATO or the EU. For them, Russia is too big and too Russian. And has anyone ever invited Moscow to be part of them?

Initially, Putin has set the bar high in relations with the EU: "Russia is an integral, organic part of Greater Europe, of broader European civilization."[141] The foreign policy directive adopted on 7th May 2012 proposed that in relations with the EU, the emphasis should be on achieving "a strategic goal – the creation of a unified economic and human space from the Atlantic to the Pacific Ocean."[142]

---

[140] Aleksey Arbatov, Vladimir Dvorkin, and Sergey Oznobishchev, *Sovremennyye yadernyye doktriny gosudarstv* (*Modern Nuclear State Doctrines*). Moscow, 2010. P. 40.

[141] Vladimir Putin, "Rossiya i menyayushchiysya mir" ("Russia and a Changing World"), *Moskovskiye novosti* (*Moscow News*), February 27, 2012 <https://www.mn.ru/politics/78738>.

[142] Decree of the President of the Russian Federation of 07.05.2012 No. 605 "O merakh po

The collaboration between Russia and the EU, even before the Ukraine crisis, was not marked by any particular dynamism apart from trade volumes. The key document that defined relations with the EU was the Partnership and Cooperation Agreement, which was a standard, non-preferential agreement – the lowest level of cooperation that the EU has with anyone. It expired in 2008. Negotiations over a new document dragged on interminably, and then stopped completely.

The concept of a strategic partnership proposed by the EU and backed by Russia in 1999 has been forgotten, as well as the concept for creating four common zones (economic; domestic security; foreign security; and science, education and culture) approved during the Russia-EU summit in Saint-Petersburgh in March 2003 and other, twice-yearly, Russia-EU summits.

The energy partnership was troubled by the gas wars. The EU's "third energy packet", adopted in 2011, stipulated that all the transportation of gas and the conveying of electricity to the EU must be kept separate, functionally and legally, from the manufacturing and sale thereof, which clearly discriminated against Gazprom. The EU is also conducting a special antitrust investigation against Gazprom. Brussels has blocked the construction of the "Southern Stream" gas pipeline through Bulgaria, which circumvents Ukraine. Moscow had to replace it with the "Turkish Stream". Subsequently, some EU countries and the USA began amicably blocking "Nord Stream 2".

There is a dividing line between Russia and Europe that runs along other lines, too: on cultural matters, associated with attitudes towards religion, morality, family values and same-sex marriages.

Now not only the USA but also the EU – for the first time – is seen as an unfriendly force. Does Russia want to be part of Europe? I do not think it does any more.

At the same time, as Putin has stressed, "Russia not only does not reject the idea of forming a unified economic and humanitarian space with the EU from the Atlantic to the Pacific Ocean, but considers it the most promising idea in the context of ensuring the long-term, sustainable development of the entire Eurasian continent."[143] The prerequisites for moving towards a normalization of relations, above all with the EU countries, exist.

----

realizatsii vneshnepoliticheskogo kursa Rossiyskoy Federatsii" ("On measures to implement the foreign policy course of the Russian Federation"). The Russian President's official website, 2012 <http://www.kremlin.ru/acts/bank/35269>.

[143] Vladimir Putin at the Soveshchaniye poslov i postoyannykh predstaviteley Rossiyskoy

The unity within Europe that was observed in the initial phase of the Ukrainian crisis, based on anti-Russian sentiment, is beginning to weaken. There is clearly a group of states that is not willing to see sanctions go on forever – Greece, Cyprus, Hungary, the Czech Republic, Slovakia, Austria, Italy, Finland. Dialogue with Moscow is being reinstated on many issues.

At the same time, the possibility of normalizing relations with Russia are now being linked, in the West, with the implementation by Russia of the Minsk Accords. Yet the Minsk Accords do not contain any provisions which have to be implemented by Moscow. And there is not a single point that Kyiv has implemented or intends to implement, for it refuses to recognise the core human rights – to self-determination and to life – of the people of Crimea and the Donetsk and Lugansk Republics. However the West still accuses Russia of violating the Minsk Accords.

Meanwhile, the EU is being left by the most significant of the states that gave the entire European Union a highly anti-Russian tone – the UK. "Putin, of course, did not cause the Brexit vote, but he and his foreign policy course objectives stand to gain enormously from it," wrote McFall. "Most importantly, one of the European Union's most principled critics of Russian aggression in Europe will no longer have a vote in Brussels. That's good for Putin's interests and bad for U.S. national interests."[144]

A policy of moving closer towards Europe contained an inherent problem: Russia found itself more closely economically bound to the hostile EU, which has brought in sanctions against Moscow, than to the dynamically growing Asia-Pacific Region, which is not hostile at all.

The United States has been seen in Moscow as the only global superpower and as an unavoidable partner in the fight against the spread of weapons of mass destruction and international terrorism. Russia's concern is associated with America's heightened military activity around the entire perimeter of Russia's borders. And the USA has been seen in Moscow as a country that still has an interest in containing, weakening and destabilizing Russia. Moreover, in American concept documents Russia is described as "enemy number one".

....

Federatsii (Speech at the Conference for Ambassadors and permanent representatives of the Russian Federation) on June 30, 2016. The Russian President's official website <http://kremlin.ru/events/president/news/52298>.

[144] Michael McFall, "How Brexit is a Win for Putin", *The Washington Post*, June 25, 2016 <https://www.washingtonpost.com/opinions/global-opinions/how-brexit-is-a-win-for-putin/2016/06/25/800e4d3c-3b06-11e6-8f7c-d4c723a2becb_story.html>.

The USA's global ABM system required the creation of bases in Poland, Romania and the Mediterranean, and this was a direct contravention of the NATO's obligation not to deploy military infrastructure on the territory of new members of the alliance. An anti-missile system is being rapidly created in North-East Asia, and now in space.

One often hears people discussing whether or not we are in a "new Cold War". In my view, under many parameters the situation today is worse than back then. During the Cold War, there were always multiple formats for dialogue – diplomatic and military avenues, dialogue between experts, parliamentary and social formats, and so on. Today, they do not exist. Personal sanctions against politicians and parliamentarians were not applied even in the worst years of the Cold War. There was no American military presence in Eastern Europe or in the Baltic states or in Ukraine, and Kyiv's policy was not determined from Washington.

"NATO had markedly increased its presence and visibility in the Baltic states, Poland and the Black Sea, where allied forces deployed for exercises on land, sea and in the air, and where new air and maritime policing missions were added to old ones. And this was only the beginning of a greater effort to revamp NATO for regional deterrence," Western military experts noted with pleasure.[145] It has also been noted in Russia that in 2017 alone, an American armoured tank brigade was deployed in Poland, with a battalion from this brigade, including other NATO countries, located in Latvia, Lithuania and Estonia. Mk 41 missile launch areas were being rolled out in Poland and Romania as part of EuroABM. In the context of the rotation of the NATO air policing mission, the number of military jets from the alliance in the Baltic countries has doubled.[146] The number of flights made by US planes near the Russian borders has increased hundreds of times over.

Washington is covertly using against Russia the military potential and territory of Ukraine, where a series of NATO military exercises have taken place. Kyiv is receiving military assistance and arms from the USA and NATO countries. "The United States is walking into a proxy war with Moscow – one that it is unprepared to win. […] Russia's interests in Ukraine are far greater and its military superiority is well established. In contrast,

---

[145] Jens Ringsmose and Sten Rynning, "Now for the Hard Part: NATO's Strategic Adaptation to Russia", *Survival*, June/July 2017. P. 131.

[146] Vladimir Mukhin, "NATO postroilo dlya Kiyeva zavody po proizvodstvu boyepripasov" ("NATO has Built Munitions Factories for Kyiv"), *Nezavisimaya Gazeta* (*Independent Newspaper*), October 2, 2017 <https://www.ng.ru/world/2017-10-02/2_7085_nato.html>.

the United States' coercive credibility in the region is close to nonexistent," warns Michael Koffman of the Wilson Center.[147]

Russia has the worst press coverage in the West in my entire conscious life. Never before have we been lied about so openly and unashamedly, never before have our leaders been insulted in such a disgusting way. A confusing web is being woven that will probably not be capable of being untangled in the foreseeable future – hackers, fake news, internet trolls, a conspiracy between Trump and the Kremlin, ambassador-spies. In Russia, all this is seen, to put it mildly, as utter nonsense.

Russia has drastically cut her investment in US debt, which amounted to over $150 billion back in 2013. Selling American government bonds worth $80 billion in April and May 2018 alone, Russia diminished her portfolio to mere $14.9 billion.[148]

From the Russian side, the door is not being closed to dialogue with Washington, either, but it is being shut ever more firmly by the American side amidst endless investigations of Moscow's alleged assaults on American democratic institutions.

And, of course, the crisis in relations with the West is accelerating the process whereby Russia is turning towards the East. This process began before now, but it was only after the crisis over Ukraine that many in the Russian elite began to understand more clearly: there is no alternative to an intensification of interaction with non-Western countries.

Multi-Dimensional Civilization

The Russian Federation has still not fully recognized its Asia-Pacific identity. At the same time, in other states in the region, Russia is often not considered to be one of them; it is often seen instead as a European country. The imperatives of the 21st century force us to look at the Russian Federation not as a European or Eurasian, but as a Euro-Pacific country. A policy aimed at strengthening Russia's position in the Asian-Pacific Region requires the completion of a trio of tasks: the modernized development of the Far East of Russia using the capabilities of the rapidly growing neighboring states;

---

[147] Michael Kofman, "For the U.S., Arming Ukraine Could Be a Deadly Mistake", *The New York Times*, August 25, 2017 <https://www.nytimes.com/2017/08/25/opinion/united-states-arm-ukraine-missiles.html>.

[148] Tat'yana Lomskaya, "Rossiya otdayet dolg SShA" ("Russia Pays Off the US Debt"), *Vedomosti*, Issue 131, July 19, 2018 <https://vedomosti.profkiosk.ru/article.aspx?aid=660515>.

the transformation of Russia into a component part of the APR economy; and increasing Russia's role in regional integration processes and security mechanisms.

Thus far, the major products Russia sells on the APR market are raw materials, primarily fuel and energy, and also metals, forestry products, and maritime bio-resources. Russia's energy strategy up until 2030 stipulated an increase in the APR's share of Russian exports of fuel and energy resources, from 8-10% to 26-27%.

An important task is the promotion of Russian hi-tech goods in the APR market. Worthy of note here are projects in the field of atomic energy and the nuclear fuel cycle. Cooperation is taking place in the space sector and the military-technical sphere. A new and significant aspect of this cooperation is linked to the promotion in Asia of the GLONASS telecommunication and navigation system.

It is in Russia's interests for the APR to acquire a multi-layered, polycentric architecture for security and cooperation, outside the bloc. Most important of all for Moscow are the East-Asia Summits, the APEC, SCO, RIC and BRICS, the ASEAN Regional Forum (ARF), ASEAN+Russia Defence Minister conferences, and the "Asia-Europe" forum (ASEM).

For Russia, the rise of Asia represents both a challenge and an opportunity. It is a challenge because for the first time in many centuries, a center of power has emerged in the East that is superior to Russia in terms of its potential. It is an opportunity because Russia could become part of this rise.

Our biggest and most important partner in Asia is China. Relations are at the highest level of partnership in their entire history. The symbol of China is the Great Wall, which protected it for millennia from the biggest threat of all – invasions from the north. The issue of the border has been settled, an issue that is of supreme importance to China: for the first time, they have a recognized, fixed and secure northern border. The two countries' interests overlap to a large extent. China shares Russia's view on global governance, which is expressed by the concept of multipolarity. Russia and China take a dim view of the pressure they face from the West.

China and Russia are the countries which initiated the establishment of BRICS, and play a leading role in it. China is also Russia's most important regional partner within the Shanghai Cooperation Organization (SCO). The Chinese highly appreciate Moscow's support on Tibet, Taiwan and Xinjiang.

China is Russia's biggest economic partner. The energy partnership between the two is a significant one: Russia is already the biggest supplier of energy to China, providing 13.8% of all its imported oil in 2016.[149] The two sides promote joint projects in civil aviation, astronautics, in other hi-tech fields, and also with regard to technology parks, industrial clusters, and special economic zones in both Russia and China. The first wide-body CR 929 airplane will take to the skies in 2023, dealing a blow to the monopoly enjoyed by Boeing and Airbus in the market for long-haul airplanes. Demand from China alone is estimated at 1500 planes.[150] On 17th July 2018, the ice-class gas carrier "Vladimir Rusanov" reached the Chinese coast to start the delivery of the Russian LNG from Yamal via the Arctic Ocean route to the PRC, thus replacing the American LNG.[151] The countries passed the $100 billion mark in bilateral trade in 2018. Agreements on payments in national currencies and the integration of the settlement system of the Bank of Russia and the Chinese equivalent of SWIFT have been prepared. A plan for the joint development of the agricultural sector of the Russian Far East and North-East China is being implemented, bans on food supplies are being lifted, and inter-university exchanges are rapidly expanding.[152] China has become the second most popular holiday destination for Russian tourists, while visitors from China lead the field in terms of the numbers coming to Russia.

Putin has spoken more than once about the need to "catch the Chinese wind in Russia's sails". During his visit to Moscow on the occasion of the 70th anniversary of Victory against Germany, Xi Jinping attended the signing of more than 30 agreements, among which were the integration of the EEU and the "B&R" projects, the construction of high-speed railways, the expansion of lending by Russian banks, and innovative cooperation. Leaders of the two countries celebrated the 70th anniversary of Victory against Japan in Beijing together as well.[153]

---

[149] Vitaliy Petlevoy, "Rossiyskiye neftyaniki sokratili eksport nefteproduktov, no zarabotali bol'she" ("Russian Oil Workers Reduced the Export of Petroleum Products, but Earned More"), *Vedomosti*, June 29, 2017 <https://www.vedomosti.ru/business/articles/2017/06/29/700959-neftyaniki-snizili-eksport>.

[150] Sergey Ptichkin and Taras Fomchenkov, "Layneru dali imya" ("The Liner has Been Given a Name"), *Rossiyskaya Gazeta* (*Russian Newspaper*), October 2, 2017 <https://rg.profkiosk.ru/593125>.

[151] Artur Toporkov, "'Novatek' proshel Severom" ("'Novatek' Runs North"), *Vedomosti*, Issue 131, July 19, 2018 <https://vedomosti.profkiosk.ru/article.aspx?aid=660516>.

[152] Dmitriy Butrin, "Rossiysko-kitayskoye prodvizheniye" ("Russian-Chinese Advancement"), *Kommersant* (*The Businessman*), Issue 205, November 8, 2018 <https://www.kommersant.ru/doc/3793107>.

[153] Kira Latukhina, "Put' Pobedy" ("The Way to Victory"), *Rossiyskaya Gazeta* (*Russian*

There are, nonetheless, areas in which China and Russia do not see eye to eye. For China, Gorbachev's Soviet Union and Yeltsin's Russia were of interest, first and foremost, as examples of how not to behave, under any circumstances, so as to avoid causing the break-up of the country and the collapse of its economy. Economic cooperation lags behind the level of political relations and mutual trust between the leaders.

Anti-China alarmism in Russia is still strong. It is fashionable to talk and write about a "Chinese expansion" that is being prepared. Meanwhile, the Chinese currently have no targeted policy of demographic expansion through migration. Bigger problems arise due to the lack of order on Moscow's side: the typical Chinese entrepreneur does not last long in Russia.

The ex-director of the Russian Academy of Science's Institute of the Far East, Sergey Luzyanin, believes that at present, the RF is practically the only major state with which China has no serious (or systemic) disagreements. "…A working mechanism has taken shape, characterized by the complementary capacities of two countries, where Russia enjoys obvious superiority in terms of strategic military potential and China has the upper hand in economic and technical potential."[154] At the same time, as Chinese experts have stressed, "China does not have a vested interest in a formal alliance with Russia or in the creation of any kind of anti-American or anti-Western bloc."[155]

That may change now with the US under Trump pursuing the policy of "double containment" of both Russia and China, and increasing sanctions pressure on both countries.

Relations with Japan are proving to be far more problematic. Anti-Russian sentiment in the Land of the Rising Sun is pretty strong: the Koreans are perhaps the only people that are less popular there than the Russians. The well-known expert on Japan, Sergey Chugrov, believes that the Japanese distrust and suspicion of Russia has a long history and was initially founded on ideas about the sheer size and unpredictability of Russia, which, the Japanese feel, could "come crushing down" on "little Japan". The concerns which arose when Russia was present in Manchuria in the late 19th century linger on in the historical memory… The USSR's declaration of war in August 1945 dealt a blow to national pride. A particularly frustrating factor was the

....
Newspaper), May 11, 2015 <https://rg.ru/2015/05/12/putin.html>.

[154] Sergey Luzyanin, *Rossiya – Kitay: formirovaniye obnovlennogo mira* (*Russia and China: Shaping the Renewed World*). Moscow, 2018. P.223.

[155] Fu Ying, "Kak Kitay vosprinimayet Rossiyu" ("How China Sees Russia"), *Rossiya v global'noy politike* (*Russia in Global Affairs*), May/June 2016. P. 188.

imprisonment of more than 800,000 Japanese prisoners of war in Siberia. "On the whole, the USSR was seen as the bearer of an evil, unpredictable will."[156] The issue of the northern territories, as the four islands of the South Kurils are known in Japan, and which Japan considers its own, is put on the agenda at every opportunity.

At the same time, as prominent Russian specialists have emphasized, "The Japanese political elite clearly would not wish to get dragged into the American strategy of containing China, since a worsening of relations with their mighty neighbor could lead to many political and economic losses. On the other hand, Tokyo is not overjoyed by the prospect of becoming 'Beijing's little brother'. Hence the talk about the need for more advanced relations with Russia, with the Chinese and Korean factors, above all, in mind."[157] During the latest high-level meetings, Abe proposed a plan for cooperation on eight different areas: energy, industry, health, agriculture, the urban environment, cooperation between small and medium-sized businesses, advanced technologies, and humanitarian exchanges.[158]

Russia and India are a unique case in world history: they are the only pair of great powers who not only have not fought each other, but have never even had a serious dispute with one another. Bilateral relations remain an important priority for both countries, as can be seen in the multiple agreements and declarations which define common approaches on a wide range of regional and global issues, including the most delicate ones. Russia supports India's efforts to achieve the status of a permanent member of the UN's Security Council, and ensured its membership of SCO. "Today, there are probably only two problems that exist between Delhi and Moscow, namely the weakening of bilateral trade ties, and the risk that Russia might do too much to strengthen the military potential of China," writes Raja Mohan.[159] Russia is a supplier of hydrocarbons, while India imports Russian liquefied natural gas from the Sakhalin-1 field, in which Indian companies have a

---

[156] Sergey Chugrov, *Yaponiya v poiskakh novoy identichnosti* (*Japan in Search of a New Identity*). Moscow, 2010. P. 214.

[157] *Sovremennyye rossiysko-yaponskiye otnosheniya i perspektivy ikh razvitiya* (*Contemporary Russo-Japanese Relations and Prospects for Development*), ed. by A. N. Panov et al. Moscow, 2012. P. 9.

[158] Kira Latukhina, "Skazano v Yaponii" ("Said in Japan"), *Rossiyskaya Gazeta* (*Russian Newspaper*), December 2016 <https://rg.profkiosk.ru/520566>.

[159] C. Raja Mohan, "Indiya i politicheskoye ravnovesiye" ("India and Political Equilibrium"), Rossiya v global'noy politike (Russia in Global Affairs), Issue 4, July/August 2006 <https://globalaffairs.ru/articles/indiya-i-politicheskoe-ravnovesie/>.

20% stake. At the Kudankulam NPP constructed by Rosatom, two units are at full capacity, and 12 power units are planned in total. The company "Russian Railways" organizes modern railway communications in India. Military-technical cooperation is not limited to the supply of Russian arms; the countries have also established joint production for military purposes. Meanwhile, relations between the two countries are far closer now than in the days of the Soviet Union.

Putin was the first Russian leader to recognize, at the highest level, that Russia "is a Muslim country, and Russian Muslims are fully entitled to feel part of the global ummah, and Russia itself has always been, and remains, a geopolitical ally of Islam."[160]

It is clear, though, that radical Islamism presents clear external security threats for the Russian Federation. Moscow has no interest in the creation of a new caliphate and a terrorist internationale, whose next target could well be Russia. Hence, the decision to become involved in the war against terrorists in Syria. "Among them are a considerable number from Russia and the CIS states," the President stressed. "They are receiving money and arms, and gaining strength. And if they grow stronger, and triumph there, they will inevitably turn up here among us, sowing fear and hatred, blowing things up, killing and torturing people. And we are obligated to find them and destroy them in the places from which they may come against us. That is why the decision was made to undertake a military operation on the basis of an official appeal by the lawful, legitimate Syrian government. In Syria, too, our Armed Forces are fighting above all for Russia; it is our citizens whose security they are protecting."[161] During this operation, Russia's Army and Navy have demonstrated a high degree of battle-readiness, and the priceless experience of applying state-of-the-art machinery and weaponry will be used in order to perfect them in the future.

Russia's decisive contribution in the battle against ISIL has significantly enhanced her authority in the Middle East, including even Saudi Arabia, whose King visited Moscow for the first time in the autumn of 2017. The

---

[160] Rinat Mukhametov, "Rossiyskiye musul'mane i vneshnyaya politika" ("Russian Muslims and Foreign Policy"), *Rossiya v global'noy politike* (*Russia in Global Affairs*), May/June, 2012. PP. 109-110.

[161] Poslaniye Prezidenta Rossiyskoy Federatsii ot 03.12.2015 g. b/n ("O polozhenii v strane i osnovnykh napravleniyakh vnutrenney i vneshney politiki gosudarstva") [The address by the President of the Russian Federation to the Federal Assembly of the Russian Federation ("On the situation in the country and the main areas of the state's domestic and foreign policy")]. The Russian President's official website <http://www.kremlin.ru/acts/bank/40542>.

Arab youth see Moscow as their main supporter in the international arena.[162] Russia has noticeably strengthened its position in relation to Egypt, Libya, Algeria, Iraq and Jordan.

Turkey, for whom Russia has become the number one trading partner, is becoming Moscow's major counterpart in the Islamic world. The construction of a nuclear power plant has begun in Mersin. Russia has been the main market for Turkish construction contractors, and Turkey is a key holiday destination for Russian tourists.[163] The actions of the Russian air force in Syria, where Erdogan backed Assad's enemies, brought about an acute worsening of his relations with Moscow. A Sukhoi-24 bomber was shot down by a Turkish plane. Moscow responded by breaking off relations on all fronts. Having acted against its own interests, Ankara apologized in June 2015. Shortly afterwards came the attempted coup in Turkey, in which some detected the hand of the United States, and Erdogan showed greater willingness to restore Turkey's partnership with Moscow on bilateral basis, as well as on a multilateral basis – in the so-called "Astana format" – with Iran.

Russia proposed that the Iranian nuclear problem should be resolved solely through peaceful means, and that Iran's right to develop a civil nuclear program should be recognized, in exchange for all of Iran's nuclear activity being put under the control of IAEA. Moscow was an active participant in the negotiations which led to the nuclear deal with Tehran. After this, Russia responded to Iran's desire for supplies of S-400 missile complexes and the construction of a second nuclear power energy bloc. Moscow harshly criticized Trump's decision to leave the nuclear deal and ignored the new American sanctions against Teheran.

Latin America is coming back into the orbit of Russian foreign policy. During the Cold War, the interest was almost exclusively an ideological and geopolitical one, the symbol of which was Cuba, where the frontline of the confrontation between the two superpowers lay. Now, the interest is more of a pragmatic and economic one. It is increasingly clear that Brazil is the key partner on the continent.

The rapprochement between Russia and Brazil began in the 1990s, and achieved its greatest intensity in the new century. The Brazilian analyst Fabiano Melnichuk explains this trend by saying that "both countries have

---

[162] Konstantin Dudarev, "Moskva – Er-Riyad: kurs na sblizheniye" ("Moscow-Riyadh: the Road to Friendship"), *Nezavisimaya Gazeta* (*Independent Newspaper*), October 2, 2017 <https://nvo.ng.ru/kartblansh/2017-10-02/3_7085_kartblansh.html>.

[163] "Russia and Turkey: Cool Pragmatism", *The Economist*, December 8, 2012. P. 36.

reassessed their identities and come closer together as partners on the basis of protecting the course of general development (in the case of Brazil) and of a multipolar world order (in the case of Russia), so as to strengthen their overlapping interests in the international arena... Both countries stepped back from being committed to an international order founded on the liberal consensus, and from recognizing the unipolar world (with the USA playing a leading role) after the Cold War."[164]

The new President of Brazil, Jair Bolsonaro, has moved in the direction of the USA. Experts from the RAS's Institute of Latin America assert that the declared "pragmatism" of Brazil's foreign policy leaves open possibilities for a productive relationship, though the pro-American orientation of Brazil and disagreements on Venezuela make Brazil-Russia ties problematic.[165]

Brazil is not interested in the "Russo-Bolivarian" axis as a counterweight to the USA. The limits of Russo-Brazilian cooperation can be seen at the point where the threat of a confrontation with Washington starts.

As for Africa, Moscow definitely left this continent after the collapse of the Soviet Union. As the President of the Africa Institute, Aleksey Vasilyev, notes, "The USSR played an outstanding role in the de-colonization of Africa, in the sense that it acted in accordance with the historical process. For precisely this reason, Russia, as the successor to the USSR, acquired a large but gradually diminishing stock of sympathy and loyalty among Africans – a basis for subsequent political and economic cooperation. Negative recollections from the past live on, too: the spreading into Africa (albeit on a limited scale) of the global confrontation between the USSR and the USA, the drawing in of the African countries into an arms race that was devastating for them."[166] South Africa is Russia's leading trade counterpart in Africa, but trade turnover is not yet very big, standing at just over 1 billion dollars.

The image of the Russian Federation has suffered in the last decade, both from centuries of historical stereotypes and the residual phobias from the Cold War era, and from new images: a country in a state of collapse, degra-

....

[164] Fabiano Melnichuk, "Rossiysko-brazil'skiye otnosheniya posle kholodnoy voyny" ("Russo-Brazilian Relations after the Cold War"), *Mezhdunarodnaya zhizn'* (*International Life*), April 2012. PP. 38, 47.

[165] Z. V. Ivanovskiy, L. N. Simonova and L. S. Okunea, *Smena prioritetov v novom politicheskom tsikle* (*Brazil: A Change of Priorities in the New Political Cycle*). Moscow, 2019. PP. 88, 91.

[166] Aleksey Vasil'yev, "Afrika nuzhna Rossii. Rossiya nuzhna Afrike" ("Russia needs Africa. Africa needs Russia"), in *Vneshnyaya politika Rossii: 2000-2020* (*Russia's Foreign Policy: 2000-2020*). Vol. 1. Moscow, 2012. PP. 196-197.

dation and abject poverty, governed by incompetent civil servants, and an aggressor consumed with plans to "restore the empire".

The German journalist O. Zinkovsky notes: "It is interesting that the West allows China, Japan, and India to be unique. No-one tells Asia how to live. But Russia is seen more as a relative who has gone astray, but whose ways can still be corrected. People learn from India. Yet they try to give lessons to the Russians. There is a certain 'family syndrome' at play here. It may be that it is based on geographical proximity, and also on shared Christian roots."[167] It is undoubtedly also true that no-one can get rid of geopolitics. Strong rivals are never looked upon with fondness. Throughout the last century, the USA and the West had far more reason to look upon Russia as a geopolitical rival than to do the same with regard, say, to China.

In the West, meanwhile, the only occasions when Russia has been applauded have been when it committed suicide – in February 1917 and in December 1991.

The image of the state is also strongly influenced by the foreign, or foreign-funded, non-governmental organizations acting inside it, particularly those whose goal is to make this image deteriorate. Western countries are fairly actively supporting the implacable anti-Russian opposition, representatives of which are the main commentators on events in Russia for the Western media, which at the same time perform the role of worldwide media organizations.

For all that, Russia has far more allies than anyone would like it to have. Russia has no unresolved image problems among most countries in Asia, Africa or Latin America. Talk of Russia's growing international isolation is nothing more than dreams in Washington. The West – and only the West – is actively trying to isolate Moscow – thus far unsuccessfully.

In relative terms, Russia is weaker than the USSR. Yet it is definitely stronger than two decades ago. It is also infinitely more monolithic in terms of the understanding of its essence, of good and evil, not distorted by Communist or pseudo-democratic dogma.

Russian-ness is something that can be understood, above all, on the basis of the essence of Russia itself, rather than that of anyone else. It is a self-sufficient cultural and civilizational phenomenon, of the kind that can only be

---

[167] O. Ye. Zin'kovskiy, "Istoki neponimaniya – genezis vospriyatiya rossiyskoy gosudarstvennosti v Yevrope (na primere Germanii)" ("The Sources of Misunderstanding – the Genesis of the Perception of Russian Statehood in Europe (Based on the Example of Germany))", in *Rossiyskaya gosudarstvennost': istoricheskiye traditsii i vyzovy XXI veka* (*Russian Statehood: Historical Traditions and Challenges of the 21st Century*). Moscow, 2013. P. 663.

described in its own terms. Russia is neither the Western part of the East, nor is it the Eastern part of the West. The historical movement of a country spread across vast expanses of Eurasia from the Baltic to the Pacific Ocean could not help but endow it with its own specific traits. It is a core state with an independent civilization, whether we call it Russian or Eastern European, to which European civilization is the closest.

And what if Russia really were to find itself in a situation where it had no allies at all? It so happens that the country has experienced what it is like to stand alone, or almost alone, against the forces of a united West. In 1812, the Grande Armée of a united Europe was led into Russia by Napoleon. In 1941, Hitler did the same thing. We know what the outcome was. Russia proved to be on the winning side. And on the right side of history.

CHAPTER 6
THE RETURN OF ASIA

After an interval of a few centuries, the Asian continent is becoming a leader in many areas of the development of modern civilization, bringing a fresh impetus to the global community. And let us not forget that it was in Asia that the history of mankind began. It was here that the first cities were built, the first political, social and economic institutions were founded, the first states were created, the first harvest of proto-wheat was gathered, the seven-day week was invented, the hour was divided into 60 minutes, and the circle into 360 degrees, the foundations were laid for the modern system of writing, and all the world's religions were founded.

The Fever of Growth

In terms of its geography and demographics, Asia is the giant of our planet. It has one fifth of the Earth's land mass. It has 29 states: 21 on the continent itself, and eight on islands and archipelagos. The most densely populated territory, with a population density three times higher than the world average, 60% of the planet's inhabitants and six of the world's ten most highly-populated countries: China, India, Indonesia, Pakistan, Bangladesh and Russia (the others in the top ten are the USA, Brazil, Nigeria and Mexico, which recently overtook Japan). By the middle of this century, admittedly, Asia's quotient will drop down to five: Russia will be replaced in the list by Ethiopia and/or the Congo.

Asia is the motherland of many civilizations and sub-civilizations, each of which is characterized by its own genetic code: Chinese, Japanese, Hindu, Islamic (with Turkish, Persian and Arabic sub-civilizations), and the civilization of South-East Asia.

Asia is a growing global player. The world's biggest economy by PPP since 2014 has been China. The biggest city in the world is Tokyo, followed by Delhi, Shanghai and Mumbai. The tallest skyscraper in the world is in Dubai, the second-highest is in Shanghai, and the third-highest is in Mecca. The biggest residential building belongs to Mukesh Ambani, from Mumbai: a 27-floor skyscraper serviced by a staff of 600. The biggest joint-stock company is a Chinese one. The largest investment fund is in the United Arab Emirates. The most extensive gold and foreign currency reserves are to be found in China and Japan. The biggest bank in the world is the Bank of China. Of the top five countries in terms of income per head of the population, four are Asian: Qatar, Singapore, Macao and Brunei (the other is Luxembourg). The biggest oil refinery complex is located in India. All the biggest factories in the world are located in China. Japan produces the largest number of patents in the world, while South Korea produces the most per head of the population. The highest proportion of GDP spent on R&D is in Israel. The largest number of mobile telephones per head of the population is in Macau.

The best airlines – based on my many years as a globe-trotter – are Singapore Airlines, Qatar and Emirates, with Korean Air not far behind. Where is the biggest airport in the world? In Beijing. What is the best airport? Changi, in Singapore, has achieved the top spot in the rankings in recent years. Three airlines – Emirates in Dubai, Etihad Airlines from Abu Dhabi, and Qatar Airways – have more wide-fuselage planes than all the American airlines combined. Where is the largest number of rocket-launchers in the world produced? At Baikonur, in Kazakhstan. The biggest casinos in the world are in Macau; often they are reproductions of casinos in Las Vegas, only several times larger. The largest number of movies are produced in India, at Bollywood, and hence it comes as no surprise that this country also has the highest attendance figures for movie theatres. The world's biggest shopping center is to be found in Beijing. The biggest Ferris wheel is in Singapore.

In the 1970s, North America consumed twice as much oil as Asia. In 2005, Asia overtook it for the first time. The United States has not built any new nuclear reactors for 30 years, while China plans to open 33 new reactors by 2030, adding, every year, capacity that is equal to all the electricity generated in India. In 1980, the US produced 100 million tons of steel, China 40 million, and India 10 million. In 2010, the USA produced 80 million tons, China 600 million, and India 65 million tons. In the mid-1960s, Western Europe was the undisputed leader in shipbuilding, producing ships with an aggregate tonnage of 5 million tons; the countries of Asia produced 3.7 million, and the USA 0.25 million. By 2009, Asia had increased production to 70 million tons, exactly ten times more than was produced by the rest of the world combined.[1]

From 2014 the Asian region became the largest investor in the world (440 billion dollars of direct foreign investment), overtaking both North America (390 billion) and the European Union (286 billion).[2] China had the second highest number of billionaires, and India was in fourth place, overtaking Russia; the USA is still in first place.[3] In terms of ethnicity, the biggest group among the billionaires are the Chinese, with 380 (just over half living in China, with the rest in Indonesia, Singapore, Malaysia, Thailand, the Philippines, the USA, Australia, and Canada), ahead of the Anglo-Saxons, with more than 300, and the Jews, with fewer than 300.[4] In Hong Kong alone, there are more billionaires than in London and Los Angeles put together.[5]

More than half the growth in the world's economy has been provided in recent years by two countries – China and India.[6] The top ten fastest-growing economies in 2017 included Yemen, Myanmar, Mongolia, Laos, India and Cambodia (the other countries were all from Africa).[7] Over the last 20 years, China alone lifted 400 million people out of poverty. Few people in Asia have any doubts about the efficiency of their own economic models.

China and India – the most populous countries in the world, as one might well have imagined – are the world's biggest producers and consumers of foodstuffs. Countries in which hunger was the norm for centuries produced the first generations which enjoyed a sufficient diet. This has led, among other things, to the average height of the population, in Japan after the Second World War for example, rising by 20 cm. Moreover, the exporting of agricultural products has become possible. At the same time, 80% of food is produced by tiny, non-mechanized farmsteads on plots of land no bigger than two hectares. Growth in agriculture is stagnating due to the degrada-

---

[1] Charles Kupchan, *No One's World. The West, the Rising Rest, and the Coming Global Turn.* Oxford, 2012. PP. 81-82.

[2] Tat'yana Yedovina, "Investitsii navynos" ("Investments to Go"), *Kommersant* (*The Businessman*), May 19, 2015 <https://www.kommersant.ru/doc/2729237>.

[3] "Brazilian Whacks", *Forbes*, March 23, 2015. P. 32.

[4] Leonid Radzikhovsky, "Geopolitika deneg" ("The Geopolitics of Money"), *Rossiyskaya Gazeta* (*Russian Newspaper*), March 16, 2015 <https://rg.ru/2015/03/17/radzihovski.html>.

[5] Nash Jenkins, "Hong Kong's Hope", *Time*, September 12-19, 2016. P. 30.

[6] Yu Lintao, "The Power of Five", *Newsweek*, August 25 – September 1, 2017. P. 15.

[7] "The World in 2017", *The Economist*, 2017. P. 93.

tion of the environment, insufficient irrigation, and also the falling level of soil fertility in many regions of Indochina, Myanmar, Malaysia, Indonesia and South China.[8] The largest number of people on the planet with not enough to eat is also in Asia: 578 million in 2010, as against 239 million in sub-Saharan Africa.[9]

Asia was for a long time the site of colonial expansion, and then of intense geopolitical rivalry among the great powers, and of some major armed conflicts. From the Second World War onwards, practically all such conflicts have taken place with the direct involvement of the United States: the wars in Korea in the early 1950s, the Vietnam War in the 1960s and 1970s, and the invasions of Afghanistan and Iraq at the start of the 21st century. The USSR also became embroiled in an unsuccessful war in Afghanistan.

An essential attribute for a state in Asia is its army: not always modern and effective, but always of large proportions. Among the 20 countries with the biggest armies in the world, only one is a Western country – the USA, which is second behind China. These two are followed by India, North Korea, Russia, Pakistan, South Korea, Iran, Vietnam, Egypt, Myanmar, Indonesia, Thailand, Turkey, and Japan. Near the bottom of the top twenty, one also finds Saudi Arabia and Taiwan, interspersed with several Latin American countries and one from Africa – Brazil, Colombia and Mexico, and Sudan. The largest European army – the French – was in a modest 24th place (if one does not count the Ukrainian army, in 22nd place), equal with Sri Lanka.[10] In 2017, defence spending in Asia exceeded that of the European members of NATO by 100 billion dollars a year.[11]

In terms of arms purchases, Asia is also significantly ahead of other parts of the world. The leading importer is India, which procures 13% of all arms in the world, followed by Saudi Arabia with 8.2%, the UAE with 4.6% and China with 4.5%.[12]

---

[8] Monika Barthwal-Datta, *Food Security in Asia: Challenges, Policies and Implications*. London, 2014. PP. 11-14.

[9] Yekaterina Kravchenko, "Sytykh stalo bol'she" ("There are More People Who are Well Fed", *Vedomosti*, September 15, 2010 <https://www.vedomosti.ru/newspaper/articles/2010/09/15/sytyh_stalo_bolshe>.

[10] *The Military Balance. 2017. The Annual Assessment of Global Military Capabilities and Defence Economics*. London, 2017. P. 553-559.

[11] Robert Ayson, "Manjeet S. Pardesi. Asia's Diplomacy of Violence: China-US Coercion and Regional Order", *Survival*, April/May 2017. P. 85.

[12] Anton Bayev, "Mir vooruzhayetsya" ("The World is Arming Itself"), *RBK*, February 20, 2017 <https://www.rbc.ru/newspaper/2017/02/21/58aad8b59a794756977f5617>.

In recent years, besides the five official members of the "nuclear club", a further four countries – India, Pakistan, Israel and North Korea – have acquired a nuclear weapon. According to current data, China has the third-highest number of nuclear warheads, that is ahead not only of the UK, but also, probably France. Japan, South Korea and Taiwan can be classified as "latent nuclear states", ones that are capable of creating a nuclear weapon of their own within a short period of time. The creation of North Korea's nuclear missile potential and the growth in China's military might are creating additional incentives for them to strive for nuclear status, and this has been kept in check by the sufficiency, thus far, of American nuclear guarantees.[13]

In an eloquently-titled article, "End of Whose History?", which played on the title of Francis Fukuyama's book *The End of History*, the dean of the Lee Kwan Yew School of Government in Singapore, Kishore Mahbubani, wrote: "[I]n the 21st century, history will unfold in the exact opposite direction of what Western intellectuals anticipated in 1991. We will now see that the 'return of history' equals 'the retreat of the West'. One prediction I can make confidently is that the Western footprint on the world, which was hugely oversized in the 19th and 20th centuries, will retreat significantly. This will not mean a retreat of all Western ideas. [...] The return of Asia will be accompanied by an astonishing Asian renaissance in which many diverse Asian cultures will rediscover their lost heritage of art and philosophy. There is no question that Asians will celebrate the return of history. The only question is: Will the West join them in these celebrations, or will they keep waiting for the end to come?"[14]

Both in the East and the West, books are published which offer the same idea. The 19th century belonged to Europe, the 20th century to the USA, and the 21st century will belong to Asia, and no-one will be able to stop this trend.[15] The USA's National Intelligence Council has concluded that by 2030, Asia will overtake the USA and the EU, combined, in terms of all the components of might: size of GDP, population, military spending and investment in technology.[16]

---

[13] Mark Fitzpatrick, *Asia's Latent Nuclear Powers: Japan, South Korea and Taiwan*. L., 2016.

[14] Kishore Mahbubani, "End of Whose History?", *The New York Times*, November 11, 2009 <https://www.nytimes.com/2009/11/12/opinion/12iht-edmahbubani.html>.

[15] Kishore Mahbubani, *The New Asian Hemisphere: The Irresistible Shift of Global Power to the East*. N. Y., 2008; Fareed Zakaria, *The Post-American World*. N. Y., 2009; Martin Jacques, *When China Rules the World: The End of the Western World and the Birth of a New Global Order*. Penguin, 2012.

[16] *Global Trends 2030: Alternative Worlds*. National Intelligence Council, 2012. P. iv.

And these forecasts may well turn out to be right. The mega-trend in recent decades has been the shifting of the global center of power towards East Asia and Asia-Pacific. In order to double their income per head of the population in the 20th century, the UK and the USA needed, respectively, 48 and 47 years, whereas Japan has done this in just 33 years, Indonesia in 17, Korea in 11, and China in 10. The Chinese economy grew by an average of 8% in the 1980s and the first half of the 1990s, and "the Tigers were close behind".[17]

In East Asia, there have been, and still are today, various economic models: post-industrial, industrial and even pre-industrial. Economic growth conformed with the concept of "flying geese" put forward by the Japanese economist Kaname Akamatsu back in the 1930s: following a more developed country and adopting its model for growing the economy after the other country moves to a new technological level. Thus, Japan, when it became involved in domestic electronics and automobile manufacturing, handed the textile industry to South Korea and Taiwan. When Japan began focusing on even more advanced technological products, South Korea and Taiwan took over the electronics and automobile industries, and the textile industry moved to Indonesia, Thailand etc. South Korea, Taiwan and Singapore have joined Japan in developing an economy of knowledge.

Differences in the levels of economic development remain huge. Powerful economies whose people enjoy a high standard of living – Japan, Hong Kong, Singapore – are alongside such poverty-stricken countries as East Timor and Papua New Guinea. Even the rapidly-growing economies – China, India, Indonesia, Vietnam – cannot yet boast of having a high volume of GDP when calculated per capita.

Asia is home to the biggest geopolitical centers of the modern world. China is considered, not without justification, as the main candidate for the title of the second superpower on the planet. India is becoming an ever more significant global and regional player. The biggest Islamic country in the world – Indonesia, with its population of 270 million – is one of the 10 countries in the ASEAN, which incorporates 651 million people.

Russia is notable in the region as a major political player, but is not seen as a significant economic or cultural factor. Certain prejudices are playing out here – not only geopolitical ones, but also racial and ethnic ones. "Historically, East Asian countries have tended to see Russia as a 'distant

---

[17] Samuel P. Huntington, *The Clash of Civilizations and the Remaking of World Order.* N.Y. et al., 1996. P. 103.

neighbor' with a distinct civilization – neither European nor Asian – and political and strategic interests at odds with their own," notes the director of the center for East Asian studies at the Monterey Institute, Tsuneo Akaha.[18]

There is serious potential for conflict in Asia. It was here, effectively, that the Second World War began – with the Japanese occupation of China and the countries of Southeast Asia. Even today, in East Asia, the memory of WWII provokes far more powerful emotions than on the European continent. There are still age-old geopolitical divisions in the region as well, dating back to even before the start of the Cold War era. There is mutual distrust between countries, and between some there is open hostility: India and Pakistan, South Korea and North Korea. There are still territorial disputes, into which almost all the countries of East Asia have been drawn. Three regions in the South China Sea (the Paracel Islands, the Spratly Islands and the Gulf of Tonkin) are the subject of multilateral disputes. Problems remain unresolved on the borders between India and Pakistan, India and China, China and Vietnam, Japan and all its neighbors, Cambodia and Thailand.

Brzezinski, commenting upon the high potential for conflict in East Asia and comparing the situation in Asia with that of Europe in the 19th century, also pointed out a host of significant differences. Firstly, Asia must still take into account the possibility of interference by a predominant force from without. Secondly, East Asia is gaining a lot from the growth in economic mutual dependency, and this is fanning the flames of nationalism. Thirdly, Asian countries have historically been able to coexist peacefully for centuries, whereas in Europe periods of peace were more the exception than the rule.[19] John Mearsheimer and Robert Kaplan have highlighted another factor: "the stopping power of water" in conditions whereby "the grand geography of East Asia is primarily maritime". Countries are divided and bound together less by dry land than by the sea, and this has the effect of slowing down and restraining the use of military force.[20]

A key question for security in the region is how relations between the two main players in the Asia-Pacific region – the USA and China – are going to develop. The very rise of China itself prompts a diverse range of opinions –

---

[18] Tsuneo Akaha, "A Distant Neighbor: Russia's Search to Find Its Place in East Asia", *Global Asia*, Vol. 7, Summer 2012. P. 8.

[19] Zbigniew Brzezinski, *Strategic Vision: America and the Crisis of Global Power*. N. Y., 2012. PP. 159-161.

[20] John J. Mearsheimer, *The Tragedy of Great Power Politics*. University of Chicago, 2001. P. 114; Robert D. Kaplan, *Asia's Cauldron. The South China Sea and the End of a Stable Pacific*. Random House, 2014. PP. 5-7.

from the hope that Beijing will use the strength it has acquired to maintain stability, to concerns about China's total strategic dominance in the region. One can increasingly sense the return of fears about a bipolar confrontation, this time between the USA and China. Countries in the region would like to avoid this, by incorporating the two powers into some form of general arrangement that would provide safeguards against a conflict between them.

The countries of Asia and the Asia-Pacific have not demonstrated any desire whatsoever to take a side in the stand-off between Russia and the West regarding Ukraine. Of the states in the region, Australia eagerly joined in with the sanctions against Moscow, while Japan did so reluctantly. Even such close allies of the USA as South Korea and New Zealand did not wish to spoil relations with Russia. Statements were made by Beijing and Delhi about Russia's rights to defend its core strategic interests. The ASEAN countries spoke out in favor of activating trade and economic cooperation with Russia. Even in Malaysia, one of whose planes was shot down over Novorossiya, a majority of public opinion was inclined towards the view that this was a provocation, with the USA behind it.[21]

A flaring up of any of the "dormant" conflicts – be it the tension on the Korean peninsula, the Taiwan problem, or the territorial dispute in the South China Sea – could lead to a major disaster. This means that a pressing matter on the agenda is to create the kind of regional architecture that might make it possible to prevent and overcome conflicts, and create incentives for cooperation. Do the contemporary realities of the Asia-Pacific region satisfy these criteria?

Attempts have been made to create regional mechanisms, starting in the late 1940s: there were the ideas of a United States of Indochina (1946), the Union of South-East Asia (1947), the Association of South-East Asia (1961), and many others. In 1954, on the initiative of the USA, the South-East Asian Treaty Organization (SEATO) was set up, and in 1966 the Asia-Pacific Conference (ASPAC) was established. On account of their military-bloc logic, however, these initiatives and organizations were not able to become universal. ASEAN – the Association of South-East Asian Nations – which came into being in 1967, and incorporated Indonesia, Malaysia, Singapore, Thailand, and the Philippines – was seen as a pro-Western grouping, re-

....

[21] Vladimir Petrovskiy, "Rossiya i Vostochnaya Aziya v kontekste ukrainskogo krizisa: 'net' sanktsiyam, 'da' novomu miroporyadku" ("Russia and East Asia in the Context of the Ukrainian Crisis: 'No' to Sanctions, 'Yes' to a New World Order"), *Mezhdunarodnaya zhizn'* (*International Life*), October 2014. PP. 52-65.

sisting the communist "hegemony" and Maoist penetration. After the Cold War, integration processes involving external blocs began to take place in the APR. In January 1989, an initiative to create the forum of the Asia-Pacific Economic Cooperation (APEC), put forward by the Australian Prime Minister Bob Hoke, was given backing.[22]

Following the Asian crisis in 1997-1998, there was a desire to develop economic integration in the region, and areas of free trade. Today, there is an alphabet soup of organizations in the Asia-Pacific Region. The biggest of these are the Association of South-East Asian Nations (ASEAN), the South Asian Association for Regional Cooperation (SAARC) and the Shanghai Organization for Cooperation (SOC). There are also multiple forums for dialogue in the region. These include the APEC, the ASEAN Regional Forum for Security (ARF), the Conference on Interaction and Confidence-Building Measures in Asia (CICA), created in 1992 at the initiative of Nursultan Nazarbayev (uniting 26 countries and 9 observers, of which even Ukraine is one), and interaction in the formats Russia-India-China (RIC), the East-Asian Three (China, Japan, South Korea), Dialogue on Cooperation in Asia (DCA), the Forum for Pacific Islands (FOPO), the Bali Democratic Forum, and others. An increasingly important role is being played by inter-regional associations – BRICS, the dialogue forums "Asia-Europe" (ACEM), "Asia-Middle East", "East Asia-Latin America" (EASLAF), and the New Afro-Asian Strategic Partnership (NAASP), etc.

The main trend in regional development is the drawing up of bilateral and multilateral free trade agreements (FTAs).

One of the paradoxes of the Asia-Pacific Region is that in a region that contains more great states than anywhere else, the kernel and driving force of integration processes have traditionally been states in the second rank, those within ASEAN. Initially, their only partners were states from the Western club. It was the countries of ASEAN, however, that were the initiators of the creation of the Conference, first of all, and then of the Council for Pacific Economic Cooperation, on the basis of which, underpinned by examples of European integration and NAFTA, the APEC forum came into being. Since 1993, the ASEAN Regional Forum has been in place (ARF), which incorporates 27 states, including the Russian Federation. It is a structure for multilateral cooperation in the field of security and

---

[22] S. B. Shipilov, *Aziatsko-Tikhookeanskoye ekonomicheskoye sotrudnichestvo: Stanovleniye, razvitiye, perspektivy (1989–2007 gg.)* (*Asian-Pacific Economic Cooperation. Rise, Development, Prospects (1989-2007)*). Moscow, 2009.

the establishment of measures designed to build trust. The ARF also has a meaningful second mechanism process called the Council for Security Cooperation in the Asia-Pacific (CSCAP). By the end of the 20th century, ASEAN stretched across the whole of South-East Asia, after bringing in, one by one, Brunei, Vietnam, Laos, Myanmar, and Cambodia, which were not initially members. There is a whole host of ASEAN+1 gatherings, with leading partner states, one of which is with Russia. Cooperation in the format ASEAN+3 (China, Japan and South Korea) is developing apace. In December 2005, a new structure was formed: ASEAN+6, or the mechanism of East-Asia Summits, which were joined by Australia, New Zealand, and India.

In the final report on the 16th summit, which took place in Hanoi in April 2010, the ASEAN countries expressed their willingness to look into the issue of expanding the EAS by including Russia and the USA (ASEAN+8). Amid the great hotchpotch of acronyms, two organizations appeared for the first time with a matching set of member states: the East-Asia Summit (EAS) and the ASEAN Defence Ministers' Meetings-Plus (ADMM+). In Bali, where the first EAS summit took place in November 2011 with the involvement of Russia and the USA, a declaration was adopted in which the overall vision of the EAS's role was emphasized, as a Leaders-led forum for dialogue and cooperation on broad strategic, political and economic issues of common concerns. The EAS has every chance of becoming a platform for strategic dialogue on key regional issues.

The aforementioned American idea of creating a regional Trans-Pacific Partnership excluding China has begun to be implemented, though without the USA. At the same time, however, the prospects for drawing up an agreement on "Regional Comprehensive Economic Partnership" (RCEP) have been discussed; this would unite in a single free trade zone – without the USA – Australia, China, India, Japan, South Asia, New Zealand, and the ten ASEAN countries.[23] The idea of the RCEP is described as a Chinese one, but in fact it was proposed by the ASEAN countries and was actively backed by the USA's partners in the region. It involves the joint drafting of pan-Asian trade rules.[24]

---

[23] Chas W. Freeman Jr., "Mir nepredvidennykh slozhnostey" ("A World of Unpredictable Complications"), *Rossiya v global'noy politike* (*Russia in Global Affairs*), Issue 3, May/June 2014. P. 32.

[24] Evan A. Feigenbaum, "China and the World. Dealing With a Reluctant Power", *Foreign Affairs*, January/February 2017. P. 38.

Of considerable interest is the rivalry between the various development institutions. The regional version of the World Bank has been the Asian Development Bank, created in 1966 with a head office in Manila. The President of this bank has always come from Japan, and the voting shares in it are distributed as follows: the USA and Japan 13% each, the EU countries 16%, China 5.5%, slightly more than Australia and Canada. It came as no surprise, therefore, that China put forward an initiative to set up an Asian Bank for Investment in Infrastructure, which the USA tried to dissuade all its partners from taking part in, but ultimately was only able to convince itself and Japan. In their absence – in accordance with the countries' weight in the global economy – China has 26% of the votes, India 7.5%, Russia 5.9%, Germany 4.2%, South Korea and Australia 3.5% each, France and India 3.2% each, Brazil has 3%, and the UK 2.9%.[25]

In terms of its scale and the sheer scope of its ambition in terms of time and space, the "Belt & Road" initiative by the Chinese leader Xi Jinping is unprecedented. "For the first time since Vasco da Gama sailed the seas, an attempt is being made to construct a system of mutual economic ties from the East to the West."[26]

Various negotiation formats have been formed for regulating conflict situations. Of particular importance among them is the mechanism for six-party talks on the nuclear problem in the Korean peninsula; the "six" are the USA, Russia, China, Japan, South Korea, and North Korea. Lately, though, this has been put to one side. Threats from the American leadership to deal with the Northern Korean regime of Kim Jong Un have given rise to the politics of "songun" – the priority of military matters, focusing on ever more active testing of nuclear missiles by North Korea, although the meetings between Trump and Kim Jong Un opened an option for political dialogue.

At the same time, it is difficult to describe this whole motley picture as fully-fledged regional architecture. Something, or someone, is bound to fall out of any of the existing formats. There are no military and political alliances, such as NATO, or continental structures following the model of the EU, OSCE or the Council of Europe. The multilateral organizations in the APR are fairly vague in nature, and the decisions they take are not

---

[25] Stephen D. King, *Grave New World: The End of Globalization, the Return of History*. New Haven, 2017. P. 140.

[26] Dmitriy Yefremenko, "Rozhdeniye Bol'shoy Yevrazii" ("The Birth of Great Eurasia"), *Rossiya v global'noy politike* (*Russia in Global Affairs*), November/December 2016. P. 30.

binding. The ASEAN countries, which are at the center of the integration processes, are suspicious and jealous about any attempts to create structures which threaten to take the steering wheel of regional integration out of their hands.

The transformation of East Asia into the engine of the world economy has led to a strengthening of national self-awareness. Ideas connected with "historical revenge" and the restoration of historical justice, trampled over by the colonial power of the Western states, are gaining in popularity.

Huntington remarked: "In the early 1990s Asian triumphalism was articulated anew in what can only be described as the 'Singaporean cultural offensive'. From Lee Kuan Yew on down, Singarorean leaders trumpeted the rise of Asia in relation to the West and contrasted the virtues of Asian, basically Confucian, culture responsible for this success – order, discipline, family responsibility, hard work, collectivism, abstemiousness – to the self-indulgence, sloth, individualism, crime, inferior education, disrespect for authority and 'mental ossification' responsible for the decline of the West."[27] Ideas about "Asian values" achieved a particular resonance.

The State Above All Else

Historically in Eastern societies, by contrast with Europe, there was indeed little evidence of political and social pluralism. There, a system of power as property was in place: power was equivalent to property, and vice-versa. The state, as an institution, stood against the owner of private property, seeing in the excessive strengthening of his position a threat to the state coffers and to political stability. There were no laws that protected private property (as there were under Roman law). This created the kind of society in which the state played the primary role, with the private sector playing a secondary role, and one that was mediated by the state.

As the knowledgeable orientalist Leonid Vasilyev has observed, "The non-European state has since time immemorial always and everywhere been not just an integral part of a body public that cannot be divided from it, but also the highest summit of that body public. By including the society within it, and marrying it, it raised itself above it and subordinated it to itself (this was least in evidence in Islamic societies). In an oriental society, the state amounts to the highest power, not limited by anything, before

---

[27] Samuel P. Huntington, *The Clash of Civilizations and the Remaking of World Order*. N.Y. et al., 1996. P. 108.

which the whole of society trembles and is obliged to tremble, from top to bottom. And whereas in antique, bourgeois Europe, power depends on the balancing of contradictory trends in the body public, in the East, the authority of power never depends on anything of the kind. Ultimately, everything is decided only by the strength of power itself, the efficiency of the administration that is in place, and the regular flow into the coffers of a guaranteed level of income."[28]

The rights of the individual, in the Orient, were protected solely in relation to another person, but not from the state. Property rights in land were never as formal in nature as they were in Europe. For the state, the question of land ownership boiled down to the question of who was paying taxes. No market for land, or system of open trade in land plots, existed.

However, the fact that Asia is now streaking ahead ought to not come as a surprise to anyone who is familiar with world history.

The history of humankind started in Asia. There is evidence suggesting that it was in the Middle East that the first sapient man appeared. It was here that the Neolithic revolution began, and the agriculture that it brought with it formed the basis for the first proto-state structures. People living in Asia built the first cities, founded the first political, economic and social institutions, created the first states and civilizations – in the valleys of the Tigris, the Euphrates, the Nile, the Indus and the Yellow River. The forebears of wheat or barley are to be sought among the wild grasses which still grow in Lebanon, Syria or Palestine. It is no coincidence that the ancient Romans, whose civilization was in many ways a daughter-civilization in relation to that of the Middle East, used to say, respectfully: "Ex Oriente lux!" – "The light comes from the Orient!"

Our seven-day week originates from the Biblical story about the Creation of the world, which, in turn, is based on the Semite system of counting, which had the number seven at its heart. The ancient Semites of Mesopotamia (the Babylonians) believed there were seven planets, to the most important of which – the Sun – they dedicated the 1st day of the week (Sunday), while the Moon was given the 2nd day (Monday), and Saturn was given the 7th (Saturday). The dividing up of the hour into 60 minutes, the minute into 60 seconds, and of a circle into 360 degrees – all this came from Mesopotamia. It was there, too, that a pictorial system of writing was devised, which was later elaborated in Egypt, and the Phoenicians – the distant forebears of the modern-day inhabitants of the Lebanon – turned

....

[28] Leonid Vasil'yev, *Istoriya Vostoka* (*A History of the East*). Vol. 1. Moscow, 2011. P. 710.

it into an alphabet and gave it to the rest of the world (the part of it which did not use hieroglyphs).[29]

Asia is the birthplace of all the world's religions, the cradle of culture and the state. Five religious or moral systems are descended from the ancient civilizations of China and India – Hinduism, Buddhism, Confucianism, Taoism, and Shintoism. Today, Hinduism is the religion of the majority in India and Nepal, and is preached in neighboring Bangladesh, Bhutan, and Sri Lanka. Shintoism is limited to Japan. Buddhism, which emerged in India in around 500 BC, by contrast, is widespread throughout Asia, and is the main religion of Bhutan, Cambodia, Laos, Mongolia, Myanmar, and Sri Lanka. In Russia, it is widespread in Buryatia, Kalmykia and Tyva. Together with Confucianism, Buddhism is the dominant religion in China, North and South Korea, Singapore, Thailand and Vietnam, and it is a significant religion in Brunei and Malaysia too.

In addition to these religions came the Abrahamic religions, nourished in the Middle East, mainly in Palestine: Judaism, Christianity and Islam, which were the product of the spiritual experience of the Semite peoples. The Jewish faith, which is preserved today mainly in Israel and the Jewish diaspora throughout the world, gave us the Bible (the Old Testament), but did not recognize the divine nature of Christ, whose life and passion were put into the Gospels written by his apostles, thanks to the alphabet, which was invented by the Phoenicians. Christianity, which was born in Asia and had a massive influence worldwide, affected Asia less than anywhere else, unless one includes Russia, of course. Even in the regions with a high percentage of people who are of the Christian faith (South Korea, where a quarter of the population are Christians, Indonesia 10%, and Malaysia 7%), it remains the second-largest religion. Islam, by contrast, which incorporated a great deal from the Jewish and Christian traditions, spread from Saudi Arabia across the continent, to Central Asia, Afghanistan and Pakistan, and further East across the sea, to Bangladesh, Brunei, Indonesia, Malaysia, and the Maldives. More than two thirds of those whose religion is Islam live in Asia. The countries with the largest Islamic populations are also in Asia: Indonesia (160 million believers), Bangladesh (125 million), Pakistan (116 million), and India (100 million).

For many centuries, Asia had an overwhelming level of military force. After the fall of Rome, the next millennium, from the 5th to the 16th centuries

---

[29] Philip Hitti, *Kratkaya istoriya Blizhnego Vostoka. Most trekh kontinentov* (*A Brief History of the Middle East. The Bridge of Three Continents*). Moscow, 2012. PP. 7-8.

CE, was a period when, as the comparative studies by Ian Morris reveal, Asia had military superiority on its side.[30] This could be seen in the successes of the Arabic caliphate, the invincible advance of Genghis Khan, the military achievements and voyages halfway around the world of China during the Ming dynasty, the destruction of the Byzantine Empire by the Ottomans, and the martial art of the Japanese samurais.

In 1500, the population of Western Europe stood at less than 50 million people, whereas in Ming dynasty China and in India under the Great Moguls, the population was 200 million and 110 million respectively.

Back in the mid-18th century, China accounted for more than a third of GDP, India had 29%, and the biggest European economy had only 5%. And that economy was Russia. China's domination, in addition to its vast internal consumption, was due to the colossal demand in the West for porcelain, silk, cotton fabrics and tea, and India rose up on the basis of its exports of tea, cotton, spices, and opium. In 1820, China's share of the planet's GDP still stood at 32.4%, the whole of Europe at 26.6%, India at 16%, Japan 3% and the USA 1.8%.[31]

Asia, many experts believe, is less a geographical, economic and political phenomenon, than a historico-cultural one. "[T]he very concept of Asia is largely a Western one," stresses Dominique Moïsi. "Asians do not naturally call themselves or consider themselves Asians – at least not nearly to the extent that Europeans consider themselves Europeans. Asians do not have a common religion […]. They do not have a common history. They do not have a common enemy (which is what Islam once represented for the Christian nations of Europe). They do not have common cultural references."[32] It is worth noting that the only museum of Asian civilization in Asia is in the Westernized Singapore, where the Chinese, Malay and Indian population are united by the official language, English.

While agreeing with this, one cannot help but observe that an awareness of Asian unity does exist, and the story of its establishment goes back well over a millennium. The oldest trading route on the planet stretched 5,000 kilometers from the mountains of Asia Minor across the interfluve of the

---

[30] Ian Morris, *The Measure of Civilization. How Social Development Decides the Fate of Nations*. London, 2013. PP. 189-191.

[31] Dambisa Moyo, *How The West Was Lost: Fifty Years of Economic Folly – And the Stark Choices Ahead*. Penguin, 2011. P. 15.

[32] Dominique Moïsi, *The Geopolitics of Emotion: How Cultures of Fear, Humiliation and Hope are Reshaping the World*. Random House, 2009.

Tigris and the Euphrates to the Gulf of Persia, and from the banks of the Indian Ocean to the banks of the Indus. It was at the crossroads on this route that the major trading cities of Ur, Akal, Babylon and Ninevah (all of which are in present-day Iraq) came into being. The flow of goods from these cities spread ever more broadly: initially to the Middle East, then to the Mediterranean, and then to the East – up to China.

More than 2,000 years ago, Chinese silk and porcelain were already being exchanged for Indian cotton and South Asian herbs and timber, along the entire length of the Great Silk Route and the waterways of South-East Asia.[33] Silk from China reached Rome at the start of the 1st century AD. Chinese merchants would load up their vessels in the southern ports; from there, they would move along the coast of Indonesia and the Malay Peninsula, across the Bay of Bengal to the ports of Sri Lanka. There, they were met by Indian merchants, who would send the fabrics on to Tamil ports. From there, via Arabic and Greek middlemen, they would be taken to the Island of Dioscorea off the south coast of the Arabian peninsula, where there was a bustling marketplace attended by Indian, Persian, Ethiopian, Arabic, and Greek entrepreneurs, who reached Egypt across the Red Sea. From there the goods would be taken up the Nile to the Mediterranean. Of even greater complexity was the route over land, along the Silk Route, opened by emissaries of the emperors of the Khan dynasty in the 2nd century AD, at whose main centers – Samarkand, Isfahan, Herat – a leading role was played by Jewish, Armenian and Syrian merchants and middlemen.[34]

The cultural ties have their roots in the 3rd century BC, when the Indian Emperor Ashoka began to spread Buddhism beyond the limits of the sub-continent.

A huge role was played in the forging of a shared Asian unity by the biggest empire in the history of mankind: the Mongol empire of the Chingizids, which stretched from the Pacific Ocean to Eastern Europe and incorporated modern-day China, Russia, Ukraine, Hungary, Iran, the countries of Central Asia and the Levant, and North India. It combined within a single state representatives of a diverse range of peoples, religions and cultures, leaving its imprint upon them. The experience of the Mongol state, whose rulers lived in China, was curious.

....

[33] William Bernstein, *The Magnificent Exchange. A History of World Trade.* Atlantic Monthly Press, 2008. P. 82.
[34] Ibid. PP. 2-4.

Carrere d'Encausse considered the most important components of the Mongol legacy to be the ideology, and the principles of the political organization of the state, and property relations: "Genghis Khan passed on to his successors political structures and a method of governance which were incomparably more efficient than any other state structure of that time. This system was the product of an ideological concept, something that was encountered extremely rarely, if it even existed at all, at the time, but which became a ubiquitous phenomenon in the 20th century. The Mongol system set itself the aim of asserting its global Empire, won by means of a series of continual wars, and it strove to establish, thanks to the power that it had won everywhere, global peace and public order, the key concepts in which were the words justice and equality, under the aegis of the all-powerful Khan. Mankind organized in this way, however, with security and equality provided, had to pay for these blessings, with constant and tireless service to the state, i.e. the Khan, who was the embodiment of the state. For his part, the Khan, the almighty ruler of the lives of his subjects, was also the owner of the land in his Empire."[35]

The Mongol Empire set an example of poly-ethnicity and a multi-faith community. Genghis Khan was respectful towards the adherents of other cults, on condition that they prayed to their gods for the health of the Mongols. The younger brother of Batu Khan, Berke, incidentally, who ruled over the North Caucasus region, was the first of the Genghis dynasty to adopt Islam as his faith.

In the Shadow of the West

When and why did the West catch up and pull ahead? I would suggest that demographics, geography and technologies turned out to be the key factors. The presence of a vast workforce in Asia, one that was often bigger than it needed to be, encouraged extensive production. There were no serious incentives for bringing in technical innovations. Academic learning in the West proved to be far more necessary for practical purposes than in the East.

The West also began to get ahead thanks to the use of firearms. One would have thought that gunpowder would have been invented in China, and that artillery would have emerged there no later than in the West. Why was it that Asia did not start developing these weapons? Kenneth Chase be-

---

[35] Helene Carrere d'Encausse, *Nezavershennaya Rossiya* (*Incomplete Russia*). Moscow, 2005. PP. 37-38.

lieves that there were greater incentives for this in Europe than in the East. In Europe, political fragmentation led to a larger number of wars. Large armies proved to be necessary, and there were not enough horses to go round, since there was nowhere for large herds to graze. The infantry therefore came to the fore, and their main tasks were to slowly destroy the advancing infantry of the enemy and to take the fortified cities. For both purposes, firearms and cannons were the most effective tools.

In Asia, wars were a rare occurrence, particularly civil wars, with the exception of the Great War in Korea in 1592-1598. China, the largest state in military terms, was mainly required to defend itself against nomadic tribes in the steppes, against whom firearms would have been ineffective. The armies of China, India, Persia and Turkey were to a considerable extent cavalry-based ones, and the expanses of the steppes, or proximity to them, made it possible to have an unlimited number of horses. The incentives for military innovation in Europe proved to be far stronger.[36]

Geography must take part of the blame, too, as Ian Morris maintains: "Back in the 15th century, new methods of sailing (pioneered in China) made it possible for ships to cross the oceans. All of a sudden, the geographical detail that the Western Europe was only 3,000 miles from America's east coast while China was 8,000 miles from its west coast became the most important factor in the world. It meant that Europeans, rather than Chinese, colonized the New World, creating new kinds of market economies around the shores of the Atlantic. These markets generated equally new incentives that drove Europeans, rather than Chinese, to harness the power of fossil fuels in an industrial revolution. This revolution's steamships and railroads further shrank the world in the 19th century, unleashing the vast industrial potential of North America's hinterland."[37]

A long-term crisis of two Asian giants – China and India – and with them, the whole of the Asian continent, arrived when the British, using the latest achievements of the industrial revolution for military objectives, occupied India and began extracting from it untold riches, and then producing opium there and trying to sell it to China. Since the Chinese put up resistance, Britain began the opium wars against them, eventually forcing them to buy the narcotics. Between 1840 and 1842, the small British fleet

....

[36] Kenneth Chase, *Firearms: A Global History to 1700*. Cambridge University Press, 2003. P. 154.

[37] Ian Morris, "Here Comes the East", *The International Herald Tribune*, December 22, 2010. P. 6.

brought China to its knees. This is an eyewitness account from Lord Robert Jocelyn: "[T]he shipping opened their broadsides upon the town, and the crashing of timber, falling houses, and groans of men resounded from the shore. The firing lasted on our side for nine minutes [...]. We landed on a deserted beach; a few dead bodies, bows and arrows, broken spears and guns, remaining the sole occupants of the field."[38] In 1890, China's share of global GDP stood at 13%, and Europe's at 40%.[39]

The peak of colonialism in Asia came in the 19th century, when several zones came under colonial control: the British zone, in the south and southwest of the continent, the Russian zone in Central Asia and the Caucasus, the French zone in Indochina, the Dutch zone in Indonesia, and an area of joint influence by Western states and Russia in East Asia. Foreign expansion disrupted the natural development of Asia, resulting in a clash of civilizations at different stages of development. Although in Europe, secular and even liberal standards had already taken root in various places, the colonial regimes were not at all concerned about adhering to them. Governance was hierarchical and authoritarian, and in this sense it was just as brutal, and at times more so, than traditional oriental systems of order.

The European states had the ability to intervene, militarily, in any country in Asia. From there, they procured an almost unpaid workforce: Indians on the Malay Peninsula, Chinese in Trinidad, and so on. From Asia, they took away cultural artefacts, with which museums and private collections in Western Europe are still filled to this day. From there, they took away, in whatever quantities they liked, the raw materials that were so vital to Western industrialization, which at the same time meant that industrialization could not get started in the East. The Asian markets were fully open to European industrial goods, and this destroyed many local artisan trades. Civilization was now identified with European forms of scientific and historical knowledge, and European ideas on morality, social order, law, and even on style of dress and religion. "This is why the European subordination of Asia was not merely economic and political and military," notes the well-known Indian analyst Pankaj Mishra. "It was also intellectual and moral and spiritual: a completely different kind of conquest than had been witnessed before, which left its victims resentful but also envious of their conquerors

---

[38] Robert Jocelyn, *Six Months with the Chinese Expedition; or Leaves from a Soldier's Note-Book*. London, 1841. PP. 55-56, 57.

[39] Dambisa Moyo, *How The West Was Lost: Fifty Years of Economic Folly – And the Stark Choices Ahead*. Penguin, 2011. P. 15.

and, ultimately, eager to be initiated into the mysteries of their seemingly near-magical power."[40]

Sun Yat-sen, the founder of the Kuomintang, would say, in 1924, that even in the last decade of the 19th century, no-one believed that liberation from the reign of the white man was even possible: "Men thought and believed that European civilization was a progressive one – in science, industry, manufacture, and armament – and that Asia had nothing to compare with it. Consequently, they assumed that Asia could never resist Europe, and that European oppression could never be shaken off."[41] For many Asian thinkers, the challenge posed by the West was not a geopolitical one: it was an existential one. A considerable number of intellectuals emerged who began preparing a revolution in the Asian consciousness. They began borrowing individual elements of Western political ideas, norms and traditions, while at the same time searching for an original path of their own, taking national traditions into account. Among them was the Chinese historian and philosopher Liang Qichao, the journalist Jamal al-Din al-Afghani, the Indian Rabindranath Tagore, and the Japanese Saseki.

What was the reason for the West's superiority? The Asian intellectuals were not happy with answers which blamed "Eastern despotism" and "racial inferiority". They found an answer in the way the Western states and societies were organized: European forms of political and military mobilization – an army with conscription, effective taxation systems, codified laws; financial institutions – along with joint stock companies, stock exchanges, and a public life and education system that were saturated with information. The first to move onto the path of borrowing the Western forms of state organization was Japan, whose role in the development of Asianism would prove to be big in future years, too. The Meiji reforms, introduced from 1868 onwards, began to transform Japan into a great power. By the end of the century, Japan itself had begun to interfere actively in colonial conflicts in East Asia, laying claim not only to its own territories, but also to completing the mission of liberating Asia from the conquerors.

In Russia and in the West, people have grown accustomed to thinking that the main events in the history of the 20th century were the two world wars, and then a bipolar confrontation and the cold war. "But it is now

---

[40] Pankaj Mishra, *From the Ruins of Empire: The Revolt Against the West and the Remaking of Asia*. N. Y., 2013. P. 45.

[41] Sun Yat-sen, *China and Japan: Natural Friends – Unnatural Enemies*. China united Press, 1941. P. 142.

clearer that the central event of the last century for the majority of the world's population was the intellectual and political awakening of Asia and its emergence from the ruins of both Asian and European empires," believes Mishra.[42]

One can identify the moment in history when the peoples of Asia sensed that the colonial oppression by European states could successfully be resisted. However unpleasant it may be for Russians to recall this, the matter in question is the battle of Tsushima in May 1905, when a small Japanese fleet under admiral Heihachiro Togo sank the majority of the Russian fleet, after circumnavigating half the world, a feat which decided the outcome of the war being fought over control of Korea and Manchuria. This event delighted an unknown Indian lawyer named Mahatma Gandhi, who was living in South Africa at the time; a 16-year-old boy named Jawaharlal Nehru, who was studying in England; a young Ottoman soldier named Mustafa Kemal, who was serving in Damascus, and who later achieved fame under the name Ataturk; and the Chinese nationalist Sun Yat-sen, who was living in London. A teacher named Rabindranath Tagore took his pupils out of their school in rural Bengal, on a victory march. Hundreds of thousands of people celebrated in China, Vietnam, Persia, Turkey and Egypt. New-born babies all over Asia were named after admiral Togo, and the main conclusion that people drew was: "White men, conquerors of the world, were no longer invincible."[43]

Students from Asian countries moved to Japan to gain experience. Asian rulers looked on Japan as an example, and began borrowing its experience and institutions. In the Ottoman Empire, young Turks forced the Sultan Abdulhamid to restore the constitution, which had been abolished in 1876. In Persia, in 1906, the National Assembly was created. In Indonesia, the first nationalist party emerged. Japan's success in the war against Russia could not disguise the reality of the military and economic superiority of the West, but it triggered the process of intellectual decolonization.

The next boost for anti-colonialism and the ideology of Asianism was the First World War, during which European Civilization lost what was left of its moral authority in the eyes of Asians. A point of agreement for Eastern intellectuals was a belief in the imperialist nature of European

---

[42] Pankaj Mishra, *From the Ruins of Empire: The Revolt Against the West and the Remaking of Asia*. N. Y., 2013. P. 8.
[43] Ibid. PP. 1-3.

slaughter, in which colonial possessions were at stake. A strong impression was made in Asia by Vladimir Lenin's book *Imperialism as the Highest Stage of Capitalism*, in which he described the skirmish among the European states, greedy for capital and resources; and Japan and the USA were in no way lagging behind the European states. The Leninist principle of nations' right to self-determination preceded its proclamation by the American President Woodrow Wilson, although Wilson had greater opportunities to convey his stance to the global community.

Asian countries were initially inspired by the principles of Wilson, who also proclaimed the right of small nations to self-determination. It soon became clear though, that this principle in Wilsonism only concerned the European peoples. As early as 1919, the British had brutally put down protest movements in the Punjab, Afghanistan, and Egypt, without encountering the slightest objection on the part of the USA. Mao Tse-tung, Jawaharlal Nehru, Ho Chi Minh, and other nationalists in Asia were convinced that empire was coming back.[44] Wilson's star fell even lower in the eyes of Asians during the Versailles Conference. Japan – the only non-white, non-Christian country represented at Versailles – put forward a proposal to include "racial equality" among the principles of the League of Nations. Wilson blocked this idea, instead proposing the principle of "open doors" in East Asia.[45] The 1910s also saw the peak of racist, anti-immigrant legislation in Australia, Canada and California, where there were concerns about an influx of "hordes of Asians".

In light of these circumstances, the sympathies of the Asian nationalists began to be inclined towards a country that had proclaimed the principle of the equality of all nations, anti-colonialism and proletarian internationalism: Soviet Russia. In 1920, the Bolsheviks organized a Congress of Peoples of the East in Baku, and the Comintern rolled out its efforts to raise the forces of national liberation in Asia. Many future leaders of the revolutionary movement in Asian and Africa completed their studies in Moscow, and in all places, communist parties were active players, if not the main driving forces, in social change.

The Chinese thinker Yan Fu, in his old age, increasingly sensed that Western "progress during the last three hundred years has only led to selfishness,

---

[44] For a discussion of self-determination of small nations, see Erez Manela, *The Wilsonian Moment: Self-Determination and the International Origins of Anticolonial Nationalism*. Oxford University Press, 2007. PP. 215-225.

[45] Mark Mazower, *Governing the World. The History of an Idea*. Allen Lane, 2012. PP. 163-165.

slaughter, corruption, and shamelessness."[46] Sun Yat-sen insisted in *The Three People's Principles* on a restoration of traditional values, which he called "the royal path" of the East: "loyalty and filial piety, then humanity and love, faithfulness and duty, harmony and peace."[47] On the other hand, imperial Japan in the 1920s and 1930s justified its predatory military actions with ideas about Asian unity, the liberation of Asian states from the Western colonial yoke, and the creation of the Greater East Asia Co-Prosperity Sphere. The war in Asia began with Japan's invasion of Manchuria in 1931, and continued until 1945.

In the three months after the attack on Pearl Harbor on 7th December 1941, Japan seized British, American and Dutch territories: the Philippines, Singapore, Malaysia, Hong Kong, the Indonesian islands, most of Siam, French Indochina and Burma, and had troops on the border of India. This was one of the most dramatic episodes of the simultaneous humiliation of almost all the great Western states. In the territories they had taken, the Japanese displayed unprecedented levels of brutality, before which even the crimes of Hitlerism pale, if one can imagine such a thing. The war cost Asia, according to the most conservative estimates, 24 million lives, including 3.5 million Indians who died of famine in 1943, and hundreds of thousands of Chinese who were shot in Nanking. Slave labor, torture and mass rapes were commonplace. People in Asia will hardly forget what the Japanese did.

Also important, though, was the fact that the Japanese – acting under the slogan "Asia for Asians" – not only overthrew the European colonial administrations in many places, expelling them or sending their representatives to prison or to concentration camps, but also triggered nationalist and pan-Asian movements across the continent. As of April 1943, Japan's official slogan became "the liberation of Asia", and in that year the Congress of Greater East Asia took place in Tokyo, showing that pan-Asianism was by no means only a Japanese idea. Nehru, who was in a British prison when the Second World War broke out, wrote that "Asiatics [was] a common bond uniting us against the aggression of Europe."[48] His vision of the future consisted of a "federation which includes China and India, Burma and Ceylon, Afghanistan and possibly other countries."[49]

....

[46] Cit. from: Pankaj Mishra, *From the Ruins of Empire: The Revolt Against the West and the Remaking of Asia*. N. Y., 2013.

[47] *Sources of Chinese Tradition: From 1600 Through the Twentieth Century*, compiled by William De Bary and Richard Lufano. Vol. 2. N. Y.: Columbia University Press, 2000. P. 322.

[48] Jawaharlal Nehru, *An Autobiography*. Oxford University Press, 1989. PP. 470-471.

[49] Ibid. P. 608.

The colonial powers were creaking at the seams everywhere, even in the places where there were no Japanese. The creator of modern Singapore, Lee Kuan Yew, would write: "My colleagues and I are of the generation of young men who went through the Second World War and the Japanese Occupation and emerged determined that no one – neither the Japanese nor the British – had the right push and kick us around. We are determined that we could govern ourselves and bring up children in a country where we can be proud to be self-representing people."[50] Japan lost the war, but by now it was impossible to restore colonial rule in Asia.

Throughout Asia, the eruption of liberation movements was preceded by extremely active nationalist agitation, aimed at consolidating the extremely fragmented, multi-ethnic, multi-faith societies that existed in all the Asian colonial and semi-colonial countries. The next stage was revolutions, which were led by nationalist and left-wing forces. In 1947, the British fled from India in a state of semi-panic, though not before separating Pakistan from India, a catastrophic event for South Asia. Burma was liberated in 1948. In 1949, the forces of Sukarno drove the Dutch out of East India, and the United States of Indonesia was created – a federation of 15 states, which became the Republic of Indonesia one year later. Malaysia and Singapore rose up against British rule. Revolution triumphed in China.

"From its zenith at the beginning of the twentieth century, Europe's hold over Asia would dramatically weaken; by 1950, with India and China already sovereign states, Europe would be reduced to a peripheral presence in Asia, shored up only by the newest Western power, the United States, and increasingly dependent on an informal empire constituted by military bases, economic pressures and political coups," writes Mishra.[51]

In 1951, the president of Iran, Muhammad Mossadegh, interrupted applause at the UN to talk about the nationalization of British oil companies, and, recalling that the Second World War had "changed the map of the world", said: "In the neighbourhood of my country, hundreds of millions of Asian people, after centuries of colonial exploitation, have now gained their independence and freedom. […] Iran demands that right."[52] In two

....

[50] Cit. from: Eri Hotta, *Pan-Asianism and Japan's War 1931-1945*. Palgrave Macmillan, 2007. P. 218.

[51] Pankaj Mishra, *From the Ruins of Empire: The Revolt Against the West and the Remaking of Asia*. N. Y., 2013. P. 7.

[52] Christopher De Bellaigue, *Patriot of Persia: Muhammad Mossadegh and a Very British Coup*. Random House, 2012. P. 179.

years' time, Mossadegh was overthrown as a result of an Anglo-American "color revolution".

The Cold War relocated to Asia, and the symbol of this was the creation, under the auspices of the USA, of the South-East Asian Treaty Organization (SEATO), in 1954. The Indian Prime Minister, Jawaharlal Nehru, described this act as "a unilateral proclamation of a kind of Monroe doctrine in relation to the countries of South-East Asia." Nehru, together with the president of Indonesia, Sukarno, were the initiators of the Bandung Conference in 1955.

At the heart of the Bandung declaration lay the idea of a joint struggle by the countries of Asia, Africa, and Latin America against Western imperialism and colonialism, which became the basis of the ideology of the Non-Alignment Movement, created at the same time. The spirit of Asian unity was also demonstrated in support for the Indonesian concept of Pancha Shila, which was roughly transformed into five principles for peaceful co-existence. A realization of the fact that the rise of the national-liberation movement, and the unambiguous support for it on the part of the Soviet Union, was depriving the West of moral leadership, forced the United States to start adopting an anti-colonial stance (which was reflected during the Suez Crisis in 1956), and to begin overcoming racial discrimination within the USA itself.[53] From the early 1960s onwards, the Afro-Asian bloc of states has determined the outcome of votes at the UN.

Independence did not come easily to the Asian states; they all experienced economic and political shocks. The goal set by Nehru, Mao Tse-tung, Ho Chi Minh and Sukarno – to catch up with the Western countries as quickly as possible – proved a rather distant one. The tasks facing the idealistic elites of the new countries, who were utterly inexperienced in matters of governance, were serious: consolidating their territory, finding money for the industrialization of the economy, creating a tax system, conducting land reform, building roads, creating a parliament and parties, building an army and a state apparatus, forming a national identity in a multi-ethnic society, writing laws, launching education and healthcare systems. All manner of political models were tried out: socialism in China and North Vietnam, parliamentary democracy in India, a secular state allied to the USA in Turkey. The Asian countries met with disappointment for at least three decades, however, with the exception once again of Japan, which rose rapidly with American assistance.

---

[53] Mark Mazower, *Governing the World. The History of an Idea*. Allen Lane, 2013. PP. 258-261.

Whichever system was adopted, however, it was inserted into the local cultural matrix, and an orientation towards the USSR or the USA did not mean automatic agreement with their policies, and servility. "Notably," writes the historian Ramachandra Guha, from Bangalore, "while classical Marxist theory disparaged nationalist sentiments, Communist regimes in Asia were deeply nationalist. In both China and Vietnam, the ruling Communists partook of a deep sense of national and even civilizational pride. The interests of one's country were usually placed above that of socialist (or proletarian) internationalism."[54] The West's Asian allies were in no hurry to become involved in their military operations in the region. A large number of Asian states preferred to remain in the paradigm of consistent non-alignment.

Asia asserted itself with particular vigor in 1973, when key oil-producing countries in the Middle East – Saudi Arabia, Kuwait, Qatar, Abu-Dhabi, Dubai, Bahrain, and also Libya and Algeria – announced a reduction in oil extraction and imposed an embargo on supplies of oil to the USA, in response to Washington's support for Israel in its war against Egypt and Syria, after which the age of cheap oil in the world came to an end.

The next phase of growth in Asian self-consciousness began with the Japanese "economic miracle" and the emergence of the "Asian tigers" (Hong Kong, Singapore, South Korea and Taiwan), which demonstrated an ability to move from an agrarian, developing economy to the level of advanced industrial states within a single generation. They were followed by other countries, including the two giants of Asia – China and India. This was seen as evidence of the superiority of their own model, and the effectiveness of returning to their Asian origins.

It has already become commonplace to refer to the current century as the Asian century. People in the West would be shocked if they found out how deeply held and powerful anti-Western feeling is, and millions "derive profound gratification from the prospect of humiliating their former masters and overlords."[55] This does not bring Mishra himself much joy, though, since there is at present no convincing, universal answer to Western ideas in politics and economics.[56]

....

[54] Ramachandra Guha, "The Politics Behind the Economics of Asia's Rise", in *Makers of Modern Asia*, ed. by Ramachandra Guha. Harvard University Press, 2014. P. 7.

[55] Pankaj Mishra, *From the Ruins of Empire: The Revolt Against the West and the Remaking of Asia*. Penguin, 2013. P. 295.

[56] Ibid.

In many countries, liberation from Western colonialism led to the development of what a researcher from Stanford, Majari Miller, who tracked the experiences of China and India, has dubbed a "post-imperial ideology". It incorporates the "collective trauma" of a victim who suffered unjustly, a desire for this fact to be recognized by others, and a desire not to be in the position of a victim again. Hence, a hypertrophied desire to maximize territorial sovereignty and status, and a marked sense of national pride and respect for one's own culture and historic legacy.[57]

Asian Community

What does the Asian code look like today? For the most general definition of the differences between contemporary Asian and Western values, I shall turn to Jörgen Möller, who identified three basic ones: less of a focus on money, social status and social stratification; a more balanced relationship between man and nature; and different ideas about what governs society – values or the law. Culture, and social and moral traditions, had and still have greater significance than legal norms, institutions and ideologies.[58]

There are significant differences at the individual level, too. To put it briefly, in European culture, "the individual is assessed as a whole, its actions in various situations are considered as a manifestation of one and the same essence. As for the Chinese, though, for example, they avoid appraisals of a person as a whole, dividing his behavior into isolated areas, each of which has its own laws and standards of behavior. In European society, a person's behavior is explained by motives… whereas in China, by general rules and norms. In the East, people are more introverted."[59]

The Asian code also incorporates certain demographic characteristics. Traditions of a strong family are ubiquitous, although they are also diverse in different cultural areas. In South Asia, marriages take place at an early age and are preceded by an engagement; the man's role is a dominant one, and the extended family is important. In East Asia, where the husband is also the head of the family, the nuclear family plays the central role. In Islamic

---

[57] Majari Ch. Miller, *Wronged by Empire: Post-Imperial Ideology and Foreign Policy in India and China*. Stanford University Press, 2013. PP. 20, 135.

[58] Jörgen Ostrom Möller, *How Asia Can Shape the World: From the Era of Plenty to the Era of Scarcities*. Singapore, 2011. P. 59.

[59] *Vvedeniye v vostokovedeniye* (*An Introduction to Oriental Studies*), ed. by Ye. I. Zelenev and V. B. Kasevich. St. Petersburg, 2011. P. 168.

countries, polygamy is permitted, and women are not always able to choose their own spouse. A notable exception is provided by the Islamic countries of South-East Asia, where, on the whole, women have broader rights than anywhere else in the East. In South Asia and China, almost 98% of men and women get married, whereas in the West, a quarter of people over 30 are still single, and half of all marriages end in divorce. In Japan, only 2% of children are born outside of wedlock, whereas in Sweden the figure is 55%, and in Iceland 66%. In East Asia, however, the same trends are starting to be seen as in the West: people are getting married later and less often, and divorces are becoming more common. These changes are related, above all, to the increased level of education and wealth among women, and the fact that they have employment outside the family home.[60]

What about demographic challenges? According to a report by the IMF, population growth in Asia is set to fall to zero by 2050, while the number of people aged 65 and over will grow by two and a half times. Some believe that Asia will get old before it gets rich.[61]

Let's start to describe Asia from the East. It should be said that with reference to East Asia, there is reason to speak of a cultural and civilizational unity, at the basis of which lay, first and foremost, the Chinese tradition. "China, thanks to the scale and ancient nature of its cultural traditions, was, in this historico-cultural region, the source of practically all cultural, scientific and technical innovations," notes the orientalist N. A. Samoilov. "The main philosophical and religious systems arrived in the other countries of East Asia either from China or through it."[62]

It is a region of hieroglyphic character-based writing, which for centuries was the source of communication in East Asia. The Chinese, Korean, Japanese and Vietnamese languages are utterly unlike one another, but educated speakers of these languages understand one another, interacting "with the help of the brush". Chinese characters were brought to Japan by Buddhist monks from the Korean Kingdom of Baekje, and they are used to this day in addition to two alphabets which were invented later. Korea and Vietnam adopted alphabets long ago, but hieroglyphic characters are still used in

....

[60] "The Flight From Marriage", *The Economist*, August 20, 2011. PP. 17-20.

[61] Enda Curran, "Parts of Asia Will Grow Old Before Getting Rich, IMF Warns", *Bloomberg*, May 9, 2017 <https://www.bloomberg.com/news/articles/2017-05-09/parts-of-asia-will-grow-old-before-getting-rich-imf-warns>.

[62] *Vvedeniye v vostokovedeniye (An Introduction to Oriental Studies)*, ed. by Ye. I. Zelenev and V. B. Kasevich. St. Petersburg, 2011. P. 396.

these countries, forming a connection to their classical culture. According to the beliefs of the East Asian peoples, culture is to be found primarily in writing, as the guardian of centuries-old traditions. Today, practically one in four people on the planet understands and uses hieroglyphics to some extent. It would seem that the Internet, too, with its unifying hieroglyphics, is creating fresh impulses for cultural unity.

In none of the countries of East Asia has the state been combined with, or even drawn closer to, the church, as happened in Europe, Byzantium, and the Islamic countries, and indeed the Church, in the canonical understanding of this word, did not feature in the East-Asian region. The states were sacrosanct in and of themselves, and had no need for legitimacy on the part of the Church. The system of religious syncretism, combined with local cults and beliefs, and the particularly esteemed cult of the ancestors, established the main cultural and ethno-psychological characteristics. "As a counterweight to the West, which differentiates sharply between the human and the divine, the Far East does not know this difference," notes Braudel. "A religious aspect permeates all forms of human life: the state is religion, philosophy is religion, morals are religion, social relations are religion. All these forms are related to the sacred. Hence their trend towards immutability, towards eternity."[63]

The increased focus on education is attributable to the Confucian emphasis on education open for all, as well as on practical experience as a resource for the development of the individual ("self-perfection") and society, in their mutual dependency. The level of literacy in a country such as Korea – where the Confucian tradition lives on in its purest form – was simply outstanding, long before the Japanese colonization and the reforms in Japan itself. Even today, East Asian countries are at the top of the global rankings for the level of education.

The concept that has developed of "East Asian values" usually includes a strong, paternalistic and illiberal state; a centralized, fiercely hierarchical bureaucracy; respect for the traditional mainstays, aimed at maintaining agreement and social harmony as a counterweight to differences and confrontation; collectivism, the notion of prioritizing collective rights over individual ones; subordination to the authority of a group; the family as the optimum model for the organization of society; a powerful clan-based system; discipline, hard work and caution; respect for one's elders, which

---

[63] Fernand Braudel, *Grammatika tsivilizatsiy* (*Grammar of Civilizations*). Moscow, 2008. P. 183.

include those in power; prioritizing social harmony over conflict; bowing down before education and knowledge; patience and caution.⁶⁴

East Asia is the site of the development of a model for modernization which is seen not as Westernization, but as a special path of development, founded on a synthesis of a sort of democracy and the local political culture. The Asian democracies may differ considerably from the European and American models, but they are still democracies. They are no "better" and no "worse", they are simply "different", and they are perhaps better equipped to solve their own political problems.⁶⁵

Characteristic of this model is the initial creation of an economic basis and the legitimate introduction of economic liberalism, then a gradual and at the same time brutal introduction of market principles, then a gradual democratization depending on the society's ability to "digest" political change. In all the countries of East Asia that have achieved economic flourishing, the forms and speed with which this took place varied, but the models remained unchanged.

This did not depend greatly on the political system, incidentally. In India, a Westminster-style parliamentary model exists side by side with the caste system; in Sri Lanka, a Buddhist state co-exists with democracy; in Malaysia, the special role of Islam co-exists with the syncretic ideology of "panca sila"; in Singapore, there are restrictions on certain freedoms and a dominant leader; in China, there is China-ized Marxism, inter-party democracy, elections at the local level, and a Confucian elite; in Vietnam, there is a Chinese-Confucian model with a Soviet political system.

The Prime Minister of Malaysia, Mahathir, expressed an attitude towards democracy that was fairly typical: "Democracy is a good system, but it has its weaknesses. You must understand the workings of democracy to make it work. […] [S]ome people seem to think that if you go to war and make such-and-such country a democratic country [U.S. in Iraq], you'll solve all their

....

⁶⁴ See, for example: *"Asian Values" and Democracy in Asia*, ed. by Takashi Inoguchi. Tokyo, 1997; Konstantin Asmolov, "Aziatskiye tsennosti kak doroga k progressu" ("Asian Values as a Road to Progress", *Rossiya v global'noy politike* (*Russia in Global Affairs*), March/April 2017 <https://globalaffairs.ru/articles/aziatskie-czennosti-kak-doroga-k-progressu/>.

⁶⁵ A. D. Voskresenskiy, "Sravnitel'nyy analiz politicheskikh sistem, politicheskikh kul'tur i politicheskikh protsessov na vostoke: obshchiye zakonomernosti i spetsifika ikh regional'noy transformatsii" ("A Comparative Analysis of Political Systems, Political Cultures and Political Processes in the East: General Patterns and Specificity of Their Regional Transformation"), in *Politicheskiye sistemy i politicheskiye kul'tury Vostoka* (*Political Systems and Political Cultures of the East*), ed. by A. D. Voskresenskiy. Moscow, 2006. PP. 20-25, 28-29.

problems. It's the wrong thing to do. People must understand democracy before they accept democracy, because there is a limit to freedom. There is no absolute freedom for anyone."[66]

Fareed Zakaria had observed: "East Asia today is a mixture of liberalism, oligarchy, democracy, capitalism, and corruption – much like the West in, say, 1900."[67] I don't think the West today is much different.

---

[66] Tom Plate, *Giants of Asia: Doctor M: Operation Malaysia. Conversations with Mahathir Mohamad.* Singapore, 2011. P. 97.

[67] Fareed Zakaria, *The Future of Freedom: Illiberal Democracy at Home and Abroad.* W. W. Norton & Company, 2007. P. 57.

CHAPTER 7
THE CHINESE PARTY

China is the most ancient of all the world's civilizations, with a history that stretches back 5000 years. The last couple of centuries, which were unsuccessful for the country, are seen there as a mere blip in the nation's history.

Henry Kissinger wrote: "No other country can claim so long a continuous civilization, or such an intimate link to its ancient past and classical principles of strategy and statesmanship. Other societies, the United States included, have claimed universal applicability for their values and institutions. Still, none equals China in persisting – and persuading its neighbors to acquiesce – in such an elevated conception of its world role for so long, and in the face of so many of historical vicissitudes."[1]

They say that the price of a millennium is not high in China.

The Shang-Yin and the Zhou

Sinanthropus pekinensis – "Peking Man" – lived on the territory of Northern China half a million years ago. Some enthusiasts put the starting date of Chinese history at 8 millennia BC, for the first archeological finds providing evidence of the remains of a civilization date to this period. The Chinese mythological tradition and modern science are more modest, estimating that the civilization emerged in the 3rd millennium BC, when a traditional calendar, a religious cult, a system of prophesying, and a social organization came into being.

In ancient times, China's territory was delineated by the middle and lower courses of two great rivers, the Yellow River and the Yangtze, with a gentle, warm and moist climate and fertile soils that were easy to till. Nature itself made it possible to provide food for a large number of people. When the

---

[1] Henry Kissinger, *On China*. Penguin, 2012. P. 2.

Bronze Age arrived, sophisticated artefacts from which have been dated to the second half of the 2nd millennium, certain aspects of the Chinese mentality start to take shape. The Sky went from being a supreme deity, like the Earth, to a natural being, to be respected rather than worshipped. To rebel against the Sky or the Earth was not so much sacrilege as a nonsensical pursuit. Man's moral imperative consisted in obeying divine commands, sent down in response to prayers, in understanding the law in a manner compatible with life in the world, and abiding by it. The search for this law and for man's place in the world lay at the heart of morality.

The new cultural phenomena that accompanied the transition from the Neolithic age to the Bronze Age are ascribed by Chinese tradition to such civilizing heroes as Yu the Great or Huang-di (the Yellow Emperor). Archeologists have uncovered a host of Neolithic cultures in Henan and in the south of Hebei, which may correspond to the first – semi-mythical – Xia dynasty, traditionally said to have lasted from 2207-1766 BC. Chinese civilization per se, with a clear sense of authentic identity, begins in the 18th century BC, a period traditionally seen as the start of the Shang dynasty. It was then that the main technical achievements of the Chinese appeared – horse-drawn battle chariots and literacy. In this epoch, a paternalistic empire emerged, creating a societal model analogous to the family model, and we see a division between the aristocracy living in the cities and the ordinary people living off the land. The empire's "familial" structure was supplemented by the absence of clergy in the strict sense of the word: the emperor himself, like the father of the family, addresses the spirits.[2]

The Chinese realm in the Shang era (the 18th – 12th centuries BC) was a system of city-states – military and religious centers, in which the nobility lived. The number of political entities gradually decreased – from several thousand in the Xia era to 1,200 by the end of the Shang era, and seven by the time of the Warring States.[3]

The Warring States period (475-221 BC) was marked by constant wars, which led to the emergence of a regular infantry, the invention of the crossbow and the catapult (5th century BC), and the creation of cavalry divisions (in the 4th century BC). Duels fought to defend honor – battles between noble warriors in chariots – gave way to battles between armies containing several hundred thousand men, in which the peasants made up the bulk

---

[2] Ivan Kamenarovich, *Klassicheskiy Kitay* (*Classical China*). Moscow, 2014. PP. 10-16.

[3] Kwang-chih Chang, *Art, Myth, and Ritual: The Path to Political Authority in Ancient China.* Cambridge, 1983. PP. 26-27.

of the soldiers. The mass cavalry developed, under the influence of those terrifying archers on horseback, the Huns, and in order to do battle against them. As a result of this, horsemen were never a noble class in China – by contrast with Europe – and they were recruited from among the peasantry, and were often of barbarian descent. And generally, by contrast with the archaic epoch, military matters began to be seen as the domain of the ordinary people. The new form of war called for focused command, highly-trained warriors, and countless reservists. Campaigns became more distant and long-drawn-out, and the art of strategy developed. The manuals of Sun Bin and Sun Tzu are still seen as important for military strategy today.

Soldiers began to take their orders not from rulers and their ministers, representing noble families, as had been the case in the past, but from professional generals. Reforms to state management were oriented towards fierce centralization. A custom was established whereby administrative units were put under the control of replaceable civil servants, who submitted detailed reports on their activities each year. Thus a professional bureaucracy was born.

The Chu and Qi kingdoms, in the 5th century BC, were the first to build defensive walls on their borders. In the next century, other kingdoms followed suit. Some of the walls protected against incursions by neighboring kingdoms, while others were designed to fend off invasions by marauding nomads from Mongolia and Manchuria. Once the walls had been extended westwards to southern Gansu and eastwards to Liaodong Bay, they formed a continuous defensive line with a length of over 3,000 km. These reinforcements were installed some distance to the north of the wall that was built in the 15th century during the Ming dynasty, substantial portions of which have survived to this day.

The wars required the rapid development of artisan crafts and agricultural production. Craftsmen's workshops depended on the palace; there were no free trades. Income from the exploitation of minerals and wood went into the state coffers. Large-scale irrigation works began, along with the construction of canals. As in the case of the walls, this involved the presence of powerful state structures, capable of mobilizing a large, disciplined workforce. Wars, which blurred state borders, led to the development of trade and the proliferation of metal coins, which first appeared around 500 BC. The development of commerce was also facilitated by written trade contracts. In the 4th and 3rd centuries BC, the merchant class took shape and, accordingly, a mindset based on calculation, far-sightedness and cunning emerged.

Confucianism, Taoism, Legism and the Empire

From the 7th to the 3rd centuries BC, in the period that Karl Jaspers called the Axial Age (*Achsenzeit*), tempestuous processes took place throughout the whole of the then civilized world, whereby elites were crystallized, and great philosophical, political and religious systems were born.[4] This was the age of Buddha, Plato, and Aristotle. In China, the most remarkable figure in the epoch of the "divided states" was Confucius (circa 551-479 BC).

Confucius was filled with moral principles that were respected by the nobility: moderation, respect for rituals, and loyalty to ancient traditions, which were preserved by the ancient fiefdoms of the Great Chinese flatlands. His teaching was based on five major formulae. First: leadership. The model man is a ruler – not an impetuous and dim-witted aristocrat, but an educated, balanced, well brought-up man, who thinks through his actions and words, which must express the reality acknowledged by everyone. Second: kindness towards living beings, founded on the foregoing; third: governance, founded on respect; fourth: an order to things that is conditioned by the rhythms of ceremonies; fifth: putting the principles of morality into action.[5]

Confucius's sayings are a good example of inductive logic. When things and phenomena are correctly classified, knowledge becomes sufficiently deep. When knowledge becomes sufficiently deep, undertakings and ambitions become sincere. When undertakings and ambitions are sincere, the heart is purified. Once the heart is purified, the personality is perfected. Once the personality is perfected, order and unanimity is established in the family. Once order and unanimity are established in the family, the state is in good order. Once the state is in good order, the Celestial Empire is at peace.

Confucius did not dwell on abstract concepts such as freedom and justice, focusing instead on the debts and obligations of a man, thanks to the discharge of which man merges harmoniously with the family, society and the state. A famous principle of Confucian thought is the following: "Preserve harmony, irrespective of differences."

Another extremely important trend in thought for the Chinese civilization was Taoism – the teachings about the Great Absolute, Tao. The founder of this teaching is considered to be Lao Tzu, who supposedly lived at the same time as Confucius (though it is not beyond the bounds of pos-

---

[4] See: Karl Jaspers, *The Origin and Goal of History*. Routledge, 1953. PP. 1-21.

[5] Danielle Elisseeff, *Istoriya Kitaya: Korni nastoyashchego* (*The History of China: Roots of the Present*). St. Petersburg, 2008. PP. 36, 39-40.

sibility that he was a mythical character, created later). The Taoists called on people to follow the Absolute, to become one with nature and avoid all that is artificial, deliberate, opposed to the natural. One of the principles of the Taoists was the concept of non-doing, the ability to build one's life in such a way that it follows the right path without the active interference of man, whether with regard to nature, people, or even state governance, and the ideological origins of anarchism or even liberalism have been seen as stemming from this. Over time – in the Han era – philosophical Taoism was transformed into religious Taoism, with the search for immortality, divine beings, heroes, fortune-telling and predictions. The Taoists and the schools of natural philosophers, which were similar to them, devised the idea of yin and yang, which is essentially about the contrasting and the constant beneficial interaction of the male (the yang) and female (yin) origins.

The Taoist school was opposed by the realistic theoreticians of the state – the legists. Order ought to be based on benefit and fear, and not on morals. There should be no reliance on the noblemen, inclined towards unrest, but the creation of a smoothly operating bureaucratic machine, precise instructions, the performance of which is well rewarded, and warnings, failure to heed which is harshly punished. The works of the legalist Han Fei are strongly reminiscent of the reasoning of Machiavelli in *The Prince*. Legism became the doctrine that most accurately reflected the imperatives of creating a centralized state.

The doctrine inspired Qin Shi Huang, who, in the 3rd century BC, created, through blood and steel, the Chinese Empire. He did not reign for long, but the administrative structure of the Chinese world and its state infrastructure had been established once and for all. Qin Shi Huang not only bequeathed China an empire, he also gave it one of its names. It is commonly thought that the name China came into being in Europe initially thanks to the silk fabrics from the Qin Empire. The Chinese referred to themselves, however, as the Han. 92% of the population of today's China consider themselves to be Han. This word comes from the Han dynasty (206 BC to 220 AD), which was the successor to the Qin dynasty.

"China was the first world civilization to create a modern state," writes Francis Fukuyama.[6] "During the Qin and Han dynasties, China developed a common culture in addition to creating a strong state. [...] But there was a strong feeling that China was defined by a shared written language, a clas-

---

[6] Francis Fukuyama, *The Origins of Political Order. From Prehuman Times to the French Revolution.* Profile Books, 2011. P. 150.

sical literary canon, a bureaucratic tradition, a shared history, empirewide educational institutions, and a value system that dictated elite behavior at both the political and social levels."[7]

In the 1st century BC, Buddhism began to move into China and India, via Central Asia. Buddhism turned out to be the only form of teaching from a foreign land (before communism) that not only took root in China, but also became an integral part of its civilization. This was helped by the fact that it was similar to Taoism. The first Chinese Buddhists were former Taoists; Taoist terms and concepts were used by Buddhist monks as the Chinese equivalents that were needed during the translation of ancient texts from Pali and Sanskrit into Chinese. From the 3rd century onwards, the term "the three teachings" began to be used in Chinese literature with reference to Confucianism, Taoism and Buddhism. A Chinaman striving to be a Confucian in public life remained a Taoist at least a little bit in his soul, while not forgetting to perform Buddhist rituals. Even today, one might come across a temple that houses a statue of Buddha, an altar to the Taoist gods, and a statue of the almost deified Confucius.

That said, Confucianism was utterly dominant in the field of state governance and in the system of regulating relations in society, in ethics, morality, and family relations. The ministry of ranks, guided by the principles of Confucius and the legists, built a strong and durable system for preparing and appointing civil servants. In the Tang era (617-907), a unified principle of competition was established once and for all, founded on a system of exams, in order to pass which one had to know the canons of Confucianism and the works of the ancient authors, and demonstrate erudition, literary taste and the ability to compose poetry. Those who achieved the best results were permitted to take an exam at a higher level, opening the way to better career opportunities.

China has long been a leader in scientific knowledge, having given the world paper, book-printing, astronomical and mechanical clocks, along with countless works on agriculture, architecture, the art of war, pediatrics, acupuncture and pharmacology. In 1014, a vaccine against smallpox was invented. Discoveries which changed the face of the planet were made in the Sun era (960-1279): the compass and powder. Under the Emperor Yongle (Zhu Di), in the 14th and 15th centuries, 2,000 academics worked on a description of the whole of human knowledge, which ultimately filled 11,000 volumes. This work remained the most voluminous encyclopedic

---

[7] Ibid. P. 149.

work on the planet for six centuries, right up until 2007, when Wikipedia overtook it in size.[8]

Yongle arranged several maritime expeditions led by a eunuch from a Muslim family, Zheng He. In the last of these, 27,000 men and 63 ships were involved, and on the flagship alone there were more than a thousand people (the crew of Columbus' *La Nina* was 24 sailors). The flotillas reached Champa (in the south of present-day Vietnam), Sumatra, Malacca, Ceylon, India, Hormuz, and East Africa (Mogadishu). Not having received any information about the existence anywhere else of a higher civilization than the Chinese one, the emperors deemed it nonsensical to spend money on seafaring, and the expeditions came to an end. And that was at a time when Europeans were only just beginning to undertake such voyages.

The Manchurian Qing dynasty, which ruled from the mid-17th century, was the last. Odd Arne Westad of the London Economic Institute has written: "The coffers were emptying out, the military was tired of engagements abroad, and the population was becoming weary of the police state that was less and less effective."[9] The Manchurian nobility wove interminable intrigues at court, along with the most senior Han civil servants and the eunuchs. Meanwhile, the Europeans were by now at the gates, offering narcotics (by the 1830s, the British were smuggling more than 30,000-40,000 cases every year). The Emperor tried to resist the poisoning of the people, by banning imports of opium, but, after losing the "opium war", China was forced to open five ports for the British.[10] And that was only the beginning of the colonizing of the country.

China turned out to not be ready to respond to the geopolitical challenge laid down by the West. The organization of armed resistance as the *raison d'être* of the Empire was not something that came naturally to Qing China, and this explained its defeat and the inefficient system of countering foreign expansion throughout the whole of the 19th century and the early 20th century.[11]

---

[8] Niall Ferguson, *Civilization: The West and the Rest*. Penguin, 2011. P. 22.

[9] Odd Arne Westad, *Restless Empire: China and the World since 1750*. Random House, 2012. P. 20.

[10] Jeremy Paxman, *Empire*. London, 2011. PP. 62-64.

[11] Dukhovnaya kul'tura Kitaya. Tom 4: Istoricheskaya mysl'. Politicheskaya i pravovaya kul'tura (*The Spiritual Culture of China*. Vol. 4: Historical Thought. Political and Legal Culture), ed. by M. L. Titarenko, A. I. Kobzev, A. Ye. Luk'yanov. Moscow, 2009. P. 194.

The Chinese Republic

The uprising by soldiers and officers in Wuchang on 10th October 1911 proved enough of a jolt for the Qing dynasty for it to collapse, and central government along with it. In the north of the country, Yuan Shikai, who was appointed prime minister in November, announced the convening of a China-wide parliament. In the south, Sun Yat-sen was elected temporary president of the Chinese Republic, with Nanking as its capital. On 12th February, 1912, the monarchy was officially abolished.

As had occurred numerous times before during crisis periods in China's history, the military came to the forefront, and it is with good reason that the period after the overthrowing of the monarchy came to be known as the "era of militarists". The temporary parliament alternated between being disbanded and reconvened. Sun Yat-sen, who created the Kuomintang party in 1913, was elected president, but then lost this post because the militarists did not want him in power. He was given support by the USSR, which helped with the forming of armed forces. In 1925, the government of the South, which was led by Sun's successor, Chiang Kai-shek, proclaimed itself a National Government and declared the start of a war for the unification of the country, undertaking the victorious Northern Expedition. Its power was gradually recognized by all the political forces, except for the Communists, who became the Kuomintang's main adversaries.

In 1931, Japan seized Manchuria, where it created the puppet state of Manchukuo, led by the last Emperor Pu Yi. Then came the attack on Shanghai and the occupation of the whole of Northern China. In 1937, the Japanese began their occupation of the East coast of China. Even before the start of the Second World War, more than ten million Chinese had been killed. Chiang Kai-shek relocated to the West – to Chongqing – and led the resistance against Japan, inviting the armed forces of the Communist Party of China, which were based near the border with the USSR, to be his ally. Initially, the Communists agreed to the creation of a unified anti-Japanese front, but when Mao Tse-tung came to power in the Communist Party, there was a series of changes to the general stance, and the Communists preferred to do battle against the Japanese separately. When the USSR declared war on Japan in August 1945 and occupied Manchuria, the armaments and stockpiles of the Kwantung Army, which had surrendered to it, helped the Communist party, as did Soviet military instructors. After the Communists' victory in 1949 and the establishment of the People's Republic of China (PRC), forcing the Kuomintang, still led by Chiang Kai-shek, to flee to Taiwan, Mao received an invitation to visit the Kremlin. The "two Chinas" had come into being.

While the world kept track of Mao's social experiment and saw in it an attempt to force the country into communism, by contrast, within China itself this process was looked upon as a normal search for social justice, for a state of superior harmony, governed by a great, charismatic leader. The strategy was a pragmatic one: "Dig tunnels deep, store grain everywhere, and never seek hegemony."[12]

In just a few years, the People's Republic of China, with Soviet assistance, restored the economy, which had been destroyed by the wars, and achieved significant results. The annual growth of the economy during the first five-year plan was 16%-18%, and GDP more than doubled.[13] The autocracy created in the PRC was reminiscent of the Stalinist system of party-state governance. The two neighboring states were never able to establish smooth relations, however, primarily because of the personal enmity between Mao and Khrushchev and their rivalry over the minds of the global communist movement. Soon after the 20th Party Congress in the Soviet Union, which Mao saw as a betrayal of the global communist movement, he proclaimed the "Great Leap Forward". This set the goal of overtaking the Soviet Union in the matter of building a new life, on the basis of enthusiasm for labor and in strict conditions. To accelerate the process of industrialization, smelting of metal took place in almost every courtyard, although the peasants, deprived of land and property, became less active, and food reserves were consumed at the people's communes. Production was disorganized.

Fighting within the party intensified dramatically; one of the consequences of this was the Cultural Revolution, the slogan for which was "the fire at the headquarters". Many representatives of party bodies, the apparatus of power and the intelligentsia suffered persecution, and were sent to the countryside to be re-educated, while young brigades of *hongweibing* monitored the purity of the ranks. The Cultural Revolution, writes Mao's biographer Rana Mitter, was "the most extreme radical anti-Confucian elements" in the entire history of the PRC.[14]

....

[12] Gucheng Li, *A Glossary of Political Terms of the People's Republic of China*. Chinese University Press, 1995. P. 403.

[13] Alexander Pantsov, *Mao Tse-tung*. Moscow, 2007. PP. 562-563.

[14] Rana Mitter, "Mao Zedong and Charismatic Maoism", in *Makers of Modern Asia*, ed. by Ramachandra Guha. Harvard University Press, 2014. P. 108.

No Matter What Color the Cat Is

Mao's successors faced the problem of recovering from an economic dead-end: workers in China received a salary that was less than 1% of the salary of a worker in the USA or Japan. China was lucky in that the man at the helm of the country was in effect Deng Xiaoping, who had actively studied the works of the ideologue behind the Soviet New Economic Policy (NEP), Nikolay Bukharin. In December 1978, at the 3rd Plenum of the Central Committee, Deng gave a speech which proved to be the most important in the modern history of China. He announced that the regime must focus on economic development, and not on ideology. "It doesn't matter whether a cat is white or black, as long as it catches mice?" Since then, China has followed a path of pragmatic modernization. Unlike the Soviet Union, incidentally, where *perestroika* brought political relations and democratization to the forefront, Beijing chose to focus on economic liberalization, with the state institutions and traditions remaining untouched.

My first visit to China took place in 1994, as part of a parliamentary delegation. Back then, there were still hardly any cars in Beijing, and one saw great flows of people dressed in blue robes moving about on squeaky bicycles. Today, China manufactures more automobiles than any other country on Earth. China set a world record that will probably never be broken: for 33 years in a row – from 1978 to 2011 – its economy grew at a rate of over 10%.[15]

The reforms approved by the Plenum of the Central Committee in 1979 stipulated the winding up of the collective farms and the handing over of land to peasants for personal use, and the legalization of free trade. The role of state planning was restricted, and opportunities were created for the development of a cooperative and individual sector in industry, trade and services. State enterprises were provided with rights and opportunities to expand production and for the free sale of products from outside the plan, including overseas.

The market reforms in the PRC were aimed less at changing the forms of property than at maintaining sustainable economic growth. The peasantry not only ensured the stable development of agriculture, but also formed a market for consumer goods, making the first accumulation of capital possible, and also became a driving force in the process of urbanization (in 1978-1998, the population of the cities rose by an average of 14.5

---

[15] Hu Angang, *Embracing China's New Normal*, Foreign Affairs, May/June, 2015. P. 8.

million people a year). An influx of foreign investment into Shenzhen, Guangzhou and other special economic zones began. Large-scale changes began after Deng Xiaoping's southern tour in 1992, as well, when he was greatly impressed by Singapore, which had been poverty-ridden not so very long before.

Furthermore, the Chinese scrutinized the Soviet reforms which had led to the collapse of the USSR, so as not to repeat the mistakes that were made.

The term "privatization" was barely used in China, and indeed it effectively did not happen. Instead, the government allowed investors to create new companies, rather than to acquire assets which had once belonged to the state. There was not a shrinking of the public sector, but rather an expansion of the private sector. Chinese companies got the opportunity to invest in their own production. The market was opened up, and from 1979 through 2008, foreign corporations invested 852.6 billion dollars in the country's economy. Most of the skyscrapers and grandiose buildings which defined the look of the new China were built by foreign architects. When the time came to choose a director for the opening festival of the 2008 Olympic Games, Beijing opted to entrust the task to Steven Spielberg. In 1977, China accounted for 0.6% of world trade; now, China is the world's leader, and with 120 countries it does more trade than those countries do with the United States.[16]

The state has not removed itself from the economy. Really large private companies are few in number - Huawei, Shagang Group, Haier, Suning, Gome. The combined profits of the 500 biggest private firms are lower than the profits of the two major state companies – China Mobile and CNPC. Private business in the PRC, moreover, faces stiff competition from foreign companies, while state corporations are in many ways protected from it.[17]

China widely applied measures of state support for national producers: tax exemptions, direct subsidies, loans at discounted rates, and limits access to imported goods on the national market, both with the help of protective tariffs and through countless requirements for the certification of supplies. The highest duties – up to 65% – are applied in relation to agricultural products.[18]

---

[16] Ian Bremmer, "The China Decade", *Time*, August 31, 2015. P. 36.

[17] Feng Shaolei, "Privatizatsiya po-kitaysk" ("Privatization, Chinese style"), *Svobodnaya mysl'* (*Free Thought*), 2011, Issue 1. P. 79.

[18] Tat'yana Yedovina, "Kitayskiy rynok ne speshit otkryvat'sya" ("The Chinese Market is

For the state, growth is first and foremost about the construction of infrastructure. Between 1990 and 2009, the railway network grew by a factor of 1.47, the number of airports by 1.76, and the road network by a factor of 3.75. Since 2005, 132,500 km of general purpose roads have been built, along with 2200 km of railways and 190 new sea ports, not to mention airports and subway systems. China survived the economic crisis of 2007-2009 relatively unscathed, after allocating 600 billion dollars to stimulate the economy through the financing of ambitious infrastructural, industrial and social projects. There are 22,000 kilometers of high-speed railways in the country, more than in the rest of the world. China is rapidly catching up with America in terms of the number of skyscrapers, and is unrivalled in terms of the speed with which it is building residential housing, and in the quality and scale of the airports, bridges and motorways it is constructing. The biggest movement of people on the planet takes place when the Chinese New Year, which starts on 13th January, is celebrated.[19]

The huge net surplus in its trade with the USA has made China a holder of vast dollar reserves, which also became its vulnerable spot. From 2003 to 2010 alone, China lost more than 270 billion dollars due to the fall in the value of the American currency. To save itself from this "dollar damnation", Beijing backed a policy of buying up raw materials which were not yet in circulation by issuing credits – the borrowers are usually national governments or companies that are close to them – against guaranteed supplies of raw material in the long-term perspective. Deals like this were done in Venezuela, Turkmenistan, and Russia (multi-billion dollar loans to Rosneft and Transneft).[20] Another of the instruments with which China is replacing its dollar assets is gold, the volumes of which, in the official storage facilities in Beijing, have risen markedly in recent years.[21] The internationalization of the yuan is actively taking place.

It is worth reminding oneself that in 2014, China became the leading country in the world in terms of GDP (in PPP terms) The USA, though,

in no Hurry to Open up"), *Kommersant* (*The Businessman*), October 2, 2017 <https://www.kommersant.ru/doc/3427477>.

[19] "Infrastructure. Hunting White Elephants", *The Economist*, January 14, 2017. P. 28.

[20] Pavel Salin, "Pekinskiy pas'yans" ("The Beijing Solitaire"), *Rossiya v global'noy politike* (*Russia in Global Affairs*), Vol. 8, Issue 4, August 7, 2010 <https://globalaffairs.ru/number/Pekinskii-pasyans-14960>.

[21] Mikhail Overchenko, "Kitayu razonravilsya dollar" ("China no Longer Likes the Dollar"), *Vedomosti*, March 2, 2012 <https://www.vedomosti.ru/finance/articles/2012/03/02/kitayu_ne_nravitsya_dollar>.

still had an income per head of the population that was four times that of China, and in the UN's human development index, China is right down in 101st place.

"China's rise has changed the world already," writes Martin Wolf and David Pilling of *The Financial Times*. "By becoming the globe's low-cost factory, it has cut the cost of manufactured goods. That has increased consumers' purchasing power, although competition from hundreds of millions of Chinese workers may have lowered western wages in the process. As a huge importer of raw materials, China has begun to alter the fates of commodity exporters from Brazil to Australia and from Mongolia to Angola. If Africa's economy is finally stirring that is in no small measure due to Chinese demand."[22] Growth was secured not only by industry: the services sector's share of GDP in 2015 exceeded 50% for the first time.[23] China's Trade and Industry Bank (ICBC) was the most valuable banking brand in 2017, overtaking America's Wells Fargo. The world's top ten biggest banks also include China Construction Bank, Bank of China, and Agricultural Bank of China.[24]

In the club of high-tech companies with a market capitalization of over 400 billion dollars, American giants like Apple or Google have been joined by Alibaba Group and Tencent Holdings, who dominate the Chinese market and whose shares are worth twice as much as those of Intel, Cisco and IBM.[25]

China is advancing to assert technological leadership in critical fields of science and technology. L. Rafael Reif, the president of the Massachusetts Institute of Technology, thinks that "in fields from personal communications to business, health and security, China is likely to become the world's most advanced technological nation and the source of the most cutting-edge technological products in not much more than a decade."[26]

---

[22] Martin Wolf and David Pilling, "China: On Top of the World", *The Financial Times*, May 2, 2014 <https://www.ft.com/content/c355e0e6-d1d1-11e3-8ff4-00144feabdc0>.

[23] Mark Magnier, "As Growth Slows, China Highlights Transition From Manufacturing to Service; Attempt to stress the positive as manufacturing output falters", *The Wall Street Journal*, January 19, 2016 <https://www.wsj.com/articles/china-economic-growth-slows-to-6-9-on-year-in-2015-1453169398>.

[24] *Moskva-Pekin* (*Moscow-Beijing*), May-June 2017. P. 36.

[25] Paul Mozur, "The World's Biggest Tech Companies Are No Longer Just American", *The New York Times*, August 17, 2017 <https://www.nytimes.com/2017/08/17/business/dealbook/alibaba-sales-revenue-first-quarter-profit.html>.

[26] L. Rafael Reif, "China's Challenge Is America's Opportunity", *The New York Times*, August 8, 2018 <https://www.nytimes.com/2018/08/08/opinion/china-technology-trade-united-states.html>.

Just how sustainable is China's growth? Is it capable of continuing to play the role of the driver of the world economy? From the outside, and in a purely visual sense, China's forward growth appears unstoppable. The Chinese socio-economic model, however, is not without its weaknesses.

There is too much borrowing in the economy. A the start of 2017, corporations' debts – primarily state debt – amounted to 153% of GDP. The deficit in regional budgets has recently reached 5% of GDP every year.[27] In many ways this is linked to the fact that, given the excessive supply to the housing market (on Beijing's orders) of more than 200 cities in recent years, apartments have been bought up from developers in empty apartment blocks (and there are plenty of them in China's cities), with people from flimsy houses and from the villages being moved into them. The program helped rescue many construction companies from bankruptcy and supported prices in the property market, which provides up to a third of economic growth, but increased the debt burden still further.[28]

The Chinese market is gradually losing one of its main competitive strengths, in the shape of the low level of salaries. Average salaries have doubled every five years, though this rate of increase has slowed of late. Chinese employers are continually being forced to improve working conditions, bring in new benefits, and increase salaries. Losses resulting from social expenditure are also growing. China has never been known for its advanced social policy, and now it is moving on.

There is a stark problem of inequality, which is only getting worse. 70% of the wealth is in the hands of the richest 10% of citizens (in the USA, the figure stands at 80%).[29] In the lifetime of the current generation, the Gini coefficient in China has almost reached Latin American levels. The fruits of economic growth are more visible in the coastal regions, and vast agricultural territories remain in many ways "lost overboard". The gap in income per head of the population can be as much as seven times greater in one province than in another. A rapid stratification of society is taking place, with new classes and groups of entrepreneurs demanding additional rights and levers of influence, including political ones.

---

[27] Louis Kurys, "China Unlikely to See Financial Crisis", *China Daily*, June 6, 2017.

[28] Ibid.; Dominique Fong, "Chinese Cities Buy Off Housing Glut With Borrowed Money", *The Wall Street Journal*, October 13, 2017 <https://www.wsj.com/articles/chinese-cities-buy-off-housing-glut-with-borrowed-money-1507887001>; "China's Fiscal System. Muddled Model", *The Economist*, November 18, 2017. P. 13.

[29] "Inequality in China. The Great Divide of China", *The Economist*, February 18, 2017. P. 63.

Low consumption by households remains a problem for China: one third of GDP, which is half as much as in developed countries, and less than in developing ones. It appears that traditional Confucian morality, with its preaching of moderation in expenditure, still dominates people's consciousness.[30]

There has been an increase in the number of social protests and demonstrations, involving hired laborers, workers, farmers and students. The context of these protests is irritation with corruption, a lack of legal protection, and the opaque bureaucratic system. The protests are far more closely related to property, though. Land disputes and litigation over loss of land are becoming more and more serious and common, owing to a harsh policy of clearing sites to suit government requirements, and as a result of the activity of land speculators (half of the biggest fortunes in the country were made through deals involving land and real estate).

In spite of measures aimed at controlling the birth rate, including the one-child policy, the population continued to grow. By 2019 it had reached 1.40 billion people. The percentage of elderly people is increasing, too. In 2014, the number of people aged over 60 crossed the 200 million mark (more than 15%), and in another ten years it is expected to be 487 million.[31] 2012 saw the first ever fall in the number of people of working age (defined by the National Statistics Office as 15 to 64). The number of young people aged between 15 and 24 is predicted to fall by 21% in the next decade. The average age in the country was 22.1 in 1980, 35.4 in 2013, and in 2050 – according to a forecast by the UN – it will be 46.3. China's demographic dividend, associated with the constant flow of cheap manpower, is gradually disappearing. "China's transformation into the 'land of the silver-haired' without an influx of fresh young strength into the labor market is becoming dangerous for the Chinese economy, which, since the reforms were introduced, has relied on unlimited labor resources as one of its most important competitive strengths."[32] It was this that forced the country to reject the policy of restricting the birth rate in 2015. That was not enough, though, because parents are not in a hurry to have more children. As of 2018, officials are looking for ways "to stimulate a baby boom, worried that a looming demographic crisis could imperil economic growth".[33]

---

[30]   *Asia Business: Kitay*, Summer 2012. P. 9.

[31]   An Fu, "Strana dolgoletiya" ("The Land of Longevity"), *Dykhaniye Kitaya* (*The Breath of China*), October 2014. P. 38.

[32]   Igor' Denisov, "Uroki politicheskoy demografii" ("The Lessons of Political Demography"), *Rossiya v global'noy politike* (*Russia in Global Affairs*), Issue 6, November/December 2015. P. 201.

[33]   Steven Lee Myers and Olivia Mitchell Ryan, "China Pushes a Baby Boom", *The New York*

Incidentally, 47% of the population are still living in rural areas, which remains an essential source of additional manpower.[34]

Urbanization is, however, continuing. 500 million people have moved to the cities over the last three decades, the equivalent of the entire US population plus the UK population three times over. By 2030, there will be 1 billion people living in China's cities – one in every eight people on the planet.[35] This is leading, on the one hand, to a rise in internal demand, and on the other hand, to an increased need in the cities for resources of all kinds. Tension between migrants from the countryside and city-dwellers continues.

Yet for all that, the Chinese economic model is highly sustainable. Xi Jinping declared that at the next stage of development "the new normal" will consist of annual growth of around 7%, which in real terms will mean greater growth than during the period of 14% growth some years ago. State debt is concentrated inside the country, and it can be serviced thanks to the gold and currency reserves. The burden of the economy is shifting from investment to growing consumption, creating a powerful foundation for the economy.

Power as Maintaining Balance

In English, the concept of "power" (as in state power) is a word that also means strength, while in Russian the equivalent term, *vlast*, is derived from the word *vladeniye*, or "possession". The meaning of the character *quan* (power) in times of yore was "a scale for weights". It later started being used as a verb. "Rule and power in China is neither force nor possession, but the observance of moderation. 'Balance', and 'determine', 'take a decision' – these are the meanings that were acquired by this hieroglyph later. He who balanced had great power, i.e. was entitled to engage in balancing. Power is not something that is fixed forever, it comes in a dynamic state, in growth," writes the St. Petersburg-based sinologist Nikolay Speshnev.[36]

Times, International Edition, August 13, 2018. P. 1.

[34] An Fu, "Strana dolgoletiya" ("The Land of Longevity"), *Dykhaniye Kitaya* (*The Breath of China*), October 2014. PP. 38-39; "China's Population: Peak Toil", *The Economist*, January 26, 2013. PP. 48-49; Baozhen Luo, "China Will Get Rich Before it Grows Old", *Foreign Affairs*, May/June 2015. P. 19.

[35] "Where China's Future Will Happen", *The Economist*, April 19, 2014. P. 8.

[36] Nikolay Speshnev, Kitaytsy: Osobennosti natsional'noy psikhologii (*The Chinese: Peculiarities of the National Mindset*). St. Petersburg, 2011. PP. 114-116.

The PRC was established as a republic of the Soviet type, in which it was customary to have formal superiority of the representative bodies and the exercising of real powers by narrower groups of party leaders or executive structures. Soviet models still permeate all the pores of "socialism with Chinese specifics". The main executive functions belong to the CPC, whose governing role is enshrined in the Constitution. An important instrument for party influence is the practice of combining the posts of main director and secretary of the party committee, and the creation of party committees and "party leadership groups" within central and local state bodies, farming and cultural institutions, and non-governmental organizations. Since 2002, entrepreneurs have been entitled to join the party. In all commercial and non-commercial structures, even in firms that are 100% foreign-owned, party cells of the CPC have been created. Membership of the Communist party has reached 90 million people (the only other party that can rival these sorts of numbers is the ruling Bharata party in India, with its far more amorphous body of members). In recent times, however, the rate of growth in the ranks of the Chinese Communist party has slowed, as part of the drive to increase its qualitative component.[37]

The party exercises fairly strict control over the information space, the internet, and the many hundreds of television and radio stations which broadcast in the country. "China has sought to promote the concept of cyber sovereignty – in effect, formal acknowledgement of states' right to determine what information passes through their national networks."[38]

Formally, the Chinese national people's Congress is the highest governing institution. It functions as a parliament and heads the system of local representative institutions, which pass 30-40 times more laws than the NPC. Usually the head of the local party unit chairs the regional legislature. In addition to the CPC, eight more political parties exist, meaning that it is not essential to be a CPC member in order to have a political career.

Positions within the civil service are popular and held in esteem. The salaries are not huge, but people are attracted by the medical and pension insurance, paid leave, and housing benefits. The size of the state apparatus is still relatively small, though: 5.1 million people. In HR policy, the government stresses three areas: constant rotation of staff, with promotions; renewal of managerial staff, so that the time people can spend even in the top posts is precisely regulated; and devolution to

---

[37] "It's Not for Everyone. The Communist Party", *The Economist*, November 25, 2017. PP. 57-58.
[38] Nigel Inkster, *China's Cyber Power*. Routledge, 2018. P. 147.

regional and local governments (in the early 1980s, centralized income amounted up to 75% of the money coming into the budget, and it is now around half that figure).

One of the main problems faced by China is corruption. Under a resolution of the National People's Congress from 1995, civil servants must declare their income twice a year; they are obliged to declare their property and that of their relatives, and their loved ones cannot engage in entrepreneurial activity in spheres or in territories which are in any way under their control. In recent years, anyone found to have taken bribes of 10 million yuan (more than $1.4 m) or more has been given the death penalty.

Under Xi Jinping, the battle against corruption took on an incredibly broad scope. Among those arrested were the former minister of the railways, the former director of the Commission for national development and reforms, university rectors, editors-in-chief of newspapers, and regional party civil servants. These activities were favorably reflected in Xi's popularity ratings.[39] In the spring of 2018, a new anti-corruption ministry was created, which brought together state and party control over civil servants within the framework of a single structure.[40]

Xi Jinping, having become General Secretary in 2012 and subsequently, in March 2013, Chairman of the PRC, belongs to the category of "princes". During the Cultural Revolution, his father was dismissed from the post of deputy prime minister of the State Council and put in prison, and Xi himself was exiled to a remote village. He escaped, and was put in prison for having done so. He continued to educate himself, though, and tried to join the party nine times, before finally being accepted.[41]

At the 3rd Plenum of the CC, held in November 2013, a plan for the deepening of reforms until 2020 was approved, and two wholly new bodies were created: a Group for leading the deepening of reforms, and a Central Committee on State Security. Both were led by Xi Jinping. "This degree of concentrating of power in the hands of the leader can be compared to the similar transformations brought in by the leaders of the Kuomintang in the

---

[39] *Strategic Survey 2014: The Annual Review of World Affairs*. Routledge, 2014. PP. 315-318; James Leung, "Xi's Corruption Crackdown", *Foreign Affairs*, May/June 2015. P. 32.

[40] Mikhail Korostnikov, "Nadzor i partiya yediny" ("Supervision and Party are a Single Whole"), *Kommersant (The Businessman)*, October 31, 2017 <https://www.kommersant.ru/doc/3454766>.

[41] Aleksey Nikol'skiy, "Chego zhdat' ot novogo kitayskogo lidera" ("Xi Jinping: What to Expect from the New Chinese Leader"), *Vedomosti*, November 19, 2012 <https://www.vedomosti.ru/opinion/articles/2012/11/19/si_czinpin>.

1950s, after a heavy defeat on the continent," write Russian sinologists.⁴² Experts have commented upon the concentrating of powers in the hands of the head of state, unprecedented since the days of Mao, as well as Xi's powerful ideological appeal. Elizabeth Economy of the American Council on Foreign Affairs, wrote: "Chinese President Xi Jinping has articulated a simple but powerful vision: the rejuvenation of the Chinese nation. It is a patriotic call to arms, drawing inspiration from the glories of China's imperial past and the ideals of its socialist present to promote political unity at home and influence abroad."⁴³

In March 2015, at an assembly of the National People's Congress, the basic political concept for the 5th generation of Chinese leadership was approved; it was dubbed "the four all-encompassing aspects": building a society of moderate affluence, deepening the reforms, ensuring the primacy of law, and strengthening party discipline.⁴⁴

At the 19th Congress of the CPC in October 2017, Xi Jinping was re-elected as General Secretary. Since there was no room in the seven-person Standing Committee for a younger candidate in the role of successor, it is not beyond the bounds of possibility that Xi will wish to stay in office for longer than two five-year terms.

In the short-term, there are no grounds for predicting any kind of fundamental shifts in China's political system. Reforms are taking place by means of the internal modernization of the CPC. The protests in Hong Kong do not challenge the political stability and structure of the mainland.

The authorities in China are placing ever greater emphasis on the revival and strengthening of national traditions. By contrast with the days of the Cultural Revolution, when the "four old things" had to be overcome – old customs, culture, habits and ideas – today, young people in China are taking up calligraphy and traditional crafts, learning how to play ancient musical instruments, and studying Confucius. Xi is highlighting the continuity in the country's history, from ancient times right up to the present day. Ancient festivals are being recreated. Right across China, a plethora of new temples,

---

⁴² Ya. M. Berger, "Vsestoronneye uglubleniye reform v Kitaye" ("Comprehensive Intensification of Reforms in China"), in *Kitayskaya narodnaya respublika: politika, ekonomika, kul'tura: K 65-letiyu KNR (The People's Republic of China: Politics, Economics, Culture. To the 65th Anniversary of the PRC)*, ed. by M. L. Titarenko. Moscow, 2014. P. 133.

⁴³ Elizabeth C. Economy, "China's Imperial President Xi Jinping Tightens His Grip", *Foreign Affairs*, November/December 2014. P. 80.

⁴⁴ Xie Ping, "Chetyre aspekta odnoy sessii" ("Four Aspects of One Session"), *Dykhaniye Kitaya (The Breath of China)*, March 2015. PP. 14-15.

churches, and mosques are opening, and the number of people who profess a religion is growing exponentially.[45]

China is a country with multiple ethnicities. Officially, there are 56 ethnic minorities, though the real number is considerably higher. 120 million people are not Han Chinese: they are Mongols, Koreans, Kazakhs, Uighurs, and so on. Although Chinese thought has traditionally been based on the idea of the superiority of Chinese culture, nationalism is not systemic.[46] Having said which, ethnic separatism in Xinjiang and Tibet represents a serious problem.

After the fall of the empire, Tibet became an independent state, but the Communists, on coming to power, brought it back within China's sway. Tibet was given autonomy, and its former system of governance, led by the Dalai Lama, was preserved. The changes wrought by the Communists provoked an anti-Chinese uprising in 1959, which was crushed by the army, and the 14th Dalai Lama and his supporters fled to India, where they established a Tibetan government in exile. The 10th Panchen Lama, who stayed in Tibet, tried to cooperate with Beijing, but in 1964 he was sent to prison. The Tibetan autonomous district was created. During the Cultural Revolution, of the roughly 3000 monasteries, just three were left standing. Serious unrest broke out in Tibet in 1989. It was decided that negotiations with the Dalai Lama would be broken off, and all references to him would be prohibited.

Xinjiang, or Chinese Turkestan, is the most westerly Chinese province, separated from the rest of the country by the Gobi desert. Xinjiang became part of China in the late 19th century, but after that it rebelled. In 1949, Mao's forces annexed the province once and for all, but the Uighurs continued to riot (there are around eight million of them, and they account for 40% of Xinjiang's population, as do the Han Chinese). In recent years, the situation in Xinjiang has become extremely volatile on numerous occasions, and violence has broken out there, which Beijing suspects may have been organized by external forces, primarily the United States and Islamists. Huge amounts of money are being put into the development of Xinjiang and Tibet, so as to quell separatism. The army and police have a strong presence in these places.

Critics of China argue that repression of the mostly Muslim minority make Western Xinjiang look like "a massive internment camp". Beijing re-

---

[45] "Reviving Traditional Culture. Making History", *The Economist*, August 19, 2017. PP. 42-43; Ian Johnson, "China's Great Awakening. How the People's Republic Got Religion", *Foreign Affairs*, March/April 2017. P. 83.

[46] Gray Tuttle, "China's Race Problem", *Foreign Affairs*, May/June 2015. PP. 39, 41.

jects the allegations and say it is trying to stamp out religious extremism and sectarianism.[47]

The New Superpower

China's historic past inspires the Chinese leaders to try to turn the country into an influential, and in the long-run, a great, dominant and flourishing state. "To be Chinese still means to exhibit proper behavior and to be part of a civilization that has primacy in the world," writes the American researcher into the Chinese soul, Perry Link.[48] The country's leadership also wants to preclude the possibility of a repetition of the more than a century-long history of "humiliation by foreign states", which are subconsciously considered barbarian.

In China, by contrast with other countries in the APR, there is a clearly defined foreign policy strategy, which can be seen less in doctrinal documents than in specific actions. Since the early 1980s, China has conducted a policy that it calls "independent and self-sustained".

In the 1990s, Deng Xiaoping issued a statement consisting of 24 characters to the effect that in China's foreign policy, there was a need to "observe cold-bloodedly", "behave modestly", "not claim a leadership role", "wait things out in the shadows", "stand firmly on its feet", and so on.

A missionary approach to foreign policy is something that is alien to Beijing: it does not strive to establish its own ideology, system of governance, or ideas about morality in other countries.

China was extremely cautious in outlining its international ambitions. In 2003, the term "peaceful rise" emerged to describe its strategic objectives, which at the time was seen as too strong, and was replaced with "peaceful growth".

At the same time, among experts, there has been much discussion about the legacy of Deng Xiaoping: new hieroglyphic characters are needed, which might shake up the country's foreign policy principles. A rapidly growing demand for a more decisive foreign policy has also been seen on the Chinese Internet. Xi Jinping is far more determined than his predecessors.

In November 2014, the Chinese leader made a speech setting out his program, in which he described the country as a "major power". This term was

---

[47] Ciara Nugent, "China Accused of Detaining Millions in Crackdown on Ethnic Minority", *Time*, August 27, 2018. P. 7.

[48] Perry Link, "What It Means to Be Chinese", *Foreign Affairs*, May/June 2015. P. 25.

then included in official documents. In August to September 2017, a series of prime time TV programs were aired entitled "Great-Power Diplomacy". The main theme: Xi is the creator of a new foreign policy, which has brought China universal respect in the world: "great-power diplomacy with Chinese characteristics". The Foreign Minister Wang Yi stresses that Xi's thinking on foreign policy "blazed new trails and gone beyond traditional Western international-relations theory of the past 300 years."[49] At the 19th party congress, Xi Jinping said: "Whatever level of development China achieves, it will never lay claim to a position of hegemony."[50]

Today, China's armed forces are the biggest in the world. In 2018, their numbers stood at 2.035 million, of which ground forces constitute 975,000, the navy 250,000, the air force 395,000, and the strategic missiles forces 120,000; the rest are in the support services. The reserve, kept in battle-ready condition, stands at 660,000 people. The level of military spending since the start of the 21st century has grown faster than GDP, amounting to 168 billion dollars.[51]

The army enjoys great authority, and is able to recruit the best personnel; however, it is subject to fierce scrutiny by the CPC. "Our principle is that the party commands the rifle; it is utterly inadmissible for the rifle to command the party," said Mao Tse-tung.[52] Historically, the army has always been seen as backup and insurance of civil power.[53]

The Chinese army is energetically devising strategies by which it can undermine the USA's ability to send troops into the region (the strategy of "isolation of the area of military actions"). China has demonstrated an ability to destroy objects flying in low orbits, and this is creating a challenge to other countries' satellite architecture. In April 2015, Beijing carried out the first landing of armed forces in a country in the grip of war – Chinese Special Forces evacuated Chinese citizens from Aden, in Yemen. In September, it was announced that its first military base overseas was to be created – a supply point for the fleet in Djibouti. In December, the National People's

---

[49] "God's Gift. China Declares Itself a Global Power", *The Economist*, September 16, 2017. P. 49.

[50] Yekaterina Zabrodina, "Pekin bez pretenziy" ("Beijing Has No Complaints"), *Rossiyskaya Gazeta (Russian Newspaper)*, October 2017 <https://rg.profkiosk.ru/597515>.

[51] *The Military Balance. 2019. The Annual Assessment of Global Military Capabilities and Defence Economics.* London, 2019. P. 256.

[52] Cit. from: Charles F. Andrain, *Comparative Political Systems: Policy Performance and Social Change*. M.E. Sharpe, 1994. P. 129.

[53] Richard McGregor, *The Party: The Secret World of China's Communist Rulers*. Penguin, 2012. PP. 117-118.

Congress set about creating the legal basis for sending troops overseas to conduct counter-terrorist operations. At the same time, radical military reforms began, intended to enhance the role of the navy and reduce the proportional share of land forces; unified command units were created, capable of leading cross-sectoral operations.

A book on military strategy released in 2015 identified the key tasks as the protection of sovereignty and territorial integrity, unification with Taiwan, protecting interests in "new spheres", "ensuring the security of foreign interests", nuclear deterrent, and the fight against terrorism and separatism. Whereas in the past, the navy's role was to defend the coastal waters, it was now tasked with "defending the open seas". The new strategy also noted the increased significance of cyber security and brought in the concept of a "computerized local war". New strategic forces were introduced in the People's Liberation Army, uniting radio-technical troops, space intelligence, cyber intelligence and radio-electronic warfare.[54]

China has gone to considerable lengths to try to regulate its numerous border disputes: with the republics of Central Asia, with Russia, and with several other neighbors (India is an exception). The Great Wall of China provides the best evidence of the fact that, since ancient times, China has always been concerned, above all else, about the threat of foreign aggression from the north, across land. That threat has now gone. And this fact is cherished in China.

On the sea, China faces an increasingly complex situation. A problem area for the Chinese navy is the so-called "first island chain": the Korean peninsula, the Kuril Islands, Japan (including the Ryukyu Islands), Taiwan, the Philippines, Indonesia, and Australia. China is embroiled in a dispute about the possession of various parts of the bottom of the East China and South China Seas.

Beijing is also preparing to challenge the USA's hegemony in the Pacific, and is growing its navy and the so-called "string of pearls" – a series of ports and military bases in friendly countries on the coast of the Pacific and Indian Oceans. Chinese naval forces are striving to spread their presence further afield than the Chinese coastline in accordance with a new strategy – "long-distance sea defence". China is preparing to accompany vessels from the Persian Gulf

---

[54] Vasiliy Kashin, "Pekin smotrit vdal'. Kak Kitay narashchivayet potentsial proyetsirovaniya sily" ("Beijing is Looking Far Ahead. How China is Growing its Potential to Project Power"), *Rossiya v global'noy politike* (*Russia in Global Affairs*), May/June 2016 <https://globalaffairs.ru/articles/pekin-smotrit-vdal/>.

to the Straits of Malacca, and also to protect its interests in the South China and East China Seas. Another aspect of Chinese military and naval strategy is the expansion of its operational capabilities beyond the South China Sea and the Philippines to the so-called "second island chain" – the rocks and atolls in the Pacific Ocean. This zone intersects with the sphere in which the American and Japanese navies dominate.

An extensive plan for the development of a fleet of aircraft-carriers matching that of America is being implemented. As the former chief of intelligence for the USA's Pacific Fleet, Captain James Fanell, observed, China is building coastline protection vessels – many of which are the biggest in the world – "at an astonishing rate". Combined with the dramatic increase in the number of non-nuclear ballistic missiles, this is undermining America's entire strategy for projecting power in East Asia.[55]

China's strategic nuclear forces include the full triad: strategic missile troops, strategic aviation, and an atomic missile fleet, which has traditionally been small and ill-suited to carrying out the first strike. The total number of strategic delivery vehicles is estimated to be 300, with the number of rapidly deployed warheads standing at 100-200.[56] It appears that China's commitment not to use a nuclear weapon first, in any situation, is by no means of an avowed nature. At the same time, China is actively modernizing and expanding its triad. These reforms are frequently associated with the deployment of the American anti-missile defence system, which poses a greater threat to China's deterrence potential, than, for instance, Russia's.[57] It is no accident that the positioning of THAAD systems in South Korea in the spring of 2017 elicited a "merciless" (as the former South Korean trade minister put it) reaction on the part of Beijing, which imposed ferocious restrictions on the activity of South Korean companies in China, and organized a boycott of goods from South Korea.[58]

China is increasing its influence in its neighboring states first and foremost through active economic integration, which is currently being accompanied by demographic expansion, to which Beijing is increasingly adding "soft power".

---

[55] Jennifer Lind, "Asia's Other Revisionist Power", *Foreign Affairs*, March/April 2017. P. 76.

[56] Jeffrey Lewis, *Paper Tigers: China's Nuclear Posture*. Routledge, 2014. PP. 148-149.

[57] Baohui Zhang, "US Missile Defence and China's Nuclear Posture: Changing Dynamics of an Offence-Defence Arms Race", *International Affairs*, May 2011. PP. 555-569.

[58] Kim Hyun-chong, "A Sound in the East", *Korea JoongAng Daily*, May 9, 2017 <https://koreajoongangdaily.joins.com/news/article/article.aspx?aid=3033171&ref=mobile>.

Chinese influence is growing as a result of its diaspora – the millions of ethnic Chinese and their descendants who have set down roots in business, culture and politics all over the world. Beijing can depend on this diaspora, particularly now, at a time of heightened national pride. Thanks to the Chinese, rapid economic growth has taken place in the Asian "tigers" (three of the four "tigers" – Hong Kong, Taiwan and Singapore – are Chinese societies), and *Huàqiào* – ethnic Chinese living overseas – have been an important source of investment in China. At the start of the 21st century, ethnic Chinese accounted for 1% of the population of the Philippines, but controlled 35% of sales there; 2-3% of the population of Indonesia, but with 70% of local capital; 10% of the population of Thailand, but with control over 50% of its GNP.[59]

China has been one of the winners of globalization. It is no accident that at the Davos Forum in 2017, Xi Jinping was one of a handful of leaders who defended globalization; he asserted that protectionism was akin to "like locking oneself in a dark room". Yet, it should be noted that China is actively protecting its domestic market.[60]

In the system of China's foreign policy priorities, relations with the great powers are coming to the fore. In first place are the USA and Russia, then the EU states (the UK, France and Germany are usually the ones mentioned). Next come Japan and India.

Competitor of the West

In the 1990s, the Chinese government based its approach on the basis that the USA, from the moment it became the only superpower, was conducting a policy of hegemony and seeking to make use of its strength. "Western hostile forces," said Jiang Zemin in 1995, "have not for a moment abandoned their plots to Westernize and 'divide' our country." [61]

Disputes between the US and China will be inevitable in the future, too, all the more so given that the USA is continuing to view the world through the prism of a stand-off between the powers of democracy and authoritar-

---

[59] Samuel P. Huntington, *The Clash of Civilizations and the Remaking of World Order*. N.Y. et al., 1996. PP. 169-170.

[60] "China's Beleaguered Liberals: The Two Faces of Mr Xi", *The Economist*, February 18, 2017. P. 10.

[61] Cit. from: Samuel P. Huntington, *The Clash of Civilizations and the Remaking of World Order*. N.Y. et al., 1996. P. 223.

ianism, free market and state paternalism. In the United States, China is looked upon as the country's main rival, in the geo-economic sense first and foremost. However, US power in the region, which was founded on its financial capabilities, is now growing weaker. China's financial capabilities are now greater than America's: "China can deploy trillions in state-backed finance, something the United States cannot do."[62] China has become the main importer of products from East Asia, where, in some countries, the subject of the Chinese threat is seen merely as an element of the American competitive battle with Beijing.

"This challenge is much more economic in nature than military as the United States continues to hold an unassailable advantage in the instruments of war."[63]

The USA and China are the biggest trading partners in the modern world, and incidentally the American deficit in its trade with China, at the end of 2016, stood at 347 billion dollars. Trump was rather bellicose in his attitude towards China, and promised to punish it as a "currency manipulator", and to protect American producers from the influx of Chinese goods. The trade war did not start immediately; at the end of the first six months of 2017, Chinese imports had risen by 18.3%, and American imports to China by 28.5%.[64] Meanwhile, a bipartisan anti-Chinese lobby was activated in the USA, led by the Republican congressman Robert Pittenger, with the primary goal of restricting Chinese investment in the USA, which in 2016 alone had tripled and reached 45.5 billion dollars.[65] During a visit by Trump to Beijing in November 2017, contracts worth a combined total of 253 billion dollars were signed. This primarily involved Chinese investment in the acquisition of energy assets on US territory.

What are the chances of the parties in a trade war? In August 2018, Trump proclaimed victory. The Chinese stock market had fallen by 27% since the beginning of the year. The negative effects of the trade war are indeed beginning to manifest themselves in China's economy. In 2018, the growth of

---

[62] Evan A. Feigenbaum, "China and the World: Dealing With a Reluctant Power", *Foreign Affairs*, January/February 2017. P. 40.

[63] Steve Chan, *Looking for Balance: China, the United States, and Power Balancing in East Asia*. Stanford University Press, 2012. P. 240.

[64] Chen Qingqing, "US Aims to Curb Deficit with China", *Global Times*, June 8, 2017 <http://www.globaltimes.cn/content/1050771.shtml>.

[65] Kate O'Keeffe, "Lawmakers Push for Tighter Scrutiny of Chinese Investment in U.S.", *The Wall Street Journal*, February 21, 2017 <https://www.wsj.com/articles/lawmakers-push-for-tighter-scrutiny-of-chinese-investment-in-u-s-1487678403>.

Chinese GDP was 6.6%, against 6.9% in 2017, and was forecast slow to 6.3% in 2019.

However, it is not clear how the confrontation will end. Capital Economics estimates that imports from China are equivalent to 2.5% of US GDP, and that the introduction of 25% duties could lead to a 0.6% increase in prices, while 10% duties might add 0.3%. Such protectionism could cost the US economy 0.2% of GDP growth. A similar assessment – minus 0.25% growth – was given by Moody's. For China, the losses might amount to 0.3-0.5% of GDP growth, but most of the losses from the increase in duties might be offset by a weakening of the yuan, which would make Chinese products more competitive.

China cannot sell its dollar assets quickly: that would bring with it the risk of the dollar collapsing, which in turn would ruin the American economy – and so lead to a depreciation of China's own international reserves and the shrinkage of its most important market. China, therefore, is going slowly: slowly, it is reducing the proportion of US securities in its international reserves.

Approximately 60% of goods exported from China to the United States are produced by non-Chinese companies, including American ones, which are suffering direct losses from the tariff barriers. Higher tariffs on Chinese goods result in higher prices for American consumers. Thus the 20% tariff on washing machines imported from China has led to a 16.4% price rise.[66]

The American market is important for Chinese producers, but not crucial. It accounts for 3% of the total industrial production of China. Products manufactured in China incorporate a large proportion of value-added components from other countries, including the United States. For example, iPhones imported to the US from China have South Korean displays, Japanese chips, and American design and software. The same sort of thing is true of any electronics goods manufactured in China. In addition, the Chinese, unlike Washington, have taken measures to further open their market to foreign companies and to attract foreign investment.

After China imposed protectionist tariffs on American agricultural products, thousands of American farmers who used to sell soybeans, wheat, corn, cotton, almond, pork, sorghum dairy and other products to the Celestial Empire found themselves on the brink of bankruptcy. Mary Lovely, of Syra-

---

[66] Tat'yana Vdovina, "SShA i Kitay vozobnovili torgovyye deystviya" ("The US and China have Resumed Trading Activities"), *Kommersant* (*The Businessman*), Issue 170, September 19, 2018 <https://www.kommersant.ru/doc/3745211>.

cuse University, is confident of China's victory in the trade war because it "is playing this game more skillfully": tariffs imposed by the United States will be paid mainly by US companies and consumers while China is retaliating with moves that soften the blow for companies in China, including those that are foreign-owned.[67]

Sebastian Mallaby wrote in *The Washington Post* that "China has moved far beyond the point of merely mimicking Western inventions. Even if Trump's trade war stopped Chinese technology theft completely, it would not change the most unsettling aspects of China's advance. […] Alibaba began as 'the Chinese eBay', but it has long since grown beyond online auctions, spawning the financial services group Ant Financial, the world's most valuable privately held tech firm, or 'unicorn'. Tencent began as a Chinese version of AOL's instant-messaging service, but now it offers everything from social networking to online gaming to music. Of the top 10 unicorns listed by Wikipedia, three are American, one is Indian, and six are Chinese. […] The United States will never match China's maniacal, frequently unethical, win-at-all-costs commercial culture. On the other hand, there is nothing to stop it from investing in smart infrastructure and recognizing the social gains from rich data before it regulates its tech titans."[68]

However, widespread fears that the US-China trade war will undermine global economic growth are not without reason.

A serious sticking point is the problem of Taiwan, which has a central place in Beijing's policy. China insists on the need for reunification with it, for the good of all Chinese. Washington maintains that America's job is to safeguard democracy, the bearer of which is Taiwan. The root of the problem lies elsewhere, though. Back in the day, General Douglas Macarthur said that Taiwan was an "unsinkable aircraft-carrier", occupying a position right in the middle of China's coastline. Only the merging of Taiwan and China would signify the emergence in East Asia of a "truly multipolar military situation".

At present, Chinese leaders prefer not to put any time-frame on a resolution of the "Taiwan problem", although it has been said in the past that that this task ought to be completed by the middle of the 21st century.

....

[67] Mary E. Lovely, "How China Wins the Trade War", *The New York Times*, August 8, 2018 <https://www.nytimes.com/2018/08/08/opinion/trump-tariffs-china-trade-war-who-will-win.html>.

[68] Sebastian Mallaby, "Trump is Rising to the China Challenge in the Worst Way Possible", *The Washington Post*, October 1, 2018 <https://www.washingtonpost.com/opinions/trump-is-rising-to-the-china-challenge-in-the-worst-way-possible/2018/09/30/b645a00e-c41f-11e8-b338-a3289f6cb742_story.html>.

After the victory by the Kuomintang party in the parliamentary and presidential elections in 2008, the prerequisite conditions were in place for reducing the conflict potential that had accumulated during the years in which the Democratic Progressive Party (DPP) was in power; the DPP had adopted a policy of sovereign-ization. The election of Ma Ying-jeou as chairman of the Kuomintang in 2009 signified an even higher level of dialogue. Every year, the island is visited by around half a million tourists from the mainland, and 750,000 Taiwanese spend at least half the year in China. The authorities in Beijing have begun investing large sums in supporting and restoring cult sites on the mainland that are popular among Taiwanese tourists.[69]

The victory by the opposition Democratic progressive party and its leader Tsai Ing-wen in the elections in January 2016 signified an obvious changing of the guard in Taiwanese politics. The DPP initially rejected all ties whatsoever with Chinese politics, putting its emphasis on the construction of a separate, strictly Taiwanese political nation. There was an active rejection of the course adopted by the Kuomintang and even of its symbols. Just as statues of confederate generals were taken down in the USA, in Taiwan, more than two hundred statues of Chiang Kai-shek were taken down, as he symbolized the tie between the island and the mainland, their common history and destiny.[70] Incidentally, 70% of the island's inhabitants consider themselves to be Taiwanese first and foremost, and Chinese only on a secondary level.[71]

Strategic dialogue between the EU and China began in the 1990s. "Europe is the main focus for China in the diversification of our currency reserves," the Chinese premier Wen Jiabao said at an EU-China summit in 2012. "China is genuinely and firmly willing to help Europe deal with its debt problems." The chairman of the People's Bank of China, Zhou Xiaochuan, added: "China will always be committed to the principles of owning assets such as the EU's sovereign debts."[72]

....

[69] Ho Ai Li, "Honoring the Gods of Cross-Strait Peace", *The Straits Times*, June 28, 2012. P. 10.

[70] Vasiliy Kashin, "Tayvan' uplyvayet ot Kitaya" ("Taiwan is Sailing Away from China"), *Vedomosti*, January 20, 2016 <https://www.vedomosti.ru/opinion/articles/2016/01/21/624836-taivan-ot-kitaya>; Austin Ramzy, "Divisive Monuments? Put Them All in a Taiwan Park", *The New York Times*, August 22, 2017 <https://www.nytimes.com/2017/08/22/world/asia/taiwan-statues-chiang-kai-shek-park.html>.

[71] "The Decline of Deterrence", *The Economist*, May 3, 2014. P. 39.

[72] Mikhail Overchenko, "Kitayu razonravilsya dollar" ("China no Longer Likes the Dollar"), *Vedomosti*, March 2, 2012 <https://www.vedomosti.ru/finance/articles/2012/03/02/kitayu_ne_

In April 2014, Xi Jinping completed an 11-day tour of Europe, which the Chinese press christened "a smiling visit with confidence".[73] The Chinese leader called on the EU to sign a free trade agreement, which would enable the launch of the "twin engines of global economic growth" and take the volume of trade up to 1 trillion dollars by 2020.[74]

Beijing lists a host of demands that it is making of Brussels. Key is EU recognition that China has a market economy, something that would deprive the EU of a justification for erecting customs barriers. Beijing wants to import more advanced technologies from Europe and acquire more European assets, and it is seeking the cancellation of the embargo that has been in place since 1989 on supplies of European arms. A report by the EU's Chamber of Commerce in China (EUCCC) in 2017 commented on a deterioration of the business climate for workers from European companies there, although most of them demonstrated respectable financial results.[75]

On 12th March 2019, the European Commission encouraged China to open its markets more widely to European countries, to protect intellectual property, and to stop subsidizing domestic companies. At a meeting with Xi, Macron and Merkel expressed their concern about the "economic expansion" of China. However, their combative mood was shaken by China's decision to buy 300 Airbuses for 30 billion Euro. At the same time, Italy joined the "Belt & Road" initiative, as Portugal, Greece, Hungary, Poland and Croatia had done before.[76]

Back-to-Back

A growing role in China's foreign policy is being played by Russia. In China, it is still remembered that in the late 1940s and early 1950s, a special model for relations was created, the essence of which lay in the division of global

---

nravitsya_dollar>.

[73] Jin Kai, Building 'A Bridge Between China and Europe' "Building 'A Bridge Between China and Europe'", *The Diplomat*, April 23, 2014 <https://thediplomat.com/2014/04/building-a-bridge-between-china-and-europe/>.

[74] "President Xi's European Visit Signals New Era of China-EU Cooperation", *China Today*, May 4, 2014 <http://www.chinatoday.com.cn/english/society/2014-05/04/content_616597_3.htm>.

[75] "China 'Welcomes' Companies from Europe", *Global Times*, June 9, 2017.

[76] Alexey Nevelsky, "Vtoroy Front Protiv Kitaya" ("The Second Front Against China"), *Vedomosti*, March 2019 <https://vedomosti.profkiosk.ru/719011>; Vyacheslav Prokof'yev, "Mini-sammit v Yeliseyskom" ("Mini-Summit in the Elysee Palace"), *Rossiyskaya Gazeta (Russian Newspaper)*, March 26, 2019 <https://rg.ru/2019/03/26/parizh-i-berlin-prizvali-pekin-nalazhivat-sviazi-s-es.html?utm_source=yxnews&utm_medium=desktop>.

and regional responsibility, and in the promotion of shared foreign policy interests based on a "back-to-back" principle. China recognized the USSR as a senior partner, and itself as an ally of the Soviet Union. "Then, after the Sino-Soviet split, it saw itself as the leader of the Third World against both the superpowers, which produced substantial costs and few benefits. After the shift in U.S. policy in the Nixon administration, China sought to be the third party in a balance of power game with the two superpowers, aligning itself with the United States during the 1970s when the United States seemed weak and then shifting to a more equidistant position in the 1980s as U.S. military power increased and the Soviet Union declined economically and became bogged down in Afghanistan," wrote Huntington.[77]

Today, Russia is the only major country on which the Chinese foreign policy elite can traditionally rely, more so than the political elite of other countries, since there is a greater level of mutual understanding, of mutual reflection, the countries have closer historical ties, and so on. Moscow – an independent center of power – is of interest to Beijing as something of a counterweight in its complex partner-rival relations with the United States, Europe and Japan, and as one of the guarantors of its own "independent and self-sustained" foreign policy. China shares the Russian view on multipolarity. Behind the idea is a simple reality: both Russia and China are strong enough to have their own approaches in international relations, but not strong enough to stand up to the sole superpower on their own.

Brzezinski noted that "China's rising importance and Russia's recovery were creating a new geopolitical power alignment, not overtly directed at the United States, like the old Sino-Soviet alliance, but driven by congruous regional interests as well as a shared (but not openly proclaimed) desire to clip America's overstretched wings."[78] Russia and China take a dim view of pressure from the West on issues related to their internal systems of governance, and to the American policy of "promoting democracy", and of course on sanctions and trade wars.

Beijing has a vested interest in securing the long-term and guaranteed supply of hydrocarbons from Russia, as it strives to reduce its dependency on supplies from the Middle East, from Africa, and now from the US. Through the use of land-based pipelines, China hopes to reduce the risks posed by

---

[77] Samuel P. Huntington, *The Clash of Civilizations and the Remaking of World Order*. N.Y. et al., 1996. P. 168.

[78] Zbigniew Brzezinski, *Second Chance: Three Presidents and the Crisis of American Superpower*. Hachette UK, 2008.

sea routes, which could be cut off by the navies of hostile states. China has an interest in border cooperation with Russia with the aim of developing its north-eastern territories, and therefore adopts a constructive approach to resolving border issues and questions of migration and bilateral trade.

The two countries' elites interact fairly well on matters of the contemporary world order, but there is a discrepancy between the agreements made "at the top" and the reality of bilateral relations. Russia is China's tenth-biggest trading partner, although for Russia, China is its number one partner.

The level of mutual complementarity of the two economies is still insufficient, as is cooperation in Russia's priority spheres – modernization and innovation. China's rapid growth is leading to the pollution of the Russian borderlands and of the river Amur. There is the problem of China's growing influence in Central Asia, although at present there is no fixed policy to push Russia out of this region, and this is precisely because the Russian factor is taken into account. China cannot officially recognize Abkhazia and South Ossetia or the reunification of the Crimea; for China, matters of territorial integrity are a sore point.

At the same time, China has adopted a generally pro-Russian stance in relation to events in Ukraine; it has not concealed its satisfaction at the fact that Russia taught the US a lesson. Putin's popularity ratings in China surged after the events in the Crimea. China officially avoids actions which could be interpreted as criticism of the Russian position, and unofficially, Moscow has been promised full moral and economic support, on mutually beneficial terms, of course.[79] A record number of Russo-Chinese agreements have been signed since 2014, with the deal concerning the "Power of Siberia" pipeline worth 400 billion dollars alone – and it's worth it!

Settlement and clearing centers have been created for operations involving national currencies. Supplies of energy carriers stand at more than half of Russian exports to China. In 2016, China, having overtaken Turkey and Egypt, became the biggest importer of Russian foodstuffs, which in China are seen as environmentally friendly. Russia has a substantial role in the Belt and Road Initiative. Its portion will be the high-speed route from Moscow to Kazan, construction of which is being bankrolled by China. The China Railway Construction Corporation is building three metro stations in Moscow. Chinese tourists have been pouring into Russia.[80]

---

[79] "Aziatskaya dialektika 'Bol'shoy igry'" ("The Asian Dialectics of the 'Great Game'"), *Russian View*, Issue 2, May/June 2014. PP. 31-33.

[80] *Moskva-Pekin* (*Moscow-Beijing*), May-June 2017. PP. 3, 10-11, 14, 48-50.

Putin emphasized that cooperation between the two states had become "better than at any time in its centuries-old history".[81]

Colossus of the Developing World

China's foreign policy agenda has become fully global. Beijing has reacted positively to signals from the Japanese government indicating a desire to conduct a policy that is less dependent on the USA. In 2010, it was declared that the priority was to achieve a format of "strategic and mutually beneficial interests" as a step towards "strategic cooperation". In the same year, China became Japan's biggest trading partner. The countries began using the yuan and the yen in their bilateral trade and investments. Japan acquired Chinese state bonds.[82] Relations between them nonetheless developed in the context of the formula "neither friend nor foe".

China and North Korea are developing their relationship as allies. China views an independent DPRK as a key link in the chain of its own security, wary of excessive American influence in any potential unified Korea. Beijing exerts its influence on Pyongyang through private contact, calling for sensible flexibility. Meanwhile, the irresponsiveness of the North Korean leadership to attempts to prompt the reform of the economy on the basis of Chinese experience, and the stagnation of DPRK, are causing irritation in Beijing, as is the unapproved policy of creating nuclear and rocket weapons. It is felt in Beijing that a full-scale and significant economic partnership between North Korea and China is hardly likely to become a reality until North Korea rejects its program to create a nuclear weapon.[83]

The dramatic deterioration in relations between the USA and North Korea, and the threats of war on the part of Trump, put China in a difficult position. Beijing, which controls 85% of North Korea's foreign trade, let it be understood that it did not approve of the creation of WMDs by Pyongyang, and supported sanctions against Kim Jong Un's regime. It was announced that joint Chinese and North Korean firms would be closed by the end of 2017, together with the closing of the accounts of North Korean individuals

---

[81] Tat'yana Zamakhina, "Sblizheniye s Podnebesnoy" ("Drawing Closer to China"), *Rossiyskaya Gazeta* (*Russian Newspaper*), May 20, 2014 <https://rg.ru/2014/05/19/vstrecha-site.html>.

[82] Margarita Lyutova, "Yuan' na ves' mir" ("The Yuan for the Whole World"), *Vedomosti*, December 28, 2011. P. 3.

[83] Zhu Feng, "The Korean Peninsula after the Tian An Incident", *CIR*, November/December 2011. P. 70.

and legal entities in China. But Beijing spoke out fiercely against a military solution, insisting on a winding down of tension on the peninsula as the main precondition for its denuclearization.[84]

Rapprochement between Washington and Pionyang would not have been possible without Chinese pressure on North Korea to accommodate the demands of the international community and without some security guarantees to North Korea being given by Beijing.

The crisis around the deployment of American THAAD systems in South Korea, which cost Seoul direct losses of 6.4 billion dollars in one year, and lost earnings of 20.3 billion due to hidden Chinese sanctions, was resolved on 31st October 2017 through the signing of an agreement on the normalizing of bilateral relations. Seoul agree to not roll out any new THAAD complexes after the first six, and not to integrate its anti-missile defence system with the American one or enter into a trilateral military alliance with Japan and the USA.[85]

On 1st January 2010, a free trade zone between China and ASEAN was opened. In its relations with the ASEAN states, China is using a tactful policy, refraining from interfering in their domestic affairs. China is providing all of them with greater access to its market, and allows a deficit in its trade with them (this has resulted in record profits for entrepreneurs from ASEAN).

All over South-East Asia, incidentally, there are concerns about being neighbors with this northern giant. China is not prepared to share the lonely Scarborough Reef (its Chinese name is Huangyan) with the Philippines, though it is valuable only as a fishing site. Relations with Vietnam are far from easy. During the American intervention, Beijing unambiguously supported North Vietnam. However, when the unified Vietnam began to lay claim to the role of leader of the communist movement in Asia and hold itself out to be a regional power, China decided to put it firmly in its place. China supported the Cambodian Khmer Rouge regime in its conflict with Hanoi, and when the Vietnamese overthrew that regime, Beijing sent troops to Vietnam, where it suffered a painful defeat.

---

[84] Andrey Lan'kov, "Pochemu Kim Chen Yn bol'she ne mozhet rasschityvat' na Pekin" ("Why Kim Jong Un Can No Longer Rely on Beijing"), *RBK*, November 27, 2017 <https://www.rbc.ru/newspaper/2017/11/28/5a1bc2409a79472bc6bb717b>.

[85] Mikhail Korostikov, "Razryadka protivoraketnoy napryazhennosti" ("The Relieving of Anti-Missile Tension"), *Kommersant* (*The Businessman*), November 24, 2017 <https://www.kommersant.ru/doc/3475937>.

In May 2014, relations with Hanoi became tense once again, after a Chinese trawler rammed a Vietnamese fishing vessel, and China established a drilling platform in the waters around Sisha, or the Paracel Islands, to which both countries lay claim. Beijing's stance was that it would make "no concessions or compromises" on the matter of territory. At the same time, Chinese leaders recognized that the intensifying of its territorial disputes with its neighbors increased the risk of isolation or of creating a united front among them, which the USA would gladly back.[86] And this is indeed already happening. In August 2014, the chairman of the Joint Chiefs of Staff, John Dempsey, was the first high-ranking American military official to visit Vietnam in over 40 years, and discussions were held about the acquisition of arms from the USA and about joint efforts to contain Chinese might.[87] Incidentally, at an APEC summit in Danang in the autumn of 2017, Xi Jinping was the guest of honor.

China's relations with India are far from straightforward. The countries, in their modern form, were formed almost simultaneously, after the Second World War, and displayed mutual sympathies, which, admittedly, were overshadowed by mutual suspicions, border disputes, by both countries' claims for leadership in the Third World, and disputes over Tibet. When Beijing abolished Tibet's autonomy in 1959, and its leader – the Dalai Lama XIV – fled to India, where he formed a government in exile, the border disputes were immediately resurrected. Nehru was convinced of the inviolability of the borders established by the British for their Empire, while Mao considered them a manifestation of unjust imperialist policy and one of the symbols of national humiliation.[88] In 1962, an armed conflict broke out, in which China prevailed, retaining control over the region of Aksai Chin, which India considers to be the territory of its state of Jammu and Kashmir. At the time, Moscow did not support China, and the USA and the UK began direct military supplies to India. In 1993 and 1996, China and India signed agreements whereby they began to respect the "line of effective control".

....

[86] Vitaliy Vorob'yev and Andrey Ivanov, "Liniya Pekina v uregulirovanii problem v basseyne Yuzhno-Kitayskogo moray" ("The Policy of Beijing towards Problems in the South China Sea Basin"), *Vestnik MGIMO-Universiteta* (*MGIMO-University Bulletin*), Issue 3, 2013. PP. 37-44; Andrey Kirillov and Aleksey Selishchev, "Nikto ne khotel ustupat'" ("No-one Wanted to Back Down"), *Ekho planety* (*Echo of the Planet*), Issue 25, 2014. PP. 15-16.

[87] Jane Perlez, "In China's Shadow, U. S. Pursue Closer Ties to Vietnam", *The New York Times*, August 17, 2014. P. A4(L).

[88] Mohan Guruswamy and Zorawar Daulet Singh, *India-China Relations: The Border Issue and Beyond*. New Delhi, 2009. PP. 68-82.

At the heart of the partnership with India lies mutual economic interest in growing trade. At the same time, both sides are aware that the basis for conflict has not gone away, but has rather been politically "preserved". The steps taken by India to draw closer to the USA, Japan and Australia, after the signing in Delhi, in October 2008, of an agreement with Washington on cooperation in the nuclear sector, did not go unnoticed in Beijing. Tension is also arising from the expansion of influence by each country in the other party's strategic "back yard" (meaning India's activities in Vietnam and Singapore, and China's in Myanmar, Bangladesh and Sri Lanka).

As far as India is concerned, particularly at the unofficial level, it has a long list of issues with China: its support for Pakistan, its desire to achieve regional hegemony, its support for the Maoists in Nepal, its suppression of protests in Tibet, its desire to control key sectors in the Indian economy, its foreign trade surplus, and so on. In 2013, there were several armed incidents on the Sino-Indian border, with deaths on both sides.[89] The tension was eased by visits from Li Keqiang and Xi Jinping to Delhi in 2013-2014, and by the Indian Prime Minister Narendra Modi's visit to China in May 2015 and the meeting between Xi and Modi at the Shanghai Cooperation Organization summit in Astana in June 2017. China welcomed the accession to the SCO of both India and Pakistan, which took place at this summit, which enabled the "cooperation" (in the context of this organization, at least) of two countries with 44% of the planet's population, and expanded China's influence in South Asia.[90]

Meanwhile, all through the summer of 2017, Chinese and Indian forces stood facing one another, yards apart, on disputed territory on the border with Bhutan, towards which the Chinese had built a cross-country road.[91]

A traditional priority for Beijing has been relations with Pakistan. Islamabad also considers China to be one of its closest partners, in spite of the fact that it is an ally of the USA. Pakistan has an interest in Beijing being more actively involved in the affairs of South Asia, and this could lead to

---

[89] Andrey Ivanov and Alexander Lukin, "Aktivizatsiya vneshney politiki Kitaya v ATR i interesy Rossii" ("The Activation of China's Foreign Policy in the APR and Russia's Interests"), *Yezhegodnik Instituta mezhdunarodnykh issledovaniy MGIMO* (*Annual of the Institute of International Research MGIMO*), Issues 3-4 (5-6). Moscow, 2013. PP. 165-167.

[90] An Baijie and Li Xiaokun, "Xi, Modi Vow Close Cooperation", *China Daily*, June 10, 2017 <https://www.chinadaily.com.cn/a/201706/10/WS59bbe4cda310ded8ac18a6eb.html>; Li Lifan, "Expansion to Add Fresh Vitality to SCO", *China Daily*, June 12, 2017 <https://www.chinadaily.com.cn/kindle/2017-06/12/content_29712455.htm>.

[91] "The China-India Border. Fisticuffs at Dawn", *The Economist*, August 26, 2017. P. 23.

an adjustment of the balance on the sub-continent that does not work in India's favor. A system of mutual support has taken shape, to promote regional organizations: with Pakistan's help, China acquired the status of an observer in SAARC (Association for Regional Cooperation), while Pakistan joined the SCO.

For China, Central Asia is a potentially important strategic rear, not least in the context of its competition with the USA, and a source of stable and growing supplies of hydrocarbons and raw materials. China has become the biggest investor in and trade partner of the countries of Central Asia, and for some of them (Kyrgyzstan and Tajikistan) it is also a crucial economic donor. China's filling of the vacuum left by "Russia's departure" seems, to a certain section of the elites of the countries in the region, preferable to increased influence from the USA, Turkey or the EU, not to mention Islamists. It cannot be said, though, that people in Central Asia are "resigned" to inevitable dominance by China. In political circles in the region's countries, there are widespread concerns over the prospect of dependency on China.

In 2013-2014, China announced some major new initiatives in the Asian area: the creation of an Asian Investment Bank, which is going to rival the World Bank, and the strategic Belt and Road Initiative. The latter is designed to bring overland transport infrastructure to dozens of states in Eurasia, and will cost 4 trillion dollars over the next thirty years. The first corridor is to unite North-East China, Mongolia and Siberia with a modern railway network. The economic corridor between China and Pakistan will link Xinjiang and the deep-water port of Gwadar in Pakistan. China's south-western provinces are opening up to the Indian Ocean, investing in railways, highways, ports, pipelines and canals to India, Bangladesh and Myanmar. A Sino-Indian economic corridor is being opened up towards the south, linking China to the ASEAN countries through investment in ports and high-speed railways. Two major railway corridors extend to Europe: one via Kazakhstan and Russia, the other via Central Asia, Iran and Turkey. There is another corridor in Africa – it links the ports of Djibouti, Kenya, Tanzania and Mozambique with the Red Sea, the eastern Mediterranean, and south-eastern and central Europe. Over time, the scale of the project and the size of the financing have become less ambitious. Obviously, this project may lay the basis for a trade bloc on the scale of Eurasia.[92]

....

[92] Feng Shaolei, "Odin put' – mnogo vozmozhnostey" ("One Road – Many Opportunities"), *Rossiya v global'noy politike* (*Russia in Global Affairs*), Issue 3, May/June 2016 <https://globalaffairs.ru/articles/odin-put-mnogo-vozmozhnostej/>; Gal Luft, "China's Infrastructure

Among experts within China, the plan was portrayed, not just from an economic standpoint but also from a geopolitical one – as a breakthrough in the "strategic environment", and as the disruption of America's efforts to contain China in the region. These plans on the part of China are naturally not going down well in the West, and Washington is doing all it can to throw a spanner in the works. "Beijing has wasted no time in laying out its own vision for a more integrated Eurasia that may exclude the United States and in which China will play the leading role," Robin Niblett notes with some displeasure.[93]

China takes a negative view of the USA's military presence in Iraq and, particularly, in Afghanistan, seeing it less in the context of the war on terror than as part of an American plan for the military encirclement of China itself. In this context, political cooperation with Tehran is important to Beijing. The Islamic republic satisfies around 11% of China's demand for imported hydrocarbons – China accounts for around 22% of its oil exports. Moreover, Beijing is one of the biggest investors in the Iranian oil and gas sector, and will be irrespective of the US sanctions on Iran. China has shown solidarity with Russia in its stance on the Middle East and Syria. At the same time, China maintains relations with the USA's allies in the region. From 2009, China has been the biggest consumer of Saudi oil. Saudi Arabian companies are investing actively in oil refining and oil and chemicals projects in China.

In November 2006, a Sino-African summit was held in Beijing, with 48 heads of state from the continent attending (Taiwan's five allies declined the invitation, as has become traditional). It was announced that relations were to be stepped up to the level of strategic partnership. China gave out loans worth 5 billion dollars, and 12 Chinese state companies signed contracts with African governments worth 2 billion dollars, the biggest of which involved taking control of oil and gas fields in Liberia, the building of a railway in Nigeria, and the construction of a hydro-electric power station in Ghana. After this, many politicians and media representatives in the West began talking about the threat of Chinese expansion into Africa and a loss of status there for the USA and the EU.

....

Play: Why Washington Should Accept the New Silk Road", *Foreign Affairs*, September/October 2016. PP. 68-75; "The New Silk Route. All Aboard the Belt-and-Road Express", *The Economist*, May 6, 2017. PP. 53-54; Andrew Browne, "China's World: Beijing Tightens Belt on Its Grand Trade Plan", *The Wall Street Journal*, May 10, 2017. P. A.2.

[93] Robin Niblett, "Liberalism in Retreat: The Demise of a Dream", *Foreign Affairs*, Vol. 96, Issue 1, January/February 2017. P. 17.

Such talk increased dramatically after a forum in Sharm-el-Sheikh in 2009, at which Wen Jiabao promised to make Africa loans worth another 10 billion dollars and to create a fund of 1 billion dollars for loans to African SMEs. Beijing brought in a zero customs tariff on 95% of goods from the poorest countries in Africa, wrote off the debts of the poorest debtors, provided medical equipment to 30 hospitals, and began building 50 schools and carrying out 100 projects aimed at producing energy using renewable sources. The program for providing tuition to Africans at Chinese universities was expanded.

China moved into first place in trade turnover with Africa in 2008. Huge amounts of investment are going into the fuel and energy and mining sectors of African countries. Investment risks are being covered by the specially created China-Africa Development Fund. In most African countries, there are permanent Chinese trade missions operating. A Chinese-African Chamber of Commerce has opened in Beijing, and negotiations are ongoing on the creation of a free trade zone with the states of Southern Africa.

The rapid strengthening of China's position in Africa, against the backdrop of the weakening influence of Western countries, is causing concern among the latter, who accuse China of conducting a policy of "new colonialism". Many African leaders also express concerns, off the record, to the effect that China's ambitious projects could lead to a new economic subjugation of Africans. And *The New York Times* asserts that "the Chinese government is basically snatching fish out of the nets of poor fishermen in Africa in order to keep fish on plates in China."[94]

Anti-Chinese feeling on the continent, incidentally, is not as strong as anti-American sentiment. A survey by PEW Research Center in Senegal found that 86% of the population took a positive view of China's role in their country, while 56% felt positive about the USA's role; in Kenya, the figures were 91% to 74%, and so on.[95] From 2000 through to 2015, Eximbank China provided 63 billion dollars' worth of loans to 54 countries in Africa, while Eximbank America provided 1.7 billion to five countries. "You can see what they are spending their money on but you can't see what the Americans are spending on. [...] Slowly but surely, the Chinese

---

[94] "China Wants Fish, So Africa Goes Hungry", *The New York Times*, May 3, 2017 <https://www.nytimes.com/2017/05/03/opinion/china-wants-fish-so-africa-goes-hungry.html>.

[95] Dambisa Moyo, "Beijing, a Boon for Africa", *The International Herald Tribune*, June 29, 2012. P. 6.

are winning in Africa," notes the editor of the biggest newspaper in Liberia, Philibert Brown.[96] Chinese investment in Africa has risen above 10 billion dollars.[97] There are 31,000 Chinese companies working in Africa and investing in the continent.

China's key relationships with Latin American countries are those with Brazil, Mexico, Argentina, and Venezuela. A key role is played by bodies set up to facilitate dialogue, such as MERCOSUR, the Andes community, the RIO group, and CARICOM. Beijing became a member of the Inter-American Development Bank, the Inter-American Investment Corporation and the Multilateral Investment Fund. In the first decade of the 21st century, the volume of trade turnover increased 10-fold as a result of cooperation in the fields of minerals mining, transport, communications, production of foodstuffs, and the associated infrastructure. A contract was signed with Brazil's Petrobras for the joint exploitation of oilfields on the Atlantic shelf. Joint projects are being carried out with Venezuela's PDVSA in the basin of the river Orinocko, and China has no intentions of abandoning them despite pressure from the Trump administration. The Chinese have acquired shares in the Argentine oil company Bridas. At the same time, Chinese expansion is causing concern here, too.

There is an increasing understanding in Beijing of the need to export ideas and cultural values. This, however, has not typically been the Chinese way, owing due to the traditional self-sufficiency of Chinese civilization and the complicated and not always adequate perception of Chinese values in other parts of the planet. The main sources of Chinese "soft power" are considered to be the culture and successes of the Chinese model of modernization. The conduits for Chinese "soft power" are large-scale events such as the 2008 Olympics and EXPO-2010, the active networks of the Confucius Institute all over the world, the ever-growing intake of foreign students, the global Chinese cultural brands that are appearing, and the creation of Chinese equivalents of CNN and Hollywood. There is an intensively growing network of Chinese newspapers, magazines, radio and TV channels, and information websites in various languages: French, English, Spanish, Arabic, Russian, Portuguese.

---

[96] David Pilling, "Ports and Roads Mean China is 'Winning in Africa'", *The Financial Times*, May 3, 2017 <https://www.ft.com/content/65591ac0-2f49-11e7-9555-23ef563ecf9a>.

[97] Adewale Maja-Pearce, "Nigeria's China Connection", *The New York Times*, May 7, 2014 <https://www.nytimes.com/2014/05/08/opinion/majapearce-nigerias-china-connection.html>.

China's presence in the global information space is growing rapidly – including show-business, animation, computer games, cinematography, TV, publishing, and advertising. The main consumers of cultural products are ethnic Chinese living overseas. The role of foreign audiences is growing, however. Chinese actors and directors (Jackie Chan, Jet Li, Zhang Yimou) have worked in Hollywood for many years.[98]

China craves peace and stability inside the country and in the international arena, so as to make up for lost time and reassemble the remnants of its ancient civilization, which has for a long time been reminiscent of a smashed Ming dynasty vase. Beijing is also hoping to achieve at least a semblance of its former glory and majesty. "China supports the old-fashioned, hackneyed, Westphalian architecture of national states which restrain one another, which Metternich succinctly and accurately compared to 'the balancing of a large candelabra,'" writes Daniel Fung.[99]

"As a result of its complex modernization, China has restored a sense of being a fully-fledged civilization, and a sense of optimism," Russian sinologists have rightly observed.[100] One would be hard-pressed to find a country that looks upon the future with greater confidence.

....

[98] Yevgeniy Yevdokimov, "Politika Kitaya v global'nom informatsionnom prostranstve" ("China's Policy in the Global Information Space"), *Mezhdunarodnyye protsessy* (*International Processes*), Issue 1, January/April 2011. PP. 74-83.

[99] Daniel Fung, "Politika v stile retro" ("Politics, Retro Style"), *Rossiya v global'noy politike* (*Russia in Global Affairs*), Vol. 9, Issue 1, February 14, 2011 <https://globalaffairs.ru/number/Politika-v-stile-retro-15110>.

[100] *Dukhovnaya kul'tura Kitaya*. Tom 4: Istoricheskaya mysl'. Politicheskaya i pravovaya kul'tura (*The Spiritual Culture of China*. Vol. 4: Historical Thought. Political and Legal Culture), ed. by M. L. Titarenko, A. I. Kobzev, A. Ye. Luk'yanov. Moscow, 2009. P. 201.

CHAPTER 8
THE COLLECTIVE OF THE RISING SUN

Japan is one of the most original countries, and one of the most complicated to understand. Japanese civilization arose in a struggle against natural disasters – earthquakes, tsunamis, volcanic eruptions. In many ways, it was nature that shaped Japan's unique culture, with its aesthetic of rising from the ashes, fostering the power of the spirit, a work ethic, a capacity for self-organization, and collective behavior. It is no accident that the Japanese say 私には日本人の血が流れている, which translates as: "Japanese blood is in my veins."

Yamato and Nippon

Huntington, in defining Japan's place in the order of civilizations, came to the conclusion: "The most important lone country is Japan. No other country shares its distinct culture, and Japanese migrants are either not numerically significant in other countries or have assimilated to the cultures of those countries [...]."[1]

There is an ancient legend about the creation of Japan: "When the gods Izanagi and Izanami came down from the heavens on a rainbow, to separate the solid ground from the depths, Izanagi's spear struck an eddy swirling downwards, and at that moment a trail of drops fell from his spear, thus forming this contorted chain of islands." The country consists of the islands of the Japanese archipelago, extending roughly 3,400 km along the Eastern coast of Eurasia. Japan's territory is 372,300 square km and consists of four main islands (Honshu, Hokkaido, Kyushu and Shikoku) and around 3,900 small or miniscule islands.

---

[1] Samuel P. Huntington, *The Clash of Civilizations and the Remaking of World Order*. N.Y. et al., 1996. P. 137.

"The path of the mountains" – that is one of the meanings of the ancient name of the country, Yamato. There are 16 mountain peaks in the country that are over 3,000 m above sea level. Of its 150 mountains, around forty are active volcanos. Hence one sees a high degree of seismic activity in Japan, particular on the biggest island, Honshu. Every year, around 1,500 earthquakes are recorded. If the epicenter of an earthquake happens to be in the sea, tsunamis are caused. Cyclones and typhoons are relatively common. Natural disasters are one of the main reasons for the Japanese people's inherent durability in the face of the vicissitudes of fate.

The historical development of the islands, until recently thought to represent the edge of the world, lagged behind the continent for many centuries. "Every element of civilization reached it with a delay, and how late it arrived corresponded exactly to its historical circumstances and geographical remoteness from the Chinese, Siberian, and Indian centers or the centers of South-East Asia. Thus, Japanese chronology always appears as a marginal one, shifted by one temporal degree from that of the continent," write the French Orientalists Vadim and Danielle Elisseeff in their classic study.[2]

The story of Japan's origins is one of the vaguer chapters in world history. It is almost as if it went straight from nothing to being a fully-formed state. Yet the continuity of events and time in their own country is a sort of *idée fixe* in the Japanese historical consciousness. The earliest information we have about Japan is given to us by Korean and Chinese dynastic chronicles and histories, written in the first few centuries AD. Japanese written sources, *per se*, appeared in the form of semi-mythical chronicles only in the 8th century: Kojiki (*Notes about Past Events*) and *The Nihon Shoki* (*The Chronicles of Japan*).

In the *Nihon Shoki* – the most historical of all the mythological sources – even the creation of man and the world happens in Japan. The ancestor of all Japanese – and only them – is the illuminating sun goddess Amaterasu. In the 7th century BC, there was a great movement of people from the tenson and izumo tribes led by her grandson, Ivaro, from the island of Kyushu to the island of Honshu. They established a state on the Yamato plain beside Mount Miva, and from here, the Japanese people were created. Starting with Ivaro, who was called "Jimmu-tenno" ("Divine" or "Heavenly" tsar, warrior), the Yamato were led by a "great prince", the okimi. The imperial family was extremely powerful, largely thanks to the beliefs about its sacred nature, although another mighty

---

[2] Vadim Elisseeff and Danielle Elisseeff, *Yaponskaya tsivilizatsiya* (*Japanese Civilization*). Yekaterinburg-Moscow, 2008. P. 28.

clan may have held real power. In the 6th and 7th centuries AD, Japan's clan-based society took on the characteristics of fully-fledged statehood. One of the main reasons for this was an encounter with China.

The might of a civilization which had already existed for millennia by the time Japan appeared on the historical horizon was witnessed by ambassadors sent to the Chinese court of the Sui dynasty by Prince Shotoku Taisi, regent under the Empress Suiko. Buddhism and Confucianism began to penetrate the country from Korea and China, along with literacy, and from these countries the Japanese learned of craftsmanship, silk production, the tea culture, and new forms of irrigation. The Japanese who visited China not only admired the luxury of the court, but also expressed concern about its military might, and this prompted radical reforms which continued throughout the 7th century, initially instigated by Prince Shotoku Taisi, and later by the Soga clan and the emperors Tenji and Tenmu. The foundations for the state structure of *ritsuryo* were laid down, which essentially reproduced Chinese customs. The Emperor's court actively supported the spread of Buddhism, which, in 594, became the state religion; at this time, the construction of temples began in Shitenno-ji and Horyu-ji, which marked the start of Japanese architecture in the Chinese style. Written characters were brought into circulation, and the Chinese language – adapted to local phonetics – became the official language (the first teachers of it were Korean).

In this period, the country acquired the name "Nihon", or "Nippon" ("The land of the rising sun"). Why not Yamato? One of the meanings of the character that was used to write this name sounded like "dwarves", while another sounded like "distant", "remote". This was not to the liking of Japan's ambitious ruling elite, which was rapidly closing the gap on the country's mighty neighbor. The new name and the flag – the red ball of the sun on a white background – are directly related to the solar symbol of state ideology.[3]

China had a huge influence on the rise of Japanese civilization. "Chinese civilization was dominant on the Japanese islands for many centuries," Fernand Braudel has asserted. "Its dawn was accompanied by so many deformations that it often became unrecognizable (an example is Buddhism, which, in the form of the teachings of Zen, became the ideology of the 'bloody Samurais', starting in the 12th century). In other cases, by contrast, Chinese civilization preserved its archaic forms in Japan, which were already

---

[3] *Vsemirnaya istoriya*: v 6 t. (*World History*, in 6 vols.), ed. by A. O. Chubar'yan. T. 2: *Srednevekovyye tsivilizatsii Zapada i Vostoka* (Vol. 2: *Medieval Civilizations of the Occident and the Orient*). Moscow, 2012. P. 309.

consigned to oblivion in China itself (e.g. Chinese music that had been lost in China lived on in Japan)."[4]

At the same time, there were significant differences between the state structures of China and Japan. In the Chinese tradition, the idea of the "Heavenly right" to rule the country had prevailed since ancient times; this right was given to specific rulers, and to dynasties as a whole, by Heaven itself. Such a doctrine could not take root in Japan due to the utterly different attitude towards the Emperor. According to Shinto, the Emperor is a direct descendant of the Goddess Amaterasu – in other words, a living deity. James George Fraser described the nature of the mikado's power as follows: "He is an incarnation of the sun goddess, the deity who rules the universe, gods and men included; once a year, all the gods wait upon him and spend a month at his court. During that month, the name of which means 'without gods', no one frequents the temples, for they are believed to be deserted."[5] The very idea of a change of dynasty was unthinkable.

Tenno, though, presided over the country without being the actual ruler of it. Representatives of the house of Fujiwara were always appointed regents under emperors who had not yet come of age, and as chancellors under adults, while the emperors themselves took wives from among this same clan, inevitably making the Fujiwara their senior relatives. Emperor Shirakawa instituted another tradition: in 1086, he abdicated the throne in favor of his son Horikawa and took his vows as a Buddhist monk. Yet Shirakawa retained political power and was the real power behind the throne. Two political sub-systems came into being: regent chancellors (seikan-seiji) and emperors who go off to live in monasteries (in-sei).[6] As we can see, real power and formal power were hardly ever one and the same thing in Japan.

Confucianism, Buddhism, and Taoism came to Japan from China, in the same way that they went to Korea and Vietnam, but Taoism was not included in the "triad of teachings"; its place was taken by an ancient Japanese religion, *Shinto* (literally: "the path of the gods") – a cult of nature and of ancestors. Shinto asserts that everything in the world has a spirit, and is thus imbued with holiness: mountains, rainbows, lotuses, and so on. Amaterasu

---

[4] Fernand Braudel, *Grammatika tsivilizatsiy* (*Grammar of Civilizations*). Moscow, 2008. P. 285.

[5] James George Fraser, *The Golden Bough: A Study in Magic and Religion*. Oxford University Press, 2009. P. 134.

[6] *Vsemirnaya istoriya*: v 6 t. (*World History*, in 6 vols.), ed. by A. O. Chubar'yan. T. 2: *Srednevekovyye tsivilizatsii Zapada i Vostoka* (Vol. 2: *Medieval Civilizations of the Occident and the Orient*). Moscow, 2012. PP. 316-318.

is the head of these 8 million deities. Shinto is the deification of nature, born of admiration for it. The Japanese worshipped objects and phenomena from the world around them not out of fear in the face of the terrifying forces of nature, but out of a sense of gratitude to it for its generosity and multifaceted beauty. Shinto does not require daily prayers from the faithful; presence at the temple on feast-days and the bringing of offerings for the rituals is sufficient. In daily life, the Shinto demonstrate their religion through the observance of cleanliness. Dirt is associated with evil, while purification is at the center of all the rituals.

"Since Shinto rituals, by and large, focused on openhearted supplications to *kami* for assistance in this world, whereas Buddhism dealt with the fate of one's soul after death, a person could participate in both faiths," the American Japanologist James McClain has emphasized. "In the centuries after Buddhism had been introduced into Japan, religious authorities and lay followers alike came to view *kami* as incarnations of specific Buddhas and bodhisattvas."[7] At the Shinto holy sites, people began building Buddhist pagodas. It was thought that the *Shinto* gods were the most effective at cleansing Buddha of evil spirits. The third component of the Japanese "three teachings" was Confucianism. During the Shogunate Tokugawa period, it was put at the heart of a child's upbringing and education.

At times, the Japanese have replaced their faith with aesthetics, the worshipping of the beautiful, the cult of beauty. Aesthetic norms in many ways define the philosophy of Japanese civilization. There is a definition of Japanese culture as the culture of the four seasons or the civilization of the pine needle (the ability to revel in the beauty of the pine cone, without trying to fit the whole tree into one's gaze). A characteristic trait of Japanese culture is mimicry of nature, and it is built on the model of nature.

The Japanese are collectivists. This is probably associated with the traditions of rice-growing, which is only effective when at least twenty people are involved. The mountainous landscape forced the people to settle in small, isolated villages pressed against the foothills. The nobility tried not to let the peasants move away to others' territories. In Japan, right up until the 19th century, they even tried to avoid building bridges over rivers, so as to make travel more difficult. All this helped to define the nation's way of life: year on year, in the same place, living door to door with the same old neighbors, subordinating one's own interests to those of the collective.

---

[7] James L. McClain, *Japan: A Modern History*. W.W. Norton & Company, Inc., 2002. P. 34.

For centuries, the patriarchal family was considered the main unit of society. The patriarchal unit "ia" ("house") stipulated proximity of people through blood, combined with the legacy of their ancestors. The registers in which the rural and urban councils recorded all important events – births, deaths, marriages, achievements, and minor offenses – were for centuries an effective method of controlling behavior: it was considered a disgrace if facts which brought shame on the family were put into the book.

The Shogunates

The deification of the Emperor, combined with military-feudal regime, predetermined the existence, for many centuries, of a system of governance known as the shogunate: dictatorships of the strongest clan in terms of military, political and economic power. Its head bore the title shogun ("warlord", "military commander"; the full name of the title is "great warlord and vanquisher of the barbarians") and had practically absolute power in the country. The shoguns, isolating the emperors from matters of governance of the country and leaving them the right "to communicate with the gods", never tried to overthrow the ruling dynasty or to proclaim a new one, as happened several times in China. The Shogun dynasties existed in parallel to that of the Emperor.[8] In Japan's history, there are three periods of rule by the shoguns: the Minamoto shogunate, during which the capital was Kamakura (1192-1333), the Asikaga shogunate, the center of which was in Muromati (1338-1598), and the Tokugawa shogunate, in the Edo period (1603-1867). The age of the shoguns is often compared to the Middle Ages in the West. "The eternal battle of elites between the *kuge*, the nobility from the imperial court, and the *bushi*, the warriors, is one of the original features of Japanese civilization. Having taken shape in the 12th century, this stand-off continued right up until the Meiji era," writes the French Japanologist Michel Vié.[9]

In Japan, by contrast with China, a strong military tradition developed. Why? In China, soldiers were never seen as a separate class, and the military was not seen as a prestigious profession. A true warrior ought to achieve victories without having to fight. Military achievements could not

---

[8] *Vvedeniye v vostokovedeniye* (*An Introduction to Oriental Studies*), ed. by Ye. I. Zelenev and V. B. Kasevich. St. Petersburg, 2011. P. 402.

[9] Michel Vié, *Istoriya Yaponii s drevnikh vremen do epokhi Meydzi* (*The History of Japan from Ancient Times to the Age of Meiji*). Moscow, 2009. P. 38.

be compared to successes in the field of state governance or in literature. In Japan, by contrast, military glory was seen as being above all else.

It can be assumed that Buddhism played its part, in its specific Japanese form of Zen Buddhism, which contributed to the upbringing of generations of samurai, who underwent training in Zen monasteries, with their harsh discipline and obedience to the tutor. Why was it, though, that Buddhism, which is essentially peaceful, became militaristic in Japan? It seems that the intense rivalry among the elite over limited resources, and for control over land and people in want of a sufficiently strong and effective central power, enabled the principle of strength to come to the fore.

The Elisseeffs emphasize: "The warriors, the *bushi*, who held power from the 13th to the 19th centuries, were not notorious militarists… but rulers, whose role in organizing civil activity such as education and trade was outstanding; being firm believers in Confucian ethics, the *bushi* were very well-educated people, and wrote political and economic works."[10] The lower part of the *bushi* class consisted of the minor military nobility, the samurai, who were warriors in the service of princes. Samurai were required to give their lives unquestioningly in the service of their sovereign, and to commit suicide in case of the slightest infringement, by putting a sword through their stomach, after writing a pre-death poem. The Samurai's code of honor, the Bushido, was considered – and in many ways is still considered – a template for dignified service.

Europeans came to Japan in the 16th century (the Portuguese arrived in 1542, followed by the Spanish), and engaged mainly in intermediary trade in goods from Asian countries, while also trying to spread Christianity. The Japanese did not understand Christianity, and did not adopt it. The idea of a single God was incompatible with their belief in the millions of Shinto deities. The missionaries launched an attack on the holiest of holies – the "Japanese soul". Moreover, their teachings were strongly at odds with the licentious behavior of the Western sailors and merchants in Japan's ports and with the selfishness of the priests themselves. From 1640 onwards, the shoguns instigated a policy of isolating Japan from the outside world. Being a Christian was a crime punishable by death. Any foreigner who set foot on the Japanese islands risked facing the death penalty. However, Japan's isolation from the European world was not absolute, and was not accompanied by an official rejection of everything originating outside Japan, or scorn

---

[10] Vadim Elisseeff and Danielle Elisseeff, *Yaponskaya tsivilizatsiya (Japanese Civilization)*. Yekaterinburg-Moscow, 2008. P. 12.

for it. On the contrary, the formation of the Japanese phenomenon was fostered by a centuries-old tendency to borrow from the outside world, in the absence of the respect characteristic of China for one's own wisdom and scorn for other cultures. Contact continued with the Dutch, thanks to which Western science came to Japan (rangaku – "Dutch knowledge"): medicine, natural sciences, metallurgy, chemistry.

Isolation from the Western world did not prevent Japan's own expansion into neighboring Asian territories. Japanese trading vessels travelled to the ports of China and South-East Asia. Manila in the Philippines, Ayutthaya in Siam, and Hoi An in Vietnam, still contain the preserved remains of Japanese settlements.[11] Foreign trade and the sponsoring of business on the part of the daimyo led, as early as in the 17th century, to the emergence of wealthy trading houses, including Mitsui and Sumitomo, which later became famous.

However, isolation from the Western world proved to be impossible. Just like China, Japan opened itself up to the colonial powers and experienced a series of national humiliations. By the mid-19th century, the United States could perceive the idea of taking their civilization across the Pacific Ocean as the "course of destiny". The American commander Matthew Perry emerged in 1854 at the head of a navy made up of eight of the biggest ships in the world, demanding that the borders be opened up for trade, under threat of the bombing and besieging of Edo from the sea. The Ansei Treaties, concluded with the USA and the European powers in 1854-1858, opened up Japan to the winds of the global market. In 1855, the first Russo-Japanese treaty was signed, marking the start of official relations between the states. In 1863-1864, clashes took place on the border between Japanese troops and Western ships, in which the *bakufu* government demonstrated its helplessness in face of the West. The reaction to Western colonization was the political coup of 1868, as a result of which power passed from the shoguns into the hands of Emperor Mutsuhito (Meiji).

The Meiji Restoration and the Empire

Japan was practically the only country in the East whose development in the period of industrial colonization and energetic Westernization did not signal a crisis, but in fact the opposite: what occurred was a period of intensive growth.

....

[11] Sergey Chugrov, *Yaponiya v poiskakh novoy identichnosti* (*Japan in Search of a New Identity*). Moscow, 2010. P. 196.

The Meiji Restoration brought some extremely important changes: the opening of certain ports to foreigners and the sending of Japanese overseas to study and gather information; the destruction of the shogunate and the restoring of centralized power in the shape of the Emperor (the restoration); and the modernization of the army, economy and state institutes, using Western achievements. Emperor Mutsuhito and his advisers liquidated the feudal apanages and the inherited privileges of the *daimyo* noblemen, and undermined the tenets of the Samurai era. Japan was divided into governorates and prefectures, headed by civil servants appointed centrally. The positions were filled by the same *daimyos* and samurais, but they were now independent aristocrats, and civil servants who were employed by the state and paid from the state coffers. What is more, they were civil servants who did not have any traditions of bureaucracy, and were therefore not mired in corruption (can you imagine a corrupt samurai?), and not schooled in bureaucratic heel-dragging.

A sturdy administrative and bureaucratic system was created, founded on equality of classes, a strengthening of the role of the state finances, and a unified financial system.

Although the samurais, as a class, were abolished, the code of the *bushido* lived on, and it allowed no room for doubting Japan's supremacy. To protect the country from Western rule, a pragmatic approach was chosen – to increase the country's might. For the Japanese, being modern began to mean being the victor in various fields of life, primarily on the battlefield. The creation of a powerful army and, in particular, navy, became the number one task, and this led to even greater industrial development. The government founded the largest enterprises who took responsibility for weapons arsenals, metallurgical plants, and wharfs, and later, under a law passed in 1880, sold them for a symbolic fee to major companies such as Mitsui, Mitsubishi and Fukawa.

In 1889, the text of the Constitution was published on behalf of the Emperor. A constitutional monarchy was created, conferring broad powers on the emperor, who also held the right to introduce legislative initiatives. A parliament of two houses was created in 1890, with no more than 1% of the country's taxpayers entitled to elect the members of its lower house, while the upper house was somewhat analogous to the UK's House of Lords.

This did not lead to the formation of a Western-style political system, however. "Prior to its encounter with the West, Japan was already endowed with a strong state that had many characteristics of Weberian bureaucracy, with a state-society 'balance' heavily weighted in favor of the state," wrote

Fukuyama. "There were different social groups – farmers, merchants, and warriors – but they were not organized for collective action in a manner comparable to Europe's independent cities, churches, guilds and the like." Civil society in Japan is to this day far weaker and less well-organized than in the West.[12]

Fernand Braudel described the essence of the changes accurately: "The Son of the Sun, esteemed in the temples for his divine origin, ordered the start of the industrialization of the country. In order to carry out his will, Japan did not need a new ideology or religion – these already existed. It was these things that made it possible to control Japan as though it were a single person."[13]

Japan is the only non-European country whose development enabled it, by the turn of the 20th century, not only to be on a par with the leading European states, but to be one of the most influential and successfully developing countries, competing for a remaking of the world order. The samurais of yesteryear, and their descendants, formed the officer corps of the new army. Whereas in the past their spirit had manifested itself in internecine wars, it was now directed outward. At the end of the 19th century, the concept of "Asianism" became widespread, reflecting nationalists' claims for Japan's role of "the elder in the Asian family". This was how the saying "eight corners under one roof" was interpreted.[14]

Japan, following the example of the European countries, formed its own colonial empire, incorporating Taiwan, Korea and Manchuria. In the lands it conquered, Japan was not seen as the bringer of a more perfect civilization, and the colonizers had to rely to a far greater degree on force – the police and the army – and conduct a more brutal policy of asserting the Japanese values and language; they also moved more Japanese people into the colonies. At the same time, while preparing for war, Tokyo industrialized the lands it conquered.[15]

Ambitions for the role of leader in Asia brought Japan into an alliance with Hitler's Germany. In July 1938, Japanese forces invaded Soviet territo-

---

[12] Francis Fukuyama, *Political Order and Political Decay. From the Industrial Revolution to the Globalization of Democracy*. London, 2014. P. 351.

[13] Fernand Braudel, *Grammatika tsivilizatsiy* (*Grammar of Civilizations*). Moscow, 2008. P. 285.

[14] Sergey Chugrov, *Yaponiya v poiskakh novoy identichnosti* (*Japan in Search of a New Identity*). Moscow, 2010. P. 197.

[15] V. A. Perminova, "Yaponskiy kolonializm: osobennosti upravleniya" ("Japanese Colonialism: Peculiarities of Management"), *Voprosy istorii* (*Questions of History*), Issue 7, 2014. PP. 129-135.

ry near Lake Khasan, but were defeated. On 11th May 1939, divisions of the Japanese Kwantung Army attacked territory in Mongolia in the vicinity of Khalkhyn Gol. General Zhukov's troops, joining forces with the Mongols, regained control by late August. After this, Tokyo began to favor the "southern" option – an invasion of the territories belonging to the European powers and the USA in South-East Asia and the Pacific Ocean.

With the outbreak of war in Europe, Tokyo decided that the time had come. After waiting for France and Holland to capitulate before Germany, the Japanese began an occupation of Indochina, proclaiming the concept of a "Greater East Asia Co-Prosperity Sphere", which in practice meant the creation of a gigantic empire. Japan's efforts were confirmed in the trilateral pact with Germany and Italy signed on 27th September 1940. Pressing ahead with expansion towards the south, Tokyo continued to prepare for a war against the USSR. In order to prevent the possibility of an attack and a war on two fronts, the Soviet government proposed that a non-aggression treaty should be signed. Japan, also concerned by the prospect of a war on two fronts, replied in the affirmative. On 13th April 1941, a non-aggression treaty was signed.

On the night of 7th and 8th December 1941, the Japanese air force and navy – a day before war was declared – attacked the American naval base at Pearl Harbor in Hawaii, and also Guam, Manila and Hong Kong. In the imperial rescript on the declaration of war, the West was called racist and imperialist, and as having "inordinate ambition to dominate the East".[16] In the initial phase of the war with the USA and Great Britain, Tokyo met with success; by the middle of 1942, Japan had occupied the Philippines, Indochina, Thailand, Burma, Malaya, and Indonesia.

Franklin Roosevelt's America proved to be a worthy adversary. The battles at the Midway Atoll and in the Coral Sea resulted in a shift in favor of the United States. Despite the difficult position on the Pacific fronts, Japan continued to hold its Kwantung Army, with around a million men, on the borders with the Soviet Union, thereby tying down in the Far East of Russia a substantial portion of the Soviet troops needed for the war against Hitler. In line with the obligations adopted at the Yalta conference, the USSR denounced, in April 1945, the non-aggression pact, and in August of that year, soon after the nuclear bombs were dropped on Hiroshima and Nagasaki by the Americans, Soviet troops laid waste to the Kwantung Army and took Manchuria, North Korea, South Sakhalin and the Kuril Islands. To avoid

....

[16] James L. McClain, *Japan: A Modern History*. W.W. Norton & Company, Inc., 2002. P. 490.

further casualties, the Emperor ordered the country to surrender. On 2nd September 1945, Japan unconditionally surrendered.

The Japanese Miracle

"The loss of the war was a complete shock to the system. In their minds the whole thing became worthless and was thrown out."[17] Japan had lost all its colonial holdings and the territories that it had conquered. The question of its status arose, and the Americans had a say in this, after occupying the country. The Japanese government was required to implement the directives of the American high command.

In October 1946, the new Constitution was adopted by parliament; it took effect on 3rd May 1947. The 9th article declared the rejection of the use of armed force as a method of resolving international conflicts and of creating armed forces with this aim. There was a purge of war criminals from the apparatus of state, a decentralization of the police system, and reforms to the education system. As George Kennan noted when he arrived in Japan, "Here SCAP [MacArthur's headquarters] had proceeded on a scale, and with a dogmatic, impersonal vindictiveness, for which there were few examples outside the totalitarian countries themselves."[18]

In large part influenced by such assessments, from late 1948 the US began introducing a "reverse policy": an "economic stabilization program" was adopted, which enabled the Japanese monopolies to regain a strong position, and in 1950 the police reserve corps was created as the foundation of the future army. On 8th September 1951, at a conference in San Francisco, a peace treaty was signed with Japan, in which, incidentally, it rejected the Kuril Islands (though the USSR refused to sign it). On the same day, a Japanese-American Security Treaty was signed, which gave the USA the right to create bases and to keep troops in Japan for an indefinite period.

The first – openly pro-American – government of Yoshida resigned from office in December 1954. The new government was led by Ichiro Hatoyama, the president of the Democratic Party, formed at the same time, which, after merging with the liberals, became known as the Liberal Democratic Party of Japan (LDP). It went on to govern for the next 54 years. The wounds of the Second World War began to heal quickly from the 1950s onwards. The

....

[17] Cit. from: Samuel P. Huntington, *The Clash of Civilizations and the Remaking of World Order*. N.Y. et al., 1996. P. 105.

[18] George F. Kennan, *Memoirs 1925-1950*. Bantam Books, 1969. P. 409.

Japanese economy started growing rapidly in the new and very favorable conditions, and this laid the foundations for the phenomenon of Japan.

Japan, unlike China or the USSR, was in no way restricted in its ability to acquire Western – above all, American – technologies and know-how, and actively bought up all over the world and actively implemented tens of thousands of patents and licenses. Land reform and the abolition of land-owning by the aristocracy led to the creation of a large number of individual freeholdings, which were highly productive. Japan was saved from having to spend too much on the military, and this increased its rate of accumulation. Meanwhile, the country received massive military and associated orders from the US during the wars in Korea and Vietnam.[19]

A role was also played by the indicative planning system, and an increase in the competitiveness of industry through the merging and unifying of companies brought to the forefront several major national leaders – Mitsui, Mitsubishi, Sumitomo, Fuji, Kawasaki, Nissan, Toyota. The behavior of the workforce, in many ways harking back to a Confucian sense of discipline, culture and work ethic, and far more interested in genuine collaboration with their firm than in doing battle with its directors in the name of asserting their rights, also made a significant contribution to the country's advancement.[20]

Japan overtook virtually every other country in the world (with the possible exception of Sweden) in creating a social safety net. From the slogan "all people are soldiers", the country moved to the slogan "all people should have insurance", actively protecting its citizens from the vicissitudes of life.[21] "If they were born sick, the state would pay", Ferguson pointed out. "If they could not afford education, the state would pay. If they could not find work, the state would pay. [...] When they retired, the state would pay. And when they finally died, the state would pay their dependents. [...] Most welfare states aimed at universal, cradle-to-grave coverage. Yet the Japanese welfare state seemed to be a miracle of effectiveness. In terms of life expectancy, the country led the world. In education, too, it was ahead of the field."[22]

---

[19] Alexander Panov, *O Yaponii: Ocherki i issledovaniya diplomata* (*On Japan. Sketches and Studies of a Diplomat*). Moscow, 2014. PP. 169-174.

[20] Leonid Vasil'yev, *Istoriya Vostoka* (*A History of the East*). Vol. 2. Moscow, 2011. PP. 332-333.

[21] Niall Ferguson, *The Ascent of Money: A Financial History of the World*. Penguin, 2008. P. 208.

[22] Ibid. PP. 207, 208-209.

From 1950 through to 1974, the economy grew at an average of 10% a year. In 1980, Japan produced 15% of global industrial output, reaching second place in the world in terms of GDP.[23] After this, its economy surged.

What did exactly happen? In 1985, the US, concerned about the poor competitiveness of American goods, convinced the biggest economies, including Japan, to reevaluate their currencies (the Plaza agreement). Japanese exporters began to make losses, and it was decided that these should be compensated for via financial speculations, after which money flowed into the Tokyo stock exchange and into real estate. Credit organizations' capital began to balloon, and Japanese investors set about acquiring foreign assets – from state bonds to skyscrapers and resorts. By 1988, the nine biggest banks in the world were all Japanese, the Nikkei index rose by 300%, and Japanese real estate was worth more, in total, than American real estate. In order to soothe the market, the Bank of Japan increased interest rates in 1989 from 2.5% to 4.25%. Investment bankers started selling up, in a panic, and the stock market lost 6 trillion dollars of capitalization in a few months.[24]

Investment fell due to the large increase in "bad debts" accumulated by the banks, and deflation began, against the backdrop of the inability of the government and bureaucracy to take decisions that would be painful for entrepreneurs. In order to revive the economy, the government resorted to increasing state spending on infrastructure, while construction was paid for by the issuing of bonds, which were mainly bought up by its own population. State debt began increasing rapidly during the depression in the 1990s, and Japan took first place by reference to the ratio of accumulated debt to GDP. It also fell victim to its excessive social obligations, against the backdrop of the reduced number of people fit for employment in the population and a higher number of pensioners and people with dependents.

The expansion of exports, as a result of its improved position in the global economy, and a large-scale program of anti-crisis measures, were the key factors behind the resurgence of the Japanese economy. On 11th March 2011, however, the north-eastern coast of the island of Honshu was destroyed by a catastrophic earthquake, and beset by a tsunami, which caused the destruction of the nuclear power station at Fukushima. This "triple blow" took the lives of more than 20,000 people, and left 150,000 without a roof over their heads. The overall damage stood at more than 430 billion dollars,

---

[23] Joseph Nye, Jr., *The Future of Power*. PublicAffairs, 2011. PP. 164-165.

[24] Mariya Prikhodina, "Skazka o poteryannom vremeni" ("The Tale of the Lost Time"), *RBK*, May 2013. PP. 46-51.

7% of Japan's annual GDP. The expectation was that it would take 30 to 40 years to overcome the consequences of the catastrophe.[25]

A complicated situation arose in respect of foreign trade. Japanese corporations conceded to companies from South Korea, Taiwan and China their global supremacy in the manufacturing of electronic components, personal computers, TVs, power equipment, black metals, and plastics. They remain leaders in the field of unique equipment (supercomputers), and in the production of medical equipment and innovative medicines, and construction vehicles.

Japan has fallen into a demographic trap. The population of working age, defined as 15 to 64, reached its highest point in 1995: 87.3 million; by 2012, though, it had fallen to 77.5 million. In the mid-1990s, the workforce grew by 2 million people every year, and it is now growing by 1.25 million a year. Japan is among the leading countries in terms of life-expectancy, and the percentage of people over 65 in the population doubled, reaching 26%. In the middle of this century, this group will make up 40% of the population. More Pampers were sold to the elderly than were bought for babies. The birth rate is 1.4, with fewer babies being born than ever before, meaning that demand for everything – from housing to automobiles – is falling. Japan has become a sort of democratic gerontocracy, in which the older generation is the decisive political force, whose political weight is significantly higher than its numbers would suggest. Firstly, pensioners take part in elections more actively than other age groups. Secondly, the electoral districts are delineated in such a way that regions with an elderly population have greater representation in parliament. Japanese corporations are full of elderly employees, who earn more money than their younger colleagues. Spending on pensions, medical services and care for the elderly amount to a third of the budget. Social mobility is blocked from above.[26]

The level of unemployment is low by international standards. For Japan, however, where, throughout the post-war years, unemployment practically did not exist, 4% was its highest figure in recent decades. The number of temporary workers, who do not have insurance or social security, has risen to 20 million people (34% of the workforce). Suicide and "karosi" (death

---

[25] "Japan After the Tsunami. Grinding on", *The Economist*, February 7, 2015. P. 44.

[26] Yoichi Funabashi, "Japan's Gray-Haired Pacifism", *The New York Times*, August 12, 2015 <https://www.nytimes.com/2015/08/13/opinion/japans-gray-haired-pacifism.html>; Robin Harding, "New World of Work: Japan's Lost Generation Struggles to Catch Up", *The Financial Times*, August 9, 2015 <https://www.ft.com/content/6f1a7626-0ade-11e5-9df4-00144feabdc0>.

caused by relentless, exhausting work) are increasingly afflicting young men. There is a growing number of "hikikomori" – this is the name given to young people who do not pass the entrance exams to prestigious universities, or do not get a job at a major corporation immediately after leaving them. These people will probably never get a "second chance".[27] The level of poverty (in Japanese terms, this means an income per head of less than 12,000 dollars a year) has reached 14%, two times higher than a decade ago.

Non-Westminster Democracy

For a long time, Japan went through a period of political instability: not a single one of the six cabinets which preceded the election of Shinzo Abe in 2012 stayed in power for more than a year. This was not unique to this period, however: since 1885, there have been 96 prime ministers in the country, meaning that the average term in office for a prime minister is 1.4 years.[28]

The problems of modern-day Japan are also a result of its specific political system. The institutions of representative democracy were injected into a country in which, before 1945, the organic prerequisites for such democracy were lacking. Japan's contemporary political system differs from the Western ones on a whole host of parameters. Although there is a multiparty system in theory, one party dominates in practice. Even the prime ministers are heavily dependent on the distribution of power between the fractions in parliament and in the LDP, and on the unchanging senior career civil servants, who have authority in society and consider themselves irreplaceable. The civil servants retain a monopoly on information and determine the level of openness of government policy. Under pressure from the government, popular TV-program hosts are routinely withdrawn from leading TV channels. Even foreign journalists complain about attempts at censorship. "Reporters Without Borders" has moved Japan 50 positions down in the rankings for freedom of speech, and it lies in 61st place.[29] Executive decisions are often

---

[27] Alexander Zotin, "Geront nashego vremeni" ("A Gerontocrat of Our Time"), *Kommersant. Den'gi* (*The Businessman. Money*), November 19-25, 2012. PP. 23-24.

[28] Mariya Prikhodina, "Akio Kawato: Populisty sil'neye zemletryaseniya" ("Akio Kawato: Populists are More Powerful Than an Earthquake"), *RBK*, May 2013. PP. 52-53.

[29] See: E. V. Molodyakova, "Politicheskaya sisema Yaponii" ("Japan's Political System"), in *Vostok i politika: Politicheskiye sistemy, politicheskiye kul'tury, politicheskiye protsessy* (*The East and Politics: Political Systems, Political Cultures, Political Processes*), ed. by A. D. Voskresenskiy. Moscow, 2011. PP. 547-568; D.V. Strel'tsov, "Sovremennaya sistema gosudarstvennogo upravleniya Yaponii" ("Japan's Modern System of State Governance"), in *Politicheskiye sistemy*

more significant than laws. The "grey zone" in decision-making, due to the mutually overlapping interests of the bureaucracy, political circles and the business world, is vast.[30] There are some influential political dynasties in Japan: four of the last six premiers – Abe, Fukuda, Aso, Hatoyama – were the children or grandchildren of former prime ministers. Two fifths of the deputies from the LDP are guaranteed to be elected, by regions which were represented in the past by their fathers, grandfathers or uncles.[31]

In 2012, Shinzo Abe brought about his "second coming" to power, calling for an "unlimited stimulating" of the economy worth 15 trillion yen (181 billion dollars), and a reduction of the threshold for corporation tax from 38% to 20%, so as to achieve 2% inflation and 3% growth in GDP.[32] The LDP's platform called for the post-war Constitution to be rejected and replaced with a document which might emphasize "Japanese honor and Japanese-ness", and for a review of the "unjust" view of the country's role in the Second World War as an aggressor. After the LDP's victory, the chairman of the Bank of Japan, Haruhiko Kuroda, announced a doubling of the cash base within two years, and investments in state bonds and assets, in order to push inflation to 2% in two years.[33] These measures resulted in 2.6% growth in 2013.

In order to solve the problem of the budget deficit, on 1st April 2014 sales tax increased from 5% to 8%. This not only displeased the people, but also led to a fall in GDP of 7.1% in a single quarter. The Moody's agency reduced Japan's credit rating to A1, which is lower than China or South Korea, and on a par with Estonia or the Bermuda.[34]

---

i politicheskiye kul'tury Vostoka (*Political Systems and Political Cultures of the East*), ed. by A. D. Voskresenskiy. Moscow, 2006. PP. 550-570.

[30] "Japanese Politics. To the District Born", *The Economist*, November 29, 2014. P. 48.

[31] "Japan's Dismal Election", *The Wall Street Journal*, November 25, 2012 <https://www.wsj.com/articles/SB10001424127887324352004578132492249786894>; Margarita Lyutova, "Borets s deflyatsiyey" ("Fighting Against Deflation"), *Vedomosti*, December 27, 2012 <https://www.vedomosti.ru/politics/articles/2012/12/27/borec_s_deflyaciej>.

[32] ""Japan's Dismal Election", The Wall Street Journal, November 25, 2012 <https://www.wsj.com/articles/SB10001424127887324352004578132492249786894>; Margarita Lyutova, "Novyy prem'yer Yaponii Sindzo Abe planiruyet vyvesti ekonomiku iz retsessii" ("New Japanese Prime Minister Shinzo Abe Plans to Pull the Economy Out of Recession"), Vedomosti, December 27, 2012 <https://www.vedomosti.ru/politics/articles/2012/12/27/borec_s_deflyaciej>.

[33] Sergey Smirnov, "Yaponiya boretsya za inflyatsiyu" ("Japan is Fighting for Inflation"), *Vedomosti*, April 5, 2013 <https://www.vedomosti.ru/newspaper/articles/2013/04/05/yaponiya_boretsya_zainflyaciyu>.

[34] Jonathan Soble, "Consumers Bolster Japan's Growth: Abenomics", *The Financial Times*, May 17, 2013. P. 5; "Coming to a Crunch. Time is Running Out for Abenomics", in *The World in 2015: The Economist*, 2015. P. 68; Ben McLannahan, "Moody's Downgrades Japan's Credit Rating", The

Analysts saw the main risks in the possibility of a debt collapse by Japan. For the time being, Japanese investors are prepared to pay back state debt at a very low interest rate (95% of the debt is in the hands of citizens, via banks, insurance companies and pension funds). If growth stops, though, the mood may change among the people. In economic science, the word "Japan" has begun to be used at times almost as a curse-word, as a symbol of economic inefficiency. Paul Krugman, wishing to emphasize the failures of Sweden's economic policy, wrote that it was being turned into Japan.[35]

State debt reached 229% of GDP in 2015, and this was a consequence of deflation, of the doubling – from 12% to 24% – of GDP, of social spending, set against stagnation in income at the level of one third of GDP, and increased spending on servicing the debt (a quarter of the budget). The budget deficit (without debt payment) stood at 6.6%, and the rise in prices was nil. Whereas house prices were falling in China, in Japan, by contrast, they were rising rapidly due to the low interest rates, the strong supply of money, and the weakening of the yen. The Japanese are buying smaller apartments than they did a few years ago.[36]

Wages still did not grow: since 1995 they have risen by 0.3%. A growing portion of corporate profits is spent on social taxes payments. The deflation trap has still not been overcome. More than 60% of GDP goes towards household consumption, yet households are reluctant consumers: both due to deflation, which forces them to wait for the prices of goods to drop, and due to a lack of confidence in any rise in their earnings. During the first quarter of 2018, Japan's economy contracted for the first time since 2015, by 0.6%.[37] That is why the Bank of Japan maintains "extremely low" interest rates, not joining other big financial regulators in rolling back crisis-era stimulus policies.[38]

....

Financial Times, December 1, 2014 <https://www.ft.com/content/eea537be-7939-11e4-a57d-00144feabdc0>.

[35] William Pesek, "Krugman's Well-Timed Wisecracks on Japan", *Gulf News*, April 28, 2014 <https://gulfnews.com/opinion/op-eds/krugmans-well-timed-wisecracks-on-japan-1.1325373>.

[36] Kirill Rodionov, "Yaponiya buksuyet" ("Japan is stalling"), *Vedomosti*, April 16, 2015. P. 5; "Economic Policy in Japan. End of the Affair", *The Economist*, April 11, 2015. PP. 48-49; Robin Harding, "Shrinking Tokyo Living Rooms Put Squeeze on Abenomics", *The Financial Times*, February 6, 2015 <https://www.ft.com/content/fec40338-a2d2-11e4-ac1c-00144feab7de>.

[37] Robin Harding, "Fall in Japan GDP Halts Longest Run of Growth since 1989", *The Financial Times*, May 17, 2018. P. 7.

[38] Leo Lewis and Kana Inagaki, "BoJ Bucks Central Bank Trend to Stick with 'Extremely Low' Rates", *The Financial Times*, August 1, 2018. P. 13.

It is not all doom and gloom, however. The economy has grown by 1.2% since 2014.[39] Despite the drop in the number of people of working age, the number of people in employment has risen by 2.2 million since 2012: more and more people are choosing not to retire, and more and more women are starting to work (though they are paid 74% of their male equivalents' earnings and do not hold senior managerial roles), and there are already 1 million foreign workers in the country. Meanwhile, the supply of jobs is growing, with 1.5 vacancies for every jobseeker, although the jobs in question are not always permanent positions. Unemployment fell to 2.8%, the lowest it has been since the early 1990s. The yen is 30% cheaper than the dollar by comparison with 2012, but the Nikkei index rose by 150% in that time.[40]

Unsinkable Aircraft Carrier

For a long time, Japan held back from taking an active part in solving global military and political problems. This was due both to the traumatic shock it had suffered (the first occupation of the country in its history, and the atomic bombs dropped on Hiroshima and Nagasaki), and the presence of the American security umbrella. Japanese policy in choosing its allies has traditionally been built on "following the strong, rather than resisting him", in "forming an alliance with the most influential force". In contemporary Japan, there is no tradition of independent foreign policy or military-political thought. All the key concepts are in many ways borrowed from the USA's national security doctrines and the plans for American military deployment. Those in favor of a stance oriented towards the Asian world are gaining in strength, but such a policy is far from simple: Japan, to put it mildly, is not loved in Asia.

For a long time, the framework of Japan's defence policy consisted of the Constitution and a host of pacifist laws, which stipulated the introduction of a purely defensive policy, the rejection of a transformation into a military state, civil control over the armed forces, adherence to the three non-nucle-

---

[39] "The Quiet but Substantial Successes of Abenomics", *The Financial Times*, May 2, 2017. P. 8.
[40] "Wages in Japan. Behind a Pay Wall", *The Economist*, September 17, 2016. P. 65; Robin Harding, "Japan's Night Workers Call It a Day", *The Financial Times*, February 22, 2017. P. 5; "Japan's Labor Market. Wanted: Stroppier Employees", *The Economist*, April 8, 2017. PP. 67-68; "The Quiet but Substantial Successes of Abenomics", *The Financial Times*, May 2, 2017. P. 8; Thisanka Siripala, "Thanks to a Shopping Spree, Japan Is Looking Up. It May Not Last", *The New York Times*, August 19, 2017. P. B4(L); "Japan. The Slow-Grilled Economy", *The Economist*, November 18, 2017. PP. 65-66.

ar principles (not to possess, not to produce, and not to allow the storage of, nuclear weapons on its territory). In formal terms, there are no armed forces in Japan, merely "self-defence forces", on which no more than 1% of GDP may be spent.

A new campaign to step up military programs began against the backdrop of the increased military potential of China and, particularly, after the nuclear missile tests conducted by North Korea in April – May 2009. The government of Taro Aso was the first to call North Korea a threat to Japan; it deployed on Japanese soil elements of the American THAAD system, and declared its interest in acquiring its own operational and tactical containment forces. The status of the Ministry of Defence was enshrined in law, a full-scale intelligence community was formed, and the legislative basis for the actions of the armed forces overseas was expanded.

In December 2010, *The Main Aspects of the Program of National Defence* was published, which declared a transition from "basic" to "dynamic" defence, designed to ensure a more flexible response to external military threats.

Even though military spending is still limited to 1% of GDP, Japan now has the fifth largest military potential in the world. There are 247,150 service men and women in its armed forces, of which 150,850 are in the territorial defence force, 45,350 are in the naval defence force, and 47,000 are in the air force. Japan has 1,600 military planes, and four gigantic helicopter carriers. The country has four military satellites. About 54,000 US servicemen and women are on assignment in Japan.[41]

Japan is capable of creating its own nuclear weapon, and has not ruled out such a possibility. By the 70th anniversary of the bombing of Hiroshima and Nagasaki, Japan had accumulated 47 metric tons of plutonium, enough to create 6,000 bombs similar to the ones that were dropped on those two cities by the Americans.[42]

Shinzo Abe declared himself in favor of reviewing Article 9 of the Japanese Constitution, but his far-reaching plans in this regard met with resistance on the part of his pacifist partner in the parliamentary coalition, the Komeito party. For this reason, the policy of re-militarization was initially adopted in a slightly toned-down form.

---

[41] *The Military Balance. 2019. The Annual Assessment of Global Military Capabilities and Defence Economics.* London, 2019. PP. 276-280.

[42] Peter Wynn Kirby, "Japan's Plutonium Problem", *The New York Times*, August 16, 2015 <https://www.nytimes.com/2015/08/17/opinion/japans-plutonium-problem.html>.

In December 2013, parliament adopted a law on the creation of a National Security Council, modelled on, and similar to, the equivalent structures in the USA and the UK. A new National Security Strategy was published. The Defence Ministry launched amended Provisions on national defence and a Medium-term Defence Program, in which they declared their intention to create "dynamic armed forces", capable of projecting power beyond the borders of the "Japanese periphery".[43]

On 1st April 2014, the ban on the exporting of weapons, which had been in place in Japan since 1976, was lifted. Tokyo is now able to offer ships, anti-aircraft systems, radio-electronic equipment, and electronic components, competing more with the USA and the EU than with Russia.[44] A concept of "limited collective self-defence" was adopted, which would be used in three cases: if an attack on another state represented an "obvious danger" to Japan's existence and to the constitutional rights of its citizens; if there was no other way of protecting Japan and its citizens; and if the use of force could be kept to a minimum. China and South Korea have already expressed their understandable concern over this.[45]

In 2015, the government brought in a series of laws which interpreted the Constitution in a spirit of what Abe called "proactive pacifism". The self-defence forces, despite opposition from the majority of public opinion, were granted the right to use military force overseas. The Prime Minister's popularity rating fell to 38% (down from 70% a year earlier).[46]

The crisis around North Korea was used to the full extent to create military hysteria and to force the issue of constitutional reform. The study of the martial art of jukendo was put back on the school curriculum; this discipline was used by the imperial army during the Second World War and prohibited thereafter. The largest helicopter-carrier, the Izumo, accompanied American military vessels for the first time. Military expenditure rose to 48 billion dollars. Major arms acquisitions from the USA are planned, including

---

[43] *Strategic Survey 2014: The Annual Review of World Affairs*. Routledge, 2014. PP. 331-332.

[44] Konstantin Volkov, "Tokio mozhet stat' ser'yeznym igrokom na rynke vooruzheniy" ("Tokyo Could Become a Serious Player in the Arms Market"), *Izvestiya*, April 1, 2014 <https://iz.ru/news/568504>.

[45] *Strategic Survey 2014: The Annual Review of World Affairs*. Routledge, 2014. P. 332-334.

[46] Robin Harding, "Abe Wraps Past War Apologies in Nationalism", *The Financial Times*, August 15, 2015. P. 3; "Japan's Security. Gloves Off", *The Economist*, Vol. 416, July 11, 2015. PP. 38-39; Inna Sidorkova and Pavel Tarasenko, "Yaponiya rasshiryayet granitsy samooborony" ("Japan Expands the Boundaries of Self-Defense"), *Kommersant (The Businessman)*, July 17, 2015 <https://www.kommersant.ru/doc/2769253>.

state-of-the-art air defence systems. The question of a significant increase in the size of the navy and of capabilities for conducting cyber-warfare has been put on the agenda.[47]

In May 2017, Abe identified, for the first time, the moment when a decision was to be taken on whether or not to review the Constitution – 2020. The idea of abolishing Article 9 is backed by 45% of the electorate according to one poll, with 46% against. A different poll had 25% in favor and 57% against, and it is worth noting that young people, who are not overly keen to see active service, tend to have particularly strong objections. The number of young people of conscription age, incidentally, is falling all the time.[48]

A characteristic feature of Japanese foreign policy in the post-war period was unstinting loyalty to its American ally, underpinned by a US military presence. Washington also sees its military-political alliance with Tokyo as the main framing structure for the system of American alliances and tools of influence in the Asia Pacific, or Indo-Pacific as it is called more and more often. Japan provided extensive political, diplomatic, material and technical support to the USA in its war with Vietnam. In 1964, Japan agreed to let American nuclear submarines dock in its ports, and in 1967 to the housing of nuclear aircraft carriers and other ships. The stance of the Japanese elite has never been unambiguous, however. There are "nationalist", "pacifist" and "mercantile" trends within the LDP, each of which had its own view of the threats and priorities. The "mercantilists" proceeded from the notion that the main security threat was caused by the country's isolation and the downturn in the system of global trade. The "nationalists" sounded the alarm about the loss of sovereignty and Japan's complete submission to its senior partner, while the "pacifists" were concerned about the risk of being drawn into an armed conflict, against the country's will.[49]

....

[47] Yokio Okamoto, "North Korea Has Forced Japan to Leave Its Comfort Zone", *The Financial Times*, April 28, 2017. P. 9; Cai Hong, "Abe Opens New Chapter on Patriotism", *China Daily Asia*, May 8, 2017 <http://epaper.chinadailyasia.com/asia-weekly/article-11960.html>; Robin Harding, "Japan Warship Escorts US Vessel for First Time in Modern History", *The Financial Times*, May 2, 2017. P. 5; Motoko Rich, "North Korea's Threat Pushes Japan to Reassess Its Might and Rights", *The New York Times*, September 15, 2017 <https://www.nytimes.com/2017/09/15/world/asia/japan-north-korea-missile-defense.html>.

[48] "Japan's Self-Defence Forces. Barmy Army", *The Economist*, February 18, 2017. P. 47; Leo Lewis, "Abe Sets 2020 Target for Amending Japan's Pacifist Constitution", *The Financial Times*, May 4, 2017. P. 4; "Japanese Politics. On the Offensive", *The Economist*, May 6, 2017. PP. 49-50.

[49] Dmitriy Strel'tsov, "Moskva i Tokio: vyyti iz spyachki" ("Moscow and Tokyo: Breaking Out of Their Slumbers"), *Rossiya v global'noy politike* (*Russia in Global Affairs*), September/October 2011 <https://globalaffairs.ru/articles/moskva-i-tokio-vyjti-iz-spyachki/>.

Abe was in favor of a close military-political partnership with the USA. The framework of military cooperation has been expanded, and tension in relation to American bases in Okinawa has been reduced for the time being. Obama was the first American President to state that the USA's obligation to protect Japanese territory extends to the Senkaku Islands. Few people in Japan believed, incidentally, that the USA would genuinely do battle against China if a conflict were to break out in connection with these islands.

During his election campaign of 2016, Trump criticized Japan on several occasions, accusing it of currency machinations, of pressing its cars through to the American market and of inadequate financing of its own defence. After Trump was elected, the level of trust in the American leadership fell from 78% to 24% in Japan. Abe hastened to salvage the relationship, and was the first head of state to meet Trump as early as in November 2016, in the most informal of settings – on the golf course. In February 2017, a three-day official visit by the Japanese premier took place in Washington, when there was talk of a new phase of "special relations". Anti-Japanese rhetoric in Washington vanished, and joint steps against North Korea welded the bilateral alliance together, helping Abe secure an increase in the military budget.[50]

A serious challenge to Japan's relations with the outside world as a whole is presented by Abe's policy of stoking nationalist sentiment. In many ways, he has changed the interpretation of the events of the Second World War, placing greater emphasis on the motives for the battle against Western colonialism and in protection of Asian values. He denied the Nanking Massacre of 1937, and Korean sexual slavery, and he regularly visited the Yasukuni shrine, where Japanese military criminals are buried, and saw the postwar occupation of Japan by the US as a humiliation. Most Japanese are not committed to nationalist feelings, however, and Abe's electoral support is more closely associated with his economic policy than with his campaign to revive the national spirit.[51]

For Japan, the US and Western Europe are not only partners, but also economic rivals, while the Asian countries are less so, since their development was in alignment with the concept of "flying geese", and they are in a different technological niche. Asia's role in Japan's foreign policy is growing steadily.

---

[50] Ian Bremmer, "Sorry, Brits: Abe and Trump Have the Real 'Special Relationship'", *Time*, February 27 –March 6, 2017. P. 8; Takako Hikotani, "Trump's Gift to Japan", *Foreign Affairs*, September/October 2017. PP. 21-23.

[51] Jennifer Lind, "Restraining Nationalism in Japan", *The International Herald Tribune*, July 25, 2013. P. 6.

The second most significant area – after the USA – in Japan's foreign policy is China. Diplomatic relations between them were only established in 1972. In 1978, Japan signed a treaty on peace and friendship with China, agreeing (with a few provisos) to the inclusion of a clause on the battle with "hegemonism", to which the Chinese leadership added an anti-Soviet meaning. At the same time, Sino-Japanese relations are characterized by profound mutual distrust and acute problems: the perception of history (diametrically opposed views of the events of the Sino-Japanese war of 1937-1945); territorial disputes (China's claims to the Senkaku Islands); the future of Taiwan; matters of human rights; illegal immigration from China to Japan; China's negative attitude towards the American-Japanese union; the dramatic increase in China's potential as a regional superpower and the possibility that Beijing will devise a concept for a "Great East Asia" without Japan.[52]

In April 2014, Japan demonstrated to China a united Japanese-Taiwanese front, by signing an agreement in Taipei to allow Taiwanese sailors into the waters around Senkaku. Abe and Xi Jinping did not meet until November 2014, at the APEC summit in Beijing; that meeting led to a thaw, to some extent, in the ice of distrust. As William Choong, who has studied the history of the two countries' bilateral relations, notes, "[a] focus solely on contemporary issues misses the fact that bilateral relations between Japan and China have always been cyclical, turning from conflict to cooperation and back again."[53] There will still be plenty of twists and turns to come.

An important place in Japan's foreign policy strategy is occupied by South Korea, both in terms of its economic interests, and as a "front-line state" in the provision of security against "threats from Pyongyang". In recent years, Seoul has been striving in an increasingly obvious way to achieve parity in its relations with Tokyo, to whom it has played second fiddle for many years. A significant irritant in the bilateral relations were Tokyo's claims in respect of Seoul, and "profound disagreements" in the assessment of the historical past. In March 2015, there was a meeting between the foreign ministers of Japan, China and South Korea, and the first bilateral Japanese-South Korean summit took place in April.[54] The period of détente ended early in 2017,

....

[52] "Bol'shaya Vostochnaya Aziya": mirovaya politika i regional'nyye transformatsii ("Greater East Asia": World Politics and Regional Transformations), ed. by A. D. Voskresenskiy. Moscow, 2010. PP. 98-99.

[53] William Choong, *The Ties that Divide: History, Honor and Territory in Sino-Japanese Relations*. Routledge, 2014. P. 14.

[54] "South Korea and Japan. Tentative Two-Step", *The Economist*, April 18, 2015. P. 35.

when a memorial was erected opposite the Japanese consulate in Busan to Korean sexual slavery during the era of Japanese colonial rule.[55]

Japan is adopting an increasingly tough stance in relation to North Korea. Tokyo supported, and still supports, the toughest sanctions against Pyongyang. Bans were introduced, unilaterally, on all imports from North Korea and on the use of Japanese ports by North Korean ships. The North Korean threat is seen by many not only as a challenge in its own right, but also as an "addition" to the Chinese threat. The deployment of THAAD by Tokyo and Washington should be seen as part of the strategy of deterring China, although formally it is aimed against threats on the part of North Korea.

One of Japan's foreign policy priorities is the deepening of relations with the ASEAN countries, the main aspects of which have been identified as "open regionalism", economic partnership, and the creation of bilateral and, if possible, multilateral free trade zones. Paradoxically, one of Japan's partners in the region is a country that was until recently a geopolitical enemy – Communist Vietnam. As part of the strategic partnership that was declared, Tokyo is helping Vietnam create a coastal defence system and to take control of its own sources of rare metals, so as to avoid a situation whereby China has a monopoly on their production.[56]

By the end of 2013 Abe finished visiting ASEAN capitals aiming at establishing a united front against China. At the ASEAN-Japan summit in December 2013 in Tokyo, 20 billion dollars of economic aid was promised to all ten ASEAN countries. However, Japan's ability to bring the South Asian countries together to counterbalance China is still questionable.[57]

The decision by the United States to walk away from the negotiations on the Trans-Pacific Partnership (TPP) forced Japan to start showing greater independence in its Asian policy. Tokyo decided first that the TPP would not make sense without American participation, but then changed its mind, proposing – successfully – that the rest of the participants go ahead. On 23rd January 2018, the remaining 11 members met in Tokyo to finalize the details of the plan which would come into force in 2019. Although, without the US, which accounted for two third of the original's block output, the TPP lost in significance.[58]

---

[55] "South Korea and Japan. Future Tense", *The Economist*, January 14, 2017. PP. 24-25.

[56] Sergey Strokan', "Yaponiya predlagayet antikitayskiye uslugi" ("Japan is Offering Anti-Chinese Services"), *Kommersant (The Businessman)*, July 17, 2012 <https://www.kommersant.ru/doc/1981978>.

[57] *Strategic Survey 2014: The Annual Review of World Affairs*. Routledge, 2014. PP. 337-338.

[58] "Trading Places. Why Free Trade Is Not a Political Milestone in Asia", *The Economist*,

Also changing his mind, and against the will of Washington, Abe did not exclude Japanese participation in the Chinese Belt and Road Project and even in the China-led Asian Infrastructure Investment Bank (AIIB).[59] "Mr. Abe has started to consider a more independent role for Japan in Asia: one that looks beyond the current White House as Japan prepares for an era in which American influence may be waning," *The New York Times* noted.[60]

A limiting factor on the rise in Japan's influence in the economics and politics of the APR is the reluctance of the countries in the region to accept Tokyo's political leadership, not to mention its military leadership. In military-political matters, Japan's neighbors are inclined to see it as no more than a body-double of the USA. Few are willing to form a new "sphere of joint flourishing" led by Japan. Tokyo does not have any friends it can count on in East Asia.

Japan is increasingly making its presence felt in Africa, and in Tokyo's opinion, the experience of the industrial advances in the Meiji era and the post-war reconstruction are very suitable for this purpose. There has been investment in the Program for the Infrastructural Development of Africa (transport, energy, water), and the Japanese have helped to provide infrastructure for 14 rapid border-crossing points between African countries. Since 2008, the Japan Bank for International Co-operation has been issuing loans, at low interest rates, to Africa, and Japanese companies are busily conducting geological surveys on the continent.[61]

The Japanese have not stepped back one iota from their position, which is that Russia is "duty-bound" to give them back all four of the Southern Kuril Islands. No interim scenarios are even discussed. A major concession by Vladimir Putin, who, displaying notable political courage, agreed to return to the formula signed and ratified by the two parties in the Joint Declaration of 1956, stipulating the handover by the Russian side of two islands after the signing of a peace treaty, met with great disquiet and was rejected by Tokyo. Since Russia represents an easy and well-targeted propaganda subject, To-

---

January 27, 2018. P. 47.

[59] "Japan Proposes a Rescue Mission for the TPP", *The Financial Times*, May 4, 2017. P. 8; Chen Yang, "Abe's B&R Decision Hinges on Washington", *Global Times*, June 9, 2017 <http://www.globaltimes.cn/content/1050889.shtml>.

[60] Motoko Rich, "Japan Still Seeks U.S. Protection but Quietly Stakes Its Own Path", *The New York Times*, August 19, 2017. P. A8(L).

[61] Yutaka Yoshizawa, "Japan Is Committed to Aiding African Development", *Independent Online*, March 12, 2013 <https://www.iol.co.za/business-report/economy/japan-is-committed-to-aiding-african-development-1484584>.

kyo cannot strike the problem of the "northern territories" off the agenda in bilateral relations. In Moscow, the belief is that the post-war regulation of the situation was resolved in the Joint Declaration of 1956 and in a series of bilateral agreements.

Does that leave Russo-Japanese relations at a complete stalemate? The situation is not quite as hopeless as that. Among the G7 countries in the 1990s, Japan was the one with the most favorable attitude towards Russia on a whole host of issues: the fight against terrorism in the North Caucasus, human rights, the provision of economic aid following the default in 1998, Russia's accession to APEC.[62] The advances made in the economy, which for long decades was a hostage to politics, are clear for all to see. Russia is an important supplier of energy resources, non-ferrous metals, seafood, and timber. Japanese companies are the leaders among Russia's foreign partners in terms of the volume of capital investment in Russian fuel and energy projects in the Far East. Japanese investment funded 30% of the Sakhalin-1 project and 22.5% of the Sakhalin-2 project. The latter gets its raw materials from Russia's LNG plant, owned by Sakhalin Energy, in the village of Prigorodnoye in the south of Sakhalin, whose capacity is 9.6 million tons a year (5% of global production of LNG), and 60% of the gas produced is contracted for supplies to Japan.[63] All the major Japanese car producers are present in Russia.

Shifts on the political front have been less noticeable. Most of the Japanese experts and leading newspapers still have a fairly negative attitude towards Russia. The level of awareness about Russia and its politics is low. There is a superiority complex in Japan in relation to Russia. As the London-based Japanologist Alexander Bukh has shown, the Japanese ascribe to Russia all the developmental shortcomings, and cultural and psychological pathologies, which one could have found in the Anglo-American discourse about Japan in the days of the Second World War. Russia, for Japan (where Western models of knowledge are dominant), just as for the West, is the Other, and "the differentness of Russia for the West has been used in the Japanese discourse to construct the idea that Japan belongs to a universal civilization, but at the same time to show its unique socio-cul-

---

[62] *Sovremennyye rossiysko-yaponskiye otnosheniya i perspektivy ikh razvitiya* (*Contemporary Russo-Japanese Relations and Prospects for Their Development*), ed. by A. N. Panov et al. Moscow, 2012. P. 27.

[63] A.V. Ivanov, "Energeticheskaya strategiya Yaponii i rossiysko-yaponskoye sotrudnichestvo v oblasti energetiki" ("Japan's Energy Strategy and Russo-Japanese Cooperation in the Field of Energy"), *Yezhegodnik IMI-2010* (*Annual IMI-2010*). Moscow, 2011. P. 261.

tural superiority not only over Russia, but over the West itself."[64] It also is commonplace to read remarks about a rise of "Russian imperialism".

At the same time, anti-Japanese sentiment has been on the rise in Russia, too. From 1995 to 2011, the level of sympathy fell from 70% to 45%, while the level of antipathy rose from 19% to 31%. More than 90% of Russians are against the handing over of the Kuril Islands. It is hard to imagine there being any fundamental advances in bilateral relations in the foreseeable future, particularly in light of the sanctions brought against Russia, and the ban imposed on importing some Japanese goods imposed by Russia in response. It should be said, however, that "to date, Japan's sanctions have been the softest of all in comparison with the measures taken by the other countries in the G7."[65] None of the joint Russo-Japanese economic projects were brought to a halt, and Putin and Abe went on official visits to one another on a regular basis and kept emphasizing their mutual aspiration to sign the peace treaty, albeit with no likelihood of success in the near future.

Japan is frequently categorized as being part of the West. From a civilizational perspective, though, as we have seen, it is definitely not part of the West.

In the 1970s and 1980s, Japan's successful economic growth, which contrasted with the decline in the American economy, caused disillusionment with Western models and fresh interest in Japan's native culture. The Japanese do not find it all that easy to "connect with Asia", though. "Japan is also perceived as 'Asian' only by the West," notes Moïsi. "In Asia today, Japan, more than sixty years after the end of World War II, is still resented as uniquely, arrogantly 'Nippon' by the majority of its neighbors. Too Western for the majority of Asians, the Japanese have remained too Asian to be fully understood by Westerners."[66]

For the Japanese, the Asian countries were for a long time "different from us, and we must differ from them". In recent years, though, a psychological shift has been seen, and some Asian countries are becoming

....

[64] Alexander Bukh, *Yaponiya: natsional'naya identichnost' i vneshnyaya politika* (*Japan: National Identity and Foreign Policy*). Moscow, 2012. PP. 83, 222.

[65] Vladimir Petrovskiy, "Rossiya i Vostochnaya Aziya v kontekste ukrainskogo krizisa: 'net' sanktsiyam, 'da' novomu miroporyadku" ("Russia and East Asia in the Context of the Ukrainian Crisis: 'No' to Sanctions, 'Yes' to a New World Order"), *Mezhdunarodnaya zhizn'* (*International Life*), October 2014. P. 53.

[66] Dominique Moïsi, *The Geopolitics of Emotion: How Cultures of Fear, Humiliation and Hope are Reshaping the World*. Random House, 2009.

"different, and we must be more like them".⁶⁷ The Japanese began going on tours to, and holidaying in, their neighboring countries. Interest in Asian culture is on the rise. Disillusionment with the West and envy of it have vanished, but there is an obvious curiosity among the Japanese about Thai and Chinese cuisine, interest in the applied art of Vietnam and the island of Bali, and in the cinema of Hong Kong, Taiwan and South Korea. There is strong interest in India as the cradle of Buddhism, in its esotericism and ancient culture. "Until recently the Japanese tended to look upon the East through the filter of the stereotypes of Western 'Asia-sceptics' – with an unconcealed sense of superiority. Now, in the main, the Japanese people's attitude to other Asians is not flavored with snobbery; they think of them as relatives."⁶⁸ Japan itself has been making stubborn use of "soft power" in East Asia. The Japanese sub-culture is increasingly taking the younger generation in East Asia under its influence. The shops Isetan and Marui are having a powerful influence on consumer tastes in the region.

The continuing economic stagnation is having a negative impact on the national sense of self. The country is unsure what its nature is and what path it should follow. It is pained by the fact that it has been pushed off its economic perch not just by China, but also by India. In political circles in Tokyo and, in particular, at the Ministry of Foreign Affairs (the Gaimusho), one can sense an obsessive fear of China.

The search for a new identity is going along a well-trodden path: the Japanese are dreaming of a "comfortable Japan", a "beautiful country", "the Switzerland of Asia", "the country of mankind's second chance", and are building "a good society", in which, however, one can still perceive the contours of the old, traditional way of life. Can Japan lay claim to the role of a superpower in the 21st century? It is hardly likely. "Roughly the size of California, Japan will never have the geographical or population scale of the United States," wrote Joseph Nye. "Its success in modernization and democracy and its popular culture provide Japan with some soft power, but ethnocentric attitudes and policies undercut it."⁶⁹

Japanese traditionalism is bowing to pressure from globalization, but preserving its hidden power. Japan is a country that one could never confuse with any other, in the same way that a kimono is an unmistakable

---

[67] Sergey Chugrov, *Yaponiya v poiskakh novoy identichnosti* (*Japan in Search of a New Identity*). Moscow, 2010. P. 196.

[68] Ibid. PP. 206-207.

[69] Joseph Nye, Jr., *The Future of Power*. PublicAffairs, 2011. P. 165.

garment; also unmistakable are the wooden sandals, the *geta*, shaped like little stools. And as for karate, katanas, ikebana, bonzais, sushi, and sake – they need no introduction. Russia is one of the few countries where Japanese cuisine is more popular than Chinese. Japanese blood is still flowing with vigor.

CHAPTER 9
THE INDIAN WAY

The second most populous country in the world, India is set to become the most populous in the near future. The third-largest economy in the world, India looks likely to become the second-biggest by the middle of this century, overtaking the United States. It is a country on which the world depends to an incredibly large extent. "As the United States and China become great power rivals, the direction in which India tilts could determine the course of geopolitics in Eurasia in the twenty-first century," Robert Kaplan believes. "India, in other words, looms as the ultimate pivot state."[1]

Indianism

India is the core state in Southern Asia. Located in tropical and sub-equatorial latitudes, fenced off by a chain of the highest mountains in the world – the Himalayas – from the winds to the North, it is one of the hottest countries in the world. It is known for the exceptional diversity of its natural beauty: snowy peaks, scorched savannahs, deserts and jungles. The Himalayas contain the sources of the streams which feed the two great rivers of the Hindustani peninsula, the Indus and the Ganges. The Indus, almost all of whose basin is situated in Pakistan in the modern era, lent its name to the country which became the focus of an ancient civilization. The Hindus themselves called the river the Sindhu, but the Persians changed the word to Hindu. From Persia, the word wandered into Greece, where it began to be used to mean the whole of Hindustan.[2]

---

[1] Robert D. Kaplan, *The Revenge of Geography: What the Map Tells Us About Coming Conflicts and the Battle Against Fate.* Random House, 2013. P. 228.

[2] Arthur Basham, *Tsivilizatsiya Drevney Indii (The Civilization of Ancient India).* Yekaterinburg, 2007. P. 15.

The mountains fostered isolation. They were never an insurmountable boundary, though. India took in plenty of waves of migration, becoming home to Dravidian and Aryan tribes, the Kushan, Huns and Hephthalites, Jews, the Parsi, and representatives of Muslims and other peoples. There were various forms of contact with Egypt, Babylon, the Greco-Roman world, and the countries of Central and South-East Asia, the Caucasus and China. From the 12th century onwards, Northern India became part of the Muslim world. From the end of the 15th century onwards, Portuguese, British, Dutch, Frenchmen, Danes, and Armenians appeared in the country.

The history of India is usually traced back to the proto-Indian, or Harappan, civilization (circa 26th to 17th centuries BC), which developed over a vast territory in the Indus valley and its tributaries, in the upper Ganges and in the modern state of Gujarat. It was an urban civilization, with a level of development not inferior to Ancient Egypt and Sumer. Its centers – the cities of Harappa (the modern name of the settlement in Punjab) and Mohenjodaro (on the right Bank of the Indus, about 400 km from the mouth) – were built up with houses of burnt bricks, often two or more floors, and provided with a water supply and sewerage. Irrigated agriculture was highly developed, and there was a culture of copper and bronze processing. Harappa used one system of writing. It remains undeciphered, although it seems that scientists are close to a solution. There is reason to believe that the harappans were the first in the world to master spinning and weaving, and maybe even wheeled transport.

Harappan civilization existed for about a thousand years and disappeared, apparently, in the 19th to 17th centuries BC, it seems even before the onslaught of the Indo-Aryan tribes that followed in the middle of the II Millennium BC from a series of floods and the decline of trade with Mesopotamia. There is no evidence of genetic continuity of modern India from the civilization of Harappa.

The invasion of the Indo-Aryans, the ancestral home of whom many scholars believe to be the South Russian steppes, lasted for centuries. Arias, says the prominent Indian historian Romila Tapar, was originally the name of the people who spoke Indo-Aryan languages, who adhered to the caste system and followed a worldview derived from Vedic literature. The settlers mingled with the local population, creating a fusion of Aryan and autochthonous beliefs, cultures and social institutions, on the basis of which the Indian tradition was formed. The arrival of the Aryans opened the so-called Vedic era (1500-600 BC), which was named after the Vedas – the oldest relics of spiritual culture, which include collections of hymns, prayers and sacrificial formulas (Rigveda, Samaveda, Yajurveda, Atharvaveda), and theological tracts ("Brahmanas", "Upanishads"). The authorship of the Vedas belongs to the priests of the Aryan tribe Bharat (from which comes the second official name of modern India – Bharat) and these texts contained the views of both the ancient Aryans and the indigenous inhabitants of the Hindustan Peninsula.

The foundation of Indian civilization is Hinduism. Its main ideas were formed from a merger of Vedism and the beliefs of the Pre-Aryan peoples, and from the end of the second millennium BC was derived from Vedic Brahmanism, having been influenced along the way by a plethora of belief systems from a vast number of sects and ritual practices. The term "Hinduism" itself, though, only appeared during a period of Muslim rule in the 14th century AD, as a way of identifying the local population, who did not profess the faith of Islam.[3]

The pantheon of Hindu gods is fairly sizeable. Each of them represents some sort of unique facet of a single, ubiquitous God. The most highly esteemed, famous trinity, consists of Brahma the creator god, Vishnu the protector, and Shiva the destroyer and restorer simultaneously. All of them are usually depicted with four arms, and Brahma also has four heads, underlining his all-seeing presence. Each of the gods has a spouse, who also has extraordinary abilities. The holy books of Hinduism are the Bhagavad Gita, the Védas, the Upanishads, the Puranas, and the epic works the "Mahabharata" and the "Ramayana".

Leonid Vasil'yev writes: "The world of everything that is alive, including people and even gods, according to the ideas of Hinduism, is a samsara, a chain – with no end and no beginning – of rebirths, the sad existence of the profane, i.e. the fate of everything that is ordinary, commonplace. The value of this world was always considered to be very relative; after all, ultimately, it is nothing but a kind of illusion, or maya. Beyond the bounds of this world, however, outside the wheel of the samsara, is the world of the great, genuine Reality, where the Absolute rules. Breaking out of the world of the samsara, reaching the highest Reality, and becoming one with the great Absolute – that is the final objective desired by the religiously active individual, the ascetic person, the yogi, the guru, the rishi, an individual greatly respected in Hinduism. It is not easy to achieve this goal; it is not something that everyone will find easy to do, far from it; to say nothing of

---

[3] Romila Thapar, *The Past as Present. Forging Contemporary Identities Through History*. New Delhi, 2014. PP. vii-viii.

the fact that to achieve this objective, one must dedicate one's entire life to doing so, making one's life a feat of selflessness, psychological training, and deadened asceticism."[4]

Life in the world of the samsara is regulated by karma, i.e. the balance of good and evil deeds in an individual's former lives. Man, like all other living creatures, is born into the world with a karma that is preconditioned by all his previous incarnations; this karma determines not only the outward appearance of the new-born creature (whether it be a person, an animal, a worm or a plant), but also its place. If the new-born creature is a person, then it finds itself in the complex, hierarchical system of varna and castes.

The first mention of varna can be found in the Rigveda. A varna – there are four in total – is a sacred concept, by contrast with the castes, of which there are a multitude within the framework of the varnas. At the top of the social pyramid are the Brahmans – priests, ministers, advisers to rulers, teachers. A Brahman was considered to be an incarnation of god on earth, and he was forbidden from doing physical labor. The representatives of the highest varna (and of a multitude of castes), the priests – the bearers of the ancient wisdom of the Veda – are incomparably better prepared than others to break free from the karmic chain of rebirths. Below the Brahmans were the Kshatriya, who were initially the military elite of the Indo-Aryans. They were responsible for state governance, military affairs, and protecting the subjects and ensuring that they adhered to the customs of their caste. Below them were the Vaishyas – merchants, moneylenders, free members of the commune, tillers of the land. These three varnas were also known as "twice-borns". Boys from these varnas were allowed to study the sacred texts in Sanskrit, which give an individual a second birth. The fourth varna – the Shudra – were not allowed to do this. They were required to serve the "twice-borns", and work the land, but they could not own any land. Outside this four-varna system were the untouchables, who had to clean up rubbish and dirt.

The representatives of each of the varnas were broken down into a plethora of castes, each of which had its own identity, expressed in special forms of worship of the gods, and specific mythologies, songs and dances. The caste was a person's constant and unchanging place in his given incarnation in the world of the samsara. And since no-one besides you is the creator of your own karma, you have only yourself to blame for the fact that you lead a miserable existence – it is the price you must pay for your past lives. If you

---

[4] Leonid Vasil'yev, *Istoriya Vostoka* (*A History of the East*). Vol. 2. Moscow, 2011. PP. 98-100.

abide by all the requirements dictated by the position of your caste, you can expect fate to be kind to you in your next incarnation.

Hinduism was a way of life in India, with its orientation towards the supreme value of non-existence and the very limited significance of the world of the samsara. For a Hindu, there is not much sense in history, and it is no coincidence that the Indian tradition, so rich with events and culturally saturated, has so few chronicles, manuscripts, historical and geographical descriptions and so on to offer. For a Hindu, calls for equality or social harmony do not make much sense, since they contradict the idea of karma, of individual responsibility for one's social inferiority in the current incarnation. For a Hindu, active social protest is an alien concept, and violence even more so, since it is a sign of worsening karma.

Meanwhile, this political and social indifference is compensated for by emotionality, the richness of aesthetics and feelings, fed by the mythologies of the epic works, the Mahabharata and the Ramayana, or the Puranas. In India, they are unrivalled in their popularity to this day. Hinduism is not even a religion in the Aramaic sense, but rather a philosophy, indeed one which has more questions than answers. In Hinduism's most important text, we find the central poem, the Hymn to Creation, which contains the lines:

> *Who knows from whence this great creation sprang?*
> *He from whom all this great creation came.*
> *Whether his will created or was mute,*
> *The Most High seer that is in highest heaven,*
> *He knows it – or perchance even He knows not.*

Compare this to the confident language of the Bible. Hinduism never had a church organized along hierarchical lines, and was known for its tolerance towards other religions. As they strive to achieve moral behavior and principles of thinking, the followers of Hinduism are provided with leeway in all other respects, including the search for their own paths to salvation. There can be no sectarianism in the strict sense of the word in Hinduism, due to the lack of a church structure or official dogma. The most vivid example of the integrating power of Hinduism is the fate of Buddhism, which has practically disappeared in India, and by no means as a result of persecution. Hinduism incorporated the premises of Buddhism within it, and in effect swallowed it up. The power and remarkable inner solidity, the vibrancy of Hinduism is explained by the fact that it relied on a community and caste-based structure, and sanctioned it.

Has Hinduism had an effect on the main characteristic of the Indian political tradition – weakness of the state, which has been expressed not only in a constant struggle and frequent changes of the ruling elite, but also in their territorial instability, "fluidity" and exceptionally communal pluralism? Without question. Hinduism is effectively indifferent to power, to the state. Its principles precluded ambition and the careerism associated with it. Governing the state is the professional occupation of the Kshatriyas and the Brahman-advisers, while the fate of the others is to perform their communal and caste-based obligations, as regulated over centuries.

Francis Fukuyama has also emphasized that in India, "Kings were thus regarded as subject to law written by others, not simply as the makers of law as in China. [...] But this huge territory was never once ruled by a single political power and never developed a single literary language as China did. Indeed, the history of India before late 20th century is much more one of persistent political disunity and weakness, with some of the most successful unifiers being foreign invaders whose political power rested on a different social basis."[5]

Indian tradition considered the ruler's main task to be supporting the *dharma* – the social order sanctioned by religion. Indian monarchs considered taxes to be their salary for performing precisely this function, and also for the work they did to expand the territories they controlled, and establish matrimonial ties. "As a rule, though, in territories inherited from the monarch's father or conquered territories, neither the monarch nor the state on his behalf, intervened in the socio-economic, political and cultural life of the communities subject to them, restricting themselves merely to supporting the dharma and the collecting of taxes. Among the institutions on which the life of an Indian depended directly, the state was far from being in first place," Boris Kuzyk and Tat'yana Shaumyan have emphasized.[6]

None of the empires that have existed on the subcontinent, even such mighty ones as the Maury Empire (4th – 2nd centuries BC), the Gupta Empire (4th – 6th centuries AD) and the Mughal Empire (16th – 19th centuries), ever included all of the territory of what is now the Republic of India. History did not allow these states enough time to consolidate their territory and form a fully-fledged national identity; a new conqueror would come along,

---

[5] Francis Fukuyama, *The Origins of Political Order. From Prehuman Times to the French Revolution*. Profile Books, 2011. PP. 151-153.

[6] Boris Kuzyk and Tat'yana Shaumyan, *Indiya – Rossiya: strategiya partnerstva v XXI veke* (*India – Russia: a Strategy of Partnership in the 21st Century*). Moscow, 2009.

incorporating into the new empire regions which were by no means striving for unity. The multiple state formations paid little attention to working on the theory and practice of administration, nor on an ideological doctrine. There was no clearly defined legal mandate of the ruler's right to all the land and resources in the country, as was the case in the classical countries of Islam or in China.

The bureaucracy was immeasurably weaker and far cheaper than in China or even in Muslim countries. The strict regulations of the caste hierarchy limited the ambitions of politicians and successful military leaders, and curbed envy and love of power, phenomena which proved so costly to other countries. The level of consumption by the main bulk of the population was always low. Clothing was minimal, people's diet was mainly vegetarian, and housing was primitive, something that was explained both by the climate and by religious requirements. Though they took little from the community, the rulers were nonetheless fantastically rich, as a result of the broad tax base.[7]

The pluralism of the social structure inherent to Indian civilization effectively laid the groundwork for later ideas formed outside Hindustan, including the concept of political representation, to take root.

The weakness of executive power and the unconsolidated nature of the elites had a negative impact on the destiny of Indian sovereignty. The colonisers – both the Muslims, and the British who succeeded them – always found countless allies among the local elites, who did not have patriotic feelings in relation to the whole of Hindustan and thought in terms of "their" distinct territories. India, Fernand Braudel has emphasized, managed to survive "like China, thanks to its overwhelming vibrancy, and also thanks to the fact that its territory was never entirely captured, as far as Kanyakumari."[8]

Conquest by the British led to a decisive breaking of India's traditional structure. The revenues, most of which had sat in the treasuries of sultans and princes, now flowed into the metropolis, going a considerable way towards enabling the British economic miracle. In the 18th century, the British proposed the concept of India being governed on the basis of its centuries-old traditions of the "classical past", trampled upon by Moghul conquerors. Later, though, concerned by the rise in national consciousness, they began actively pushing Indian culture aside in the 19th century, replacing

---

[7] Leonid Vasil'yev, *Istoriya Vostoka* (*A History of the East*). Vol. 1. Moscow, 2011. PP. 484-485.
[8] Fernand Braudel, *Grammatika tsivilizatsiy* (*Grammar of Civilizations*). Moscow, 2008. P. 180.

it with slogans about the civilizing mission of the superior race on untamed lands.⁹

Britain did not construct a unified system of governance for its largest colony. Some of India's provinces found themselves ruled over directly by the East India Company, and after 1858 by the crown. In 500 territories, maharajahs, nizams and the like remained in place, with genuine power, while some border regions found themselves under the control of special British military administrations.¹⁰

India was forced to familiarize itself very quickly with new forms of societal relations: machine-oriented manufacturing, achievements in science and technology, liberal democracy, parliamentarianism, and active involvement in the global market. The British built railways and industrial concerns, and created a colonial administration and a postal service. English began to serve as a unifying language, helping with the consolidation of a multi-ethnic country.

Hindu civilization resisted, passively but stubbornly, as it had done previously in relation to its Muslim rulers, and adapted. A process of Westernization took place among the Brahman elite: the children of those at the top received a European education, both in India and in England, served in the institutions of British India, and peopled the ranks of the burgeoning Indian intelligentsia and bourgeoisie, oriented towards the European way of life. As this adaptation took place, though, resistance grew as well.

The British authorities sought to get across the idea, without success, that colonial rule had saved India from "chaos" and enabled the establishment of state unity. This gave rise, in the minds of educated Indians, to the notion of a common country, in which a united nation resided. The Indian National Congress (INC) – the first nationwide party, created in 1885 – defended, right from the outset, the concept of a single India and claimed to represent all Indians, irrespective of their home region or faith.

The leading role in India's acquisition of independence was played by Mahatma Gandhi, who was educated as a lawyer in England and made a name for himself, selflessly – in the face of beatings and arrests – defending Indians' rights in South Africa. At the heart of his ideology lay the "Bhagavad-Gita", the teachings of Tolstoy (with whom he entered into a correspon-

---

⁹   David Day, *Conquest: How Societies Overwhelm Others*. Oxford University Press, 2013. PP. 144-145.

¹⁰   Jurgen Osterhammel, *The Transformation of the World: A Global History of the Nineteenth Century*. Princeton-Oxford: Princeton University Press, 2014. P. 581.

dence), Jesus's Sermon on the Mount, and the poem *The Light of Asia* by Sir Edwin Arnold. His method of struggle, which is often called the method of non-violence, is more accurately described by the term that Gandhi himself used for it, "satyagraha": "sat" means truth, and "agraha" means steadfastness in Sanskrit. "Non-violence, in its active form, consists… in benevolence towards all that is essential," wrote Gandhi. "It is love in its purest form. I read about this in the Hindu Sacred Writings, in the Bible and in the Koran… Each time I suffer a defeat, and precisely because of the defeat, my efforts only become more decisive."[11]

The Indian Civil Service, created in the mid-19th century, was a corps, tightly-knit through the corporate interests and ideals of "honest administration", consisting of several hundred (and later growing to around 2,000) authoritative and highly-paid civil servants, who were known as the "steel carcass" of the British colonial regime. By 1947, Indians constituted more than half of the workforce in the civil service, enabling them to take over the reins of power from the British when they left India.[12]

After the Second World War, the British prime minister, Clement Attlee, was in a hurry to get rid of India, and gave Lord Mountbatten powers to determine its fate; Mountbatten had been dubbed the "master of disaster" at the British Admiralty on account of the number of accidents that had occurred on board ships under his command. It was he who came up with the idea of dividing the country into India and two Muslim states, which would later be called Pakistan and Bangladesh. Precise figures for the number of people killed in the ethnic and religious violence that followed this decision cannot be ascertained. Estimates range from 20,000 to 2 million, while somewhere between 10 and 20 million people were forced to leave their homes. Gandhi was shot dead on 30th January 1948 by a religious fanatic, because he had defended the cause of an India for all Indians (including Muslims), not just for Hindus.[13]

---

[11] Christine Jordis, *Makhatma Gandi* (*Mahatma Gandhi*). Moscow, 2013. PP. 104-105.

[12] Leonid Alayev, "Politicheskaya sistema i politicheskaya kul'tura Indii" ("India's Political System and Political Cullture"), in *Politicheskiye sistemy i politicheskiye kul'tury Vostoka* (*Political Systems and Political Cultures of the East*), ed. by A. D. Voskresenskiy. Moscow, 2006. P. 398.

[13] Alex von Tunzelmann, "Who Is to Blame for Partition? Above All, Imperial Britain", *The New York Times*, August 18, 2017 <https://www.nytimes.com/2017/08/18/opinion/india-pakistan-partition-imperial-britain.html?searchResultPosition=2>; Gopalkrishna Gandhi, "Gandhi Won't Leave India", *The New York Times*, August 14, 2017 <https://www.nytimes.com/2017/08/14/opinion/gandhi-wont-leave-india.html?searchResultPosition=1>.

The Biggest Democracy

The political course chosen by independent India carried a strong imprint of the personality of Jawaharlal Nehru, who, from 1947 to 1964, was Prime Minister and Foreign Minister. His political foundation was the left wing of the Indian National Congress (INC), which was determinedly fighting for independence, and a host of political forces which were even more left-wing, including the communist party. There was much talk of a non-capitalist and even a socialist path of development. "Nehru was a socialist in economics but a democrat in politics," emphasizes the historian Ramachandra Guha. "As one 'bred up in the Ghandhian tradition', he could not appreciate the violence generated by the Russian Revolution. […] At the same time, Nehru was attracted by the promise of planning, of using science and technology to promote economic growth and end poverty."[14]

India's political structure, enshrined by the Constitution of 1950, was highly democratic. Nehru insisted on a right to vote for all, although many tried to persuade him not to introduce it in a country in which two thirds of the population were completely illiterate. People enjoyed freedom of religion, and many had been given the opportunity to get an education in their mother tongue. Women, whose status had traditionally been low, in both Hindu and Muslim traditions, were given full civil rights. Early in 1952, the Indian National Congress and its allies easily secured a majority in the first parliamentary elections, marking the start of a long period of dominance by the INC.[15]

"The 'Nehruvian' state was a compromise which was fronted by Nehru; it was inefficiently capitalist, fiercely nationalist and increasingly parochial despite its public rhetoric of socialism, internationalism, justice and tolerance," writes his biographer, Benjamin Zachariah.[16]

The strategic goal of India's foreign policy – transformation into a world-class state – was determined immediately after the country obtained independence. There were initially three main aspects to Indian's foreign policy, three concentric circles: building up relations with the superpowers, alongside a general striving towards equidistance and non-participation in any possible conflict between the two blocs; a strengthening of ties with

---

[14] Ramachandra Guha, "Jawaharlal Nehru: A Romantic in Politics", in *Makers of Modern Asia*, ed. by Ramachandra Guha. Harvard University Press, 2014. P. 133.

[15] Ibid. PP. 125-129.

[16] Benjamin Zachariah, "The Importance of Being Nehru", *Frontline*, December 12, 2014. P. 6.

developing countries, with the aim of becoming a leader of the Southern hemisphere; and reinforcing its dominant position in South Asia.[17] Foreign policy was rendered more complex by the lack of clarity over the fates of the territories which were disputed by Pakistan, and by the end of the 1950s, China was making territorial claims against India too. The upshot was that Kashmir found itself divided between three states.

Nehru was an idealist, a moralist, and was in favour of a policy of non-alignment and against the Cold War. Following the maxims of his teacher, Mahatma Gandhi, Nehru rejected alliances, pacts and agreements, seeing them as part of the old "realpolitik": he was not interested in the military aspects of politics. A week after he came to power, Nehru spent some time at the Ministry of Defence and was enraged to find professional soldiers among his colleagues. From that time onwards, the entire staff of the "South Block" in Delhi went to work in civilian dress.[18]

In the selection of a foreign policy direction, a big helping hand was provided by the United States. In the search for partners in the Cold War, John Foster Dulles's gaze fell on Pakistan, and President Eisenhower sanctioned the supply of weapons to the country. The USA created SEATO, which India and other Asian countries saw as a direct challenge, responding by creating the Non-Alignment Movement. In January 1955, a session of the Indian National Congress proclaimed a "socialist society" in India. In 1955, Nehru was given a very warm welcome in Moscow, and during Khrushchev and Bulganin's return visit to Kolkata, the two were given a rapturous greeting by a two-million-strong crowd. India, which always thought highly of the Soviet Union's efforts with regard to decolonization, began to look on the USSR as a reliable friend.[19]

Disagreements with China over the disputed territory worsened dramatically, however. "Mao's China did not accept imperialist demarcations of its territory," notes John Keay.[20] Divisions from the PLA swept aside the Indian forces with ease, then hurried into the strategic corridor which linked West Bengal to Assam. "Although *Hindi-Yankee Bhai Bhai* was never an officially

---

[17] Sergey Lunev, "Indiyskaya tsivilizatsiya v globaliziruyushchemsya mire" ("Indian Civilization in a Globalizing World"), *Mirovaya ekonomika i mezhdunarodnyye otnosheniya* (*World Economy and International Relations*), Issue 3, 2003. P. 80.

[18] Fareed Zakaria, *The Post-American World*. W. W. Norton & Company, 2008. PP. 147-148.

[19] Ramachandra Guha, "Jawaharlal Nehru: A Romantic in Politics", in *Makers of Modern Asia*, ed. by Ramachandra Guha. Harvard University Press, 2014. P. 132; K. P. Fabian, "The Middle Path", *Frontline*, December 12, 2014. PP. 27-28.

[20] John Keay, *India: A History*. Grove Press, 2001. P. 516.

endorsed slogan, non-alignment was clearly in tatters." Nehru was obviously shaken by the fact that Mao had rudely rejected his utopian internationalism, and he never quite recovered from this shock. Early in 1964, he was struck by a disease of the liver, and in May of that year, he died.[21]

Today, India is the biggest democratic state in the world. There are more than 1.37 billion people living there. A country which takes up 2.5% of the earth is home to one sixth of the world's population. The anthropogenic pressure on the natural and ecological system is among the highest in the world, and is still growing stronger.

For many centuries, the average number of children born to each woman was at least six or seven. The policy of birth control became a priority after independence was obtained, but in fact what followed was a demographic explosion in the 1950s and 1960s: an increase in quality of life and better healthcare led to a dramatic decline in infant mortality and infectious diseases. Average life expectancy rose almost 3-fold. Yet infant mortality remains high, as does mortality among females of reproductive age, and the structure of mortality is not "modern", with 40% caused by infectious and parasitic diseases.

Not until the 1980s did the stereotype of large families start to surrender its position. The number of children born to each woman is still twice as high as the desired figures, though. The birth rate is kept high by low levels of urbanization, literacy and employment levels among women (two to three times lower than among men), and of social welfare and pensions.

Until recently, the dominant view was that population growth was having a negative impact on the country's development. There is an increasingly widespread view, however, that this massive human potential is an advantage. The median age is around 25 (the average in Asia is 30, and in Europe 40), which, in circumstances of rapid growth in the economy and in employment, makes it possible to achieve a demographic dividend. "[T]he hope is that China will get old before it gets rich, and India will reach middle-income status while it is still young," as Ruchir Sharma put it. The country has the chance to achieve zero natural growth no earlier than by the middle of the 21st century, when the population will stand at 1.6-1.7 billion and India will overtake China."[22] To turn its demographic problems into an

....

[21] Ibid.

[22] Boris Kuzyk and Tat'yana Shaumyan, *Indiya – Rossiya: strategiya partnerstva v XXI veke* (*India – Russia: a Strategy of Partnership in the 21st Century*). Moscow, 2009. PP. 205, 140, 207, 215, 249, 216-217, 229, 236-237, 259; Yelena Bragina, "Indiya – inoy sredniy klass?" ("India – a

advantage, though, India must resolve a host of complex problems: employment, poverty, education.

In India, almost 500 million people are younger than 30.[23] Of the 25 million born each year, 15 million join the workforce (the rest do not work or are involved in domestic agricultural work), of whom 6.6 million have completed their education.[24]

At present, one third of the population are illiterate. 27% of pupils do not complete elementary school, while 40.6% drop out of primary education and 49.3% drop out of secondary education. In the system of the Ministry for the Development of Human Resources, there are 40 central universities (there are 712 in total), 30 national technological institutions, and 1.4 million schools. There is a shortage of schoolteachers, though, with 38% of teaching posts at higher education institutions vacant; nor are standards are high: none of the universities are among the top 200 in the world.[25] Of the 16 million young people that flood the labor market each year, only 10% have some level of professional training.[26]

It is abundantly clear that there are two Indias. One is a land of developing entrepreneurialism, growing cities, growing classes of rich and affluent people. Entrepreneurs, qualified workers, the civil service, peasants with a degree of wealth, the owners of small businesses, and small-time tradesmen constitute around a third of the population – 400 million people. Affluent India is separated from the crowds, the dirt, the heat and the poverty in a way that is not seen anywhere else – by limousines whose drivers do not make the slightest noise, by homes in gated districts. The other India is that of 580,000 villages and hundreds of millions of poverty-stricken people. The only thing these two Indias have in common is their love for the game of cricket.

....

Different Kind of Middle Class?"), *Mezhdunarodnaya zhizn'* (*International Life*), February 2014. P. 137; Ruchir Sharma, *Breakout Nations: In Pursuit of the Next Economic Miracles*. Penguin, 2012. P. 38.

[23] Ejaz Syed Ghani, "How Policymakers Can Transform Rural India as a New Driver for Job Creation", *Business Standard*, January 17, 2018 <https://www.business-standard.com/article/opinion/how-policymakers-can-transform-rural-india-as-a-new-driver-for-job-creation-118011701502_1.html>.

[24] Soumya Ghosh and Pulak Ghosh, "Jobless Growth in India: Truth or Hoopla?", *The Times of India*, January 18, 2018 <https://timesofindia.indiatimes.com/blogs/toi-edit-page/jobless-growth-in-india-truth-or-hoopla-to-know-the-answer-we-need-better-payroll-reporting/>.

[25] Anubhuti Vishnoi, "Can She Deliver?", *India Today*, December 15, 2014. P. 25.

[26] Chandrika Bahadur, "Quality of Education for All: Can It Be Done?", in *Global Goals, National Actions: Making the Post-2015 Development Agenda Relevant to India*. Delhi, 2016. PP. 35-37.

There are poor people in every country. The poor of Europe and the poor of India are utterly different people, though. A typical poor person and his family in India is as follows: below average height, underweight, suffering from chronic illnesses due to constant malnutrition, subsisting only on seasonal or incidental income. He needs to send his children to work, rather than to school. There is an excessive burden placed on women, who must not only work in the field, but also fetch fuel many kilometres from home and look for drinking water. There is a lack of normal housing: in the cities, the homeless – the "pavement dwellers" as they are known, live in slums; in the villages, people live in "katchas" – one-room clay structures, with bin-liners for doors. In 2017, the government announced that 29 billion dollars of funding was to be made available as part of the "Clean India Mission" programme, to be spent on the construction of toilets (not necessarily with water closets), and on persuading people to use them rather than spend a penny somewhere else.[27]

30% of the population lives below the poverty line, a percentage that is higher than in all 26 of the countries of sub-Saharan Africa.[28] 40% of all children do not get enough food, and 36% of women have a body-mass index that is below the critical level. India accounts for one quarter of all the people suffering from malnutrition on the planet, while one third of children have a critically low weight.[29] Due to the weak system of healthcare, two children under the age of five die every minute.[30] In India there is a chronic shortage of doctors and nurses.

The poor live in a world without electricity, and without basic knowledge about the outside world. They are unfamiliar with the mass media, i.e. they have never seen a newspaper, listened to the radio, or watched TV. 300 million people have to make do without electricity altogether, while 800 million endure regular power cuts. Only 23% of elderly people who are not working receive a pension.

The government is implementing mass programs of food aid, and the social welfare system is growing – it is one of the biggest in the world. It is

---

[27] "Missing the Mark; Sanitation in India", *The Economist*, August 19, 2017. P. 40.

[28] Pankaj Mishra, "Games India Isn't Ready to Play", *New York Times*, October 2, 2010 <https://www.nytimes.com/2010/10/03/opinion/03mishra.html>.

[29] Sadaf Javed, "New Road to the Old Destination: Analysing the Hunger Goal", in *Global Goals, National Actions: Making the Post-2015 Development Agenda Relevant to India*. New Delhi, 2016. P. 24.

[30] Samar Halarnkar, "Can India Stop Its Children From Dying?", *The New York Times*, August 24, 2017 <https://www.nytimes.com/2017/08/24/opinion/india-child-mortality-hospital.html>.

still not sufficient, though, and implementation of these programs is complicated by corruption, a lack of targeting, and delay. A further hindrance is the caste system. Dominique Moïsi has noted: "Rich Indians tend not even to see the huge masses who live in poverty. Their selective eyes go across or above them with a serenity of mind that may be at least in part due to the existence of the caste system. The implicit attitude is: Of course they are very poor, but what can you expect? It has always been like this, and at least there are fewer of them today, and they don't die of starvation any longer."[31]

India remains a rural country – three quarters of its population live in rural areas, but the population of the cities is comparable to the population of the USA. In 1900, Kolkata was the only Indian city with more than 1 million inhabitants; in 1951 there were five such cities, in 2001 35, and in 2011 53. More than 500 cities have a population of over 100,000. Orangi Town in Karachi and Dharavi in Mumbai are among the biggest urban slums in the world: each has more than a million people living in it.[32]

An analysis of the ethnic composition of the population of India is problematic, since, in the censuses, nationality is not indicated, and only linguistic differences are recorded. Officially, Hindustanis, Telugu, Bengali and Marathi are not representatives of nationalities, but expressions of the cultural diversity of the unified Indian nation. Unofficially, there are more than 450 ethnicities and ethnic groups within the country. Four families of languages are spoken: Indo-European (India-Aryan), whose languages are spoken by 76% of the population; Dravidian (21.6%); Austro-Asiatic (1.2%) and Tibeto-Burman (1.0%). The official national languages are Hindi and English.

Hindi came into being on the basis of Sanskrit, and has at least 13 dialects, each of which lays claim to independent status. It is the native tongue of 30% of the Indian population. In the north of India, Muslims from Iran and Central Asia also adopted one of the dialects of Hindi, giving it Arabic, Persian and Turkic words, as a result of which the language of Urdu came into being, using the Arabic alphabet, rather than the Sanskrit alphabet of Devanagari. Since Hindi and Urdu have the same grammar and a common set of words in day-to-day use, they are often seen as two literary forms of the single language of Hindustani.

---

[31] Dominique Moïsi, *The Geopolitics of Emotion: How Cultures of Fear, Humiliation and Hope are Reshaping the World*. Random House, 2009.

[32] Bhuma Shrivastava and Sheridan Prasso, "In India, Slum Dwellers Move into High Rises", *Bloomberg Businessweek*, September 1-7, 2014. P. 14.

Along with the Hindustani, such large ethnic groups as Bengali, Marathi, Gujaratis, Oriya, Punjabi, the Assamese, and the Kashmiri speak languages of Sanskrit origin. All these people have European appearance. Ethnic groups of Southern India speak Dravidian languages. These are Telugu, the Kanarese, Tamils and Malayali. The have darker skin and Australoid traits. Central regions of India are inhabited by Australoid peoples who speak Munda languages of the Austro-Asiatic family. The north-eastern states of India are inhabited by small Mongoloid ethnic groups (3% of the population) such as Manipuri, Tirpa, Garo, Naga, Mizo and others. They speak Tibeto-Burman languages.[33]

Arnold Toynbee once wrote: "The cultural gulf between the Hindu society and the Modern West was no mere diversity; it was an outright contradiction; for the Modern West had fabricated a secular version of its cultural heritage from which religion was eliminated, whereas the Hindu society was and remained religious to the core [...]."[34] Hinduism is professed by 80.5% of the population; 13.4% are Muslims, 2.3% are Christians, 1.9% are Sikhs, and the rest are Jains, Buddhists, and followers of Zoroastrianism, Judaism and local cult-like faiths.[35]

One would think that the fact that the vast majority of the population share the same religion ought to serve as a unifying force. Hinduism, though, is a phenomenon that incorporates a vast number of diverse cults, rituals and ways of life. That said, there are growing forces that are striving to transform Hinduism into a single religion, like Islam, and to bring Hindus together on the basis of shared values. The rise in Hindu fundamentalism in recent years "sounded like a kind of response to the strengthening of manifestations of Islamic radicalism in the regions adjoining India, and indeed in the Muslim community within India itself."[36]

India is one of the biggest Islamic countries. "Islam in India has been altered through its contact with Hinduism, becoming less Abrahamic and more spiritual." Indian Muslims worship saints and relics, they glorify music

---

[33] Gleb and Irina Ivashentsovy, *Indiya: vkrattse obo vsem* (*India: A Concise Guide*). Moscow, 2009. PP. 75-76.

[34] Arnold Toynbee, *A Study of History: Abridgement of Vols. VII-X*. Oxford University Press, 1987. P. 162.

[35] Gleb and Irina Ivashentsovy, *Indiya: vkrattse obo vsem* (*India: A Concise Guide*). Moscow, 2009. PP. 75-76.

[36] Gleb Ivashentsov, "Rossiya – Indiya: novyye formaty davnego partnerstva" ("Russia – India: New Formats for an Old Partnership"), *Mezhdunarodnaya zhizn'* (*International Life*), February 2016. P. 8.

and art, and they have a more practical view of life than most of their fellow Muslims across the border.[37]

Officially, everyone in India is equal, regardless of nationality, race, religion or caste. The significance of the relations between the castes is still great, though. The precise number of castes is not known. A recent study found that there were 4,635 "communities" – castes and tribes (this number is very conservative; some experts suggest there are as many as 15,000 castes). They are divided into sub-castes, which genuinely exist as separate communities.[38] The Brahmans make up 5.5% of the population, the middle castes (non-Brahman, but "clean") constitute more than 40%, and the untouchables 17% (the total is less than 100% because it does not include the highest non-Brahman castes, or the Muslims, Christians, tribes etc.).

Caste differences continue to play a sizeable role in everyday life. A person belonging to a high or even a middle caste would rather go hungry than work as a rubbish collector or furrier, jobs which must be done by the untouchables. The word "untouchable" itself is not used: it has been replaced by the term "Harijans" ("Children of God"), which was the name proposed by Mahatma Gandhi. Or Dalits. Their situation has, however, changed over time. There are 84 Dalits in the Parliament (out of 545 deputies), they are represented in the Chamber of commerce, and their interests are defended by influential non-governmental organizations. But they remain less educated, poorer, and 30% more likely to go to prison than the average Indian. According to one study, 98% of other castes will not offer tea to a Dalit in their home. Inter-caste weddings are to this day extremely rare, and in most cases it is the parents who choose the bride or groom, rather than the young people themselves.

Hindu tradition prohibits divorces and second marriages by widows, and, although laws passed in independent India have abolished these ancient prohibitions, the majority of the population still stick to them. Tradition lives on in the fact that the bodies of the dead are set alight in funeral fires, and the ashes are scattered. Hindus believe a number of animals to be sacred, above all cows and oxen of the Zebu breed. To Hindus, the killing of cows and the consumption of beef is a sin.

....

[37] Fareed Zakaria, *The Post-American World*. W. W. Norton & Company, 2008. P. 156.

[38] Leonid Alayev, "Politicheskaya sistema i politicheskaya kul'tura Indii" ("India's Political System and Political Cullture"), in *Politicheskiye sistemy i politicheskiye kul'tury Vostoka* (*Political Systems and Political Cultures of the East*), ed. by A. D. Voskresenskiy. Moscow, 2006. P. 399.

Outside the country today, there is an Indian diaspora numbering around 20 million people. "Hindus are deeply practical. They can easily find an accommodation with the outside reality," observes Fareed Zakaria. Indian businessmen – most of them Hindus – will thrive in any atmosphere that creates an opportunity for trade and commerce. Indian merchants have excelled in whichever country fate has scattered them. As long as they can put up a figure of an idol in their own home, so as to pray or meditate, their sense of Hinduism is fully satisfied.[39]

Indians living in other countries send billions of dollars to their native land, hold shares in joint enterprises, and finance projects. The most dynamic and affluent of them live in the USA, the UK and Canada. A large number of Indians live and work in the Persian Gulf states, in Malaysia, Singapore, the countries of the Caribbean basin, and in Africa, particularly in South Africa.[40] There has been a sharp increase in the number of Indians living in the USA (they are the third biggest "Asian" group among the population, behind only the Chinese and the Filipinos), and this was linked to the development of information technologies.

According to its Constitution, India has the "Westminster system" of governance. The head of state is the President, who acts "on the advice of the prime minister". Real power is in the hands of the prime minister, who is backed up by a majority in the lower chamber of parliament – the Lok Sabha. Indian general elections are not so much national elections than a collection of regional and local campaigns.

India is defined in the Constitution as "a union of states", i.e. it is officially a federation. In the states, which retain a significant amount of autonomy, legislative councils are elected, which form governments led by the main ministers. The president (i.e. the federal government) appoints governors, who are representatives of the center in the provinces. Heads of districts are also appointed, as are heads of regions (tehsils in the north, and taluks in the south). All these officials are members of the Indian Administrative Service, a colonial legacy. Their lives are subject to strict rules: a pay-rise every year; a promotion once every three years; and retirement at the age of 55. In the villages, or groups of villages, central power is in the hands of "civil servants for development" (gram sevaks). Local autonomy is developing, built up from the bottom, at the level of the village, the tehsil and the

---

[39] Fareed Zakaria, *The Post-American World*. W. W. Norton & Company, 2008. PP. 155-156.

[40] Boris Kuzyk and Tat'yana Shaumyan, *Indiya – Rossiya: strategiya partnerstva v XXI veke* (*India – Russia: a Strategy of Partnership in the 21st Century*). Moscow, 2009. P. 331.

district.[41] A major role is played by "panchayats", self-governing communities which have existed in India since ancient times, state interference in whose affairs has always been very limited. The extent to which the "panchayats" are integrated into the political system reflects a kind of "know-how" with regard to the Indian model of democracy.

"The durability of Indian parliamentarianism is striking, for a third-world country," writes the orientalist Larisa Yefimova. "There have never been attempts to establish a one-party system in India… or a military dictatorship. And this durability is based in many ways on the traditionally Hindu tenets – on the striking pluralism of Hindu sects and castes, the tolerance traditional in the Hindu worldview, smoothly connected to the sustainability of the caste structure, on the charismatic authority of Mahatma Gandhi and other great figures in Indian parliamentary democracy, and the traditional authority of those representatives of the Brahman princely elite, who have continually, and in a way that is utterly disproportionate to their relative weight, found themselves at the top of the political hierarchy…"[42]

The party-based system with domination by one party, which existed in the first decades of independence, has been consigned to history. Since the end of the 1980s, two coalitions have been formed, between whom power has alternated: the Indian National Congress (INC) and the Bharatiya Janata Party (BJP). The former is associated with Westernization, progressiveness, and secularism; the latter – with nativism, religiosity, with calls to find the "Indian way" and to build an "Indian kingdom". The disagreements between the two should not be exaggerated, though. The political parties are in fact groups which are united around their leader more than anything else. A significant role is played by familial nature and charisma, seen as qualities which come from above and are passed on as an inheritance. Therein lies the reason for the role played by the family of Jawaharlal Nehru, whose charisma was "passed on" to his daughter, son, widow and grandson.

All the parties are for democracy, but for their own version of it, not the Western version. Liberal ideas are confined to the Indians. The Indian newspapers and NGOs raise the same questions and concerns as the Western

---

[41] Leonid Alayev, "Politicheskaya sistema i politicheskaya kul'tura Indii" ("India's Political System and Political Cullture"), in *Politicheskiye sistemy i politicheskiye kul'tury Vostoka* (*Political Systems and Political Cultures of the East*), ed. by A. D. Voskresenskiy. Moscow, 2006. P. 399.

[42] Larisa Yefimova, "Osobennosti politicheskoy kul'tury sovremennogo Vostoka" ("The Peculiarities of the Political Culture of the Contemporary East"), in *Vostok i politika: Politicheskiye sistemy, politicheskiye kul'tury, politicheskiye protsessy* (*The East and Politics: Political Systems, Political Cultures, Political Processes*), ed. by A. D. Voskresenskiy. Moscow, 2011. PP. 82-83.

ones. This stance probably reflects the views of the Anglophone elite in India, though – still a minority – which feels more comfortable in the Western world than in its own world.

The bulk of the population are not interested in politics. At the same time, during the years of its independence, there have been 18 rounds of parliamentary elections in India (for the Lok Sabha) and more than 120 elections for the states' legislative councils, with up to 60%-70% of the electorate usually taking part in them. These high turnouts are ensured by the same illiterate masses who, according to the surveys, have no interest in politics.

India's judicial branch is unique in the sense that the higher judiciary appoints itself. In 1993, the so called collegium was set up, consisting of the Chief Justice of India and the two most senior judges, who make the selection. "There are widespread insinuations of favouritism, nepotism, groupism, victimisation and ego clashes, which have sometimes prevented outstanding candidates from being selected as high court or SC judges."[43]

Another paradox of India's political culture is the perception of corruption. On the one hand, as in all eastern countries, it is an important built-in element of political and economic life. On the other hand, though, the country is shaken by the constant corruption scandals, which are similar to what happens in the West. Ministers accused of corruption resign, and are pursued by the courts. In 2000, the former Prime Minister, Narasimha Rao, was given a prison sentence for financial machinations in support of the INC.

Indian democracy is so peculiar that a host of academics are stating that it does not exist, because it simply cannot exist. Some describe the country as a "functioning anarchy", others as "parliamentary authoritarianism". Yet for all that, the system that operates in India is most definitely a democratic one, although it is a very unusual and not entirely Western one. In December 2013, India's Supreme Court overturned a 2009 decision of a lower court, which decriminalized homosexual activity between consenting adults. The Supreme Court, provoking masses of objections on the part of the Western press, cited a formula from the Indian colonial code, drawn up by the British in 1861, which prohibited sexual ties that were "against the order of nature".[44]

....

[43] Baijayant Panda, "Not Very Collegial: The Supreme Court is Split Wide Open Today Due to Its Opaque Collegium System", *The Times of India*, January 18, 2018 <https://timesofindia.indiatimes.com/blogs/toi-edit-page/not-very-collegial-the-supreme-court-is-split-wide-open-today-due-to-its-opaque-collegium-system/>.

[44] Ira Trivedi, "The Indian in the Closet: New Delhi's Wrong Turn on Gay Rights", *Foreign Affairs*, March/April 2014. P. 21.

The alliance of Prime Minister Singh's INC and nine other parties became mired in scandal after scandal. The government's popularity fell against the backdrop of the slowing of economic growth. The INC, on the eve of the election campaign in 2014, backed Raul Gandhi, who led its youth organization and preached ideas about restoring the spirit of the great Mahatma. Back in 2013, however, opinion polls were already showing that he lagged behind the leader of the BDP, Narendra Modi, who was at times characterized by the press as "a blend of Putin and Lee Kuan Yew".[45] Modi positioned himself as a "statesman" and an "effective manager", who had achieved successes as head of the state of Gujarat. Admittedly, he was accused of having been involved in anti-Muslim attacks in 2002 which claimed the lives of thousands of Muslims. In connection with these events, Modi was sanctioned by the USA – he was banned from entering the country. Until late 2012 the same sanctions were in force in the EU as well.

The party whose official color is orange, symbolizing the cleansing flame and sanctity, and whose symbol is the lotus flower, on which Brahma and Shiva sat solemnly, put huge faith in the religious majority – the Hindus. The BJP's campaign slogan was: "Nationalism is our inspiration. Growth and good governance is our goal."[46] Modi himself preferred to avoid polarizing subjects, emphasizing his desire for change, growth and the creation of jobs. In the elections of May 2014, the Indian National Congress not only lost, it suffered the most devastating defeat in history, securing only 44 seats in the Lok Sabha (it had held 206). The BJP won enough seats in parliament to form the government on its own – 272 of the 543 seats, and together with its partners in the 11-party National Democratic Alliance, a total of 336 seats.

Two important political forces were initially unhappy with Modi's policies in power. The first was the press, which has always been pro-Western and liberal, and in the press's eyes, Modi is a behind-the-times nationalist. A vast array of causes of dissatisfaction was cited. The minister for the development of human resources – the former waitress, model and TV presenter Smriti Irani – consulted a Vedic astrologer. Sanskrit is now being taught in a large number of schools. There is talk of the need to develop education in the languages of the peoples of India (and not just in English), in which,

---

[45] James Traub, "The End of the Gandhis", *Foreign Policy*, May/June 2013. PP. 90-95.

[46] Sergey Strokan', "Sobiratel' indiyskikh zemel': K vlasti v Indii idet natsionalist i gosudarstvennik" ("The Collector of Indian Lands: A Nationalist and Statesman is Heading to Power in India"), *Kommersant* (*The Businessman*), April 1, 2014 <https://www.kommersant.ru/doc/2442690>; Boris Volkhonskiy, "Prem'yer iz ognennykh trushchob" ("A Premier from the Fiery Slums"), *Ekho planety* (*Echo of the Planet*), Issue 24, 2014. PP. 6-9.

it is felt, there are no normal educational resources.⁴⁷ "The future is lost, a mythical past is upon us, the barbarians are at the gates. Where is my ticket to a genuinely liberal American East Coast campus or think tank?" writes the well-known journalist Shekhar Gupta, describing the mood among the liberal intellectuals.⁴⁸ Modi responds to the liberals in kind, calling them a relic of the colonial era, the "Delhi club", of which he has never been, nor ever will be, a member. "He breathes Hindu culture and history and values its benefits in his own life and the life of the country," writes his biographer, Andy Marino. "But he says he has no use for ritual or ritual observance."⁴⁹

The second unhappy political force is the old career civil service. The BJP had a small number of experienced statesmen. The Ministers were not very well-prepared for their role. Career civil servants, however, believed that Modi and his team did not consult with them enough.

Modi's popularity increased rapidly against the backdrop of the rise in economic indicators and the improvement in the national mood, reaching 87% in 2016, but then fell to 81%. His well-funded, disciplined party faces an opposition that is more divided than ever before.

The INC continued to exist as a Gandhi family business, so a change of leadership was not an option. Congress was unable to make up its mind over its own ideology and leadership. Sonya Gandhi's health was fragile, and she had a reputation as somewhat of a "foreign origin". Raul Gandhi did not elicit enthusiasm either from the party's supporters, or from the INC's potential partners. The parliamentary election of 2019 gave BJP and its allies 362 seats, and the United Progressive Alliance headed by the INC 94 seats.⁵⁰

Modi's government and the Indian political system are being subjected to ever fiercer criticism on the part of the Western media for their perceived

....

⁴⁷   Victor Mallet, "Mystics Distract Ministers from Modi's Development Drive", *The Financial Times*, December 1, 2014. P. 2; Tejaswini Niranjana, "Beyond the Language Tussle", *The Hindu*, December 6, 2014 <https://www.thehindu.com/opinion/lead/beyond-the-language-tussle/article6665681.ece>.

⁴⁸   Shekhar Gupta, "Saving Indian Liberalism from its Left-Liberal Elite", *India Today*, December 15, 2014. P. 20.

⁴⁹   Andy Marino, *Narendra Modi. A Political Biography*. HarperCollins, 2014. PP. 260-261.

⁵⁰   Nida Najar, "Modi Retains Broad Support in India Despite Criticism, Poll Finds", *The New York Times*, September 19, 2016 <https://www.nytimes.com/2016/09/20/world/asia/narendra-modi-support-pew-poll.html>; "Indian Politics. Non-Stick PM", *The Economist*, January 14, 2017. P. 49; Amulya Ganguli, "Who Will Stop the BJP? No One in Sight", *Gulf News*, April 29, 2017 <https://gulfnews.com/opinion/op-eds/who-will-stop-the-bjp-no-one-in-sight-1.2019155>; Amulya Ganguli, "Sonia's Unifying Role Is Unlikely to Succeed", *Gulf News*, May 6, 2017 <https://gulfnews.com/opinion/op-eds/sonias-unifying-role-is-unlikely-to-succeed-1.2022704>.

lack of democracy. Among the claims most often heard are Hindu nationalism – the sowing of traditional Indian values instead of liberal ones; a ban on publications deemed to be anti-patriotic; monitoring of NGOs; attacks by Modi on those who enjoy hearty beef steaks, particularly among Muslims; and restrictions on pornographic websites.[51]

India Grows at Night

A period of rapid economic growth began in India on the basis of state capitalism in the 1980s, when GDP rose by an average of 6% a year, mainly through growth in industrial production. In the early 1990s, the country faced a crisis, caused by problems in the energy market and the collapse of its main partner, the Soviet Union. The transition to a new growth model was announced in June 1991, when the government proclaimed economic reforms: providing greater freedom to the market and to private enterprise, and the internationalization of the economy. The architect of the economic reforms was the Finance Minister Manmohan Singh, who later became prime minister.

At the same time, the preservation of basic industries and instruments of state regulation in the hands of the state enabled India to avoid a fall in production and in the volume of capital investments while the reforms were being implemented, and to get through the Asian financial crisis of 1998 successfully. In the 2000s, India's GDP rose by more than 7% each year. Growth continued during the global recession, as well. Incidentally, the accuracy of economic statistics is highly questionable, due to the existence of a vast informal sector in the economy.

Indian economic growth is taking place from the bottom up – it is tangled, chaotic and largely unplanned. The famous publicist Gurcharan Das writes: "Indians wryly admit that 'India grows at night' when they sit down to sip chai and talk about their country's messy road into the future. But that is only half the saying. The complete sentence is: 'India grows at night while the government sleeps,' meaning that India may well be rising despite the

---

[51] "India's Government Censorship", *The New York Times*, August 17, 2015 <https://www.nytimes.com/2015/08/18/opinion/indias-government-censorship.html>; Ashutosh Varshney, "The Illiberal Drift of Modi Threatens India's Democracy", *The Financial Times*, August 18, 2017. P. 9; Amy Kazmin, "Modi Stakes His Claim for a New, Conservative India", *The Financial Times*, August 22, 2017. P. 8; Kiran Stacey, "India Right to Privacy Ruling Deals Blow to Biometric ID System", *The Financial Times*, August 25, 2017. P. 2.

state. Prosperity is, indeed, spreading across the country even as governance failure pervades public life. It is a tale of private success and public failure."[52]

Indian capitalism is very different from the market-based models that one can read about in American or French textbooks. In Western economies, considerably more than half of the profits made on the stock market go to companies controlled by institutional investors; however, in India, it accounts only for one eighth. 344 of the 500 biggest Indian companies are owned not by their shareholders, but by their founders.[53] 40% of profits go to state corporations. These carry out two thirds of the country's financial operations, and produce two thirds of its energy and mineral resources.

Despite India's reputation for high-tech start-ups and new entrepreneurs, a dominant role in the country's private sector is played by old family firms, which, flouting the classical Western textbooks, are involved in a multi-profile business: from cigarettes and spices to noodles and hotels. Among the leading oligarchs are Ratan Tata, who represents the fifth generation of owners of the Tata Sons conglomerate; Anand Mahindra, the director of the Mahindra Group, founded by his grandfather; and Anil Ambani, who inherited from his father part of the Reliance Empire. They continue to make most of their money from the construction of roads and property, and the extraction of minerals and energy. One could live in a house, drive a car, talk on the telephone, have lunch, take out insurance, get dressed, wear a watch, stay at a hotel – and do all this using services provided by the company Tata. It accounts for 7% of the capitalization of the stock market and 3% of corporate taxes.

The concentration of capital is exceptionally high. By the standards of the biggest economies in the world, though, the giants of Indian business are not so big. The State Bank of India, the biggest bank in the country, is one tenth the size of the biggest Chinese bank in terms of its profits. Reliance, the largest company in India in terms of capitalization, and the most serious player in the chemical and energy industries, is one third the size of the French company Total.[54] "In the past decade Indian business has not been on a journey towards someone else's economic model," *The Economist* concludes. "Instead it seems to have established its own equilibrium."[55]

....

[52] Gurcharan Das, *India Grows at Night. A Liberal Case for a Strong State*. New Delhi, 2012. P. 1.

[53] "Indian Business. Toppling the Tycoons", *The Economist*, August 26, 2017. P. 12.

[54] "Special report: Business in India", *The Economist*, October 22, 2011. PP. 3, 4, 5, 17; "Ratan Tata's legacy; Capitalism in India", *The Economist*, December 1, 2012. P. 12.

[55] "Special report: Business in India", *The Economist*, October 22, 2011. P. 4.

The most impressive characteristic of today's India is its human capital: the vast and ever-growing number of entrepreneurs, managers and resourceful one-off businessmen. Their number is increasing at an unimaginable rate, in part because they speak English. They do not need translators in order to find out about computers, management theory, market strategy, or the latest innovations in science and technology. 37% of India's GDP is made up by micro, small and medium enterprises.[56] The role of the consumer is significant in India's growth. Young Indian professionals do not save up money to buy a house, they take out a mortgage. The number of credit cards issued is growing at 35% a year. Private consumption accounts for an incredible 67% of GDP, a good deal higher than in China (42%) or any other Asian country. The only country in which the share of private consumption is even higher – at 70% – is the USA.[57]

The most successful and dynamic sector in the modern "knowledge economy" is the production of software products and the exporting thereof to the USA and Europe. Annual growth in profits in this sector in the 2000s surpassed 50%. The companies Infosys, Wipro, and Tata Consultancy Services have become global giants in computer programming. Bill Gates has called India a "software superpower". Many American companies hire staff from India, who work for them without having to leave their home country. Hundreds of thousands of Indians answer calls from customers all over the world, or make cold calls them themselves, in order to sell credit cards, offer mobile phones at discounted prices, or remind people about overdue payments. A low-paid and far from prestigious job at an American call center is becoming a well-paid and prestigious job at an Indian one.[58] Although the number of Internet users is less than a quarter of the population, that still equates to around 400 million people, and more than a billion people in India own a cell phone.

India has an advanced space program. In February 2017, it set a new record by sending no fewer than 104 satellites into orbit using a single rocket-launcher (the previous record had been 37 satellites, set by Russia in 2014).[59] India has achieved full independence in terms of planning, building

---

[56] Nalin Mehta, "Only Micro, Small and Medium Businesses Can Provide Maximum Jobs, Entrepreneurs and Products for India", *The Times of India*, May 10, 2017 <https://timesofindia.indiatimes.com/blogs/academic-interest/only-micro-small-and-medium-businesses-can-provide-maximum-jobs-entrepreneurs-and-products-for-india/>.

[57] Fareed Zakaria, *The Post-American World*. W. W. Norton & Company, 2008. P. 136.

[58] Thomas L. Friedman, *The World is Flat: A Brief History of the Twenty-First Century*. Penguin Books, 2006. PP. 28-29.

[59] "Milestones", *Time*, February 27 – March 6, 2017. P. 19.

and servicing nuclear power plants; it is conducting research in the Arctic and Antarctic, and produces a quarter of all the medicines supplied to the global market.

It is still difficult to describe the structure of the economy and of employment as modern, though. According to data from the World Bank, more than 30% of Indians aged 15 to 29 are "not in education, employment or training". This may be something of an exaggeration, though, in a country where 86% of workers operate in the "informal employment", where they pay no taxes and do not enter into labor contracts.[60] 90% of firms operate in this shadow sector and it produces half of GDP. 40% of Indian tea is sold there, along with 85% of jewelry and 70% of dairy products.[61] According to estimates, 49% of people are employed in the field of agriculture, forestry or fishing, which account for 13.7% of GDP. Industry produces 21.5% of GDP and gives work to 20% of those in employment. The fastest-growing sector of the economy – the services sector – accounts for 64.8% of GDP and provides 31% of jobs. Only 4% work in the rapidly growing sector of information and other modern technologies.

Exports are worth around 450 billion dollars, of which 300 billion is provided by goods: software programs, foodstuffs, petrochemicals, jewelry, medicines, and textiles. The goods mainly go to Europe (17%), the USA (13%), the UAE (13%), China (6%), and Singapore (5%).[62]

India has a large resource potential. The country is 3rd in the world in terms of the mining of coal, lignite and barites. India accounts for a quarter of global reserves of iron ore, which ensures the development of black metallurgy. Large amounts of magnesium ore and bauxites are mined (though the growth of aluminum manufacturing is restricted by a shortage of energy capabilities).[63] Meanwhile, the country is facing an acute energy shortage. Most of the country's rural population still has no access to electricity. Coal is the primary fuel, accounting for around half of all energy consumption. Oil accounts for around a third. 80% of oil and natural gas is imported by sea.[64]

....

[60] "Just the Job; India's Economy", *The Economist*, September 16, 2017. P. 52.
[61] "Making Money in India; Schumpeter", *The Economist*, August 26, 2017. P. 58.
[62] Leon F. Wegner, "India. The Fascinating Country", *La Vie Diplomatique*, Issue 2, 2014. P. 27.
[63] Boris Kuzyk and Tat'yana Shaumyan, *Indiya – Rossiya: strategiya partnerstva v XXI veke (India-Russia: A Strategy of Partnership in the 21st Century)*. Moscow, 2009. P. 166.
[64] A. K. Alekseyev et al., *Problemy sovremennoy Azii: istoriya, konflikty, geopolitika (The Problems of Modern Asia. History, Conflicts, Geopolitics)*. St. Petersburg, 2009. P. 65.

India achieved outstanding successes in agriculture in the 1970s and 1980s (the time of the "green revolution") by cultivating high-yielding types of wheat, rice and other crops, when there was an abundant harvest. More than a third of the area under crop produces a harvest more than once a year. The rate of growth in agricultural production is falling, though, due to degradation of the land and water resources. Almost half of the territory of India is in the grip of erosion processes. And global warming makes the situation more dramatic. According to the World Resources Institute, over half of India now faces high or extremely high water stress. Levels of the sacred Ganges are declining – by a fourth at some estimates. 15 million farmers have already abandoned their land because of a shortage of water drought.[65]

India is one of the countries that has suffered the most deforestation in the world: the area covered by forests is being cut by 1.5 billion hectares a year. 500 species of mammal are under threat of extinction, as are 100 species of fish and 1000 species of bird.

The scale of annual emissions of domestic and industrial waste is leading to the pollution of such deep and sacred rivers, for the Hindus, as the Ganges. India faces problems both with drinking water and with water for irrigation: 84% of all spring water goes towards irrigation, industry consumes 12%, and the populace 4%. The main source is underground water, reserves of which are diminishing with each passing year.[66] The polluted waters are reaching the ocean, including the zone in which fish are traditionally caught, which is moving further and further away from the coast. Large amounts of gases are being pumped into the atmosphere by numerous chemicals companies. The disaster in 1984 in the city of Bhopal, during which over 2,500 people died and 35,000 suffered poisoning, is in the Guinness Book of Records as the biggest man-made catastrophe of all time.[67]

Thirteen of the world's 20 most polluted cities are in India. The most gas-polluted city in the world is Delhi, where levels of greenhouse gases are six times higher than the maximum recommended amount.[68] The main

---

[65] Mary Schilling, "Dust to Dust", *Newsweek*, August 31, 2018. PP. 32-33.

[66] Amitabh Kant, "India's Great Drying Out", *The Times of India*, September 21, 2016 <https://timesofindia.indiatimes.com/blogs/toi-edit-page/indias-great-drying-out-cauvery-dispute-manifests-growing-water-shortage-how-does-india-tackle-it/>.

[67] T. P. Petrova, "Ekologicheskiye problemy v stranakh BRIKS" ("Ecological Problems in the BRICS Countries"), in *Voskhodyashchiye gosudarstva-giganty BRIKS: rol' v mirovoy politike, strategii modernizatsii* (*The Rising Giant-States of BRICS: Their Role in World Politics, Strategies for Modernization*). Moscow, 2012. PP. 129-130.

[68] "Air Pollution in India. Breath Uneasy", *The Economist*, February 7, 2015. P. 47; Jason Burke,

source of air pollution is the millions of vehicles of various kinds on the city's streets (cars, trucks, buses, motorized rickshaws, motorcycles, and so on). I hardly saw any cars in India without scratches. 20%-30% of the country's entire urban population live in the slums (and in the biggest cities, 30%-40% of the population), with practically no basic sanitary and hygienic conditions whatsoever. The shortfall in residential housing in the cities is estimated at 20 million buildings.[69]

The arrival of Modi as prime minister inspired enthusiasm in Indian business. A set of ambitious programs was initiated: "Make in India" – the transformation of the country into an industrial giant, "Skilled India" – the training of human resources for the modern economy; "Digital India" – the task of giving 250,000 out of 640,000 villages, and a quarter of all schools, access to the Internet; "Smart Cities" – the erection, from scratch, of 100 modern cities; "Startup India" – a program that gave tax exemptions for three years to startups created after 1st April 2016; "Clean India", and others. Modi announced plans to bring about an infrastructure boom in India, similar to the one in China, and announced the aim of providing everyone with housing, within eight years, in which they would have water, electricity and sewage systems. Land reforms involved, first and foremost, the restoring of order to the extremely muddled system of land ownership and land use. Experts noted the absence from Modi's plans of measures to simplify the taxation system and reduce the budget deficit.[70]

Modi brought great disappointment to supporters of a market economy when he decided, in November 2016, to take 86% of paper money out of circulation – by destroying the old 500 and 1,000 rupee banknotes (equivalent in value to 7.5 and 15 dollars) and replacing them with new denominations with a face value of 500 and 2,000 rupees. The aim was to punish rich tax-avoiders. In a country where more than 90% of the people have never

---

"Indian Minister Promises to Tackle Country's Acute Air Pollution Problem", *The Guardian*, April 5, 2015 <https://www.theguardian.com/world/2015/apr/05/indian-minister-promises-acute-air-pollution-world-health-organisation>; "Polluting Vehicles Turn Delhi into Toxic Hotspot", *Gulf News*, May 7, 2017. P. A1.

[69] Rumir Aijaz, "Adressing Urbanization", in *Global Goals, National Actions: Making the Post-2015 Development Agenda Relevant to India*. New Delhi, 2016. P. 71.

[70] *The Economist: The World in 2015*, 2015. P. 97; James Saft, "India Benefits from Reform and a Bit of Luck", *Reuters*, February 24, 2015 <https://www.reuters.com/article/markets-india-james-saft/column-india-benefits-from-reform-and-a-bit-of-luck-james-saft-idINKBN0LS0A320150224>; "India 'Bright Spot' in Asia", *The Asian Age*, February 27, 2015. P. 15; Amy Kazmin, "Modi Stumbles Over Land Reform", *The Financial Times*, August 10, 2015. P. 5.

made a cashless payment in their lives, this move caused chaos. Huge lines were formed at the banks, and many ATMs simply did not have the new banknotes.

People hurried to withdraw their savings, and by March 2017, somewhere between 44 and 67 billion dollars had been withdrawn (estimates vary). By the end of 2016, sales of automobiles had fallen by 19%, and sales of houses by 44%. Another blow was dealt to business in the shape of the ban on the sale of alcohol in shops, bars and hotels located less than 500 meters from a motorway (in an effort to counter drink-driving; some 400 people are killed on India's roads every day).[71]

Many expected Modi's popularity to wane, but despite fierce criticism from liberal circles, this did not happen. People looked on the prime minister as someone who was protecting the interests of the little man from the tax-dodgers and those with vast sums of money stashed away in safes.[72] And by the late summer of 2017, the amount of money in bank accounts had risen by 13%, the number of electronic payments had increased by 40%, accompanied by a reduction in the amount of cash in circulation from 12% to 10% of GDP, and the number of taxpayers had almost doubled.[73] The government returned to large-scale privatization – to the tune of 11 billion dollars in 2017, including a controlling share of the Hindustan Petroleum Corporation.[74]

India's economy is one of the fastest growing in the world, even if the growth rate is slightly declining. Since 2003, an increase in GDP of 9% per year has been considered normal. In 2015-2016 (fiscal year in India ends on 31st March) growth was 8%, in 2016-2017 7.1%, in 2017-2018 6.5%. The reasons usually mentioned for the slowdown are macroeconomic imbalances, lack of adequate infrastructure, high interest rates, and weak tax collection. Per capita income is 1,700 dollars a year, almost one fifth of that in China.[75]

---

[71] "India Pays Steep Price for Cash Withdrawal", *Time*, November 28 – December 5, 2016. P. 9; Ruchir Sharma, "The Boom Was a Blip. Getting Used to Slow Growth", *Foreign Affairs*, May/June 2017. PP. 104-108; Simon Mundy, "India's Financial Sector Grapples With Effects of Demonetisation", *The Financial Times*, August 23, 2017. P. 12; "Government Caprice in India. Bar Wars", *The Economist*, April 8, 2017. P. 51.

[72] "Indian Politics. Non-Stick PM", *The Economist*, January 14, 2017. PP. 23-24.

[73] "Making Money in India; Schumpeter", *The Economist*, August 26, 2017. P. 55.

[74] Kiran Stacey, "India's Privatisations Back on Track", *The Financial Times*, August 26, 2017. P. 11.

[75] Surjit S. Bhalla, "Tax-Fruits of Demonetisation", The Indian Express, January 17, 2018 <https://indianexpress.com/article/opinion/columns/tax-fruits-of-demonetisation-5027534/>; Jahangir Aziz, "A Testing Time", India Today, January 22, 2018. PP. 35-37.

Strategic Autonomy

Dominique Moïsi writes: "If 'China is back', India is arriving on the world stage for the first time. It does not feel like an old empire recovering its central status, but like a new nation [...]."[76] India has the same number of diplomats as New Zealand. However, nowadays, few doubt that India has the economic, demographic, cultural and civilizational prerequisites to become one of the biggest sovereign centers of power in the 21st century. Works are also being published in which a more active foreign policy strategy is being formulated. Worthy of note among them is a book by the security expert Raja Menon and the economist Rajiv Kumar, *The Long View from Delhi*, published in 2010. It marked an obvious change of focus – to a desire to play an increasingly active role and take on ever more responsibility in the world. At the center of attention are the United States and China.[77]

Does Indian foreign policy have a special style all of its own? Shivshankar Menon, who served as National Security Advisor to the Prime Minister for many years, said that answering this question was "just as it is hard to put into words what makes a person Indian, since we base our nationhood not on religion, ethnicity, language, or any of the standard nineteenth-century criteria but on an idea of India. [...] If there is an Indian way in foreign policy, it is marked by a combination of boldness in conception and caution in implementation, by the dominant and determining role of the prime minister, by a didactic negotiating style, by a fundamentally realistic approach masked by normative rhetoric, by comfort in a plural and diverse world or multiverse, and, most consistently, by a consciousness of India's destiny as a great power."[78]

A unipolar world is unacceptable to India, above all because the country is itself staking a claim to be one of the world's leaders. "The key to understanding Delhi's policy today is the declared foreign policy course of supporting 'strategic autonomy'. Despite the fact that Modi's new government has chosen, due to the domestic political environment, not to use this term in his rhetoric, the foreign policy imperative of retaining a degree of

---

[76] Dominique Moïsi, *The Geopolitics of Emotion: How Cultures of Fear, Humiliation and Hope are Reshaping the World*. Random House, 2009.

[77] Raja Menon and Rajiv Kumar, *The Long View From Delhi: To Define the Indian Grand Strategy for Foreign Policy*. New Delhi, 2010.

[78] Shivshankar Menon, *Choices: Inside the Making of India's Foreign Policy*. Brookings Institution Press, 2016. P. 132.

distance from the main centers of global politics and the principle of a 'free hand' continue to dominate the Indian leadership. Behind this term stands nothing other than a declaration of the policy of balancing between China and the USA with the active cooperation of other centers of power (Russia, the EU, Australia, Japan, the ASEAN states)."[79]

A popular concept is that of the three bangles of Indian strategy in foreign policy. The first ring incorporates India's immediate neighbors. Here, Delhi is striving to achieve supremacy and non-interference by third-party countries. The second ring incorporates India's "extended neighborhood" in Asia and along the edge of the Indian Ocean. The third is the entire global arena.

The priority is South Asia, a region which also includes Pakistan, Bangladesh, Nepal, Sri Lanka, Bhutan, and the Maldives. India has around three quarters of Southern Asia's territory and population, and around 80% of its GDP. The dominance of one country leads to a natural sense of unease for others. India is categorically against the bringing in of external forces, particularly other greater powers, to resolve regional problems. India's neighbors, by contrast, see no security threats outside the borders of the region, accusing India of trying to have a hegemony: interference in the internal affairs of Nepal and Bangladesh, supporting the Tamil insurgents in Sri Lanka or the separatists in the Baluchistan region of Pakistan.[80] The contradiction between the economic benefits of cooperation with India and fear of it is determining the political dynamics in the region.

Therefore, in South Asia, all the negative factors which usually hinder the development of integration processes are present: a dominant regional power, the lack of a common enemy, and economies which do not mutually benefit one another sufficiently. The largest regional organization is the South Asian Association for Regional Cooperation (SAARC), created in 1985 in Dhaka. In 1993, an agreement was adopted on mutual trade preferences. In 2004, the SAARC countries agreed on the formation, in the long-term, of a free trade zone in South Asia, but the Pakistani government is continuing to restrict imports from India. South Asia remains the least integrated part of the planet. 0.5% of Indian imports and 4% of its exports involve its neighbors in SAARC.[81]

---

[79] Rostislav Lenchuk, "Tseli i zadachi vneshnepoliticheskoy strategii Indii na sovremennom etape" ("Aims and Objectives of India's Foreign Policy Strategy at the Present Stage"), *Mezhdunarodnaya zhizn'* (*International Affairs*), March 2016, PP. 35-36.

[80] "The Elephant in the Region; India and Its Near-Abroad", *The Economist*, February 18, 2012. P. 14.

[81] Sergey Lunev, "Region Bol'shaya Vostochnaya Aziya i politika Indii" ("The Region of Great East Asia and the Politics of India"), *Vestnik analitiki* (*Analytics Bulletin*), Issue 3, 2008. PP. 66-

Relations between India and Pakistan shape the situation in South Asia. Although Pakistan has only one eighth of the economic, territorial and demographic potential of India, it is a fairly powerful state, whose population is larger than that of Russia. The main bone of contention in their relations is the unresolved problem of Kashmir. After three armed conflicts, India's relations with Pakistan have become frozen at the negotiation stage.

In 1998, India became a nuclear state, convinced that only by doing so could it achieve the status of a global power. The "Chinese threat" was identified as the main reason that compelled it to cross the "nuclear threshold", but the issue was primarily about Pakistan, which responded with a test of its own. The two countries' transition to the category of *de facto* nuclear states caused serious damage to the policy of non-proliferation. Neither of them have signed the Non-Proliferation Treaty, and the continued confrontation between them provides ground for concerns about a nuclear conflict. So as not to allow the worst-case scenario to unfold, Indian and Pakistan agreed that neither would attack the nuclear facilities of the other, and information is exchanged each year about the number and location of such facilities. In 2005, an agreement came into force on keeping one another informed in the event of test launches of ballistic missiles capable of carrying nuclear warheads.

Pakistan's nuclear potential is estimated to be 110-130 warheads. Some experts believe that the correct figure is double this, if weapon-usable nuclear materials are included.[82] Experts are of the view that "at present, there is rough nuclear parity between India and Pakistan, with Pakistan having a larger arsenal and India having more advanced air- and sea-based capabilities."[83]

When he came to power, Modi confirmed that relations with the South Asian countries were a priority, and invited all the leaders of SAARC to his inauguration, including the leader of Pakistan, Nawaz Sharif. The Indian prime minister announced his wish to open a new chapter in relations with Islamabad.[84]

69; "The Elephant in the Region; India and Its Near-Abroad", *The Economist*, February 18, 2012. P. 14.

[82] Mark Fitzpatrick, *Overcoming Pakistan's Nuclear Dangers*. London, 2014. PP. 21-22.

[83] Michael Krepon, "Nuclear Race on the Subcontinent", *The New York Times*, April 4, 2013 <https://www.nytimes.com/2013/04/05/opinion/global/nuclear-race-on-the-subcontinent.html>.

[84] *Strategic Survey 2014: The Annual Review of World Affairs*. Routledge, 2014. P. 295.

When tensions rose in the fall of 2016, with Pakistani forces opening fire on a military camp in Uri, 67% of Indians were in favor of the use of military force against Pakistan, and senior figures in the military declared that they had the right to use force at any time and place, at their own discretion. Indian experts estimate their armed forces to be considerably better than Pakistan's, but this, in their view, means only one thing: if a war were to break out, Karachi would use a nuclear weapon at an early stage of the conflict.[85]

The political crisis in Pakistan, which put Nawaz Sharif in the dock for corruption, and the July 2016 election won by Pakistan Tehreek-e-Insaf party (Movement for Justice), led by Imran Khan, a former cricket star and Oxford graduate, shuffled the deck. Two political dynasties that have long fought for the leadership of Pakistan – The Pakistan Muslim League (Nawaz), controlled by the Sharif family, and the Pakistan Peoples party of the Bhutto family – have united in the fight against Imran Khan.[86] Khan kept sending signals that he was eager to improve relations with India; however, a new armed conflict in early 2019 nearly led to a full-scale war.

The most significant region for India, outside South Asia, is East Asia. As early as the start of the 1990s, the policy of "Look to the East" was proclaimed, with the ambition of becoming a leading regional player. In 1995, India acquired the status of a full-scale partner with ASEAN. In November 2002, the first ASEAN-India summit took place. The country was among the 16 participants in the first East Asia Summit, held in Malaysia in December 2005. The Mekong-Ganges forum has come into being, uniting India and five ASEAN countries – Cambodia, Laos, Myanmar, Thailand, and Vietnam. In 2009, India signed a free trade agreement with ASEAN. In 1997, the Bay of Bengal Initiative for Multi-Sectoral Technical and Economic Cooperation (BIMSTEC) was launched, uniting India, Bangladesh, Sri Lanka, Nepal, Bhutan, Myanmar, and Thailand. The Indian government also agreed to the new BCIM format (Bangladesh – China – India – Myanmar), but not as another sub-regional organization, but in order to carry out specific joint projects.[87]

---

[85] "PM Clears Effective Response, Army Says It's Ready & Willing to Hit Back", *The Times of India*, September 20, 2016; Air Marshal PS Ahluwalia, "Air Option Better Than Ground Option", *The Economic Times*, September 20, 2016 <https://economictimes.indiatimes.com/blogs/et-commentary/air-option-better-than-ground-action/>.

[86] Farhan Bokhari and Kiran Stacey, "Pakistan Dynasties to Join Forces over 'Rigged' Khan Victory", *The Financial Times*, August 13, 2018. P. 4.

[87] *"Bol'shaya Vostochnaya Aziya": mirovaya politika i regional'nyye transformatsii* ("*Greater East Asia*": *World Politics and Regional Transformations*), ed. by A. D. Voskresenskiy. Moscow,

A particularly important and intriguing development has been the evolution of Indo-Chinese relations, in which the main trend has been a radical – though far from complete – lessening of tension. The Indian journalist and politician Jairam Ramesh coined the term "Chindia" in connection with this, as a way of denoting both of these rapidly growing and densely-populated Asian countries. The size of Chinese-Indian trade has seen a 20-fold increase since the start of the century. "China and India each are starting to exert powerful influence in virtually every dimension of global business," writes the editor of the book *Chindia*, Pat Angardio, of *Business Week*. "In the coming decades, they will likely be the biggest forces reshaping the world economy."[88]

Relations between the two can be described as a "collaborative rivalry", which is reflected in the stances of various groups within the Indian elite. The pragmatists – a portion of the members of congress and of the business elite – are in favor of cooperation. The realists – representatives of BJP, the security structures, and the Foreign Ministry – are inclined towards a tougher policy in relation to China. The "peacemakers" – members of the communist (Marxist) party and other left-wing organizations – see no particular threat on the part of China.[89] India is not happy with its deficit in bilateral trade, nor is China content with Delhi's refusal to grant China the status of a country with a market economy. Chinese-Indian rivalry is intensifying, meanwhile, over foreign (African) and internal Indian markets.

There is serious concern in Delhi about the military-political cooperation between China and Pakistan, however much Beijing claims that the "Indian factor" is not part of Pakistani-Chinese relations. China recently admitted the need to regulate the Kashmir problem on a bilateral basis, without being unambiguously on the side of Islamabad. Beijing is also concerned by the strengthening of cooperation between America and India, in which it perceives a plan to contain China.

India is extremely cautious about the Chinese Belt and Road Initiative. It is seen as an instrument for expanding China's geopolitical influence. Moreover, one of the transport corridors that Beijing is proposing to use

....
2010. P. 96; "India in Asia. Eastern Promises", *The Economist*. August 30, 2014. P. 11.

[88] *Chindia: How China and India Are Revolutionizing Global Business*, ed. by Pete Engardio. McGraw-Hill Education, 2007. P. 13.

[89] Tat'yana Shaumyan, "Faktor dvustoronnikh otnosheniy v formate BRIKS: opyt Indii" ("The Factor of Bilateral Relations in the BRICS Format: India's Experience"), in *Strategiya Rossii v BRIKS: tseli i instrumenty* (*Russia's Strategy in BRICS: Aims and Instruments*). Moscow, 2013. PP. 132-133.

would pass through a part of Kashmir claimed by India. It was for this very reason that Modi turned down an invitation to attend a summit on B&R in Beijing in 2017.[90]

China is being accused of busily "buying friends in the Maldives and the Seychelles and investing in Mauritius – all for the purpose of securing its 'maritime silk road' that cuts right across the Indian ocean, which India has long considered 'its lake'. With China's economic expansions come political clout and, eventually, military presence. Chinese submarines are being spotted on a regular basis in an ocean where no Chinese naval ships have been present since Zheng He […]."[91] The Doklam standoff in the summer of 2017, when Indian and Chinese troops were standing eyeball-to-eyeball in the Himalayan wilderness after Beijing decided to build a road through an area disputed by China and Bhutan, visibly demonstrated the vastness of conflict potential.

Japan has become an important partner for India, particularly since Junichiro Koizumi became prime minister; he announced a "strategic partnership", wary of China and envious of the alliance between Washington and Delhi. This took place despite Tokyo's sharply critical response to India's nuclear tests in 1998, which led to Japanese sanctions. Meanwhile, India is actively smoothing over ties with Japan, specifically in the field of nuclear and other new technologies. Some people among India's foreign policy elite openly state that they would not object to Japan becoming a nuclear state (as a counterweight, obviously, to China). Tokyo has begun sending some of its foreign investment to India, which is now in first place among the recipients of Japanese aid for developmental needs. Moreover, Japan is showing growing interest in expanding its military cooperation with India, particularly at sea. India bought its first consignment of amphibious aircraft from Japan, and has placed an order for six silent submarines.[92] The navies of Japan, India and the USA conducted joint exercises in the Bay of Bengal in July 2017.[93]

The countries of the Persian Gulf are emerging as important partners for India; up to two thirds of India's oil imports come from the region. The

---

[90] "Forget India", *The Times of India*, May 10, 2017.
[91] Bertil Lintner, "Not a Border Dispute", *India Today*, January 22, 2018. P. 43.
[92] Rajat Pandit, "Wary of China, India and Japan Set to Forge Aircraft Deal", *The Times of India*, February 26, 2015 <https://timesofindia.indiatimes.com/india/Wary-of-China-India-and-Japan-set-to-forge-aircraft-deal/articleshow/46375098.cms>.
[93] Valeriy Kistanov, "Yaponiya i Indiya sozdayut al'yans s oglyadkoy na Kitay" ("Japan and India are Creating an Alliance with China in Mind"), *Nezavisimaya Gazeta* (*Independent Newspaper*), October 2, 2017 <https://www.ng.ru/dipkurer/2017-10-02/9_7085_japan.html>.

volume of trade has long exceeded 200 billion dollars. More than 7 million Indian citizens live and work in the region, mostly in construction and in the services sector.[94]

Relations between Russia and India quickly deteriorated after the collapse of the USSR, when Moscow simply walked away from India. In 1991, foreign trade stood at 7.6 billion dollars (10.3% of India's trade), and a year later – 862 million. India is now in 18th place among Russia's trade partners, with 7.7 billion dollars of trade turnover.[95] As for Indian imports from Russia, 60% are ferrous and non-ferrous metals, mineral fertilizers, and paper for newspapers; only 8% consists of machines and equipment. The bulk of Indian exports to Russia (65%) consists of cotton items, tea, coffee, and medicines.

An important place in Russo-Indian relations has traditionally been held by military and technical cooperation. India accounted for 50% of all arms sales contracts concluded by Russia in the 2000s. India is still first in terms of buying Russian arms. Almost 70% of the weaponry used by India was made in Russia. Agreements have been signed on the acquisition, and production in India under Russian licenses, of state-of-the-art Russian tanks, armored vehicles and fighter jets, and also on the sale to India of the aircraft-carrier the "Admiral Gorshkov" ("Vikramaditya"), the contract for the renovation of which was worth more than 2.2 billion dollars. In 2012, two frigates were supplied with a value of over 1 billion dollars, along with the "Nerpa" nuclear submarine. India is using Russian know-how to create its own submarines and reactors for them, and is renting nuclear submarines from Moscow so that it can use them to train Indian naval officers.[96]

The joint designing and production of a fifth-generation military jet is taking place, and of a multi-purpose transport plane, and the licensed production of T-90 S tanks and SU-30 MKI planes, with jointly-created "BrahMos" cruise missiles which are taken into service by the navy of both countries and are used in SU jet fighters' equipment. Today, almost all major contracts between Russia and India stipulate the simultaneous handover of arms production technologies, even the most cutting-edge.[97] Coopera-

....

[94] *West Asia in Transition*, ed. by Arundhati Ghose. New Delhi, 2014. PP. 114-115.

[95] *Rossiya v tsifrakh. 2017* (*Russia in Figures. 2017*). Moscow, 2017. PP. 479, 481.

[96] Aleksey Nikol'skiy, "Plan perekryli na $1,5 mlrd" ("A Plan Covered for $1.5 Billion"), *Vedomosti*, February 16, 2012 <https://www.vedomosti.ru/newspaper/articles/2012/02/16/plan_perekryli_na_15_mlrd>; Yogesh Joshi and Frank O'Donnell, "India's Submarine Deterrent and Asian Nuclear Proliferation", *Survival*, August/September 2014. P. 159.

[97] G. A. Vlaskin, S. P. Glinkina, and Y. B. Lenchuk, "Sotrudnichestvo so stranami BRIKS v interesakh modernizatsii rossiyskoy ekonomiki" ("Cooperation with the BRICS States in the

tion in the field of space exploration has centered on plans for manned space flights. Russian specialists participate in the creation of orbital spaceships, and training centers for astronauts in India, and are working with their Indian counterparts on the creation and launch of satellites, and on the use of the Russian GLONASS navigation system.[98]

Moscow and Delhi are cooperating ever more actively in multilateral formats. The RIC (Russia – India – China, the "Primakov triangle") has played the role of a restricting force on traditional Sino-Indian disagreements. Within the context of the RIC, Russia has managed to initiate trilateral discussions, partially neutralizing the tension between Beijing and New Delhi.

Reportedly, Modi was planning to make his first foreign trip a visit to Moscow, but the visit did not happen. Several experts relate this to Russia's intention to resume military and technical cooperation with Pakistan, which was discontinued after the collapse of the USSR, and to sell MI-35 attack helicopters to Islamabad.[99] As a result, Modi's first state visit was to Bhutan, and he met Putin at the BRICS summit in Brazil; the Russian leader was first to make a state visit, going to India in December 2014.

During the meeting, Modi said: "President Putin is the leader of a great country, to which we are tied by unique relations, founded on friendship, trust and goodwill. Our strategic partnership is unprecedented… And in the future, the significance of these relations for both countries will grow in many ways." During the summit, agreements were reached on the diversification of mutual trade and the growing of investment using national currencies. Consultations began on the signing of agreements on a free trade zone between India and the Eurasian Economic Union. A document was signed on the strengthening of cooperation in the use of nuclear energy: the construction in India of more than 20 nuclear energy blocs, cooperation in the kitting out of nuclear power plants following Russian designs in third-party countries, the joint mining of uranium, and the production of nuclear fuel. Rosneft and Gazprom drew up joint plans with their Indian partners on the exploitation of the Russian Arctic shelf, and the expansion of supplies of compressed natural gas.[100]

Interests of Modernizing the Russian Economy"), in *Strategiya Rossii v BRIKS: tseli i instrumenty* (*Russia's Strategy in BRICS: Aims and Instruments*). Moscow, 2013. PP. 338-339.

[98] Ibid. P. 337.

[99] Sergey Strokan', "Ot vorot vertolyot: Voyennaya sdelka s Pakistanom mozhet rassorit' Rossiyu i Indiyu" ("A Brush-Off: A Military Deal with Pakistan Might Lead to Tension between Russia and India"), *Kommersant* (*The Businessman*), June 9, 2014 <https://www.kommersant.ru/doc/2489427>.

[100] "Zayavleniya dlya pressy po itogam rossiysko-indiyskikh peregovoro" ("Press Statements

In the Indian civil service, among professional diplomats and the intelligence community, there is an understanding of the need for India – in the interests of maintaining the global and world equilibrium – of maintaining amicable relations with Russia. There is a large reserve of trust and goodwill. There is an anti-Russian campaign in the press not dissimilar to the Western, but it is by no means dominant.

Among the Indian elite, there is high regard for the potential of BRICS, which is also seen as an instrument for restoring global historical justice, and as an opportunity for revenge on the part of developing countries. Modi came down in favor of closer cooperation within BRICS. At a summit in Fortaleza, Brazil, it was he that proposed calling the newly-created BRICS bank the New Development Bank, and giving it equal capital for all three countries amounting to 50 billion dollars.[101]

India's relations with the USA are far from straightforward. The two nations began to draw closer after the conflict with China, mentioned earlier, in 1962.[102] In September 1963, the countries held joint military and aerial exercises, but there was no serious progress in relations. Washington still had a preference for Pakistan, and from the early 1970s onwards, for China. Delhi, in turn, was on the side of the Soviet Union.

During Bill Clinton's administration, the White House was full of determination to restrict, reduce and ultimately destroy India's nuclear potential. Sanctions were brought in, in response to nuclear weapons tests. Even while facing sanctions, however, India announced that it was a natural ally of the United States, and in 2000 the first visit to India by a US president in 22 years took place. The strategic context of relations was altered by the administration of George Bush Jr., who, under the influence of his advisor Robert Blackville, who later became ambassador to Delhi, cancelled many of the sanctions, opened the door for cooperation on advanced technologies, provided support in India's struggle against terrorism, ended the unambiguous support for Pakistan on Kashmir, and took up a stance that was closer to Delhi in the India-China equation. In response to this, India supported the USA on anti-missile defence and in its operations in Afghanistan, protecting the US military cargo moving there through the Straits of Malacca.

....
Following the Russian-Indian Talks"), The Russian President's official website, December 11, 2014 <http://news.kremlin.ru/transcripts/47221>.

[101] Andy Marino, *Narendra Modi. A Political Biography*. HarperCollins, 2014. P. 277.
[102] See John Keay, *India: A History*. Grove Press, 2001. P. 516.

Washington acknowledged India's special role in the region and the world. In 2004, relations between India and America were for the first time described as a "strategic partnership" in a joint declaration by Bush and the premier from the BJP, Vajpayee, in which the parties called for the taking of the next steps in strategic partnership.

In 2005-2006 there was a qualitative breakthrough in relations, evidence of which was provided in the "nuclear deal". In July 2005, an agreement was signed by Bush and Manmohan Singh on cooperation in the nuclear sphere. The USA undertook to take part in assisting India with the development of a peaceful nuclear program, and to supply India with nuclear reactors and fuel. In response, Delhi agreed to divide its nuclear program into a peace-time and a military one, extending to its civil nuclear power stations international safety measures and taking on a host of non-proliferation obligations. "The deal was the culmination of our efforts to improve relations between the world's oldest democracy and the world's largest democracy," stressed George Bush. "I believe India, home to roughly a billion people and an educated middle class, has the potential to be one of America's closest partners. The nuclear agreement was a historic step, because it signaled the country's new role on the world stage."[103]

Evidence of a change of American policy in South Asia was provided by Washington's refusal to supply nuclear material to Pakistan, which was linked, among other things, to its view of it as an unreliable partner who had allowed nuclear technologies to be leaked to third-party countries (such as North Korea). In the changing nature of bilateral relations, a role was also played by the Indian diaspora in the USA, which numbers around 2 million people, with an aggregate income of around 300 billion dollars a year.[104]

The partnership between India and America also has an anti-Chinese dimension. India welcomes the US's military presence in the Indian Ocean as an important factor in ensuring stability in the transportation of oil from the Persian Gulf.[105]

The US concept of Indo-Pacific bears a clear anti-Chinese connotation. New Delhi's interest in Quad, which also includes USA, Japan and Australia, has its limitations. "India's engagement with the Indo-Pacific framework will

---

[103] George W. Bush, *Decision Points*. Random House, 2010. P. 214.

[104] C. Raja Mohan, "Indiya i politicheskoye ravnovesiye" ("India and Political Equilibrium"), *Rossiya v global'noy politike* (*Russia in Global Affairs*), Issue 4, July/August 2006. P. 22.

[105] *Safeguarding Prosperity in the Indian Ocean: Exploring India-US Cooperation*. New Delhi: Observer Research Foundation, 2012. P. 25.

remain largely diplomatic, economic and rhetorical. India's core strategic focus lies west of the Strait of Malacca."[106]

In recent years, the USA has been one of the biggest suppliers of arms to India. There is a firm belief in Washington that the strengthening of the Indian state, and support for the development of a strategic and military culture of collaboration, will meet the USA's national interests. However, there are still a host of restrictive factors on American-Indian relations. The USA is hardly likely to agree to provide India with a permanent seat on the UN Security Council. It is also doubtful whether or not they would be willing to recognize India's nuclear status *de jure*. In spite of a certain lowering of Pakistan's role in the US's foreign policy priorities, Washington has not abandoned the "Pakistan card" altogether.

India is still, albeit less actively now, positioning itself as the leader of the Non-Alignment movement. In the UN, India voted in the same way as the US in only 25% of cases. Delhi takes an extremely dim view of how the USA is playing with the Taliban in Afghanistan, fearing that the Taliban might seize power there once American troops have pulled out. India has always been against the breaking of trade and economic ties with Iran, and against the US policy of sanctions.

The election of Narendra Modi, who had been subjected to American sanctions, did not promise anything positive in this regard. After the election, though, in May 2014, the USA decided to cancel existing visa restrictions, and in September, Modi visited the General Assembly of the UN and had a meeting with the American president. Obama became the first American president ever to be invited as a special guest at the Independence Day celebrations, in 2015. He did look somewhat melancholy though, it must be said, as he watched the parade of military equipment, mostly consisting of Russian-made tanks, going past. Nonetheless, a fresh round – the fourth, this time – of efforts to draw America and India closer together has begun.[107]

Alyssa Ayres of the Council on Foreign Relations notes: "Working with a rising India will not always be easy. The country remains fiercely protective of its policy independence, shuns formal alliances, and remains ever willing to break global consensus, as it has done most famously on trade negotia-

---

[106] Rahul Roy-Chaudhury and Kate Sullivan de Estrada, "India, the Indo-Pacific and the Quad", *Survival*, June/July 2018. P. 181.

[107] Shekhar Gupta, "Obama at Rajpath: Not Just Another Selfie Moment", *India Today*, December 8, 2014. PP. 20-21; Nikhil Kumar, "India Rising. A Meeting Between the Leaders of U. S. and India May Cement a Surprising New Partnership", *Time*, February 9, 2015. P. 10.

tions. It can be a close defense partner, but not in the familiar template of most US alliances."[108]

India's economic and political ties to the European states – above all, France and the UK – are becoming deeper, too. Paris stole a march on Washington in backing the idea that an emergent India would be a good market in which to sell high-tech goods. France protected Delhi from the wrath of the G8 after Delhi conducted nuclear tests. Latterly, the UK has also begun to acknowledge the regional and global ambitions of its former colony.

India has traditionally been one of the key initiators of cooperation along the South-South axis.

In October 2011, the fifth IBSA summit was held in Pretoria. It confirmed that in spite of the formation of BRICS, Brazil, India and South Africa had no intention of ending their cooperation in the "trio" format. Moreover, they intended to activate their cooperation, positioning themselves as "genuine big democracies" (a hint that they do not see China and Russia as such), and striving for the status of permanent members of the UN Security Council.[109]

One sometimes hears the view: "India is coming to Africa in China's shadow." Delhi prefers a less public, more subtle approach, aimed at creating the conditions in African countries for the development of human and technological potential. India's Trade Minister Jairam Ramesh, at the first India-Africa summit in April 2008, maintained: "The first principle of Indian policy in Africa is its ambition not to be like the Chinese. China is exploiting the natural resources in Africa, whereas our strategy consists in adding to its wealth."[110]

Since 1964, India has provided help to developing countries (mainly in Africa) in training experts – in the field of IT and the services sector – as part of the ITEC program (Indian Technical and Economic Coopera-

---

[108] Alyssa Ayres, "Will India Start Acting Like a Global Power? New Delhi's New Role", *Foreign Affairs*, November/December 2017. P. 84.

[109] Pyotr Yakovlev, "Braziliya v BRIKS: modeli dvustoronnikh svyazey" ("Brazil in BRICS: Models for Bilateral Ties"), in *Voskhodyashchiye gosudarstva-giganty BRIKS: rol' v mirovoy politike, strategii modernizatsii* (*The Rising Giant-States of BRICS: Their Role in World Politics, Strategies for Modernization*). Moscow, 2012. PP. 170-171.

[110] Vyacheslav Usov, "Sozdaniye BRIKS i problemy proniknoveniya Indii v agrosektor afrikanskikh stran" ("The Creation of BRICS and the Problems of Penetrating India in the Agricultural Sector of African Countries"), in *Voskhodyashchiye gosudarstva-giganty BRIKS: rol' v mirovoy politike, strategii modernizatsii* (*The Rising Giant-States of BRICS: Their Role in World Politics, Strategies for Modernization*). Moscow, 2012. PP. 270-271.

tion). In March 2012, it was announced that more than a hundred science and innovation centers would be built, for the development of human resources, including such institutions as the Indian-African Institute of Planning and Management in Education, the Institute of Diamonds, the Institute of Information Technologies, the Institute for the Development of Agriculture, the Center for Medium-Term Weather Forecasting, and the Academy of Civil Aviation.[111] Indian companies have purchased or acquired under long leases thousands of hectares of fertile land in Ethiopia, Kenya, Madagascar, Mozambique and Senegal, where the Indians are growing rice, sugar cane, maize and other crops, which, as a rule, are exported to India.

India's biggest partner in Africa is South Africa, thanks to long-established historical ties, and the presence there of an Indian diaspora numbering 1.3 million people. Indian capital investment has been made in many sectors of the South African economy, primarily in agriculture, and it is coming from the private sector, by contrast with Chinese investment.[112] South Africa's state oil company, PetroSA, and the Cairn India Group signed an agreement regarding extraction from the oil and gas fields in the valley of the Orange River on the east coast of South Africa.

"India itself cannot be viewed only as a bundle of the old and the new, accidentally and uncomfortably pieced together, an artificial construct without a natural unity," claims Rajiv Malhotra. "Nor is she just a repository of quaint, fashionable accessories to Western lifestyles; nor a junior partner in a global capitalist world. India is its own distinct and unified civilization with a proven ability to manage profound differences, engage creatively with various cultures, religions and philosophies, and peacefully integrate many diverse streams of humanity. These values are based on ideas about divinity, the cosmos and humanity that stand in contrast to the fundamental assumptions of Western civilization."[113]

....

[111] Vyacheslav Usov, "Afrikanskaya strategiya Indii i formirovaniye BRIKS" ("India's African Strategy and the Formation of BRICS"), in *BRIKS i Afrika: sotrudnichestvo v tselyakh razvitiya* (*BRICS and Africa: Cooperation with the Aim of Development*). Moscow, 2013. PP. 162, 164-165.

[112] Eleonora Lebedeva, "YUAR v BRIKS: perspektivnoye sotrudnichestvo?" ("South Africa and BRICS: A Cooperation with Good Prospects?"), in *Voskhodyashchiye gosudarstva-giganty BRIKS: rol' v mirovoy politike, strategii modernizatsii* (*The Rising Giant-States of BRICS: Their Role in World Politics, Strategies for Modernization*). Moscow, 2012. PP. 234-235.

[113] Rajiv Malhotra, *Being Different: An Indian Challenge to Western Universalism*. HarperCollins, 2013. P. 4.

India, Fareed Zakaria believes, can still capitalize on its strengths: a large-scale and growing economy, political democracy, anti-clericalism and tolerance, a subtle understanding of the East and the West, and special relations with America. If all these forces are mobilized and used as intended, India will once again be able to claim its place among the leading countries. This could be second, third or fourth place in the world.[114] Indeed, India is clearly lacking what it takes to become the number one. Strength of the state.

---

[114] Fareed Zakaria, *The Post-American World*. W. W. Norton & Company, 2008. P. 165.

CHAPTER 10
THE ISLAMIC FACTOR

Since the start of the 21st century, Islam has been a genuine hit in global politics: the Taliban, Afghanistan, 9/11, Al-Qaida, the war in Iraq, the Uighur separatists in China, Kosovo, the Arab-Israeli conflict, the Intifada, Jihad, Chechnya, the "Arab Spring", the wars in Libya, Syria and Yemen, Iran's nuclear ambitions, Islamic State, and regime change in Algeria and Sudan. We sometimes hear about all this more often than about the events taking place in the great powers.

The Six Pillars of the Faith

Islam could be considered the strongest and most fit-for-purpose religion of our times. Growth in the numbers of Muslims, who already account for a quarter of all people of faith on the planet (Christians account for less than a third) is going to be twice as high over the next 20 years in comparison to the increase in the non-Muslim population.[1] No other faith has the same number of followers who are dedicated to their faith quite so passionately and selflessly. They feel Islam to be a way of life, the measure of all things. We know of a large number of cases when people have converted to Islam from other faiths, including Christianity, but cases of Muslims converting to other beliefs are incredibly rare. The clarity of this religion's tenets, its ability to give its followers an integral and comprehensible picture of the world, society and the structure of the Universe – all of this makes Islam attractive to new followers.

Islam has its roots back in the 7th century AD, in the sands of the Arabian Peninsula. The founder of the faith, Muhammed (Mohammed, Moham-

---

[1] "Briefly. United States: Growth of Muslim Population Seen Outpacing Non-Muslims", *The International Herald Tribune*, January 28, 2011. P. 5.

mad) was descended from a prominent but poverty-stricken clan from the Quraysh tribe. According to the prominent British expert Peter Mansfield, he "was a man of genius and inspiration who helped to transform the history of mankind – a fact which is acknowledged not only by the one fifth of the human race who subscribe to the faith that he founded."[2] For one and a half decades, Muhammed travelled with his caravans between the oases of Arabia and the Syrian Desert "ports" of the Byzantine Empire. He was a well-educated man, who knew the religious teachings and political orders of the neighboring states, particularly Byzantium, where his attention was caught by two particularities that were lacking entirely in Arabia: monotheism in religion, and law and order in governance. Muhammed made it his life's work to move both of these elements of the "Rum" system of public order to the local Arab soil, and to bring an Arabianized monotheism and the Arabianized Empire together into a unified institution: the all-encompassing institution of Islam.[3]

His religious activity began when he was roughly forty years old, in 609-610. Muhammed spent a good deal of time at ascetic vigils in a cave on Mount Hira near Mecca, where the archangel Jabrail (known to Christians as Gabriel) appeared to him, and began revealing to Muhammed the text of the Book that was stored beneath the heavenly throne of Allah (the Koran), and on behalf of Allah imposed on Muhammed the obligation of informing his fellow-countrymen about the instructions of the Almighty.

Muhammed began to preach, but this prompted resistance on the part of the merchant oligarchy of Mecca, who exiled the prophet from the city. Muhammed and his followers migrated to Medina, and the day on which this journey (the Hegira) began, 22nd September 622, is the starting point of the Muslim era. After an absence of seven years, he returned to Mecca, not as a pardoned exile, but as the lord. In the 630s, Muhammed subdued the whole of Saudi Arabia, attracting more and more followers acting with fire and sword, and became the head of the new theocratic state. In the course of a decade's rule in Medina, he led or organized troops for 80 large and small battles.[4]

---

[2] Peter Mansfield, *A History of the Middle East*. Penguin Books, 2019. P. 14.

[3] Arnold Toynbee, *A Study of History: Abridgement of Vols I-VI*. Oxford University Press, 1987. PP. 227-228.

[4] Ali Akbar Velayati, *Islamskaya kul'tura i tsivilizatsiya* (*Islamic Culture and Civilization*). Moscow, 2011. PP. 23-24.

Islam borrowed a great deal from the dogmatic teachings of both Judaism and Christianity. The first few lines of the Koran contain numerous references to the books of the Old Testament and the Gospels. At the same time, Islam is a succinctly compiled and developed religion with its own tenets and principles, founded on the Koran and on the Sunna (a collection of Muhammed's utterances, which was initially passed on orally and was only written down in the 8th and 9th centuries). These principles are usually set out in the form of the six "pillars of the faith" (the tenets of doctrinal theology) and in five or six "pillars of Islam" (the tenets of confessional practice).

The first and most important of the pillars of the faith is belief in Allah, the one God, the creator of everything, and the identifying of him with the one and only truth. "That is because Allah is the Truth, and that what they call upon other than Him is falsehood […]" reads the Koran.[5] The most fearful sin of all, for Islam, is polytheism, and Christianity – with its teachings about the divine trinity – falls under this concept. Islam is a religion that is unambiguously monotheist. "The Lord needs absolutely nothing, but everyone needs Him. The Lord is omniscient and all-powerful. He is everywhere, and there is no place where He is not present. For Him, the heavens and the earth are one, and whichever way we turn, we shall be standing before Him. He knows the secrets of our hearts, our thoughts, the intentions and concerns of all of us. He is closer to man than his carotid artery. He is a collection of perfections."[6]

The second pillar is belief in the angels. There are references to angels in the Koran and the Sunna who are particularly close to Allah, above all Jabrail, who delivered the divine revelation to the prophet; there is also a devil in Islam – Iblis, who disobeyed Allah and was banished to the earth. The third principle is faith in the Holy Scriptures, sent down by Allah: the divine revelation, which no-one can challenge. The fourth is belief in the prophets, the emissaries. There were a lot of them. Only 28 are mentioned by name in the Koran, but it is believed that Allah spoke to the people through the mouths of 124,000 emissaries. Many of them are well-known Biblical figures. For example, Nuh (Noah), who was warned by Allah about the Flood, or the eighth of the nine "major prophets", Isa (Jesus), son of Mary, who, Muslims believe, also received part of the divine revelation. Bringing up the rear of this list is Muhammed, as the last prophet, the "seal of the

---

[5] The Koran. Surah Luqman [31:30].

[6] Morteza Motahhari, *Islamskoye mirovozzreniye* (*The Islamic Worldview*). Moscow, 2010. P. 24.

prophets", to whom Allah sent down the Koran, i.e. the full version of the divine revelation. The fifth pillar of the faith is belief in the end of the world, in the Day of Judgment, in the existence of Heaven and Hell. The sixth is belief in divine pre-determination: Muslims must believe that everything that happens in the world happens through the will of Allah.

The five pillars of Islam are "Shahada" – the preaching of the faith ("There is no God besides Allah, and Muhammed is His prophet"); "Salat" (or, in Persian, "Namaz") – the complex prayer rituals; "Zakat" – a tax paid to Muslims in need; "Sawm" (or "Uraza") – the practice of fasting in the month of Ramadan (the ninth month in the Muslim calendar); and "Hajj" – a pilgrimage to Mecca, which every Muslim is required to undertake, if he can afford to do so. Finally, the concept of Jihad is often referred to as the "sixth pillar of Islam" – the need to fight for the faith. The various interpretations of this concept will be examined in more detail below.

In Islam, there are none of the institutions of the church and the priesthood that are customary for Christians. "Islam has no clergy which is in possession of the 'means of grace', so it has no dogmatic magisterium, no pontifical authority, no Council which is responsible for defining dogma."[7] Anyone at all can be an imam – that is, a supplicant – after being elected to the role by his peers. Roughly speaking, it is fair to say that with all other things being equal, an imam ought to be more knowledgeable than other Muslims, and be able to convey this knowledge to the community of believers. On the one hand, this appears very democratic, but on the other, it creates big difficulties for the world of Islam, since there is no-one who, by dint of his "office", has authority over everyone else in the interpretation of religious law. In other words, there was no-one who could say that Osama bin-Laden was wrong, since he was an imam, respected in the same way as any other.

From the Muslims' point of view, the expansion of the Islamic world was a noble cause. "The world that Islam was to conquer was living in a dispirited state, amid a decline in tolerance and moderation," writes the Iranian religious expert Abdolhossein Zarrinkoub. "… Islam breathed new life into this world, which was a prisoner to religious and ethnic fanaticism. A common Islamic 'house' was created, the center of which was the Koran (rather than Syria or Iraq), which cured the diseases of racial and ethnic enmity."[8]

---

[7] Henry Corbin, *History of Islamic Philosophy*. Routledge, 2014. P. 2.

[8] Abdolhossein Zarrinkoub, *Islamskaya tsivilizatsiya: velikiye otkrytiya i dostizheniya chelovechestva* (*Islamic Civilization: Great Discoveries and Achievements of Mankind*).

The "people of writing", as the Jews, Christians, Zoroastrians and Sabites (Iraqi Mandeans, a Harran community in Mesopotamia) were known, were acknowledged and not forced to adopt Islam, but cases in which they voluntarily converted to the religion of their vanquishers were fairly frequent.

The Rise and Fall

During the first few centuries of its history, Islam was dominant in the global political scene, in culture, and in international relations. The new creed promised victories, and they began occurring – indeed, they were victories over ancient, hitherto invincible empires: the Byzantine and Sasanian Empires, whose vast territories fell under the sway of the Muslims. In the 8th century, from their bases in North Africa, the Arabs, together with the Berbers, whom they had converted to Islam, conquered Spain and Portugal and invaded France. Afghanistan, Uzbekistan, Turkmenistan, and South Pakistan found themselves under the control of an Arabic-speaking elite. In the 9th century, Arabian troops seized Sicily, invaded Italy, and besieged Ostia and Rome. An ambassador had been sent to China as early as under the third Caliph, Usman, and in the 9th century a colony of several thousand Muslims lived in Guangzhou.

We know of other famous examples of rapid conquest and expansion in history: the empire of Alexander the Great, or that of Genghis Khan. In the territories that they conquered, however, Greek and Mongol are not the languages spoken today. The Arabic conquest was notable for its enduring influence. Many of the indigenous peoples adopted Islam, and in the Middle East and North Africa they switched to the Arabic language, which would later become the native language there. Only Spain, Portugal, and Sicily returned to their almost original condition.[9]

It was during the era of the Caliphate that Arab-Muslim culture took shape. "Each and every Muslim was first and foremost a member of the Muslim community, and only after that a resident of a particular city or province, or a member of a particular ethnic group… Literary Arabic was in effect 'denationalized', and began to be seen not only as the language of the conquerors, but above all as the language of a common culture. Any educated Muslim, whether an Iranian or a Turk, someone living in distant

----

St. Petersburg, 2011. PP. 19-20.

[9]   Hugh Kennedy, *The Great Arab Conquests: How the Spread of Islam Changed the World We Live In*. Da Capo Press Inc., 2008. P. 3.

Andalusia or in India, strove to learn the language of the Holy Koran and the extensive theological literature."[10]

The Islamic countries seized control for several centuries over traditional world trade. This was the most advanced economic force in the world, which conducted trade over an incredibly large territory in Asia, Europe, and Africa, exported slaves from South Africa, and took wool to Europe.

The languages of the Arabic peoples have given us not only terms such as caravan and bazaar, but also tariff, check and magazine (in the sense of a "storage place", and in the meaning it has in modern Arabic, French, Italian, Catalan and Russian, namely "store" or "shop"). The Islamic world also achieved a magnificent level of development in science, art and philosophy, inheriting a body of knowledge from the Middle East, Byzantium, Persia and India, and adding many innovations of its own to it. Islamic culture was a synthesis of elements of ancient Semite, specifically Judeo-Christian culture, and Greco-Roman culture.[11]

At a time when Charlemagne was finding it hard to find a handful of literate men in the empire of the Franks, at the court of the Abyssinian Caliph, Ma'mun, there were discussions about the works of Plato, Aristotle and Euclid, the structure of the earth's core, and the planets; the surface of the Earth was measured, and paper was manufactured (the first European paper mill was established in Italy in the 13th century). Under Harun al-Rashid, of *The One Thousand and One Nights* fame (8th – 9th centuries), the "House of Wisdom" was created in Baghdad, and this became the first and the largest public library and academic institution. At the Fatimid House of Knowledge, in Egypt, there were almost a million books, while at the House of Science in Tripoli there were 1.6 million. In Cordoba, the Umayyad caliph Hakim II built a library of 400,000 works, and in Granada alone there were 70 public libraries. When the French king Charles the Wise (1364-1380) began compiling a library four centuries later, he could not even find a thousand books, and a third of the ones he did find were theological works. The Arabs began creating higher education institutions, the madrasahs, where science was taught alongside the Koran (Nizamia, Mustansiriya, Halaviya, Jawziyyah), and these were an early prototype for European universities. The word "baccalaureate", indeed, is derived from

---

[10] Isaak Fil'shtinskiy, *Istoriya arabov i Khalifata (750–1517 gg.)* [*The History of the Arabs and the Caliphate (750-1517)*]. Moscow, 2008. PP. 299-300.

[11] Philip Hitty, *A Short History of the Near East*. D. Van Nostrand, 1966.

the Arabic phrase "Bihaqq al-riwayatt" (meaning "the right to restate the learning to someone else").[12]

Jabir ibn Hayyan, who lived in the 8th century and is known in Europe as Geber, is considered the father of both chemistry and alchemy. We use Arabic numbers, even though they first came into being in India and are known as Indian numbers in Islamic countries. These digits themselves became famous thanks to the translation from the Sanskrit by Muhammed Farazi of a book about astronomy, *Stenhend*, and thanks to the later works of Al-Khwarizmi. The word "algorithm" is quite simply a distortion of his name. Al-Khwarizmi's most important work, Al-Jabr w'al Muqabala ("The Compendious Book on Calculation by Completion and Balancing") was the first book about algebra and trigonometry, and gave this branch of mathematics its name. Algebra lay at the heart of astronomy, which had been developed earlier in Indian and Persian studies. The biggest observatories in the world were located in Samarkand and Maragha. Azimuth and zenith are Arabic words. The most significant work on medicine in the Middle Ages was the Al-Qanun (the Medical canon) by Ibn Sina, better known as Avicenna, whose works in translation, in the 16th century alone, had more than 20 editions in Europe.[13]

Europe in the Middle Ages not only learned about science and the arts from Muslims, but also, to a certain extent, was culturally dependent on them, relying on Arabic translations of ancient texts of which the originals had been lost. Chinese inventions – the compass, powder, book-printing – were also things that the Europeans borrowed from the Muslims. The languages of the Islamic peoples' countries have given us the Turkish word "tulip", the Persian word "peach" and the Arabic word "kahva" (coffee).

In the 11th century, the first attempts by Western Europe to strike back against the Muslims took place. The Crusades in Palestine lasted from 1096 to 1270, and were led by French knights, and it is because of this that Europeans are known in the Middle East as "farangs", i.e. "franks". Officially, the purpose of the Crusades was to conquer the Tomb of Our Lord in Jerusalem, but in the Middle East they were unambiguously in-

---

[12] Abdolhossein Zarrinkoub, *Islamskaya tsivilizatsiya: velikiye otkrytiya i dostizheniya chelovechestva* (*Islamic Civilization: Great Discoveries and Achievements of Mankind*). St. Petersburg, 2011. PP. 93, 40, 41, 43, 47, 48; Ali Akbar Velayati, *Islamskaya kul'tura i tsivilizatsiya* (*Islamic Culture and Civilization*). Moscow, 2011. PP. 28-41.

[13] Abdolhossein Zarrinkoub, *Islamskaya tsivilizatsiya: velikiye otkrytiya i dostizheniya chelovechestva* (*Islamic Civilization: Great Discoveries and Achievements of Mankind*). St. Petersburg, 2011.

terpreted as Western aggression and the brutal devastation of the lands of the Muslims and Eastern Christians – Byzantium. The ransacking of Muslim holy sites was accompanied by the destruction of cultural centers and libraries, and the burning of books, which were of the least interest for the Crusaders.

The main event in the history of the Islamic world in later centuries was the rise of the Ottoman Empire, which grew out of a small Turkmen kingdom. The Ottomans triumphed thanks to the exceptionally mobile nature of their cavalry, and none of their innovations could compare with the creation of the homogeneous corps of the janissaries, the forerunner of all modern armies, which was made up of prisoners of war captured on Christian lands and then supplemented through the imposition of the youth-levy upon the Balkan vassals.[14] In 1389, Sultan Bayezid, in a battle fought on the Kosovo plain, brought Serbian independence to an end, and then invaded Bulgaria, on the Danube, and Macedonia, and attacked Hungary and Wallachia. In 1453, Sultan Mehmed, with a 160,000-strong army, began the thirteenth Muslim siege of Constantinople, which was defended by fewer than 5,000 Romans and a few thousand "Latins". Promises to save the city, which were made by the Pope and the European capitals after the Byzantine Emperor agreed to a union with the Catholics in 1439 (prompting a split in the Orthodox Church), proved to be a fiction. The Great Eastern Roman Empire fell. After storming Constantinople, the Ottomans continued their expansion into the Balkan Peninsula, and threatened the center of Europe, reaching Vienna. The time of the Great Ottoman Empire had arrived, and its sultans took the title of caliphs from 1517 onwards.

The Central Asian Turks, meanwhile, conquered India, founding the empire of the Great Moghuls. During the flourishing of the Islamic civilization, only the Chinese civilization could compete with it in terms of population numbers and cultural achievements. Chinese civilization came into being as a local civilization, however, limited to a single region and a single racial group. Islam created a civilization of global scale: poly-ethnic, multi-racial, and intercontinental. Islam had at that time the greatest military might on the planet, and its armies were able to march into Europe, Africa, India and China simultaneously.[15]

---

[14] Caroline Finkel, *Osman's Dream: The Story of the Ottoman Empire 1300-1923*. London, 2005. PP. 5-6, 28, 74-75.

[15] Bernard Lewis, *What Went Wrong? Western Impact and Middle Eastern Response*. Oxford, 2002. P. 6.

And suddenly this period of flourishing and might came to an end. The Europeans began making significant headway. The Renaissance, great geographical discoveries, the rise of Russia, and the start of the industrial revolution enabled a gradual overcoming of the situation. In the 1550s, Ivan IV inflicted defeats on the khanates of Kazan and Astrakhan, which were allied to the Ottoman Empire. At the end of the 17th century, a peace agreement was signed for the first time between a defeated Islamic state and Christian governments – the Treaty of Karlowitz. At the same time, Peter the Great ventured to the Sea of Azov, and under Catherine II, Russia conquered the Black Sea region, the Crimea, and then in the 19th century the Caucasus and Central Asia. Napoleon, whose incursion into Egypt, Palestine and Syria in 1799 was seen as another Crusade and resulted in a Jihad in response, conquered these countries without any problems, even though the English navy was fighting on their side. In 1830-1847, Algeria was conquered by the French. The ports of the Islamic nations became a field of activity for European companies and the place from which the influence of the Western governments began to spread to the capitals of Muslim countries. Tunisia, Morocco and Libya fell under European control.

As a result of the First World War, the Ottoman Empire disappeared, and Turkey arose from the remnants of it, while the Arabic-speaking part of the empire was now fully under British and French control. By 1920, only four Islamic states remained free from some form or another of non-Muslim rule: Turkey, Saudi Arabia, Iran, and Afghanistan.

What had suddenly gone so wrong? Various answers to this question were put forward. The Islamic leaders could not see the causes of their failures in the successes of Western civilization: their whole previous history had convinced them that there was not, nor could there be, anything of value in the world of the infidels. For a society that was used to looking down on everyone else, the idea of learning from others was unacceptable. Admittedly, life had forced them to borrow military equipment from the Europeans, but they were lagging behind them even in this regard. A society that had coped admirably with the challenges of the Middle Ages now found itself extremely unresponsive to the imperatives of modernization, against which the public consciousness put up active resistance.

The West experimented with new institutions, laws, political and scientific theories, and artistic concepts. In the world of Islam, meanwhile, the response came in the shape of tradition. Hence, the desire to preserve knowledge, rather than to create or multiply it, hence the notion of science as the veneration of that which has already been proven. It is only recently, by historical standards, that the Islamic world has begun to overcome its scorn for secular education and the study of the languages of the Christian peoples.

The isolation of women not only deprived half the population of the ability to contribute to social development and to production, but also resulted in them having a low level of education, and therefore an inability to bring up their children in the best possible way. Uneducated mothers are hardly likely to have super-educated children. In Islamic society, there was no understanding of freedom as a value, either, nor of the concept of civil society.

Furthermore, the collapse of the Ottoman Empire left the Islamic world without a core state. As Huntington has emphasized, in the 20th century "no Muslim country has had both sufficient power and sufficient cultural and religious legitimacy to assume that role and be accepted as the leader of Islam by other Islamic states and non-Islamic countries."[16]

A considerable number of Muslims saw the main reason for their sudden lagging behind as their retreat from their traditions. Thus it was that Islamic fundamentalism came into being, oriented towards the past, towards early Islam. Another trend – towards the modernizing of Islam, towards adapting it to the modern reality and striving to create an industrial, secular civilization, took shape later – in the early 20th century. The most striking representative of modernist Islam was Kemal Ataturk, the founder of the modern state of Turkey. Building the state in accordance with Western patterns was the key trend in its development. Practically all the known Western ideologies and institutional systems were experimented with, including fascism.

The first serious cracks in Western domination began to appear in 1940, when France suffered defeat at the hands of Germany, and Italy threatened British interests in the deserts of Western Egypt, Ethiopia, and on the southern borders of the Sudan. WWII undermined the position and prestige of all the former colonial powers, and a parade of independence proclamations followed. The Suez crisis of 1956 and the war in Algeria in 1954-1964 were London and Paris's last attempts to hold on to their status. There was one place where, after the departure of the British, the Arabs suffered a defeat: Palestine, where the state of Israel was established.

Is it possible, today, to talk about the Islamic world as a single entity in global politics? Yes and no. This world consists of multiple and very heterogeneous actors. There are Muslim communities in practically every country in the world. In 35 countries, the majority of the population is Muslim, and

---

[16] Samuel P. Huntington, *The Clash of Civilizations and the Remaking of World Order*. Simon & Schuster, 1996. P. 177.

in 29, they constitute an influential minority; in 28 countries, Islam is recognized as the state religion or as an official religion.

Muslims are also trying to form their own economic system, and a growing number of their leaders are in favor of creating a common Arabic or common Islamic market. In the context of the League of Arabic States, efforts are being made – without much success, to date – regarding the economic integration of the countries that are members. Economic integration is being hindered in many ways by the fact that Islam does not welcome the development of a host of market institutions. The Koran, for example, directly prohibits the charging of interest, and therefore it is simply not possible to have a fully-fledged banking system in the Islamic world. Banks exist, but they operate in a very specific way: their profits are not measured in terms of interest rates, but through participation in the profits of the bank.

The Islamic world as a whole is the poorest part of the planet after sub-Saharan Africa. It has not provided any impressive examples of economic flourishing, if one discounts the relatively secular Turkey and the absolute monarchies of the Arabian Peninsula, which dig for oil.

The self-definition of the Islamic world as a player in international relations stems in no small part from the way it contrasts itself to the rest of the world, and this sometimes manifests itself in displays of solidarity with Islamic states. An example was Kosovo, where resistance to the Serbian government forces was put up (with decisive support from NATO), not only by the Albanian fighters of the Kosovo Liberation Army, but also by Mujahidin volunteers and by officers on active military service from the United Arab Emirates, Kuwait, Qatar, and Oman.

At the same time, the Islamic world is not one that is of a common accord on all things, of course, and it is driven by serious disagreements. One of these is the continuation of the ancient historical conflicts between the civilizations of the Nile and Mesopotamia. Others are the conflicts between radical and more moderate, secular regimes; between fundamentalist and relatively secular states; between Arabs and Persians; between Sunnis and Shiites. There are vast differences of opinion within the Arab world. The Secretary-General of the Arab League, Ahmad Aboul Gheit, said in 2017: "We as Arab nations have a lot in common such as language and culture, but we don't appreciate our common ground, and have failed to understand our full potential and strength. Under this fragmentation, national interests will be lost and we will continue to live in these wars, deaths, and divisions for another century. We must not let this happen."[17]

---

[17] Cit. from: Jumana Khamis, "Arab Nations Need to Establish Joint Armed Forces: Arab

There are various ideological trends within Islam. There is a tendency to identify three of these as core: liberal Islam, traditional Islam and radical or Jihadi Islam.

The liberal project, which is of elite character in the main, involves the shifting onto Islamic soil of so-called common human – essentially Western – forms of social life, from parliaments to birth control, with simultaneous changes to Islam itself, in order to make it the driving force of development.

Traditional Islam amounts, to a far greater degree, to a layer of people's consciousness, and is the justification for the status quo and does not stipulate a need for any transformations whatsoever. Mansfield believes that, strictly speaking, "[A]ll Muslim believers are fundamentalists, because they know that the Holy Koran was God's final message to mankind. The triumph of the West in the last two or three centuries is seen by Muslims as an aberration of history."[18] Traditionalists adopt the view that everything that is necessary is written down in the Koran, and that the problems of the Islamic world are brought about solely by a departure from the principles which were laid down in the 7th century. The most extreme expression of this trend was the Taliban in Afghanistan, who banned the radio, TV, photography and other "demonic inventions" from the West, just as traditionalists in the 17th to 19th centuries had banned the use of clocks.

The third movement, the Jihadist movement, is founded on the idea that Islam must actively wage war so as to expand its influence in the world.

How do the three ideological trends relate to one another today? The position of modernist Muslims, who were fairly numerous in the 1920s to the 1960s, is becoming increasingly complicated and unenviable. Society increasingly looks on them as renegades, encroaching on the inviolability of tradition, although in actual fact there are already many Muslims who do not fully adhere to this tradition. Liberal Muslims, who were cheering when the "Arab Spring" was in full swing, are, in the main, feeling a deep sense of pessimism at the moment, and stepping back. Meanwhile, the traditionalists (and, until recently, Jihadists) were on the rise. A process of re-Islamization is taking place, at the heart of which lies deep disillusionment, brought about by the fact that the Muslim community has been forced to look on powerlessly while others rule the world. The solution to these problems is in returning to them, under the slogan "Islam as the answer" to the challenges of the modern world.

....

League Chief", *Gulf News*, May 1, 2017 <https://gulfnews.com/uae/government/arab-nations-need-to-establish-joint-armed-forces-arab-league-chief-1.2020256>.

[18] Peter Mansfield, *A History of the Middle East*. Penguin Books, 2019. P. 15.

Re-Islamization

If one were to try to identify the factors and events which have made the greatest contribution towards the process of re-Islamization in recent decades, I would put in first place the rise in the influence of a certain relatively young, fundamentalist state: Saudi Arabia.

In the 13th century, practically the entire Arabian Peninsula came under Egyptian rule, and then from 1517 onwards fell under the rule of the Ottoman Empire. At the start of the 20th century, Abd al-Aziz ibn-Saud captured Riyadh and secured recognition from the Turkish sultan for his state of Najd. Relying on the teachings of the medieval religious leader Sheikh Muhammad ibn Abd al-Wahhab, ibn-Saud united the country under his rule. Wahhabism exists within the framework of *hanbali* – the most strictly orthodox *madhab* (interpretation) of Sunnism. It came into being as a protest against the Ottoman Empire, which upset the Arabic population with its luxury, debauchery and departure from the canons of Islam. The Wahhabis looked on the Koran as the highest degree of knowledge, not allowing any interpretations, thus objectively turning the Wahhabis into the adversaries of most Muslims, who belong to the various other *madhabs*.[19]

In 1926, the USSR became the first country to give Saudi Arabia diplomatic recognition, and in 1932 it was officially recognized as the Kingdom of Saudi Arabia. Abd al-Aziz had more than 300 wives. By the time of his death in 1953, he had officially fathered 34 sons, from 14 different mothers. His sons continue to rule over the kingdom, as was their father's will: the throne is passed down from one to the next in order of seniority. In *The Tenets of the System of Power in the Kingdom of Saudi Arabia*, written in 1992 – a constitution based on Sharia law – there is the following line: "Power belongs to the sons of the King – the founder of the state, Abd al-Aziz ibn Abd ar-Rahman ibn Faisal Al Saud, and to the sons of his sons… The King chooses the prince who shall be his heir, and may replace him by royal decree… The supreme instance of all kinds of power is the King."[20]

In the 1930s, oil was found in the country, and immediately, a concession was granted to Standard Oil, which became the core component of the Ar-

---

[19] Igor' Mel'nikov, "Evolyutsiya vakhkhabitskogo faktora v Saudovskoy Aravii" ("The Evolution of the Wahabi Factor in Saudi Arabia"), *Rodnaya Ladoga*, Issue 2, 2016. PP. 251-261.

[20] V. Ye. Dontsov and T. A. Churilina, "Politicheskiye sistemy monarkhiy Araviyskogo poluostrova" ("Political Systems of the Monarchies of the Arabian Peninsula"), in *Politicheskiye sistemy i politicheskiye kul'tury Vostoka* (*Political Systems and Political Cultures of the East*), ed. by A. D. Voskresenskiy. Moscow, 2006. PP. 154-160.

ab-American Oil Company (Aramco). The company was a source of money for modernization, and Saudi Arabia was transformed into the USA's closest partner. The Kingdom was of huge significance for Washington as the main importer of Saudi oil, profits from the sale of which were mostly deposited in American banks and on stock markets (up to 1 trillion dollars at the start of this century). Saudi Arabia also became strategically vital for the US, providing a base for US troops and ships, and access to American military bases in Qatar, Kuwait and Bahrain.[21] However, the huge weight that Saudi Arabia carries in the Islamic world stems less from its wealth and its special ties to Washington than from the fact that the most important Muslim holy sites – Mecca and Medina – are located on its territory.

Oil is a crucially important factor in re-Islamization. For the first time in the modern age, the Islamic world operated as a cohesive, independent and, essentially, anti-Western force in the early 1970s, when it provoked a shock in the oil market. The policy of raising prices was begun by the young leader of Libya, Colonel Muammar Gaddafi, who, in 1970, invited a representative of the US company Occidental Petroleum to meet him over a cup of coffee, and, placing a pistol in front of him, asked for an increase of 30 cents a barrel in the price of oil. It was hard to say no to such an offer, and this was followed by the nationalization of American companies. Things like this are not easily forgiven. In 1973, the key oil-producing countries in the Middle East – Saudi Arabia, Kuwait, Qatar, Abu-Dhabi, Dubai, Bahrain, Libya and Algeria – announced a cut in oil extraction and imposed an embargo on supplies of it to the USA, in response to Washington's support for Israel in its war against Egypt and Syria, after which the age of cheap oil came to an end.[22]

This dramatically enhanced the financial capabilities of a host of Muslim states. Effectively, re-Islamization can also be said to have started in the 1970s, when oil prices shot up and Saudi Arabia, the flagship of the proliferation of Islamic ideas in traditional and radical forms, obtained large sums of money. Many of the thousands of new mosques which have sprung up latterly, for example, on the territory of the former USSR, were built using Saudi oil money.

A powerful boost to the return to fundamental tenets was provided by the Iranian Revolution of 1979, prompted by a protest of traditionalism against

---

[21] Mark Hollingsworth and Sandy Mitchell, *Saudi Babylon: Torture, Corruption and Cover-Up Inside the House of Saud*. Edinburgh; London, 2010. PP. 79-81.

[22] Andrew Scott Cooper, *The Oil Kings: How the U.S., Iran and Saudi Arabia Changed the Balance of Power in the Middle East*. Oxford, 2012. PP. 108-124.

Westernization, the driving force behind which were the Islamists. "Only they were united; only they truly knew what they wanted; only they had the courage to lay down a challenge to the Sheikh… only they amounted to an organized force, with its own hierarchy, the foundation for which was the mullahs (of which there were tens of thousands), and at the top were the ayatollahs, who held themselves apart, incidentally, and to whom the people paid heed. The government, without being aware of it, gave them something more than a leader – a hero: the Ayatollah Khomeini, who had been arrested in 1963, then exiled," wrote the famous French orientalist Jean-Paul Roux.[23]

A massive role in the Islamic revival was played by the USSR's war in Afghanistan. It was at that moment, in that country, that radical, Wahhabi Islam, which engendered Al-Qaida and many other extremist organizations, came into being. At first, the organizing of resistance to Soviet troops in Afghanistan was a routine Cold War operation. The logic was simple: if pro-Russian Marxists from the People's Democratic Party of Afghanistan were to come to power in Kabul, then they should be resisted by Islam and the Muslims.

According to the official version of events, the CIA began helping the Mujahedeen only from 1980 onwards, but Brzezinski has since confirmed the existence of a directive on secret aid to Afghan opposition forces, signed by President Carter as early as 3rd July 1979. When asked later whether he regretted this policy of encouraging future terrorists, Brzezinski said that he still considered it to be an "excellent idea": "What is more important in world history? The Taliban or the collapse of the Soviet empire? Some agitated Moslems or the liberation of Central Europe and the end of the cold war?"[24]

The operation was carried out by the USA (it was personally coordinated by the director of the CIA, William Casey), Pakistan, Saudi Arabia, France, Egypt, and a host of other states. "Casey committed CIA support to a long-standing ISI initiative to recruit radical Muslims from around the world to come to Pakistan and fight with Afghan Mujaheddin," confirms the well-known Pakistani author Ahmed Rashid. "President Zia aimed to cement Islamic unity, turn Pakistan into the leader of the Muslim world and foster an Islamic opposition in Central Asia. Washington wanted to demonstrate that the entire Muslim world was fighting the Soviet Union

---

[23] Jean-Paul Roux, *Istoriya Irana i irantsev: Ot istokov do nashikh dney* (*The History of Iran and the Iranians: From the Origins to Our Times*). St. Petersburg, 2012. PP. 338-339.

[24] Cit. from: David N. Gibbs, "Afghanistan: The Soviet Invasion in Retrospect", *International Politics*, Issue 37, 2000. P. 242.

alongside the Afghans and their American benefactors. And the Saudis saw an opportunity both to promote Wahhabism and get rid of its disgruntled radicals. None of the players reckoned on these volunteers having their own agendas, which would eventually turn their hatred against the Soviets on their own regimes and the Americans."[25]

The Mujahedeen forces were led by a Palestinian named Abdullah Azzam, who was employed by the League of the Islamic World (effectively the Ministry of Religious Affairs in Saudi Arabia), but the leadership role was later passed on to Osama bin Laden. At least 15,000 men joined his Arab expeditionary corps in Afghanistan, 5,000 of whom were Saudis. The war in Afghanistan was, among other things, a war of Muslims fighting on the side of the Soviet Union, against Muslims who were enemies of the Soviet Union. In order to send people to such a war, where they would be required to kill their brothers in the faith, it was necessary to acquire, in essence, a new ideology. The Muslims, against whom the faithful Mujahedeen Jihadist fighters fought, were denounced as kaafirs, i.e. as unbelievers who had fallen from Islam.

When the Arabic "Afghan war veterans" returned to their countries, however, they discovered that there were Muslims there, too, who were not adhering to Sharia law and were communicating with the West, above all, with its leaders. It was on these people that the veterans of Jihad unleashed their wrath.

We cannot but take into consideration the obvious re-Islamization of the influential country that is Turkey, following the victory by the Party of Justice and Development led by Recep Tayyip Erdogan in the elections of 2002. The status of the military, which had always been the main pillar of the policy of Westernization, was dramatically reduced through a series of much-hyped trials, during which hundreds of them suffered persecution. A new concept for foreign policy was formulated by the prominent political scientist, and then head of the Foreign Ministry, Ahmet Davutoglu, in his book *Strategic Depth*. He proposed that Turkey should undergo a grandiose political transformation in its immediate vicinity, and to do so it needed to reject the policy of the status quo in respect of its contemporary borders, and adopt an expansionist, pan-Turkist policy, founded on the principles of the Americans who were the founding fathers of geopolitics – Mahan, Mackinder, Haushofer and Spykman.[26]

....

[25] Ahmed Rashid, *The Taliban: Islam, Oil and the New Great Game in Central Asia*. I.B. Tauris & Co Ltd, 2010. P. 129.

[26] Behlut Ozkan, "Turkey, Davitoglu and the Idea of Pan-Islamism", *Survival*, August/September 2014. PP. 119-140.

In 2014, Erdogan introduced constitutional reforms that enabled him to stay on as head of state after his term of office came to an end. The main executive powers were now concentrated in the hands of the president, and Erdogan proclaimed a "new era" in Turkish politics, defined as a "holy conquest", which was to bring Turkey greater flourishing, piety, and global influence.[27] Many of Turkey's neighbors saw in this the resurrection of the ghost of the Ottoman Empire.

Turkey opted to draw noticeably closer to Russia, with Erdogan concluding a deal with Putin on large-scale energy projects capable of turning the country into a gas hub for Europe. However, Moscow and Ankara supported different sides of the conflict in Syria; moreover, the shooting down by Turkey of a Russian bomber caused a rupture in the relationship.

Ankara responded to unrest and pressure from the West with sweeping measures against opponents of Erdogan's regime, particularly the supporters of Fethullah Gülen, a preacher living in the US, who was accused of trying to organize a coup.

Ankara's desire to strengthen its international position and to participate in shoring up "Assad's inheritance" brought about results opposite to those intended. "Instead of expanding its influence all over the region, Turkey itself was engulfed by regional instability – the infiltration of extremists over the Southern border, radicalization, a refugee crisis, a sharp escalation of the Kurdish problem, a deterioration of relations with foreign partners, dissatisfaction with the ruling party policy among pro-Western voters, and unrest in the army and in the security agencies."[28]

On the night of 15th July 2016, armored tanks came out onto the streets of Turkish cities. The president's palace was stormed, shots were fired at the Turkish parliament, TV stations were seized; the soldiers behind the coup appeared to be gaining the upper hand. However, Erdogan succeeded in suppressing the attempted coup, and managed to ensure that not only did the rebels lay down their arms, but so too did all those opposed to his chosen course.[29] Mass purges ensued in the armed forces and law enforcement agencies.

---

[27] "Turkey's New Government. Davitoglu's Moment", *The Economist*, August 30, 2014. P. 24.

[28] Fyodor Luk'yanov, "Volna Varvarstva" ("A Wave of Barbarism"), *Rossiyskaya Gazeta (Russian Newspaper)*, 20 December 2016 <https://rg.ru/2016/12/20/lukianov-ubijstvo-posla-priznak-podnimaiushchejsia-volny-varvarstva.html>.

[29] Ivan Safronov, "Noch' dlinnykh posledstviy" ("The Night of Long Consequences"), *Kommersant. Vlast'* (*The Businessman. Power*), Issue 29, July 25, 2016 <https://www.kommersant.ru/doc/3042411>.

Erdogan went on to hold – and win – a referendum on the constitution on 16th April 2017, which authorized an increase in the president's powers. Another wave of mass arrests followed.

Erdogan announced a program entitled "Vision 2023" (the year in which the Turkish Republic will celebrate its 100th anniversary), under which he plans to take the country into the top ten economies of the world and even into the European Union.[30]

Erdogan's political reforms were seen as stifling democratic freedoms and asserting authoritarianism, and a tough campaign in the Western media began against him. In addition, the Turkish leadership greatly angered the US by its decision to buy an anti-missile system S-400 from Russia, and the arrest of the Protestant pastor Andrew Brunson for participating in the Gülen conspiracy. Turkey, for its part, criticized the United States for supporting the Kurds.

The US raised tariffs on Turkish steel and aluminum, and sanctions under the Magnitsky Act were introduced against the Turkish Minister of Justice and Minister of the Interior. Congress voted to withhold delivery of a consignment of F-35 jet fighters, and urged international financial institutions to cut off loans to Turkey. Ankara responded with mirror counter-sanctions. The pro-government Turkish media have called for the closure of an American military base in Incirlik.[31]

Erdogan openly warned: "Unless the United States starts respecting Turkey's sovereignty and proves that it understands the dangers that our nation faces, our partnership could be in jeopardy. [...] Failure to reverse this trend of unilateralism and disrespect will require us to start looking for new friends and allies."[32] This is perhaps the most serious conflict within NATO

---

[30] Timur Akhmetov, "Pochemu turki golosuyut za Erdogana" ("Why Turks Vote for Erdogan"), *RBK*, Issue 112, June 26, 2018 <https://www.rbc.ru/newspaper/2018/06/26/5b30de619a7947d924962556>; Sergey Strokan' and Kirill Krivosheyev, "Kul't yedinolichnosti" ("The Cult of the Individual"), *Kommersant* (*The Businessman*), Issue 109, June 26, 2018 <https://www.kommersant.ru/doc/3668401>; Sergey Strokan', "Turtsiya dlya odnogo" ("Turkey for the One"), *Kommersant* (*The Businessman*), Issue 119, July 10, 2018 <https://www.kommersant.ru/doc/3681913>.

[31] Amberin Zaman, "Understanding the Failed Deal With Turkey That Sparked Trump's Fury", *The New York Times*, August 7, 2018 <https://www.nytimes.com/2018/08/07/opinion/turkey-andrew-brunson-prison.html>; "Turkey's Downward Spiral", *The New York Times*, August 10, 2018 <https://www.nytimes.com/2018/08/10/opinion/turkey-united-states-trump-erdogan.html>; Ruchir Sharma, "Worried About Turkey's Economic Problems? China's Could Be Worse", *The New York Times*, August 15, 2018 <https://www.nytimes.com/2018/08/15/opinion/turkey-economy-lira-china-currency-erdogan.html>.

[32] Recep Tayyip Erdogan, "How Turkey Sees the Crisis With the U.S.", *The New York Times*,

since France's withdrawal from NATO's integrated military command in the 1960s.

Muslim society in recent decades has been subjected to a good deal of re-Islamization, even in its outward appearance. The number of people who have begun wearing the niqab or growing a beard has risen dramatically. Re-Islamization has taken place in a whole host of areas.

There has been a big increase in the number of private or state-owned religious schools and universities where Islam is taught. One of the consequences of this has been the emergence of a huge number of unemployed graduates from academic institutions who know the Koran by heart, speak Arabic, but may not necessarily have a good grasp of arithmetic. These are the individuals who have formed the basis of many groups of guerrilla fighters and even whole armies. The word "Taliban" itself translates as "studenthood", and it was these students that seized, and for a long time controlled, Afghanistan.

A process is taking place whereby the legal foundations of states are being moved towards Sharia principles. In the last decades, Kuwait, Pakistan, Algeria, Yemen and Libya have all rejected written constitutions and recognized the Koran as their constitution. The idea that Sharia law should be the main law of the land is one that over 80% of people in Afghanistan, Iraq, Malaysia, Pakistan and Morocco, and over 60% of people in Egypt, Indonesia and Jordan, subscribe to.[33]

The creation of so-called official Islam has begun: states are starting to coalesce with Islamic organizations, and in many countries, special government bodies are appearing which deal with religious matters. Nothing of this kind used to exist in Islam, where, it is worth reiterating, there is no hierarchy among spiritual leaders. In Egypt, Syria, and all the ex-Soviet states, the official post of mufti has begun to be introduced. In Turkey and Jordan, ministries for religious affairs have sprung up. Spiritual leaders in offices of state have been given exclusive powers, for example, to promote imams to the biggest mosques and to manage religious education. This is how things stand in Morocco, Algeria, Tunisia, Egypt, Syria, Turkey, Uzbekistan, and so on. In many countries, religious education has been made compulsory – even in Turkey, which still has the reputation of being one of the most secular of all the Islamic countries.

....
August 13, 2018 <https://www.nytimes.com/2018/08/10/opinion/turkey-erdogan-trump-crisis-sanctions.html>.

[33] "Muslim Democrats, Inshallah", *The Economist*, August 26, 2017. PP. 19-20.

At the same time, re-Islamization has in many ways fallen outside the control of the state as such: the ruling regimes are often subjected to strong criticism from the representatives of radical Islam, who accuse those in power of not showing enough commitment to Muslim norms.

The penetration of modern learning into the Islamic world still comes up against restrictions even today. By way of example, only 1% of all the scientists in the world are Muslims. In Israel alone, there are more people involved in science than in the whole of the Arab world. Investment in scientific research and development is very low, if one excludes the countries of South-East Asia and Iran. Engineering is not a popular subject. The extraction of oil by the Arab countries is conducted mainly through the efforts of foreigners. The Emirates is finding work for European and American architects and Indian manpower. The subway system in Mecca is being built by Chinese workers.

Traditionalists often lay the blame for the failures in development at the door of external forces, above all the USA, the "Great Satan", which is exploiting the whole of humanity, engendering poverty and other problems in the Islamic world. Israel tends to be seen as the next most significant enemy, the "Small Satan". Its sovereignty over Jerusalem, which is the third most significant holy city in Islam, is not recognized. There are two particularly sacred mosques there, both of which are associated with the legendary Muhammed's journey by night from Mecca to the Palestinian land, during which the prophet was raised up the heavens, to Allah's throne. Now, though, these holy sites are controlled by Israel, which, in the eyes of Muslims, is a Western outpost.

A much more violent Islamization model has a number of names: Salafism, Wahhabism, Islamism, radical Islam.

The three main postulates of radical Islamism are as follows. Firstly, Jihad is understood solely as an armed battle. There can be no spiritual or verbal Jihad – anyone who has opted for the path of Jihad must take up arms. Secondly, every Muslim is duty-bound to wage this kind of Jihad. Thirdly, Jihad is directed against kaafirs – infidels, which includes all non-Muslims and all those who do not accept the first two postulates.

It is very hard to imagine the inner world of people like this. For us, life is preferable to death. For someone who has embarked on the path of Jihad, this is not the case. True life is not the here and now: the real world begins after death. And the transient earthly world is the field of a most bitter struggle between genuine Muslims and infidels. The outcome of this conflict is predetermined: the true believers will win it, without question, and this victory will confirm the superiority of Islam. As Bin Laden used to say, "To fight in the defense of religion and belief is a collective duty; there is no other duty after belief than fighting the enemy who is corrupting the life and the religion."[34] The Jihadi mission is to create a universal caliphate.

Practical attempts to implement these postulates are being taken in a variety of areas: the promotion of Islamic clergy and the expulsion of those who do not preach radical forms of Islam; the creation of religious-political organizations opposed to both the modernization of political systems and the local Islamic spiritual leaders; and the creation of footholds in areas where the central governments of various states do not have firm control: examples would be the south of the Lebanon, where the Shi'ite group Hezbollah has its base; the south of the Philippines; the northern part of the island of Sumatra in Indonesia, where the Islamic Free Aceh Movement operates; a considerable portion of Indonesia's Maluku Islands, and large areas not only in Syria, Iraq and Libya, but also in Algeria, Mali, Sudan, Nigeria and Somalia. The area of the Afghan and Pakistani border is not controlled by any central government whatsoever, only by local power brokers, and that is where the training centers for terrorists are concentrated; they were created back in the 1980s to train the Mujahedeen to do battle against the Soviet forces. In Russia, areas like this were created in the Kadar region of Dagestan, and in Chechnya, which, in the period between 1996 and 1999 was effectively transformed into an Islamic republic.

The sources of financing for Islamic extremism are certain countries in the Persian Gulf, for whom this, among other things, is a way of ridding themselves of Wahhabis and a way of fighting against Shi'ite regimes. The USA does not shy away from funding extremists, either, if the extremists are fighting against governments disliked by Washington – as in Syria or Libya. The role of internal sources is very large, too, for example ISIL controlled a sizeable portion of the Iraqi and Syrian oil industry.

There is also the invisible source of funding known as "hawala" – an utterly informal Islamic financial network, operating purely on the basis of trust. For centuries, this network has made up for the lack of a developed banking system in the Islamic world, replacing official channels for the transfer of money. If there is a need to wire money from Paris to Algeria, no problem: just find the right person in Paris, and in a few hours another trusted per-

---

[34] Cit. from: Michael Scott Doran, "Somebody Else's Civil War", *Foreign Affairs*, January/February 2002 <https://www.foreignaffairs.com/articles/united-states/2002-01-01/somebody-elses-civil-war>.

son will pass on the sum to the recipient in the Algerian countryside. This system, which is used throughout the entire Muslim world, leaves no traces whatsoever. The terrorist organizations are not going to be short of money in the foreseeable future.

Technologies that would not have looked out of place in the Middle Ages go hand in hand with cutting-edge ones. The Jihadists use the Internet a great deal to promote their ideas, raise funds and attract supporters; they hold online forums and training sessions, and organize terrorist communities using Twitter and Facebook.[35]

The biggest irritant for the Islamist terrorists is the United States. On 11th September 2001, the USA suffered the most serious terrorist attack ever, as a result of which more people died than during the Japanese attack on Pearl Harbor. It was subsequently discovered that a huge proportion of the Muslim preachers operating on the territory of America itself were representatives of radical Islam.

The USA declared a global war on terror. The war in Afghanistan significantly weakened the position of the Taliban, though it by no means killed them off entirely. Thereafter, Iraq found itself in America's sights, though Iraq had nothing to do with Islamist extremism. The USA quickly took Baghdad, but was then confronted by major problems when it tried to "win the peace". The withdrawal of American troops from Iraq in 2011 looked more like flight than anything else.

David Gardner of *The Financial Times* wrote: "When future historians date the end of the brief, post-cold war, unipolar moment, they will surely pinpoint Iraq."[36]

The Spring Turmoil

Starting in early 2011, the Arabic East began to witness turbulent changes, which became known as the "Arab Spring". The first was the "Jasmine Revolution" in Tunisia, as a result of which President Zine el Abidine Ben Ali, who had ruled the country for over 23 years, was overthrown. After this first toppling, a "domino effect" ensued – a chain reaction among the Arabic countries: a revolution in Egypt, protests in Algeria, Morocco, Mau-

---

[35] Aaron Brantley, "Innovation and Adaptation in Jihadist Digital Security", *Survival*, February/March 2017. PP. 79-102.

[36] David Gardner, "Iraq: a Display of Declining US Power", *The Financial Times*, March 8, 2013 <https://www.ft.com/content/1805afe2-869a-11e2-b907-00144feabdc0>.

ritius, Jordan, Yemen and Bahrain, civil wars in Libya, Syria and Iraq. The government crisis that broke out in the Lebanon has begun to be seen in this same context, as has the collapse of Sudan, where the first precedent in post-colonial Africa was set for the dividing up of a country via a nationwide referendum. Never, since the days of the collapse of socialism in Eastern Europe in the late 1980s and early 1990s, had such a large number of simultaneous popular demonstrations been seen.

The causes of the "Arab Spring" are greatly disputed: what was it that forced the population of a host of countries to act in a way that went utterly against the traditional stereotypes of Arab behavior? The explanation most commonly put forward is that popular revolution took place, prompted by the democratic deficit and the difficult economic position. The masses did indeed play a major role in the events, and all is not well with democracy and the economy in the Arabic world. It should be noted, though, that in those Arabic states where they have never even heard of democracy – in Saudi Arabia, the Emirates – there were no protests. Absolute monarchies, particularly those whose ancestry can be traced back to the Prophet, face virtually no threat at all. Whereas Tunisia and Egypt, which began the "Arab Spring", were, in all regional measures – Arabic, African, Muslim – among the freest and most dynamically growing states.

In actual fact, a whole range of factors were at play.

Without question, protests against living conditions were a factor. The overall problem is that the existing political and economic order in the Arab world is unstable and it cannot be maintained, because it does not satisfy the majority of the citizens, as the Jordanian journalist Rami G. Khouri wrote, when the events began.[37] The rise in food prices (caused in part by the drought in Russia in 2010) lessened the possibility of the state subsidizing prices for foodstuffs. The rise in unemployment also played a role: the number of young people out of work reached 42.8% in Egypt, 30.4% in Tunisia, 24.4% in Syria, 30% in Libya.[38] The global economic crisis, which resulted in a downturn for everyone, affected the Arab world too, for it is heavily dependent on the tourism industry.

A "color democratization" also took place in the Arab world. Regimes were overthrown in countries where elections regularly took place, where

---

[37] Rami G. Khouri, "Transformation Worth Watching", *The Jordan Times*, January 21-22, 2011.

[38] Marina Sapronova, "Genezis arabskikh revolyutsiy" ("The Genesis of the Arabic Revolutions"), *Mezhdunarodnyye protsessy* (*International Processes*), September/December 2011. P. 129.

there were relatively independent media organizations, where the Internet had developed, and where street demonstrations were permitted. The protesters drew up joint plans and received instructions via social networks, or using mobile phones and text messages. The Tunisians found out from the Internet site WikiLeaks about some telegrams from the American embassy, which contained references to the corruption of the president, his wife, and her numerous children. Al-Jazeera – an influential Qatari TV channel – broadcast a live report on the protests from the moment they began, and did so in a distinctly anti-government tone.

There were also a few Arab states behind the "Arab Spring". For Saudi Arabia and Qatar, the influential autocracies, the most important targets were the secularized regimes with the rudiments of democracy, and the aim was regime change. Iran, too, has never said no to the exporting of Islamic revolution – in Shi'ite form – and sees countries with a Shi'ite population or government as zones of interest: Iraq, Syria, Lebanon, Bahrain, Kuwait, Saudi Arabia, Yemen.

And finally, Western influences. For the US, and for its leading European allies – the UK and France – the target was, and remains, the same regimes as for the Saudis, though not because of their secularism, but rather because of their anti-Western or insufficiently pro-Western stances, and their strategic, political and/or economic significance, or their significance for the energy industry.

Western countries also showed a tendency to fit what was taking place into the Procrustean bed of the formula "democracy versus dictatorships".[39]

The "Arab Spring" did not justify the hopes of its instigators, or of Western governments. Elections that followed did not prove to be a panacea. Openly Islamist groups came to power in Tunisia, Egypt and Morocco. In both Tunisia and Egypt, demonstrations attended by many thousands of people have continued, demanding a deepening of the revolution, and tougher punishments for representatives of the old regime. The devastation has increased, meanwhile. Protests occurring everyday have caused economic losses running into hundreds of millions of dollars, a sharp reduction in the number of foreign tourists, and the bankruptcy of SMEs, which in some cases die on the same day they are born. Unemployment has doubled and foreign investment has dried up throughout the Arab world. Revenues from tourism have fallen sharply.[40]

---

[39] Ibid. PP. 130-132.

[40] Adeel Malik and Bassem Awadallah, "An Arab Marshall Plan is Needed", *Today*, May 12,

The Tunisian writer Souhir Stevenson has argued: "A year later, we have no democracy, no trust in elected officials, no improved constitution. Human rights and women's rights are threatened. The economy is tanking. Tourism is dwindling. Who wants to vacation among bands of bearded savages raiding embassies, staking their black pirate flag over universities or burning trucks carrying beer?"[41] And this in a country which, in the Western press, is portrayed as a success story for democratization in the context of the "Arab Spring".

In Libya, the USA, France, the UK, Qatar and Saudi Arabia all mobilized against Gaddafi. The Arab monarchies financed the military operation, the Americans provided the military and technical equipment and the reconnaissance, and Paris and London conducted the aerial raids and secret missions on the ground. Most of the insurgents were separatists from Cyrenaica and Al-Qaida fighters. Muammar Gaddafi was torn to pieces by a crowd – an altogether un-Muslim-like death. The newly created administration has little control over the country. The US ambassador was killed. In Benghazi, where the Libyan revolution began, explosions and gunfire are still heard, with Egyptian workers, French engineers and Turkish managers among the victims.[42]

The first elected prime minister of Libya, Mustafa Abushagur, stayed in office for just one month, and as of the summer of 2015, there had been seven different prime ministers. Islamists were the dominant force in the General National Congress – the first post-war parliament. Naturally, efforts to disarm the armed bands which fought against Gaddafi have not succeeded. American policy in Libya was characterized by analysts as an absolute failure.[43] The parliament, recognized by the international community, was housed in Tobruk and controlled only part of Cyrenaica. Its Libyan National Army fought against divisions of Jihadists, and its commander, field marshal Khalifa Haftar, laid claim to the role of the dictator of Libya. The Tobruk government was opposed by the Islamist government, with its parliament in Tripoli – the New General National Congress. In December 2015, a Gov-

---

2013 <https://www.todayonline.com/commentary/arab-marshall-plan-needed>.

[41] Souhir Stephenson, "Tunisia, a Sad Year Later", *The International Herald Tribune*, November 1, 2012. P. 6.

[42] "Libya's Eastern City. If Only the Bombs Would Go Away", *The Economist*, April 19, 2014. PP. 30-31.

[43] Alan J. Kuperman, "Obama's Libya Debacle. How a Well-Meaning Intervention Ended in Failure", *Foreign Affairs*, March/April 2015. PP. 67-68.

ernment of National Accord was created in Tripoli, led by Fayez al-Sarraj, recognized internationally as the only legitimate power in the country on the basis of an agreement signed in Skhirat, Morocco. Neither the parliament in Tripoli, nor the one in Tobruk, recognized it.[44]

A far more influential figure, as it turned out, was Haftar, who defeated the Islamists in Benghazi and gained control over the main oilfields and ports. Haftar "has a deep hatred for the Muslim Brotherhood and he talks about his conviction that he has been called by the people to save the country."[45] At first he acted like a stooge of Egypt and the UAE, but he also became a frequent visitor to Moscow. Washington has refrained from backing Haftar. In July 2017, Haftar and Sarraj agreed to a ceasefire and that elections should be held if an opportunity arose.[46] However, in spring 2019 Haftar lead his forces to Tripoli, and fighting broke out around the city.

In Yemen, revolutionary events led to a humanitarian disaster. 13 million have no access to clean drinking water, and 10 million do not have enough to eat.[47] In Yemen, the activity of Al-Qaida was curbed by attacks on it by unmanned American drones. Yemen has had more rockets fired on it by these drones than any other country, surpassing Pakistan.[48]

On 6th February 2015, the Houthis – members of the Shi'ite organization Ansar Allah – proclaimed victory over President Hadi's Sunni authorities. The Houthis' main political slogans are: the USA and Israel are the devil incarnate, and so too are any other governments which cooperate with them. This brought an end to the USA's policy of many years, whereby Yemen, until recently, was seen as a template for a successful American anti-terrorist strategy.[49] A 10-state coalition was formed, with Saudi Arabia and the

---

[44] Sergey Manukov, "Ataka klonov" ("Attack of the Clones"), *Kommersant. Vlast'* (*The Businessman. Power*), April 4, 2016. PP. 36-39; Johannes Makar, "Libya's Lasting Transition", *New African*, August/September 2016. PP. 16-17.

[45] Laurent de Saint Perier, "Khalifa Haftar", *The Africa Report*, Issue 97, February 2018. P. 14.

[46] "Islamic State in Libya. Down but Not Out", *The Economist*, May 27, 2017. P. 31; Marianna Belen'kaya, "Fel'dmarshal soblaznyayet kontraktami" ("The Field Marshal Seduces with Contracts"), *Profil'* (*Profile*), August 21, 2017. PP. 14-15; Andrey Ontikov and Tat'yana Baykova, "Faktor Khaftara" ("The Haftar Factor"), *Izvestiya*, October 2, 2017 <https://iz.ru/651267/andrei-ontikov-tatiana-baikova/liviiskomu-pravitelstvu-dobaviat-voennyi-faktor>.

[47] Cit. from: Saeed Al Batati, "50 Per Cent of Yemenis Need Urgent Assistance – UN Official", *Gulf News*, April 27, 2014 <https://gulfnews.com/world/gulf/yemen/50-per-cent-of-yemenis-need-urgent-assistance--un-official-1.1324969>.

[48] "Yemen, America and al-Qaeda. Droning On", *The Economist*, April 26, 2014. P. 36; Peter Mansfield, *A History of the Middle East*. Penguin Books, 2019. P. 524.

[49] Ivan Groshkov, "Postupilis' printsipami: Yyemenskiy krizis zastavlyayet SSHA stat'

UAE playing the most active roles; this coalition started a war against the pro-Iranian Houthi government, with the aim of restoring Hadi, who had fled the country, to office. Air and land operations were coordinated from the coalition's center in Riyadh, where American and British advisers were based.[50] Air strikes in the late summer of 2017 left around 8,000 people killed and 42,000 wounded. Over three million people became refugees. Riyadh shut down air and sea links to Yemen entirely, cutting its population off from all humanitarian aid whatsoever. The Houthi's forces struck back at Saudi Arabia, causing shock waves over the energy markets.

Egypt has suffered, the country that "has always considered itself central to the Arab world, the country that has the longest history of self-government, and therefore an almost innate sense of nationalism."[51] After 2011, Egypt – with the acknowledged connivance of Islamists – has lost more archaeological, architectural and cultural treasures than throughout the rest of the country's centuries-old history. A Scientific Center in Cairo, built in the time of Napoleon, was destroyed, and a substantial part of the library burnt down in a fire – 160,000 ancient manuscripts, and 200 unique folios.[52] On 30th June 2012, the first civil president to be elected in free elections in 60 years, Mohamed Morsi, swore his oath of office; he was the candidate of the Muslim Brotherhood. Rule by the Islamists did not last long. The policy founded on the slogan "Islam is the solution" prompted resistance among traditionally secular army circles, a substantial portion of the urban youth, Christians (10% of Egyptians), and the business community, particularly the tourist industry, which suffered from the Islamists' view of tourism as a kind of prostitution.[53]

The coup on 3rd July 2013, which brought an end to Morsi's rule, was led by the Defence Minister Field-marshal Abdul-Fattah el-Sisi. The military, on coming to power, declared the Muslim Brotherhood to be a terrorist

....

soyuznikom terroristicheskogo Islamskogo gosudarstva (IG)" ("Giving up the Principles: The Yemen Crisis is Forcing the USA to Become an Ally of the Terrorist Islamic State"), *Mir i politika (The World and Politics)*, March 2015. PP. 20-23.

[50] Peter Salisbury and Simeon Kerr, "UAE Forces Help Saudis Make Gains in Aden and Shift momentum in conflict with Houthis", *The Financial Times*, August 12, 2015. P. 7.

[51] Ben Fishman, "North Africa in Transition", *North Africa in Transition: The Struggle for Democracies and Institutions*, Vol. 55, 2015. P. 11.

[52] Dina P'yanykh, "Strana piramid vlipla v istoriyu" ("The Land of Pyramids has Got Stuck in History"), *Ekho Planety (Echo of the Planet)*, Issue 6, 2013. PP. 46-47.

[53] Vladimir Belyakov, "Yegipet: rozhdeniye 'vtoroy respubliki'" ("Egypt: 'The Birth of the 'Second Republic'"), *Mezhdunarodnaya zhizn' (International Life)*, November 2012. PP. 130-140.

organization. Show trials began, and hundreds of the organization's activists were given the death penalty. The Brotherhood's remaining leaders fled to Qatar, prompting a crisis within the Gulf Cooperation Council (GCC). On 5th March 2014, Saudi Arabia, Bahrain and the UAE, as a sign of protest against the cooperation between Qatar and the Muslim Brotherhood, recalled their ambassadors from Doha. Qatar was forced to hide the leaders of the Muslim Brotherhood in Libya.[54]

Whereas the USA and Western Europe saw the overthrowing of Morsi as a banal military coup and stopped providing aid to Egypt, the reaction of Russia and China was a more positive one, laying the groundwork for closer ties between Cairo and both Moscow and Beijing. Meanwhile, el-Sisi managed not only to consolidate his power, but also to restore economic growth.

"The resilience of the Egyptian state during this turmoil has been remarkable but unsurprising. A high degree of institutionalisation meant that the state could weather the upheaval – in contrast with Libya and Syria [...]. Size, history and geography make it [Egypt] a giant of the modern Middle East. However, as it faces internal upheaval and reordering, it appears to be culturally and economically dormant and to have retreated from its role as a dominant power," contemporary Egyptologists suggest.[55]

Syria fell victim not so much to internal disagreements as to external interference, organized by the USA, the Saudis, Qatar and Turkey. The total number of anti-government troops, at the height of their activity, was estimated at 100,000, of which only a third could be categorized as "moderate secular revolutionaries", who were supported by the Western countries. 40,000-45,000 were radical Islamists, with 10,000 of these affiliated to Jabhat-an-Nusra and the Islamic State in Iraq and the Levant.[56]

In September 2013, Putin proposed a formula for resolving the conflict: putting Syrian chemical weapons under international control, and subsequently destroying them. For the first time in many years, Russia and the Western states succeeded in devising a joint position on regulating an extremely acute international conflict. In April 2014, the Agency for Chemical Disarmament announced that 86.5% of all of Syria's chemical weapons had

---

[54] "Brotherhood Leaders Leave Qatar for Libya: Report", *Gulf News*, April 25, 2014 <https://gulfnews.com/world/gulf/qatar/brotherhood-leaders-leave-qatar-for-libya-report-1.1324196>.

[55] *Egypt after the Spring: Revolt and Reaction*, ed. by Emile Hoyakem and Hebatalla Taha. Routledge, 2018. P. 11.

[56] Maxim Yusin, "Siriyskaya oppozitsiya terpima na tret'" ("The Syrian Opposition is One Third Tolerable"), *Kommersant (The Businessman)*, September 17, 2013 <https://www.kommersant.ru/doc/2280577>.

been handed over to it, but the accusations that Assad had used chemical weapons continued to pour in.[57]

Presidential elections held on 3rd June 2014 brought together the enemies of Assad regime once again. Prominent opposition leaders labeled these elections as "a cheap performance" and called on the West for military intervention.[58]

Northern regions of Syria became the targets of bombing raids by the US and its allies during operations against IS. Washington claimed that the man to blame for the spread of radical Islam was… Bashar Assad, and statements were made to the effect that victory over Islamic State would be impossible without political change in Syria.[59] 6.3 million Syrians have become refugees in their own country, 5 million have fled overseas – 3 million to Turkey, and more than a million to EU countries. More than 500,000 have died, hundreds of thousands have been wounded, 13.5 million people needed humanitarian aid.[60] Of the historic legacy of Syria, little remains of the ancient cities of Damascus and Palmira.

The armed conflict in Syria has developed into a regional war. In the autumn of 2013, a new front was opened in Iraq. The Islamist uprising captured a substantial part of the Iraqi province of Anbar and the cities of Falludjah, Ramadi and Abu-Ghraib. Insurgents from the Islamic State in Iraq and the Levant carried out military actions not only against their traditional enemies, the Shi'ites, but also against the Kurds.[61]

In Iraq, the regime of al-Maliki, put in place by the Americans, tried to build up its power not on a religious basis, but on a nationalist one. It did not stick with it for long, though, and, with the support of Iran, placed its bets firmly on the Shi'ites, pushing itself away from the Sunnis, who had ruled

....

[57] "Eliminating Syria's Chemical Weapons. Getting There", *The Economist*, April 26, 2014. P. 26.

[58] Pavel Tarasenko, "Sirii dobavili kandidatov" ("More Candidates Added in Syria"), *Kommersant (The Businessman)*, April 22, 2014 <https://www.kommersant.ru/doc/2457673>.

[59] Yevgeniy Shestakov, "Asada sdelali 'kraynim'" ("Assad has been Made an 'Extremist'"), *Rossiyskaya Gazeta (Russian Newspaper)*, November 14, 2014 <https://rg.ru/2014/11/13/obvineniye-site.html>.

[60] Louise Callaghan, "Syrian Refugees Return to Ruins of Their Homes, Exhausted and Broke", *The Sunday Times*, August 20, 2017 <https://www.thetimes.co.uk/article/syrian-refugees-return-to-ruins-of-their-homes-exhausted-and-broke-2nxslv7k5>.

[61] Olga Kuznetsova, "Irak vtyanulsya v dve grazhdanskiye voyny" ("Iraq Got Dragged into Two Civil Wars"), *Kommersant (The Businessman)*, October 2, 2013 <https://www.kommersant.ru/doc/2309991>; "Siriyskaya voyna – ot Beyruta do Bagdada" ("The Syrian Civil War – from Beirut to Baghdad"), *Nezavisimaya Gazeta (Independent Newspaper)*, January 13, 2014 <https://www.ng.ru/editorial/2014-01-13/2_red.html>.

under Saddam, and also the Kurds.⁶² Al-Maliki's policy of dallying with both Washington and Tehran simultaneously led to the collapse of his regime. In August 2014, Haider al-Abadi was appointed prime minister of Iraq; under Saddam, he had led the biggest Shi'ite opposition party, Ad-Dawa.⁶³ The biggest threat to Iraq's survival became ISIL.

Through a series of military operations in the summer of 2014, starting with the taking of Mosul on 30ᵗʰ June, ISIL, over one hundred days, inflicted defeats on the Iraqi armed forces (a 350,000-strong army, with 41.6 billion dollars spent on it since 2011), on divisions of the Kurdish Peshmerga in Iraq, on the Syrian army, and on the Syrian rebels. The combination of religious fanaticism and a well-oiled military organization, which was provided by officers formerly exiled from the Iraqi army (Saddam's army was fully disbanded by the Americans), led to a result that shocked the whole world. A Caliphate was proclaimed, led by Caliph Abu Bakr al-Baghdadi, in a territory one hundred times bigger than any territory Bin Laden ever controlled. The world had never seen such barbaric methods of establishing power and conducting public executions, at least not since the times of the Khmer Rouge in Cambodia 40 years earlier.⁶⁴ IS acted like a mafia, with no scruples whatsoever: it engaged in an illegal oil trade, the hi-jacking of cars, racketeering, and kidnappings for ransom. Local state banks and private companies were robbed of all they had.

Islamic State also had its own manufacturing capabilities, ministries, courts, taxation systems and communal payments systems.⁶⁵ It could no longer be classed as a terrorist organization, claimed the American expert on the problem, Audrey Cronin: "ISIS, on the other hand, boasts some 30,000 fighters, holds territory in both Iraq and Syria, maintains extensive military capabilities, controls lines of communication, commands infrastructure, funds itself, and engages in sophisticated military operations. If

---

⁶² See: Joel Rayburn, *Iraq After America: Strongmen, Sectarians, Resistance*. Hoover Institution Press, 2014.

⁶³ Stanislav Ivanov, "Kart-blansh: Iraktsy zhdut ot novogo prem'yera reshitel'nykh mer" ("Carte Blanche: The Iraqis are Awaiting Decisive Measures from Their New Prime Minister"), *Nezavisimaya Gazeta* (*Independent Newspaper*), August 19, 2014 <https://nvo.ng.ru/world/2014-08-19/3_kartblansh.html>.

⁶⁴ Patrick Cockburn, *The Rise of Islamic State: ISIS and the New Sunni Revolution*. London, 2015. PP. x-xi.

⁶⁵ Rinat Mukhametov, "Fenomen 'Islamskogo gosudarstva'" ("The Phenomenon of 'Islamic State'"), *Rossiya v global'noy politike* (*Russia in Global Affairs*), Issue 5, September/October 2014. PP. 134-135; Ivan Gorshkov, "Okhotniki i sobirateli" ("Hunters and Gatherers"), *Mir i politika* (*The World and Politics*), November 2014. P. 11.

ISIS is purely and simply anything, it is a pseudo-state led by a conventional army. And that is why the counterterrorism and counterinsurgency strategies that greatly diminished the threat from al Qaeda will not work against ISIS."[66] At the peak of its influence, according to American intelligence, ISIL had 42,000 people in its ranks, from 120 countries – including 7,600 fighters from Western states.[67] Jihadist groups from North Africa to Pakistan declared their allegiance to the self-proclaimed Caliph, Abu Bakr; these groups include some former sections of Al-Qaida.

The international coalition that faced it, meanwhile, was a long way from having achieved unity. The Americans were fighting against both ISIL and the Assad regime in Syria, which was the strongest opponent to Islamic State. Iran supported Assad, the Iraqi government, and Shi'ite forces in Iraq, as well as groups attached to Hezbollah and operating from Lebanon. Saudi Arabia, the UAE and Turkey, considered Assad and the Syrian Kurds enemies to no less an extent than IS itself.[68]

The USA was obviously not in a great hurry to destroy ISIL. During the bombing campaign against Yugoslavia, the American air force carried out 250 sorties a day; in Afghanistan, in the opening phase of the war, there were 83 a day; against ISIL in Iraq and Syria, there were just 10 a day.[69] The territory under ISIL's control was only growing larger. In September 2015, *The Financial Times* wrote that the military operation against it was "locked in a stalemate, and criticism is mounting across the 60-nation coalition pledged to combat the group that Washington's strategy to defeat the jihadis is failing."[70]

In the autumn of 2015, Russia entered the fray with its air force, providing decisive support to the Syrian army and destroying ISIL's economic and military infrastructure. Russia was accused of humanitarian crimes, and

---

[66] Audrey Kurth Cronin, "ISIS Is Not a Terrorist Group", *Foreign Affairs*, March/April 2015. P. 88.

[67] Eric Schmitt, "Caliphate in Peril, More ISIS Fighters May Take Mayhem to Europe", *The New York Times*, September 17, 2016 <https://www.nytimes.com/2016/09/18/us/politics/caliphate-in-peril-more-isis-fighters-may-take-mayhem-to-europe.html>.

[68] "The War Against Islamic State. Creeping Toward Damascus", *The Economist*, April 11, 2015. P. 34.

[69] David Kilcullen, "I See no Alternative to a Larger, More Intense Conventional War against Isis", *The Guardian*, July 10, 2015 <https://www.theguardian.com/commentisfree/2015/jul/10/i-see-no-alternative-to-a-larger-more-intense-conventional-war-against-isis>.

[70] Sam Jones and Erika Solomon, "Coalition United in Impotence Against ISIS", *The Financial Times*, September 19, 2015. P. 4.

attempts were even made to blame it for the Assad regime's alleged use of chemical weapons (which, it seems, were used by the terrorists).

In May 2017, the Memorandum on four zones of de-escalation was adopted following talks in Astana between representatives of the Russian Federation, Iran, and Turkey. The plan was, on the whole, positively responded to in the West, but not among the enemies of the Assad regime in the Middle East.[71] In October 2017, Syrian troops, with Russian air support, liberated Deir ez-Zor and pushed on to the Euphrates, while the Americans and Kurds took back Raqqa. In December, Putin declared victory over ISIL and said that a substantial portion of the troops in Syria would now be withdrawing.

There has been a dramatic deterioration of the problem of the Kurds – a nation of 30 million, the largest ethnic group in the world that does not have its own state, with its people divided between Iraq, Syria, Turkey and Iran. In 2014, Baghdad stopped financing Iraqi Kurdistan, and the Kurdish regional government began independently disposing of the oil extracted there. The Kurdish Peshmerga (literally "those who face death") shouldered the main burden of the war on ISIL. In September 2017, a referendum was held in Iraqi Kurdistan, in which, as expected, 98% voted in favor of the creation of an independent state (although the results of the referendum were not recognized internationally). Syrian Kurds demanded independence as well.

Growing Kurdish activities led to Turkish military intervention in the Northern Syria. As the Astana process continued, it gave way to a political solution to the conflict which was quite acceptable to the Assad government but not to Washington and several groups of Syrian opposition locked in Idlib with the remnant Islamist forces.

Obviously, military victory over ISIL – primarily through the efforts of Russia and its allies – has been achieved. Rebuilding the devastated Syria is now on the agenda. Interestingly, in announcing the withdrawal of their troops, the USA threatened to impose sanctions against anyone who assists the Syrian government.

A humanitarian catastrophe caused by the Syrian war has begun in Lebanon, a country with a population of 4.5 million people, whose border,

---

[71] Yuriy Gavrilov, "Mir v ukazannykh granitsakh" ("The World in the Borders Indicated"), *Rossiyskaya Gazeta* (*Russian Newspaper*), May 5, 2017 <https://rg.ru/2017/05/05/v-sirii-sozdadut-chetyre-zony-deeskalacii.html>; "A Syrian Plan Worth a Look", *The New York Times*, May 9, 2017 <https://www.nytimes.com/2017/05/09/opinion/a-syrian-plan-worth-a-look.html>; Sami Moubayed, "The Many Loopholes of a Syrian Ceasefire Deal", *Gulf News*, May 5, 2017 <https://gulfnews.com/opinion/op-eds/the-many-loopholes-of-a-syrian-ceasefire-deal-1.2022320>.

in April 2014, was crossed by the one millionth refugee from Syria. The Lebanese Sunnis showed solidarity with the Syrian opposition, whereas the Shiites officially support Damascus, while the most belligerent Shiite group, Hezbollah (meaning Party of Allah), supported by Iran and included in the Lebanese government of national unity, has also been engaged in military operations. In response, the forces of the radical Syrian opposition began firing on Lebanese territory.[72] In March 2016, the League of Arab States declared Hezbollah a terrorist organization, whereupon the ministers of Libya and Iraq walked out of the conference. Saudi Arabia, which traditionally financed the Lebanese army and special services, cut off the allocation of funds to Lebanon, enabling Hezbollah to consolidate its position still further. Political life was paralyzed by the battle on the part of the pro-Syrian parliamentary coalition against Hezbollah and the anti-Syrian "14 March", sponsored by the Saudis.[73] After two and a half years of resistance, at the end of October 2016, the parliament, on the basis of a compromise by all parties, at the forty-sixth attempt managed to elect a president, General Michel Auon, the leader of the Free Patriotic Movement. However, in November 2017, the Saudis announced that they were going to consider Lebanon a hostile state, until Hezbollah joins the ruling coalition.

Morocco withstood the general chaos. It is a close partner of the USA, and facilitates the maintenance of CIA prisons on its territory. King Mohammed VI, whose ancestry goes back to the Prophet, moved towards much-vaunted democratization by allowing parliamentary elections to take place, and these were won by the moderate Islamist Party, and its leader Abdelilah Benikrane became prime minister.[74] Algeria maintained stability for many years; there, the government managed "to direct its hydrocarbon wealth to increased government spending that addressed protesters' concerns."[75] However, in February 2019 riots broke out, preventing Abdelaziz Bouteflika, who was head of state from 1999, from running for a new presidential term. After that, protesters demanded the rotation of the whole ruling elite.

---

[72] "UN Chief: Syria War Threatens Lebanon's Stability", *Gulf News*, April 25, 2014 <https://gulfnews.com/world/mena/un-chief-syria-war-threatens-lebanons-stability-1.1324190>.

[73] Shamsudin Mamayev, "The Redrawing of the Conflict", *Kommersant. Vlast'* (*The Businessman. Power*), April 4, 2016. PP. 32-34.

[74] Jonathan Broder, "Jihad vs J-Lo: How Morocco is on a Knife-Edge Between ISIS and the West", *Newsweek*, July 24, 2017. P. 14.

[75] Ben Fishman, "The Challenges on Implementing Institutional Reform", *North Africa in Transition: The Struggle for Democracies and Institutions*, Vol. 55, 2015. P. 135.

The absolute monarchies appeared to be less vulnerable; they are not experimenting with democracy. There is a wide range of scenarios that could play out in Saudi Arabia, from stability to an Islamist Caliphate and a state on the wane.

At present, it is a rentier-state, whose economy boils down in many ways to the allocation of oil profits, which made it possible for a long time to impose no taxes, to provide free education and healthcare, to subsidize the prices of water, fuel and electricity, to provide grants for training overseas, and to attract workers from abroad. In 2014-2015, oil incomes dropped. A sharp fall in spending followed, creating serious social tension.[76] At the same time, opportunities for public protest are seriously limited: in practice the country is governed by the Committee for the Promotion of Virtue and the Prevention of Vice. Firing squads carry out executions on the central squares, people have their heads cut off, hands are chopped off for stealing (an anesthetic is administered); people can face beatings for having beer in the fridge, or be put in prison for posting the wrong thing on social media.[77]

In late 2014, the Saudis were one of the instigators of the creation of a unified military command to coordinate the defensive efforts of the Union of Gulf States, aimed less against the Islamic State than against Iran (the Saudis feel as if they are surrounded by enemies who are subordinate to Tehran – in Bahrain, Syria, Yemen and Iraq). ISIL's ambitions of creating a Caliphate involve it taking control of Mecca and Medina. Half a dozen IS willayahs were established in the country. Under these circumstances, Riyadh opted not to support the Syrian opposition, and to switch its focus to the fight against terror and to collaboration with Moscow.[78]

Saudi Arabia's fight for regional leadership led to the creation of a coalition with Egypt, Bahrain and the UAE, which, in early June 2017, halted diplomatic relations and brought in a transport embargo on Qatar, accusing it of supporting the Muslim Brotherhood and Hamas, and of making over-

---

[76] "Economic Reform in the Gulf. Time to Sheikh it Up", *The Economist*, September 10, 2016. PP. 13-14; "Gulf Budget Deficit Seen Peaking This Year", *Gulf News*, September 20, 2016 <https://gulfnews.com/business/gulf-budget-deficit-seen-peaking-this-year-1.1899506>.

[77] John Sfakianakis, "Drill Deeper Than Oil for Saudi Prosperity", *The Financial Times*, May 20, 2015. P. 9; Mikhail Zotik, "Na zolotoy trube sideli: Novaya mirovaya pridet s Araviyskogo poluostrova" ("Sitting on the Golden Pipe: The New World War will Come from the Arabian Peninsula"), *Mir i politika* (*The World and Politics*), March 2015. PP. 52-55.

[78] Ravil' Mustafin, "U Moskvy mogut perekhvatit' initsiativu po Cirii" ("Moscow Might Have the Initiative Seized from it on Syria"), *Nezavisimaya Gazeta* (*Independent Newspaper*), September 14, 2017 <https://www.ng.ru/kartblansh/2017-09-14/3_7073_kartblansh.html>.

tures to Iran. Qatar, where the US Central Command in the Middle East is headquartered, responded by expanding its ties with Turkey, Iran and neighboring Oman, and also with Moscow.[79]

In the summer of 2016, the Kingdom's Council of Ministers adopted an ambitious program, "Saudi vision-2030", which was presented by the young heir to the heir to the throne (this is his official status), Mohammed bin Salman, known as MBS for short. The country's Constitution was declared to be Islam, but experts noted that the document suggests not Wahhabism, which is at present the official religion, but "the Islam of the center", as reformers see it. A clear leaning towards Arab nationalism (pan-Arabism) could also be seen.[80] At the same time, persecution was stepped up inside Saudi Arabia, and this affected a considerable circle of clergy and academics.[81]

Many members of the royal family and representatives of big business were arrested, accused of corruption. The overwhelming majority of those arrested agreed to hand over their fortunes (estimated at a total of 100 billion dollars) in exchange for their freedom.

The murder and dismemberment in the Saudi Consulate in Turkey of the leading analyst and columnist for *The Washington Post*, Jamal Khashoggi, led to a similar conflict with the West. All the evidence pointed to the involvement of the Crown Prince Mohammed bin Salman, but Trump preferred not to disrupt relations with Saudi Arabia; his stance received fierce criticism.

As a result of the tumultuous events in the Middle East, thousands of people hastened, on whatever vessels were available, makeshift or otherwise, to escape across the Mediterranean to Europe. Italy and its islands, jutting out far into the sea to the south of the continent, had to bear the heaviest burden. Now, though, quotas have been set for accepting refugees from Libya and other countries, for all the member states of the EU, including the Eastern European newcomers. For the first time since World War Two, France suddenly found itself participating in four wars at once – in Afghanistan, in Libya (where Nicholas Sarkozy personally managed to involve in the whole of NATO), in Cote d'Ivoire, where president Gbagbo refused to admit his defeat at the elections and had to be urgently removed, and in Mali.

....

[79] Simeon Kerr and Ahmed Al Omran, "Qatar Set to Inflame Regional Tensions by Restoring Diplomatic Ties with Iran", *The Financial Times*, August 25, 2017. P. 1.

[80] Alexander Ignatenko, "Gologramma dlya ocherednogo naslednika prestola" ("A Hologram for the Next Heir to the Throne"), *Nezavisimaya Gazeta* (*Independent Newspaper*), July 14, 2016 <https://www.ng.ru/faith/2016-07-14/3_kartblansh.html>.

[81] Ben Hubbard, "Saudi Arabia Detains Critics of Crown Prince", *The New York Times*, September 15, 2017. P. A4(L).

Thomas L. Friedman wrote: "The term 'Arab Spring' has to be retired. There is nothing springlike going on. [T]he 'Arab Awakening' also no longer seems valid, given all that has been awakened."[82]

The traditional hotspots in the Arab world are continuing to flare up, too. The Arab-Israeli conflict is far from being resolved. In April 2014, negotiations between Israel and Palestine, brokered by the USA, were discontinued after Hamas Islamists and the moderate wing of Fatah, headed by Palestinian President Mahmoud Abbass, agreed once again to merge the Palestinian administrations on the West Bank and in the Gaza Strip. Hamas resolved to ally itself with a moderate government mostly because it had lost the support of its main sponsor – the Islamic Brotherhood from Egypt. The American stance on regulating the situation in the Middle East remains unchanged since 2006: recognizing Israel, condemning violence, and recognizing all the agreements previously signed between Israel and the PLO. As for Israel, it is taking actions which are unacceptable for the Arabs, including the making of a demand that it be recognized specifically as a "Jewish state" (in order to sign peace treaties with Egypt and Jordan, Israel required only that it be recognized as a state), and the establishment of new settlements in the territories it has captured in the West Bank and East Jerusalem.[83]

Israel is far from ecstatic about the successes of the regime in Damascus, and of Hezbollah, in Syria, and is taking all possible measures to ensure that Hezbollah in Lebanon does not get its hands on missiles, air defence systems and drones, conducting air strikes to this end across Syrian territory.[84]

The situation in the region was made dramatically more acute by Trump's decision to move the American embassy to Jerusalem and to recognize Jerusalem as the official capital of Israel, something that the rest of the international community does not accept. A third intifada has begun, and the Organization of Islamic States officially recognized East Jerusalem as the capital of Palestine on 13th December 2017. Trump has threatened to withhold aid to the Palestinians if they do not establish peace with Israel. However, the Palestinian President Mahmoud Abbas said the United States had taken

---

[82] Thomas L. Friedman, "The Arab Quarter Century", *The International Herald Tribune*, April 11, 2013. P. 7.

[83] "The Palestinians. Glimpses of Unity", *The Economist*, April 26, 2014. P. 35; "Netanyahu to Abbas: 'Tear up' Pact with Hamas", *Gulf News*, April 27, 2014 <https://gulfnews.com/world/mena/netanyahu-to-abbas-tear-up-pact-with-hamas-1.1325112>.

[84] Marwan Kabalan, "Israel's Syria Red Lines", *Gulf News*, May 4, 2017 <https://gulfnews.com/opinion/op-eds/israels-syria-red-lines-1.2021967>.

itself "off the table" as a peace mediator.[85] A Palestinian bid to repeal the US decision in the UN Security Council was vetoed by Washington. Edward Luce rightly observed, "By taking the Holy City's final status off the table, Mr Trump has all but guaranteed the Palestinians will not come to the table. He is also making life tougher for his Arab friends."[86] Trump's decision to recognize Israel's sovereignty over the Golan Heights in March 2019 exacerbated regional tensions even more.

The Iran situation is worsening as well, though quite recently the chances of resolving the Iranian nuclear problem peacefully were unprecedently high. After the resignation of Ahmadinejad in the summer of 2013 and the elections which brought the moderate Hasan Rouhani to power, the 5+1 talks (the members of the UN Security Council + Germany) were resumed. Iran agreed to reduce its uranium enrichment and make its nuclear program transparent for MAGATE. This made it possible to secure a "nuclear deal", involving the cancellation of most of the Western sanctions against Iran. Against this backdrop, the Iranians have clearly strengthened their position in Iraq, Syria, Lebanon and Yemen, causing consternation among the Sunni monarchies and in the United States. Meanwhile, the Saudis and their partners in the GCC – and Israel – could not forgive Washington for having begun to draw closer to Tehran.[87]

As a result of the removal of sanctions, the Iranian economy (equivalent in size to Austria's in terms of the exchange rate and to Australia's in terms of purchasing power parity) was able to breathe again. French, Italian, German, Chinese, Russian and South Korean companies all hurried to Iran. Tehran managed to attract foreign investment to the tune of 12 billion dollars in the Iranian year 1395 (which ended on 20th March 2017).[88]

The coming to power of Trump, who had called Tehran the biggest problem in the Middle East, if not the world, brought the disagreements between Iran and the USA into sharp focus once again. In Washington, there was talk of a fresh round of sanctions. Anti-American rhetoric was stepped up in Tehran, too, and

....

[85] "Abbas Committed to Serious Negotiations", *Gulf Times*, February 3, 2018 <https://www.gulf-times.com/story/580347/Abbas-committed-to-serious-negotiations>.

[86] Edward Luce, "Trump is Playing with Matches in the Middle East", *The Financial Times*, May 17, 2018. P. 9.

[87] Matthew Rosenberg and Ben Hubbard, "Middle East Allies See Heightened Peril in Newly Empowered, Emboldened Tehran", *The New York Times*, July 15, 2015. P. A9(L).

[88] "Zarif: Sanctions Impaired Iran's Economic Transparency", *Tehran Times*, April 15, 2017 <https://www.tehrantimes.com/news/412642/Zarif-Sanctions-impaired-Iran-s-economic-transparency>.

the budget adopted in 2017 stipulated an increase in military allocations from 6% to 9% of total spending.[89] The newly deteriorated economic situation had to do with the fact that at the end of the year, Iran faced street protests, which, according to the authorities, were inspired by the United States, Great Britain, Israel, Saudi Arabia and the radical organization "Mujahedin-e-Hulk" based abroad.[90]

Nevertheless, in early May 2018, Trump announced his withdrawal from the JCPOA and offered to start discussing a new deal. The United States put forward 12 conditions for Iran to conclude a new agreement, which were no longer limited to Tehran's refusal to create nuclear weapons, but provided for a review of the entire foreign policy of the Islamic Republic: to stop the program of ballistic missiles, to withdraw support forces from Syria, to stop support for Hezbollah and Hamas. Otherwise, "unprecedented financial pressure" was promised.

Tehran responded with a clear denial, not seeing the slightest reason for the USA's abandonment of the JCPOA. IAEA Director General Yukiya Amano confirmed that Iran is fully complying with its obligations under the nuclear deal. On 7th July, in Vienna, Iran, Russia, China, Germany, France and the United Kingdom confirmed their readiness to comply with the agreements reached in 2015.[91]

Trump signed an executive order restoring sanctions. The EU instructed European firms not to comply with the sanctions, but firms are taking them seriously.[92] However, France and Germany decided to establish a special mechanism allowing European companies to interact with Iran and evade American sanctions.

Sanctions and capital flight have exacerbated a currency crisis in Iran. Ayatollah Ali Khamenei banned any negotiations with the Trump administration as he attacked the US for being "a bullying and deceitful regime".[93]

---

[89] "Defence Ministry Displays Latest Achievements", *Financial Tribune*, April 15, 2017 <https://financialtribune.com/articles/national/62464/defense-ministry-displays-latest-achievements>.

[90] Sergey Strokan', "Iran ustal ot islamskoy revolyutsii" ("Iran is Tired of the Islamic Revolution"), *Kommersant (The Businessman)*, Issue 1, January 9, 2018 <https://www.kommersant.ru/doc/3514770>.

[91] Pavel Tarasenko and Yelena Chernenko, "Partneram Irana dali 180 dney na razmyshleniye" ("Iran's Partners were Given 180 Days to Think"), *Kommersant (The Businessman)*, Issue 78, May 10, 2018 <https://www.kommersant.ru/doc/3623837>; Igor' Dunayevskiy, "Sanktsii vmesto strategii" ("Sanctions Instead of Strategy"), *Rossiyskaya Gazeta (Russian Newspaper)*, Issue 109, May 23, 2018 <https://rg.profkiosk.ru/article.aspx?aid=646853>; Yuriy Kogalov, "Sdelka budet zhit'" ("The Deal will Live"), *Rossiyskaya Gazeta (Russian Newspaper)*, Issue 146, July 9, 2018 <https://rg.profkiosk.ru/article.aspx?aid=657545>.

[92] "America and Iran. The Pain of No Deal", *The Economist*, August 11, 2018. P. 29.

[93] Najmeh Bozorgmehr, "Iran Supreme Leader Bars Talks with 'Bullying' US", *The Financial*

Russia and China said that they continue to adhere to the commitments made in the framework of the JCPOA. Moscow has also fulfilled its promise to Israel to have Iranian forces pull back from Syrian territory close to the Israeli border, 85 km behind an armistice line that Syria and Israel agreed to in 1974. At the same time, Russia has deepened co-operation with Iran and Central Asian neighbors through a landmark deal on carving up the Caspian Sea, paving the way for long-stalled energy projects and confirming Moscow's military domination over the biggest lake on earth by banning any military presence on the Caspian by non-signatories.[94] Russia is not going to discontinue its cooperation with Iran.

In Afghanistan, the start of the withdrawal of American troops coincided with the end of the 12-year era of Hamid Karzai, who was replaced by Ashraf Ghani. In late 2014, there was a contingent of American troops numbering more than 10,000 there. The strategic significance of this country, which has borders with Iran, China, Central Asia, India and Pakistan, is simply too great. It is a geostrategic Klondike, which, admittedly, has the reputation of being the graveyard of empires, and deservedly so. The country is in a desperate condition. Foreigners have either fled, or are sitting it out in heavily protected districts of Kabul. It "is a violent and dysfunctional country," wrote *The Economist*. "It is also the poorest in Asia and one of the world's most corrupt."[95]

By the end of Obama's presidency, his policy in Afghanistan was deemed to have been a complete failure. The attempts to create a government that was fit for purpose had proved so unsuccessful that the definitive withdrawal of American troops, it was felt in Washington, would lead to an immediate victory for the Taliban. The decision was taken to maintain a limited military presence and finance of 10-20 billion dollars a year, to prevent the regime from collapsing.[96] Trump, in essence, continued the previous policy, with the same result. After the announcement of his plan for Afghanistan, *The New York Times* wrote: "Its combination of state collapse, civil conflict, ethnic disintegration and multisided intervention has locked it in a self-perpetuat-

---

Times, August 14, 2018. P. 2.

[94] Henry Foy, "Russia Woos Iran to Boost Caspian Clout", *The Financial Times*, August 13, 2018. P. 7.

[95] "Afghanistan. So Long, Good Luck", *The Economist*, November 29, 2014. PP. 35-36.

[96] Max Fisher, "15 Years into Afghan War, Americans Would Rather Not Talk about It", *The New York Times*, September 20, 2016 <https://www.nytimes.com/2016/09/21/world/asia/afghanistan-war-15-years-americans.html>.

ing cycle that may be simply beyond outside resolution. [...] American-led efforts, despite some successes, have ended up reinforcing and accelerating the broader cycles of violence and fragmentation that have been growing since the state's collapse in the early 1990s."[97]

The Middle East has always had its fair share of conflicts and disagreements. Never before in history, however, have there been so many, and never have they been of such an all-encompassing, profound and extremely acute nature. And this happened immediately after the USA arrived in the Middle East to wage war on terrorism.

It is not surprising that relations between the Islamic world and the West are far from ideal. Muslims' distrust of the West, writes the Oxford professor Tariq Ramadan, "is fueled by America's decades-long support for dictators who accommodated its economic and security interests; by the invasions of Iraq and Afghanistan; by the humiliating treatment of prisoners at Abu Ghraib and Guantánamo Bay; and by America's seemingly permanent and unconditional support for Israel. [...] Withdrawing from Afghanistan, respecting United Nations resolutions and treaty obligations with regard to Palestine, calling back the killer drones and winding up the 'war on terror' would be excellent places to start."[98]

The Moscow Factor

Vladimir Putin has said a number of times that there are more than 20 million Muslims living in Russia. I do not know where he found this figure. If one counts the Muslims of all representatives of the nationalities which are traditionally considered to be Islamic, the total comes to around 13 million people. If one takes only those who actively profess the Islamic faith, i.e. those who perform the religious rituals, the maximum figure is no more than 5% of Russia's population. But even if there are only 13 million, or 9 million, that is still more than enough to think of Russia as one of the biggest Islamic countries, particularly given the large number of migrants from Central Asia. At present, 57 ethnicities associate themselves with Islam, and they are the titular ethnicities in eight subject entities of the Federation.

---

[97] Max Fisher, "Recipe for an Endless War in Afghanistan", *The New York Times,* August 25, 2017. P. A4(L).

[98] Tariq Ramadan, "Waiting for an Arab Spring of Ideas", *The New York Times,* September 30, 2012 <https://www.nytimes.com/2012/10/01/opinion/waiting-for-an-arab-spring-of-ideas.html>.

Moscow is the biggest Islamic city, not only in Russia, but in the whole of Europe (if one excludes Istanbul, again). According to various estimates, there are between 800,000 and 1.5 million Muslims living in Moscow. Most of Russia's Islamic communities are either modernist or traditionalist. The Council of Muftis of Russia has declared *fatwas* numerous times (theological interpretations of Sharia), condemning manifestations of Islamic radicalism. The problem is not Islam itself, but Islamist extremism.

Relations between Russia and Islam beyond the borders were, for several centuries, limited to relations with the Ottoman Empire, and, to a lesser extent, with Persia. The Soviet Union set itself a significantly wider set of objectives: it established contact with the whole of the Muslim world in the fields of economics, scientific and technical cooperation, culture, and education. "The politics of the former colonial powers, and then of the USA, prompted a whole range of Arabic countries to cooperate with the USSR," Yevgeniy Primakov noted. "The growth of the Arab-Israeli conflict had the same effect. Soviet aid to the Arab world, and the stance adopted by Moscow at critical moments in the confrontation between the Arab countries and Israel, meant that the Arabic monarchies, with their close links to the West, were favorably disposed towards the Soviet Union… Yet it was the Arab states led by revolutionary nationalists that became partners with the USSR."[99] Or, as Mansfield noted, the Soviet Union, in the post-war years, backed "popular national leaders who were prepared to show independence from the West. Nasser of Egypt was such an Arab leader *par excellence*."[100]

When the Cold War ended, the "external battlefield" of Soviet-American rivalry was destroyed. Israel and the "conservative" states became more interested in developing contact with Russia. Meanwhile, the former Soviet partners began to look towards the USA. And modern Russia was seen as an unsustainable product of the collapse of the Soviet Union, whose future, and foreign policy orientation, was not entirely defined.

In Russia, people have observed events in the Arab world with great consternation. "The 'Arab Spring' was initially interpreted as giving rise to hope for positive changes," observed Putin. "On the whole, what is taking place in the Arab world is very instructive. The events show that the desire to introduce democracy through forceful methods may – and often does – lead to the diametrically opposite result. Forces rise up from the bottom, includ-

---

[99] Yevgeniy Primakov, *Konfidentsial'no: Blizhniy Vostok na stsene i za kulisami* (*Confidential: The Middle East on Stage and in the Wings*). Moscow, 2012. PP. 68-69.
[100] Peter Mansfield, *A History of the Middle East*. Penguin Books, 2019. P. 286.

ing religious extremists, which try to alter the very course of the countries' development, the secular nature of their rule."[101] The prospect of the energy of terror being directed at the Caucasus and Central Asia, and indeed to the rest of the country, represents a serious threat.

In 1994, emissaries of Al-Qaida were found, for the first time, on the territory of the Russian Federation. Five years later, this presence took on visible forms: the uprising in Dagestan in 1999 began not under the banner of Chechnya, but under the black banners of Al-Qaida. Al-Qaida's black banner hung above the stage at the stage of the Dubrovka Theater in Moscow, captured by terrorists. Emissaries of Hizbut-Tahrir al-Islami hastened to Russia. When the Americans, while entering Afghanistan, cleaned out Bin Laden's training camps, and then took the people they arrested to Guantanamo, they discovered a considerable number of Russian citizens during the filtration process. There are quite a few volunteers from Russia fighting for ISIL, too.

In recent years, Moscow has tried to restore the set of mutual ties that existed in the past, attempting to relate to the Muslim world with respect.

Russia has noticeably enhanced its prestige in the Islamic world, by making a decisive contribution to the destruction of ISIL in Syria. It is no accident that in a poll conducted in the spring of 2017 among Arab youths in 16 countries, Russia came first among the external forces considered as friendly states, notably moving ahead of the United States (Russia, indeed, came third among all the countries in the world, behind only the UAE and Saudi Arabia).[102]

The President of the Institute for Eastern Studies at the Russian Academy of Sciences, Vitaliy Naumkin, thinks it is important that "Russians have similar moral ideals which draw them closer to the Islamic world. These are man's responsibility to society and the state, and a moral approach to international relations, and much else. One can say there is a civilizational proximity between our peoples… Russia and the Islamic world jointly have at their disposal the bulk of the world's resource and energy potential. We will be in the same boat for some time to come – and preferably for as long as possible."[103]

---

[101] Vladimir Putin, "Rossiya i menyayushchiysya mir" ("Russia and a Changing World"), *Moskovskiye novosti* (*Moscow News*), February 27, 2012 < https://www.mn.ru/politics/78738 >.

[102] Simeon Kerr, "Young Arabs Turn to Russia as Region's Best Allies amid Waning US Influence", *The Financial Times*, May 4, 2017. P. 4.

[103] Vitaliy Naumkin, *Blizhniy Vostok v mirovoy politike i kul'ture* (*The Middle East in World*

CHAPTER 11
LATIN-AMERICAN CHARISMA

Latin America is becoming one of the key poles in the present and future world order. Yet Latin America's sense of self-identity as a civilization is still in the process of coming into being, although efforts to recognize itself as a separate world, to be defined in relation to the cultural traditions which took shape there – Ibero-European, Indian and African – were seen in Latin America back in the colonial era. A Latin American civilization certainly existed on the continent, incidentally, even before the Europeans arrived in America.

Conquistadors and Caudillo Realm

After Christopher Columbus's expedition, which, between 1492 and 1504, discovered the islands of the Caribbean Sea (the archipelago of the Antilles), and also the coast of Central America and Venezuela, the first Spanish settlements were established on the Espanola islands (modern-day Haiti) and in Cuba. These would later become key support points for future expansion deep into the American continent.

The European colonizers arrived too late to encounter the Mayan civilization (on the territory of present-day Guatemala, Belize and Southern Mexico), whose classical period lasted from 250 to 900 AD. In the middle of the 9th century, for a reason as yet unknown to scientists – theories suggested include population movement, political infighting, or a lengthy drought – the cities of the classical epoch went through a period of chaos and then a mass exodus. When the conquistadors arrived there were other civilizations for them to discover, however.

Politics and Culture). Moscow, 2011. PP. 18, 19.

The cavalry, firearms, and infectious diseases that the Europeans brought with them helped to reduce the indigenous population of Mexico at the time from 25 million to 9 million in less than 50 years.

The state and civilization of the Aztecs, who in cultural terms were in many ways superior to the Spanish (if one overlooks the human sacrifice rituals used by the former), and who, unhappily for them, proved to have too much gold, were destroyed by an expedition of conquistadors led by Hernan Cortes (1519-1521) and by the colonial Spanish rule that followed it.

The Inca culture was also destroyed, and the state of Tawantinsuyu was plundered in 1532 – 1536 by the Spanish conquistador Francisco Pizarro. He died soon afterwards in skirmishes with his colleagues, who continued to devastate the continent.

By the start of the 17th century, Spanish rule had been established on the territory of Mexico, California, Florida, Central America, and throughout the entire continent of South America, with the exception of Brazil. Brazil had been conquered by Portugal, and Guinea had been divided up between England, Holland and France. The resistance that was put up by the indigenous people was crushed by gunfire and the sword, with the brutality extending to indiscriminate slaughter.

The West Indies and the coastal parts of Venezuela and Brazil were turned into settlement colonies used predominantly for slave plantations, for which the importing of slaves from Africa was required.

In areas with a long tradition of agriculture, where the indigenous peoples had lived in territorial communes, the colonial administrations bound them to the land and brought in labor conscription, which became known as a system of encomienda. In Paraguay and parts of Brazil and Argentina, where Jesuit missionaries were active and able to enjoy complete freedom in their actions, unlike in Europe (until the order's activities in Spain itself and in her colonies was banned in 1767), attempts were made effectively to restore the caste-based system from the Inca empire. As they sought to bring Christianity to the local populace, the Jesuits paid off the local leaders (the *caciques*), even giving them Spanish titles and calling them *hidalgos*, and taught the people agronomy, artisan trades and musical culture. The far south of the continent and the majority of the internal parts of South America were not settled by the Europeans until the 19th century.

Following the abolition of the encomienda in the 18th century, the lands that had belonged to the communes came under the ownership of the major latifundistas, and the indigenous people moved to the position of being tenants, or moved to the cities, where contraband trade was flourishing and industry had come into being. Settlers from Spain and Portugal mixed with creoles (their direct descendants, who were born in America), indigenous people, negroes and mulattos.

For the continent's inhabitants, the idea that they could identify with the metropolis, which looked on its colonies across the ocean as a source of riches and of the gold that was necessary, not least, for wars on the European continent, was something that became less and less evident. The struggle for independence was on the agenda, and it was led by creoles who were inspired by the successful War of Independence waged by Great Britain's North American colonies, and by the French Revolution.

For the leading ideologues of Latin American liberation – Venezuelan-born Francisco de Miranda and Simon Bolivar, natives of Argentina José de Saint-Martin and Mariano Moreno and others – very consonant were the slogans of freedom, equality and fraternity. They were disgusted, however, by the radicalism of the French Jacobins and the model of the United States, since for them slavery was unacceptable.

The first country to strike out for independence was Haiti, a land over which a war broke out in 1793 between France, Britain and Spain. A local army made up of former slaves and led by Toussaint-Louverture became involved in the war, initially fighting on the side of revolutionary France, which had proclaimed the abolition of slavery, before later driving the French off the island as well. On 1st January 1804, Toussaint-Louverture's successor, Jean-Jacques Dessalines, proclaimed the establishment of the Republic of Haiti. It was the first to abolish the institution of slave-owning in the Western hemisphere. This was the first example of freedom being won, and before long other nations were following suit.

The mainland now began to follow Haiti's example. They were helped by the fact that at the beginning of the 19th century the countries of the Iberian Peninsula were greatly weakened as a result of the conquest of their Napoleonic troops in 1808, when king Ferdinand VII was arrested and held prisoner for six years in the French city of Bayon. At this time, patriotic juntas were created both in the metropolis and in the colonies, and they fought for the liberation of the king. From 1810, though, some juntas in the colonies turned into centers of struggle for independence from the powerless Spain. Three hotbeds of the war for liberation were formed: La Plata (modern Argentina), Paraguay, and Uruguay; the "Andean countries" – Venezuela, New Granada, Peru, Chile, and Quito; and New Spain – Mexico. The rebellion had no single center, but its leaders from various parts of the vast continent were familiar with one another, and had met in London, which was an important center of anti-Spanish conspiracies.

Between 1810 and 1830, Venezuela, Paraguay, Argentina, Chile, Colombia, Mexico, Brazil, Bolivia, Peru, the countries of Central America, Uruguay, and Ecuador obtained independence, and finally, in 1844, the Dominican Republic did too.

The wars fought for independence in the early 19th century – with the exception of Brazil, where everything was limited to dynastic agreements – were bloody ones. This was particularly true of Mexico, where the war was led by Miguel Hidalgo y Costilla and Jose Maria Morelos, who were executed by the Spanish. Of the roughly 6 million-strong population of Mexico at the time, more than 300,000 had died by the time independence was achieved in 1821. Spain continued to make attempts even later than that to win its American colonies back.

The desire to realize itself as a separate world, to determine the cultural traditions encountered there – Ibero-European, Indian, African – manifested itself in Latin America in the colonial era. By the end of the War of independence, there emerged not so much local national identities as regional identity, reminiscent of the experience of the North American colonies of England, which created the United States. The struggle with the European (Spanish) crown became a symbol of unity, and the concept of "patria" began to spread throughout the continent.

In the first decades of independence, there was a continental concept of "Americanism", based on the idea of a united "our America", proposed by Simon Bolivar. The question of the creation of a common state was repeatedly raised, as reflected in the creation, by the Liberator himself, as Bolivar came to be called, of the great Colombia of 1821-1830. There was the Peruvian-Bolivian Confederation in 1836-1839, the Federation of the United Provinces of Central America in 1823-1839, and then again the Central American Union in 1873-1885. The sense of statehood still prevailed, however. In his "Letter from Jamaica" of 1815, Bolivar admits: "Personally, more than anyone else, I would like to create a great nation in America, which would be famous for its size and wealth, as much as freedom and valor. However, although I dream of the most perfect form of government for my country, I am unable to assert that the New World could become at the present moment a single great Republic, and as this is impossible, I dare not think of it." [1]

---

[1] *Politicheskaya istoriya stran Latinskoy Ameriki v XIX veke* (*The Political History of the*

However, the principles of constitutional order laid down by Bolivar were to become a reference point for many generations of Latin American politicians. He stressed that "laws must be born of the People who obey them; that only in extremely rare cases are the laws of one country suitable for another; that laws must correspond to the physical conditions of the country, its climate, the properties of its land, its location, size, and the features of life of the people; that the laws should reflect the degree of Freedom which the Constitution allows, taking into account the religion of the inhabitants, their inclinations, their standard of living, their number, occupation, customs, and education! This is the code by which we should be guided, not the Code of Washington!"[2]

The event that finally brought down the Spanish empire was the Spanish-American war of 1898, which, in 1902-1903 – the third wave of the liberation – brought independence to Cuba and Puerto Rico, but immediately put them under the strict control of the USA (as well as the Philippines).

The fourth wave of the struggle for independence would not arrive until the period 1962-1981, when Jamaica, Guyana, Trinidad and Tobago, Barbados, the Commonwealth of Bahamian Islands, Grenada, Dominique, St Vincent and the Grenadines, Saint Lucia, St Kitts and Nevis, Antigua and Barbuda, and Belize, all proclaimed their independence.

Independence, as is often the way, did not bring immediate happiness. Of course, in the decades that followed, republics were put in place, democratic institutions were tried out, and noble titles were abolished, as was the levy imposed on indigenous Americans. Slavery was abolished in Mexico and Central America in the early 1820s, in most other countries between 1830 and the 1850s, and in Cuba and Brazil in the late 1880s. A huge number of constitutions were drawn up: in Bolivia alone, there were 11 between 1826 and 1880; in Peru, there were 10 between 1821 and 1867.[3] This by no means led to genuine constitutionalism being established, however.

The industrial revolution only began in the final third of the 19th century, and was limited mainly to the construction of railways. Mexico, by way of example, did not manage to restore the level of GDP seen under colonial times until the 1880s. This was followed by a three-decade-long period of

....
Countries of Latin America in the 19th Century), edited by Ye. A. Larin. Moscow, 2012. P. 10.

[2] Simon Bolivar, *Izbrannyye proizvedeniya. 1812-1830 (Selected Works. 1812-1830)*. Moscow, 1983. P. 82.

[3] Jurgen Osterhammel, *The Transformation of the World: A Global History of the Nineteenth Century*. Princeton-Oxford: Princeton University Press, 2014. P. 598.

stability under the dictatorship of general Porfirio Dias, finally brought to an end by the first socialist revolution of the 20th century, which began in 1910 and was inspired by the ideas of Trotskyism. During the revolution, some 700,000 people died (out of a total population of 15 million), and a further 250,000 fled to the USA.

Military coups and dictatorships were not uncommon. An exceptionally brutal one was the rule of Juan Manuel de Rosas in Argentina in 1829-1852. In practically every state on the continent, the phenomenon of caudillismo had emerged: the local leaders or even church priests, who wielded great authority, made particular territories subordinate to themselves, usually so as to protect the land boundaries, titles and privileges of the landowners. To this end, they created their own armies, which were sometimes on a par with the national armed forces. Even without that, military regimes held sway in more than half of the countries in South America for more than half of the century. There were civil wars in Mexico, Argentina, Colombia, Venezuela, Uruguay and Guatemala. Conflicts between states occurred occasionally, too, the most notable ones being the war of the Triple Alliance – Brazil, Argentina and Uruguay – against Paraguay in 1864-1870, and the Second Pacific War of 1879-1884, which pitted Chile against Peru and Bolivia.

The emancipation of the civilization of Latin America, the drive towards which had been set in motion by the independence movement, was held back in the 19th and 20th centuries by continuing Westernization, which happened in two main ways. Firstly, mass immigration of Europeans started. By the late 19th century, the population of Latin America had reached 60 million, as a result of a sharp increase in the number of immigrants, most of whom headed for Argentina, Uruguay, Brazil and Chile, and later to Venezuela. The Italian, new Spanish, German and Slavic immigration (particularly to Argentina and Uruguay) moved these countries away from the "creole" path. "In the cultural consciousness, under the pressure of the new priorities, one can identify a painful polarization between the traditional Hispanic and creole culture, which was founded on creole lore, 'mixed' métis forms, related to the indigenous culture, and the very new, shared European, cosmopolitan influences."[4]

Secondly, the role played by the United States increased dramatically; in the 1820s, the US had proclaimed the "Monroe doctrine": "America

---

[4] *Istoriya literatur Latinskoy Ameriki* (*The History of the Literatures of Latin America*), ed. by V. B. Zemskov. Moscow, 1994. P. 9.

for Americans". Initially signifying resistance to any kind of European interference in the continent's affairs, this doctrine later became the basis for growing interference in them by the US itself. On the whole, those in Washington tended to see Latin America as their back yard by rights. The foundations for this were laid by the war with Mexico in 1846-1848, in which the USA occupied Texas and California and made them its own – 2.5 million square kilometers of territory that had originally belonged to Mexico.

There was intense competition over the continent between the USA, Spain, England, France, and later Germany. In the field of American influence were Mexico, the Central American nations, the Isthmus of Panama, and Venezuela. The European grandees competed with one another in Brazil, Argentina, Chile, and Uruguay.

This economic competition was accompanied by a conflict between geopolitical concepts: Hispanicism, pan-Americanism, Latinism, and then pan-Germanism. The numerous attempts that were made to develop a common platform for uniting the continent started to look increasingly idealistic. The blurred nature of state borders, which did not coincide with ethno-cultural ones, became a source of inter-state conflicts (Mexico/Guatemala, Argentina/Uruguay/Brazil/Paraguay, Chile/Bolivia/Peru), which made the continent even more vulnerable to penetration from without.

In 1889, at the initiative of the United States, the Pan-American Union was created in Washington, and declared that its priority lay in peaceful economic and cultural ties. Yet things did not turn out like that. At the turn of the century, the concepts of Hispanicism and North American pan-Americanism clashed in a battle for Cuba and Puerto Rico.

Meddling in the liberation struggle in Cuba, the USA crushed Spain, occupied Cuba, annexed Puerto Rico, and provoked the break-up of Colombia, which had resisted the construction of a canal between the oceans. President Theodore Roosevelt – the first American to win the Nobel Peace Prize – facilitated the revolution of November 1903, "gifted" independence from Colombia to Panama within two weeks, and secured permission from its new government for the building of the canal. In 1915, American troops occupied Haiti, and in 1916 Santo Domingo and Nicaragua, and the same year committed an incursion into Mexico.

Thereafter, the Americanization of Latin America took place in a rather more peaceful way, for the most part brought about via the activity of transnational corporations and a military-political partnership.

"[H]e's a son of a bitch, but he's our son of a bitch."[5] These words, uttered by President Franklin Roosevelt with reference to the Nicaraguan dictator Somoza, became the quintessence of the United States' relations with the majority of the regimes in the region, where democracy remained a rarely-seen guest.

At the same time, the American notion of South America's place in the world as a God-given appendage, essential if the great North American democracy was to flourish, began to diverge, ever more noticeably, from the Latin American people's own understanding of their destiny. In his famous article *Our America*, the Cuban José Martí wrote: "We were a masquerader in English breeches, Parisian vest, North American jacket, and Spanish cap. The Indian hovered near us in silence, and went off to hills to baptize his children. The Negro was seen pouring out the songs of his heart at night, alone and unrecognized among the rivers and wild animals. The peasant, the creator, turned in blind indignation against the disdainful city, against his own child. […] Let the world be grafted onto our republics, but the trunk must be our own."[6]

By the mid-20th century, the countries of Latin America had stepped into the arena of global politics of their own accord. During the Second World War, all the countries of Central America and Ecuador entered the war against the axis states, at the same time as the USA, in December 1941; Mexico, Brazil, Bolivia and Colombia later did likewise. The last country to enter the war was Argentina, which had supported Germany until February 1945. Brazilian troops fought on the Italian frontline, and the Mexican air force took part in battles against Japan in the Philippines and in Taiwan. It was in this period that the military and political union between the Latin American states and the USA commenced, a union that was strengthened by the creation of the Inter-American Defence Union, headquartered in Washington. Of the 50 original members of the UN, created in the spring of 1945, 20 countries came from Latin America.

The war also strengthened the influence of leftist forces, with membership of communist parties increasing from 90,000 to 370,000. In Chile, Ecuador, Costa Rica and Cuba, Communists were included in the government, and they were represented in the parliaments of 12 countries. This

---

[5]   Cit. from: David Close, *Latin American Politics: An Introduction*. University of Toronto Press, 2017. P. 110.

[6]   José Martí, "Our America", in *The Cuba Reader: History, Culture, Politics*. Duke University Press, 2003. PP. 125, 124.

could not be anything but a source of concern to the United States, which put a great deal of energy into its efforts to shift the continent back to the right of the political spectrum. In September 1947, the United States and 20 countries from the continent signed the Inter-American Treaty on Reciprocal Assistance – the Rio Pact. This was supplemented by the creation, at an inter-American conference in Bogota in 1948, of a political union in the shape of the Organization of American States (OAS), whose tasks included countering "the Communist threat".

In April 1947, Communists in Chile were dismissed from the government and purged. This was followed by physical harassment of Communists all over Latin America – thousands were killed or arrested. This oppression led to uprisings and civil wars in Colombia, Paraguay and Costa Rica, which were crushed by the army. As a result of military coups in the late 1940s and early 1950s, dictatorships were established in Peru, Venezuela, Panama, Bolivia and Cuba. In 1954 General Stroessner established a dictatorship in Paraguay that would last for 35 years. At the same time, with support from the USA, a revolution was put down and a dictatorship established in Guatemala. A coup took place in Honduras, and then in Brazil, where the military overthrew Vargas's government. Peron lost power in Argentina in 1955 in a similar scenario. Military coups and dictatorships strengthened the role of the army, and the number of anti-communist measures introduced was off the charts. By the mid-1950s, the only countries that maintained diplomatic relations with the USSR were Mexico, Argentina and Uruguay. The theory of "geographical pre-determination" became popular, according to which the USA was the leader and guiding star for the whole of the Western hemisphere, and all Soviet scheming and plotting was doomed to failure.[7]

This only served to make the Cuban Revolution of 1959 even more surprising; it led to an alliance between Havana and Moscow, and prompted a host of countries from the continent to attempt to choose a socialist path of development. The expansion of the Soviet presence and influence in the Western hemisphere enabled the Latin American countries to expand the field of their political maneuvering, thereby forcing the USA to pay more attention to its "back yard". The situation changed after the break-up of the USSR and the Warsaw Pact, when Latin America lost the role of a strategic "near abroad" for the USA, in its confrontation with an opposing global

---

[7] Alexander Stroganov, *Latinskaya Amerika: Stranitsy istorii XX veka* (*Latin America: Pages from the History of the 20th Century*). Moscow, 2011. PP. 42-46.

bloc. The region descended even further down the list of Washington's foreign policy priorities after 9/11 2001.

Latin-American Spirit

A characteristic feature of the political culture of the Latin American states was "presidentialism", fierce loyalty to a charismatic leader. "The image of the leader, endowed, in the eyes of his followers with an authority founded on the exclusive qualities of his personality, a leader who projected power throughout the whole country, who embodied responsibility and legitimacy; this image had no competitors, and was imbued with ideas of charisma," says Lyudmila Okuneva, a professor at MGIMO. "Charisma, in turn, was an integral part of executive power."[8] The notion – traditional in Latin America, and borrowed from the USA – that the posts of head of state and leader of the government should be combined in one person, served to strengthen the idea of the national leader as a driver of change, an inspirer of reforms, as someone taking the fight to centrifugal trends, regionalism and private interests. The Latin American people were not frightened by strong executive power.

Throughout the whole history of the Latin American states, intellectual discussions about the reasons why they lag behind the USA and Canada, socio-economically, have continued. Various answers have been put forward. In the early 19th century, the blame tended to be placed on the Iberian legacy, with its intolerant Catholicism. By the middle of the same century, more and more people subscribed to the view that a large proportion of the indigenous population were not inclined towards progress. In the first two decades of the 20th century, particularly during the Mexican revolution, there was a widespread belief that extreme poverty and developmental problems stemmed from the unjust distribution of wealth and the fact that the peasants had no land. Later, these problems were explained with ever greater intensity as being connected to imperialist exploitation, primarily "Yankee imperialism".

One of the most oft-quoted Spanish-speaking analysts – Carlos Alberto Montaner – linked the failures of the Latin American model of development to the characteristics of the elite, which bore within it specific traits of the continent's political culture.[9]

....

[8] Lyudmila Okuneva, *Braziliya: osobennosti demokraticheskogo proyekta* (*Brazil: The Peculiarities of a Democratic Project*). Moscow, 2008. P. 255.

[9] Carlos Alberto Montaner, "Culture and the Behavior of Elites in Latin America", in *Culture Matters: How Values Shape Human Progress*, ed. by Lawrence E. Harrison and

The political class was traditionally very corrupt, and the majority of the population endured corruption with patience, considering it to be a natural part of life. The corruption came in extremely diverse forms: from banal bribe-taking to preferential treatment for people close to you, and clientelism – attempts to buy the loyalty of large groups of voters. Ideas about the common good do not have much currency. The military often took upon themselves the role of saviors of the nation from incompetent politicians and politicians who were for sale to the highest bidder, often acting, incidentally, as they would in an occupied country. The caudillo provoked a fair number of civil wars in the 19th century, and created numerous dictatorships in the 20th century. "The *caudillo* is more than a simple dictator who exercises power by force. He is a leader to whom many citizens, and practically the entire power structure, delegate full power of decision and control of the instruments of repression. The result is not only antithetical to democratic development but is also extremely costly in an economic sense, and inevitably causes confusion of public and private property."[10]

Businessmen were less like entrepreneurs believing in risk, than cautious speculators, who preferred to invest in property and receive a stable income. The growing of business from the top of the state led to a monopolization of the economy under the pretext of protecting national interests, and this was accompanied by tax breaks, subsidies and special interest rates for friends. "The fact is, with few exceptions, Latin America has never experienced the modern capitalism combined with political democracy […]."[11]

The Catholic Church, which had lost most of its property during the second half of the 19th century, had a very anti-capitalist stance, condemning the race for profits, consumerism, competition, and more recently "savage neoliberalism" as well.[12]

Intellectuals have always played a particularly large role in Latin America. "Once a writer and an artist has achieved fame, he or she becomes an expert on all subjects, including war in the Balkans, the virtues of in vitro fertilization, and the disaster that is caused by privatizing state enterprises."[13] The non-professional opinions of celebrities formed the basis of the Latin American worldview, and were given pride of place in university courses.

....

Samuel P. Huntington. Basic Books, 2001. PP. 56-64.

[10] Ibid. P. 60.
[11] Ibid. P. 61.
[12] Ibid. PP. 61-62.
[13] Ibid. P. 62.

Moreover, a huge number of Latin American intellectuals hold views which are strongly anti-Western, anti-American and anti-market (making them radically different from the Russian intelligentsia, who are at times more pro-Western than the West itself).

The labor unions are extremely strong, and they speak out against market freedom. In many countries, meanwhile, a category of professional revolutionaries exists, for whom Ernesto Che Guevara remains an icon and an example to strive to follow in the battle against capitalism and the Yankees.[14]

Latin America leads in the crime figures. The continent accounts for 8% of the world's population and 33% of all homicides. Brazil, Argentina and Colombia have turned to their armed forces for domestic security. Military operations in the favelas are commonplace in Brazil, where the army is currently in charge of Rio's police force. Argentina deployed troops in the northern border region to counter illicit trafficking. The logic behind this is that the underfunded and often corrupt police has failed to provide citizen security.[15]

If this is the West, then it is a way too specific kind of West.

And nonetheless it is obvious now that a region whose countries, in the 20th century, were bogged down in the middle or near the bottom of the developing world, and suffered multiple crises and defaults and were constantly in need of Western or Soviet aid, is today being transformed into a dynamic pole for global development.

A Continent on the Rise

Modern-day Latin America incorporates 25 states, and also the remnants of the colonial lands owned by the United Kingdom, France, the Netherlands and the USA. On an area covering some 21 million square km – roughly the same size as the USSR – there now live more than 626 million people. The population is not expected to continue growing rapidly: whereas in the 1960s the birth rate stood at six children per woman, in the 2010s it was around two children per woman, and in Brazil and Chile 1.8.[16] In 18 countries, the state language or official language is Spanish; in Brazil it is Portuguese; in

---

[14] Ibid. P. 64.
[15] Rebecca Bill Chavez, "The Return of Latin America's Military", *The New York Times*, August 14, 2018 <https://www.nytimes.com/2018/08/14/opinion/mattis-latin-americas-military.html>.
[16] "Demography in Latin America. Autumn of the Patriarchs", *The Economist*, June 1, 2013. P. 47.

Haiti it is French; in the Bahamas, Barbados, Guyana, Trinidad and Tobago, Jamaica, and the British colonies, it is English; in Suriname and the other Dutch colonies, it is Dutch. Over 10% of the population still speak indigenous languages.

Latin America is rich with natural and human resources. It has approximately 20% of the planet's natural resources, including oil, gas and other strategic minerals, vast resources of fresh water, extensive areas of agricultural land with favorable climactic conditions for food production. It has superb conditions for agriculture. I recall travelling around Uruguay once with a colleague, a member of parliament from a Russian farm area, who muttered: "And they call that agriculture?" Huge herds graze on endless fields all year round, not requiring any particularly intensive supervision by the few gauchos that could be seen. The way in which the continent was populated, indeed, began like this: a handful of oxen and cows were unloaded from a ship that had sailed up to the coast. Five years later, people could return to the same spot and establish a settlement, for it now boasted a well-fed herd.

Latin America has a voluminous and high-potential market that is well-integrated, with a total GDP of over 5.6 trillion dollars. The region's share of the global population is 8%-9%, and it has 7%-8% of the world's GDP.[17] It is the demand – demand that has been rising rapidly and steadily – of the Asian markets for iron ore, tin, gold and foodstuffs that was seen as among the leading reasons for the Latin American economic miracle.[18] 90% of the roses sold in Russia and half of the bananas come from Ecuador. At the same time, industrial production is growing in Latin America too. By way of example, until recently, oil accounted for 75% of Mexican exports, but now industrial goods account for the same percentage, i.e. three quarters of the country's exports.[19]

"The distribution of income in the Latin America has improved in the last decade," observes Luis Lopez-Calva from the World Bank. "This has resulted in an impressive movement of people out of poverty, which represents a positive trend." There is a growing middle class, which, by Latin American standards, means those who earn 10 to 50 dollars a day. In 2011, the number

---

[17] Ye. M. Astakhov, "Perspektivy razvitiya Latinskoy Ameriki i yeye mesto v budushchem miroustroystve" ("Prospects for the Development of Latin America and Its Place in the Future World Order"), *Vestnik MGIMO-Universiteta* (*MGIMO-University Bulletin*), Issue 4 (13), 2010. P. 37.

[18] Simon Romero, "Latin American Economies Find a Way to Thrive with Resources", *The International Herald Tribune*, July 2, 2010. PP. 1, 16.

[19] Shannon K. O'Neil, "Mexico. Viva las Reformas", *Foreign Affairs*, January/February 2014. P. 11.

of people in the middle class rose above the number categorized as poor, but still does not amount to a third of the population.[20]

There is serious inequality between the regions, and even inside each of the countries. Mexico's industrial state of Nuevo Leon, for example, which is adjacent to the US border, has a standard of living similar to that of South Korea, while the standard of living in Mexico's southern states is like that of Honduras.[21]

The Left Turn and *Indigenista*

A leading left-wing sociologist from Yale University, Immanuel Wallerstein, observed in 2010, with a clear sense of satisfaction: "Latin America has been the success story of the world left in the first decade of the 21st century. [...] The first and most widely noticed way is that left or left-of-center parties have won a remarkable series of elections during the decade. And collectively, Latin America governments have established for the first time a significant degree of distance from the United States. Latin America has become a relatively autonomous geopolitical force. Moreover, movements of the indigenous populations of Latin America have asserted themselves politically almost everywhere and have demanded the right to organize their political and social lives autonomously."[22]

The *indigenista* movement loudly announced itself for the first time in 1994, in the Mexican state of Chiapas. It then spread throughout the whole continent, forming a unified Latin American network with key hubs in Bolivia, Ecuador, Guatemala and Mexico. Reforms were introduced in all the countries of Latin America, aimed at taking ethnic diversity into account: amendments appeared in the constitutions everywhere, acknowledging the rights of indigenous peoples; laws were adopted in support of education in people's native languages, and to ensure that ethnic minorities were represented in the institutions of power. Evo Morales and Ollanta Humala, both of indigenous origin, were elected presidents of Bolivia (in 2006) and Peru (in 2011), respectively.[23]

---

[20] Luis F. Lopez-Calva, "A New Economic Framework to Analyse the Middle Classes in Latin America", *Poverty in Focus. On the Middle Class*, Issue 26, October 2013. PP. 16, 15.

[21] "Development in Mexico. Of Cars and Carts", *The Economist*, September 19, 2015. P. 20.

[22] Immanuel Wallerstein, "Latin America's Leftist Divide", *The International Herald Tribune*, August 18, 2010. P. 6.

[23] Deborah J. Yashar, "Does Race Matter in Latin America? How Racial and Ethnic Identities

The *indigenista* movement, with its combination of elements of socialism and a return to the people's roots, manifested itself not only in the countries of the distinctly anti-American "Bolivarian group", or the Bolivian alternative for Latin America, which included the Venezuela of the late Hugo Chavez and his successor Maduro, Cuba under the Castro brothers, the Nicaragua of Daniel Ortega, the head of the Sandinistas, who has returned to power, the Ecuador of Rafael Correa, and the Bolivia of Evo Morales. A shift to the left was also characteristic, to a large extent, of such grandees of the continent as Brazil under the workers' party of Lula da Silva and his successor Dilma Rousseff, and the Argentina of Cristina Fernandez (Kirchner).

Left-wing Latin American leaders tend to be seen as dictators, who suppress freedom inside their countries and run the economy into the ground. The leaders of Venezuela have suffered particularly from this for a long time; the country had the most pro-American politics on the continent (second only to Colombia), but then – under Hugo Chavez, who proclaimed a "Bolivarian revolution" – became Washington's biggest headache, overtaking even Cuba in that regard. "The Bolivarian revolution has promoted the destruction of democracy and has set afoot an authoritarian socialist movement throughout Latin America that despises the market economy, liberal democracy and the political, and U.S. political and cultural hegemony."[24] Washington attempted numerous times to effect regime change in Venezuela, but without success (some American researchers categorically deny this, it should be said).[25] I shall, however, quote an article written by Mark Weisbrot, which was printed in *The International Herald Tribune* after Chavez's re-election as President of Venezuela in the autumn of 2012: "Since the Chávez government got control over the national oil industry, poverty has been cut by half, and extreme poverty by 70 percent. College enrollment has more than doubled, millions of people have access to health care for the first time and the number of people eligible for public pensions has quadrupled. So it should not be surprising that most Venezuelans would reelect a president who has improved their living standards. That's what has happened with all of the leftist governments that now govern most of South America. This is despite the fact that they, like Chávez, have most of their countries'

Shape the Region's Politics", *Foreign Affairs*, March/April 2015. P. 33.

[24] Luis Fleischman, *Latin America in the Post-Chávez Era: The Security Threat to the United States*. Washington: Potomac Books, Inc., 2013. P. 212.

[25] Javier Corrales and Carlos A. Romero, *U. S.-Venezuela Relations Since the 1990s*. Abingdon, 2013. P. 5.

media against them, and their opposition has most of the wealth and income of their respective countries."[26] In the first decade of the 21st century, over 70 million people in Latin America broke out of the poverty trap.[27]

Everywhere, though – irrespective of the ideological inclinations of the ruling establishment – government policy was increasingly framed by the phraseology of independence, by criticism of "imperialism", "global capitalism" and even globalization, from which the countries of Latin America can be said to have gained more, objectively, than almost anyone else.

It is interesting that the *indigenista* movements were involved in a confrontation not only with conservative governments, as in Mexico, Colombia and Peru, but also with regimes which ostensibly appeared to express their interests directly, such as those in Brazil, Venezuela or even in Bolivia, and also in Ecuador, where the left-wing government of Rafael Correa came to power with the support of the *indigenistas* at the outset, after proclaiming the second and final liberation of Latin America. As it turns out, the *indigenistas* are even more radical than the left-wing regimes.

A subject that unified the whole of Latin America is the story of the founder of WikiLeaks, Julian Assange, who lived in the embassy of Ecuador, where he was given refuge, but whose use of the embassy was opposed by the British government. London's stance was unilaterally condemned not only by the Bolivarian alliance, but also by the entire Union of South American Nations, UNASUR (the foreign ministers of the member states needed only eight minutes to come to that decision).[28] An even more shocking effect was created by the revelations made by Edward Snowden, not least with regard to the fact that the USA had been spying on heads of state, particularly in Brazil. The decision taken by France and Portugal to close its airspace to the airplane of the president of Bolivia, Evo Morales, because they suspected that Snowden was on board, sent shockwaves right across Latin America. An emergency summit was once again convened for the 12 countries of the Union of South American Nations, which condemned the European governments in sharp tones as American puppets.[29]

---

[26] Mark Weisbrot, "Why Chavez Was Re-elected", *The International Herald Tribune*, October 10, 2012. P. 8.

[27] Shannon K. O'Neil, "Latin America's Populist Hangover. What to Do When the People's Party Ends", *Foreign Affairs*, November/December 2016. P. 31.

[28] Pavel Tarasenko, "Dzhulian Assanzh ob"yedinil Yuzhnuyu Ameriku" ("Julian Assange has United South America"), *Kommersant (The Businessman)*, August 21, 2012 <https://www.kommersant.ru/doc/2005466>.

[29] Mariya Yefimova and Pavel Tarasenko, "Samolet prezidenta Bolivii zaderzhali iz-za Edvarda

The sense of self-respect in Latin America was enhanced after Jorge Mario Bergoglio was elected as Pope in March 2013. He assumed the name of Francis I and was the first non-European to be Pope; he is the most influential Argentine in the world, and the first Jesuit pope. Latin America is the most Catholic continent of all: 72% of the population are Catholics (this figure stood at 90% in 1910, admittedly).[30] It is no accident, therefore, that the choice fell on a man who represents a continent that has 40% of all the Catholics on the planet, rather than on someone from a Europe that is becoming ever more atheist. This was also a response to the increased influence in recent years of protestant denominations (mainly due to scandals related to paedophile priests and bans on abortion within the Catholic Church). The country with the largest population of Roman Catholics – 123 million believers – is Brazil, and it is no coincidence that Pope Francis chose that country for his first pastoral visit in July 2013.[31]

A Shift to the Right

In recent years, the turn to the left was replaced by an obvious tilt to the right.

It is worth noting that the failures of the left-wing governments were connected not only with their own mistakes, but also with the targeted resistance to them on the part of Washington – whether that be efforts to discredit them, economic sanctions, or support for the opposition. Argentina was cut off from international capital markets, Venezuela was subjected to rounds of sanctions and, like Brazil, came up against targeted efforts to bring about a change of their governments.

Largely in order to hinder the drift to the left, George W. Bush proposed that a Free Trade Area of the Americas (FTAA, or ALCA in Spanish) should be created, but the initiative was torpedoed by Brazil and Argentina. Obama proposed a less ambitious project: with his direct support, an organization was created in 2012 with four states that had pro-American and pro-centrist governments: Mexico, Colombia, Peru and Chile, who formed the Pacific Alliance, members of which had free trade agreements with the USA and with each other.[32]

....
Snoudena" ("The Bolivian President's Plane was Detained Because of Edward Snowden"), *Kommersant* (*The Businessman*), July 4, 2013 <https://www.kommersant.ru/doc/2225562>.

[30] "A Pope for the Poor", *Time*, July 29, 2013. PP. 14-17.

[31] "Religion in Brazil. Earthly Concerns", *The Economist*, July 20. 2013. PP. 41-42.

[32] Vladimir Sudarev, "Vashington v poiskakh novykh podkhodov k Latinskoy Amerike"

In Argentina in 2015, the leader of the center-right Cambiemos ("let's change") bloc and former president of the football club Boca Juniors, Mauricio Macri, defeated Kirchner's anointed successor, Daniel Scioli, promising to steer the country down a more market-oriented path. Macri abolished restrictions on the movement of capital, took aim at the Central Bank in the battle against inflation, and held talks with international creditors, enabling the country to return to the international credit market.[33]

In Bolivia, Morales lost a referendum in February 2016, in which the people were asked to vote on whether or not to abolish restrictions on the number of terms of office that the president could have.

Raphael Correa announced that he did not intend to stand for re-election in Ecuador in 2017, and in May of that year he was replaced by the candidate he had put forward, Lenin Moreno, who was considered a less radical politician.[34] It was Moreno who took the decision to deliver Julian Assange to the British authorities in April 2019, under American pressure.

In June 2016, a 77-year-old banker named Pedro Pablo Kuchinsky became president of Peru, finishing just ahead of Keiko Fujimori, the daughter of the former populist president, in the polls.

In August 2016, the Senate dismissed Dilma Rousseff from her post as President of Brazil through the impeachment procedure. The new president was Michel Temer, representing the centrist Party of the Brazilian Democratic Movement. And at the end of 2018, right-wing conservative politician Jair Bolsonaro was elected president, as will be discussed below.

The left-wing, pro-American president Michelle Bachelet, whose second term of office as president of Chile ended in March 2018, left his compatriots disappointed. The economy stagnated, reforms to education, the tax system and employment laws failed to bear fruit, and her son was embroiled in corruption scandals. By the end of her presidency, Bachelet's popularity rating stood at 32%.[35] Thus, Sebasian Pinera Echenique made a comeback in March 2018.

In Colombia in June 2018, the election was won by the 42-year-old leader of the right party Democratic Center Ivan Duque. A man with a Russian

---

("Washington in Search of New Approaches to Latin America"), *Mezhdunarodnaya zhizn'* (*International Life*), March 2016. PP. 47-54.

[33] Ian Bremmer, "Argentina's Mauricio Macri on the Challenge of Change", *Time*, October 31, 2016. P. 8.

[34] "Ecuador. Breaking Glas", *The Economist*, August 12, 2017. P. 36.

[35] "Chile. Term Ending", *The Economist*, August 12, 2016. P. 36.

name, elite upbringing and pro-American credentials, he is close to the former President Alvaro Uribe.³⁶

Chavism maintained its strong position in Venezuela, but is experiencing increasingly serious difficulties. In March 2015, Obama made the assertion (though he soon disowned it) that Venezuela was a threat to the USA's national security. In the parliamentary elections, the opposition, backed by the USA, won a majority, and street protests were held by those opposed to President Maduro. The government believed that the protests were to a huge extent organized by Washington. As they were portrayed by the Venezuelan opposition groups and the American media, the protests reflect "the conviction that the 21ˢᵗ-century socialism begun by former President Hugo Chavez has failed and has left the country in ruins. And there are other, darker new elements involved – police brutality, mass detentions and the use of paramilitary groups armed by the government to carry out the dirty work the military doesn't want to handle: murdering people. [...] At long last, liberty and democracy have become an existential struggle, a matter of life and death."³⁷

Real opposition candidates were not admitted to the presidential elections held in May 2018, and Maduro easily won. The United States, the EU, and 15 Latin American countries declared non-recognition of the vote and threatened new sanctions that could lead to a drop in oil production by more than half. Opponents of the government started yet another round of strikes and protests.³⁸

On 23ʳᵈ January 2019, National Assembly interim speaker Juan Guaido declared himself president of Venezuela, and within several hours was recognized as such by Donald Trump. After that, about 50 American allies (including half of the Latin American allies) also recognized Guaido as the legitimate Venezuelan leader. Maduro refused to yield the presidency, and with support from Russia, China, India, Cuba and other countries fought

---

36   Yekaterina Mareyeva, "Kolumbiya progolosovala protiv Venesuely" ("Colombia Voted Against Venezuela"), *Kommersant* (*The Businessman*), Issue 104, June 19, 2018 <https://www.kommersant.ru/doc/3661928>; Irina Akimushkina, "Novyy prezident Kolumbii – predstavitel' elity s russkim imenem" ("The New President of Colombia is a Representative of the Elite with a Russian Name"), *Nezavisimaya Gazeta* (*Independent Newspaper*), July 31, 2018 <http://www.ng.ru/vision/2018-07-31/6_7278_view.html>; Rebecca Bill Chavez, "The Return of Latin America's Military", *The New York Times*, August 14, 2018 <https://www.nytimes.com/2018/08/14/opinion/mattis-latin-americas-military.html>.

37   Hugo Prieto, "Chaos Looms Over Venezuela", *The New York Times*, May 3, 2017. P. A27(L).

38   Gideon Long, "Venezuela Devalues Currency by 95% in Effort to Stave off Collapse", *The Financial Times*, August 21, 2018. P. 1.

back against "the American puppet". The USA retaliated with tough sanctions against oil companies and Venezuela's financial institutions of, ruining its economy. At the same time, the USA brought up the possibility of using force for a regime change not only in Venezuela but in Cuba and Nicaragua as well. Not yet.

However, even Cuba is now changing. In April 2018, Raúl Castro handed the presidency to Miguel Díaz-Canel, and started working on the new constitution. The text was approved by the National Assembly on 22nd July. The constitution reorganized the national and local governments, and legalized private property and same-sex marriage. A clause on Cuba's progress towards a communist society has been dropped. Yet the Communist Party's monopoly on power and the government's domination of the economy remain in place.[39]

As Shannon O'Neil of the Council on Foreign Affairs has remarked, not without some satisfaction, "even as populists are surging throughout the rest of the world, such voices have fallen conspicuously silent in Latin America. The region's grandiose strongmen, with their cults of personality, have largely faded away."[40]

The more right-wing politicians also proved to be fairly ineffective, however. Support for Temer's government in Brazil has melted away dramatically.

Peña Nieto's government in Mexico was extremely unpopular, and Trump's belligerent rhetoric and his promises to punish the country economically and, to all intents and purposes, bury NAFTA, are making Mexico far from the most attractive country for investment at a time when its economy is limping as well.[41]

The election campaign of 2018 became extremely stormy. In its course, more than 100 politicians were killed in Mexico, 46 of them real or potential candidates. The victory was won by the person who challenged the system – the leader of the left coalition: "Together we will make history," said Andres Manuel Lopez Obrador. The familiar accusations of the candidate about his relations with Moscow, which were made from the US Senate, did not help. Obrador received 53.5% of the votes in the first round,

---

[39] "Cuba's New Constitution. Less than Meets the Eye", *The Economist*, July 28, 2018. PP. 36-37.

[40] Shannon K. O'Neil, "Latin America's Populist Hangover: What to Do When the People's Party Ends", *Foreign Affairs*, November/December 2016. P. 31.

[41] Jude Webber, "Mexico's Multiplying Problems Threaten to Undermine NAFTA Talks", *The Financial Times*, May 9, 2017. P. 4.

while the center-right Ricardo Anaya received 22.6%, and the candidate from the ruling Institutional Revolutionary Party, ex-foreign minister Jose Antonio Mida – 15.8%.[42]

Macri's market reforms have not brought tangible results in Argentina, and economic growth has not begun. Inflation amounted to 40% in 2016, and stayed at the level of 26% in 2017 and 30% in 2018. The refinancing rate amounted to 26.25%, which made state bonds very attractive for wealthy speculators, who returned to Argentina feeling amicable, but it did not allow investment in the real economy to appear. The protest movements were not long in coming.[43]

The destinies of governments in Latin America depend to a large extent on the economic situation. Six years of stagnation, linked to a fall in prices of raw materials, went a long way towards facilitating the defeats of the left-wing governments. The slow economic recovery, however – 1% in 2016 and a little more than that in 2017-2019 is now challenging the right-wing governments also.[44]

At the same time, the swing to the right has already gained institutional implementation and consolidation. Until recently, the Union of South American Nations (UNASUR), established on a wave of leftist revival through the efforts of Lula da Silva, Ugo Chavez and Evo Morales, played a prominent role among many regional organizations. UNASUR has ceased to exist, but in March 2019 the right-leaning leaders of Chile, Colombia, Brazil, Argentina, Paraguay, Peru and Guyana established instead the Forum for the Progress and Development of South America (FPDSA). Guaido was invited to join as well.[45]

---

[42] Yekaterina Mareyeva, "Latinskaya Amerika mozhet stat' chut' boleye krasnoy" ("Latin America May Become a Little More Red"), *Kommersant* (*The Businessman*), Issue 109, June 26, 2018 <https://www.kommersant.ru/doc/3668741>; Yekaterina Mareyeva, "Meksika nabrala golosov na bor'bu s korruptsiyey" ("Mexico Voted to Fight Corruption"), *Kommersant* (*The Businessman*), Issue 114, July 3, 2018 <https://www.kommersant.ru/doc/3675467>.

[43] Benedict Mander, "Macri to Tout Reforms at Trump Summit", *The Financial Times*, April 27, 2017. P. 4; "Argentina's Beef Export. Bull Market", *The Economist*, August 4, 2018. P. 37.

[44] Michael Reid, "Red Retreat. South Americans Will Turn Away from the Left", *The Economist: The World in 2017*. P. 55.

[45] Emil' Dabagyan, "V Latinskoy Amerike rodilsya novyy regional'nyy blok" ("A New Regional Organization has Sprung Up in Latin America"), *Nezavisimaya Gazeta* (*Independent Newspaper*), 25 March 2019 <https://yandex.ru/turbo/ng.ru/s/vision/2019-03-24/6_7538_view.html>.

The South-Western Pole

The continent is undoubtedly becoming one of the poles of the contemporary and future global system. The identity of Latin American civilization is not yet very well expressed, however. "Subjectively, Latin Americans themselves are divided in their self-identification," observed Huntington. "Some say, 'Yes, we are part of the West.' Others claim, 'No, we have our own unique culture,' and a large literature by Latin and North Americans elaborates their cultural differences."[46] In Brazil, the multiplicity of identities is plain to see. Many representatives of the elite consider the country to be a Western country. Almost half the population describes itself as "black", or "not White". "Brazilians think of themselves less as Latin Americans and more as Brazilians: a hodgepodge of African, European, Middle Eastern, Asian, and indigenous cultures."[47] The well-known Brazilian sociologist and philosopher Gilberto Freyre observed, in the 1960s: Some Brazilians themselves believe that their culture is characterized by a particular form of civilization. They feel that this civilization [...] is able to project onto other continents the values which were received as a result of the adaptation of standards from contemporary civilization to other, more backward regions, without damaging the cultures and customs of the local population.[48]

The typical Argentinian, nowadays, is known as a *criollo*. In terms of identity, however, one is struck by the clear duality: in the internal regions, the Spanish and indigenous culture prevails, while the capital is more cosmopolitan, similar to European culture. In Mexico, they talk of *Mexico profundo* – the part of society that feels a strong sense of being the cultural heir to the Mesoamerican civilization. And that does not just mean the 7 million people who speak the languages of the Native Americans, but also the tens of millions of *mestizo*, for whom family and community values, associated among other things with small business and farming, are very important.[49]

As it becomes a civilization, Latin America has not yet completed the task of becoming aware that it has this quality. Latin America is starting to

---

[46] Samuel P. Huntington, *The Clash of Civilizations and the Remaking of World Order*. Simon & Schuster, 1996. P. 46.

[47] Julia E. Sweig, "A New Global Player: Brazil's Far-Flung Agenda", *Foreign Affairs*, November/December 2010. PP. 174, 182.

[48] Gilberto Freyre, *Brazil*. Washington, 1993. P. 23.

[49] "Development in Mexico. Of Cars and Carts", *The Economist*, September 19, 2015. P. 21.

look less and less like an area in which the USA has the prevailing influence. "The United States is no longer the only go-to power for resolving crises, providing security, or setting the development agenda for Latin America," observed the American expert Julia Sweig in 2010.[50] In many countries, people are unable to forgive the United States for their support for dictatorial regimes, which continued for decades. People did not like their overly harsh stance in relation to Cuba, which, outside the USA, no-one in the Western hemisphere considers to be a black sheep. People do not like the attempts inspired from Washington to overthrow local regimes. In many countries, the expansion of the USA's military presence at bases in Colombia provokes resentment. People do not like the brutal obstructions that are put up in the path of migration flows into the United States. America's global "war on terror" was hardly supported, nor did the results of the implementation of neoliberal economic recipes.

The USA also had a growing list of claims against Latin America, the first of which was the shift to the left. Its objections are not limited to the left-wing, populist regimes, however. As far as Brazil is concerned, the Americans feel discomfort with "a rising power in their extended neighborhood."[51] On the border between the USA and Mexico, not only is a wall being built, but for many years now a genuine war has been fought between armies of Mexican drug cartels, on the one hand, and the armed forces and police of two countries, on the other.

The coming to power of Barack Obama's administration gave rise to high hopes. As Obama quickly understood, however, obstacles to the path of effective diplomacy in the Western hemisphere should be sought not in "bad left" countries, but far closer, at home. These were the National Rifle Association, the anti-Castro Cuban lobby, the agricultural industry, anti-Latino jingoism and also the State Department and the Department of Commerce.[52]

It was the complete isolation of the USA in relation to Cuba, which became a stumbling-block in Washington's relationships with all countries of the Western hemisphere, that forced Obama, at the end of 2014, to announce that diplomatic relations with Cuba had been restored. He emphasized,

---

[50] Julia E. Sweig, "A New Global Player: Brazil's Far-Flung Agenda", *Foreign Affairs*, November/December 2010. P. 182.

[51] Julia Sweig and Matias Spektor, "Mr. Obama, Meet the New Brazil", *The International Herald Tribune*, March 19-20, 2011. P. 6.

[52] Greg Grandin, "Playing Catch-Up in Latin America", *The International Herald Tribune*, March 19-20, 2011. P. 6.

admittedly, that the United States would not step back from its efforts to undermine the Cuban regime.

At the end of September 2017, the Trump administration decided to call home 60% of its diplomatic staff in Havana due to concerns over their health, in connection with some mysterious "acoustic attacks", and also to stop issuing entry visas to the USA to Cuban citizens. The State Department called on Americans to refrain from travelling to Cuba.[53]

Trump has done significant damage to relations with Mexico. "The Mexicans think we are domineering and imperialist, and we think they are corrupt," an American expert put it, explaining the essence of the dispute.[54] Trump declared NAFTA to be "the worst trade deal in history" and announced that Mexico is "killing us economically". He called Mexican immigrants "criminals" and "rapists", who steal jobs from Americans and pose a threat to their lives. He has spoken in favor of the mass deportation of "criminal aliens", and demanded that the Mexican government pay for the construction of a wall along the USA's southern border.[55]

"The United States seems to continue to apply toward its Latin American 'backyard' (itself a condescending term) the same attitude it severely denounced when it was applied by European powers to their former African colonies," remarks Dominique Moïsi. "Although U.S. interventions are now usually indirect, America remains both a vital balancer and a resented source of outside interference throughout Latin America."[56] The economies of Central America and the Caribbean are effectively a continuation of the American economy. America has invested much more money in the region than China or any other country. The USA has strong channels of influence on internal processes in Latin American countries and a long history of *coups d'états* that were conceived in Washington. Cristina Kirchner once explained why there could never be a coup d'etat in the USA itself: because there is no American embassy there.

---

[53] Yevgeniy Bay, "Amerika razorvala otnosheniya s kubintsami" ("America has Torn up Its Relations with the Cubans"), *Kommersant* (*The Businessman*), October 2, 2017 <https://www.kommersant.ru/doc/3427451>.

[54] Cit. from: Azam Ahmed and Damien Cave, "'El Chapo' Guzmán's Escape in Mexico Adds to Strains with U.S.", *The New York Times*, July 14, 2016 <https://www.nytimes.com/2015/07/15/world/americas/mexico-hunts-joaquin-chapo-guzman-united-states-offer-help.html>.

[55] Shannon O'Neil, "The Mexican Standoff. Trump and the Art of the Workaround", *Foreign Affairs*, September/October 2017. PP. 43-44.

[56] Dominique Moïsi, *The Geopolitics of Emotion: How Cultures of Fear, Humiliation and Hope are Reshaping the World*. Random House, 2009.

The USA retains a military presence in a host of countries, and keeps up intense military and technical contact with most of them. The Latin American sphere of vitally important interests is under the patronage of the US Southern Command (SOUTHCOM), headquartered in Miami. There are military bases in Cuba (Guantánamo) and in Honduras. A real stronghold is Colombia, where the USA has several military bases. The US Fourth Fleet has full control over the waters of the western hemisphere. The emergence of new players in the region – China, India, Russia, even the EU – causes strong resentment in Washington. Yet the reserves of strength of American influence are still huge.

The interests of the Latin American countries are increasingly extending beyond the limits of the Western hemisphere, and China is strengthening its position as a rising geo-economic player in the region. Unlike the USA, China is not able to have a military and strategic projection on the continent, and the increase in Chinese influence is causing unrest among American strategists. As Zbigniew Brzezinski observed, "This not to suggest that China would seek to dominate this region, but it obviously could benefit from receding American regional power, by helping more overtly anti-American governments in their economic development."[57] An example is Beijing's plan to invest $50 billion in the construction of a canal between the Atlantic Ocean and the Pacific Ocean, via Nicaragua.

India is taking on the role of a major player in the region, buying up more and more oil, soybeans and copper. India is becoming "the next China" as a market for Latin American raw materials, and India's industrial exports to the region are also growing. Indian IT firms have hired tens of thousands of programmers in Latin American countries. The Reliance Industries Corporation receives a quarter of its oil from Latin America. ONGC Videsh has invested $2.2 billion in oil extraction in Venezuela. Jindal is developing one of the world's biggest sources of iron ore, and building a steel smelting plant there. India is displaying interest in the experiences of Latin American companies in urbanization, developing the food industry, and the banking sector.[58]

Latin America is returning to the orbit of Russian foreign policy. Its interest in doing so now is probably a pragmatic and economic one rather than anything else.

---

[57] Zbigniew Brzezinski, *Strategic Vision: America and the Crisis of Global Power*. Basic Books, 2013. PP. 108-109.

[58] Jude Webber, "Subcontinent Prepares to Be Next China", *The Financial Times*, April 26, 2011. P. 4.

In Mexico, contracts are being concluded for the supply of turbines for power stations. Russian specialists are taking part in the development of the Mexican space program. Russia is actively collaborating with Argentina in the field of hydroelectric energy, and Rosatom is supplying isotope production and preparing to build a nuclear power plant. In Venezuela, Russian companies are involved in the development of the Khunin-6 oilfield and a host of other energy projects. Helicopters and Lada automobiles are being supplied to Peru. Russia is sending equipment for the construction of the power station on the rivers Toachi and Pilaton in Ecuador. Russia's biggest partners on the continent are Brazil and Argentina.[59]

In the arms and ammunitions markets in Latin America, Russia has many serious competitors: not just the USA, but also France, and China, which is offering military equipment and armaments modelled on the Russian ones, but at a more advantageous price.

In July 2014, Putin went on a tour of Latin America, visiting Cuba, Nicaragua and Argentina, and then made an official visit to Brazil, staying in Rio de Janeiro, Brasilia and Fortaleza. The president of Russia attended a BRICS Summit, at the end of which the Fortaleza declaration and the Fortaleza action plan were adopted. Putin held bilateral meetings not only with his colleagues in the BRICS countries, but also with Latin American leaders: the presidents of Venezuela, Bolivia, Uruguay, and on the sidelines of the summit with the presidents of Peru, Chile, and Colombia. Putin watched the final of the football World Cup, following which Russia was handed the baton for the hosting of the tournament in 2018. In some countries of Latin America, the channel RT is available in Spanish.

Obviously, Russia is suspected of proceeding with geopolitical games. The recent demonstrations of the Russian flag in Cuba, Venezuela and Nicaragua were not greeted with a universally positive response by the Latin American establishment, let alone by Washington. There is a degree of caution in relation to supplies of Russian arms to Venezuela and its support for the Maduro government. "The only Russian plea that provokes a response in the region is the plea to put an end to American uni-polarity," writes Joao Fabio Bertoni of Brazil's Maringa University.[60]

---

[59] Pavel Tarasenko, "Rossiya vnedryayetsya v Latinskuyu Ameriku" ("Russia is Laying Down Roots in Latin America"), *Kommersant* (*The Businessman*), June 13, 2013 <https://www.kommersant.ru/doc/2210364>.

[60] Cit. from: Andrey Davydenko, "ZH. F. Berton'ya: Konets amerikanskoy gegemonii v Yuzhnoy Amerike?" ("Joao Fabio Bertonha: The End of American Hegemony in South America?"), *Mezhdunarodnaya zhizn'* (*International Life*), May 2011. PP. 150-159.

Latin Americans are against unilateral and forceful methods of ensuring security, and against the activation of existing military blocs or the creation of new ones. They have raised the matter of securing greater representation on the Security Council of the United Nations. The countries have not yet been able to reach an agreement amongst themselves on this matter. Brazil's ambitions for a place on the Security Council are challenged by Mexico and Argentina, which are in favor of the region being represented on a rotating basis.

The European Union has fairly good relations with the Latin American states. A serious advantage Europe has is its cultural proximity. "In various countries in the region, approximately 30 million Italians, 25 million Spaniards, around 15 million Germans, and 50 million Portuguese, not to mention immigrants from Poland, Scandinavia and Russia, have become assimilated and started to think in a Brazilian way or, let's say, in an Argentinian way."[61] A mechanism is in place for holding summits between the European Union and CELAC, which take place once every two years. Relations with the Pacific Alliance are developing successfully: the EU has free trade agreements with all four of its members.[62]

Latin America is not greatly affected by the militarization trend. The average level of defence spending on the continent has in fact fallen slightly: from 1.42% of their combined GDP in 1999 to 1.35% in 2008 and 1.18% in 2018. At the same time, only 5 countries – Brazil, Colombia, Mexico, Chile and Argentina – account for nearly 90% of military spending on the continent. Venezuela's military spending is not precisely known, but it has the fourth largest army (after Brazil, Colombia and Mexico) on the continent, comprising 123,000 soldiers.[63] In March 2009, the 12 defence ministers of the South American Defence Council met for the first time in Santiago. The Council was created to maintain dialogue and ensure coordination in matters of security on the continent. For the time being, however, military cooperation is still in its initial phase.[64]

So, where is Latin America going? Many experts and politicians on the continent would give you the following response: wherever Brazil is going.

....

[61] Cit. from: Ibid.

[62] "Latin American Integration. Past and Future", *The Economist*, February 2, 2013. P. 40.

[63] *The Military Balance 2019: The Annual Assessment of Global Military Capabilities and Defence Economics*. London: IISS, 2019. P. 380, 384.

[64] *The Military Balance 2010: An Annual Assessment of Global Military Capabilities and Defence Economies*. London: IISS, 2010. P. 59.

The Brazilian Model

Brazil is the largest country in Latin America (8.5 million km², the fifth largest country in the world). Its geographical position, as Robert Kaplan emphasizes, "offers less of a comparative advantage. It lies isolated in South America, geographically removed from other landmasses."[65]

The transformation of Brazil not only into an economic, political and civilizational leader in Latin America, but also into one of the global leaders, is one of the most interesting trends in the planet's development in the 21st century. A country which, for 300 years, lived under colonial rule, and then, for more than a century, demonstrated mediocre indicators under weak democratic or insolvent authoritarian governments, has acquired dynamism and self-confidence.

The territory of modern Brazil became Portuguese… before its discovery. After Columbus's first voyage, Spain and Portugal preferred to separate their domains in the Western hemisphere. The demarcation line established by the Treaty of Tordesillas of 1494 (in force until 1777) was drawn across both poles and would appear to cut South America from North to South. Land to the East of it departed to Portugal, to the West – Spain.

The indigenous population had better luck than in those parts of the New World invaded by the Spanish or the British. Unlike the Spanish, who came up against organized resistance by the developed civilizations of the Aztecs and Incas, the Portuguese in Brazil only encountered scattered Tupi-Guarani tribes, who had nothing that could have been expropriated from them, and managed to conquer the territory without undue bloodshed.

By contrast with the British, who did not see the indigenous Americans or blacks as people worthy of being converted to Christianity, or, to an even lesser extent, worthy of marrying them, according to the Brazilian sociologist and historian Sergio Buarque de Holanda, "[t]he complete, or nearly complete, absence of any racial pride – or at least the obstinate and uncompromising pride characteristic of northern countries – among the Portuguese is another, quite typical, aspect of the social adaptability of the Portuguese This side of their character, which approximates that of other nations of Latin origin and, even more, of Muslims of Africa, is explained to a large extent simply by their being Portuguese and also by the fact that

---

[65] Robert D. Kaplan, *The Revenge of Geography: What the Map Tells Us About Coming Conflicts and the Battle Against Fate*. Random House, 2013. P. 31.

they were already a mixed people at the time of Brazil's discovery."⁶⁶ Indeed, Portugal's policy with regard to the natives was reminiscent of the country's approach to the Moors within the country before the 15th century, when the Moors were considered equal to whites in all civil acts, including marriages. In Brazil too. However, the indigenous population fell dramatically as a result of diseases and the capturing of territory by the colonialists – from 5 million in the early 16th century, when the Portuguese conquest began, to 300,000 today.⁶⁷

The Catholic ideal, in the form in which it was brought to Latin America by Portuguese missionaries, implied the Christianization of the local population and did not present any obstacle to mixed marriages between Portuguese colonialists and women from the indigenous population. Portuguese Catholicism proved to be so pliant that in the Brazilian churches, even the portraits of the saints and the Virgin Mary herself took on a swarthy skin tone. As the Russian expert on Latin America, Boris Martynov, emphasizes: "The special synergy between races, civilizations and cultures which occurred in Brazil in the 15th to 17th centuries, must, by the start of the next century, have created a new characteristic that was already fundamentally different. Having been absorbed into the local milieu, among the local peoples, having adopted their traditions, customs and culture as their own, the Portuguese, by that time, could no longer avoid turning into Brazilians." The vast expanses of Brazil were discovered not by the Portuguese, but by the local people born there, who had no need to resort to large-scale violence. "In this sense, the 'conquering' of Brazil by the Portuguese would be more aptly dubbed a 'mastering', and in this, there was much in common with the process of mastering Siberia and the Far East in the 16th to the 18th centuries."⁶⁸

Brazil's culture and her demographic make-up were defined by a synthesis of European, African and indigenous American (Tupi e Tapuia, Arawak, Carib) components. Brazilian folklore combines themes from indigenous American and African fairytales, and legends about earliest explorers – *bandeirantes*. The country's music was strongly influenced by African melodies, and Brazilian songs – mod – are derived from Portuguese ones. To what

....

⁶⁶ Sergio Buarque de Holanda, *Roots of Brazil*. University of Notre Dame Press, 2012. P. 23.

⁶⁷ Michael Palin, *Brazil*. London, 2013. P. 4.

⁶⁸ Boris Martynov, *Braziliya – gigant v globaliziruyushchemsya mire* (*Brazil – a Giant in a Globalizing World*). Moscow, 2008. PP. 19, 17.

other culture, though, can one link the colorful carnivals, during which a king of samba is elected?

In 2012, Brazil's population passed the 200 million mark, making it the fifth most-populated country in the world. 55% of the population are Europeans and their descendants, 38% are Metis and Mulatto, 6% are black, 1% are Japanese, Arabs and indigenous Americans. The Brazilian variant of the Portuguese language has three dialects: northern, north-eastern and southern. Among the Metis and the indigenous Americans, a language known as lingua geral is also spoken. Some black Brazilians also speak the African languages of Kimbundu and Yoruba. 90% of those with a religious belief are Catholics, while the rest are Protestants or spiritualists.

Several cycles can be identified in Brazil's economic history. The first was associated with the exporting to Europe of red wood (pau brasil), from whence the country took its name. The second cycle – the 16th century – is associated with the growing of sugar cane and the exporting of sugar, when Brazil was able to satisfy practically 100% of the global demand for this product. The third began in the 18th century, when plentiful sources of gold and diamonds were discovered, becoming key items for export. The fourth, in the following century, brought cotton and coffee to the fore. At the turn of the 20th century, a brief period began when Brazil had a monopoly on the production of natural rubber. Of all these cultures, coffee and sugar have retained great significance to this day.[69]

In Brazil, the struggle for independence was a relatively calm one, as has been noted. After Napoleon Bonaparte set off for Portugal in 1808, the Royal Court moved to Brazil, which acquired a status equal to that of the metropolis in the United Kingdom of Portugal, Brazil and the Algarve. When the King returned to Lisbon after the defeat of Napoleon and attempts were made to remove this status from Brazil, the heir to the throne, Don Pedro, who had stayed on in Rio, proclaimed Brazil's independence in 1822, and was crowned as its first Emperor. Essentially, gaining independence became a kind of compromise within the Royal House of Braganza. Under Pedro I and his successor Pedro II, who governed for almost half a century (1831-1889), a fairly advanced constitution was adopted, and a competent state administration was created. Brazil remained an independent monarchy right up until 1889, when the Regent Isabel, to the consternation of the landowning nobility, abolished slavery,

....

[69] Yevgeniy Larin, *Vseobshchaya istoriya: latinoamerikanskaya tsivilizatsiya* (*Universal History: Latin American Civilization*). Moscow, 2007. PP. 231-232.

and the military overthrew the Emperor. Brazil acquired the status of an independent republic with a federative structure (the provinces of the empire were renamed states), a presidential system of government, and a Congress with two chambers.

The "old republic" existed until 1930, when, by revolutionary means, it was replaced by the "Estado novo" ("new state") of Getulio Vargas, who soon declared a state of emergency and disbanded Congress. The import-replacement industrialization policy that he introduced, when the government concerned itself with the construction of industrial facilities and hydroelectric power stations, led to rapid industrial growth. Labor and social legislation appeared, as did pensions, but all strikes were banned and state-controlled labor unions were not allowed to participate in a political struggle. Vargas dispatched a 25,000-strong corps to the European theater during the Second World War, meaning Brazil thus entered the arena of global politics. In February 1945, democratic freedoms were restored and legitimate parties came into being; diplomatic relations with Moscow were restored.

In the elections of 1950, Vargas secured victory once again. In October 1953, he signed a law on the creation of the national company Petrobras, which obtained a monopoly on the extraction and refining of oil. "He adopted a nationalistic line in the economic sphere and blamed foreign capital for Brazil's balance of payment problems," writes the Brazilian historian Boris Fausto on reasons for the problems Vargas soon faced. "When American and Canadian electric energy firms were reluctant to make new investments, Vargas reacted, in April 1954, with a bill creating a state firm for this area – Eletrobras."[70] In August of that year, US-connected military presented him with an ultimatum, and Vargas shot himself in the heart in the private apartments of the Catete Palace.

Brazil's development was accelerated by Juscelino Kubitschek, elected president in 1956, whose slogan was "50 years in five", and who undertook to turn the idea of creating a new capital, one that was written into the first constitution, into a reality. Thus, a new capital was born: Brasilia (the first capital having been Salvador, the second Rio) – an urban utopia, the chief architect of which was the Communist Oscar Niemeyer. In terms of its shape, the city resembled an airplane with the Monumental axis as its fuselage; the government buildings are located along this road, while the parliament and the presidential palace are situated at its western end. The

....

[70] Boris Fausto, *A Concise History of Brazil*. Cambridge Uniersity Press, 1999. P. 249.

streets are numbered, and there is a hotel sector alongside the banking sector and cultural sector, and so on. This was the symbol of the new Brazil. Which does not look very much like the rest of Brazil.

In 1964, the military seized power once again, after which the five subsequent presidents in the period up to 1985 were all generals. In 2014 – after many months of work, accompanied by sabotage on the part of civil servants and the military – a 4400-page report was finally completed by a government commission set up to investigate the crimes of the military dictatorships. The report documented hundreds of murders, disappearances, incidences of torture, and the concealment of bodies. President Dilma Rousseff, who was herself a victim of torture, could not hold back her tears when she read the report.[71] "A growth spurt in the mid-twentieth century was financed with foreign debt within a semiclosed economy, which collapsed among the oil shocks of the 1970s. Two volatile decades of rampant inflation followed, reaching more than 700 percent a year by the early 1990s," observed Joseph Nye.[72]

Important milestones were the adoption of the new constitution in 1988 and the first presidential elections in three decades, in 1989, which resulted in a victory for Fernando Collor de Melo. The authors of *Why Nations Fail*, Daron Acemoglu and James Robinson, have commented that Brazil's subsequent rise "was not engineered by economists of international institutions instructing Brazilian policy-makers on how to design better policies or avoid market failures. It was not achieved with injections of foreign aid. It was not the natural outcome of modernization. Rather, it was the consequence of diverse groups of people courageously building inclusive institutions. Eventually these led to more inclusive economic institutions."[73]

Brazil's economic miracle is associated in no small degree with the ambitious and rational policies of two of its presidents: the leader of Brazil's Social Democratic party, Fernando Henrique Cardoso, and the leader of the Labor Party, Luiz Inácio Lula da Silva (better known among the people as Lula), whose student was Rousseff.

The 1990s became known in Brazil as "the decade of reform". At the time of the elections in 1994, there was still a mood of depression and pes-

---

[71] Maxim Makarychev, "Kogda plachet prezident" ("When the President Cries"), *Rossiyskaya Gazeta (Russian Newspaper)*, December 11, 2014 <https://rg.ru/2014/12/12/brazilia.html>.

[72] Joseph S. Nye, Jr., *The Future of Power*. PublicAffairs, 2011. P. 175.

[73] Daron Acemoglu and James A. Robinson, *Why Nations Fail: The Origins of Power, Prosperity, and Poverty*. Profile Books, 2012. P. 457.

simism across the nation: the economy had been going through a lengthy period of stagnation, national debt was growing hopelessly high, inflation averaged 30% a month, and the country was cut off from the international capital markets, since it had refused to service its foreign debt. The election was won by the then finance minister – a liberal sociologist and political scientist of international renown, from a family whose previous generations had served in the military and the civil service. His policies were based on liberal, macro-economic principles, with a simultaneous increase in social programs, designed to enable an increase in purchasing power among the people.

State-owned property was privatized for a total sum of $100 billion (more than anywhere else in the developing world), and this helped to balance the budget. "Plan real", related to the introduction of a new currency, made it possible to halt inflation within a few months. The bailout and privatization of the banks, which belonged to the states, a general modernization of the banking system, partial de-monopolizing of the oil and gas industry and the provision of access to it for foreign investors, privatization of the telecommunications sector, and the adoption of laws on concessions gave a serious boost to the influx of private investment, including foreign investment. Serious reforms began in the tax and pensions systems, and the transformation of the agricultural sector commenced. The results proved to be impressive. Macroeconomic stability, the targeting of inflation, a floating currency exchange rate, the accumulation and investing of gold and of currency reserves received from the sale of natural resources, and the climate of political stability made Brazil stand out sharply, in a positive sense, among its Latin American neighbors.

Power to the Left

Despite the undoubted successes of the liberal policies of Cardozo's government, in 2002 the social democrats were forced to concede power to the leftists. Why? In his memoirs, Cardozo explained this by saying that his fellow countrymen were not fond of capitalism: "The parliamentarians, the journalists, the professors do not like this system. And within this system they particularly do not like the banks, the financial markets and the speculators… They love the state, they love state interference, overall control and control over currency operations… They do not like domestic capital, but they are even less keen on international capital. The ideal, in their minds, is an isolated, non-capitalist regime with a powerful state and expensive social programs…

The government which offers to integrate Brazil into a new international distribution of labor is considered a neoliberal one. This label presupposes that it has no wish to solve social problems."[74]

The new president – Lula – appeared to be the polar opposite of his predecessor. Lula was born into a poor working-class family in the backward north-east corner of the country; he grew up without a father, left school early and dedicated his entire life to an organization responsible for labor unions and strikes. His rise to Brazil's political summit was one of the manifestations of the continent's "left-wing Renaissance".

When he took up office, Lula did not bring Cardozo's macroeconomic policy to an end. The only main difference was the complete turnaround in subsequent privatization. By 2007, the rate of economic growth averaged 5.4%.[75] Then, due to a fall in global prices and in the demand for raw material, the partial paralysis of the international credit mechanism and a considerable leakage of capital, GDP fell to 3.5%, but by 2010 it had reached a record level of 7.5%; in 2011, 4% growth was observed. Between 2000 and 2008 the primary surplus in the federal budget amounted to between 2.2% and 2.8% of GDP, and even in the crisis year of 2009 it was above zero (0.64% of GDP). Direct foreign investment rose by 26% each year over five years, reaching $48.5 billion in 2010. Between 1998 and 2008, 31.3% of all foreign investment in Latin America went to Brazil ($274 billion).[76] Inflation fell from 200% in 1990 to 4.8% in 2008.

Far greater emphasis was placed on social programs, the most famous of which was Bolsa Familia – "the family purse". Payments to the poorest families were tied to whether or not their children attended school and received regular vaccinations. Pensions were increased, as was the minimum wage. The central aspect of the policy of stimulating economic growth was a series of infrastructural programs. Social and construction projects increased the share of state expenditure in GDP from 21.7% to 23.8% in the period 2002

---

[74] Cit. from: Sergey Vasil'yev, "Epokha dvukh prezidentov: Braziliya na puti modernizatsii" ("The Epoch of Two Presidents: Brazil on the Road to Modernization"), *Rossiya v global'noy politike* (*Russia in Global Affairs*), Issue 5, 2010 <https://globalaffairs.ru/articles/epoha-dvuh-prezidentov/>.

[75] E. I. Pankov, "Braziliya: stremleniye v budushcheye" ("Brazil: Striving for the Future"), *Vestnik MGIMO-Universiteta* (*MGIMO-University Bulletin*), Issue 4, 2010. P. 200.

[76] V. M. Davydov and A. V. Bobrovnikov, *Rol' voskhodyashchikh gigantov v mirovoy ekonomike i politike (shansy Brazilii i Meksiki v global'nom izmerenii)* [*The Role of the Rising Giants in Global Economics and Politics (Brazil and Mexico's Chances in the Global Dimension)*]. Moscow, 2009. P. 46.

to 2008.⁷⁷ In 2004, the Ministry of social development and the fight against hunger was created; it operated in all 5,563 municipalities, its scope covering 68 million people (37% of the population). From 1995 to 2005, the amount spent on social aid to the poorest increased by 13 times. Between 1990 and 2005, the number of Brazilians whose income was less than a dollar a day fell to 4% of the population, and infant mortality was almost halved.⁷⁸

It is thought that thanks to Lula's social programs, 20.5 million Brazilians were helped out of poverty, and 40 million – the equivalent of the population of Argentina – joined the middle class between 2003 and 2011, when the average wage rose by 4.61% a year.⁷⁹ This laid the foundations for political stability and the continuation of reforms under the administration of Dilma Rousseff (a Bulgarian with Russian ancestry).

In 2011, Brazil's state statistics committee put Brazil's GDP in terms of purchasing power parity higher than both Russia and Germany. Brazil is Russia's biggest competitor for the title of the world's fifth or even fourth biggest economy. GDP per head of the population is slightly lower than that of Russia with its smaller population, and amounts to 91% of the average global level. Its Gini inequality index almost coincides with the global average.

Today, Brazil meets 90% of the needs of its domestic market through its own manufacturing, 80% of which consists of automobile and equipment manufacturing. Modern industry is growing quickly, with the resulting products accounting for 30% of exports.⁸⁰ The Embraer Corporation, created at the end of the 1970s, was transformed into the world's third biggest manufacturer of aviation technology (after Boeing and Airbus). There have been major achievements in electronics, IT, biotechnologies and nanotechnologies, genetics, and nuclear research. Three nuclear reactors were launched in Brazil, after which the country obtained full cycle uranium enrichment. There are plans to launch a further four reactors by 2030. Today, Brazil has the sixth largest proved reserves of natural uranium, which are mainly sent

....

[77] Ibid.

[78] A. Yu. Borzova, "Podkhody Brazilii k probleme 'ustoychivogo razvitiya' v ramkakh BRIKS" ("Brazil's Approaches to the Problem of 'Sustainable Development' in the Context of BRICS"), in *Voskhodyashchiye gosudarstva-giganty BRIKS: rol' v mirovoy politike, strategii modernizatsii* (*The Emerging Giants of BRICS: Their Role in World Politics, Strategies for Modernization*). Moscow, 2012. PP. 180-181.

[79] Marcelo Neri, "The New Brazilian Middle Class and the Bright Side of the Poor", *Poverty in Focus. On the Middle Class*, Issue 26, October 2013. P. 18.

[80] E. I. Pankov, "Braziliya: stremleniye v budushcheye" ("Brazil: Striving for the Future"), *Vestnik MGIMO-Universiteta* (*MGIMO-University Bulletin*), Issue 4, 2010. PP. 200-201.

overseas – to Canada and Europe – for enrichment.[81] Brazil's military-industrial complex is the undisputed leader on the continent, and many types of weapons are eagerly purchased from it by other countries. Major infrastructure projects are being implemented, including the construction of a high-speed rail connection between Rio and São Paulo at a cost of $22 billion.

Recent decades have seen fundamental changes to the energy situation in Brazil, which imported 85% of its fuel as recently as the 1970s. The reason for this is bioethanol and oil. Brazil was traditionally one of the world's leaders in ethanol production (it is known simply as alcohol there). Back in the days of the Great Depression, surplus sugar was transformed into ethanol; it was compulsory to add it to engine oil. After WWII, cheap oil made the production of it irrelevant, right up until the oil crisis of 1973.

By the mid-1980s, 95% of new cars sold in Brazil ran on "alcohol". At the start of the 21st century, three factors once again made ethanol popular: the rise in oil prices; breakthroughs in science, which made ethanol production significantly cheaper; and the manufacturing of engines capable of running on various kinds of fuel. If ethanol is produced not from corn, but from sugar cane (as it is most commonly produced today), there is not even a need to cut down rainforests, in which the cane grows remarkably well.

For a long time, it was thought that there was no oil in Brazil. Nowadays, the Brazilian oil and gas company Petrobras is already the biggest global player, with operations in 27 countries, and in terms of identified oil reserves, Brazil has moved from 24th position to 8th in the world.[82]

The government of Dilma Rousseff, like that of her predecessor, operated on the assumption that the state should play an active role in stimulating economic growth.

In 2011 the 20% tax on salary was abolished for the four sectors creating the largest number of jobs: the manufacturing of clothes, shoes, furniture and software. The policy "Buy Brazilian!" also involved stricter measures for tackling dumping by importers, monitoring the origins of products (many Chinese goods were entering the country free of customs, via third-party countries), and the ability to make purchases for the needs of the state from local producers at 25% more than the market

---

[81] Julia E. Sweig, "A New Global Player: Brazil's Far-Flung Agenda", *Foreign Affairs*, November/December 2010. P. 178.

[82] Daniel Yergin, *The Quest: Energy, Security and the Remaking of the Modern World*. London, 2012. PP. 657-661.

price. Construction and the services sector grew as a result of powerful domestic demand.[83]

Brazil is the world's fourth biggest exporter of foodstuffs, the world leader in the production of sugar cane, coffee and beef, and one of the leaders in the exporting of soy, poultry, pork and concentrated orange juice. Incidentally, only a quarter of the country's area is currently set aside for agriculture, and there are reserves available for future growth. According to data from the World Bank, Brazil will be capable of feeding more than 1 billion people "on its own".

The country is an ecological superpower. Along with Siberia, the region of the Amazon is one of the "lungs of the planet", and three fifths of the Amazon rainforest is in Brazil. The priority in environmental policy is the preservation of the unique Amazon rainforests, where there are as many as 4,000 valuable species of tree, and also the biodiversity of the river itself, in which there are 2,000 species of fish. On a single tree in the Amazon rainforest, scientists counted more species of birds, butterflies, ants and other fauna, than in all the woodlands of England. This is the world's natural storehouse, for the preservation of which many Latin American countries are assuming responsibility.

In terms of its reserves of pure water, Brazil (18% of the global total) is ahead even of Russia. Hydroelectric power stations produce 40% of the energy the country needs, and the same amount is produced by biofuel. According to international surveys, Brazilians are more concerned about environmental matters than any other people in the world.

Brazil is described as a model of "globalization with social responsibility". Housing credits started being provided by the state, and the minimum wage is constantly being increased. From the start of Rousseff's presidency, a "Brazil Without Poverty" program was implemented. Some 22 million people have been lifted out of complete poverty, meaning that this issue has effectively been solved.[84] In the late 1990s, only 2% of non-white Brazilians had been through university education, whereas in 2013 that figure stood at 6%.

The percentage of GDP allocated from the budgets stood at 35% – the highest percentage in Latin America. No less than 13% of GDP – an extraordinarily high percentage – went towards pensions.[85] The Brazilian middle

---

[83] "Brazil's Industrial Policy. Dealing with the Real", *The Economist*, August 6, 2011. P. 39.

[84] *Bolsa Familia Program: A Decade of Social Inclusion in Brazil. Executive Summary*, ed. by Teresa Campello and Marcelo Cortes Neri. Brasilia, 2014. PP. 14-15.

[85] Michael Mandelbaum, "BRIC Bust?", *The American Interest*, May/June 2014. P. 78.

class, defined as those with an income of 131 dollars a month, now includes a hundred million people, and the percentage of people in this category has risen since the start of the century from 38% to 53%. At the same time, the increase in the size of the middle class is also creating growing expectations within it, which the government is by no means always able to satisfy, creating the conditions for social protest.[86]

For all that, a huge number of problems remain. The quality of education remains low: 16% of the population are illiterate, and 26% of the population are still living in slums. In Rio de Janeiro alone, one million people – one in five – live in sprawling favelas, where criminal gangs often rule the roost. After it was announced that Rio was to host the Olympics, some of the favelas were subjected to "pacification", which included not only raids by armed police, but also the installation of water pipes and sewage systems, Internet cables, the installing of streetlights, the creation of social and educational services. Unemployment is high.[87]

Tropical Democracy

According to the constitution of 1988 (as amended), Brazil is a democratic state with the rule of law, a federative Republic, consisting of 26 states, with Brasilia as its capital federal district. It is a clearly expressed presidential republic.

The constitution enshrined that the president, vice president, deputies, senators, governors, members of the legislative assemblies of states, mayors and global judges must be directly elected. The voting age is 16, and for those aged between 18 and 70, it is compulsory to vote. A minimum of 30% of the places in the representative bodies is reserved for women. Brazil is the first country to switch to electronic voting. Political parties have a monopoly on political representation, and candidates who are not affiliated to a party are not allowed to take part in elections.

Brazil's party political system is considered to be one of the factors of instability. The Labor Party of Lula and Rousseff, created in 1980 at a congress of metalworkers in São Paulo, initially incorporated a broad range

---

[86] Antonio Sampaio, "Brazil's Angry Middle Class", *Survival*, August/September 2014. PP. 108-109.

[87] Carlos Henrique Corseuil, Miguel Foguel, Gustavo Gonzaga, and Eduardo Ribeiro, "A Brief Overview of Youth Turnover in the Brazilian Formal Labor Market", *Policy in Focus. Youth and Employment Among the BRICS*, Issue 28, April 2014. P. 10.

of left-wing forces – from Guevarists, Trotskyists and Maoists, to radical university intelligentsia and moderate social democrats. Rejecting class warfare, the party's declared aim was democratic socialism and building a society free of exploitation. In the Congress elected in 2011 to 2014, 27 parties were represented. The Rousseff administration was supported by a coalition consisting of more than a dozen of these parties – from Communists to right-wing populists. Many of these parties, however, were interested less in ideology and legislation than in being given positions in the state apparatus, in which the president appoints up to 25,000 civil servants, and government contracts.

A serious boost to the opposition arrived in the form of the mass protest movement that began in June 2013, initially prompted by an increase in prices for journeys on public transport, and also by consternation at the vast sums being spent on the 2014 World Cup. Sport is an extremely powerful nation-building factor for Brazil. The fact that Brazil was chosen as the host of the World Cup in 2014, and of the Summer Olympics in 2016, gave the country a massive boost in terms of its national self-esteem. Yet, at the same time, only 34% of Brazilians were of the view that hosting the championships would be useful for the economy on the grounds that it would create jobs, while 61% thought it would be a bad thing for the economy, because it would divert resources away from more pressing needs.[88]

I would suggest that all the costs and inconveniences brought about by the preparations for the championships would have been forgiven, had Brazil's national team won the tournament; but the team's crushing defeat in the semi-final caused shock. At the head of the protest movement was the "creative middle class", displeased by the government's policy as a whole. The protests did not take place without the influence of external forces and social networks, the number of users of which rose from 6 million in 2010 to 83 million in 2014.

Rousseff's popularity fell dramatically, but she still won, with 52% of the vote. Her second term had a heavy shadow cast over it by the corruption scandal involving Petrobras, which only served to fan the flames of the mass protests. On 12th April 2015, 660,000 people took to the streets in 152 cities. Three quarters of Brazilians supported the anti-government protests, and 63% felt it was necessary to commence impeachment proceedings against

---

[88] "Most Say Hosting World Cup is Bad for Brazil: 2014", Pew Research Center, June 2, 2014 <https://www.pewresearch.org/global/2014/06/03/brazilian-discontent-ahead-of-world-cup/brazil-report-03/>.

Rousseff.[89] Her rating fell to 13%.[90] Although there was no proof that Rousseff herself was corrupt, the basis for her impeachment was the fact that Petrobras funds had been used in her presidential election campaign.

The vice-president Michel Temer, who took charge of the country, immediately found himself embroiled in a corruption scandal with the very same oil company. In February 2017, 65% of Brazilians agreed that Temer's cabinet was no less corrupt than his predecessor. And only 10% of the electorate approved of his activity.[91]

In 2016 a record 62,500 Brazilians were murdered by criminals. The *Lava Jato* ("Car Wash") corruption cases investigation led to the indictments of leading figures in every major political party, and discredited the entire political class. Temer has avoided prosecution only because congress voted to protect him from it. Just 13% of Brazilians said they were satisfied with their democracy.

The economy was not in the best shape. From late 2014 to 2016 the GDP shrank by 7.7%, the longest contraction ever. In 2017 there were signs of an economic recovery – by 1% a year.[92]

People in the streets became nostalgic about Lula, although he was not the preferred choice of the government. Lula was arrested in April 2018 after a dramatic standoff with police, when he stated: "I won't be stopped because I am not a human being, I am an idea. And going forward all of you will become Lulas."[93] The Supreme Electoral Court had banned Lula from running for a third term in the October election. The Workers' Party, though, insisted that he was the only name it would put on the ballot, and it officially nominated Lula as its candidate at the party convention in August. Lula was leading electoral polls with 30% of Brazilians saying they would vote for him, and 47% for a candidate endorsed by him. This

---

[89] Joe Leahy, "Rousseff Accused of Outsourcing Government", *The Financial Times*, April 17, 2015. P. 4.

[90] "Protests in Brazil. Tropical Tea Party", *The Economist*, April 18, 2015. P. 44.

[91] Brian Winter, "Brazil's Never-Ending Corruption Crisis", *Foreign Affairs*, May/June 2017. P. 88.

[92] "Brazil's Economy. When Will the Future Arrive?", *The Economist*, August 19, 2017. P. 35; Joe Leahy, "Brazil Offerings Flow After Four-Year Drought", *The Financial Times*, August 17, 2017. P. 18; Vinod Sreeharsha, "Brazilian Hedge Funds Are Flourishing Despite a Rocky Political Environment", *The New York Times*, August 23, 2017. P. B3(L); "Brazilian Banks. In the Doldrums, with Full Sails", *The Economist*, August 4, 2018. PP. 36-37.

[93] Shasta Darlington, "As 'Lula' Sits in Brazil Jail, Workers' Party Nominates Him for President", *The New York Times*, August 6, 2018. P. A8(L).

made the WP's nominee for the vice-president very important. That was Fernando Haddad, a former mayor of São Paulo.[94]

Lula spoke out from the jail in Curitiba where he was serving a 12-year sentence for corruption: "President Dilma Rousseff was impeached and removed from office for an action that even her opponents admitted was not an impeachable offence. Then, I, too, was sent to prison, after a dubious trial [...]. My imprisonment was the latest phase in a slow-motion coup designed to permanently marginalise progressive forces in Brazil."[95]

In this context, Jair Bolsonaro, described by the liberal media as "a flame-throwing right-winger", a master of "outrageous provocation" became a front-runner in the race for the presidency. He once said he would "prefer a dead son to a gay one", that a "policeman who doesn't kill isn't a policeman". He also proposed to reduce the age of criminal responsibility to 14.[96]

Bolsonaro pulled ahead in the polls, though, campaigning as the "Brazilian Trump". Similarities with Trump were "conscious and deliberate", said Guilherme Casarões, a comparative politics professor at the Getulio Vargas Foundation. "Five years ago, he was just another congressman with anti-gay views. Now Bolsonaro, like Trump, has become a larger-than-life figure. Bolsonaro uses well-crafted rhetoric – his slogan is 'Brazil before everything, and God above all.' He has been able to reach out to different groups of voters who feel abandoned by the political class. They are now blind to the negative things he says and does, and tend to overlook any aspect that speaks against their candidate."[97]

His talk of bringing back family values has been appealing to conservative Catholics and evangelicals, even though he is currently married to his third wife. After an unsuccessful assassination attempt in September, some Brazilians proclaimed his survival a divine sign. Many argued that

....

[94] Ibid.; "Brazilian Politics. The Plot Thickens", *The Economist*, August 11, 2018. PP. 38-39.

[95] Luiz Inacio Lula da Silva, "There is a Right-Wing Coup Underway in Brazil", *The New York Times*, August 14, 2018 <https://www.nytimes.com/2018/08/14/opinion/lula-brazil-candidacy-prison.html>.

[96] "Brasília, We Have a Problem", *The Economist*, August 11, 2018. PP. 10-11.

[97] Anthony Faiola and Marina Lopes, "'Just like Trump': Bolsonaro Leads Brazil's Presidential Race With Right-Wing Populist Pitch", *The Washington Post*, October 4, 2018 <https://www.washingtonpost.com/world/the_americas/just-like-trump-bolsonaro-leads-brazils-presidential-race-with-right-wing-populist-pitch/2018/10/04/c4ba3728-c65c-11e8-9c0f-2ffaf6d422aa_story.html>.

Bolsonaro's rhetoric is hate speech, bringing racism and homophobia into mainstream dialogue.[98]

Bolsonaro took office on 1st January 2019, and solemnly declared that the national flag "will never be red again, unless it is necessary to shed blood for it to remain green and yellow."[99] He urged his opponents to unite to implement the right-wing conservative development strategy of the country, which will be based on Judeo-Christian traditions. Representatives of the Workers' Party pointedly ignored the inauguration ceremony.

Among the 22 members of the new Cabinet, 7 are retired military, something which did not happen even during military dictatorships. The Economy Minister was Paulo Gedes, graduate of the University of Chicago, student of Milton Friedman, professor of the University of Chile during Pinochet's rule, banker, multimillionaire. His priorities – pension reform and large-scale privatization, from which it was planned to exclude China.[100] I wonder how.

The Century of Brazil?

Ideas of creating the Great Brazil as an independent center of regional and global development had been present in the minds of the leaders of the country for many decades, and was discernible in the concepts of the "New State" of Vargas or New Pan-Americanism of Juscelino Kubitschek. The military regimes that ruled in the 1960s to 1980s were less ambitious, and preferred to position Brazil as a non-aligned country and a partner, though not an automatic one, of the United States.

Everything has changed since Cardoso and Lula. First came the concept of Brazil as the "United States of the South". Then Cardoso spoke of "tropical Russia". Under Lula, a new paradigm was formulated, which he modestly voiced in Rome in October 2005: "The 19th century was the century of Europe, the 20th century of the USA. The 21st century will be the century of Brazil."[101]

....

[98] Ibid.

[99] "Brazil Turns Right", *Daily Management Review*, September 1, 2019 <https://www.dailymanagementreview.com/Brazil-turns-right_a5187.html>.

[100] Aleksey Alekseyev and Sergey Strokan', "Braziliya vklyuchila pravyy povorot" ("Brazil has Made a Turn to the Right"), *Kommersant (The Businessman)*, Issue 1, January 9, 2019 <https://www.kommersant.ru/doc/3849668>.

[101] V. M. Davydov and A. V. Bobrovnikov, *Rol' voskhodyashchikh gigantov v mirovoy ekonomike i politike (shansy Brazilii i Meksiki v global'nom izmerenii)* [*The Role of the Rising Giants in Global*

Rousseff declared her intention to build productive relations with the United States, on an equal footing, rejecting all US attempts to talk to Brazil with the tone of a mentor, and avoiding ideological discussions. "Brazil will turn down any proposals to become a formal ally of Washington. But as a major beneficiary of globalization, it will not seek to overturn the existing rules of the game. Rather it will strive to adapt them smoothly to a changing world" – concluded Julia Sweig and Matias Spektor, who runs the Center for International Relations of Getulio Vargas Foundation.[102]

The USA were becoming more and more aware of the value of Brazil as a key state in Latin America. From harsh criticism of the Brazil that had "turned red" after the election of Lula da Silva as president, the USA has moved on to conversations about the need for bilateral strategic cooperation, and Brazil has even been asked to help moderate the "anti-American radicalism" of left-wing regimes, particularly in Venezuela. However, the USA played a role in removing Rousseff from power.

Bolsonaro's presidency might well usher in a new honeymoon in relations between Brazil and the USA. Visiting the inauguration ceremony, Secretary of State Mike Pompeo called for a joint struggle with the main Russian allies in the region – Venezuela, Nicaragua and Cuba. Bolsonaro did not exclude the possibility of the establishment of a US military base on the territory of Brazil. Trump even brought up the subject of Brazil's possible membership of NATO, to the confusion of his European allies and the Brazilians themselves. The new Brazilian administration has readily joined America's harsh campaign against Venezuela, though Brazilian generals disapprove of the idea of US bases in Brazil or a military intervention in Venezuela.

With regard to its membership of (what was then) BRIC, Brazil initially expressed considerable doubt. However, the organization, which became BRICS when South Africa joined it, continued to arouse more and more interest and enthusiasm. As the famous diplomat and analyst Gelson Fonseca observed, "the five States would play some role in any equation on the international order. [...] [T]he transformation of BRICS into a political instance, albeit informal, enshrines the idea that they already exerted influence separately; together, they could influence even more [...]."[103] Brazil

....
Economics and Politics (Brazil and Mexico's Chances in the Global Dimension)]. Moscow, 2009. PP. 27-28.

[102] Julia Sweig and Matias Spektor, "Mr. Obama, Meet the New Brazil", *The International Herald Tribune*, March 19-20, 2011. P. 6.

[103] Gelson Fonseca Jr. "BRICS: Notes and Questions", in *Brasil, BRICS and the International*

could play a special role within BRICS, according to the former diplomat Rubens Barbosa, since it has the greatest potential for building consensus and leading the group along a course of "soft power" deployment.[104]

With the help of BRICS, Brazil is striving to secure a permanent seat on the UN's Security Council, and to strengthen its role in the formation of a new, "just" world order, in reforming the main global financial institutions, and in the G20, which also offers Brazil an important opportunity to strengthen its status as a regional power and a representative of the interests of the countries of South America in the key international forums. This explains why Bolsonaro is continuing to work within BRICS; Brazil, indeed, has been acting as BRICS Chairman in 2019.

Since 2009, China has been Brazil's primary trading partner, having overtaken the USA. China has a strong interest in stable supplies of iron ore (27% of Brazilian exports go to China), soy (23%), and oil (6%). Chinese exports to Brazil are dominated by industrial goods, and inexpensive consumer items (textiles, clothes, shoes, children's toys, and goods for the home and leisure) are increasingly being pushed aside by industrial equipment, vehicles, chemical products, domestic goods and computers.

In 2010 agreement was reached on the construction in Brazil of metalworking facilities worth $5 billion, and Petrobras began a collaboration with the Chinese Corporation Sino Pak in the field of hydrocarbon extraction on the Brazilian shelf. Investment also flowed into ports, railways, and reactors. Numerous Chinese companies are engaged in wood processing, the catering industry, telecoms, and the production of electrical devices. A host of Brazilian companies, in turn, are carrying out projects in China, particularly in the field of hydroelectric energy. Embraer built a plant there for the assembly of its civil aircraft, and a Brazilian-Chinese agreement is in place for the production and launch of China-Brazil Earth Reconnaissance Satellites. One new trend is the use of national currencies in mutual transactions.

Brazil has a deficit in trade with India, something that is uncharacteristic of Brazil. A strategic collaboration has begun between Petrobras and Indian energy companies. Cooperation is developing in the fields of science, education, advanced technologies, IT, bio and nanotechnologies, space ex-

---

Agenda, ed. by José Vicente de Sá Pimentel. Brasilia, 2013. P. 25.

[104] "Roundtable at FIESP", in *Debating BRICS*, ed. by José Vicente de Sá Pimentel. Brasilia, 2013. P. 107.

ploration, metallurgy, aviation and automobile construction, and in military technologies.[105.]

Brazil was the first South American state with which Russia established diplomatic relations – in 1828. However, there was contact between the two countries long before official relations began. In 1804, the ships *Nadezhda* and *Neva*, which were taking part in round the world expeditions, stopped off in Brazilian ports. The men who contributed to the relationship were the famous Russian academic and diplomat Grigory Langsdorf and the founder of the Brazilian school of diplomacy Baron de Rio-Branco, who visited Russia in 1884.[106] For a long time afterwards, however, relations remained in stagnation, in no small degree due to the fact that Brazil was in the sphere of influence of the USA.

The relationship was given a boost under president Cardoso. In October 1994, the first visit to Russia by a Brazilian Foreign Minister took place. Yevgeniy Primakov made an official visit to Brazil in November 1997. Early in 2002, the president of Brazil – Cardoso – made the first ever visit to Russia, where he declared that both countries were in favor of a multipolar world. In 2004, Putin became the first Russian leader to visit Brazil. In October 2005, Lula and Putin signed an agreement on cooperation in space, and shortly afterwards Marcos Pontes became the first Brazilian astronaut. The further development of Russo-Brazilian ties is facilitated by the start of collaboration between Russia and MERCOSUR on the basis of a memorandum of understanding signed in 2006.

Latterly, Russia has been among the leading importers of Brazilian foodstuffs, particularly raw sugar, coffee, beef, pork, poultry, fruit juices and spirits. When sanctions were introduced against Western foodstuffs, Brazil's share in the Russian market grew further. Russia, for its part, supplies Brazil with mineral fertilizers, which account for up to 90% of the value of Russian exports to the Brazilian market.[107] In 2014, Rosneft obtained a

---

[105] Tat'yana Shaumyan, "Faktor dvustoronnikh otnosheniy v formate BRIKS: opyt Indii" ("The Factor of Bilateral Relations in the BRICS Format: India's Experience"), in *Strategiya Rossii v BRIKS: tseli i instrumenty* (*Russia's Strategy in BRICS: Aims and Instruments*). Moscow, 2013. P. 127; P. P. Yakovlev, "Braziliya v BRIKS: modeli dvustoronnikh svyazey" ("Brazil in BRICS: Models of Bilateral Ties), in *Voskhodyashchiye gosudarstva-giganty BRIKS: rol' v mirovoy politike, strategii modernizatsii* (*The Emerging Giants of BRICS: Their Role in World Politics, Strategies for Modernization*). Moscow, 2012. PP. 165-166.

[106] Sergey Lavrov, *Mezhdu proshlym i budushchim. Rossiyskaya diplomatiya v menyayushchemsya mire* (*Between the Past and the Future. Russian Diplomacy in a Changing World*). Moscow, 2011. PP. 669-670.

[107] P. P. Yakovlev, "Braziliya v BRIKS: modeli dvustoronnikh svyazey" ("Brazil in BRICS:

controlling share in a joint project with HRT to develop oil and gas fields in the Solimoes. The cost of the project is estimated to be $14 billion, taking the construction of the oil and gas pipelines into account.[108]

Brazil is increasingly making a name for itself as a leader of the entire developing world. Back in 1987, the Brazilian agency for cooperation was established, with a view to coordinating and financing technical assistance for developing countries in agriculture, staff training, the enhancement of education systems, the rule of law, health care, environmental protection, IT, the harmonizing of infrastructure and town planning, culture, and the protection of human rights. The agency is implementing a host of projects in 81 southern hemisphere countries. Most of the assistance has gone to countries in Latin America and sub-Saharan Africa, particularly those in which Portuguese is spoken.[109] The Brazilian National Bank for Economic and Social Development (BNDES) grants credits for infrastructure development, energy and agriculture.

Cooperation with African countries is also seen by Brazil as important political capital, necessary, among other things, in order to strengthen its support at the UN.[110] Africa's share of total Brazilian imports has reached 10%, and exports currently stand at 6%. Brazil has the second-largest black population in the world after Nigeria. Brazil's biggest investments were initially made in Portuguese speaking countries – Angola, Mozambique and Guinea-Bissau – and a host of countries possessing natural resources. Later, South Africa, Nigeria and Algeria became major partners. Petrobras has invested more than $2 billion in projects associated with oil, gas, coal and biofuel in Nigeria, and is conducting research into oil on the shelf of Angola. The Brazilian company Vale has invested in the mining industry in Mozambique, and, in conjunction with the construction company Odebrecht, is erecting a hydroelectric power station and ports there, and building a rail-

---

Models of Bilateral Ties), in *Voskhodyashchiye gosudarstva-giganty BRIKS: rol' v mirovoy politike, strategii modernizatsii* (*The Emerging Giants of BRICS: Their Role in World Politics, Strategies for Modernization*). Moscow, 2012. PP. 172-174.

[108] Lyudmila Podobedova, "'Rosneft' poluchila kontrol' v brazil'skom mestorozhdenii" ("'Rosneft' has been Given Control of a Brazilian Oilfield"), *Izvestiya*, March 24, 2014. P. 1.

[109] A. Yu. Borzova, "Rol' brazil'skogo agentstva po sotrudnichestvu (ABC) v razvitii sistemy zdravookhraneniya v Afrike" ("Role of the Brazilian Cooperation Agency (BCA) in the Development of Health the System in Africa"), in *BRIKS i Afrika: sotrudnichestvo v tselyakh razvitiya* (*BRICS and Africa: Cooperation with the Aim of Development*). Moscow, 2013. PP. 144-145.

[110] Joe Leahy, "Brazil Seeks to Triumph in New Great Game for Africa", *The Financial Times*, April 26, 2011. P. 4.

way line. Odebrecht has become the biggest non-governmental employer in Angola, growing its business in the food industry, ethanol production, and the construction of office blocks, factories and supermarkets.

Brazil is clearly diversifying its foreign arms suppliers. The German-made Leopard-1 has become the army's tank of choice. Russian Mi-35 helicopters are being used in the fight against drug trafficking in the Amazon. Up to 50 Cougar helicopters have been procured in France. As part of the strategic order plan 2011, the territorial forces were relocated from southern and south-eastern regions, where they have traditionally been situated, to the central part of the country and to the Amazon in the north.

In December 2012, the Ministry of Defence called for the creation of a military system of cyber defence. In connection with the revelations made by Snowden, it set the task of developing a system of satellite communications, to "untie" Brazil from the US fiber-optic network, for which a special cable is being laid to South Africa. Brazil is actively supporting the idea of global rules regulating the Internet and preventing cyber-attacks.

Brazil has fairly sizeable, albeit decreasing, military spending – 28 billion dollars (45% of the total military spending of the Latin American countries). The Armed Forces comprise 335,000 personnel, of whom 198,000 serve in the army, 69,000 in the Navy, and 67,500 in the air force, with a further 395,000 in the semi-military units. There are 1.34 million reservists.[111] Strong emphasis is placed on compulsory military service, which, among other things, is seen as a way of creating greater national and social unity. Brazil's global ambitions are beginning to take on a military component as well.

As for whether the 21st century will be the Brazilian century – we know not. But as for the idea that Brazil has taken its place in the club of leading powers of the world – of that there can be no doubt.

---

[111] *The Military Balance 2019: The Annual Assessment of Global Military Capabilities and Defence Economics.* London, 2019. PP. 384, 400.

CHAPTER 12
THE AFROCENTRISM OF HOPE

In the 21st century, Africa may well become a dynamically growing region; the character and tempo of the planet's development might come to depend on it to a considerable extent, for the provision of raw materials, energy resources and human resources. The people of Africa themselves probably see their mission as being to restore unity between mankind and nature.

The Uncomfortable Cradle of Humankind

People rarely appreciate just how big Africa is – even those who live there. It has an area of 13,000,000 km², which is bigger than the territory of the USA, Western Europe, India, China and Argentina combined. There are roughly 1.2 billion people on the continent, and this number will be far higher in the future, as Africa's explosive population growth continues.

Paleoanthropologists are in little doubt that Africa was the cradle of mankind. Geneticists have established that Africa was the home of the man and woman – dubbed Adam and Eve by scientists for obvious reasons – from whom everyone alive today on the planet is descended.

When people talk about African civilization, they usually have in mind ancient Egypt, the city of Carthage founded by the Phoenicians, the Arab Maghreb. The many other states that existed on the continent at one time or another are remembered less often, if at all; the history of the people that lived to the south of the Sahara is known to a far lesser extent, the main reason for this being the lack of literacy among those peoples. It is true nonetheless that Africa has not shown itself to be a place where a large number of states have come into being. One of the main reasons has been identified by the political scientist Jeffrey Herbst. The fundamental problem for creators of states in Africa – whether they were colonial kings, colonial governors or presidents in the era of independence – was how to propagate power in inhospitable territories with a relatively low population density.[1]

A significant part of Africa is scarcely suitable or not suitable at all for life. The Sahara – the biggest desert on the planet, equivalent in size to the USA together with Alaska – is one of the driest places on the planet. Only 8% of the continent is in the tropics, while 50% of its surface receives such a small amount of precipitation that no husbandry of the land can be carried out there. The climate, in which there is no winter, creates exceptionally favorable conditions for the spreading of parasites; this means that some kinds of agriculture are precluded, first and foremost in animal rearing: a third of the continent's surface area to the south of the Sahara is unfit for breeding cattle due to the tsetse fly (which is particularly dangerous for horses). For centuries, famine was the main distinguishing feature of African history.

In Africa, there are few rivers; rivers, in theory at least, make it easier to project power and create states. There are few paths over the dry land: whereas the roads paved by the Romans could be used for a thousand years, in Africa, tropical rainstorms wash away any roads in just a few years. The coastline is only 30,000 km long, half the length of that of Asia. It is continuous, meaning that there are none of the naturally occurring bays and coves that are necessary for seafaring.[2]

The evidence suggests that the ancient Egyptian state came into being in the 4th millennium BC on an autochthonous basis, and only later separated, culturally, from the rest of Africa, interweaving its history with the fate of Western Asia and the Mediterranean. Yet to the west of Egypt, as early as in the 13th and 12th centuries BC, there existed the state of the Garamantes, with Garama as its capital, on the territory of modern-day Libya. To the south of Egypt – in what is now Sudan – the kingdom of Kush came into being in the 2nd millennium BC; this kingdom at some point went so far as to conquer Egypt, and founded the 25th (Ethiopian) dynasty there. The kingdom of Kush, with Meroe at its center, existed for more than 1000 years and was only destroyed in the 4th century AD by the forces of the Aksumite Empire, which emerged in the middle of the 1st millennium BC, in the northern part of modern-day Ethiopia.

In the 7th and 8th centuries AD, Egypt and the whole of North Africa was conquered by the Arabs, entered the Arabic caliphate, and then, 800 years later, was swallowed up by the Ottoman Empire. The deserts of the Sahel,

---

[1] Jeffrey Herbst, *States and Power in Africa*. Princeton, 2000. P. 11.
[2] Tom Young, *Africa: A Beginner's Guide*. Oneworld Publications, 2010. PP. 4-8.

however, presented insurmountable obstacles to would-be invaders, even for people as accustomed to the sands as the Arabs; invaders were thus unable to spread their influence deep into the heart of the continent. The line between the desert, with its nomadic tribes, and the African Savannah, where there were settled tribes and their states, along which the border between Islam and paganism also ran, was transformed into an arena of constant battle, which has not ceased even in our times.

The states to the south of the Sahara were a long way from our present-day understanding of a state; often, it was a matter of recognizing the power and authority of a "great chief" and a certain set of customs and norms among village communities over a large territory, rather than the presence of political institutions or a codified law. In Nubia, in the 7th to the 16th centuries, there were the Christian states of Dongol, Mukurra and Aloa, which were later heavily Islamized. A center of culture in West Sudan was the state of Kanem-Bornu, which emerged in the 9th century on the north-eastern shore of Lake Chad.

From roughly the 9th century AD onwards, there existed a powerful state known as Auker (Ghana), whose territory stretched from Senegal to the middle course of the Niger. In the mid-13th century, the state of Mali appeared, and became the largest trader in gold of that era. In the 14th century, the ruler of Mali, Mussa, when he set off on a pilgrimage to Mecca in the 1320s, took with him an entourage consisting of 500 camels loaded with gold, and gave this gold away to the priests and dignitaries, causing inflation in the Arab world.[3] In the 15th and 16th centuries, the entire middle section of the Niger was part of the state of Songhai, with Timbuktu as its capital; in 1591 the city was destroyed by the Moroccans, who were attracted to it because of its riches.

By the time Europeans arrived on the territory of Nigeria, inhabited by the Yoruba, the city-states of Ile-Ife, Ilorin and Ibadan existed; in the southern course of the Niger was the state of Benin. In the basin of the River Congo were the states and tribal associations of Congo, Lunda, Ndongo, and Bushongo. In the confluence of the Zambezi and the Limpopo was the proto-state of Monomotapa. And there were Buganda (in the south of present-day Uganda), Unyuro, Rwanda, Burundi, Ankola, and in Madagascar – Imerina. On the coastline of East Africa were the cities of Sofala, Kilva, Lamu, Mombasa and Zanzibar, which took part in maritime trade in the

....

[3] Felipe Fernández-Armesto, *Civilizations: Culture, Ambition, and the Transformation of Nature*. Simon and Schuster, 2001. P. 91.

Indian Ocean. In the late 15th century almost all of the people were familiar with ironmongery, with the exception of the bushmen of South Africa, the pygmies in the tropical rainforests of the basins of the River Congo and the River Ogawa, and the inhabitants of the island of Fernando Poe, who still used stone implements. Sub-Saharan Africa did not bring any great civilizations to the world in the Middle Ages, and was a long way from being considered a separate civilization. Yet at the same time, it was not merely a jungle with wild men climbing in the trees when the Europeans arrived.

Colonialism and Independence

The Europeans did not hurry to colonize the continent, as they had done in America: there was not a critical amount of wealth ready for immediate plundering, and the climate was unsuitable for mass resettlement. For this reason, Africa was transformed, for several centuries, in the words of the indignant founder of theoretical communism, Karl Marx, "into a warren for the commercial hunting of black-skins".[4] The first slave trade – back in the 15th century – was begun by Portugal. In the 17th century, this lucrative business and the task of colonizing the continent attracted Great Britain, followed by the Netherlands, France, Denmark, and finally the USA. The slave traders were interested in young, strong and intelligent men and women, capable of enduring, among other things, the voyage itself – in holds where they were packed together like sardines – across the ocean. Only a small number were still alive at the other end.

According to official statistics from the countries affected by the slave trade, up until the 1870s, a total of 10 million slaves were taken to America from Africa, and a further 2 million died during the journey.[5] Clearly, though, most of the slave trade was unofficial in nature, and therefore we can only guess at the true figures. By the 18th century, the whole of the western coastline of Africa – from Senegal to the south of Angola – was transformed into a coastline of slaves. The Europeans did not generally hunt them down themselves. As a rule, they founded forts on the coastline, from which they forced and incentivized the local rulers to supply them with their fellow men and prisoners of war, in the form of a ransom or as goods sold to

---

[4] Karl Marx, *Capital*. Vol. 1, <https://www.marxists.org/archive/marx/works/1867-c1/ch31.htm>.

[5] Jurgen Osterhammel, *The Transformation of the World: A Global History of the Nineteenth Century*. Princeton-Oxford: Princeton University Press, 2014. P. 150.

professional slave traders.⁶ Those sold into slavery were seen not as people, but as property, akin to domestic capital. From an economic perspective, it was cheaper to bring in new slaves than to allow the ones you had to have offspring: if one did so, the women would be unfit to work for a long time, and the children would need to be fed for many years before they could work on the land. Arabic countries also lived off the labor of slaves – on a large scale, incidentally – as did Ethiopia, and the main hunting ground for these countries was East Sudan and the Horn of Africa, while East Africa supplied slaves to both America and the Islamic world.⁷

According to the calculations carried out by the well-known American William Dubois, who fought to protect the rights of the black population, and made public at the Versailles conference in 1919, the slave trade took from Africa some 100 million people who were killed during the reckless hunt for slaves, taken away, or died while in transit.

The colonial conquest of the continent happened very quickly, taking just over three decades in the late 19th century. Reloading shotguns and light artillery meant that resistance was futile for the Africans. Since the prevailing ideas about 'civilization' precluded non-Europeans, and the ordinary laws of war, as it was thought, did not apply to them, the European forces used such practices as destroying property and killing prisoners, which were considered inadmissible among themselves, observes Tom Young.⁸ Another factor that helped was that one group of Africans could be encouraged to wage war against another, thus making it easier to conquer the continent through the efforts of the local population as well. There was only one successful attempt at resistance against the colonialists, when in 1826 the Emperor of Abyssinia, Menelik II, crushed an Italian expeditionary force near Adwa and even managed to force the aggressor to pay compensation.

In 1876, 10% of the territory of the continent was under colonial rule, and by 1900 90% of it, with the only exceptions being Ethiopia and Liberia, which was under the patronage of the USA. The imperial powers saw their mission, as British Prime Minister Lord Palmerston put it, as being to restore fallen worlds and raise up those that have never risen up before.

In practice, this took the form of a mass resettlement of indigenous people from their lands. The Maasai were driven from their land between 1904

---

⁶ Kevin Shillington, *History of Africa*. Palgrave, 2012. P. 181.

⁷ Jurgen Osterhammel, *The Transformation of the World: A Global History of the Nineteenth Century*. Princeton-Oxford: Princeton University Press, 2014. PP. 150-151.

⁸ Tom Young, *Africa: A Beginner's Guide*. Oneworld Publications, 2010. PP. 43, 30.

and 1911. In South Rhodesia, the colonialists occupied half the territory. The inhabitants of Southern and Eastern Africa were exiled to "native reserves", which, as a rule, were located on the land that was the least suitable for use. The indigenous peoples were forced to pay taxes, and to do so they had to produce goods they could sell, rather than goods for their own consumption. Millions died of famine in East Africa in 1898-1900, and in West Africa in 1913-1914. The colonial powers also introduced forced labor, particularly in the construction of roads and railways. A 450 km railway was built from Congo to Brazzaville using the forced labor of 120,000 Africans, half of whom died.

The struggle for the redistribution of the colonies that was waged by Germany at the start of the 20th century was one of the (manifold) causes of the First World War. During the war, the colonial powers brought in conscription for their subjects; hundreds of thousands of Africans took part in military action in Europe and in Africa itself, many of whom later settled in Europe's metropolises. The time they spent in the trenches alongside Europeans turned their ideas about the world upside down: it transpired that the all-powerful white man was a mere mortal after all, and could be cowardly, venal and weak! The moral justification for colonialism seemed to be thrown into doubt.

At the Paris Peace Conference of 1919, there were Africans present who also attended the First Pan-African Congress, where the tone, admittedly, was set by African-Americans, led by William Dubois. In the French capital, speeches were made about the African people's rights, about autonomy for the colonies, which were supported enthusiastically by the Japanese (who were themselves treated little better than the blacks at the time) and the Americans, whom the older colonial powers had not permitted to enter markets in their possession. The Pan-African congresses that took place thereafter played a significant role in shaping the first generation of African politicians. Another factor that contributed to the toppling of the colonial system was the Comintern, which saw the struggle against the colonialists as part of the struggle against imperialism. Dozens of African leaders studied at the Communist University of Workers of the East in Moscow, including the man who would go on to be the first president of Kenya, Jomo Kenyatta.

The liberation of Africa was accelerated by the Second World War, which required, to an even greater extent than the first one, the use of all the resources in the colonies of the fighting nations. In order to ensure the uninterrupted supply to the metropolises of growing quantities of raw material and foodstuffs, there was a need to speed up the construction, in Africa, of roads, ports, airfields and refineries. Politically, the process of national self-determination was supported by the Atlantic Charter, in which Franklin Roosevelt and Winston Churchill, in August 1941, proclaimed the right of the peoples themselves to decide their own destiny. Strictly speaking, the declaration concerned the colonies belonging to Germany and Japan, but the other colonies took it to mean them as well.

At the forefront of the decolonization movement was the national African intelligentsia, which had been fostered by the colonial powers themselves. Among the plus sides of colonialism, as was the case on other continents, one should include the education system, initially the one established by the missionaries, and later ordinary schools, where many future members of the African elite received their schooling. Some of them took up civil service jobs in the colonial administrations, or became lawyers or journalists. The burgeoning middle class in Africa adopted many of the colonial powers' traits: their language, their names, their fashions, the nature of their familial relations. By the mid-1950s, political parties had been formed in most African countries, which armed themselves with notions of African nationalism.

The struggle against colonialism was made easier by the fact that the metropolises were greatly weakened by the Second World War. The two superpowers that had arisen – the USSR and the USA – spoke out amicably against colonialism, each for their own reasons. The United Nations, created in 1945, became an important platform for discussing the horrors of colonialism. In the first decade after the war, anti-colonial demonstrations in Africa were still put down brutally: the Mau Mau uprising in Kenya, unrest in Cameroon (a French colony), and the strikes in Nigeria and South Africa. In 1957, the British created the first precedent, by granting independence to their most developed colony, the Gold Coast, which was renamed Ghana, and where a graduate of a local teaching college, Kwame Nkrumah, came to power. 1960 became known as the year of Africa: no fewer than 17 colonies obtained independence, and the UN adopted the Declaration on the granting of independence to colonial countries and peoples.

In the parts of the world where the Europeans were not ready for decolonialization at all (which was particularly true of the territories owned by Spain, Portugal and Belgium), they were forced, on pain of death, to evacuate their colonies entirely, for they had turned into arenas for bloody and long-drawn-out conflicts (Angola, Guinea-Bissau, the Democratic Republic of Congo, the Western Sahara, Mozambique).

The African states which had acquired independence suddenly found themselves in the same position as the heirs of a millionaire, who discover, when the will is read out, that they have inherited debts running into the millions. They had no economic basis to work from, no trained workforces, no infrastructure, no healthcare, no education system, no international ties. Many peoples found that they had been deliberately divided up by the departing colonizers between several different countries. By way of example, the Somali people had been divided between Somalia, Djibouti, Ethiopia and Kenya. Meanwhile, sworn enemies discovered that they were now living within the same borders as one another: the Hausa and the Fulani, for instance, now faced the prospect of building an independent Nigeria alongside their traditional enemies, the Yoruba and the Ibo (who did not see eye to eye with one another anyway). One can only wonder how it was that there were so few inter-ethnic conflicts in subsequent years.

A number of the new regimes, incidentally, went so far as to destroy their own people – for reasons related to their race, religion, class or other traits. The most well-known example is probably the Central African Republic, which was proclaimed an empire by its president, Jean-Bédel Bokassa, who declared himself to be its king. For the coronation ceremony in France a diamond crown was ordered, along with a throne of gold in the shape of an eagle, a 6 m long velvet cloak lined with ermine, an ancient horse-drawn carriage, and so on and so forth. Equally interesting were Uganda under Idi Amin, the "ideal socialist state" of Guinea under Sékou Touré, and Equatorial Guinea under Macías Nguema, who surpassed even the Khmer Rouge in Cambodia by killing a third of his subjects and forcing another third to leave the country.

In all the outwardly democratic republics, it was clear that power was in the hands of a single individual. The president of the Ivory Coast, Félix Houphouët-Boigny, turned his native village of Yamoussoukro into a big city and made it the country's capital. The streets of Ghanaian cities were filled with colorful slogans: "Nkrumah is the new Messiah", "Nkrumah will never die", and an Institute for the study of Nkrumahism was founded. Ghana's president was to get quite a surprise when he was toppled following a military coup in 1966. Incidentally, political longevity was also in the normal run of things. Léopold Sédar Senghor was in power in Senegal for 20 years, Nierere ruled for 21 years, and Houphouët-Boigny for 33 years. In 2017, after 38 years in charge of Angola, the leader of the Marxist MPLA José Eduardo dos Santos announced that he would be giving up his powers and putting forward his successor. In November 2017, what effectively amounted to a military coup in Zimbabwe, and was met with delight in the West as a miraculous moment of salvation, brought an end to the 37 year, inglorious rule of the 93-year-old Robert Mugabe. Admittedly, his successor was a man who had until recently been a close adviser of his and former vice-president (dismissed on the whim of Mugabe's wife), Emmerson Mnangagwa, whose nickname, somewhat alarmingly, is "Crocodile", one acquired during his younger years as a member of a criminal gang.[9]

In independent South Africa, the system of apartheid continued to be in effect, whereby the black population were deprived of most of their civil rights. The white minority held onto power in Rhodesia, where model farms supported a flourishing economy and helped to feed the surrounding countries.

From the moment they acquired independence and right up until 1991, there was not a single incidence in any of the African countries of power changing hands as a result of an election. After this, when it began to be considered *de rigueur* to adhere to democratic principles, changes of government began to take place. The elected regimes, however, continued in many ways to use the same methods as the single party governments, and election results were distorted and falsified in many countries. "Suspicious of plots to overthrow them, the elite fill strategic positions in the police and military with personally loyal relatives and fellow tribesmen. Economic reforms that would strip out state controls and eliminate scarcity are opposed because the controls are the source of the rents that are extracted by the ruling elites. Since political defeat could mean exile, imprisonment, starvation and the confiscation of all property and wealth, ruling elites refuse to relinquish or share political power. Those who are excluded from power resort to violence, insurgency and civil war."[10]

The judicial system is extremely weak. In Uganda, only one in every hundred civil or administrative disputes actually reaches a lawyer. You could fit all the lawyers in Sierra Leone onto a couple of buses. In Malawi, murder trials were brought to a halt in the spring of 2016, because there was no money left to pay the lawyers allocated to them: there are just nine such lawyers, four of whom enhanced their qualifications abroad.[11]

---

[9] "A Coup in Zimbabwe. Fall of the Dictator", *The Economist*, November 18, 2017. P. 12; Jason Burke and Emma Graham-Harrison, "Mugabe Resignation Ushers in New Era for Zimbabwe", *The Guardian*, November 22, 2017 <https://www.theguardian.com/world/2017/nov/21/robert-mugabe-resigns-as-president-of-zimbabwe>; Dave Pilling, "The Crocodile Snatches the Top Job", *The Financial Times*, November 25, 2017. P. 13.

[10] Stuart S. Yeh, "Ending Corruption in Africa Through United Nations Inspections", *International Affairs*, Vol. 87, Issue 3, May 2011. P. 631.

[11] "Justice in Africa. Poor Law", *The Economist*, October 22, 2016. P. 30.

It is quite a stretch to describe this as democracy. There are some encouraging signs, however. Kenya's presidential elections in 2017 were won by the incumbent head of state Uhuru Kenyatta, and even Western observers declared the vote to be free and fair. Raila Odinga, however, whom he defeated, contested the validity of the vote in the Supreme Court. What would you expect to happen in such circumstances? Well, on this occasion, the highest court in the land ruled – in something that was a first in African history – that the election should be re-run, and it duly was![12]

The Labor Resource of the Planet

After they obtained independence, some of the African states were of a capitalist persuasion and others were of a socialist orientation; this was related less to the essence of the regimes than to the source through which they received foreign aid. In the countries that were more oriented towards the USSR and China, an active policy of industrialization was put into effect by means of the creation of large state-owned enterprises, which occasionally achieved very good results. The Aswan Dam in Egypt and the Akosombo power station in Ghana are still the primary sources of electric energy in those countries today. There were obvious failures as well, however. The gigantic steel smelting plant in the Nigerian city of Ajaokuta, built with Soviet help, never made any money, as a result of a shortage of iron ore. The textiles firms that were created often suffered from a shortage of cotton, the tobacco firms did not have enough tobacco, and so on. The local administrations often had grandiose plans but the managerial talents and capabilities of the new elites proved to be rather limited.

Rapid growth of the public sector was seen everywhere. From the 1960s to the 1980s, the number of civil servants rose 3-fold. Between 1950 and 1975 the continent's economy grew by an average of 2.4%, although some countries saw even faster growth: 5% in Kenya, while the Ivory Coast doubled the size of its economy in the 1960s and 1970s. The number of students increased from 25,000 for the whole of Africa around the time when independence was obtained to half a million by the mid-1980s. The quality of education left a great deal to be desired, however. The level of literacy rose from 27% in 1960 to 45% in 1990. By that time, a third of the population had access to

---

[12] "Kenyan Courts Should Scrutinise Election Result", *The Financial Times*, August 14, 2017. P. 8; Ian Bremmer, "The Saga of Kenya's Disputed Election is a Good-News Story", *Time*, September 25, 2017. P. 8.

normal drinking water, as compared with 10% in colonial times. This fact, along with vaccination programs, helped to lay the foundations for reducing infant mortality and increasing life expectancy from 40 to 52. The population began to grow quickly, often surpassing the growth rates of the economy, meaning that quality of life did not improve.

By the end of the 20th century, Africa had an entrepreneurial class of its own, which had experience of working in international markets and solid capital, though that capital itself was sometimes of dubious origin. This section of society, which had an interest in there being political and economic predictability on the continent, was one of the reasons for the restructuring of the public sector, and for the neoliberal economic reforms whose scope extended to almost the entire continent.

The IMF and the World Bank put forward their universal recipes: removing the government from the economy, deregulation, openness to foreign markets, creating mechanisms for competition, weakening currencies in order to stimulate domestic manufacturing. With a low and unchanging level of income, such a policy could be implemented by reducing state expenditure, including expenditure on social costs, reducing imports, and high inflation. "What was not taken into account, however, were the civilizational, psychological and socio-economic characteristics of the Africans, the closer bond between the people and the state, the preference for familial or clan and ethnicity-based ties rather than individual enrichment, the tendency of the overwhelming majority of the population to invest their free financial resources not in banks, shares and securities, but in prestige consumer goods, real estate, trade."[13]

The results of neoliberal policies proved to be woeful for Africa. In spite of the $170 billion received for the purposes of development, the economy of the sub-Saharan states deteriorated. Between 1982 and 1992, income per head of the population fell on average by 1.1% each year, whereas in the other developing countries it rose by 0.8%. In 1993, the combined GDP of all the countries to the south of the Sahara, which had a population of some 600 million people, was equal to that of Belgium. Their foreign debt increased 3-fold from 1980 and surpassed $180 billion, or 100% of GDP. Of the 20 poorest countries on the planet, 18 were located in Africa.[14] In the 1990s,

---

[13] A. L. Yemel'yanov, "Politicheskiye sistemy Afriki" ("The Political Systems of Africa"), in *Politicheskiye sistemy i politicheskiye kul'tury Vostoka* (*Political Systems and Political Cultures of the East*), ed. by A. D. Voskresenskiy. Moscow, 2006. P. 268.

[14] Ibid. PP. 268–269.

average economic growth on the continent amounted to 2.2%, while average annual inflation stood at 27% a year.

In the 21st century, all that changed. The African economy constantly grew at a faster rate than the global economy (the only countries whose economies grew more quickly were those in East Asia), and it grew 3-fold in size. We already know where the largest number of films are produced on the planet – in India's Bollywood. Who do you think is in second place, though? Hollywood? You would be wrong. It is in fact Nigeria's Nollywood, where between 1000 and 1500 movies are filmed each year, not including TV shows. This is cinema about Africans for Africans. Horror flicks related to the subject of witchcraft are popular. The films not only spread like wildfire across the continent, but also find audiences in countries with large African populations – in the USA and the UK.[15]

In the first half of the 2010s, the GDP of sub-Saharan Africa rose by an average of 4.8%. What were the main factors in this growth? At the top of the list we should put the rise of China, and the other major developing economies, which required a large amount of resources.[16]

In 2016, however, growth fell to 1.5%, and in 2017 it did not rise above 2.5%. There was a clear manifestation of Africa's "two-speed" growth. The downturn was put down to the fall in the price of raw materials, which led to the stagnation of the biggest exporter countries – South Africa, Nigeria and Angola. The Afro-pessimists who predict a dismal future for the continent raised their heads once again. Yet the economies of several states grew by more than 6% in 2017 – this applied to Burkina Faso, Ivory Coast, Senegal and Tanzania, while Ethiopia, with its market of 100 million people, saw growth of 7.5%.[17] Their growth was attributed not only to external reasons, however, but also to internal ones. According to IMF data, eight of the twelve fastest-growing economies in sub-Saharan Africa were not resource-based economies, and they included a host of the very poorest countries – Burkina Faso, Ethiopia, Mozambique, Rwanda, Tanzania and Uganda. These coun-

....

[15] Irina Lyubarskaya, "Dobro pozhalovat' v Nollivud" ("Welcome to Hollywood"), *Russian View*, May/June 2014. PP. 58-63.

[16] John O'Sullivan, "Digging Deeper: Some of the World's Fastest-Growing Economies in 2014 Will Be in Africa", *The Economist: The World in 2014*. P. 77; Konstantin Poltev, "Afrikanskoye safari" ("African Safari"), *Russian View*, July/August 2014. P. 44.

[17] Jonathan Rosenthal, "Lifting the Curse", *The Economist: The World in 2017*. P. 74; David Pilling and Maggie Fick, "Two-Speed Africa on Course for Modest Growth Rebound", *The Financial Times*, May 10, 2017. P. 3; "Africans Are Leaving Fields, but Not Flowing into Factories", *The Economist*, August 19, 2017. P. 58.

tries typically adopted growth strategies which allowed for macro-economic stability, investment in infrastructure and development of human capital.[18] The Nigerian-American journalist Dayo Olopade believes that the African countries' successes are related less to the implementation of schemes borrowed from the West or to the government's policies, than to the efforts of the Africans themselves; they learned to survive in extremely complex and specific conditions (the concept of *kanju*), through family values and connections brought about by the need for inventiveness.[19]

The continent satisfies more than 90% of the needs of the global industry in metals in the platinum group, 70% in diamonds and cobalt, 48% in chromite, 19% in gold, and so on.[20] 9.7% of the known oil reserves around the world are in Africa, as is 7.8% of the world's natural gas. Sources of these have been discovered in 19 countries on the continent, and it is here that up to 40% of direct foreign investment in Africa is made. Most of the hydrocarbon reserves that have been discovered – over 90% – are located on the territory and ocean shelf of seven African countries: Algeria, Sudan, Equatorial Guinea, Nigeria, Angola, Tunisia, and the Congo. African oil is high in quality, even by comparison with oil from the Middle East. International corporations are striving to secure a firm foothold in the field of refining, transportation and "downstream" logistics, while the African countries are mainly in charge of supervising the extraction and initial refining of raw materials "upstream".[21]

In 2006 to 2007, the Seychelles and Ghana became the first countries – after South Africa – to offer government bonds on the global market. Since then, a plethora of other states – from Nigeria to Rwanda and from Zambia to Angola – have followed suit, and this money was used less for investment than to subsidize prices and the salaries of civil servants.[22] In the course of a decade, the volume of bonds issued rose from 1 billion to 20 billion dollars in 2014, at a time when the ratio of state debt to GDP

---

[18] *Strategic Survey 2014: The Annual Review of World Affairs.* Routledge, 2014. P. 285.

[19] Dayo Olopade, *The Bright Continent: Breaking Rules and Making Change in Modern Africa.* Houghton Mifflin Harcourt, 2014.

[20] Vadim Zaytsev, "Rabotayte, nedra" ("Work, You Deep Depths"), *Kommersant. Vlast'* (*The Businessman. Power*), February 4, 2013. PP. 32-33.

[21] Ye. F. Chernenko, "Afrika v orbite energeticheskikh interesov Kitaya" ("Africa in the Orbit of China's Energy Interests"), in *BRIKS i Afrika: sotrudnichestvo v tselyakh razvitiya* (*BRICS and Africa: Cooperation with the Aim of Development*). Moscow, 2013. PP. 168-172.

[22] "Africa Must Invest Borrowings Wisely", *The Financial Times*, April 14, 2014. P. 12.

rose on average across Africa from 30% to 70%.[23] The risks of the bonds markets for African countries are growing. It is not quite clear how the borrower states are going to pay out, if and when an outflow of capital begins.[24]

In Africa, there are more than 1,000 public companies, and more than a hundred of them have an annual income in excess of $1 billion. 400 companies have a turnover of more than one billion dollars, while more than 700 companies have a turnover between 500 million and 1 billion dollars. Most of these are in South Africa.[25] There is a class of billionaires, the most famous of whom are the Nigerian Aliko Dangote, who amassed his capital in the cement, sugar and flour industries; his compatriot Tony Elumelu made his fortune in finance and electricity; one could mention Kenya's king of foodstuffs, Chris Kirubi, and others.[26] Most of the luxury stores in Lisbon's main shopping street, along with some enormous condominiums in the Portuguese resort of Cascais, belong to the billionaire Isabel dos Santos – the richest woman in Angola, and the daughter of the country's ex-president.[27] Meanwhile, the lion's share of production and, in particular, trade on the continent is accounted for by extremely small firms, usually run by just one person. In Nigeria alone, there are 37 million firms with fewer than ten employees, most of which are not even registered.[28]

More than 20 stock exchanges are in operation, the biggest of which are in South Africa and Nigeria. Every year, Africa loses around $150 billion as a result of the outflow of capital, with 60% of this figure attributable to tax evasion by corporations. There are a fair few "tax havens" and offshore zones, with Mauritius among the leading ones. It is worth noting that 43% of foreign investment in India in the first decade of this century was taken up by Mauritius, and 37 of the 100 biggest American companies had their affiliations on the island.[29]

---

[23] Richard Walker, "The Coming African Debt Crisis", *The Economist: The World in 2015*. P. 79.

[24] Ralph Atkins, "Reasons to Be Wary of African Debt Expansion", *The Financial Times*, May 2, 2014. P. 20.

[25] "Industry in Africa. In or Out?", *The Economist*, September 17, 2016. PP. 32-33.

[26] Andrew England, "A New Generation Leads the Way", *The Financial Times*, July 17, 2015. P. 1.

[27] Norimitsu Onishi, "Role Reversal for Angola", *The New York Times*, August 23, 2017. P. 1.

[28] "Red Tape in Nigeria. Of Mandarins and Men", *The Economist*, August 26, 2017. PP. 29-30.

[29] "Onshore Is the New Offshore", *The Africa Report*, Issue 26, December 2010 – January 2011. P. 19.

The percentage of adult Africans with a bank account exceeds one third of the continent's population. The number of mobile phone owners on the continent stood at 630 million in 2017, which meant a coverage of 50% (the average around the world was 68%).[30]

That said, the level of energy provision is extremely low. For 600 million people living in sub-Saharan Africa, life comes to a stop after the onset of nightfall. The region (if you exclude South Africa) consumes as much electricity as Vietnam. This means that children cannot do their homework, food goes off, women have to give birth by candlelight, and the cooking is done using firewood or pressed dung. Leaders in African business refer wryly to this shortage of electricity as the main obstacle on the path to economic growth.[31]

If one considers Africa as a whole, agriculture is growing slowly, and the use of fertilizers has remained the same since the mid-1990s. In recent years, manufacturing in the agricultural sector has seen growth in Angola, Mozambique, Senegal, South Africa and Zambia, but it has fallen to a 20-year low in Burundi, Cameroon, Equatorial Guinea, Madagascar, Uganda and the Seychelles. Agricultural production provides half of all jobs, but only around 20% of the region's GDP.[32] Half of all the land on the planet that is suitable for farming, but goes untilled, is in Africa. This can be explained in large part by the lack of roads, ports or storage facilities for agricultural products; farmers lose up to 50% of their produce simply in their attempt to get it to market.[33] Pestilence causes huge losses. In 2017, for instance, more than 20 African countries were afflicted by an attack of armyworms that was brought over from America.[34] The land is not very fertile, and fertilizers are mostly imported, and are therefore twice as expensive as they are in the USA. Africa currently imports a third of the food and water people drink, far more than the developing countries of Asia or Latin America. The exporting of foodstuffs from sub-Saharan countries has fallen 4-fold in the last 50 years, and is now lower than exports from Thailand alone.[35]

---

[30] "Big Data: The Hunt Begins", *The Africa Report*, Issue 93, September 2017. PP. 22-23.
[31] Michael Elliott, "Lighting up Africa", *The Economist: The World in 2014*. P. 80.
[32] *Strategic Survey 2014: The Annual Review of World Affairs*. Routledge, 2014. P. 287.
[33] Ngozi Okonjo-Iweala and Dilip Ratha, "Homeward Bound", *The International Herald Tribune*, March 16, 2011. P. 9.
[34] John Aglionby, "Hungry Invader: Armyworm's March across Africa Leaves Destroyed Crops in Its Wake", *The Financial Times*, April 29, 2017. P. 4.
[35] "Agriculture in Africa. Wake Up and Sell More Coffee", *The Economist*, September 19, 2015.

The best transport artery for journeys from the North to the South, as was the case many centuries ago, is still the Nile; roads across the Sahara are either missing or destroyed, and are very dangerous. Inter-continental trade accounts for only 13% of the total volume (53% inside Asia). Transport costs account for 50%-75% of the retail prices of goods in Malawi, Rwanda and Uganda. Shipping an automobile from China to Tanzania costs 4,000 dollars, and it will cost a further 5,000 dollars to transport it to the neighboring country, Uganda. Countless checkpoints demand bribes and slow down the movement of goods.[36]

Air links between the continent's countries are underdeveloped. In most of them, the flight schedules are as unreliable as the airplanes themselves. Many states have still not reached agreements with one another on the opening of flight routes. Airline tickets are so expensive that it is often cheaper to travel via Europe or Dubai when flying between African countries. Most airlines make a loss and are kept afloat through government subsidies.[37]

Africa is, for the time being, not taking part, to any strong degree, in global trade – only 2% of the total volume is accounted for by the continent. The explanation for this lies in no small part in the fact that there is still a degree of discrimination in trade on the part of the West. The EU provides a right to trade without customs and quotas to only the 27 poorest countries in Africa, while a host of former metropolises give out less generous preferences to their former colonies on a bilateral basis. The USA bestows favors on 40 countries in Africa, but rules out giving preferential treatment to any kind of agricultural products which are capable of competing with those produced inside the USA, such as cotton.[38]

Just as was the case in the past, economic growth is not keeping pace with the growth of the population. 65% of the population of Africa lives on less than 2 dollars a day, with 290 million people going hungry. At the same time, the continent has seen growth of 21% in overall working resources, and this figure will rise to as much as 30% in the next decade. In 1950, 9% of the Earth's population lived in Africa; by the middle of this century, the continent will be home to one in four people on the planet. It is the youngest continent: 43% of people in sub-Saharan Africa are under 15, and only 3%

....
PP. 33-34.

[36] "Transport in Africa. Get a Move On", *The Economist*, February 16, 2013. PP. 29-30.

[37] "Travel in Africa. Let Africans Fly", *The Economist*, February 13, 2016. PP. 9-10.

[38] K. Y. Amoako, Daniel Hamilton and Eveline Herfkens, "A Trans-Atlantic Deal for Africa", *The International Herald Tribune*, May 8, 2013. P. 6.

are over 65. After 2050, Africa will account for more than 90% of population growth, and a 65% increase in labor resources on Earth.[39] The quality of that human capital remains extremely low, however.

The level of illiteracy for the continent, on average, is 40%. 43 million Africans are infected with HIV, around 4 million have tuberculosis, and more than 90% of all deaths from malaria around the world occur in Africa. Average life expectancy is the lowest in the world – 53. And this is despite the developments in healthcare that have been achieved: the last case of poliomyelitis was recorded in 2014, for instance.[40] Unemployment is high, with the official figure (15%) not reflecting the true statistics. Labor migration is also high: 35 million migrants, out of a total of 200 million in the world, are Africans.[41] The people's standard of living remains the lowest in the world: 2,500 dollars in terms of purchasing power parity.

Africa is undergoing a tumultuous period of urbanization. In the 1950s, there was not a single city in sub-Saharan Africa with a population of 1 million; today, there are more than 50. A third of Africans already live in cities, and by 2030, one in two will do so. Unlike other parts of the world, urbanization has not been accompanied by industrialization, and is not leading to a visible rise in living standards. Why is that? Africa's cities are places where the rich spend the money they have made from natural resource royalties. Due to the weakness of the states, tax revenues are extremely low, and this explains the lack of their own investment in infrastructure or major industry. Even in the districts for the wealthy, residents have to take care of the electricity supply, and other things such as like ensuring the driveways to their villas are covered with asphalt, themselves. The poor, meanwhile, are tucked away in tiny dwellings; 40% of city-dwellers do not have a toilet, and official jobs are a rarity. Hence the

---

[39] I. O. Abramova and L. L. Fituni, "Afrikanskiy region v kontekste fundamental'nykh trendov i formiruyushchikhsya ugroz v mirovoy ekonomike i politike" ("The African Region in the Context of Fundamental Trends and Emerging Threats in the Global Economy and Politics"), *Vestnik Rossiyskogo gumanitarnogo nauchnogo fonda* (*Bulletin of RGNF*), Issue 4, 2015. PP. 58-59.

[40] Donald G. McNeil, "In a First, Africa Goes One Year Without Finding a Case of Polio", *The New York Times*, August 11, 2015 <https://www.nytimes.com/2015/08/12/health/a-milestone-in-africa-one-year-without-a-case-of-polio.html>.

[41] I. O. Abramova, "Demograficheskiye protsessy v stranakh BRIKS: posledstviya dlya Afriki" ("Demographic Processes in the BRICS Countries: Consequences for Africa"), in *BRIKS i Afrika: sotrudnichestvo v tselyakh razvitiya* (*BRICS and Africa: Cooperation with the Aim of Development*). Moscow, 2013. PP. 39-40.

fairly considerable scale at which modern housing is being constructed, for which no buyers can be found.[42]

The people of Africa charge the West with having destroyed Africa, and, furthermore, with failing to help the continent today. There are certain grounds for drawing such conclusions. According to a report published in 2016 by the organization War on Want, 101 British companies controlled resource assets in Africa worth over 1 trillion dollars. They invested 134 billion dollars in the continent in a year in the form of loans, foreign investment and aid. But they took 192 billion dollars out of Africa in profits. That represents a direct outflow of capital of 58 billion dollars. Ross Hemingway, in a special report, claimed: "Today, the African continent is facing a colonial invasion no less devastating in scale and impact than the one it suffered during the nineteenth century."[43]

Meanwhile, does the average European or American know very much about the incredibly brutal civil wars in Sudan, Angola, the Congo, Rwanda, Burundi, Sierra Leone, Liberia, Somalia, Mali and the Central African Republic, or the wiping out of a third of the population of Equatorial Guinea? And yet the conflicts in the Middle East, the "Arab Spring", and Afghanistan are talked about all the time…

After they obtained independence, the African countries also began to demonstrate a desire to achieve solidarity. In May 1963, the Organization of African Unity was established, which was later transformed into the African Union (AU), headquartered in Addis Ababa. The idea was put forward by Muammar Gaddafi – the main driving force behind integration on the continent – at the 4th extraordinary assembly of the OAU in Sirte, in September 1999. The organizational structure of the AU was in many ways modeled on the mechanisms within the European Union: an Assembly consisting of the heads of states and governments, a Commission formed of ten people, subordinate to an Executive Council. In 2004, the Peace and Security Council was created, which even had its own troops. At the same time, the Pan-African parliament was convened, with the purpose of performing mainly consultative functions. The AU's financial institutions are the African Central Bank, the African Currency Fund and the African Investment Bank. Continental solidarity can be seen in the harmonized stances adopted and joint

---

[42] "African Cities. Left Behind", *The Economist*, September 17, 2016. PP. 31-32.

[43] Ross Hemingway, "UK's New Scramble for Africa", *New African*, August/September 2016. P. 18.

voting conducted in the UN's General Assembly and the World Trade Organization.[44]

The political and economic development of Africa, after it achieved independence, has been characterized by countless peaks and troughs. All this has been accompanied by military coups, of which Africa has now had almost as many as South America. Whereas in the East, access to power was one of the ways to get rich, in Africa, it was the only way, and this determined the ferocity of the struggle for power, the brutality of the ruling regimes, the multiplicity of coups and the waves of nationalism. Corruption and displays of luxury became widespread. A new tribe emerged in Africa – the *vabenzy*, a Swahili neologism, derived from the word "Mercedes-Benz". Members of parliament in Gabon decided to pay themselves salaries that are far higher than those earned by the MPs in the UK parliament. Almost every leader ordered the construction of a huge stadium in his honor.

Afrocentrism

The majority of Western experts on matters of civilization, apart from Braudel, have failed to acknowledge the existence of a separate African civilization. Samuel Huntington was cautious: "[C]onceivably sub-Saharan Africa could cohere into a distinct civilization […]."[45] At the same time, there is good reason to consider sub-Saharan Africa in many respects as a single whole. The population, for all its ethnic diversity, is, in the main, homogeneous, and bound by a common destiny. For the Cameroonian Daniel Etounga-Manguelle, who wrote the relevant chapter of *Culture Matters*, "[T]here is a foundation of shared values, attitudes and institutions that binds together the nations south of the Sahara, and in many respects those to the north as well."[46]

A particular feature of African society is its capacity to survive, to adapt itself to extremely difficult circumstances. Ideas of private ownership of land are alien, for the land ultimately remains the property of the community. Low population density has meant that the key problem is not so much

---

[44] Reuben E. Brigety, "The New Pan-Africanism: Implications for US Africa Policy", *Survival*, August/September 2016. PP. 159-160.

[45] Samuel P. Huntington, *The Clash of Civilizations and the Remaking of World Order*. Simon & Schuster, 1996. P. 47.

[46] Daniel Etounga-Manguelle, "Does Africa Need a Cultural Adjustment Program?", in *Culture Matters: How Values Shape Human Progress*, ed. by Lawrence E. Harrison and Samuel P. Huntington. Basic Books, 2001. P. 67.

ownership of land, as the search for a workforce to work the land. Societies were preoccupied with the problem of reproduction, of having children, and polygamy was widespread. Marital life was less a private association between two people than a matter of relations between households and complex intra-community relations.

The battle for control of the land, disputes with regard to sovereignty or the demarcation of borders, which have played such a big role in world history, were not very significant in Africa, due to people's ability to migrate elsewhere. The high mobility of the population has also made it difficult to establish what is generally known as national identity. Among the 1,000 to 2,000 languages spoken in Africa, only 50 of them are spoken by more than a million people. In Sierra Leone alone, 16 different languages are in use, four of which are official state languages.

In Africa, outside the realm of Islam, there is no single religion that dominates. There is a mixture of Islam, Christianity and traditional beliefs. Faith in dark forces only grew stronger as people became familiar with the Bible and the Koran, which assert the existence of diabolical origins. The fortunes of a football team are as much in the hands of the minister of a cult as they are in the hands of the team's coach. The concept of a higher reasoning co-exists with a world of spirits of nature, ancestors, heroic soldiers and witches, on which fertility and the flourishing and prospering of the community depend. The division between the political and the religious, so important for Western consciousness, does not make much sense in the African one.[47] It is entirely run-of-the-mill for an African leader to talk about having magic powers: faith in the leader as the source of the country's power is tied up with this.

Etounga-Manguelle identifies the following typology in the "African cultural reality": a great deal of vertical differentiation, a small amount of national wealth concentrated in the hands of the few; strong faith in the idea that God alone is capable of altering the logic of the world, which he himself created for eternity; the African was enslaved by nature, which determines his fate; the African sees time and space as an unbroken whole ("A watch did not invent man"); the past can only repeat itself.[48] Prosperity is possible through community and family, and skepticism and individualism are alien

....

[47] Tom Young, *Africa: A Beginner's Guide*. Oneworld Publications, 2010. PP. 10-15.
[48] Daniel Etounga-Manguelle, "Does Africa Need a Cultural Adjustment Program?", in *Culture Matters: How Values Shape Human Progress*, ed. by Lawrence E. Harrison and Samuel P. Huntington. Basic Books, 2001. P. 69.

to African thought. Society is structured around celebrations: the birth of children, baptisms, weddings, birthdays, promotions at work, elections, the opening of parliament, arrivals and departures, traditional and church-related festivities. The African works in order to live, rather than living for work. Saving up is far less important than spending immediately. In this sense, the government and the *nouveaux riches* are not very different from the ordinary citizens.

At the same time, Etounga-Manguelle considers African culture to be one of the most humane kinds: with this is solidarity, love for one's neighbors regardless of age and status, respect for nature as something to be enjoyed by everyone.[49] And the matter of whether or not Africa has its own distinctive civilization, and of whether it is superior to the others, does not even arise for supporters of the ideas of Afrocentrism and negritude.

Afrocentrism (also Afrocentricity) is a response to long years of humiliation and oppression, to European arrogance and imperialist racism. African schoolchildren in the colonial era were forced to study not the history and culture of their peoples, but the history of the United Kingdom, France, Belgium or Portugal. Action gave rise to counter-action. Way back in 1923, Marcus Garvey, the founder of the "Back to Africa" movement in the US, asserted that Africans had mastered the arts, science and literature at a time when Europe was populated with nothing more than cannibals, barbarians and pagans.[50]

Afrocentrism began to take shape as a developed ideological movement in Afro-American circles in the USA in the early 1980s, and later became more widespread among parts of the African intelligentsia as well. One of its main theoreticians – Molefi Kete Asante, a professor from Philadelphia – writes: "Afrocentricity maintains intellectual vigilance as the proper posture toward all scholarship that ignores the origin of civilization in the highlands of East Africa. [O]nly one ancient civilization could be considered European in origin, Greece. And Greece itself is a product of its interaction with African civilizations. Among ancient civilizations Africans gave the world, Ethiopia, Nubia, Egypt, Cush, Axum, Ghana, Mali, and Songhay. These ancient civilizations are responsible for medicine, science, the concept of monarchies and divine-kingships, and an Almighty God."[51] Afrocentricity,

---

[49] Ibid. PP. 68-75.

[50] *My Soul Looks Back, Lest I Forget: A Collection of Quotations by People of Color*, ed. by D. W. Riley. N. Y., 1998. P. 7.

[51] Molefi Kete Asante, *Afrocentricity: The Theory of Social Change*. African American Images,

in his opinion, "can stand its ground among any ideologies and religion: Marxism, Islam, Christianity, Buddhism, or Judaism."[52]

In parallel to this, the ideas of negritude began to take shape: the exclusive nature, the special psychological makeup of the "negro soul", which cannot be understood and explained from the point of view of Western rationalism. The white man, according to negritude, gave in to materialism, became a slave to technology and machines, while the black man preserved his ties to nature, his emotional, sensitive perception of reality. One of the founders of negritude, the poet and first president of Senegal, Léopold Sédar Senghor, believed that the mission of black people was to restore unity between mankind and nature, in the multi-faceted spiritual development of mankind. He asserted, meanwhile, that pride in one's race is the first requirement of negritude.[53]

A striving for self-assertion leads to a rapid increase in the level of interest in one's own culture and traditions. Instead of reading about the lives of Napoleon and Queen Victoria, they now study the biographies of their own rulers and are dismayed to see them being described, in Europe, not as kings but as chiefs. From this, it is but a small step to promoting various kinds of "reverse discrimination" – discrimination against white and mixed-race people. The most striking example was Zimbabwe, where Mugabe allowed the "spontaneous" seizure of farms belonging to whites. The result was the collapse of agriculture, famine, rising levels of crime, and people fleeing to neighboring countries.

Conflicts Non-Stop

In the first two or three decades of independence, the African nations got on reasonably well with one another. The terrifying civil war in Nigeria in the late 1960s, and the bloody inter-ethnic conflicts in Rwanda and Burundi, were the exceptions. Today, Africa is the least stable region on the planet, even leaving aside all the revolutions and wars in the Maghreb, which were discussed earlier. More people are killed in wars and inter-ethnic conflicts in Africa than anywhere else in the world. Half of all the UN's peacekeeping missions take place on the continent.

2003. P. 50.

[52] Ibid. P. 56.

[53] Cit. from: Ibid. P. 90.

Along the tenth parallel north – a border between the desert worlds and the savannah, between Islam and other faiths, between cattle raisers and farmers, Arabs and blacks – there stretches an unprecedented belt of anarchy, lawlessness, famine and almost continuous bloody conflicts. Here, the tone is set not so much by governments but by clans, tribal leaders and soldiers, who often have their own agenda. In times gone by, however, there were also attempts to establish a *modus vivendi*, to take the interests of the nomadic and farming tribes into account. Today, this does not happen. As a result of global warming, droughts have become more frequent, intensifying the struggle over the water, land and food resources that are growing ever scarcer. Those working the land must struggle to prevent it being turned into a steppe, trampled upon by cattle; they must fight to save their pastures and prevent theft of their crops by hungry animals. On the nomads' traditional routes, fenced farmland and rivers are appearing.

Ideas associated with religious extremism are met with a very favorable response in some areas. Al-Qaida has become noticeably active in the countries of the Islamic Maghreb; it is working to topple all the secular regimes in the region. Up to half the population owns a weapon, mainly the tried and tested Kalashnikov. In some places, it appeared as a result of civil wars which lasted decades (Somalia or Sudan), while elsewhere governments opted to arm the people themselves (Kenya or Ethiopia).[54]

In Somalia, commanders of rebel groups, pirates and Islamists from the Al Shabaab group brought the country to a state of chaos. Kenya, which for many years was presented as a model democracy, is waging a long-drawn-out war against the Islamists. The Turkana and Dassanech tribes, which co-existed peacefully for centuries on the border between Kenya and Ethiopia, are now battling for control over Lake Turkana, whose waters are rapidly growing shallower, and the governments of both countries have armed "their" respective tribes.

A war has been going on for many years in the Sudan, in which there has been a precise division into the Muslim Arabs of the North and the black Christians and Animists in the South. The war, which has taken more than 2 million lives, ended in a referendum in 2011, in which 99% of southerners voted for independence. The vast nation of South Sudan, which was welcomed amid much fanfare by the UN, had 40 km of asphalt roads, and outside Juba and Malakal there were no visible signs of governance, or of po-

---

[54] Horand Knaup, "Epidemiya AK-47" ("The AK-47 Epidemic"), *Profil'* (*Profile*), Issue 11, 2012. PP. 28-31.

lice stations or hospitals (80% of medical assistance was provided by foreign NGOs). The country nevertheless has 75% of the oil that was once shared by the whole of Sudan, one of the largest volumes in Africa. All the oil pipelines go towards the North. Without having reached an agreement about the price of transit, the former field commander and now president of South Sudan, Salva Kiir, decided to end exports of hydrocarbons, prompting multibillion dollar losses and a new war. He relied on the support of the USA, which is lobbying for the construction of a new oil pipeline to the Kenyan port of Lama, and declared the President of Sudan, Omar Bashir (he was more friendly with China and Russia) to be a sponsor of international terrorism because of the genocide in Darfur. Fierce fighting ensued, with thousands killed on both sides.[55]

Inside South Sudan, a Civil War has been raging since December 2013 over control of oil between the government forces of Kiir, who is from the Dinka tribe, and the former vice president Riek Machar, of the Nuer people. UN peacekeepers have been trying unsuccessfully to restore order. Of the 6 million inhabitants of South Sudan, 1.8 million have left the country, including more than a million children, while tens of thousands have been killed. 75% of the children still in the country do not go to school.[56]

In North Sudan, in April 2015, Bashir was re-elected for another five-year term amid scenes of triumph, whereupon his foreign policy activity shifted towards countering the Houthis in Yemen and the Islamists in Libya, in a coalition with Egypt and the Saudis.[57] In November 2017, Bashir visited Russia for the first time and, laying the blame for all the continent's woes at the door of the Americans, invited Moscow to install a Russian military base in Sudan.[58] He also made peace with the USA, who demanded to end fuel and wheat subsidies in return for international

....

[55] Jody Clarke, "A Country Starting from Scratch", *Mail & Guardian (South Africa)*, January 14-20, 2011. P. 21; Maxim Yusin, "Na dva Sudana nefti ne khvatilo" ("There wasn't Enough Oil for Two Sudans"), *Kommersant (The Businessman)*, April 18, 2012 <https://www.kommersant.ru/doc/1917892>.

[56] "South Sudan. A New Depth of Horror", *The Economist*, April 26, 2014. P. 33; "South Sudan – Chronology of a Struggle, and a Conflict", *New African*, August/September 2016. PP. 34-35; "Children Worst Victims of S. Sudan Conflict", *Gulf News*, May 10, 2017.

[57] "Sudan's Politics. May the Only Man Win", *The Economist*, April 18, 2015. P. 36.

[58] Andrey Kolesnikov, "Tudan-Sudan: Kak dlya Vladimira Putina podbirali klyuchi k Afrike" ("Tudan-Sudan: How the keys to Africa were Picked for Vladimir Putin"), *Kommersant (The Businessman)*, November 24, 2017 <https://www.kommersant.ru/doc/3475891>.

assistance. At the end of 2018 mass protests erupted against skyrocketing prices for food and gas. On April 2019 Bashir was removed by the military.

In Mali, in 2012, the government of Amadou Toumani was removed from office, after being unable to protect the country from the Tuaregs, whose activity had been restrained prior to that via monetary aid from Gaddafi. When Gaddafi died, the Tuaregs and their Islamist allies from Al-Qaida in the Islamic Maghreb occupied northern Mali and proclaimed the establishment of a new state on a territory twice as big as Germany – Azawad. In Bamako, a military junta came to power following a coup, and set about the task of liberating the country from the Tuaregs, but this regime was not recognized by the outside world. The leaders of the Economic Community of West African States (ECOWAS), which includes 15 countries, announced that, together with the French, they were going to defend the territorial integrity of Mali.[59] Mali's neighbors themselves, however, could not control their own territories.[60]

A nation that is extremely unstable is the gigantic Nigeria, the continent's most highly-populated country – with 200 million people – and one that is competing with South Africa for the title of Africa's largest economy. In Nigeria, the group Boko Haram (its name means "Western education is a sin"), relying on support from the Kanuri tribes, established a self-proclaimed state in the poorest Islamic state, Borno. Under the law there, it is forbidden to take part in elections, to be given a secular education, or to walk around in Western clothes. In thousands of Muslim schools, the only subjects are Koran studies and Arabic, and the pupils are penniless children with unemployed parents (their fathers may have two to three dozen such children from four different wives).[61] The size of this "caliphate" is larger than the area of Belgium, having also incorporated the states of Yobe and Adamawa. Early in 2015, a wave of explosions, murders and kidnappings flared up in regions of Cameroon, Chad and Niger, adjacent to Nigeria. In March, Boko Haram officially announced that it was in a union with IS, declaring itself to be a "West African province" of ISIL's

---

[59] Anatoly Maximov, "Interventsiya protiv dzhikhada" ("The Intervention Against Jihad"), *Kommersant* (*The Businessman*), April 9, 2012 <https://www.kommersant.ru/doc/1911453>.

[60] Maxim Yusin, "Voyna v Mali idet po voskhodyashchey" ("The War in Mali is Stepping up a Gear"), *Kommersant* (*The Businessman*), February 25, 2013 <https://www.kommersant.ru/doc/2134361>.

[61] Horand Knaup, "Epidemiya AK-47" ("The AK-47 Epidemic"), *Profil'* (*Profile*), Issue 11, 2012. PP. 28-31.

global "caliphate".[62] By the end of 2017, more than 20,000 people had already been killed by its reign of terror, with 2 million becoming refugees.[63]

The elections in 2015 boiled down to a clash between the failed president Goodluck Jonathan and the former dictator, General Muhammadu Buhari, who won the election with a large majority.[64] The losing side acknowledged Buhari's victory, and this was the first case of power being handed from one party to another in Nigeria's history.

Thereafter, however, profits from the sale of oil, which account for 70% of all the money coming into the budget and 90% of exports, fell sharply, prompting a crisis in 2016 (a fall of 1.5%), which was replaced by growth of less than 1% in 2017. 66% of budget income had to be used to service the country's debt, forcing the ratings agencies to lower the country's credit rating to five degrees below the "garbage" level. Hopes for fresh growth are tied to a rise in the price of oil and major Chinese investment in infrastructure projects.[65]

The situation was made worse by problems with Buhari's health: for months at a time, he was not only away from his desk, but away from the country, undergoing treatment in London. Under these circumstances, there was talk of the country being divided in two – the mainly Muslim North and the mainly Christian South, which is represented among the country's political elite by Vice-president Yemi Osinbajo, the man actually running the country.[66]

The coastline of Africa has become the major site for piracy in the world. Until quite recently, the leading area for this was the equatorial Indian Ocean

---

[62] Ivan Ivanov and Igor Kryuchkov, "Black Flags over Africa", *Mir i politika* (*The World and Politics*), April 2015. PP. 59-61; "Nigeria's Insurgency. Bombs Are Back", *The Economist*, July 11, 2015. PP. 32-33.

[63] Ruth Maclean, "Suicide Bomber Kills Dozens at Mosque in North-East Nigeria", *The Guardian*, November 22, 2017.

[64] "Nigeria's Election. The Least Awful", *The Economist*, February 7, 2015. PP. 10-11; "Nigerian Politics. Please Don't Expect Miracles", *The Economist*, April 11, 2015. P. 36.

[65] "Nigeria Sues Oil Firms for $12.7bn in Illegal Exports", *The Financial Tribune*, September 21, 2016 <https://financialtribune.com/articles/energy/50229/nigeria-sues-oil-firms-for-127b-in-illegal-exports?utm_campaign=more-like-this>; Maggie Fick, "Nigeria Seeks $6bn China Loan to Modernise Railways", *The Financial Times*, April 26, 2017 <https://www.ft.com/content/9a3b9b20-2aa1-11e7-bc4b-5528796fe35c>; Maggie Fick, "Nigeria Pins Hopes on Big Projects to Reverse Drop into Recession", *The Financial Times*, May 5, 2017. P. 4.

[66] Dionne Searcey and Tony Iyare, "Appearance by the Ailing President Hardly Reassures Many in Nigeria", *The New York Times*, May 9, 2017. P. A5; Ian Bremmer, "Will Nigeria's Ailing President Name a Successor?", *Time*, September 4, 2017. P. 8.

and the Gulf of Aden not far from Somalia, where attacks were made on ships practically on a daily basis. Through the efforts of the military and the Navy, however, piracy has been reduced to a minimum there, after which first place in the piracy stakes went to the Gulf of Guinea in the Atlantic, and in particularly Nigeria's waters.[67]

The instability has fueled militarization, though not on a large scale, because of the general level of poverty in the countries on this continent. The total military spending of all Sub-Saharan countries is $17 billion, which is less than the defence budget of Israel alone. Surprisingly, the rankings in terms of military spending and army size do not fully coincide. The largest defence budgets are in Algeria ($9.93 billion), South Africa ($3.68 billion), Morocco ($3.63 billion), Egypt ($2.9 billion), and Angola ($2.22 billion). The most numerous armies are in Egypt (439,000), Eritrea (202,000), Morocco (196,000), South Sudan (185,000), and Ethiopia (138,000).[68] Algeria became the first country in Africa to spend more than $10 billion a year on defence, with Angola not far behind.[69]

A Crafty Choice

Africa is of unquestioned and ever-growing interest to all the global players, as a result of its economic potential and its overall political influence. The continent's countries have 27% of the votes in the UN.

The end of the Cold War was not greeted with enthusiasm in Africa. Having concluded that the West won it, the African countries made haste to declare their loyalty to the West. No real response was forthcoming, however. It was not until the start of the 21st century that the developed countries proposed the program "A New Partnership for African development" (NEPAD). With the aim of implementing it, at the G8 summit in Kananaskis (June 2002), an action plan for Africa was adopted. However, the aid thus far has boiled down to the West sending surplus agricultural products, and also allocating credit which is returned to the West to purchase goods there and pay for the services of specialists. The products that are grown by the Africans themselves are not competitive, since

---

[67] "Piracy in Africa. The Ungoverned Seas", *The Economist*, November 29, 2014. PP. 33-34.
[68] *The Military Balance 2019: The Annual Assessment of Global Military Capabilities and Defence Economics*. London, IISS, 2019. PP. 515-518.
[69] "Comme à la guerre", *Russian View*, July/August 2014. P. 4.

they, unlike Western farmers, do not receive government subsidies.[70] In October 2008, the United States officially opened the Africa Command (AFRICOM) of their Armed Forces, with headquarters in Stuttgart. Concerned about criticism of their military policy, particularly in the Muslim world, the USA stressed that their aims in Africa were to prevent wars rather than to wage them, the long-term development of military capabilities, and the maintaining of stability.[71]

Under Obama, it appeared that the USA, considering that the President's father was from Kenya, would not need to do anything to safeguard its position and its sympathies on the continent. It turned out that this was not enough against the backdrop of other states' activities (Chinese trade with Africa was already twice as big as that of America). In August 2014, a three-day American-African summit was organized in Washington, for which some 40 African leaders travelled to the country. The USA presented itself as a partner in creating jobs, resolving conflicts, and developing human capital.[72] It transpired, however, that Washington saw its role, primarily, in the arming of African armies. Obama promised $5 billion to fund a "counter-terrorist partnership", which supports the Pentagon's programs in 35 states on the continent. The largest resources went to two countries – Nigeria and South Sudan, whose militaries are particularly famous for corruption. "America's diplomacy is becoming a handmaiden to Africa's generals," joked well-informed analysts.[73]

At first, Trump simply neglected Africa. However, in 2019 he sent the First lady Melania on a goodwill tour to four African countries, which was intended to emphasize his concern for the continent.

The European Union adopted a new strategy in its relations with Africa in 2005. Under this strategy, at least half the resources from the general European assistance funds were directed towards Africa, and the volume of these grew from 17 billion in 2003 to 25 billion Euros in 2010. Special attention was paid to supporting forward-looking projects, aimed at reducing

....

[70]   Nikolay Alekseyev-Rybin, "Pyat'desyat let muchitel'noy svobody" ("Fifty Years of Tortuous Freedom"), *Vokrug sveta (Around the World)*, November 2010. P. 92.

[71]   *The Military Balance 2010: An Annual Assessment of Global Military Capabilities and Defence Economies*. London: IISS, 2010. P. 288.

[72]   "Obama's Africa Summit", *The New York Times*, August 5, 2014 <https://www.nytimes.com/2014/08/06/opinion/obamas-africa-summit.html>.

[73]   Alex de Waal and Abdul Mohammed, "Handmaiden to Africa's Generals", *The New York Times*, August 15, 2014 <https://www.nytimes.com/2014/08/16/opinion/handmaiden-to-africas-generals.html>.

dependency on foreign investment. Europe remains the largest market for African exports.

The attitude of modern Europeans to Africa is fairly well encapsulated by this passage from Dominique Moïsi: "Among Europeans, especially those whose countries were former colonial powers in Africa, the attitude toward Africa includes both a real concern for the future of Africans and a similar blend of greed and fear. In the European case, it is the fear of having too many Africans rushing to Europe to escape lives of misery at home. The Mediterranean Sea, no longer the 'cradle of civilization' French historian Fernand Braudel described, has become a lake where the world's well-off, cruising in their yachts, can briefly glimpse the refugees from the other side of the water, clinging to their precarious craft as they risk their lives to reach the 'European paradise.'"[74]

Events in Libya – until recently the most affluent country on the continent – have had a negative impact on people's attitude towards the involvement of Western countries in Africa. The mechanism of the African Union, specially created for diplomatic and peacekeeping efforts, was demonstratively ignored in the capital cities of NATO. A panel of five African presidents, led by Jacob Zuma of South Africa, proposed that Col. Muammar Gaddafi should "go into exile in an African country and then setting up an interim government. But the plan was spurned by NATO, which preferred regime change by way of foreign intervention."[75]

Is it any wonder that the BRICS countries, particularly China, are playing an increasingly serious role on the African continent? Unlike the West, China does not impose any conditions on cooperation, and does not try to teach anyone how to live. Deng Xiaoping, in a conversation with the leader of Ghana during a visit to the country in 1985, observed: "Please don't copy our model. If there is any experience on our part, it is to formulate policies in light of one's own national conditions."[76] The president of Uganda, Yoweri Museveni, talked about the difference between the Chinese and Western approaches: "How can you have structural adjustment without electricity? The Chinese understand the basics. […] You can't impose middle-class values

---

[74] Dominique Moïsi, *The Geopolitics of Emotion: How Cultures of Fear, Humiliation and Hope are Reshaping the World*. Random House, 2009.

[75] Alex de Waal and Abdul Mohammed, "Handmaiden to Africa's Generals", *The New York Times*, August 15, 2014 <https://www.nytimes.com/2014/08/16/opinion/handmaiden-to-africas-generals.html>.

[76] Cit. from: Joshua Kurlantzick, *State Capitalism: How the Return of Statism is Transforming the World*. Oxford University Press, 2016. P. 109.

on a pre-industrial society. How can you make peasants have middle-class values? They are peasants. Many of them are pre-capitalists. How can you make them have values such as liberalism? The Chinese don't have these."[77]

Securing access to Africa's mineral resources was the key objective only in the first stage of China's penetration into Africa in the 1990s. At that time, thanks to the issuing of credit and arms supplies, Beijing quickly established amicable ties with African regimes which the West considered to be dictatorships and tried to isolate. Chinese state-owned companies were granted the right to develop hydrocarbons and minerals in places where Western companies could not work. As a result, Africa now supplies a third of the oil imported into China. Later, China started to make large development investments and to establish its own businesses on the continent.

Another serious player on the continent is India, which has a long history of being present in Africa. The Dutch brought Indian slaves to their colony on the Cape in the mid-17th century. By the 1980s, there were almost 800,000 Indians living in South Africa, yet their numbers then fell to 350,000: most of them, under the pressure of the apartheid regime, moved to Europe.[78] The countries with the closest ties to Delhi are Angola, the Congo, Gabon, Cameroon and Nigeria. By 2014, India controlled 7% of the African market for telecommunications services, 5% of consumer goods, and 10% of the energy sector. In terms of the amount of investment in the continent, it was in sixth place, and in terms of the size of foreign trade – third.[79]

In recent times, Russia has begun a gradual return to Africa, the start of which was initiated by Putin and Medvedev's visit to Morocco, South Africa, Libya, Algeria, Angola, Namibia, Nigeria and Egypt. Since the turn of the century, trade turnover has risen 10-fold, reaching 12 billion dollars, but this is only half as much as Brazil's, a quarter of that of India, and one sixteenth of that of China. 70% of Russia's trade with the continent involves the countries of North Africa, with food products and raw materials dominating, along with arms.[80]

....

[77] Cit. from: James Kynge, "Uganda Looks to China for Investment: Sub-Saharan Africa", *The Financial Times*, October 22, 2014. P. 2.

[78] Boris Kuzyk and Tat'yana Shaumyan, *Indiya – Rossiya: strategiya partnerstva v XXI veke* (*India – Russia: A Strategy of Partnership in the 21st Century*). Moscow, 2009. P. 331.

[79] Victor Mallet, "African Growth Opportunities Entice India", *The Financial Times*, March 12, 2014. P. 4.

[80] Aleksey Vasil'yev and Yevgeniy Korendyasov, "Afrikanskiy gambit" ("The African Gambit"), *Russian View*, May/June 2014. P. 41.

Russia is contributing to programs aimed at supporting development. African debt to the tune of 20 billion dollars has been written off, including 4.8 billion dollars owed by Ethiopia, 4.5 billion dollars by Libya, 4.3 billion dollars by Algeria, and 3.5 billion dollars by Angola.[81] There are more than 6500 African students studying in Russia, half of them for free.[82]

"Russia is returning to Africa from a 'low start,'" observed the former special representative of the president on ties with the continent, Mikhail Margelov. "Soviet influence, founded on loans at discounted rates and gifts in the form of dams and so on, is not something that is within the power of Russian business to provide, and the state is not engaging in this... A state economic strategy is required, for the development of which efforts by the state are needed."[83]

Does African civilization exist? I suppose, it does. And if not, then it is emerging. The leader in this process of African civilization formation is South Africa.

South African Path to Freedom

Situated on the southernmost tip of Africa, the Republic of South Africa is the 24th largest country in the world in terms of territory (1.2 million sq. km., immediately behind Mali). It has a very varied climate: from the dry deserts of the Namib to sub-tropical conditions in the East, on the border with Mozambique, and the coast of the Indian Ocean. The Western part of the country, consisting of the Kalahari Desert and the marshy lowlands bordering the Atlantic, is not very suitable for habitation. The Western coastline is a plain, where the tsetse fly reigns supreme; travellers are best advised to get through this part of the country rapidly, in order to reach the regions further inland. There, the landscape changes quickly, forming the Drakensberg and crossing into a large internal plateau, known as the veld. The lands

---

[81] Yevgeniy Korendyasov, "Interesy Rossii v Afrike" ("Russia's Interests in Africa"), in *BRIKS i Afrika: sotrudnichestvo v tselyakh razvitiya* (*BRICS and Africa: Cooperation with the Aim of Development*). Moscow, 2013. PP. 190-193; N. A. Volgina, "Rossiyskiye investitsii v Afrike" ("Russian Investment in Africa"), in *BRIKS i Afrika: sotrudnichestvo v tselyakh razvitiya* (*BRICS and Africa: Cooperation with the Aim of Development*). Moscow, 2013. PP. 174-175.

[82] Sergey Lavrov, "Rossiya i Afrika k yugu ot Sakhary: otnosheniya, proverennyye vremenem" ("Russia and Sub-Saharan Africa: Relations That Have Stood the Test of Time"), *Russian View*, May/June 2014. PP. 11, 13.

[83] Mikhail Margelov, "Vozvrashcheniye v Afriku" ("Return to Africa"), *Rossiya v global'noy politike* (*Russia in Global Affairs*), Vol. 11, 2013. P. 189.

that are best-suited for living, fertile and abundant in natural resources, are to be found here, and also in the southern plains, adjacent to the Atlantic and Indian oceans.

The first reference to a permanent settlement of Europeans dates from 1652, when Jan Van Riebeeck, on behalf of the Dutch East India Company, founded a village on the "Cape of Storms", which later became known as the Cape of Good Hope. Engaged in trade operations in India and Indonesia, the company was not greatly interested in Africa at that time, and looked upon the stop-over point known as Capstad, Capshtadt or Capetown, as nothing more than a resting place where sailors could get some rest and ships could be repaired, on the long journey from Europe to the East and back.

It was to this port – one of the most favorable parts of Africa in terms of climate – that, in the 17th and 18th centuries, colonists from the Netherlands, Germany and Britain began to arrive, along with French Huguenots, who were fleeing religious persecution in their homeland. They tilled the land along the coast, and founded cattle-rearing farms. Gradually, the Boer settlers (from the Dutch word "boer", meaning "peasant") moved deeper into the continent, uprooting and exterminating the local population, primarily the Hottentots. Slaves from other Dutch colonies were also taken to the colony at the Cape, including many from Indonesia and Madagascar. Slaves made up a quarter of the population of the Cape colony.[84] Their descendants are known as "coloreds".

Constant clashes with the British forced the Boers to set off on the so-called Great Trek, deep into the continent, to the plains of the veld. "Broad expansion, which began with the Great resettlement, was an extremely important event in the history of the Afrikaners, comparable to the conquering of the Far West in the USA," wrote Fernand Braudel.[85] Their strongest adversary was the Zulu state, in the province of Natal, which was ruled by King Shaka – now one of the key national heroes, after which Durban airport is named – and which managed to create a powerful, battle-ready army. Needless to say, Shaka was painted in the European press, and thought of by the general public, as the most bloodthirsty monster on the planet.[86] Shaka was defeated in battle in 1838. In the places to which the Bantu-speaking

---

[84] Jurgen Osterhammel, *The Transformation of the World: A Global History of the Nineteenth Century*. Princeton-Oxford: Princeton University Press, 2014. P. 152.

[85] Fernand Braudel, *Grammatika tsivilizatsiy* (*Grammar of Civilizations*). Moscow, 2008. P. 491.

[86] Jurgen Osterhammel, *The Transformation of the World: A Global History of the Nineteenth Century*. Princeton-Oxford: Princeton University Press, 2014. P. 583.

tribes were resettled in the mid-19th century, the independent republics of Transvaal and Orange were established. In the South, where the British lived and where Boer colonialists remained, the territory of the Cape colony was expanded as a result of wars with the Zulus and the Khosa, and the colony of Natal was created on the South-Eastern coast. South Africa was effectively split in two: the Boers in the North, and the British in the South.

The discovery in the late 1860s of the diamond deposit of Kimberley (named after the British Colonies Minister) and gold in the Transvaal in the 1880s prompted a diamond and gold rush and an influx of gold diggers from all over the world, which gave a huge boost to economic growth. Cities and railways were built, and companies were founded. Powerful corporations were created, one of which, De Beers, directed by the governor Cecil Rhodes, practically had a monopoly over the diamond trade.

The Boers valued their own independence and became accustomed to treating black laborers however they saw fit, while actively resisting pressure from the British. In 1880-1881, the first Anglo-Boer war took place, in which the Boers triumphed. In 1899-1902, there was a second war, which became famous around the world thanks to the novels of Louis Boussenard, *Le Capitaine Casse-Cou* and *Les Voleurs de Diamants*, in which the Boers were portrayed as the victims of Great Britain's violent colonialist policy, and also thanks to the historical work by Arthur Conan-Doyle, *The War in South Africa*, which defended the British policy. It should be said that in Russia, public sympathy was on the side of the Boers.

Russian volunteers set off for South Africa, among whom was a man who would go on to lead the Octobrists, to become the speaker of the State Duma and Defence Minister in the Provisional Government, Alexander Guchkov. He was wounded and captured by the British. The part-time Boer troops, in spite of their initial successes, nonetheless lost to the better-trained and better-armed British, who also had an overwhelming numerical advantage. After that, the Boers resorted to the tactic of guerrilla warfare, in response to which the British created a network of blockhouses, and also began sending Boer women and children to newly invented concentration camps.

After lengthy negotiations, the South African Union was formed in 1910, incorporating the Cape Colony, Natal, the Orange River Colony, and the Transvaal. Although the Union was a dominion of the British empire (and as such took part in the First World War), the Boers, who were by now increasingly referred to as Afrikaners – not only became involved in the governance of the SAU, but in many ways set the tone for its domestic policy. The system of Apartheid came into being, based on racial discrimination.

"The South African Union was a unique phenomenon, not just in Africa but in the whole world," writes Leonid Vasil'yev. "It was a multi-racial state, with the superiority of the European population in political, legal, and socio-economic matters enshrined in law, despite the fact that fewer than 20% of the country's population were European (coloreds and Indians, who were granted certain rights, by contrast with the Africans, but were also discriminated against in relation to the Europeans, made up roughly 30% of the population)."[87]

Under a law adopted in 1913, the whites were given 87% of the country's territory, while the blacks were forbidden to acquire land outside their reservations. They could only leave these designated areas if they had special permits. They were allowed to have plots of rented land on condition that they worked on the owner's land. The blacks were treated as though they were a different species of human. The battle for the political rights of the non-white population was led by national intelligentsia, at the forefront of which, from 1912 onwards, was the African National Congress (ANC).

The apartheid policy was given a definitive legal backing after the victory by the National Party in the general election in 1948, under the slogan "South Africa for whites". The law on the registration of the population in 1950 stipulated that race must be recorded, with the people officially divided into four groups: whites, Africans ("Bantu", in the terminology of the day), coloreds, and Asians (mainly Indians). Blacks were partially or fully deprived of rights to citizenship, to participation in elections, to freedom of movement (they were forbidden from going outside after sunset, and from being present in white areas – i.e. in the cities – without special permission from the authorities), to mixed marriages, to normal medical care and education (the main health and educational institutions were in "for whites only" districts). At the same time, the black majority, among whom were itinerant workers from tropical Africa, had a relatively high quality of life by African standards.

A leading role in the resistance movement was played by black activists, such as Steve Biko, Archbishop Desmond Tutu and Nelson Mandela. Armed brigades from the ANC, relying on active support from the surrounding countries in the "frontline zone", were a force to be reckoned with. ANC activists were arrested and harassed, so that they went underground, and the Communist Party, an ally of the ANC, was banned. In July 1963, Mandela was arrested at a farm where there is now a museum that commemorates his

---

[87] Leonid Vasil'yev, *Istoriya Vostoka* (*A History of the East*). Vol. 2. Moscow, 2011. P. 127.

life. During his trial, he declared: "I have fought against white domination, and I have fought against black domination. I have cherished the ideal of a democratic and free society in which all persons live together in harmony and with equal opportunities. It is an ideal which I hope to live for and to achieve. But if needs be, it is an ideal for which I am prepared to die."[88]

In 1961, the South African Union became an independent republic (the Republic of South Africa), which left the British Commonwealth, largely due to the fact that the other members of the Commonwealth did not accept the policy of apartheid (South Africa's membership of the Commonwealth was restored in 1994). The UN, in its resolutions, repeatedly declared apartheid to be "South African fascism" and called unsuccessfully for the policy of racial discrimination to be ended, threatening to impose sanctions.

South Africa is the only country to have developed a nuclear weapon and later voluntarily rejected it under pressure from two superpowers at the same time – the Soviet Union (whose satellites managed to locate the nuclear facilities), and the United States.

After the collapse of the Portuguese empire in 1974, the zone controlled by the Europeans, which had separated South Africa from independent black Africa, disappeared. In neighboring Angola and Mozambique, Marxist governments with ties to Moscow emerged, which were happy to provide refuge to members of the ANC and give them training in armed conflict, as well as Cuban forces supported by the Soviet Union. The capital of Mozambique, Maputo, located less than 50 miles from the South African border, became the main center of operations for the ANC.[89]

The collapse of the Soviet bloc in 1989 meant that the ANC was deprived of its main sources of financial and military aid. Yet it also rescued the Congress from having the reputation of a "Trojan horse", promoting Soviet interests.[90]

In September 1989, Frederik de Klerk was elected president of the country. He began taking active steps to bring the system of apartheid to an end. A large number of discriminatory laws were abolished, Nelson Mandela was released from prison and so were other freedom fighters. In 1993, after a series of negotiations and agreements, a Constituent assembly was convened,

---

[88] Cit. from: Martin Meredith, *The State of Africa: A History of the Continent since Independence*. Simon & Schuster, 2011. P. 127.
[89] Ibid. PP. 425-426.
[90] Ibid. PP. 434-435.

which adopted a transitional constitution, the text of which was published on 1ˢᵗ January 1994.

Sobornost' in the African Way

The leaders of modern-day South Africa see their history as having begun in April 1994, in the same way that the Soviet Union saw its history as having begun in October 1917. In 1994 the first general elections were held, with the African National Congress securing victory. The pre-election manifesto had talked of a new nation, constructed as a result of the development of our different cultures, faiths and languages, as the source of our common strength.[91] The president was Mandela, and the vice president was De Klerk, who left office voluntarily in 1996. The moderate wing of the ANC also secured a majority in Parliament.

Mandela himself, who was 76 at that time, allowed the leaders of the ANC to persuade him to be president for one term only. He formed a government of national unity and proclaimed a policy of national reconciliation. The objectives of the National Democratic Revolution conducted by the ANC consisted in achieving improvements in the position of the non-white majority with the help of socialist ideas. The most radical recipes, however, associated with modernization and expropriation of the property of whites, were rejected. Contemporary experts maintain that the almost peaceful transformation of South Africa from a racist, authoritarian state into a multiracial democracy is one of the most unexpected political events of the 20ᵗʰ century.[92]

Mandela's goal was a transition from a racist society not to a multiracial one, but to a race-less one.[93] In 1996, the vice president, Mbeki, in a speech about the adoption of the constitution, included all those who lived in the Republic – the Zulus, the Xhosa, the Khoi, the San, the coloreds, the Afrikaners and even the Chinese – in the single image of the African.[94] Mbeki was elected leader of the ANC and became president in 1999.

The constitution asserted that everyone was equal before the law, but at the same time, in the Bill of Rights, it was stipulated that there was the

---

[91] *A Better Life for All: Working Together for Jobs, Peace and Freedom*. Johannesburg, 1994.

[92] James L. Gibson, "Apartheid's Long Shadow. How Racial Divides Distort South Africa's Democracy", *Foreign Affairs*, March/April, 2015. P. 41.

[93] Nelson Mandela, *Conversations with Myself*. London, 2010. P. 118.

[94] Thabo Mbeki, *Africa: The Time Has Come: Selected Speeches*. Cape Town, 1998. PP. 31-36.

possibility of adopting legislative and other measures, aimed at protecting or promoting individuals or categories of individuals, suffering from unjust discrimination. Beginning in 1996, the government dramatically accelerated its policy of "affirmative action". Over the course of 18 months to two years, 22,200 civil servants in the central administration, 25,800 civil servants in the provincial administrations, and 15,500 teachers were put on state pensions. In 1997 to 1998, the entire senior leadership of the army and military intelligence were replaced; the overwhelming majority of them were white. In the late 1990s, "European" symphony orchestras and theatre troupes began to close down. Approximately a million whites left South Africa, mainly in the under-40 age bracket, along with many Indians.

Mbeki – Xhosa by ethnicity – was the architect of the new system of cultural transformation, which he called "the African Renaissance". Its objectives were: to counter the opinion that Africa was different from the other continents and was behind them in terms of development; to demonstrate that Africa could change and to restore African dignity; to show that Africans were taking responsibility into their own hands, acknowledging mistakes and working to correct them.

It was in this period that the promotion of "Ubuntu" began; this term translates from Zulu as "humanity", "togetherness" (it is similar in meaning to the Russian word *sobornost'*, i.e. 'unity'). "I am because we are." Archbishop Tutu, a winner of the Nobel peace prize, explained: "A person with Ubuntu is open and accessible to others, he does not suffer from the fact that others are better and more capable, and all this is founded on a deep conviction, stemming from the understanding that he belongs to a great whole."[95] Today, "Ubuntu" is considered to be an African ideology and an African way of life which supposedly existed before the white man arrived.

Growth in the economy in the period from 1995 to 2005 amounted to 3.5% a year, and over the next two years rose to 4.5%; each year, approximately 300,000 new jobs were created in the legal sector of the economy and another 200,000 in the raw materials sector. Free basic school education was introduced, medical points were set up in agricultural areas, and the poor were given free access to a minimum level of electricity and water. The percentage of students who were black rose from 42% to 60%. As part of the program of reconstruction and development, the government built more than 1 million residential homes. Around 10 million people were giv-

---

[95] "V stile ubuntu" ("In the ubuntu style"), *Russian View*, March/April 2015. P. 83.

en benefits and grants of various kinds. Mbeki's critics painted a different picture, however: the murder rate in the country was 50 people a day on average; 1000 people died of AIDS every day, and Mbeki was held personally responsible, because for a long time he refused to recognize the methods used throughout the world to treat this disease and to introduce them into the healthcare system; there were colossal levels of unemployment and social inequality (93% of white families owned a car, while only 10% of black families owned one).[96]

At an assembly of the ANC's National Executive Committee on 20th September 2008, a majority insisted upon "the stepping down of Comrade Mbeki" from the post of president, and he duly stepped down.[97] In the parliamentary elections in 2009, the ANC secured 65.9% of the vote, with most of the support coming from black voters, and Zuma became the head of state. The political base of his government outside the ANC included the biggest professional union, the South African Communist Party, and the youth branches of the ANC and the SACP.

Zuma's supporters were so bold as to declare that a new political era had begun, in which Zulus would govern the country. He also confirmed his commitment to Zulu traditions, including polygamy (he has six official wives, and eight in total).

The Continental Leader

Modern-day South Africa positions itself as a leader of the continent. And it has good reason for doing so. The country has the most highly developed economy in Africa. Although South Africa's territory only covers 3% of the African continent, it is the focus of 40% of industrial production, 30% of GDP, half of all the actual energy produced, and 45% of all the minerals extracted on the continent. South Africa's share of exports from African countries amounts to roughly 17%, and in overall imports 18%. South Afri-

---

[96] I. I. Filatova and A.B. Davidson, "Kakogo tsveta 'yuzhnoafrikanskoye chudo'? Natsional'no-demokraticheskaya revolyutsiya i natsional'nyye otnosheniya v YUAR v kontse XX – nachale XXI v." ("What is the Color of the 'South African Miracle'? National Democratic Revolution and National Relations in South Africa in the Late XX – Early XXI Centuries"), in *Pax Africana: kontinent i diaspora v poiskakh sebya* (*Pax Africana: A Continent and a Diaspora in Search of Themselves*), ed. by A. B. Davidson. Moscow, 2009. PP. 188-189.

[97] A. A. Arkhangel'skaya and V. G. Shubin, "YUAR – novyy chlen BRIKS" ("South Africa – a New Member of BRICS"), in *Strategiya Rossii v BRIKS: tseli i instrumenty* (*Russia's Strategy in BRICS: Aims and Instruments*). Moscow, 2013. PP. 144-145.

ca is the only African country in the G20. The number of South Africans living in a state of extreme poverty has fallen from 41% to 31%.[98]

For its development, South Africa is in many ways indebted to its abundance of natural resources. The country's government estimates these reserves to be worth $2.5 trillion, and there is more than enough to last a century. 30% of exports are accounted for by the mining industry.[99] The country's share of the worldwide production of platinum is as high as 79%, of kyanite 60%, chrome ore 42%, palladium 41%, vermiculite 40%, vanadium 35%, zirconium 32%, rutile and iron-titanium oxide 19% each, manganese ore 14%, and gold 9%.[100] The plentiful resources of diamonds, asbestos, nickel, lead, uranium and coal have not yet been exhausted. The most important export in terms of value is platinum. The key imported items are oil and products for the chemicals industry.

Unlike many other African countries, South Africa has well-developed infrastructure: the country has 25% of the total length of railways and 20% of all the asphalt roads in Africa. South African Airlines is the biggest airline on the continent. The country can boast of considerable achievements in veterinary science, agrobiology, biotechnologies, chemistry, energy, geophysics and astrophysics, metallurgy and engineering. Around 30% of the liquid fuel required by the country is produced from coal at the plants of the SASOL Corporation, which is the world leader in this field. Active research is under way in the field of solar energy, nanotechnologies, and the creation of super-strong and super-lightweight composite materials.[101] 81% of the country has access to electricity, and considerable progress has been made by comparison with the year 2000, when this figure stood at 63%.

South Africa's financial system is the most developed in Africa. 10 South African banks regularly make it into the 500 biggest banks in the world. They hold the top five positions in the ratings for the biggest banks in Africa. Meanwhile, under conditions of low growth, the banks faced problems with bad loans, and were accused by the antitrust bodies of

---

[98] "South Africa. Time to Ditch Mandela's Party", *The Economist*, May 3, 2014. P. 12.

[99] "Jacob Zuma, 'State of the Nation', February 10, 2011", South African History Online <https://www.sahistory.org.za/archive/2011-president-zuma-state-nation-address-10-february-2011>.

[100] A. A. Arkhangel'skaya and V. G. Shubin, "YUAR – novyy chlen BRIKS" ("South Africa – a New Member of BRICS"), in *Strategiya Rossii v BRIKS: tseli i instrumenty* (*Russia's Strategy in BRICS: Aims and Instruments*). Moscow, 2013. P. 148.

[101] Ibid. P. 153.

manipulating the exchange rate.[102] The stock exchange in Johannesburg is one of the 15 biggest in the world. The aggregate capitalization of South African companies has surpassed 1 trillion dollars, almost three times as much as in 1994.[103]

South African firms manage the national railway in Cameroon, and electricity companies in Tanzania, Rwanda and Cameroon. They own electrical power stations in Zimbabwe, Zambia and Mali and are mining gold in Mali and surveying for oil in Equatorial Guinea. They are building roads and bridges in Malawi and Mozambique, and a pipeline between the continental shelf of Mozambique and South Africa. They control banks, telecommunications companies, breweries, supermarkets and hotels all over Africa. They create TV programs for most of the countries on the continent. The railway company Spurnet has contracts in more than 15 countries in Africa. The company Shoprite Holdings is the biggest supplier of foodstuffs on the continent. South Africa's mining companies, the biggest of which is Anglo-American, have invested over 5 billion dollars in manufacturing in a host of countries: Ghana, Tanzania, Mali, Zambia, Zimbabwe, Namibia and Botswana.[104]

South Africa's main trading partners outside Africa have traditionally been the USA and the EU, and among the EU's member states, the UK and Germany first and foremost. That said, South Africa is increasingly banking on cooperation with the BRICS countries. China, which initiated the inclusion of South Africa in the association, is a key trade and economic partner and investor. As part of the "all-encompassing strategic partnership", China makes huge investments in the construction of nuclear power stations and the passing on of nuclear technologies.[105]

South Africa meets its domestic food needs in full, and is also one of the leading exporters of agricultural goods. 140 different types of fruit are exported and this despite the fact that only 15% of the land is suitable for use.

....

[102] "South Africa. Downgrade Doldrums", *The Africa Report*, September 2017. PP. 80, 86.

[103] Andrew England, "Time to Change Track?", *The Financial Times*, May 2, 2014. P. 9.

[104] V. A. Sidorov, "YUAR v ekonomike Afriki" ("South Africa in the Economics of Africa"), in *BRIKS i Afrika: sotrudnichestvo v tselyakh razvitiya* (*BRICS and Africa: Cooperation with the Aim of Development*). Moscow, 2013. PP. 128-130.

[105] Eleonora Lebedeva, "YUAR v BRIKS: perspektivnoye sotrudnichestvo?" ("South Africa and BRICS: A Cooperation with Good Prospects?"), in *Voskhodyashchiye gosudarstva-giganty BRIKS: rol' v mirovoy politike, strategii modernizatsii* (*The Emerging Giants of BRICS: Their Role in World Politics, Strategies for Modernization*). Moscow, 2012. PP. 180-181.

It is thought that white people own 80% of the country's agricultural land. In fact, this figure does not take into account the territory of the former Bantustans, the majority of the land in which is in "traditional use" by communities which raise livestock. The Constitution confirmed the principle of private ownership, including ownership of land. Despite this, the authorities set out a goal of reallocating to black people 30% of the farms, which is forcing the opposition to talk about a threat of the "Zimbabwe-ification" of South Africa. In 2016, parliament approved a law on the expropriation of land "for public purposes, or in the public interest".[106] No mass expropriation has yet taken place, it should be said.

The country's demographic structure is favorable: the number of people of working age is far greater than the number of children and elderly people dependent upon them. The birth rate among white people began to fall back in the 1950s and 1960s, and among black Africans in the 1970s and 1980s, falling to 2.5 children per woman by the time the country gained independence. The population is growing by less than 1% a year, and its growth is continually slowing.[107]

The employment situation is close to catastrophic, however. Unemployment is at its highest level ever – between 25% and 43%, depending on how it is calculated. This is a source of protest among young people. A wave of strikes was spurred on by the police killing miners during an illegal strike in August 2012. 80,000 miners at platinum mines went on a month-long strike, demanding higher pay.[108]

The AIDs epidemic hit South Africa very hard (it was worse only in Swaziland, Botswana and Lesotho). The number of people infected reached 18% of the adult population, and has now stabilized at the level of 10% following the measures that were taken. Average life expectancy in the country is 49, which is higher than in 2000, when it was 43.

The level of social division in South Africa is among the highest in the world. Approximately 15% of the population are able to indulge their every desire: the huge estates and plantations and the villas in luxurious districts beside the coast are a sight to behold, even for those who think they have

---

[106] Marian L. Tupy and Michael Kransdorff, "The Zimbabwe-ification of South Africa", *The Wall Street Journal*, July 16, 2009. P. 15; Kirill Krivosheyev, "Yuzhnaya Afrika doshla do peredela" ("South Africa has Reached a Point of Being Remade"), *Kommersant (The Businessman)*, June 9, 2016 <https://www.kommersant.ru/doc/3008220>.

[107] *National Development Plan: Vision for 2030*. National Planning Commission, 2011. PP. 6-7 <https://www.gov.za/sites/default/files/gcis_document/201409/devplan2.pdf>.

[108] *Strategic Survey 2014: The Annual Review of World Affairs*. Routledge, 2014. PP. 281, 276.

seen it all. A large number of world-famous stars have residences in Cape Town and its suburbs, including Elton John and Leonardo DiCaprio.

At the same time, half the population – mainly black people – live in abject poverty, or in primitive conditions in the bush, the bare desert, or in dirty townships – agglomerations of boxes made of sheet metal, which are put together on the outskirts of the major cities. For those who make it out of the bush, the townships, where free water and electricity have been made available, provide a powerful social lift. Residents of the townships are being given the chance to find work in the city, and thereby break out of poverty. The townships are being emptied, and demand for the housing that is being built where they once stood is extremely high – probably thanks to former residents who are feeling nostalgic.[109] 85% of the black population are categorized as poor, whereas 87% of whites are considered to be in the middle class or higher.[110]

Roughly 15 million South Africans receive social grants from the state. Child benefit payments are paid out *en masse*. Meanwhile, Zuma kept repeating that South Africa was not a "state of prosperity", but a "state of development", where help must be given to those who want to help themselves.

Crime rates are extremely high, particularly in poor areas. Although the murder rate has halved in the last 20 years, it is still one of the highest in the world: 30.9 for every 100,000 people (as compared with 4.7 in the USA).[111] Visitors are strongly recommended not to go near the townships. Walking in the streets in the big cities is relatively safe, although this is mainly thanks to the large number of police posts and patrols.

A subject of much controversy was the "economic empowerment of blacks" program. Some acerbic critics even dubbed it the "economic empowerment of Zuma" program, since a couple of major programs in the coal sector were of great benefit to two members of the president's family. That said, successes have clearly been achieved. In 2014, 40% of the managers of South African companies were black, compared to only 4% in 1994.

A genuine moment of triumph for the national spirit was the World Cup in 2010. The whole world heard the sound of the legendary vuvuzelas. The organization of the championship was first-rate, although most of the profits, as is always the way, were pocketed by FIFA. As for the country's leading cities, where the main matches took place, they were left wondering

---

[109] "South African Property. Trendy Townships", *The Economist*, August 22, 2015. P. 42.
[110] Andrew England, "Time to Change Track?", *The Financial Times*, May 2, 2014. P. 9.
[111] "South Africa's Trial. Justice, After All, Is Being Done", *The Economist*, April 19, 2014. P. 31.

how they could fill in the resulting holes in their budgets, holes left by both the construction of the sports and other venues, and by growing demands, while the championship was taking place, for higher wages, which were amicably made by all the biggest unions of the state and municipal employees (at the time, no-one dared say no). It remains the case, though, that as the first country in Africa to host this sporting event, one that means so much to hundreds of millions of people, South Africa has written its name into history, a fact that has only served to strengthen its claims to leadership of the continent.

Many experts, Russian included, are predicting that the country may slide into a systemic crisis. Among the causes cited are the depreciation of the industrial equipment left from the time of apartheid; the dependency of economic demand on raw materials; the rapid development of the services sector to the detriment of industry; a fall in foreign investment; an outflow of qualified staff, particularly white staff; chronic poverty and unemployment; vast spending on social programs; and the high levels of crime and violence.

A fall in prices for raw materials slowed down the economy significantly. Growth in GDP in 2017 was at the level of 1.4%, with inflation at 5.64% and the budget deficit at 1.34%. GDP per head of the population is estimated at $5430 (13.86 in terms of purchasing power parity). State expenditure amounts to 31.5% of GDP.[112]

South Africa has the 26th largest population in the world: 58 million people. It is one of the most ethnically diverse countries in Africa. The first census was held in 1911. Back then, the proportion of white people was 22%. By 1980, it had fallen to 18%. According to a census in 2010, whites accounted for 9.2% of the population, blacks 79.4%, colored (mulattos and descendants of people from South-East Asia) 8.8%, and Indians 2.6%. The white population is falling, chiefly due to emigration to North America, Europe, Australia and New Zealand. Meanwhile, the black population is growing more than the others, thanks to an influx of people from the countries of tropical Africa. It is no coincidence that anti-immigrant sentiment is rife: in 2015, pogroms took place against stores owned by people from neighboring African countries.[113]

This ethno-cultural diversity makes it difficult to establish a common identity. Soon after freedom was obtained, surveys showed that an absolute

---

[112] *The Economist: The World in 2017*, 2017. P. 101.

[113] Andrew England, "Zuma Urges End to Attacks on Immigrants", *The Financial Times*, April 17, 2015. P. 4.

majority of South Africans considered themselves Africans, Zulus, Xhosa or Christians, etc., first and foremost. Only a very small proportion – mainly Anglophone whites and a small number of coloreds – called themselves South Africans. A decade later, another survey showed that 72% of the population rarely interacted, or had no interaction at all outside of work, with people from other racial groups, and 40% said they did not trust such people. At the same time, there were now more people who felt it was important to create a unified nation: 76%.[114]

There is no dominant religious majority in the country. According to data from 2010, 10% of the population are members of the Zion Christian Church; 7.5% belong to the Pentecostal Church, 6.5% are Catholics, 6.8% Methodists, 6.7% followers of the Dutch Reformist Church, 3.8% Anglicans, 1.3% Muslims, and so on. Under the Constitution, there are 11 state languages in South Africa (it is the third-highest country for this parameter, behind India and Bolivia). Accordingly, South Africa has 11 official names. Despite this broad selection of names, incidentally, South Africans with the strongest nationalist feelings prefer a 12th option: Azania, which contains no reminder whatsoever of the colonial era.

In theory, all the languages have equal rights, but in practice this is not the case. No noticeable development of the Bantu languages is taking place, although Bantu-language schools and a TV channel have appeared. The position of Afrikaans (which is the local version of Dutch), which is seen as a language of colonizers, has changed for the worse, although it is the native language not only of Afrikaners, but also of most coloreds. Afrikaners complain that their forefathers have been "erased from history or portrayed as the only villains of history". A campaign to rename the cities, streets, airports and so on, which was launched in 2008, was deemed by the Afrikaners to be a "deliberate slap in the face".[115] The English language has begun to flourish, on the other hand. In the first five years of freedom alone, the number of publications printed in Afrikaans fell by 70%, and in Zulu by 60%, while the number printed in English rose by 60%. By the turn of the century, more than 70% of all TV and radio programs were in English, with

---

[114] I. I. Filatova and A.B. Davidson, "Kakogo tsveta 'yuzhnoafrikanskoye chudo'? Natsional'no-demokraticheskaya revolyutsiya i natsional'nyye otnosheniya v YUAR v kontse XX – nachale XXI v." ("What is the Color of the 'South African Miracle'? National Democratic Revolution and National Relations in South Africa in the Late XX – Early XXI Centuries"), in *Pax Africana: kontinent i diaspora v poiskakh sebya* (*Pax Africana: A Continent and a Diaspora in Search of Themselves*), ed. by A. B. Davidson. Moscow, 2009. P. 214.

[115] Cit. from: Ibid. P. 179.

8% in Afrikaans and 3.5% in the languages of the Sotho-Tswana group. At 80% of secondary schools, lessons are taught in English, while in 16% the teaching language is Afrikaans.[116]

The political and legal systems in South Africa are very interesting, starting with the fact that the country has several capitals. The "main" capital is Pretoria, where the government is located. The two other branches of power are located in cities which are also called capitals: the parliament is in Cape Town, while the Supreme Court is in Bloemfontein. This abundance of centers of power is explained by the circumstances of the creation of the South African Union – from the British holdings with their capital in Cape Town, the Orange State with its capital in Bloemfontein, and the South African Republic (the Transvaal) with its capital in Pretoria. Prior to 1994, South Africa was a federation and was divided into four provinces: the Cape, Natal, the Orange Free State and the Transvaal. Modern-day South Africa is a unitary state which has nine provinces on its territory.

South Africa's legal system incorporates elements of no fewer than three legal families: the Romano-German, the Anglo-Saxon, and the traditional. South Africa is one of a handful of countries in the world where the British model of criminal law is in effect. It is not codified. The judicial system consists of the Supreme Appellate Court, the high courts and the magistrates' courts. In the country's laws, one finds, in startling proximity, a degree of liberalism that is unprecedented by African standards, and some regulations that are far from modern. In the 1990s, for instance, South Africa was the only country on the continent where same-sex marriages were legal. At the same time, corporal punishment is still given out to minors, in the form of whipping.

On 5th December 2013, at the age of 95, Nelson Mandela passed away, and his passing was a great loss for South Africa, and indeed for the wider world. On 7th May 2014, a general election was held in the country for the fifth time. Once again, the ANC were victorious. And this was not thanks to any great affection for Jacob Zuma, who was in the middle of yet another scandal, this one involving $20 million that he spent on the construction of his own villa. It is the ANC that is popular, for it is Mandela's party.

The main opposition party – the liberal Democratic Alliance – won 22% of the vote. Half of its electorate were white, with 27% colored, 20% black, and 3% Indian. In May 2015, the party's leader for many years, Helen Zille, retired, and for the first time, a black politician took over its leadership:

---

[116] Ibid. PP. 208-209.

34-year-old Mmusi Maimane, something which ought to have made the DA a competitive force, not only in the Western Cape, where it is the ruling party, but also in the country as whole. The ANC's monopoly was also threatened by the Economic Freedom Fighters, led by the former leader of its youth wing, the populist Julius Malema.[117]

Economic difficulties and corruption scandals (783 accusations of bribe-taking were made against the president) caused a long-drawn-out political crisis in the latter stages of Zuma's second term. There were several attempts to hold a vote of no confidence in the president. The ill-feeling worsened in the spring of 2017 after the president dismissed his finance minister, Pravin Gordhan, and his deputy, who were liked by opposition politicians and Western investors, and international credit agencies downgraded South Africa's credit rating to "junk".[118] Mmusi Maimane called Zuma "a corrupt and broken president".[119] Malema indulged in even more colorful language. Even the ANC's partners in its ruling coalition – the South African Communist Party and the Congress of South African Trade Unions – called for Zuma to resign. Former presidents de Klerk and Mbeki joined in with these demands.[120] The Western media jumped on the bandwagon and attacked Zuma, too.

In December 2017 the ANC expressed its lack of confidence in President Zuma and elected the vice-president Cyril Ramaphosa as their leader. In February 2018 the party proposed an ultimatum to Zuma demanding his resignation, and he had nothing to do but comply. Ramaphosa became president. Within a month Zuma was charged with corruption, extortion and money laundering.

Diplomacy of Ubuntu

South Africa has an original foreign-policy doctrine. The report on this subject published by the Department of International relations and cooperation – the name of the Foreign Ministry since 2009 – was called *Building a Better World: the Diplomacy of Ubuntu*. This means the following: "South Africa is a

---

[117] "South Africa's Opposition. Black Star Rising", *The Economist*, May 16, 2015. P. 34.
[118] "South Africa. Dump Jacob Zuma", *The Economist*, April 8, 2017. P. 12.
[119] "Long Walk to Cronyism. South Africa", *The Economist*, Aug 12, 2017. P. 8.
[120] Joseph Cotterill, "South Africa's Zuma Chided for 'Politics of Patronage' as ANC Battle Looms", *The Financial Times*, April 27, 2017. P. 3; Joseph Cotterill, "Mbeki Warns of Crisis in Rebuke to Zuma", *The Financial Times*, May 6, 2017. P. 4.

multifaceted, multicultural and multiracial country that embraces the concept of Ubuntu as a way of defining who we are and how we relate to others. The philosophy of Ubuntu means 'humanity' and is reflected in the idea that we affirm our humanity when we affirm the humanity of others. [...] This philosophy translates into an approach to international relations that respects all nations, peoples and cultures. It recognises that it is in our national interest to promote and support the positive development of others. Similarly, national security would therefore depend on the centrality of human security as a universal goal, based on the principle of Batho Pele (putting people first)."[121]

The African continent, where South Africa claims not only economic but also political leadership, is the main priority of the country's foreign policy. In recent years, soldiers from South Africa have taken part in peacekeeping and restoration missions in Burundi, Ivory Coast, the Democratic Republic of Congo, Ethiopia, Eritrea, Nepal and Sudan, and also in operations aimed at maintaining order during the elections on the Camoros, in Madagascar and in Lesotho.[122] They have also carried out auxiliary operations in the Central African Republic, and helped Mozambique fight piracy in the Mozambique Channel.[123] South Africa's ambitions to be a leader in Africa have been the main driving force behind the strengthening of its defensive capabilities.

The key priority of military development was the light motorized forces, reconnaissance and engineering divisions necessary in order to support border operations, and air delivery forces. The second level of tasks was a mechanized infantry, artillery, armored vehicles and other components for waging normal land operations.[124] The armed forces contained 65,350 people in 2019, of whom 40,200 served in the army, 7,100 in the navy, 9,900 were in the air force, and 8,150 in the ranks of the South African military-medical service. The military budget amounted to 50.5 billion rand, which is close to 3 billion dollars.[125]

---

[121] *Building a Better World: The Diplomacy of Ubuntu*. White Paper on South Africa's Foreign Policy. P. 4 <https://www.gov.za/documents/white-paper-south-african-foreign-policy-building-better-world-diplomacy-ubuntu>.

[122] *The Military Balance 2010: An Annual Assessment of Global Military Capabilities and Defence Economies*. London: IISS, 2010. P. 290.

[123] *Safeguarding South Africa for a Better Life for All: Annual Report 1 April 2010 to 31 March 2011*. Department of Defence, 2011. P. 6 <https://www.gov.za/sites/default/files/gcis_document/201409/dodanrpt20101119oct-2.pdf>.

[124] *The Military Balance 2010: An Annual Assessment of Global Military Capabilities and Defence Economies*. London: IISS, 2010. PP. 290-292.

[125] *The Military Balance 2017: The Annual Assessment of Global Military Capabilities and Defence Economies*. London, 2017. PP. 534-535.

The second most significant priority in foreign policy, after Africa, is relations on the South-South axis. Commanding most attention here is co-operation in the formats of IBSA (India, Brazil, South Africa), The African, Caribbean and Pacific Group of States (ACP), and the British Commonwealth.

In the context of a multi-polar world, the role of BRICS is rated highly. "The original concept of BRIC has evolved into a multi-sectoral diplomatic force, promoting qualitative and quantitative changes in global governance," emphasized Zuma in April 2011 at a summit in Sanya, where South Africa acquired full membership of BRICS.[126] He also issued a reminder that "just two decades ago, South Africa was still in the throes of its liberation struggle. Brazil, the Russian Federation, India and China firmly supported our quest for freedom. Today we have met as one, we have met as partners."[127]

The next priority is Asia, where China, India and Japan are singled out for special attention, since they have been the leading investors in South Africa and among its biggest trade partners. Active ties are also being kept up with the ASEAN countries, particularly with Indonesia, Malaysia and Vietnam, and also with South Korea.

Relations with the West are ambiguous. South Africa's leadership is criticised for a lack of democracy and for corruption, and also for supporting national liberation movements and their leaders even after they had turned into authoritarian rulers or even dictators. Not everyone in the West liked the fact that South Africa tried to act as a middle-man in the Libyan conflict. "[T]he AU [African Union] efforts were never given a chance. Military actions were preferred over peaceful means," complained Zuma at the UN's General Assembly in September 2011.[128]

The countries of the EU are very significant for South Africa: they account for a third of its foreign trade, 40% of exports, and 70% of direct for-

---

[126] Statement by South African President Jacob Zuma during the joint press conference by BRICS Heads of State at the Third BRICS Summit, Sanya, Hainan Island, People's Republic of China, April 14, 2011. The website of the Government of South Africa <https://www.gov.za/statement-south-african-president-jacob-zuma-during-joint-press-conference-brics-heads-state-third>.

[127] Address by President Jacob Zuma to the Plenary of the Third BRICS Leaders Meeting, Sanya, Hainan Island, People's Republic of China, April 14, 2011. The website of the Presidency of the Republic of South Africa <http://www.thepresidency.gov.za/speeches/address-president-jacob-zuma-plenary-third-brics-leaders-meeting%2C-sanya%2C-hainan-island%2C>.

[128] Statement by President Jacob Zuma to the General Debate of the 66th United Nations General Assembly, UN Headquarters, New York, September 21, 2011. P. 3. <https://gadebate.un.org/sites/default/files/gastatements/66/ZA_en.pdf>.

eign investment. Aid aimed at development is continuing to come into South Africa from the EU. The relationship with the EU and its member states is defined as a strategic partnership. Also viewed in the European context are relations with Russia and Turkey, which are deemed to have an "important role in global and regional politics".

South Africa is moving into the role of Russia's key partner on the continent. However, relations remain at a lower level than was expected, given the prestige that Russia enjoyed during the liberation struggle. Boris Yeltsin, even before April 1994, actively toyed with, and then hastened to establish, diplomatic relations with the "old regime", and this could not have failed to have a negative impact on the development of bilateral relations with South Africa once it had broken free of the apartheid regime. It took a few years for South Africa to overcome its distrust of liberal Moscow. Nelson Mandela did not visit Moscow until 1999.[129]

A landmark event in bilateral relations was the official visit by President Putin to South Africa in September 2006. This was the first trip in history by a leader of the Russian state to sub-Saharan Africa. In August 2010, the president of South Africa, Jacob Zuma, made a state visit to Moscow, bringing with him 11 ministers and more than a hundred people representing the banking, finance, defence and aerospace sectors, and the spheres of energy, engineering, information and communications, and education.

The main share of Russian exports is accounted for by ferrous and non-ferrous metals, fertilizers, instruments, artificial rubber, equipment, and optical and medical devices. Dominant in Russian imports from South Africa are foodstuffs, black metals, ores, products from the chemical industry, and alcoholic and non-alcoholic drinks.[130] Russia is offering assistance in the creation of an atomic industry in South Africa – from the mining of uranium, the construction of atomic power plants and investigative reactors, to the planning and production of atomic energy equipment.

The political attack on Zuma also damaged the cooperation between Russia and South Africa, incidentally. The Western Cape high court in Cape Town, a region opposed to the president, ruled that the deal between Zuma and Putin on the construction of nuclear reactors was illegal, since it did

---

[129] A. A. Arkhangel'skaya and V. G. Shubin, "YUAR – novyy chlen BRIKS" ("South Africa – a New Member of BRICS"), in *Strategiya Rossii v BRIKS: tseli i instrumenty* (*Russia's Strategy in BRICS: Aims and Instruments*). Moscow, 2013. PP. 164-165.

[130] A. A. Arkhangel'skaya, "South Africa: The 'Gateway to Africa'? The Results of the BRICS Summit in Durban", in *BRIKS i Afrika: sotrudnichestvo v tselyakh razvitiya* (*BRICS and Africa: Cooperation with the Aim of Development*). Moscow, 2013. PP. 108-109.

not take the country's financial capabilities into account (the objections to the financial aspect of the deal were allegedly the very thing that led to the dismissal of Minister Pravin Gordhan).[131]

Huntington once wrote: "Size, resources, and location make Nigeria a potential core state, but its intercivilizational disunity, massive corruption, political instability, repressive government, and economic problems have severely limited its ability to perform this role, although it has done so on occasion. South Africa's peaceful and negotiated transition from apartheid, its industrial strength, the higher level of economic development compared to other African countries, its military capability, its natural resources, and its sophisticated black and white political leadership all mark South Africa as clearly the leader of southern, probably the leader of English Africa, and possibly the leader of all sub-Saharan Africa."[132]

A quarter century later it is fair to say that the professor – alas now deceased – was right.

---

[131] Joseph Cotterill, "Pretoria's Nuclear Plans Hit by Court Ruling on Deal with Putin", *The Financial Times*, April 27, 2017. P. 3.

[132] Samuel P. Huntington, *The Clash of Civilizations and the Remaking of World Order*. Simon & Schuster, 1996. P. 136.

EPILOGUE

The end of history? Hardly.

The march of world events is speeding up dramatically. The world is changing more rapidly than ever. It is becoming more dangerous. There are more and more unresolvable tensions, unsolvable global problems, independent players, and more ungovernability in the international system.

We are at the turn of the ages, when former hegemons are doing all they can to reverse the onward march of history. And the rising powers are not sure of the irreversibility of their successes, and do not know exactly how to utilize their fruits. "Structurally, the situation inside the West is full of such tensions that it becomes a serious challenge to international security. If ten or fifteen years ago the goal of the international system was to manage the rise of the 'new', now, it seems, it is time to talk about the management of the decline of the 'old,'" wrote Sergey Karaganov.[1]

There is a sharp ideological confrontation within the Western elites, who see the world in increasingly gloomy tones and are trying to stop the degradation of their recently dominant positions. The upsetting of the world balance after the Soviet withdrawal from the world arena turned NATO, formerly a defensive Alliance, into a fighting Alliance, an aggressor – in Yugoslavia, Iraq, Libya – which continues to expand.

Globalization and an open world have ceased to suit Washington. Anti-globalization, symbolized by walls and protectionist tariffs rather than open borders and free trade, has replaced it. America requires the rest of the world to act in a way that is solely in the interest of the United States. It offers to make America great again at the expense of the rest of humanity.

Diplomacy, in its traditional form, no longer exists. Winston Churchill said that diplomacy is the art of telling the truth without being offensive.

---

[1] Sergey Karaganov, "Mir na vyrost. Politika na puti v budushcheye" ("World for Growth. Policy on the Way to the Future"), *Rossiya v global'noy politike* (*Russia in Global Affairs*), Issue 1, January/February 2018. P. 121.

Modern Western diplomacy has undergone an inversion. Now its essence, it seems, is to shamelessly lie in an extremely offensive form. All this against the background of the collapse of the existing system of arms control and an absence of substantive strategic dialogue. New threats are not seriously discussed at all.

The Cold War 2.0 is a reality, but the environment has changed drastically. To keep global dominance and to turn history back – to the period of Western triumphalism after the end of the Cold War, which is regarded as a golden age in the West – is hardly possible.

There is a big difference between the period after the end of the Cold War and the present. It is not even that it is no longer a conflict between the ideologies of capitalism and communism. Previously there was the idea of the West as a carrier of advanced civilization. Today, the factor of Western superiority is absent. In recent centuries, the West has only communicated with representatives of all other civilizations from this position of superiority. These days, none of the major civilization centers – Russia, China, India – feel the slightest inferiority, and value their own traditions. They do not consider the West worthy of worship.

Today, even Americans tell monstrous stories about themselves, and show their ugly side to the world. Trump and the conservatives accentuate the themes of a country in decline, the corrupt "Washington swamp", the shameless and lying media, moral degradation. Liberals and leading media paint pictures of an anti-democratic, racist power, of the complete inadequacy of the country's top leadership, which acts in the interests of Moscow and preaches medieval obscurantism. The country is so divided that the representatives of the two camps have stopped talking to and hearing each other. For an external observer it is extremely unsightly. Previously, many nations sought to emulate the United States. No-one wants to emulate THIS AMERICA.

In the Cold War 1.0, the West was admired as a showcase of consumption. The Soviet Union was defeated primarily by pictures from Western supermarkets and shopping centers. It was a triumph not of ideas, but of demonstrated consumer choice. Today, supermarkets and shopping centers in Moscow or Beijing are clearly better than in the West: there is more choice, there is a sense of scope, and many outlets work 24 hours a day, 7 days a week.

In those days, the Western media were banned in Communist countries, and forbidden fruit is always sweet. It was perceived as the ultimate truth. Today, the global information market is open... and it is the West that is starting to impose bans, for example on Russian media such as RT or Sputnik, while in Russia the freedom of the media is complete. 20,000 Russian TV channels, 60% of them private, and 2,000 foreign TV channels in cable networks. People can compare. And they are well aware that Western media is not the ultimate truth and not even a source of information, but what it has always been – first of all, a propaganda tool, and very crude ones at that.

In those days, the West dominated economically, it accounted for 80% of world GDP. It's now almost half of that. Now it is no longer the West driving growth, but China and India, while other developing countries are now overcoming their technological inferiority to the West.

Previously, the West was perceived as an intellectual leader, a source of important knowledge and information. Western intellectual life is very intense and interesting. If, however, we take a look at political thought, it is increasingly drawn into the narrow framework of tunnel thinking, and the beginning of this tunnel was the Cold War and the era of American unipolarity.

The United States has officially chosen China and Russia as its enemies. I think this is a huge American strategic miscalculation. The US seems to overestimate its power, primarily military power. Its military budget is huge because of the maintenance of military bases in more than 130 countries. At the same time, the US does not have many combat-ready units. It has not won a single war recently. The bombing of Belgrade, followed by Milosevic's request for peace, can hardly be considered a victory. Vietnam, Laos, Cambodia, Afghanistan, Iraq, Libya – they are more like defeats. Even a military operation against North Korea would be highly problematic for America.

In a number of parameters, Russia has gained a qualitative superiority in key weapons systems, primarily in deterrents. And it is now confirmed in the status of not only a key regional power, but also a global player. Beijing bypasses the United States on a wide range of indicators of aggregate strength, primarily economic. Russia and China have begun to act on the formula "back to back", as Stalin and Mao did in the early 1950s. America is incapable of double containment of Russia and China.

The old world order is crumbling. It is clear that a new one is needed. It may be multipolar. It may be mildly bipolar: one pole around the US, and the other in Greater Eurasia, with China as economic leader but not hegemon; China's power will be balanced by other Euro-Pacific centers of power. There is a possibility of returning to the concept of a "Concert of Nations", based on the balance of power and interests of the leading powers, which are also the main centers of civilizational gravity.

However, if this happens, it will not happen soon. A combination of interaction and conflict – with conflict prevailing – will be the main feature of world politics for several decades, until a new global balance of power is formed. I think it will be in favor of the new centers of power to the detriment of the old ones. But the old do not intend to give up. And this foreshadows extremely turbulent, unstable decades, full of challenges and threats.

The main thing is not to allow a new big war; that is unthinkable, and could put an end to history, together with the human race.

Given the accumulated nuclear arsenals, the stakes in this ongoing Great Game are not just enormous.

Everything is at stake.

ABOUT THE AUTHOR

Born on June 5, 1956 in Moscow, Vyacheslav Nikonov graduated from the History Faculty of Moscow State University (MSU) in 1978. He taught Modern and Contemporary History at MSU from 1978 to 1989. While there, he was awarded a Ph.D. in History in 1982 and received a second Doctoral degree in 1989. Between 1989 and 1991, Nikonov worked at the Central Committee of the Communist Party of the Soviet Union, first as an assistant to the Head of the USSR Presidential Administration, then as an assistant to the Head of the KGB. Since 1992 he has worked for the Reforma foundation, established by the academician Stanislav Shatalin, and taught at the California Institute of Technology (Caltech); he also established the Politika foundation. He served as an MP of the State Duma of the first convocation between 1993 and 1995, and later as Chairman of the Committee of Education of the State Duma of the sixth convocation (2011-2016). Since 2016 Nikonov has been Chairman of the Committee of Education and Science of the State Duma of the seventh convocation, Chairman of the Executive Board of the Russkiy Mir foundation, and Dean of the School of Public Administration at MSU. He has been President of the Polity and Unity for Russia foundations, and a member of the Presidium of the General Council of the United Russia political party. He is the grandson of the renowned Soviet politician and diplomat, Vyacheslav Molotov. Nikonov has authored more than 1,200 publications.

MEBET

by Alexander Grigorenko

Mebet concerns a man of the taiga, a hunter, in a moving narrative that blends ethnographic detail, indigenous mythology, and the snowy landscapes of the Arctic. The protagonist is a Nenets, a member of one of the peoples who call far northern Russia home. Dubbed "The Gods' Favorite" for his seeming imperviousness to harm or grief, Mebet earns the envy and derision of his fellow tribesmen. He lives that carefree and blessed life until his old age, when one day a supernatural messenger arrives to lead him to where the realms of the living and the dead meet. Now the God's Favorite must confront the price to be paid for his elevated position, and a series of dread trials that lie in store.

Called a dark and terrifying fantasy and the Nenets *Lord of the Rings* by Russian writer and journalist Sergey Kuznetsov, Grigorenko's *Mebet* is a powerful story about humanity, personal fate, and responsibility. Leading Russian literary critic Galina Yuzefovich welcomed *Mebet* as a true epic for the Nenets, a book that is profound, thrilling and vibrant. Whether the book will earn that lofty place within Nenets culture remains to be seen, but the very publication of the book marks a watershed event.

Buy it > www.glagoslav.com

AN ENGLISH QUEEN AND STALINGRAD
THE STORY OF ELIZABETH ANGELA MARGUERITE BOWES-LYON (1900–2002)

The author traces the Queen Mother's formative years, her family life in the palace environment, her growing adoration and ascension to the British throne, how she arranged aid to Stalingrad and was ultimately named an honorary citizen of that city, and other little-known details from the life of the Queen and her circle.

With a foreword by Yuri Fokin, Russia's ambassador to the UK in the period 1997–2000, who was personally acquainted with the Queen Mother, the book will undoubtedly appeal to the British public and to anyone interested in Russian-British relations and the two countries' World War II history. Illustrated with photographs from private collections and from the Battle of Stalingrad Museum, some of which readers will see for the first time.

Buy it > www.glagoslav.com

Nikolai Gumilev's Africa

Gumilev holds a unique position in the history of Russian poetry as a result of his profound involvement with Africa. He extensively wrote both poetry and prose on the culture of the continent in general and on Ethiopia (Abyssinia, as it was called in Gumilev's time) in particular. During his abbreviated lifetime Gumilev made four trips to Northern and Eastern Africa, the most extensive of which was a 1913 expedition to Abyssinia undertaken on assignment from the St. Petersburg Imperial Museum of Anthropology and Ethnography. During that trip Gumilev collected Ethiopian folklore and ethnographic objects, which, upon his return to St. Petersburg, he deposited at the Museum. He and his assistant Nikolai Sverchkov also made more than 200 photographs that offer a unique picture of the African country in the early part of the century.

This volume collects all of Gumilev's poetry and prose written about Africa for the first time as well as a number of the photographs that he and Nikolai Sverchkov took during their trip that give a fascinating view of that part of the world in the early twentieth century.

Buy it > www.glagoslav.com

A Brown Man in Russia
Lessons Learned on the Trans-Siberian
by Vijay Menon

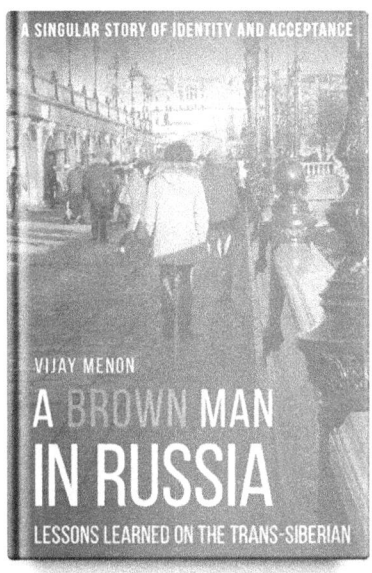

A Brown Man in Russia describes the fantastical travels of a young, colored American traveler as he backpacks across Russia in the middle of winter via the Trans-Siberian. The book is a hybrid between the curmudgeonly travelogues of Paul Theroux and the philosophical works of Robert Pirsig. Styled in the vein of Hofstadter, the author lays out a series of absurd, but true stories followed by a deeper rumination on what they mean and why they matter. Each chapter presents a vivid anecdote from the perspective of the fumbling traveler and concludes with a deeper lesson to be gleaned. For those who recognize the discordant nature of our world in a time ripe for demagoguery and for those who want to make it better, the book is an all too welcome antidote. It explores the current global climate of despair over differences and outputs a very different message – one of hope and shared understanding. At times surreal, at times inappropriate, at times hilarious, and at times deeply human, A Brown Man in Russia is a reminder to those who feel marginalized, hopeless, or endlessly divided that harmony is achievable even in the most unlikely of places.

Buy it > www.glagoslav.com

Dear Reader,

Thank you for purchasing this book.

We at Glagoslav Publications are glad to welcome you, and hope that you find our books to be a source of knowledge and inspiration.

We want to show the beauty and depth of the Slavic region to everyone looking to expand their horizon and learn something new about different cultures, different people, and we believe that with this book we have managed to do just that.

Now that you've got to know us, we want to get to know you. We value communication with our readers and want to hear from you! We offer several options:

— Join our Book Club on Goodreads, Library Thing and Shelfari, and receive special offers and information about our giveaways;

— Share your opinion about our books on Amazon, Barnes & Noble, Waterstones and other bookstores;

— Join us on Facebook and Twitter for updates on our publications and news about our authors;

— Visit our site www.glagoslav.com to check out our Catalogue and subscribe to our Newsletter.

Glagoslav Publications is getting ready to release a new collection and planning some interesting surprises — stay with us to find out!

Glagoslav Publications
Email: contact@glagoslav.com

Glagoslav Publications Catalogue

- *The Time of Women* by Elena Chizhova
- *Andrei Tarkovsky: The Collector of Dreams* by Layla Alexander-Garrett
- *Andrei Tarkovsky - A Life on the Cross* by Lyudmila Boyadzhieva
- *Sin* by Zakhar Prilepin
- *Hardly Ever Otherwise* by Maria Matios
- *Khatyn* by Ales Adamovich
- *The Lost Button* by Irene Rozdobudko
- *Christened with Crosses* by Eduard Kochergin
- *The Vital Needs of the Dead* by Igor Sakhnovsky
- *The Sarabande of Sara's Band* by Larysa Denysenko
- *A Poet and Bin Laden* by Hamid Ismailov
- *Watching The Russians (Dutch Edition)* by Maria Konyukova
- *Kobzar* by Taras Shevchenko
- *The Stone Bridge* by Alexander Terekhov
- *Moryak* by Lee Mandel
- *King Stakh's Wild Hunt* by Uladzimir Karatkevich
- *The Hawks of Peace* by Dmitry Rogozin
- *Harlequin's Costume* by Leonid Yuzefovich
- *Depeche Mode* by Serhii Zhadan
- *The Grand Slam and other stories (Dutch Edition)* by Leonid Andreev
- *METRO 2033 (Dutch Edition)* by Dmitry Glukhovsky
- *METRO 2034 (Dutch Edition)* by Dmitry Glukhovsky
- *A Russian Story* by Eugenia Kononenko
- *Herstories, An Anthology of New Ukrainian Women Prose Writers*
- *The Battle of the Sexes Russian Style* by Nadezhda Ptushkina
- *A Book Without Photographs* by Sergey Shargunov
- *Down Among The Fishes* by Natalka Babina
- *disUNITY* by Anatoly Kudryavitsky
- *Sankya* by Zakhar Prilepin
- *Wolf Messing* by Tatiana Lungin
- *Good Stalin* by Victor Erofeyev
- *Solar Plexus* by Rustam Ibragimbekov

- *Don't Call me a Victim!* by Dina Yafasova
- *Poetin (Dutch Edition)* by Chris Hutchins and Alexander Korobko
- *A History of Belarus* by Lubov Bazan
- *Children's Fashion of the Russian Empire* by Alexander Vasiliev
- *Empire of Corruption - The Russian National Pastime* by Vladimir Soloviev
- *Heroes of the 90s: People and Money. The Modern History of Russian Capitalism*
- *Fifty Highlights from the Russian Literature (Dutch Edition)* by Maarten Tengbergen
- *Bajesvolk (Dutch Edition)* by Mikhail Khodorkovsky
- *Tsarina Alexandra's Diary (Dutch Edition)*
- *Myths about Russia* by Vladimir Medinskiy
- *Boris Yeltsin: The Decade that Shook the World* by Boris Minaev
- *A Man Of Change: A study of the political life of Boris Yeltsin*
- *Sberbank: The Rebirth of Russia's Financial Giant* by Evgeny Karasyuk
- *To Get Ukraine* by Oleksandr Shyshko
- *Asystole* by Oleg Pavlov
- *Gnedich* by Maria Rybakova
- *Marina Tsvetaeva: The Essential Poetry*
- *Multiple Personalities* by Tatyana Shcherbina
- *The Investigator* by Margarita Khemlin
- *The Exile* by Zinaida Tulub
- *Leo Tolstoy: Flight from paradise* by Pavel Basinsky
- *Moscow in the 1930* by Natalia Gromova
- *Laurus (Dutch edition)* by Evgenij Vodolazkin
- *Prisoner* by Anna Nemzer
- *The Crime of Chernobyl: The Nuclear Goulag* by Wladimir Tchertkoff
- *Alpine Ballad* by Vasil Bykau
- *The Complete Correspondence of Hryhory Skovoroda*
- *The Tale of Aypi* by Ak Welsapar
- *Selected Poems* by Lydia Grigorieva
- *The Fantastic Worlds of Yuri Vynnychuk*

- *The Garden of Divine Songs and Collected Poetry of Hryhory Skovoroda*
- *Adventures in the Slavic Kitchen: A Book of Essays with Recipes*
- *Seven Signs of the Lion* by Michael M. Naydan
- *Forefathers' Eve* by Adam Mickiewicz
- *One-Two* by Igor Eliseev
- *Girls, be Good* by Bojan Babić
- *Time of the Octopus* by Anatoly Kucherena
- *The Grand Harmony* by Bohdan Ihor Antonych
- *The Selected Lyric Poetry Of Maksym Rylsky*
- *The Shining Light* by Galymkair Mutanov
- *The Frontier: 28 Contemporary Ukrainian Poets - An Anthology*
- *Acropolis: The Wawel Plays* by Stanisław Wyspiański
- *Contours of the City* by Attyla Mohylny
- *Conversations Before Silence: The Selected Poetry of Oles Ilchenko*
- *The Secret History of my Sojourn in Russia* by Jaroslav Hašek
- *Mirror Sand: An Anthology of Russian Short Poems*
- *Maybe We're Leaving* by Jan Balaban
- *Death of the Snake Catcher* by Ak Welsapar
- *A Brown Man in Russia* by Vijay Menon
- *Hard Times* by Ostap Vyshnia
- *The Flying Dutchman* by Anatoly Kudryavitsky
- *Nikolai Gumilev's Africa* by Nikolai Gumilev
- *Combustions* by Srđan Srdić
- *The Sonnets* by Adam Mickiewicz
- *Dramatic Works* by Zygmunt Krasiński
- *Four Plays* by Juliusz Słowacki
- *Little Zinnobers* by Elena Chizhova
- *We Are Building Capitalism! Moscow in Transition 1992-1997*
- *The Nuremberg Trials* by Alexander Zvyagintsev
- *The Hemingway Game* by Evgeni Grishkovets
- *A Flame Out at Sea* by Dmitry Novikov
- *Jesus' Cat* by Grig
- *Want a Baby and Other Plays* by Sergei Tretyakov
- *I Mikhail Bulgakov: The Life and Times* by Marietta Chudakova
- *Leonardo's Handwriting* by Dina Rubina

- *A Burglar of the Better Sort* by Tytus Czyżewski
- *The Mouseiad and other Mock Epics* by Ignacy Krasicki
- *Ravens before Noah* by Susanna Harutyunyan
- *Duel* by Borys Antonenko-Davydovych
- *An English Queen and Stalingrad* by Natalia Kulishenko
- *Point Zero* by Narek Malian
- *Absolute Zero* by Artem Chekh
- *Olanda* by Rafał Wojasiński
- *Robinsons* by Aram Pachyan
- *The Monastery* by Zakhar Prilepin
- *The Selected Poetry of Bohdan Rubchak: Songs of Love, Songs of Death, Songs of the Moon*
- *Mebet* by Alexander Grigorenko
- *The Lawyer from Lychakiv Street* by Andriy Kokotiukha
- *The Orchestra* by Vladimir Gonik
- *Slavdom: A Selection of his Writings, in Prose and Verse* by Ľudovit Štúr
- *Everyday Stories* by Mima Mihajlović
- *Subterranean Fire* by Natalka Bilotserkivets
- *Duel* by Borys Antonenko-Davydovych

More coming soon...

www.ingramcontent.com/pod-product-compliance
Lightning Source LLC
Chambersburg PA
CBHW071723080526
44588CB00013B/1877